THE
ALASTAIR CAMPBELL
DIARIES

Praise for *Volume Four, The Burden of Power*

'If I can use the word in its strictest form, these diaries are unique. They are a contemporary record of the intimate decisions of historic figures as set down by one who was a shrewd and straightforward chronicler of what he saw around him . . . Authenticity adheres to these pages like oil on an engineer's rag. They haven't been prettified, intellectualised or gathered second hand. This is the real thing.' *The Times*

'Memoirs and the rest are written through the self-justifying lens of hindsight. Campbell's contemporaneous jottings take the reader behind the grand sweep to capture the texture and grit of events as they were lived during the most tumultuous years of Blair's premiership.' *Financial Times*

'The final months leading to the Hutton inquiry into the circumstances leading to the death of David Kelly are riveting. Campbell himself comes across as a flawed genius, more spinned against than spinning . . . He is a man of excellent strategic and tactical judgement (it is easy to see why Blair became so dependent on him), brutally honest, occasionally self-indulgent and jealous of his undoubted integrity' *Guardian*

'As a first draft of history, albeit a highly partial one, this account is hard to beat. Campbell packs in all the events and the colourful cast of characters, enhanced often by caustic one-liners . . . Campbell's evident personality flaws, coupled with his political passions, made him a far more intriguing character than most around him. They have equally ensured that his diaries will be required reading for the New Labour era.' *Observer*

'As happens with many long-running series, the latest instalment is the author's darkest work yet . . . As ever, the immediacy of Campbell's account is engrossing. It is yet again a reminder of the salutary fact of history: that its actors do not know what is coming next.' *Independent on Sunday*

'[Campbell] was perhaps the most naturally gifted of all Blair's advisers . . . conveys very well the intolerable pressures under which prime ministers and their immediate staff work . . . It is worth getting this book for one absolute gem: Bill Clinton's mini-lecture to Campbell in early 2003 on where New Labour had gone wrong and what it needed to do to get back on track. It is a masterclass in democratic politics, which David Cameron would do well to read today.' *Evening Standard*

Praise for *Volume Three, Power & Responsibility*

'The great challenge of history is to recapture things as they really were, when the outcome of wars was unknown, deaths were not foretold and things that "everyone knows" were known only to Time Lords . . . Campbell's four-volume monsterwork is the best record of what it was like at the centre of politics at the time.' *Independent*

'Campbell had a Manichaean single-mindedness and the most extraordinary energy. After working similar hours to him, I would read a book and go to sleep. Campbell, who was ever accompanied by a thick A4 daybook in which he constantly scribbled his contemporaneous record of the day's events, would then write up his diaries at length, fail to sleep properly, and then rise early to deal with the next day's events . . . This is a serious work, lightened occasionally by hilarious episodes . . . instructive as both an example to follow and a sign of the pitfalls to avoid.' Jack Straw, *Guardian*

'As with earlier volumes, the pace is relentless. This is a warts and all account. Campbell spares no one, not even himself . . . One can't help admiring Blair and Campbell for their extraordinary resilience, somehow managing to keep their eyes on the big picture while all around them mayhem reigns.' *Observer*

Whatever you think of Blair and the Blair years, this is what it was like at the time.' *Independent on Sunday*

'Although there has been no shortage of memoirs from the New Labour era, this is without doubt the most authoritative. Campbell is no ordinary spin doctor. He enjoyed total access not only to Tony Blair and the New Labour court but also to just about every mover and shaker in the global power elite up to and including the US President.' *The Times*

Praise for *Volume One, Prelude to Power*

'Hugely gripping . . . all of human life is here. It makes *The Thick of It* look tame. And sane.' *Sunday Times*

'Campbell is a compelling diarist . . . *The Campbell Diaries* provide the fullest insider account so far of New Labour's ascent to power.' *The Times*

'Campbell's world is the brutal, angry, hard-driven, jokey, football-crazed and intensely male world of tabloid journalism. He is a fluent and industrious reporter, with amazing stamina.' *Daily Telegraph*

'There are plenty of nuggets here that are fascinating, some passages that make you wince and others that are gripping. It has historical value.' *Observer*

'Campbell's great strength is that he tells it like it is . . . This is as near as we are ever likely to get to the definitive account of the Blair governments up to the moment of Campbell's departure in August 2003. A brutally honest, relentless roller-coaster by a man who enjoyed total access.' *Spectator*

THE
ALASTAIR
CAMPBELL
DIARIES

Volume 4

THE BURDEN OF POWER

COUNTDOWN TO IRAQ

Edited by
ALASTAIR CAMPBELL
and
BILL HAGERTY

arrow books

Published by Arrow Books 2013

3 5 7 9 10 8 6 4 2

Copyright © Alastair Campbell 2012

Alastair Campbell has asserted his right under the Copyright, Designs
and Patents Act, 1988, to be identified as the author of this work

First published in Great Britain in 2012 by
Hutchinson
Random House, 20 Vauxhall Bridge Road,
London SW1V 2SA

www.randomhouse.co.uk

Addresses for companies within The Random House Group Limited can be found at:
www.randomhouse.co.uk/offices.htm

The Random House Group Limited Reg. No. 954009

A CIP catalogue record for this book
is available from the British Library

ISBN 9780099514732

The Random House Group Limited supports the Forest Stewardship Council® (FSC®),
the leading international forest-certification organisation. Our books carrying the FSC
label are printed on FSC®-certified paper. FSC is the only forest-certification scheme
supported by the leading environmental organisations, including Greenpeace. Our
paper procurement policy can be found at www.randomhouse.co.uk/environment

Typeset in Palatino by Palimpsest Book Production Limited,
Falkirk, Stirlingshire

Printed and bound by
CPI Group (UK) Ltd, Croydon, CR0 4YY

To Philip Gould (1950–2011),
because friendship matters in politics,
and team players are the best players of all.

Contents

Acknowledgements

Many thanks once more to Bill Hagerty, who took over the task of editing these diaries after the sad death of our friend and colleague Richard Stott, and to Mark Bennett, who was with me in Downing Street and has also been with me on the long and sometimes tortuous road to publication.

Both through my diaries, and the two novels and ebook I have published, I have come to appreciate the professionalism and kindness of many people at Random House. I would like to thank Gail Rebuck, Susan Sandon, Caroline Gascoigne, Joanna Taylor, Charlotte Bush, Emma Mitchell and the team of 'spin doctors', Martin Soames for his legal advice, David Milner, Mark Handsley, Vicki Robinson, Helen Judd, Sue Cavanagh, and Jeanette Slinger in reception for always ensuring one of my books is at the front of the display cabinet downstairs – at least when I am visiting the building. My thanks, as ever, to my literary agent Ed Victor, to his PA Linda Van and to his excellent team.

I want to thank Tony Blair for giving me the opportunity he did, and thank the many friends and colleagues who have helped me in good times and bad.

Finally, thanks to my family. As these diaries show, the pressures of the job I did also fell on Fiona and the children, and I thank them for their love and support. I know that they too will be happy to acknowledge our debt to Philip Gould, to whom I dedicated this volume shortly before his death, and who was an enormous support to all of us.

Introduction

At the risk of offending purists, pedants and history scholars, I have taken the liberty of beginning this volume with the same diary entry with which I ended the last one: September 11. Though this volume is the fourth in a series of the full diaries of my time working for Labour in opposition and in government, it also stands alone as a record of the most difficult and controversial period of Tony Blair's premiership. It is an intimate portrayal of Blair the war leader, with conflict in both Afghanistan and Iraq taking place during the two years covered, and September 11 is the most suitable place to begin that account.

The Taliban in Afghanistan, Saddam Hussein in Iraq, and the fear of terrorist organisations getting hold of weapons of mass destruction (WMD) with the help of rogue states, had been on TB's agenda well before September 11. Indeed, subsequently Mike White of the *Guardian* reminded me that TB had raised the issue as 'a coming challenge' at a meeting at the newspaper's head office the day before the Twin Towers fell. But without the events of that day, it is at least plausible to imagine that neither war would have taken place, certainly in the way they did. As the ten-year anniversary showed, it is a date so much now part of the public consciousness, and so central to many strategic, religious and geopolitical debates around the world, that it seems almost otiose to add the year: September 11, 2001. More than a decade on, we say 'September 11', or its American variant, '9/11', and there are very few people who don't immediately know where, when and what you mean, and summon up images of planes hitting buildings, people fleeing in terror, families grieving in all parts of the world, politicians struggling to catch up. There have been terror attacks since, but none which has made such a powerful impact, which is still felt today.

World leaders are fond of stating, in the immediate aftermath of terrorist outrages, that we must and will not let the terrorists deflect us or change our way of life. But they can, and they do. It is something I reflect on every time I go through an airport security check. But September 11 did more than see increased bag checks, belt and shoe removals and toothpaste confiscation at airports. It recast the foreign policy of major powers. It tested relationships between them. It tested the UN. It brought to a head debates which had been simmering within and about Islam. Most importantly for this book, it came to be a defining moment in Tony Blair's premiership, George Bush's presidency, the relationship between the two, the reputation of both.

The day began with TB worrying about a speech he was due to make to the Trades Union Congress in Brighton about public service reform. It was being set up as something of a 'lion's den' moment. The speech was never delivered: the first attack on the Twin Towers in New York took place as we put the finishing touches to it in a hotel suite overlooking a calm and beautiful sea. The day ended with TB back in London directing the UK end of a global crisis management response, which would subsequently see the domestic side of his job dwarfed by the consequences of the attacks.

The Burden of Power charts in sometimes minute detail what happened around TB on September 11, and every day thereafter: the initial response, the globetrotting diplomacy as the case for action was built, the decision to use military force to remove the Taliban regime in Afghanistan, a war still going on in somewhat different form today. Then not long afterwards the war in Iraq, undoubtedly the most difficult and the most controversial decision of the Blair government. In military terms, the wars were successful and, in terms of meeting the initial objectives, relatively swift. The Taliban fell. Saddam fell. But we all know that is only part of the story. The Taliban were toppled, but never really went away. Afghanistan remains far from secure, with perilous consequences for the region. Saddam was toppled, but after the initial celebrations, chaos ensued, and the controversy over the decision to commit troops to action did not disappear with the dictator those troops brought down. The stated purpose of the action was to remove what the government believed to be a growing threat from Saddam's WMD programme. Of course Saddam's long and wretched history of rule, his brutality, the wars he started, his defiance of the UN, these were all factors. But the answer to the specific question 'Why Iraq, why now?' was his continued development of a WMD programme, and the post-9/11 threat the US, the UK and others believed this posed. The fact that the weapons did not materialise in Iraq after Allied troops entered the country merely fuelled the controversy, unsurprisingly, over the original decision.

The Burden of Power seems a fitting title for a book dominated by Tony Blair's handling of these events. See the front covers of the four volumes and you see first a young and vibrant Opposition leader, then a young and jubilant prime minister taking the reins of power with an enormous landslide and huge goodwill, then a prime minister beginning to age as always they do – but still smiling – and finally, on the front of this volume, the Burden of Power. These were momentous decisions, taken amid enormous pressure and often with much else going on. It is why, though I disagree with his politics and oppose many of the things he has done, I have respect for the fact that the current prime minister, David Cameron, does the job he does. The pressures are unique to that post. Only five people alive today know what they are.

When I was asked by a newspaper to choose a defining photograph, as part of the enormous 'a decade on' coverage of September 11, I opted not for the obvious ones, but for a photo of TB sitting alongside John Monks, the general secretary of the TUC. Minutes earlier, John had said to me that it was on days like this that you realised the enormity of the responsibility that goes with the prime minister's job. The picture was used in *The Blair Years*, the extracts of my diaries published in 2007, and I have used it again in the first plate section of this volume too. TB looks focused and distracted at the same time. I know him well enough to see that his mind is whirring, thinking through the many things he will need to deal with once he has announced to the Congress that he must head back to London – his brief statement on events in the US, his expression of solidarity, his warning that the extremism behind the attacks had to be confronted, and his announcement that he would not be making the speech led to his first and last full standing ovation from a TUC event. John Monks meanwhile, also someone in a leadership position, is looking empathetically at TB, sensing the additional burdens falling on the shoulders of the man sitting next to him.

For some of his enemies, Iraq defines TB. The three election wins, a peace agreement in Ireland, record investment in schools and hospitals, Bank of England independence, devolution to Scotland, Wales and London, Sure Start, the minimum wage, civic partnerships, the New Deal, Kosovo, Sierra Leone, debt relief, securing the Olympics for London, all these and many more get parked and forgotten by those who wish only to see that when it came to Iraq, he did the wrong thing and for the wrong reasons. They see it as nothing short of a disaster, regardless of the fact that one of the most brutal dictators in history was felled after his years of defiance of the UN and brutality against his own people. It was about oil. It was about Israel. It was because TB was craven in his relationship with George Bush in particular and the US in general. It was because he had been in power too long and it had all gone to his head. For some these are unshifting and unshiftable views which, if anything, harden with time. And though TB led Labour to a comfortable third election victory even after the war in Iraq, and all the controversy that involved, I know there are people who deserted Labour on the back of it. But I hope a fair reading of my diaries shows that he took real care over all of the decisions which faced him at this time. I don't object to people disagreeing with the decisions he took. As so often in politics, things were never black and white. There was always another course that could have been taken, and I have never considered it dishonourable to hold a different view. Indeed Robin Cook expressed such a view brilliantly when he resigned from the government over Iraq. But as someone who was alongside TB as much as anyone, I know the care he took over the decisions, and the sincerity of his view that he was doing what he believed to be the right thing for Britain, British people and their security. He wasn't elected to hold views, but to take decisions based upon them, and whilst people may disagree with the conclusions he reached, they should not doubt his sincerity in the beliefs that drove him to them, not least his long-standing concerns about the threat of Islamic extremism, nor his conviction that not to have taken those decisions would have been wrong. Very little is heard in the UK media of the Iraqis who supported what we did, and who at least now have the beginnings of democracy. Those who opposed the war must at least reflect, surely, that had their position held sway, Saddam and his sons would have prospered for even longer. That was a danger TB believed the world should not countenance. It is why, despite the controversy, despite the opprobrium he has faced over Iraq, he nonetheless believes world leaders have a duty to face up to the threat of Islamic extremism, and why the conduct of Iran will at some stage have to be properly addressed too.

There was a point at which, in the run-up to the war in Iraq, I asked him if the war was really worth it if – as I feared it would – it led to him being driven out of office before his time. He said it was always worth doing what you thought was the right thing, and that Saddam was a threat the world had ignored for too long, and that included Britain. Those two insights were never far from his thinking throughout. As was clear from his evidence to the Chilcot

Inquiry into the Iraq War, he accepts mistakes were made, but he does not accept that the decision to remove Saddam was the wrong one, or that all the chaos which ensued was alone the responsibility of those who took the action to remove him. He thinks it was right, too, to be supportive of the US, not just because they came under attack on September 11, or even because we share so much in terms of values and history, but because he believed the only way to have any influence on President Bush privately – for example in getting him to take the issue of Iraq down the route of the UN, or get fresh US engagement in the Middle East Peace Process – was via maximum public support. It was to some extent a trade-off, for which he was willing to take the 'Bush's poodle' jibes.

Back in late 2001, with the memories of September 11 fresh in people's minds, and with the Taliban clearly not facing up to the challenge of helping to deliver up Osama Bin Laden and other perpetrators of the attacks, public and political support for action was stronger than it was for action in Iraq, though it is worth remembering that from some on the right in Britain, we faced the charge of being too cautious, and public support was greater at the time than it was after the event. I should make clear at this juncture that I am not linking Iraq to the September 11 attacks, in the sense of claiming Iraq played a role in them, and it was unhelpful of some in the US system to seek to do so. But where the link exists is here: until September 11, the threat posed by Iraq and WMD was one that the US and its closest allies were willing to tolerate. After September 11, the mindset shifted. To quote the phrase used often at the Chilcot Inquiry, the calculus of threat changed.

For those who think the government did the wrong thing, so much has been said and written, the arguments have been played out so volubly, that it is unlikely anything I say here, or which I wrote at the time and publish now, will persuade them otherwise. But when TB was being briefed at the Ministry of Defence on military preparedness in the event of our forces coming under attack from biological or chemical weapons, there was not a person in that room who did not consider the threat to be real. I can remember feeling a sense of fear which was matched by the looks on some of the faces in the room. I can remember TB pressing until he was as assured as he could be that our troops were as prepared as possible to face this threat if and when it came. No prime minister would commit troops to any action, let alone to the potential horror being described in that room, without thinking through the consequences, and unless they were sure there was no other way. Also, I know it is not the done thing in polite circles to speak well of George W. Bush, but I thought he made a very good observation in his book, *Decision Points*, when he said, 'If I wanted to mislead the country into war why would I pick an allegation that was certain to be disproven publicly shortly after we invaded the country?' Both he and TB, and the people working for them, believed the WMD threat was real. People are entitled to disagree with the decisions. But there was no lying, there was no conspiracy. There was a set of difficult decisions that had to be taken.

Of course the portrait of Tony Blair is the most intimate here. But I saw a good deal of Bush, of Vladimir Putin, of Jacques Chirac and other world leaders during this time. Bill Clinton still figures large, a good and sometimes critical friend to TB and his team. The night out with him and actor Kevin Spacey in a McDonald's restaurant in Blackpool was one of the more memorable meals of my life. Unforgettable too was the meeting at which he gave fellow Labour strategist Philip Gould and me a masterclass in political strategy, complete with very personal advice about my own by then difficult situation. Many on both sides of the Atlantic find it odd that TB could be close both to Clinton and to Bush, two very different leaders from different sides of the political divide. I think TB would argue that with the US the only superpower at the time, he had a duty to have good relations with its leader. Also, he genuinely got on with Bush. The Texan certainly had a cowboy touch about him, at times right down to the boots on his feet. But he has more intelligence, more charm and greater political skills than most are prepared to credit him with. It has also been interesting to note, as the Republicans have lurched through the process of trying to find a candidate to take on President Obama at the next election, that by the standards of most of the contenders, Bush is something of a moderate. Many modern politicians are more impressive in public than in private. The media age has forced politicians as a breed to communicate more and to think about how they do so. They can turn a switch and go into public mode. David Cameron is a good example of this. George Bush's switch seemed sometimes to go the other way. He would express himself less well in public than he did in private. At least he was aware that his image gave other leaders in other countries problems. I don't think the same could always be said for his vice president Dick Cheney or defense secretary Donald Rumsfeld.

Just as Iraq will always be one of the issues most associated with TB, so the issues of communication surrounding the war will always be with me, as someone somewhere reminds me online most days. As I said to the Chilcot Inquiry, I stand by everything I said and did in relation to the September 2002 dossier on WMD presented to Parliament by the Prime Minister. Being asked to give my diaries to Lord Hutton's inquiry into David Kelly's death, as this volume shows, was something of a terrifying moment. As anyone who has read my diaries now knows, I can be very frank, I can say very harsh things, I can be hard on myself and on others. I confess to being so worried about what I might have written that when I drove from our holiday home in Provence to Marseilles airport to collect my diaries so that I could transcribe them and send them to Lord Hutton in advance of my first evidence session, I had one of those momentary reflections that life might be easier all round if I just careered off the motorway. Yet as it turned out, I think the diaries may have helped our case. They showed that we took rather more care over that dossier than the BBC journalist took over his report which led to my being called to select committee inquiries, ultimately to Kelly's death, and the inquiry into that.

I never met David Kelly, but I think about him often, and whether I could have done anything differently that might have stopped him from taking his life. With the exception of the deaths of family and close friends, the day his body was found was perhaps the worst of my life, certainly the worst of my time with TB. Had it not been for Fiona, and Philip Gould who came round to the house on hearing the news, I would almost certainly have resigned there and then. I was frankly beyond caring if it meant the blame would come my way. So far as many in the media were concerned, that was going to happen anyway. I just felt the whole thing had become like a horrible, dark novel and I wanted out of it. Ironically, the night before, we were felt to be 'winning' the battle with the BBC, its reporter having been strongly criticised by the Foreign Affairs Committee. But by the morning, all that had changed. It was horrific. The feelings I had then are among the reasons why, despite always staying involved, and going back to help out in two general elections, I have never really wanted to return to a full-time position in the front line of politics.

When I gave evidence to the Leveson Inquiry into media practices in 2011, I made the point that much of today's media like to act as judge and jury on those in public life. The coverage of the Hutton Inquiry, whose deliberations are covered in this volume, but whose conclusions came after I resigned from Downing Street, is a good example. The inquiry shone a microscopic light on both the process of communication in the run-up to war, and the circumstances surrounding Dr Kelly's death. When Lord Hutton was putting government witnesses through their paces, and ministers and officials from the prime minister down were being questioned and cross-examined, day in and day out, media reporting was largely slanted to show the government in a bad light, and Lord Hutton in a good light because of the rigour of his inquiry. The bits of the evidence that suggested wrongdoing by the government led bulletins and newspapers. Anything that fitted with the government account tended to be relegated. The moment Lord Hutton concluded that the central charges against the government were not borne out by the evidence, he was condemned as Lord Whitewash. Hundreds, thousands of reports have subsequently sought to convey the sense that the BBC report was essentially true. It was not; and as Lord Hutton said at the time, even if it emerged there were no WMD in Iraq, that would not make the reporting true. It is important to remember what the accusations against us – and me in particular – were: that we inserted false intelligence into the WMD dossier, knowing it to be false and against the wishes of the intelligence agencies. To this day, I fail to see how a government can simply ignore claims as serious as that. Indeed, had the inquiry found against us, it would not just have been the end for me, but more importantly for TB. Though no WMD have been found, the BBC report is as untrue today as it was when it was first made, despite the constant attempts by many in the media to rewrite what was broadcast, or to confuse and conflate the WMD dossier with the so-called 'dodgy dossier', which was a different paper, which attracted next to no attention at the time, on which someone working for me made an error for which I apologised.

It is fair to say that in this volume, most of the personal satisfaction, even happiness I managed to get from working for TB in the early years has gone. The twin pressures of a 24–7 job of real intensity and scrutiny, and a home life where pressure was mounting on me to leave, at times felt like a living nightmare. I was glad to have discovered a new obsession in running. My sons persuaded me to go for a long run in the summer of 2002. By the end of the holiday I had decided to do the London Marathon, which coincided with a very busy time in relation to Iraq. TB felt the whole thing was a bit of a distraction; to me, it was something of a saviour. At the time I took up running, I could do the job, but I didn't feel I was doing it as well as before. I was resenting the workload, and resenting those on our own side who so often made life harder than it should have been. TB was convinced that I could and should stay, and he is a very skilful manager when it comes to getting his own way. Also, even when we fell out, as over the role of Australian con man Peter Foster and Carole Caplin when Cherie bought two flats for her son Euan, I always felt a strong sense of loyalty to TB, and I still do. It was that loyalty, in addition to the sense of being involved in such significant events, with the chance to make a difference, which made it so hard to leave. When finally I did, I knew it was the right time, even if I fell into a pretty awful depression not long afterwards.

I had forgotten until transcribing the diaries just how long I had been trying to get out. Ironically, the controversy over the communications on Iraq kept me in post for longer. TB finally agreed to my departure in May 2003, shortly before the BBC report I describe above, and yet I didn't leave until August, as the intervening months came to be dominated by the fallout. I suppose it is also something of an irony that TB hired me to take charge of his media relations and yet my own relations with the media became as bad as they did. Partly this was because I often played the role of lightning conductor. But also I was one of the few people able and willing to articulate what I believed to be a set of damaging trends in the way the media and its effect upon democratic debate were developing. I think one of the reasons I became so high profile and so controversial is that I was doing the job at a time the media age was becoming a reality. The media sought to position themselves as the sole purveyors of truth (ironically at a time when standards were falling). In their minds, what they did was truth; what we did was spin. We made mistakes, certainly, not least my colleague Jo Moore's infamous 'good day to bury bad news' email of 9/11. But in general I believe we applied far higher standards to what we said and did than many journalists applied to what they wrote or broadcast.

By the time of this volume we are certainly on the receiving end of the culture of negativity which is powerfully unique to the UK media. I'm not quite sure I would go as far as Derry Irvine's description of the press as 'Satan's people on earth' – some of them were out for Derry's son at the time – but I thought David Blunkett summed up the new media mood well when he said if TB had found a cure for cancer they'd report his failure to do anything for victims of meningitis. TB shared my analysis that the media had become a problem not just for politicians but for our culture and therefore our country. But as I said to the Leveson Inquiry, whereas I felt we had to do something about it, he continued to feel that with all the other priorities the government faced, the public simply would not understand if we launched an overhaul of press standards and regulation as another plank of reform. It was a fair point. But there was always going to come a time when the media reformed and hopefully phone-hacking has brought us to that moment. We will see.

Beyond growing disenchantment with the political media, certain other domestic themes recur in this volume: TB's frustrations at the pace of delivery; something of a culture clash with parts of the Civil Service; continuing difficulties with matters Royal; another media frenzy erupting from false charges that TB sought a bigger role in the Queen Mother's funeral, clearly being fuelled by members of the establishment, some of whom never quite reconciled themselves to a long-running Labour government; TB and his fashion sense – my determination not to let him wear a coat Cherie wanted him to put on in Russia led to one of my biggest rows with her; and of course the TBGBs. John Holmes, formerly TB's foreign policy adviser, made an interesting observation: that TB's problems are caused by his relations with two GBs – George Bush and Gordon Brown. They certainly figure large in his thinking and in any history of this remarkable period. Yet again the two sides of Gordon Brown – the brilliant and the impossible – are on show. But by now TB seems to feel the impossible outweighs the brilliant. Even at the height of international crisis, GB is asking TB for a date of departure (much as Fiona was asking the same of me). The battleground is as much about policy as simply the ambition to be PM. The euro, for example, with TB still keen that Britain should step up preparations to join the single currency, and concerned that GB's scepticism is a tactic to court the right-wing media, the left already supportive of him because of his approach to poverty. There are some fairly extraordinary scenes resulting from GB's attempts, often without consultation with the ministers concerned, to direct policy in other departments. Ministers are often unsure of what their instincts are expected to be, always a sign of division at the top.

The policy differences are exacerbated by what became a largely dysfunctional working relationship, the management of which consumed extraordinary amounts of time and energy. TB talks of GB waging a war of attrition. Jonathan Powell at one point says it is like watching a failed marriage disintegrate. John Prescott says it is all about TB's guilt at becoming leader ahead of GB, and GB's never forgotten sense of betrayal. At times GB could not even bring himself to look at TB in meetings. It all got so bad that TB, fed up with what he sometimes called GB's 'destabilisation strategy', came back from one holiday determined to sack him. It never happened. At another point a small number of his inner team are asked to reflect on what became known variously as his *grande stratégie* and *le grand projet* (he and I often spoke in French for some reason, particularly when he was nervous) – namely announcing that he would not fight the

Introduction

next election, but would stay on until that point. I think it is possible that had GB been more co-operative and more of a team player, TB might have executed that strategy. But things seemed to get worse not better. More even than in previous volumes, TB, his ministerial colleagues, I and my colleagues in the TB team are worrying about what GB would be like as PM. Yet when it came to it, there was enough of the good amid the bad to have most of us supporting him when he took over. TB says at one point that GB is a 'malign force but head and shoulders above the rest'. Back to the 'brilliant and impossible' prism.

There have been plenty of books written about the Blair/Brown era, and the Blair/Brown relationship, and there will doubtless be many more. Most of the memoirs, biographies and autobiographies of our time in government have been written with the benefit of hindsight, and some of them to suit a single view or perspective. I hope that one of the advantages of a diary from the centre, in terms of its potential contribution to historical debate and analysis, is the lack of such hindsight.

This volume brings to an end the detailed daily account of my time working for TB, in opposition and in government. I have kept a diary ever since, continue to do so and one day may publish my post-Number 10 diaries, where from a slightly different perspective I took part in and recorded two more election campaigns, between them the transition from one PM to another, and many of the ups and downs along the way, as I sought to build a different sort of life, but found myself drawn back in again and again. Re-reading this volume now, and gathering the impressions of those who have read it during the editorial process, I do understand why some people ask the question: 'Why on earth did you go back to help GB?' I understand too why they point to some passages and say it was obvious he was not temperamentally suited to the job of prime minister, or to leading Labour through a general election campaign. But look elsewhere, and it is not quite so evident. He had huge residual strengths and a political appeal which made him hard to resist when, despite all the differences between the Blair and Brown teams, as Prime Minister he was asking me, Peter Mandelson and Philip Gould to return to the fold to help him out in the run-up to the last election. Peter Mandelson returned full time, and full on, back in the Cabinet. Partly because of my views on the Lords, and partly because I didn't want to go back full time to the front line, I turned down the offer of a peerage and ministerial post but did go back to help plan the election campaign, and support GB during it. And despite being ill for much of the time, Philip made his usual big contribution on polling and strategy. As Philip wrote in his revised *Unfinished Revolution*, published shortly before his death last November, I had predicted a hung Parliament from some way out. For much of the campaign, however, I had felt the Tories were on their way towards securing a majority, and I think we surprised ourselves in preventing them from getting one. But when, after several days of post-election wrangling, the time finally came for Gordon to leave Downing Street for Buckingham Palace to offer his resignation to the Queen, I did get the very strong feeling that, politically, we had for the time being run our course. Shortly before, he spoke on the telephone to TB, from the desk in the corner of his office. It was my old office, which he had taken over when he turned 12 Downing Street into what he believed was a more modern set-up for a PM. As he and Tony chatted, Peter Mandelson and I sat and listened. All of the relationships had been tested at times, but there remained a togetherness of sorts, and certainly the sense of a remarkable shared journey that changed Britain, and British politics, for good and, in my view, for the better.

That moment also reminded me of another insight that has deepened with time and experience: that politics, at its best, is a team game. TB once said we were at our best when we were at our boldest. In what was widely seen as a dig at New Labour, by way of response GB said we were at our best when we were Labour. I felt we were always at our best when we were together, united, pulling in the same direction. When it happened, it felt like we were unstoppable. But it didn't happen all of the time; far from it.

Whenever I was under the cosh, my mother-in-law was fond of reminding me of the old Harry Truman quote, 'If you want a friend in Washington, get a dog.' But friendship in politics is possible, and can be real. Teamship is vital. It is because Philip Gould was both a great friend and a great team player that I chose to dedicate this volume to him. He more than any of us understood that politics is a team game, and right up to his death was trying to heal some of the wounds that came with the pressures of power. He died proud of the role he had played in helping to get Labour back into power, and in helping TB and his team do the job we did. I publish this full account humble enough to know we didn't get everything right, but proud of the overall story it tells, and happy to share it.

Alastair Campbell
January 2012

Who's Who

September 2001–August 2003

The Cabinet

Tony Blair	Prime Minister (TB)
John Prescott	Deputy Prime Minister and First Secretary of State (JP)
Gordon Brown	Chancellor of the Exchequer (GB)
Jack Straw	Foreign Secretary (JS)
David Blunkett	Home Secretary (DB)
Margaret Beckett	Environment, Food and Rural Affairs Secretary (MB)
Charles Clarke	Labour Party Chair 2001–2, Education Secretary from 2002
Estelle Morris	Education Secretary 2001–2
Patricia Hewitt	Trade and Industry Secretary, Minister for Women (Pat H)
Robin Cook	Leader of the House of Commons 2001–3 (RC)
Clare Short	International Development Secretary
Alistair Darling	Work and Pensions Secretary 2001–2, Transport Secretary from 2002 and Scottish Secretary from 2003 (AD)
Stephen Byers	Transport, Local Government and the Regions Secretary (SB)
Alan Milburn	Health Secretary 2001–3 (AM)
Tessa Jowell	Culture, Media and Sport Secretary
Geoff Hoon	Defence Secretary
John Reid	Northern Ireland Secretary to 2002, then Labour Party Chair 2002–3, Leader of the House of Commons 2003, Health Secretary 2003–5

Paul Murphy	Welsh Secretary 2001–2, Northern Ireland Secretary from 2002
Helen Liddell	Scottish Secretary 2001–3
Lord (Gareth) Williams	Leader of the House of Lords 2001–3
Lord (Derry) Irvine	Lord Chancellor 2001–3
Hilary Armstrong	Chief Whip (Commons)
Andrew Smith	Chief Secretary to the Treasury 2001–2, Work and Pensions Secretary from 2002
Lord (Bruce) Grocott	Chief Whip (Lords)
Lord (Peter) Goldsmith	Attorney General

Additional Cabinet changes 2002–3

Peter Hain	Welsh Secretary from 2002, Leader of the House of Commons from 2003
Paul Boateng	Chief Secretary to the Treasury from 2002
Baroness (Valerie) Amos	International Development Secretary 2003, Leader of the House of Lords from 2003
Hilary Benn	International Development Secretary from 2003
Lord (Charlie) Falconer	Lord Chancellor from 2003

10 Downing Street

Andrew Adonis	Head of Policy Unit
Alison Blackshaw	AC's personal assistant
Cherie Blair	Wife of TB (CB)
David Bradshaw	Special adviser, Strategic Communications Unit
Alastair Campbell	Director of communications and strategy
Magi Cleaver	Press officer, overseas visits
Hilary Coffman	Special adviser, Press Office
Kate Garvey	Events and visits team
David Hanson	Parliamentary private secretary to TB
Jeremy Heywood	Principal private secretary
Robert Hill	Political secretary
Anji Hunter	Director of government relations
Peter Hyman	Strategist and speechwriter
Tanya Joseph	Press officer
Tom Kelly	Prime Minister's official spokesman (with Godric Smith)

Liz Lloyd	Special adviser, Policy Unit
Sir David Manning	Chief foreign policy adviser
Pat McFadden	Deputy chief of staff
Fiona Millar	AC's partner, aide to CB (FM)
Sally Morgan	Director of political and government relations
Jonathan Powell	Chief of staff
Terry Rayner	Driver
Catherine Rimmer	Research and Information Unit
Matthew Rycroft	Private secretary, Foreign Affairs
Martin Sheehan	Press officer
Godric Smith	Prime Minister's official spokesman (with Tom Kelly)
Clare Sumner	Private secretary, Parliamentary Affairs
Sir Andrew Turnbull	Cabinet Secretary from 2002
Simon Virley	Private secretary
Anna Wechsberg	Private secretary
Ben Wilson	Press officer
Sir Richard Wilson	Cabinet Secretary to 2002 (RW)

HM Treasury

| Ian Austin, Ed Balls, Spencer Livermore, Ed Miliband, Sue Nye | Special advisers |

Whitehall/Security Services

Admiral Sir Michael Boyce	Chief of the Defence Staff 2001–3
Sir Richard Dearlove ('C')	Head of the Secret Intelligence Service (MI6)
Sir Jeremy Greenstock	UK ambassador to the United Nations
Sir Stephen Lander	Director general of the Security Service (MI5)
Dame Eliza Manningham-Buller	Lander's successor, 2002
Chris Meyer	UK ambassador to Washington
Sir Richard Mottram	Permanent secretary, DTLR
Sir David Omand	UK security and intelligence co-ordinator
John Scarlett	Chairman, UK Joint Intelligence Committee
Sir John Stevens	Metropolitan Police commissioner

United States

Dan Bartlett	Communications adviser to GWB
George W. Bush	43rd President of the United States (GWB)
Andrew Card	White House chief of staff
Dick Cheney	Vice President
Bill Clinton	42nd President of the United States
Hillary Clinton	US senator and wife of Bill Clinton
Ari Fleischer	White House press secretary
Karen Hughes	Communications adviser to GWB
Colin Powell	Secretary of State
Condoleezza Rice	National Security Advisor (Condi)
Karl Rove	Senior adviser to GWB
Donald Rumsfeld	Defense Secretary
George Tenet	Director, CIA

International

Kofi Annan	UN Secretary General
Yasser Arafat	President of Palestine
José María Aznar	Prime Minister of Spain
Silvio Berlusconi	Prime Minister of Italy
Osama Bin Laden	Militant Islamist, founder of al-Qaeda (OBL)
Hans Blix	Chief UN weapons inspector
Jacques Chirac	President of France
Jean Chrétien	Prime Minister of Canada
Catherine Colonna	Chirac's press secretary
Mohamed ElBaradei	Director general, International Atomic Energy Agency
Saddam Hussein	President of Iraq (SH)
Lionel Jospin	Prime Minister of France
Hamid Karzai	Chairman of the Afghan Transitional Administration from December 2001
General Pervez Musharraf	President of Pakistan
Mullah Omar	Taliban leader, Afghanistan
Romano Prodi	President, European Commission
Vladimir Putin	President of Russia
Gerhard Schroeder	Chancellor of Germany
Ariel Sharon	Prime Minister of Israel

Hutton Inquiry

Gavyn Davies	BBC chairman
James Dingemans QC	Senior counsel to the inquiry

Greg Dyke	BBC director general
Andrew Gilligan	Reporter for the BBC's *Today* programme
Lord Hutton	Law Lord, former Lord Chief Justice of Northern Ireland
Dr David Kelly	Biological weapons expert, Ministry of Defence
Richard Sambrook	Director of BBC News
Jonathan Sumption QC	AC's, and later government, lawyer at the inquiry

The Labour Party

Douglas Alexander	Minister of State, DTI, and party strategist
Stan Greenberg	US pollster
Glenys Kinnock MEP	Wife of Neil Kinnock
Neil Kinnock	Labour Leader 1983–92
Michael Levy	Businessman, Labour Party fundraiser
Peter Mandelson	Labour MP for Hartlepool, former Cabinet minister
David Triesman	General secretary

Parliament

Iain Duncan Smith	Leader of the (Conservative) Opposition (IDS)
Charles Kennedy	Liberal Democrat Leader
John Major	Former Prime Minister (1990–97)
Margaret Thatcher	Former Prime Minister (1979–90)
Lt Gen Sir Michael Willcocks	Black Rod, House of Lords

The Media

Guy Black	Press Complaints Commission
Adam Boulton	Sky News political editor
Rory Bremner	Impersonator and satirist
Michael Cockerell	BBC political documentary maker
Paul Dacre	*Daily Mail* editor
Richard Desmond	Owner of Express Newspapers
Sir David Frost	Broadcaster
Trevor Kavanagh	*Sun* political editor
Donald Macintyre	*Independent* political commentator
Andrew Marr	BBC political editor

Piers Morgan	*Daily Mirror* editor
Rupert Murdoch	Chairman, News Corporation
Andrew Rawnsley	*Observer* political columnist
John Sergeant	ITN political editor
Rebekah Wade	Editor, *News of the World*
Philip Webster	*Times* political editor
Michael White	*Guardian* political editor
David Yelland	Editor, *Sun*

Family and Friends

Donald and Betty Campbell	Parents of AC
Rory, Calum and Grace Campbell	Children of AC and FM
Alex Ferguson	Friend of AC, manager of Manchester United
Philip Gould	Political pollster and strategist, adviser to TB (PG, Philip)
Audrey Millar	Mother of Fiona
Gail Rebuck	Publisher, wife of Philip Gould

The Diaries

Tuesday, September 11, 2001

I woke up to the usual blah on the radio about TB [Tony Blair, Prime
Minister] and the TUC [Trades Union Congress] speech, all the old
BBC clichés about us and the unions, the only new thing GMB
[trade union] ads asking if you trust TB not to privatise the NHS.
Peter H [Hyman, policy adviser and speechwriter] and I went up to
the [12 Downing Street] flat. TB had done a good section on public-
private, an effective hit back at the John Edmonds [GMB] line. With
the economy, public services, Europe/euro and a bit on asylum which
was really worrying, we had a proper [TUC] speech. We sharpened
it and honed it a bit. He was furious at the GMB ads, said he intended
to give Edmonds a real hammering. We finished it on the train to
Brighton, were met and driven to the hotel. We were there, up at the
top of the hotel putting the finishing touches to the speech, when the
attacks on the New York Twin Towers began.

Godric [Smith, deputy press secretary] was watching TV in the
little room where the Garden Room[1] girl had set up, came up to
the top of the little staircase leading to the bit where TB and I were
working, and signalled for me to go down. It was all a bit chaotic, with
the TV people going into their usual breathless breaking-news mode,
but it was clearly something way out of the ordinary. I went upstairs,
turned on the TV and said to TB he ought to watch it. It was now even
clearer than just a few moments ago just how massive an event this
was. It was also one that was going to have pretty immediate implications for us too. We didn't watch the TV that long, but long enough
for TB to reach the judgement about just how massive an event this
was in its impact and implications. It's possible we were talking about
thousands dead. We would also have to make immediate judgements

[1] Offices of the Downing Street secretarial support

about buildings and institutions to protect here. TB was straight on to the diplomatic side as well, said that we had to help the US, that they could not go it all on their own, that they felt beleaguered and that this would be tantamount to a military attack in their minds. We had to decide whether we should cancel the speech.

There was always a moment in these terrorist outrages where governments said we must not let the terrorists change what we do, but it was meaningless. Of course they changed what we did. At first, we felt it best to go ahead with the speech but by the time we were leaving for the venue, the Towers were actually collapsing. The scale of the horror and the damage was increasing all the time and it was perfectly obvious he couldn't do the speech. We went over to the conference centre, where TB broke the news to [John] Monks [TUC general secretary] and Brendan Barber [Monks' deputy] that he intended to go on, say a few words, but then we would have to head back to London. We would issue the text but he would not deliver the speech. John Monks said to me that it's on days like this that you realise just how big his job is. TB's mind was whirring with it. His brief statement to the TUC went down well, far better than his speech would have done.[1] We walked back to the hotel, both of us conscious there seemed to be a lot more security around. We arranged a series of conference calls through Jonathan [Powell, Chief of Staff] with Jack S [Straw, Foreign Secretary], Geoff Hoon [Defence Secretary], David B [Blunkett, Home Secretary]. We asked [Cabinet Secretary Sir] Richard Wilson to fix a Cobra[2] meeting as soon as we got back.

We set off for Brighton station. He said the consequences of this were enormous. On the train he was subdued, though we did raise a smile when someone said it was the first and last time he would get a standing ovation from the TUC. Robert Hill [TB's political secretary] was listening to the radio on his earpiece and filling us in every now and then. TB asked for a pad and started to write down some of the issues we would have to address when we got back. He said the big fear was terrorists capable of this getting in league with rogue states that would help them. He'd been going on about [Osama]

[1] Blair told trade union delegates 'This mass terrorism is the new evil in our world today. It is perpetrated by fanatics who are utterly indifferent to the sanctity of human life and we, the democracies of this world, are going to have to come together to fight it together and eradicate this evil completely from our world.'

[2] The committee intended to lead responses to national crises; named after the Cabinet Office Briefing Room.

September '01: Scale of the horror increases

Bin Laden for a while because there had been so much intelligence about him and al-Qaeda. He wanted to commission proper reports on OBL and all the other terror groups. He made a note of the need to reach out to the British Muslim community who would fear a backlash if this was Bin Laden. Everyone seemed convinced it couldn't be anyone else.

We got back and before Cobra he was briefed by Stephen Lander [director general of MI5], John Scarlett [chair of the Joint Intelligence Committee], RW. DTLR [Department of Transport, Local Government and the Regions] had closed airspace over London. There had been special security put around the Stock Exchange and Canary Wharf. The general security alert had been raised to Amber. Three hundred companies were being contacted to be given advice. Scarlett said OBL and his people were the only ones with the capability to do this. Neither he nor Lander believed other governments were involved. TB said we needed a command paper of who they are, why they are, what they do, how they do it. He said at the diplomatic level he felt the US would feel beleaguered and angry because there was so much anti-Americanism around. Lander felt the pressure on the Americans to respond quickly, even immediately, would be enormous. Afghanistan was the obvious place. Iraq, Libya, Iran, the Americans will be trying to find out if they helped in this. He said there were a lot of people sympathetic to Bin Laden, more than we realised. TB said they will move straight away to the international community and their response. If I were [US President George] Bush, I would demand the Taliban deliver him up.

Scarlett and Lander were both pretty impressive, didn't mess about, thought about what they said, and said what they thought. Scarlett said this was less about technology than it was about skill and nerve. Lander said this was a logical step up from the car bomb. Turning a plane into a bomb and destroying one of the great symbols of America takes some doing but they have done it and they have been able to do it because they have any number of terrorists prepared to kill themselves. TB's immediate concern, apart from the obvious logistical steps we had to take, was that Bush would be put under enormous pressure to do something irresponsible. If America heard the general world view develop that this happened because Bush was more isolationist, there would be a reaction. He felt we had to take a lead in mobilising diplomatic solidarity in the rest of the G8 and the EU. We had to start shaping an international agenda to fill the vacuum. He spoke to [Chancellor of Germany, Gerhard] Schroeder, who wanted a G8 meeting, [President of France, Jacques] Chirac and [Prime

Minister of France, Lionel] Jospin, who were not so sure, and then [Vladamir] Putin [President of Russia], who had a real 'I told you so' tone, said he had been warning us about Islamic fundamentalism.

TB and I both pressed Scarlett and Lander on why they were so sure there were no rogue governments involved in this. They said because Bin Laden was able to do it himself and that suited his purposes better. We all trooped over to the Cobra meeting, which was a bit ragged, but that was to be expected given what people were having to deal with. There were contingency measures that had gone into effect. Private flights had been stopped. There were no commercial flights to go over the centre of London. All small-plane flights were being grounded unless they had specific clearance. Security was being stepped up around financial centres and major computer sites. The Met [police] were raising numbers on visible patrols, particularly at Canary Wharf, Heathrow and in the North London Jewish areas. We had upped protection on our premises in the Middle East. There was talk of moving some of the planes based at RAF Leuchars to London in the event of a hijack. Jack S said the EU GAC [European General Affairs and External Relations Council] was planning to meet. Geoff Hoon gave a briefing on what troops were where in the Middle East.

TB did a very good summing-up, first going through all the different measures that I should brief, then on the specific reports he wanted to commission, then on the importance of a diplomatic strategy to support the US. He said they would feel beleaguered and all the tensions that had been apparent before would now become more open, whatever the warm words around the world. He asked Jack and Geoff to come through to Number 10, said it was vital that we worked up an international agenda that went beyond the US just hitting Afghanistan. He felt NMD [National Missile Defense] would quickly rise up the agenda.

He intended to say to Bush that he should deliver an ultimatum to the Taliban to hand over Bin Laden and his people and then hit them if it didn't happen. He had been reading the Koran over the summer. [The Prophet] Mohammed had lost battles but there was a belief that if you died in the cause that you believed in then you went straight to heaven. That was a very, very powerful thing to work against. TB's public words were very much in total support of the US. He said this was going to be a nightmare, as big and as bad as any we had endured. It was interesting that he had not asked GB [Gordon Brown, Chancellor of the Exchequer] to come back for the smaller meeting. I asked him why and he said because in their recent discussions he had been monosyllabic. The Israelis were making massive attacks on the terror groups. TB said we were going to have to work exceptionally hard on the international response. Bush was getting it in the neck for not being in Washington.

Everyone was in bed when I finally got home, and Fiona [Millar, AC's partner and adviser to CB] had fallen asleep watching it all on the TV. I did a call with Jonathan to go over how much we would need to kick out of the diary in the coming days. Pretty much all of it, at least for a while. Jonathan said the Americans would be unlikely to let Bush travel – it was a bit much that he couldn't even go to his own capital – but the fallout from this was going to need an awful lot of diplomatic activity. I think we're going to be seeing a lot of the insides of planes, he said.

I turned off the TV in the bedroom and went downstairs to channel-hop while writing it all up. The TUC felt a bloody age ago. Some of the footage of the aftermath, clouds of dust and debris literally rolling down streets, was extraordinary. So were the eyewitness accounts. Gut-wrenching. What was amazing about this was that people like Bush, TB, Chirac and the rest were having to react and respond in exactly the same time frame, and with pretty much only the same knowledge of the incident as people watching on TV. The difference was they were going to have to take some huge decisions about it too.

Wednesday, September 12

Bush did a broadcast at 2am, said all the things you'd expect but looked a bit shaky. TB was generally thought to have handled it well yesterday and also got a fairly good press for the TUC speech that never was. I got in early and read the overnight intelligence reports, everything pointing now to Bin Laden. TB was starting to think about the long term and what to do about the whole terrorism agenda. It had clearly moved up to a different level. The day was taken up almost exclusively with the attack. TB wanted as much information as possible and he wanted to be in a position to work out Bush's likely reaction. He felt it likely that Bush would feel the pressure for an early response. The full enormity of what had happened was only now really sinking in. TB was pretty clear that we would end up going for the Taliban. At Cobra there was a review of the security procedures put in place. RW [Richard Wilson] and others wanted to reopen City Airport but [Stephen] Byers [Transport Secretary] objected and TB, with GB and JS [Jack Straw] in full support, agreed to keep the airport shut and the flyover path over London shut too. GB at Cobra contributed when asked to, but otherwise pretty much sat there, or muttered out of the side of his mouth to Jack. He clearly hated it, possibly hated the fact that TB was so clearly in charge in these crisis management situations.

Lander said that Bin Laden was last thought to be in Kandahar three days ago. John Stevens [Metropolitan Police commissioner] said there were more than a thousand extra police officers on the streets. TB said he had talked to the Governor of the Bank of England [Eddie George] and they were keeping in contact about how to maintain confidence in the financial system, while the supply of oil was also being constantly monitored. Jack said that we should not get ahead of the US in terms of what we say. He felt our best role was to stay close and try to exercise influence privately. Afterwards there was a smaller meeting in TB's office with Richard Dearlove (C) [chief of the Secret Intelligence Service (SIS), MI6], Lander, Hoon, Jack and Kevin Tebbit [permanent secretary, Ministry of Defence]. C said there was a significant international operation going on by us and the Americans and others that he was confident would show who was behind it.

TB commissioned a note on what Bush's options were, saying he had to get inside his mind if he could. Hoon said al-Qaeda tentacles were all over the place – Africa, Chechnya, this wasn't just about Afghanistan. There was also the view that the intelligent thing would be to wait several weeks but TB pointed out things were likely to move much more quickly than that. If the Americans are as convinced as we are that this is Bin Laden, there should be pressure put on to yield him up and if they refuse to co-operate, then he would be entitled to hit them. TB warned, following on from his phone call with Putin, that the Russians would essentially co-opt this whole event as justification for what they were doing in Chechnya. There was a discussion about recalling Parliament.

Later TB saw Scarlett and Lander and others to get a fuller briefing on Afghanistan and Bin Laden and how he operated. One of the experts from the FCO [Foreign and Commonwealth Office], a total Arabist, came very close to saying the attack was justified, saying the Americans should look to their own policy on the Middle East to understand why so many people don't like them. Scarlett said it wasn't clear that OBL controlled all the training camps, but what he did know was that there was a very large supply of young men ready to die for the cause. It was also clear that there were likely to be would-be terrorists here as asylum seekers. Both C and Lander were very good on big picture and detail. They both felt Bush would need a few days for the Americans properly to assess all this stuff. TB and I agreed he should do a press conference, saying that Cabinet would meet tomorrow and Parliament on Friday. We worked on the script and went through various options of how to express the support he would give to Bush, which was pretty full on.

We got a message that Bush wanted to speak to him. It was a good call, Bush was pretty calm and TB very supportive. Bush said he was the first foreign leader he was speaking to and he would value staying in touch. He said the American people would give him a bit of time. TB said there might be a case for a G8. TB went over some of the things he had been saying to us, and Bush said he was grateful for the help and would appreciate if he put some of those thoughts in writing. Bush said the UN and NATO statements were 'useful cover for the work that we would have to do', by which I think he meant continuing intelligence gathering and then attack. He said this was 'a new war, Pearl Harbor in the twenty-first century'. He said these people had to come out of their holes sometime. TB said he felt for him personally and Bush replied 'I know what I've got to do. I'm not a good mourner. I'm a weeper. I'll weep with the country but then act, but I don't just want to hit cruise missiles into the sand.' TB was a bit worried that the longer he waited, the more he would be expected to do.

TB wrote off a note for Bush's eyes only, which spelled out some of the problems we were facing and where Bush might go to build useful alliances. I felt Bush was almost Zen-like, almost too calm. Maybe he had decided he could wait longer than we thought. TB was sure we would need to do a lot more than just take out OBL. There was a second Cobra meeting with another discussion about whether to lift some of the restrictions. John Stevens said that the casualty figures were very vague but the UK casualties could be up to a thousand. TB agreed we should get out the possibility that figures could go into the hundreds. TB and Blunkett had a meeting on asylum with DB pushing hard for ID cards and detention centres. The general feeling was that TB was doing well. He was constantly telling us about bits of the Koran. Earlier we got the Muslim Council to condemn the attacks. Ben Wilson [press officer] started in the press office. What a day to start.

Thursday, September 13
TB's worry was that GWB would turn inwards. He had sensed a bit of resistance to the G8 idea, which he felt was a big mistake. He felt now was the time to bind in as much international support as possible. He felt a big military hit combined with a big international effort of support and a long-term agenda for terrorism was the way to go. There was a whole load more intelligence all pointing towards OBL.

We went through to the Cobra meeting where we agreed we could wind down the emergency response. TB's note to Bush was strong but he was not sure he would be receptive. TB had a meeting pre Cabinet with Jack S, Geoff [Hoon], [Admiral Sir Michael] Boyce [Chief of the Defence Staff, CDS] – who had replaced [General Sir Charles] Guthrie. I felt that with all the focus on the States, there was a danger we would neglect the Brits involved, and the fallout, which would be substantial, so suggested Tessa [Jowell, Culture Secretary] be used to sort out all that logistically etc. but also to be a kind of minister for helping families and victims. Jack was worried it would cut across the FCO stuff but I felt it needed a specific minister, specifically deputed. The Palace played the US national anthem at the Changing of the Guard while Prince Charles was visiting the embassy to sign the condolence book.

Cabinet was very sombre, though Clare [Short, International Development Secretary] did her usual bit. TB was very much in charge. He said it was an act carried out in America which should be seen as an attack on the democratic world. Of the thousands killed, he feared several hundred would be British. He said all the evidence pointed to OBL. He said long term there had to be a strategy for dealing with Islamic fundamentalism but for the moment the focus was on finding the perpetrators, putting in place the security measures needed here, and assessing the financial implications for the world economy.

Jack went through the diplomatic activity, said the UNSC [United Nations Security Council] had been easier to mobilise than the EU in some respects. On security, he said the problem was security is only as good as the weakest link. Blunkett went through all that was being done to protect public buildings, big computer installations and infrastructure sites. He said suicide bombers are notoriously difficult to plan for. He pointed out, as did others, the importance of reaching out to decent British Muslims. TB said there were three areas to focus on – whatever US military response is made, and our participation within it. Politics and diplomacy and in particular trying to get impetus into the Middle East peace process [MEPP]. And practical security arrangements. Clare said the real problem was lack of progress in the Middle East, the fact that so many people were willing to be suicide bombers, and she asked if we had the will to improve life for the Arab world. Patricia [Hewitt, Trade and Industry Secretary] briefed on oil and energy supplies, and was fairly confident. It was a good meeting, and I think people sensed TB was going to have an important role, not just here. Jack was doing fine on the media but agreed we would need to broaden the field.

September '01: TB: attack was on the democratic world

TB and I then spent a while working on his statement for tomorrow, though getting the right balance and tone would be the hard bit. Both Hilary Armstrong [chief whip] and Robert Hill warned him that the PLP [Parliamentary Labour Party] may be a bit dodgy on this and TB said 'Are they mad? Do we just let these people get away with killing thousands of people?' He said if this had been on British soil, just imagine the pressure for a swift response. Jonathan had brought in some interesting books on the Taliban which we were trying to read in addition to the material being provided by the spooks. TB sent a message to all Arab leaders. We did a TB article for about fifty regional newspapers in areas with large numbers of Muslims. There was the beginning of talk in the States about how TB's response was better than Bush's, which made him a bit anxious, and he recalled how [former US President Bill] Clinton had got a bit jumpy during Kosovo.

Friday, September 14

David Manning [Blair's newly appointed senior foreign policy adviser], who had been in the States at the time of the attacks, was now back. Quite a baptism. He gave a very good assessment of where the various bits of the American set-up were. He felt Bush was being fairly restrained but at some point that would stop. We had a meeting with TB, C, Lander, Francis Richards [director] of GCHQ [Government Communications Headquarters, intelligence monitoring agency]. Everything pointed to OBL, training camps, possibly some help from the Taliban. The US clearly believed there was real evidence but we agreed it would not be possible to publish much of it. We left for the Commons, got the tone of the statement right and went over the difficult questions. TB did fine. IDS [Iain Duncan Smith, new leader of the Conservative Party] was OK but there were too many clichés and not enough smart questions. TB felt he was perfectly bright but lacking in real imagination. Our backbenchers were fine, and the Tories and Lib Dems basically onside for the approach he set out. TB was sure that ultimatum followed by attack if no response was the right way. Anji [Hunter, head of Downing Street presentation and planning] took a call from Will Farish, the new US ambassador [to London], specifically inviting some of us to the service at St Paul's. We travelled up with Richard Wilson and John Gieve [permanent secretary, Home Office] and ended up in the front row, which was a bit embarrassing. [John] Major, [Margaret] Thatcher and [James] Callaghan [former Prime Ministers] were all there. GB was sitting next to IDS. It was a nice service. I chatted with Jamie Rubin [former

US State Department chief spokesman, 1997–2000] at the end, who said the American right would use this as an excuse to do all sorts of things right round the world. Be very careful of these people, he said.

Back at Number 10, TB, Jonathan, David Manning and I had a session pre TB's phone call with Bush. TB was worried by the reluctance to have a G8, felt it showed they were looking inwards when they should be looking outwards. They should be using now to bind in Russia and France. He also felt we had to do more to bind in Pakistan, who were going to be absolutely vital in all this. The call took place at 1.45. It was clear that the wobbly Bush of the last call had become the hawk again. He said this was a war and they would win. They wanted OBL dead or alive. Afterwards TB seemed a bit alarmed, said 'My God, fasten your seatbelts.' He said people would understand Afghanistan, but if he went for Afghanistan and Iraq together, it would be absolute madness. He was quite troubled, said we had to think of a way of getting to the US for a face-to-face meeting. He said he needed to see him in a room, and look in his eyes, not do all this on phone calls with fifteen people listening in. Bush would be getting lots of conflicting advice, and TB said he could sense that in the change of tone from call to call. We had to persuade Bush that we had to go for OBL and the Taliban but if he went for Iraq the Russians and the French would peel off. He asked DM to make sure he stayed in permanent contact with Condi [Condoleezza Rice, US National Security Advisor] and make sure they did nothing too rash. We got over Geoff H, Jack S and CDS.

TB went through his assessment of the US plan – ultimatum to yield up OBL and then let outside body move in to get rid of the camps. Alternatively, hit OBL straight away possibly going for the Taliban. And the next step is to look to other countries, including Iraq, and other countries not even linked to OBL. He said their instinct was to resolve the WMD [weapons of mass destruction] question quickly. We needed to consider what such a strategy would be and what part we would play in it. He said his advice very strongly will be to deal with Afghanistan very distinctively, whereas to go for Iraq would be certain to lose Russia and France from any international support. He said they had definitely moved to action mode but we still had an opportunity to mould things in the right direction. He said he was confident he could persuade him that to go beyond Afghanistan for four countries at once was World War territory.

CDS asked if there was any indication of how they intended to hit Afghanistan. TB was not aware they were currently planning anything beyond missile attacks. Geoff said there had been talk of special forces going into Afghanistan. CDS said it was possible to attack mountain camps as a way of showing we were not scared of putting our boots on their soil. Geoff said [Donald] Rumsfeld [US Defense Secretary] had been looking for reasons to hit Iraq. They definitely wanted regime change and that was the channel of advice that Bush had been getting since the election. Jack said they would be mad to do Iraq without justification because they will lose world opinion. TB said 'My job is to try to steer them in a sensible path.' He said we had to separate these two missions. He said their line of argument will be that it does not matter whether you did the Trade Center, if you are in the business of terrorism, then we are going to put you out of business. It's possible to be sympathetic to that but the political consequences are all too obvious. We cannot ignore that's where they are. We are talking very big issues here. He said even in the most benign circumstances this is going to be difficult.

TB said they all needed to keep in close touch with opposite numbers. He was worrying about which camp would be having most influence on Bush. We also agreed it might be sensible for Guthrie to go to see [General Pervez] Musharraf [President of Pakistan]. TB said afterwards he felt Bush was getting bad advice, that we had the right strategy and we had to persuade him of that. He would feel so much better if he could see him face to face. It was a bit alarming just how different the two calls had been. After the first, TB was worried he wasn't doing enough, and now he was talking about taking out anyone who might harbour terrorists. TB asked CDS to refine the paper on military options. Ed Richards [senior policy adviser on media business issues] came to see me about Gavyn Davies[1] getting the BBC chairmanship, which was likely to break next week.

Saturday, September 15

The aftermath of the attacks was still totally dominating the media, stories moving more to the human tragedy as well as the diplomacy. TB had a meeting first thing with C, Lander, [Francis] Richards, Scarlett, Wilson, Jonathan, Manning and me. They kept saying there was more and more evidence pointing to OBL. But as TB and I agreed later, nothing that would stand up in a court of law. There was real unease among our side now, that the Americans would do something to fracture the coalition that was being built up. Scarlett said there

[1] Goldman Sachs economist, unofficial policy adviser to Blair, and husband of Sue Nye, personal aide to Gordon Brown.

was evidence of real tensions in Pakistan. Lander reported three people arrested with false passports at Gatwick. Manning said Colin Powell [US Secretary of State] had spoken to Jack and sounded worried. There was no doubt some in the US had an agenda, led by Rumsfeld and Paul Wolfowitz [Deputy Defense Secretary], to see this as a revenge against Iraq for not finishing the Gulf War. Lander briefed TB on some of the difficulties we were facing on the issue of people using the UK to plan terrorism. TB just sat shaking his head when he told him about someone who we knew to be planning terror in India, that this was accepted by the tribunal, but we couldn't kick him out. We discussed the need for changes to human rights law and civil liberties. DM had mentioned to Condi that TB thought they should meet soon. TB, Jonathan and I were all casually dressed. The spooks were all in dark suits and carrying their battered briefcases. TB said to them, if I didn't know you were all so young, I'd say there was a generational gap.

He felt he should probably see Schroeder on Wednesday, Chirac Thursday, then the US. He called a couple of times later when I was out running, was now at that stage where he was testing his own thoughts by constantly setting out the same position and trying to find weaknesses. It was basically ultimatum, act, follow-through short, medium and long term. But we would need to be building support at every stage and he was obviously worried about the American capacity on that front. TB was getting a good press here and even more so overseas, especially the States. I couldn't help thinking that though this was a total disaster, and was going to wipe out chunks of his domestic diary, if leadership was important, here was a real opportunity to show it. The Sundays arrived, wall to wall on the attacks. The main live news story was Bush's meeting at Camp David, where he said the US must get ready for war and that OBL was the prime suspect. TB was getting a good press, GWB a bad press. [James] Naughtie's second instalment [of his serialised Blair/Brown book, *The Rivals*] was running which focused on me, and GB's fears about my diary.

Sunday, September 16

TB was doing CNN so I went in for a pre-meeting with him and David Manning. DM said they were looking at an ultimatum followed by a 48- or 72-hour wait. The noises from the Taliban were getting more and more aggressive. Thousands of refugees were pouring over the border. Pakistan was clearly going to have a hard time whatever. Robin [Cook, former Foreign Secretary, now Leader of the House of

Commons] was on *Frost* for us and the BBC were really pissed off that TB did CNN. It was a good interview. We went over all the really tough questions, but a few of them never came. I had an argument with CNN who were initially refusing to release the whole interview to other broadcasters but in the end they did.

TB said he sensed Bush would end up in the right place, that some of the stuff on the phone calls had clearly been for the benefit of internal consumption, which was why he really wanted to meet him soon, without anyone else there. 'I hope to God he's not listening to some of the people round him, because we need to be wary of them.' He was more confident. Chirac was pretty clear that they could hit Afghanistan but no further. Schroeder was in a bit of a problem at home and not quite so strong. Jospin was all over the shop because of his coalition [government] situation and Chirac was going to make it as hard for him as he could. TB wanted to get a message of support for Musharraf. He later called me to say we must get out the message about how closely the Americans were consulting us, as whatever they thought about them, that would make the other Europeans want to get closer.

Monday, September 17
Up to the flat to see TB and told him that the US were suggesting that he went to Congress with Bush. 'Oh yeah,' said TB. I said it was serious and I was worried about it because it would play into the whole poodle thing. John Kerr [permanent secretary, Foreign and Commonwealth Office] called to say it would be ghastly, that the whole thing would become an orgy of US patriotism, with TB in a kind of nod-along role. I felt we should only do it if TB also spoke, but wasn't sure if that was even doable. Charles Clarke [Labour Party chairman] told him later that there were real anxieties around about Bush and that people around the world saw TB as the only person who could restrain him. He said it was an awesome responsibility. Clare Short had gone on [Andrew] Rawnsley's [BBC Radio 4 *Westminster Hour*] programme last night and had said something that let them write government split and tension headlines. TB later wrote to her. He was really angry, said it sent exactly the wrong signal to the Taliban about our seriousness of intent. Jack and I had a long chat before his *Today* programme interview and agreed he should move the story on by echoing the line on OBL and saying that we had our own evidence that all pointed his way.

TB spoke to Musharraf later who said the risks he was taking were real and he needed real help. He seemed keen on the suggestion of

Guthrie going out. At the 8.30 intelligence meeting, there was no real knowledge of where OBL was. Lander reported on some of the people under surveillance here. There was a really gloomy mood. There was talk from the US of concerns that OBL had acquired some kind of basic nuclear capability, and worries of a possible chemical, biological or radiological attack. At TB's military meeting, Geoff Hoon and CDS were both focusing on the difficulties of any military offensive. Boyce was very unlike Guthrie as CDS, who had always been pretty can-do. Boyce was quite soft-spoken, very polite, but I wondered if he wasn't something of a fellow depressive. Geoff said he had had some difficult chats with Rumsfeld. CDS said only six per cent of Afghans have electricity. They don't even have fuel dumps that we would recognise as such. There's nothing really there, very few targets. TB said they had to know that we would hurt them if they don't yield up OBL. David Manning said we had to do more to help the Northern Alliance.[1] Lander and CDS said the heroin trail should also be hit. They said more people had been killed by heroin than died last Tuesday.

We were now planning a series of visits for TB, Berlin, Paris, Washington, New York. He was worried about Congress unless he spoke. Then came news there would be an EU summit on Friday. All a bit of a nightmare. TB had lunch with [Italian Prime Minister Silvio] Berlusconi who was wearing a pile of make-up and his hair was dyed jet black. He was reasonably supportive on the idea of military action 'provided not too many people die'. TB said there was no such thing as a painless war. He said either the US will see the international community rallying to them or there will be a battle internally and the isolationists will win. His worry was people show support up to the point where the shooting starts. He said we had to divide this into two – Afghanistan, and the broader terrorist apparatus. In respect of the second part, the decisions are for the long term.

Berlusconi emphasised that we had to make clear this was not a war against Islam. TB said it was important we got Arab countries as part of our coalition. The best signal of all would be a restart of the Middle East peace process. There was a real risk that [Israeli Prime Minister Ariel] Sharon sees this as an opportunity to say that [Palestinian leader Yasser] Arafat equals OBL. He said it was important we all made clear to Israel this should not be an opportunity to settle scores but on the contrary we should have the objective of reinvigorating the peace process. There was something very odd about Berlusconi. He didn't seem quite in control of his body, his arm

[1] The coalition of disparate opponents of the Taliban.

movements were a bit weird and most of the time he addressed himself to the interpreter rather than TB. They had a fairly lacklustre discussion on Europe and the euro. The Federal Reserve cut interest rates while they were having lunch. TB then had a big Africa meeting and we had a discussion of sorts on his [party] conference speech.

Sandy Berger [former National Security Advisor to Bill Clinton] was in town. He was looking a lot thinner, younger and happier, said he was exercising five days a week. He felt TB was doing well, that a position of total support was the best because he could influence from that position in private. He felt TB had a lot of respect because of our experience re the IRA and we should be saying this is not a war that you just win or lose, but a war you constantly manage. The New York Stock Exchange reopened but the economic impact was growing.

Tuesday, September 18

TB was at Chequers for a meeting with a group of officers. He had a chat with Jiang Zemin [Chinese premier]. He was getting a very good press as a kind of international interlocutor. Bush was going down pretty badly everywhere apart from the States. We were getting more and more work done on the nature of the Taliban. There was a bit of a discussion as to whether it was the kind of trip Cherie [Blair, TB's wife] should go on. I did the morning meeting. Geoff Hoon was doing fine. Tessa told me relatives were getting more and more angry but not with us so much as with the general situation. GB went up after interest rate cuts and the economic scene was getting more and more difficult. I started work on a note for Karen Hughes [AC's opposite number in the White House] about the system we had put in place for Kosovo. If anything, this situation was going to be even more complicated and difficult. There were a stack of meetings to plan visits, particularly the US. I was really worried about him looking like a poodle at Congress. There was to be a church service and also a visit to 'Ground Zero'. The main news story of the day was the toing and froing of the Taliban about whether to hand over OBL. They prevaricated by saying 'clerics' would decide.

TB saw Guthrie to brief him on his mission to see Musharraf. I suggested he tell him that his visit was the first step towards Britain moving to Pakistan-style rule. TB did the World Service, trying to push the line that the coalition was strengthening. David Blunkett was round for dinner. He was a bit down about the whole asylum mess and was vicious about the inability of the Home Office to do what we asked them to. He was convinced reception centres and ID cards were the answer. He said he hoped TB would stay for a long time but also asked when I thought JP [John Prescott, Deputy Prime Minister] would go. I asked if he ever thought he could be leader of the Labour Party. He said no, he could be deputy. Deputy leader or deputy PM with a department? He laughed. It was basically the latter, and I imagine he wanted it fed back. He believed we had lost our way a bit and were slightly losing the plot on public services but he was very pro TB at the moment. He said [Alan] Milburn [Health Secretary] was probably the best current bet as a non-GB [leadership] candidate. The anti-Bush feeling in the press was getting way over the top. The liberal press was revolting, the *Mirror* moronic, the *Mail* poisonous.

Wednesday, September 19

I went to see TB who was with Jack Straw discussing MEPP and saying farewell to [John] Sawers.[1] John was telling him he was going to the Middle East and he didn't want Michael Levy [Lord Levy, Labour fund-raiser, Blair's personal envoy to the Middle East], anywhere near him. I was winding up Jack [a supporter of Burnley's local rivals, Blackburn Rovers] about Burnley's latest win – eight out of nine – when Geoff Hoon and CDS came in, looking grave. CDS said that on a very unofficial net he had got hold of what the Pentagon were proposing – Tomahawks followed by 1,000 missiles raining down on various targets. He was very sceptical, said it sounded basically political and it would mean hitting a lot of sand. TB was keen for their take on what we should advise them militarily. He said he was clear what needed to be advised diplomatically but we needed to give them a military plan too. CDS felt what was needed was surgical strikes and special forces.

Then to a broader meeting with C, Lander, Scarlett, GH, JS, CDS, RW and our lot. Depressing. Lander felt that if there was a big attack we just could not predict the response. He said there was a definite rise in Islamophobia since the attacks. Nobody had a clue where OBL was and nobody was hopeful about finding out. They were also checking whether the Pennsylvania plane [United Airlines Flight 93] had been designated to hit a nuclear power plant.[2] There were quite

---

[1] Sawers, Blair's foreign affairs adviser, had been appointed UK ambassador to Egypt.

[2] The intended target of the hijacked plane remains unclear. It has been assumed that the four terrorists intended to crash into Washington's Capitol building, or perhaps the White House. The most likely nuclear power plant would have been Three Mile Island, south of Harrisburg, Pennsylvania. However, passengers, aware of attacks on the World Trade Center and Pentagon, overwhelmed the hijackers. The Boeing 757 crashed in a field at Stonycreek, Pennsylvania, killing all forty-four people on board.

a few OBL people in the UK and Europe and they understood they were currently planning attacks. We were also worried that Bush's 'dead or alive, head on platter' type of rhetoric would not be helping in Pakistan, which had the potential to be a tinderbox.

We could only get at Mullah [Mohammed] Omar [Taliban leader] and OBL with Taliban and Pakistan co-operation and even that was doubtful unless we gave them Kashmir. As the discussion wore on, CDS finally articulated what I had been thinking – namely that we had to start to prepare people for a very long-term operation, possibly taking years and years. OBL was travelling most of the time. There was no sign of a shift in the Taliban's position and any plan to divide them would take an age. I asked whether there was a public enemy number three, four, five so that the focus and the judgement wasn't solely on whether we got OBL.

Afterwards, I had a meeting with another expert just back from Islamabad, who said that the only thing OBL feared was the opprobrium of clerics. He could not care less about Western opinion because he hated the West. He said OBL had a tough, nasty, dedicated group of people around him which was virtually impossible to penetrate. They were ultra careful, especially in their travel and communications. He could probably slip to Pakistan but it was unlikely. He agreed with the guy on CNN yesterday who said the only way to get to OBL was through saying, and getting clerics to say, that he was not Islamic, that what he was doing was contrary to Islam.

TB saw some of the delivery ministers and had a meeting on Railtrack before we set off for RAF Northolt.[1] I told him what Blunkett had said about being deputy leader. He said JP had said that if it helped with Gordon he would stay on. JP was pretty down on GB at the moment, said he had told him he would support him if he sorted himself out but not if he carried on the way he was. TB admitted there was a part of him that felt it would be irresponsible to back GB for the succession. On Bush, TB said he's basically bright but he's just not good with words.

We flew out to Berlin and TB and [Gerhard] Schroeder spent most of the meeting one-on-one with an interpreter. They did a brief door-step together, and Schroeder was very strong, considering how difficult this was for him with less than one in three Germans supporting military response, but he said he was keen to lead them towards it.

[1] Railtrack plc, the company operating much of Britain's rail infrastructure, had been bailed out by the government after reporting a huge loss following extensive repairs to the network – a result of the Hatfield rail crash in 2000. It was about to be placed in administration by Transport Secretary Stephen Byers.

He gave a very good description of his own situation and felt they had to be part of the response. But for sixteen years, he said, the SPD [Social Democratic Party of Germany] was basically a peace party. Ditto the Greens. The churches were against war and culturally it was very difficult for them to go for conflict but he felt they had to. He said his situation was very different to Britain. 'You have polls where seventy-five per cent condemn the attacks and seventy-five per cent say yes to action. We have seventy-five per cent condemn the attacks but thirty per cent saying yes to action.' He was pretty relaxed and philosophical about it. We had dinner up at the top of the new swanky building that housed his new office [the Bundeskanzleramt, eight times larger than the White House], much nicer than Bonn, with great views. He talked about his own political situation. He could always go for a grand coalition but he preferred what he had and said he owed a lot to [Joschka] Fischer [Green politician, Vice Chancellor and minister for foreign affairs in Schroeder's coalition government] because he took the Greens with him. They had a bizarre love-hate relationship but they basically knew they could rely on Fischer. He said that whilst TB was building a coalition of nations, he had quite enough to do in building a coalition inside Germany.

He was much more likeable when he was open and expansive, as he was on Europe as well as Afghanistan. He had nice friendly eyes, a warm smile and easy manner, and seemed to understand and appreciate the scale of what TB was trying to do. His lovely interpreter was with him who told me not to lose any more weight. I was definitely becoming addicted to running. We got back on board the 146 to a message that Cherie had spoken to Laura Bush [George Bush's wife] who was keen for her to go to Washington. Flew to Paris.

Thursday, September 20

Paris. Up for a run in the embassy gym. Over breakfast, TB set out the approach he intended to take with Chirac, the need to separate the short-term response from the long-term agenda to deal with the deeper problems. Chirac had coincidentally been to the States and Catherine Colonna [his spokeswoman] suggested it had been helpful in that he had got a real sense of how deep it went for the Americans. For a while, he would probably curb his basic anti-American feelings. It was clear he wanted to be involved but it was also likely the Americans had remained suspicious. They did a brief doorstep together and there was a flurry of excitement because TB said at one point 'within the next few days' and we had a major job to smooth it over, make clear he was talking diplomatic not military.

We headed for the plane to meet up with Cherie, the rest of the staff and the press corps coming with us to New York. I had just about finished the note I was doing for Karen [Hughes] setting out the need for really tight co-ordination structures between all the key players, and the need for a really thought-through strategy for reaching moderate, mainstream Muslim opinion. Before dinner, TB had a long session with C and the military planners. They were looking at specific targets based on information they had obviously garnered from their various discussions with opposite numbers. What was very clear was that the US were well advanced. These were detailed plans. After an hour or so with them, TB said at least he got the sense that these guys knew what they were doing. I had a good chat with C, who said that in some ways the brave thing would be to do nothing, hold tight until we were absolutely sure of where OBL was. I was worried that the focus was so much on OBL that success or failure would be judged solely according to that.

TB did a briefing on the plane, cranking up the sense we were heading towards action and playing up solidarity with the US. TB worked on a new note for Bush with two aims – first, bringing OBL and al-Qaeda to justice, and second, going after international terrorism in all its forms. The ultimatum, and help for the Northern Alliance, remained central. He felt we should use air strikes to demolish the camps, support the NA, gather intelligence to designate high-value targets, hit the drugs trail, go for OBL, strong forward base in Uzbekistan and the Afghan border, a deal for Pakistan, help Musharraf, help Afghan people, new relations with Iran, support from Russia and Arabs. He set out too a number of things in the practical fight against terrorism – the disruption of groups from their travel. Extradition laws. He said we needed: 1. an integrated and streamlined military planning operation, binding in other allies too; 2. detailed work on the long-term agenda; 3. a well-staffed US–UK-led propaganda team, and 4. the political, military and media operations linked between us.

We landed in New York and though we had an escort, the combination of bad weather, dreadful traffic and continuing post-September 11 chaos meant that sadly we had to cancel the visit to a fire station. I was able to rescue it a bit when Clinton agreed to go instead of TB and take Cherie with him. TB was getting frantic because we were so late but we finally reached St Thomas' Church and then a mild panic because there were suggestions that the reading, which had been suggested to me by Paddy Feeny [Tessa Jowell's press officer], was not appropriate because it was about bereavement and some of the people there did not believe they had yet lost their loved ones. It suggested they were all emotionally shot to pieces. TB was in the front row with CB, Kofi Annan [United Nations Secretary General], Bill and Chelsea [Clinton]. TB's reading[1] went fine as did the message read out by [UK ambassador Sir Christopher] Meyer from the Queen, including the brilliant line 'Grief is the price we pay for love.' Bill C asked me if I wrote it. I said I'd love to take credit, but no. He said find the guy who did, and hire him.

After the national anthems we had a brief meeting with Bill and Kofi who both warned of real dangers from Pakistan if we weren't careful. Then we were taken up to the room where all the relatives were gathered. The contrast, the moment you entered the room, was palpable. We had been engaged in the normal diplomatic chat that goes on even in these circumstances, humour included, and now into this dreadful, dreadful atmosphere, haunted eyes, faces drained of blood, lips quivering. Most said it was all made worse by the fact they had no bodies to take home. Most carried pictures which they showed to TB and Bill as they moved through the room. Bill was absolutely terrific when he stood in for TB at the fire station. By now we were running really late and I felt terrible constantly reminding TB, but it was impossible to leave without him going round to speak to everyone. And they all just wanted to pour out their stories. These were in the main just ordinary people caught up in one of the most extraordinary things ever to hit anyone.

We finally got out to the airport and discovered that all the press luggage was being thoroughly searched so we were delayed even further. Meyer was next to useless at trying to cut through it. David Manning was on the phone trying to organise helicopters and warning them how late we might be. TB said he wanted a real inquiry into how we had managed to get into a situation where we spent half an hour sitting on a fucking plane while the president was in Washington waiting for us. Meanwhile Jonathan sent Meyer off the deep end when he had told him that the White House had said the meeting was one plus three, and TB wanted Jonathan, David Manning and me. Meyer threw an absolute tantrum, said he would be a laughing stock in Washington, threatened to resign on the spot. Jonathan did his usual

[1] Blair read a passage from *The Bridge of San Luis Rey*, a 1927 novel by American author Thornton Wilder. Prefacing the reading, Blair said 'We wanted to be here today, to offer our support and sympathy to the families of the lost ones. Many are British. Amid the enormity of what has happened to America, nobody will forget that this was the worst terrorist attack on British citizens in my country's history.'

unflappable bit, just let him let off steam and eventually it was resolved by David M asking Condi if she could slip in an extra place. It was all a bit silly and as TB said, leaders couldn't give two tosses which officials from the other side were there, but it made sense to him to have the three people he would be working most closely with not just here but everywhere.

When we landed, we headed straight to the White House to be met by GWB, Powell, Condi and Dan Fried [senior director for European and Eurasian affairs, National Security Council]. We were taken upstairs to one of the bigger rooms and TB went over to the corner with Bush and they clearly embarked straight away on a very tough conversation. He said later it had started fine, GWB saying how dreadful the events had been but now something good had to come out of it. The focus was OBL and the Taliban and tonight when he spoke to Congress he was going to deliver the ultimatum. But he also talked about how they could go after Saddam's [Saddam Hussein, President of Iraq] oilfields. TB emphasised the need for a measured response. Jonathan said later it was funny how [Margaret] Thatcher had gone to see Bush Senior to say 'This is no time to wobble' while TB was visiting Bush Junior – 'This IS a time to wobble.'

We went through for the dinner, scallops, veal, salad, Bush and TB doing most of the talking. Powell, Condi, Fried, Jonathan, DM and me, with Meyer stuck on the end desperately taking notes. I couldn't work out if he was embarrassed or not by his tantrum. Bush was pretty much directing the conversation, said he was grateful for our support, said Britain was a true friend and we were going to win. He said anyone could join the coalition provided they understood the doctrine – that we were going after terrorists and all who harbour them. Obviously the wider the coalition the better, but they were going to do this anyway. When the scallops arrived, there was a thin ring of pastry on top which he picked up and said 'God dang, what on earth is that?' The waiter said it was a scallop. He said to him it looks like a halo and you are the angel. I think he meant the waiter. It was a bit alarming how loudly they all laughed, including Powell, at his jokes, like when he said he wouldn't do questions at the door-step because he had his speech later and he was never allowed to say more than one thing a day. I sensed sometimes he was taking the Mickey out of himself, other times out of his team.

When he chose to be serious, he was fine. He said it was interesting Putin himself made sure the Russians didn't react last week, a clear sign the Cold War was over. Both he and Powell were really worried about Pakistan and wanted TB's take on how best to help. When we were talking about Uzbekistan, he said some of their people were 'throat cutters extraordinaire' then said don't write that down, then said if it ever came out he would say it was Powell, and they all started laughing again. He said they were going to go for the Taliban after the ultimatum, said the country was run by a bunch of nuts and we had to get a new government in there. He said he had really beaten up on Sharon who was clearly trying to use this to go after Arafat. 'I said Arafat is not Bin Laden and you do nothing.' Putin wanted to use it to go after Chechnya even harder. He said they feared Hollywood was the next target because it was high-profile, Jewish and decadent. They also had intelligence they would go for Air Force One [presidential plane]. He talked us through a fairly graphic account of what happened, how he was told of the first attack at the meeting at the school and he thought it was an accident at first, then how Andy Card [White House chief of staff] whispered to him about the second attack and said to him 'America is under attack, sir,' and he said he knew there and then this might be the biggest challenge he ever faced. We agreed the need for written shared objectives and a big public information campaign stressing the long haul.

He told the story of one day when he was playing volleyball and his dad came in and said they had got [Manuel] Noriega [dictator overthrown following US invasion of Panama] and it was 'like VE Day' and the truth was it had never just been about Noriega. On Iraq, he said there was no point denying there were differences in the administration. TB said it was easy to sense that every time the subject came up. Reading between the lines, I sensed Bush was with the doves but he enjoyed teasing Powell. I think the mood might have been different if Cheney and Rumsfeld had been there.

TB talked about the need to be sure of his ground, that we needed public opinion with us the whole time. Bush said yes, but when I am speaking tough I'm speaking to Middle America, most of whom have never heard of Bin Laden, they just know someone attacked their country and killed their fellow citizens, and they say hey, Mister President, go get someone and why ain't you done it the day before yesterday? He was in some ways much more impressive than the image, and very straightforward and self-deprecating, which is always a good trait in a leader, but the cumulative effect of the jokes, the asides and the trivial points left you feeling a bit uneasy by the end. It was the cowboy bit. He did, however, as he had over Putin when we first met, show signs of adaptability and intelligence. When TB said he had spoken to [Mohammed] Khatami [President of Iran] on the plane, Bush laughed out loud, assumed it was a joke. But when

TB said he was sending Jack S to Iran on Monday, Bush suddenly got serious, discussed Iran in some detail and then set out the kind of message he would like Jack to deliver. TB was making a point of praising Powell. He was going to be key in keeping strategy on the right track. It was still hard to work out who was calling the shots.

Bush was also graphic on the sophistication of the attacks and the technical ability of the pilot who hit the Pentagon. He seemed to have a certain admiration for the fanatic. Said the timing and the execution were sophisticated, brilliant. He said there are Muslims so dedicated they are prepared to drink to pretend to people around them they are not Muslims. They did a brief doorstep, TB fielding most of the questions and then he and GWB went up to the Bush flat before heading out to Congress. Bush and TB travelled together in the presidential limo. Jonathan, DM, Meyer and I were taken up to the First Lady's box, with the press gallery to our right, the Congress down below. TB came in with Laura, [Rudolph] Giuliani [mayor of New York], [George] Pataki [governor of New York] and the guy who was going to be the new homeland security minister [governor of Pennsylvania, Tom Ridge]. It was all a bit Politburo, standing ovations constantly interrupting the speech, rapturous applause for good lines, off the radar if they were really good. Because TB was next to Laura, he had to get up every single time that she did, which was every time anybody else did. Anji was watching me from the other side of the gallery and said I looked like I had swallowed a lemon. It was grim. Poodle-ology gone mad. But it was an excellent speech for all that, very well crafted. The story was ultimatum and telling the US troops to be ready. We met up with Bush afterwards, and he gave TB an enormous bear hug. This was getting worse. He was very warm to me as well but I couldn't wait to get out. Things hadn't been made easier by a couple of dreadful conversations with Fiona who said she could see Kosovo coming all over again, and I'd never be there. TB was drained by the whole thing. He kipped a bit on the drive out to the plane. We had a bit of debrief and TB said I had to seize the opportunity to co-ordinate strategy. It was now 4am UK time and everyone was shagged out. I slept most of the way back.

Friday, September 21

TB liked the note I had given to Karen Hughes and wanted me to get going on it. C wanted a copy, saying there was all manner of stuff they could do with us. We landed in Brussels and drove to [UK ambassador to the EU Sir Nigel] Sheinwald's residence. Stryker McGuire called from *Newsweek* and said there was a buzz going round that someone had overheard one of our people saying it was all a bit of a disaster, Bush was really alarming and planning to do far more than we wanted. I just about persuaded him it wouldn't have been any of the key people. But I agreed with Godric I should probably do a briefing, and we also pushed the line about changing UK law on terrorism. I was trying to pull them back from the sense of imminent military action. I went for a run and then back from TB's TV interviews where he was very good on the empathy and some of the personal stories from New York.

The summit [European Council emergency meeting on terrorism] was straightforward enough, and the text OK. TB wanted me to work on the US press to get them to see it as significant. Jack arrived and agreed to do the press conference rather than TB, who, thank God, wanted to leave early. I got home about midnight. Chris Patten [former Conservative Cabinet minister, now a European commissioner] hitched a lift back with us and said he was really worried about the Tories now but resisted my blandishments about defecting. The trip had gone well. TB was getting an amazing press at the moment. GWB had also turned things around with his speech which most of our media thought was very powerful, and some printed the whole thing in full.

Saturday, September 22

We were really just in military build-up mode now, plus I was keen to get coverage in the mainstream media for what we were trying to do to reach Muslims at home and abroad. TB called from Chequers and clearly thought now we should probably go to Pakistan. We set off for Norwich vs Burnley and met Charles Clarke and family for lunch. Charles felt that our politics were fine and TB was getting real strength out of this. He felt Clare should have been sacked years ago, that he never saw why Neil [Kinnock, former Labour leader] tolerated her and the same went for TB. Almost two weeks on now, the media was still totally dominated by the attacks, particularly now the anti-terror laws and military build-up. I did a conference call for the ministers on programmes tomorrow stressing that we praise Pakistan and talk up OBL as being un-Islamic. We lost 2–1. Generally, I felt the mood was pretty good considering. Certainly no grief and if anything a sense that TB had done well. The Sundays arrived late, millions of words of fuck all.

Sunday, September 23

TB called before a round of calls with Kofi [Annan], [Jean] Chrétien [Canadian Prime Minister], [Atal Bihari] Vajpayee [Indian Prime

Minister]. We briefed up TB's meeting with the chairs of select committees tomorrow, Home Affairs, Defence, Foreign Affairs, International Development. We needed to show we were building a domestic coalition as carefully as the international coalition. TB was sure now he needed to go overseas again but both of us were worried we were losing sight of the domestic agenda. Philip [Gould, pollster, strategist and adviser to TB] did a good note on the conference speech. We had dinner with the Goulds, Tessa [Jowell], David [Mills, Jowell's husband] and Jessie [Mills, their daughter]. David and Jessie were both very heavily against military action. Jessie was very anti-American, and said most young people were.

Monday, September 24
At the intelligence meeting, John Scarlett presented more evidence of OBL's involvement. But they were still no clearer on exact current whereabouts. He went through what they knew of the kind of security operation that existed around Bin Laden, which meant he basically never stayed in the same place twice, and apart from a few who were with him the whole time, the others would rotate. The intelligence picture was very patchy and I had a lot of doubts about whether we could get to the stage where any of this was publishable. The feeling was military action next week rather than this. Boyce said the US were realising they did not have the targets they thought they might have. TB was interested in what more we could do for Pakistan. Lander briefed on the people who had been arrested, also on the intelligence that the UK could be the next threat, up to and including anthrax.

TB and I had a long chat later re GB. TB had asked him what he thought of what was happening, and got the monosyllabic treatment. Eventually he said 'How am I supposed to know what to think? I don't know what is going on.' TB said there was not a word of support, or a hint of understanding of how tough this was. He even got back to the point of demanding a date for TB's departure, at which point TB snapped, said he was fed up of the way he spoke to him, the way he treated him. 'You say I have a choice about when to go. It's you that has a choice, about whether you work with me or against me, and get it into your head that if you work against me, you'll get no help from me.' He said GB was also urging him to cut loose the IRA from the peace process, which was ridiculous. I sometimes wondered whether he wouldn't actually be a total disaster as prime minister and whether in fact we weren't duty-bound to ensure it didn't happen. John Rentoul had a very good line on the 'psychologically flawed relationship' and it wasn't far wrong.[1] The main issue to be resolved today was the recall of Parliament, and what to do about party conference. TB wanted it all kept under review. He was worried about the meeting with the Foreign Affairs, Defence and Intelligence select committees but in the end it went extremely well.

TB went through four separate areas – diplomatic, action being taken, evidence re the attacks, implications for domestic law. He said we were sure the Taliban knew something was happening. He made clear military action would follow if they do not comply in yielding up OBL. He went over some of the long-term issues, money laundering, shutting down the camps, the trade in WMD capability, including the involvement of what he called responsible business people. He said a lot of people had expected the US to go straight in but they didn't. They want to get it right. Even the Tories were effusive in their praise for his handling. Questions were intelligent and sensible and as an exercise it was definitely worth doing. Chris Mullin [Labour MP, chair of the Home Affairs select committee] said afterwards he had found it extremely useful. TB was on good form and they sensed he was in charge and in control of all the arguments. On conference, we agreed it would be difficult to do normal traditional conference-type announcements but we should not imagine the whole flavour had to be foreign affairs.

TB had a meeting with IDS, who did a very supportive doorstep. TB felt he was a reasonably nice guy but very right wing, e.g. already trying to link OBL to Iraq. I went home for a run with Rory [AC's elder son] then back for TB's dinner with Blunkett, Milburn, Estelle [Morris, Education Secretary], Steve Byers, Cherie and Sally [Morgan, political secretary]. Both Alan and Estelle felt they didn't have the money to deliver and needed to press for more, that the tax credits agenda was doing them in. They both seemed demoralised. They also feared that even if we met the targets, people would not see it as a transformation of public services. Blunkett had a right old rant at the Civil Service.

Tuesday, September 25

Jack Straw was involved in a diplomatic row with Israel as he arrived in Iran because he talked about Palestine in an article for an Iranian

---

[1] Rentoul, author of *Tony Blair: Prime Minister*, wrote in the *Independent* that while Blair was successful and feted abroad 'at home his style is cramped by his psychologically flawed relationship with Gordon Brown'.

newspaper. TB said the FCO sometimes lacked subtlety. Sharon cancelled his meeting with Jack and it took a call with TB to get it back in his diary. We needed TB up today so I spent much of the day putting together a script in three parts: 1. Taliban are our enemy as diplomatic effort intensifies; 2. we are addressing the humanitarian crisis, and 3. we will report on any change to domestic law within two weeks. We announced the recall of Parliament.

At my morning meeting, I asked who was the minister responsible for the civil contingencies situation and was told Chris Leslie [junior minister]. Lovely bloke, but the public would be shocked, I reckoned, that it wasn't a big hitter. I spoke to JP after speaking to TB and we agreed Blunkett should lead on the issue. JP came to see me later, concerned he had not been visible, but there was going to be plenty of deputising work to be done, for example CHOGM [Commonwealth Heads of Government Meeting] if TB didn't go. TB was talking to Sharon, [Syrian President Bashar al-] Assad and later giving a polite bollocking to Jack. He then spoke to [Junichiro] Koizumi [Japanese Prime Minister] before he did a doorstep with the main political editors out on the terrace overlooking the garden. He was on form, strong on the Taliban and good on the humanitarian too. I did a background briefing for the broadcasters. We were having to chop and change his diary the whole time.

Wednesday, September 26

Jack called from Israel, convinced that we were briefing against him and that the idea of Number 10 charging in to rescue ministers was bad for everyone. I think I managed to assure him that we weren't, and he accepted there had been a fuck-up but wanted me to make it more clear that Sharon called TB, not the other way round, and that there had been no question of him having to apologise. Jack and I usually managed to straighten things. TB had done a draft outline for conference and we were now into pre-speech mode, what was the argument, what was the idea, what was the narrative. I really liked the power of community as a force for change at home and abroad. I was getting more alarmed about the lack of civil contingencies planning.

I had a meeting with heads of information [Civil Service communications chiefs], did my usual spiel about the need for co-ordination, did a Q&A, but it was pretty clear we were going to need to strengthen things again. The MoD and the FCO were basically OK, though the FCO had a real problem with gabbiness, everyone thinking they needed to get their own point across to the press. Within two hours, the *Guardian* had been briefed on the meeting and what I had said to them. TB spoke to Major and Thatcher, thought there may be a role for Major in this. He said Thatcher had totally gone off on one, said 'the English-speaking peoples' would have to win this despite the weakness of the continental mainland. 'We will win this like you and I defeated socialism, she said.' TB replied he would have to give her exclusive credit for that.

Thursday, September 27

Sixteen days on, after all the bellicose talk, there was still no sign of US action. Bush was leading the news with talk of tougher airline security. Our main story was going to be TB's meeting with Muslim leaders. The press had been complaining about lack of access and with Philip's note saying that TB was being seen by the public as 'a rock', and calling for him to be more not less visible, we agreed that he should do a press conference. He was worrying about Clare. I was trying to get her to do something publicly on the humanitarian front, possibly on the lines of building a humanitarian coalition alongside the military coalition. I worked on TB's script – not a war on Islam, humanitarian coalition, domestic work goes on. There was some polling showing quite a dip in economic optimism. Julian [Braithwaite, press officer] was due off next week on a management course which was bad news because he was generating some terrific stuff on the anti-OBL front.

TB's meeting with the Muslim leaders went pretty well and his message was clear at the press conference. Then a somewhat alarming meeting with the defence chiefs and the spooks. It was pretty clear the US remained undecided, could not find that many good targets, and didn't have the bases in the region. Hoon said there was a lack of clarity which made it difficult to plan. TB was getting a bit alarmed that the Yanks didn't seem to get why they needed better co-ordination. TB said we needed joint planning cells, not just with the military, but the political and the propaganda, and we needed something similar with Europeans. Equally, the humanitarian effort was going to have to be co-ordinated internationally. TB said the humanitarian operation was every bit as important as the military. Boyce said the only viable bases will have to be in a contiguous country. Iran is a no-no, the Americans won't go near Pakistan. The 'Stans were being difficult, messing us around. Condi Rice was sure the Russians were playing games. Boyce warned that the Taliban were brutal if they got their hands on enemy forces, capable of skinning them alive. It's called a hair-shirt policy. General [Anthony] Pigott [Deputy Chief of the Defence Staff (Commitments)] did a really interesting presentation setting out the concept of military action working at various levels, including the psychological and the need to win hearts and minds, but again there was no sense of the Americans getting how to do that in a joined-up way.

TB felt that Bush could afford to wait if he gave a sense of forward strategy but it was lacking at the moment. We went straight from that to Cabinet which was really TB, Jack, Clare, Geoff and DB briefing them. TB on the overall strategy, Jack on the Middle East peace process, Blunkett on civil contingencies and race relations, in which he expressed his anger at the BBC constantly giving lunatics a platform, and Clare on the humanitarian effort, and Geoff giving a military update. Then GB doing a big number on the economy, including, as he had already briefed to the press, that the reserve was pretty much gone and they would have to stick to their spending plans. Foot and mouth had already cost us £2 billion extra. He rattled through some bad figures from Europe and America, said we were better protected than most economically but we still had to bear down on spending. TB's view, expressed on the basis of what they briefed, was that it was a silly message because it would add to public concern and lack of confidence.

I grabbed Clare as she left and said we needed her out motoring on the humanitarian effort. Later she announced more money for Pakistan. Just as GB was demanding a date for TB's departure, so Fiona was asking me for a date too. She feared we were heading for another period of international crisis when I would be anywhere but home. She had become really bitter and angry about TB, and I wondered if that wasn't just an easy way of making it not about me.

Friday, September 28
Went in to work on the conference speech, worked up the script for the Sundays to keep the focus on the nature of the Taliban. There was a growing sense of drift, that the US didn't really know what to do. Peter Hyman and I went home to work on the speech.

Saturday, September 29
TB spoke to Bush and felt he was still unclear on his own strategy. The media here and there was pretty much geared up, with wall-to-wall war build-up. TB was working on the speech at Chequers and felt comfortable with the draft so far. I took Rory to Spurs vs Man U who came from behind to win 5–3.

Sunday, September 30

Up at 6 and off at 7 to Chequers with Peter H. We arrived to the sight of TB still not dressed and fretting about difficult questions of domestic terror and what more we could do to deal with those successfully abusing our laws here. Peter and I had worked up a new ending for the conference speech and TB was by and large perfectly happy with what he had done. Peter was trying very hard to get him to drop stuff that he felt was basically just whacking the party but TB was adamant there had to be a sense of him challenging the party. We set off for *Frost* and in the car went through the lines on extradition, asylum etc. Chris Patten was there reviewing the papers.

TB had his frightened-rabbit look up to the last minute but the interview went fine even if he got a bit jargonistic, e.g. talking about 'UBL' (OBL). We stayed on for breakfast and TB gave Patten and Edward Llewellyn, his right-hand man, a bit of advice about what to do with the Tory Party, basically stay in there and make them come to their senses. He thought Patten was absolutely top drawer, and if we had a few like him, we would be in much better shape. Back at Chequers, he, Peter H and I went through the speech line by line. At one point he admitted that part of the purpose of constantly challenging the party was to remind the public that he was not a traditional Labour leader, and that was in many ways his main selling point. He wanted a more forward section on the euro, including the prospect of it happening in this parliament. He had done a good section about the notion of solidarity as an international doctrine. The speech was a lot better for the fact that we didn't feel the need to touch every policy base going. Later we left for Brighton.

Monday, October 1

Most of the day stuck in the hotel, working on the speech, and also on a briefing script which I wanted to push out as interdependence/power of community. We had fallen back on the speech and having spent the weekend thinking we wouldn't have the usual last-minute bollocks, that's exactly what we did. I got Hilary [Coffman, special adviser] to do the briefing and by the time the press had finished with it, it was taken as a declaration of war. The main arguments we were still having were just how close to be to the US, and how to frame the public services section. TB wanted to hit the reform message, whereas I was arguing for a greater focus on the values underpinning the reform. It was very much his speech though, much more than any other conference speech we had done. He was comfortable in the argument and confident about the way he was putting it. Most of

September '01: TB's frightened-rabbit look

the speech team went over for [the speech by] GB. I carried on working and had it on in the background. It would be seen as a pretty good and wide-ranging domestic speech and because he allied himself to the main domestic ministers, it was likely he would get written up as the domestic PM to TB's foreign affairs PM.

We had the usual toing and froing, writing and rewriting, but TB only wanted polishing and honing from us now. It was his speech, and it was pretty well done. I had a semi-altercation with JP just before midnight when he popped in. Cherie and Sally were also there and I made a crack about GB being the domestic PM and JP snapped that even in these circles, we shouldn't be slagging him off. It was a bit much on one level, as he and I had had a session in the afternoon where he had been raging about him every bit as much as I did, but he had a point. He was worried that the tensions and the frustrations both between the principals and their teams meant that the divisions just became a given. [Gerhard] Schroeder was the main international speaker and got terrific applause for his reference to Old Labour. He went down pretty well and I think enjoyed coming over.

TB and Bush agreed TB should go to see Putin to try to secure bases and then to Pakistan to try to get a proper fix on Musharraf. It was a perfectly friendly conversation with the usual joshing and laughter amid the heavy stuff, but TB admitted he was worried they didn't seem to have a grip on things. Schroeder had felt Putin would help if we really pushed and if there was a gain in it for him. The pre-speech briefing led ITN ahead of GB which was likely to have pissed him off big time. The big message of the speech was coming together fine, international solidarity, the power of community at home. I didn't leave the hotel all day. We got to bed just after 2, which was early by comparison with most of these conference speeches.

Tuesday, October 2

TB was up at 6 and I went in to find him with the usual mass of paper all over the place, but he seemed OK with things. He had reordered things, cut down a lot of the middle section on domestic policy. There were still one or two bits that read too much like they had been done by committee, which we fixed. It was a very New Labour speech, and authentic for his voice. The overnight briefing had gone very big on the idea we were declaring war on the Taliban. It was leading the news not just in the UK but in the States too, so much so that as we were going through the autocue rehearsal at 12, Jonathan came in to tell us that David Manning had read the words on Afghanistan to the White House, who were worried about what we were saying about the nature of military action. They felt it was too forward, too clear re what we intended to hit, with the reference to camps and military installations. But that was the section we had briefed which would make it hard to pull back even if we wanted to. We toned it down a little and got it just about in the right place. TB asked Jonathan and I to go through to his room and go over the final version with the words on Afghanistan. He was getting a bit exasperated with it all, said this was like Kosovo all over again. 'What on earth do they think we are going to hit? They just aren't clear about what they want to do.' I think Hilary [Coffman] was feeling a bit stressed out at the thought that a briefing I had written and she had read out to a few journalists was now leading the news here and in different parts of the world, so much so that we had a sudden blitz of TV channels in the US and elsewhere wanting to take the speech live.

It was inevitable that foreign policy would get the main coverage but it was a strong domestic speech too. We also had extensive discussion about whether we should show the euro section to GB. It was a sign of how bad things were at the moment. The basic view was GB would take it, demand a change, then brief that he had done so to show that he could, so in the end we agreed simply to send the text through once the speech was pretty much done. As ever, his people were assuming a great plan had been unleashed to draw attention away from his speech. In reality, the briefing we did was pretty minimalist. TB had not spoken to him, so far as I knew, since we got to Brighton, which was ludicrous when I thought of the issues he was addressing.

When it came to the delivery, he got the tempo right, a bit slower and more measured, not worrying too much about reaching the heights. [BBC political editor] Andrew Marr's reaction was that it was as though he had levitated above the party, and indeed just before I left the hotel, I had said to him I got the sense that this year he needed us less, and he needed his colleagues less. The clap lines were good, the mood was good, nobody seemed to get overly alarmed at the public services section and all in all, it went down fine. The party loved the stuff on Palestine, Africa, the environment and the central idea of community driving through the whole policy agenda was strong. The euro was the only bit I felt tricky at the briefing afterwards. We left not long after to get the train back. TB called later, worried about the advice we were getting on security re the trip to Pakistan. But he was pretty keen to go, and very keen to go to Russia. The speech was getting huge play everywhere, including one headline in the States that it was TB's 'pitch for world leadership'. We would have to watch it.

Wednesday, October 3

Extraordinary press for TB's speech, though some found it a bit preachy and there was a real danger of overreach. We had a real problem with the Indians over the planned visit to Pakistan. Vajpayee was on the phone, totally adamant that if TB went to Pakistan without also visiting India, it would be a real disaster for him. He was normally so quiet and soft-spoken but there was both panic and a bit of anger in his voice. TB said that having listened to him, there was no way we could do one without the other. It was not impossible that if OBL successfully launched another hit then the Indians could launch a strike at Pakistan. The security committee, which advised on TB's own safety, had met yesterday and basically would prefer that he didn't go to Pakistan, but if he did, they wanted us to use the [Royal Air Force] VC10.

We had endless coming and going on that, including at one point Cherie coming to see me, quivering with rage, bottom lip trembling, telling me I was mad to allow it and 'Do you want to be a martyr or what?' She said it was the most stupid visit there had ever been and I should be telling him I'm not going. I pointed out that we had all seen the advice, but that he had decided to go, that therefore I should probably go too, and that if we all went down, I didn't think it would be me qualifying for martyrdom. Fiona later discovered TB and CB had had another row about Anji, which maybe explained why she was so angry. At 2.40, TB saw Geoff H and CDS. There was an outside chance the Americans might go in the next twenty-four hours because of intelligence on OBL's whereabouts.

At 4pm, the top defence and intelligence people went through what the US were asking for from us on the military side and TB gave his go-ahead. C, Scarlett and Jack set out the thinking about India/Pakistan. Jack felt we had to go for Musharraf over the help given to terrorists in Kashmir. Scarlett felt that any heavy pressure at the moment on Kashmir was a deal breaker and if our aim was to keep Musharraf on board, we should avoid it. Lander said that the Indians and Pakistanis effectively fought a proxy war over Kashmir and if you removed the proxy, there was a danger they would fight a real war with nuclear weapons. The VC10 plan meant that we had to cut down on the number of journalists we could take which led to lots of rows, all a bit pathetic. The VC10 was a bit of a nightmare because it was so old [first flown in 1962] and slow. I wrote to all media outlets pointing out that there could be no speculation as to where we were going.

Thursday, October 4

Fiona was demanding a date again, and it was obvious there was going to be an awful lot of travelling. TB and I had worked on his Commons statement late but the US intelligence agencies had taken out four of the seven pieces of information we had hoped to put in as evidence. TB was still keen to do it. We went through the statement one more time. The story was the assertion that it was definitely Bin Laden and al-Qaeda.[1]

I had running battles through the day with the BBC over them constantly saying where we were going in Pakistan. I travelled out to the airport with TB. He was very up for the visit. He had just briefed JP who told him he was really taken aback by my attitude to GB at Brighton. TB said I had to watch what I said, which was fair enough. TB had filled JP in on all the diplomatic manoeuvring and the military planning, with the strikes planned for Saturday. We went over what we needed from Putin. Something strong on OBL's involvement would be a start. TB was looking at it also from the point of view of developing a deeper relationship.

TB said he feared the Indian leg of the trip most. We were warned that the point of maximum vulnerability on the plane was on arrival and departure from Pakistan. C joined us on the plane. He would be seeing his opposite number in Russia later, as well as [Russian defence minister Sergei] Ivanov. I picked his and David Manning's brains on Kashmir. I had read up some of the disasters on previous visits. The problem was that both sides regularly just briefed that we shifted our line even if we didn't. The general feeling on the evidence document was that it was OK but there was no smoking gun. Both IDS and [Liberal Democrat leader Charles] Kennedy said they were convinced though.

On arrival, Rod Lyne [UK ambassador to Russia] came on the plane to brief us, then off to the residence and a brief meeting on Putin. TB

---

[1] Blair told the House of Commons 'Our findings have been shared and co-ordinated with those of our allies, and are clear. They are: first, it was Osama Bin Laden and al-Qaeda, the terrorist network which he heads, that planned and carried out the atrocities on September 11; second, that Osama Bin Laden and al-Qaeda were able to commit these atrocities because of their close alliance with the Taliban regime in Afghanistan which allows them to operate with impunity in pursuing their terrorist activity.'

was beginning to wonder whether the conference speech hadn't put him too far out in front. I said I feared it did and he was going to have to do this stuff anyway. We set off for the Kremlin. The meeting was largely one-on-one, plus interpreters, and then David Manning in for a bit before Tom Kelly [AC's deputy], Magi [Cleaver, press officer] and I were taken to meet him. Putin spent a lot of the time talking about how TB might go tomorrow to Tajikistan to persuade them to let us use their bases. The problem was the US would be opposed because it would mean the Russians effectively controlling our bases.

The joint press conference was OK if a bit dull but TB warmed up towards the end. Putin was very warm about TB, though his interpreter was poor and the press couldn't really hear him and when they did couldn't really understand him. Tony Bishop [interpreter], who had done them all right back to Stalin, was a different class by comparison. TB then set off for Putin's dacha while I went for a run with Rod before dinner. TB got back at 1am, Russian time. He said they had a good time, if a bit surreal at times. They played some form of Russian snooker and he said he won. Bush had called halfway through and spoken to them both. TB reckoned they were deadly serious about helping but felt that the US didn't really want them closely involved.

Friday, October 5

Very little sleep. I had breakfast with Rod who was not just very good at his job but very human with it and willing to engage on different levels according to different needs. TB was up late and we set off immediately for the airport. He said that Putin's problem was that he felt he was pushing out the boat but the Yanks were not responding and it made life difficult for him. On the flight to Islamabad, he said he was glad to have made the initial investment in Putin and felt they got on well. He was trying to work out what outcomes we wanted from Pakistan. I felt there was a danger now that the British public started to ask what is this all about, and why is he spending all his time on the needs of other countries not our own?

I really felt for David Manning on the flight out. He had pages and pages of notes to do on the Putin meeting, plus trying to debrief TB, who was always notoriously difficult to debrief because he would be straight on to focusing on the next thing. TB briefed the press on the plane, talking about the trap we were laying around the Taliban. TB's words in Pakistan were going to be important and we took a bit of time to work on that. I talked to C about what might follow any military attack. He believed there would almost certainly be some kind of al-Qaeda retaliation, possibly London, more likely a lesser-known European city. We flew over Everest at one point. The arrival was covered live with TB, straight into the cars and off to Musharraf's palace. They seemed to have shut down pretty much every road and the crowds were also kept well away. It was about as big a security operation as we'd had. They started off one-on-one.

TB reckoned him [Musharraf] to be a very tough character. I think their basic hope was that we wipe out the Taliban leadership, felt that if we did the whole show would crumble. They seemed pretty keen to get OBL, but you could never be absolutely sure who was saying what for what reason. He told TB we shouldn't underestimate how unpopular the Americans are here. He said Mullah Omar was impossible to talk to because he is a mystic, constantly talking about the afterlife. TB's impression was that he was determined to hold firm but it would get very difficult once military action started and he would need a lot of hand holding. Guthrie had done a good job laying the ground for the visit. He thought it sensible not to come to India with us because he was keen to be seen as Pakistan's man within the equation. It was amusing to watch him operate. He had been placed on the seating plan next to TB. When I suggested he might not want to be spotted, which he clearly would be as the cameras were due in, he was clearly not keen to move. And then when he and I were chatting and I asked him why he wasn't coming to Delhi, he said, just loud enough for them to hear, 'I think it's very important that the Pakistanis know I'm basically their man.'

There was something of an irony in Musharraf saying military takeovers and military dictatorships were not accepted in the world.[1] He talked over his road map for the introduction of democracy. TB did lots of warm words, made clear how important Pakistan was to this situation. We then got ready for a joint doorstep with a joint lectern which was a bit weird. I said to Musharraf he would be asked about the evidence we had presented and whether he accepted it. When he came over as a bit equivocal TB immediately stepped in at the lectern and said he strongly welcomed what Musharraf said.

At dinner I was between two five-star generals who spent most of the time listing atrocities for which they held the Indians responsible, killing their own people and trying to blame 'freedom fighters'. They were pretty convinced that one day there would be a nuclear war because India, despite its vast population and despite being seven

[1] Musharraf, as a general, had led a military coup in 1999, deposing elected prime minister Nawaz Sharif.

times bigger, was unstable and determined to take them out. When the time came to leave, the livelier of the two generals asked me to remind the Indians 'It takes us eight seconds to get the missiles over,' then flashed a huge toothy grin. We arranged it so that we had an early dinner there and then flew to Delhi but I sensed they were holding us back as long as possible. The service was unusually slow, especially after the starters, and I could sense that they were sensing that we were getting a bit impatient, and wanting to move on. We started to chivvy TB a bit, and he did his 'Oh, is it time to go, I'm having such an interesting time' look, which they took as the chance to start up a whole new strand of conversation.

As we took off, there was a lot of black humour flowing around about the prospect of us being downed by a stinger [anti-aircraft missile]. I think all of us, other than the experts, had been a bit taken aback at just how much Kashmir defined their relations and just how deep the mutual hatred and obsession was. We arrived in Delhi and TB, one of the cops and I got in with the ambassador [High Commissioner Sir Rob Young] and drove into town. TB motioned to the ambassador, asking if the car was bugged. He gave a kind of non-committal no. I was given my own valet, Sunil, who just would not leave me alone. He followed me to the gym and I literally had to tell him to disappear. He was waiting at my door when I got back.

TB, Anji and I had a chat over a drink but it was odd. I didn't feel as much part of things as I was, how often I was thinking and asking myself whether I really wanted to be there, or whether I was only there because he wanted me to be, and because I had grown used to it. As ever, we ended up talking about GB, TB saying he was biding his time, knowing that in politics, nobody walked on water forever. C and I had a great laugh about the name of the Indian security service – namely RAW [Research and Analysis Wing]. I said I intended to rename R&I [Number 10 Research and Information Unit] and we would have RAW Domestic, RAW International, and the really secret stuff would be handled by a tiny elite team called RAW Hide. He was a bit like Guthrie in the way he had got himself close to TB and used that to generate support at the top for the service as a whole. He was astutely political in his grasp of issues and very good at sorting the point that TB would most likely want to zone in on.

Saturday, October 6

Sunil was driving me bananas. Everywhere I went, he was there. I was beginning to wonder whether he had been put there either by the spooks or a paper. I told him at one point I was a tea-aholic, and he kept making me tea after tea and bringing it in. When I came back from the gym, by the time I got out of the shower, my running gear had been picked up and folded. We set off for the prime minister's residence, yet another purpose-built, well-equipped building, far better and more practical than Downing Street. Vajpayee was frail and his voice was weak, but in part because he had no fear of silence, there was a quiet force to him when he spoke. TB went through the mantra about military, diplomatic, humanitarian, and the need for restraint by India to build stability in the region. He said he had been very forceful with Musharraf over the attacks on the Kashmir Assembly.[1] The Indians were very steamed up and you couldn't help feeling that if a real refugee crisis absorbed Pakistan's forces, the Indians would go for them on the other front.

TB said that what had happened to the US had the same psychological effect as if we had lost Parliament or Buckingham Palace. It had touched every nerve. Vajpayee was pretty frank about what he thought of Pakistan and Musharraf and how he came to power, kept emphasising he on the other hand led a democracy, and TB said 'With humility, I think it's important to continue with restraint.' Jaswant Singh [foreign affairs minister] said it was not possible to separate the Taliban and OBL, they were totally interdependent. This was, as the general told me last night, a two-front war.

Singh did a lot of the talking. I sat next to him at the breakfast later and he was enormously charming. The joint press conference was in a beautiful garden setting which was home to all manner of exquisite brightly coloured birds flying around and singing. TB and Vajpayee were such different breeds of politician, TB all drive and words and desperate to get everything right, Vajpayee calm, something almost mystical about him.

We set off for the airport and, using the Kosovo statement we did in Berlin, I started work on a draft of a TB statement in the event of military action. TB was pretty anxious about the India–Pakistan situation. We were also still unclear when the US were going to strike. TB slept for a good bit on the way back and I had a chat with C who told me we were very loose on our mobiles during the Kosovo crisis. I chatted to Manning and enlisted his support in persuading the Americans, not least in his link to Condi and TB's to Bush, of the need to get far better media co-ordination in the coming days. TB

---

[1] On October 1, Pakistani terrorist group Jaish-e-Mohammed had killed thirty-eight people in a suicide and car bombing attack on the Jammu and Kashmir State Legislative Assembly in Srinagar.

October '01: Still unclear when the US will strike

had found the visit absolutely fascinating, said it was one thing to read all the briefs and listen to all the experts but you didn't have to be there for long to get a sense of just how dangerous and volatile it was. And it was clear too that we were able to exercise some influence in stopping them. They were adamant that, helped by Pakistan, OBL had successfully made Kashmir terrorism worse than ever.

They were coming up to local elections in India in which 160 million people would vote. C said to me he saw TB's strengths as many and varied but one of them was his ability to be nice to people whoever they were, however much was going on. We got back into Number 10 for TB's phone call with Bush which began with GWB saying we were definitely going to launch the strikes tomorrow, that he would get his speech over and Karen and I should discuss the various statements and timings. I faxed over the TB draft. TB briefed him on the last couple of days and laid it on thick about his worries re India and Pakistan and the importance of trying to calm it all down. He suggested to Bush he speak to Vajpayee.

Fiona was in a foul mood when I got home, said she assumed that I was going to be off fighting another war again. I had a laugh with the boys about Sunil. About the only time he left me alone was when we left and he had disappeared and despite him driving me crazy, I had been hoping to see him to give him a large tip for at least enlivening the visit.

Sunday, October 7

I was out playing football with Calum [AC's younger son] when TB called, really worried about Pickett's Lock[1] and what it said about Britain and our potential for sport. I agreed with him, but it was an odd thing to be obsessing about given what else he had on his mind. Karen Hughes called and said my note had really got them thinking about how to do the media in what was obviously going to be a cross-national media operation. I went in for Geoff Hoon's PINDAR [Ministry of Defence crisis management centre] meeting in the bunker. I chatted to CDS about exactly how to pitch our involvement. We had three Tomahawks let off and support staff not yet being used. I set out the timing of the Bush and TB statements. Then news came through that they were going early so we had to cobble together the final drafts taking in a few of Condi's changes, including them not wanting to say that action would be proportionate. I was up and down to the

---

[1] Abortive site of a National Athletics Stadium. Cost and inadequate transport links made the site, in North-East London, unviable.

flat to get the final changes in and signed off and then downstairs to do the statement to the media.

JP, Jack and Geoff were there to flank him and it was going to be important to get away from some of this presidential stuff that was surrounding him. He looked absolutely fine, but just minutes earlier, as Bush was starting his speech, TB was not even dressed, his hair was wet. He was pretty nervous about the whole thing, was sweating and later beating himself up over not having prepared properly for the statement. At least it suggested there was still humility in there. I was sure he had made the right decisions though but as ever, nobody could accurately predict exactly what would happen when the shooting started.

Monday, October 8

Several of the papers ran TB's words alongside GWB's and noted the similarity of language and message. The coverage was wall to wall of course. I was in early and the first meeting was with the intelligence and defence people. I was beginning to feel a bit sorry for Lander at the way TB asked him whether there was any sign of an attack on the UK, as though Lander was expected to know the answer in yes or no terms. He had a mischievous little face, a bit of a cross between Ian Hislop [editor of satirical magazine *Private Eye*] and Richard Stott [former tabloid editor turned irreverent *Sunday Mirror* columnist]. He said there were a large number of people 'who worry us', that sixty had been interviewed in the past three weeks, that the ones they were really worried about were under permanent surveillance. [Admiral] Boyce went over some of the thirty-two attacks launched in the immediate wave, and some of the planned targets tonight. These were likely to go on for three to five days in the first instance. Scarlett said all planes came back safely.

There was a pretty clear impression the operation had not been as effective as being hoped. [Sir John] Kerr said the Israelis were not being helpful. There were also real concerns about what reactions there might be against some of our [diplomatic] posts, especially in Indonesia. There were legal difficulties being raised re targeting some of the Afghan TV output. Both Harriet [Harman, Solicitor General] and the Attorney General [Lord Peter Goldsmith] had seemingly raised concerns. TB was clear post Kosovo that their media machine was a part of their military machine and a legitimate target. Afterwards, Richard W, Jonathan and I persuaded TB that there should be regular meetings of a War Cabinet – TB, JP, GB, JS, GH, Clare, RC, CDS and the main agencies. TB was reluctant at first, probably because of his

October '01: Air strikes 'not as effective as was hoped'

ongoing arguments with GB. RW said he was worried about the 'presidential' tag, and he was right, though his concerns – that his strictures were not always being followed – were maybe not the same as mine, though they were linked – namely that we needed a cadre of ministers bound in to the decision-making and able to go out and explain properly to MPs and public.

I got TB to agree to do Al Jazeera [Arabic news network] whose coverage was causing a lot of concern. What with that, Church leaders coming in, Cabinet and a statement in the House, there was plenty going on to brief the media and keep them busy. The Al Jazeera interview was difficult, as expected, and with a lot of focus on the Palestine question. It pretty much went to the heart of every question and managed to create the sense TB was on the defensive, though he did get over some of the key messages for the Arab world. In the pre-briefing, a couple of ultra-Arabists from the FCO had been urging him to use the interview to dump on Israel, or at least distance ourselves as much as possible. I spent a fair bit of time working on the statement for the House, in which he was able to announce the second wave had started. He did fine, though it was all a little bit flat.

Cabinet was largely just TB and the other ministers involved reporting to the rest of them. By and large they were supportive. TB went through the three different planks – military, diplomatic and humanitarian. The aim was to put a ring round the Taliban regime, undermine them militarily and politically, and meanwhile show this was about the regime not the people. He went through how we were working with the Northern Alliance, but stressed any future rule had to be broad-based. On the diplomatic front, we had a lot of allies wanting to join up in some way. But we had big problems in the Arab world and there was going to have to be a major propaganda effort to reach them. We cannot say often enough that 'This is not a war on Islam.' He said the strong message from the Church leaders, and from many Muslims, was that now we had started it, we should finish as quickly as possible. He also emphasised that we had continually to make the link to domestic policy – that this had implications for our fight against drugs and terrorism; that it was important to restoring confidence in the economy; the sooner we act, the more likely we will be to contain a refugee crisis. Geoff made clear we were able to study all of the targets because some of the planes came out of Diego Garcia [Indian Ocean military base].

Clare reported on the humanitarian situation, said even before all this Afghanistan was heading towards famine. Five million were going hungry, nothing like enough food was getting through and in six weeks the roads will be impassable. Air drops and leaflets were not enough. We must get back to convoys. She said the US were being 'more generous than usual', and money was less of a problem than logistics. GB, just back from the G7 meeting, said consumer spending was holding up, but recent company performance was not good. Tessa said the latest estimate had 120 British people killed on September 11. A lot of relatives and the process of identification and the return of remains was clearly difficult. I sent through a follow-up note to Karen Hughes on co-ordination. I saw GB re the PBR [Pre-Budget Report]. At TB's office meeting, he was just railing at the lack of progress on the domestic agenda and worrying that because he would be forced to focus on the international, departments would be taking their feet off the accelerators again.

Tuesday, October 9

I was getting into a much better rhythm with Karen Hughes. If anything, the need for proper co-ordination was going to be even greater than Kosovo because there were more and different communications challenges. For Kosovo, we had a bigger alliance, and we were fighting for Muslims. We now had a lot of anti-Americanism running around, despite Sept 11, and we had a particular problem with some of the Arab media and the way they were fuelling the idea of a war on Islam. It was going to be important to get the Americans not to think they were just talking to America the whole time. We got big play home and abroad for the Al Jazeera interview, and we were going to need to do a lot more with the Arab media. TB was seeing [Gerry] Adams and [Martin] McGuinness [leading Sinn Fein politicians in Northern Ireland] at 8 and we had to choreograph the arrivals to avoid any crossover with the War Cabinet – not what we needed right now.

At the morning meeting, there were two immediate problems to address – the first was that the BBC were reporting TB was going to Oman. They just would not listen to our concerns on this. And the second was the leak of a Jo Moore [special adviser to Stephen Byers] email from September 11 saying that it was a good time to 'bury bad news'. I didn't allow much discussion of it at the morning meeting. It was perfectly clear someone inside had leaked it and it was a classic Civil Service move on a special adviser. It was a stupid thing to say, and knowing Jo she would be mortified, but I didn't like the idea of her being hanged, drawn and quartered for it. I also knew it would unleash another avalanche of bollocks about spin, me, culture of blah.

I spoke to Byers and he asked if I thought she would have to go. I was worried it might end there. But after talking to TB, we agreed there should be a reprimand and an apology. TB felt Jo was basically a decent person, very committed and professional, and it was a bit much to destroy her career over one leaked email that she should never have sent. Tom [Kelly] came back from the eleven o'clock a bit taken aback by the ferocity over it. TB was clear that she had given us great service down the years, and it was not a hanging offence.

I did a conference call with her and Steve and we agreed there would be no budging from that line. My only question mark was whether she was really up to facing the shit that was coming her way. She sounded OK, and she had always struck me as pretty good under pressure, but who knows? I got SB to organise [Richard] Mottram [permanent secretary, Department of Transport, Local Government and the Regions (DTLR)] to do the official reprimand bit. I wrote to Greg Dyke [BBC director general] complaining about the BBC – Kate Adie [BBC chief press correspondent] – doing a number re TB and the forthcoming trip to Oman. The War Cabinet was OK. It was remarkable how quickly these extraordinary meetings became almost routine in their nature, TB wandering in with us lot, ministers chatting a bit, the spooks and defence guys sitting up straight and getting ready to do their stuff, Scarlett, C, Lander, CDS, all chipping in, very matter-of-fact and straightforward. Scarlett was meticulous in his presentation. It was again not exactly clear how successful the strikes had been. They almost got Mullah Omar. He was injured, might be dead.

Jack S and Clare both pressed Lander on what was happening re suspects here, and he was clear that though a lot of them were covered, there could be no guarantees, because a threat might well be coming from people we do not know about. They were both worried about Pakistani opinion in the UK really becoming inflamed. Blunkett really went off on one about the cops, e.g. John Stevens wanting to surround shopping centres with machine-gun-toting officers. He really let rip, and there were a few raised eyebrows, including TB's. David clearly didn't take much to the cops, made a point of saying the Security Service had been terrific, but there had to be better co-operation with the Special Branch and the police more generally. There was a lack of hard-headed clarity, and it was really annoying him, he said. The US was in the lead for attack but the UK and Israel were not far behind. The US were in no doubt there were a number of al-Qaeda 'unexpired events' still to be completed. TB said to Lander he should give us a shopping list of anything they felt would help. He didn't want them to hold back for fear that things would be politically difficult. He said give us a list of what you would want in an ideal world and we can decide what is politically possible. There was a discussion of the Saudi oilfields, what would happen to the oil price and the world economy if they went up under attack. Lander and C both said it was as well to be prepared for something pretty serious, up to and including WMD.

Ed Balls [special adviser to Gordon Brown] came to see me. He was worried re where TB was on the euro, said some of the recent noise about it was 'dangerous'. He felt TB was trying to set a political timetable for an economic union. I asked if GB was on a different track to TB. He said he didn't want to make the same mistake as the last lot made re the ERM. GB thought we had an agreement to shut down debate on the euro and couldn't understand why we had opened it again. I said it would help if they could discuss it without shouting at each other about every slight, real or imagined, going back years. Ed said we would get brownie points from the Hugo Youngs [*Guardian*] and the Phil Stephenses [*FT*] for opening it up again, but did we really think it was the right course to go down at this stage?

There was a review of security in the event of a major attack. Fiona and I were both in the red team that would be taken to the underground place with TB, but we agreed we should not be in there together, that one of us should be with the kids if at all possible. TB did the BBC World Service Pashto service, who were clearly thrilled to be asked. The interview was done by a young woman called Nijiba who afterwards told us some horrific stories re the kind of thing that went on inside Afghanistan. TB suggested I try to get her out on our airwaves too. I was determined that TB keep up a voice on the Arab and Muslim media.

We left for the airport at 6, and in the car TB asked me when I thought was the best time for Anji to leave. I felt soon. It just hadn't worked out as he had hoped for the second term. There was too much baggage in all the difficult relationships and the recent trip had shown that for all she brought to the table, Anji needed a clear role to be effective and it wasn't there at the moment. I felt he had been wrong to stop her leaving earlier when she had basically wanted to. He said how impressed he had been with David Manning. He was doing a superb job with Condi, and he was also such a nice guy to have around. TB was still worried that the Yanks were on a slightly different track, wanting to broaden this out. He was worried re the domestic agenda suffering with all of us focused elsewhere. The Jo Moore furore was really building and the hacks on the plane were trying to get us going.

We landed [in Geneva] and set off for the Intercontinental to meet Sheikh Zayed [al-Nahyan, President of the United Arab Emirates]. He was around eighty, surrounded by zillions of hangers-on, one or two of whom had a bit of a gangsterish feel to them. In the meeting, SZ said it was a battle of humanity and inhumanity, sanity and insanity. There was a TV screen in the background with pictures of a giant green parrot and some pretty girls. The parrot squawked regularly. After a while, one of the sheikh's flunkeys got up and motioned for David Manning, Anna [Wechsberg, private secretary, foreign affairs] and I to leave so that they were one-on-one. Christ knows what they would talk about. TB came out with a huge grin, and said they had resolved the problems of the world. They had brought an Abu Dhabi TV reporter with them, having promised him a TB interview and when I said nobody had mentioned it to me, they started to cut up a bit rough and unpleasant. One of them said, we are aware of your reputation but I should know the sheikh would take it as a personal slight if this didn't happen and there would be a diplomatic incident. Then another came in with a rather menacing smile and muttered something about whether the IRA really were quiet, and whether they were linked into Bin Laden and so on. In the end, partly because it allowed us to keep going with the Arab media strategy, we agreed. As it happened, it was his best interview yet and gave us live words for the travelling hacks too.

Wednesday, October 10

We landed [in Oman] in beautiful sunshine with a full red-carpet welcome, bands, national guard, the Omani works. We then headed for the guest house, set way back in its own grounds close to one of the sultan's residences. The place itself was about as ornate as anything we had seen. My bedroom had two gold-plated chandeliers hanging from a ceiling that must have taken months to paint. The bath was surrounded by more perfumes and toiletries than I knew existed. It was apparently the room normally reserved for visiting spouses so God knows what that made me. There was a lovely open-air swimming pool so I had a quick swim before doing a note to the MoD on my plan to brief the travelling press on the overall strategic direction based around the 'objectives of military action' document. We were running into a problem with the sense being communicated by the US that they were constantly trying to link Iraq into the equation.

TB was keen to pull it back and through a mix of my briefing and his interviews at the army base, we just about did that, but it was difficult to do while simultaneously avoiding US–UK split stories.

TB's room was even more luxurious, a carpet that your feet seemed to disappear into, paintings and statuettes that were both gaudy and somehow conveying a certain style. We went out to the poolside to go over what he would say to the UK troops, then set off by helicopter. I was always impressed by the way the military could set up home anywhere. Their base was pretty much a desert, but you had the sense of being in a very British, very well-organised operation. While TB was shown around, I did a background briefing on the objectives document, which they saw as substantial and newsworthy. But I stupidly referred to it as a 'policy bible' which had a touch of Bush's 'crusade' reference, which I tried to pull back from later. We rejoined TB who was getting a good response from the troops. There were several Burnley fans there, including one with the club crest tattooed on his shoulder. The speech to the troops was excellent, both in terms of its actual impact on the troops, and in media terms.

Flew back by helicopter. It was now almost unbearably hot. We got back to a couple of immediate problems. It emerged TB had told some of the squaddies, who had passed on to the press, that he had said one of the kids was thinking about the military as a career. I got Godric to call around and try to get them not to run it. Meanwhile, the BBC was reporting already that we were going on to Cairo. The others were not unreasonably pissed off that they were abiding by the agreement while the BBC seemed to be making a point of breaking it. Also, TB had been pictured with a guy wearing a T-shirt with the slogan 'We came, we saw, we kicked ass', which might go down better in the US than the UK.

I was getting pressed the whole time about the Yanks and Iraq, which was difficult. We got a report through on Battle Damage Assessment which showed the strikes had not been as effective as planned, but TB's bigger worry was the overall strategy. Then news came through that Iraq had shot down a Predator [unmanned surveillance plane]. The Americans were bound to react. The Taliban told OBL that he was free to fight Jihad. Bush publicly raised fears that OBL was using videos to send coded messages to terrorists already in the US. He also announced the '22 Most Wanted'.[1] I went out for a run on the sultan's private beach. It was hot, but that wonderful dry heat that meant that once I was into a rhythm, I was running well and felt privileged to be out on my own in such beautiful surroundings. I had a quick swim in the sea before going back for TB's bilateral with the sultan and then

[1] FBI list of twenty-two terrorist hijackers and bombers, including Bin Laden. Bush said 'Eventually, no corner of the world will be dark enough to hide in.'

an extraordinary dinner where wave upon wave of food came towards us. I noticed for the first couple of courses the sultan and his colleagues just picking, and after a while it became clear why. We were on the fifth course before I realised we were still on the appetisers. By the end, we had been served twenty-one courses. The sultan said he had a little surprise for us and out of nowhere came a pipe band, Omanis dressed in kilts serenading us with pipes and drums from the balcony above the dining room. They weren't bad.

On the substance, the Palestine problem came through every part of the discussion. He said Israel had to give. He was obviously aware of the tensions over Iraq, said they were happy to support us for now, re Afghanistan, but if the US went for Iraq, they would flake away and so would others, pretty quickly. David, Jonathan and I later had a go at TB, tried to get him to speak to GWB, but he felt he should wait for a face-to-face meeting. His bigger concern was whether they had thought through the military strategy, that they had been bombing without putting troops in sufficient numbers near the targets, or thinking through counter-attacks.

Thursday, October 11

I went for a run on the beach first thing. I hadn't slept well, partly because I felt a bit uncomfortable with the over-the-topness of the luxury. I was used to sleeping in some big beds, but this was like sleeping in a field with a duvet. TB was in the gym when I got back, again a word which understates its luxury. He was worried about the Americans, worried about the military campaign, concerned the CIA were actively looking for reasons to widen and hit Iraq. The damage was being done by bombing but where were the ground forces ready to move in and mop up? He also felt the US were paying insufficient attention to pubic opinion outside America. He felt he should go to Washington soon. He, Jonathan and DM thought there was a case for me going ahead to try to get them in a better place on their global communications strategy.

After breakfast, we set off for the airport surrounded by outriders with machine guns and tanks carrying anti-aircraft missiles. We had to have a meeting with one of the sultan's courtiers as part of the protocol, then on to the plane and on to Cairo. TB did an on-the-record briefing broken down into three parts: 1. a strong hint about the use of ground forces; 2. we had to do far better at the propaganda war in the Arab world, and 3. as important as anything, that the Middle East peace process was the key to solving all this. We had a problem with the Saudis apparently putting it out that they had postponed

TB's visit after the bombing started because it was too difficult for them. We tried to make the case that it was more about logistics than diplomacy, but they were pretty unshiftable and the Saudi snub story was a big part of the media mix.

TB was doing well and was still getting a very good press, still showing strong leadership, but he was also very conscious of the danger that he was setting himself up for a fall by being in such a position of international leadership. But he felt he was getting somewhere with Bush, and also felt strongly that he had to do it. He spent much of the flight writing a personal note to GWB to send when we got back to London. We were never quite sure how widely these notes were circulated in the US system. He wanted to be as frank as possible, but was always conscious of the strains in Washington. He was clear that we needed more special forces and more ground troops quickly. We needed bases in Uzbekistan and stronger links into the Northern Alliance. He was emphasising as well the need to deliberate with colleagues and strengthen the coalition at every phase of the campaign. He really laid it on about the importance of MEPP, and also that if there was any sense of trying to use this to go for other countries, it would play into Bin Laden's claim that this was not about September 11, or about the Taliban, or about him, but a war by the West on the Arab world. Get that wrong, and there was a danger of losing any chance of support from Russia, the Arab world, half the EU. He also felt, whatever they thought, we should not be lumping Syria in with Iraq.

On MEPP, he stated clearly it was the single biggest thing to get right, and his rebuke of Sharon had helped him in the Arab world, but that he needed a major new initiative, that talks had to get going again, that there had to be an acceptance at the outset that there would be two states at the end of it. He recommended a role for the EU as a way of lifting some of the load on the US. On the issue of propaganda, he said we needed to understand that the Arab world was on a different media planet, and Palestine was at the heart of it. He said we needed a dedicated, tightly knit unit for the war generally and for the Arab and Muslim world in particular. We have to reframe the way we think about reaching out to them. It was a very strong note, quite difficult to write because he had to be firm without seeming to be talking down to him, or not deferring to what was clearly a stronger power. We got back to London and I wrote a note to Karen to develop what TB was saying on communications. Bush did a press conference in the early hours and the story was he was giving a second chance to the Taliban, that the bombs would stop if they handed over OBL. They were slightly getting their messages mixed again.

Friday, October 12

I spoke to Byers and said he had to get out and do the media on Railtrack, even if it meant taking questions on Jo [Moore]. I felt the best thing was to do clips before the Railtrack meeting, where he could say something on Jo, then go out again after the Railtrack meeting, but only talk about rail. He sounded down and the press on this had been worse than I had realised just from the media brief. His clips were fine but I could tell from how often he was calling how nervous he was. I was starting to put my mind to a much bigger operation re the Arab media. We just weren't at the races on this. We had had the occasional reasonable one-off hit, but a strategic operation was non-existent. Julian was nagging me about it and was right. I planned a brainstorm on it.

Colleen Harris [Prince of Wales' staff], called saying that Charles was really keen to help. I said what about a visit to Bahrain, UAE, etc.? They said what about Saudi? I said we were already planning to go there. It would be great in some ways if they went together but would it mean TB could not do the politics properly. That would be the fear. I also suggested that in the UK, he could do more regional visits, mosques in particular, as we could not say often enough that it was not a war on Islam. TB, Jonathan and I met and agreed we should aim for a Saudi visit this week, Washington the week after. Re Byers and Jo, he said before leaving for Chequers that they had to tough it out.

Jonathan Prince [US Democrat adviser] called from Washington, said Hillary Clinton [former First Lady] had suggested he call because the Americans just were not at the races in the media war at the moment. She was worried the administration was constantly putting out mixed messages, e.g. when Bush had said on the same day both that it was safe to fly, and that we were facing a one hundred per cent threat. TB felt the problem was they lacked absolute clarity in their aims and strategy. He and Bush chatted on the phone for fifteen minutes or so but didn't achieve much. We had heard the Taliban were planning to invite in selected film crews, and I put in a warning about the importance of them being aware of the dangers of being used.

Saturday, October 13

TB was at Chequers and he and I both had the same feeling, it just wasn't clear where this was heading. He said Bush would be getting fed up about all the talk of splits between [Colin] Powell and the Pentagon, so it was hard for TB to push himself even further in the task of trying to get GWB in a better place. He said there was a real danger he was beginning to be seen as a pain in the arse. The sooner they met the better, he said. I had a couple of conversations with Colleen Harris and then with the creepy Mark Bolland [deputy private secretary to the Prince of Wales] who emphasised that the prince was really keen to get more involved. I sensed there was a bit of an operation to try to get back in with us a bit after all his countryside outbursts. I did a note to TB on what Charles might do, from articles, speeches and visits to a fully fledged joint visit to Saudi which would clearly be a very big step.

On the Jo Moore front, he felt that part of the problem was quite a lot of our ministers probably did treat civil servants like dirt, so when the more malign of them saw the chance of revenge, they would take it. He said we were fine because he always tried to be nice to them and they saw me as a character who at least had ability to match authority and who was always nice to the support staff and messengers. But a lot of the real civil-servant types would not take kindly to a lot of our people. He reckoned Boyce [CDS] was someone who probably believed a lot of the propaganda against us, that we basically listened the whole time to focus groups, that I was just a brutal apparatchik, etc.

On the Americans and their communications, he said it was so obvious what they needed to do. He said the sooner I went out to Washington the better, but he was conscious of not wanting to impose me or for it all to become part of a narrative about him overreaching himself. Condi called David Manning at 5pm to alert us that they were about to admit to a stray missile. I said we would put out the line that it was the right thing to admit it. She also said the Americans were worried about TB's security because he was right out there in front of the assassination queue. I worked on a note on Arab opinion, really laying it on the line about how far removed we were from a proper operation. I got into my stride, set out five pages' worth of possible ideas then called Karen Hughes to discuss it. She always sounded grateful for support and surprised at how many ideas it was possible to generate, but equally she always sounded annoyed when you got into the territory of the need to understand why anti-US feelings were so strong. I picked up, for example, a kind of revulsion in the Arab world at the sight of Bush urging American kids to send a dollar for the Afghan children. She couldn't understand it. I told her the *Guardian* had reported on this as being all about America and the mighty dollar, and they just had to understand better how they were seen outside. I agreed to send her my note, she said she would hold a similar brainstorm and we would swap notes afterwards.

Sunday, October 14

Chris Meyer sent a telegram from which it was clear the State Department were also worrying about the scale of the Islamic opinion problem. I did a note to Chris and sent him a copy of my letter to Karen Hughes. I went for a run with Rory and missed JP on *Frost*. JP called me afterwards beating himself up, saying he had been bumbling. Audrey [Millar, Fiona's mother] had watched it and said he was fine. Byers was on the phone, as was Jo [Moore], and I told them both they should keep their heads down till Tuesday and his statement on Railtrack should be sufficiently robust and substantive to get above the noise. He sounded very fed up and isolated. I was also busy sorting through a few problems pre Arafat. TB said he was willing to do a joint press conference provided he didn't just use it to trot out all the old lines about Israel. I felt if we could get Arafat to echo strongly what his spokesman said, namely that OBL could not speak for Palestine, that would be progress. We were getting heavier warnings about TB's own security. Jack called me re my note on Arab opinion, said we were on exactly the same wavelength and I should use whatever FCO resources I needed.

I went out to play football for an hour with Calum, then in for TB's War Cabinet meeting, TB, Jonathan, DM, AC, RW, AH, C and CDS. TB said he did not want the full War Cabinet daily, maybe two or three a week, but he would speak to Geoff and Jack separately. CDS was going to Tampa tomorrow and was hopeful we would get a fuller and better assessment after that. TB was pretty open about his worry about a lack of a clear overall strategy. There had to be ways of showing progress being made according to an understood plan. He was clearer than ever after the recent visits that our role had to be being in a position to give the Americans advice which they accepted, and adopted, as we were currently doing on Iraq, humanitarian, propaganda.

CDS set out where our forces were operating, and how we were liaising with the Russians. TB felt the division between Powell and Rumsfeld was raw and difficult. He said on the military, humanitarian, diplomatic, propaganda, post-Taliban planning and MEPP, there had to be far greater clarity and unity. I did a conference call and agreed with the Palestinian team that TB would push the boat out re the Palestinian state question if Arafat would condemn OBL, say he had no right to speak for Palestine and that this was an important message. The Taliban took a group of journalists into Afghanistan to Karam [village near Jalalabad, Nangarhar province], which they said had been destroyed by the US. The press were sceptical but even so I called Karen Hughes and said they must get out a response on it. It was perfectly clear after a while that she didn't know what I was talking about. I was surprised she hadn't been told, and a bit worried about whether they were really at the races.

Monday, October 15

The press was all a bit ragged but it felt like we were losing the media battle. I was determined to get going on a proper operation for Muslim and Arab opinion, and also to strengthen US–UK operations. 8am, War Cabinet. Jack was worried that we were too lax on targeting and said that at the risk of being unpopular, he felt we should be thinking about it more carefully. TB listened for a bit and got a bit irritated, said our job was to set the overall strategy but you could not have a campaign run by committee because it will not work. John Vereker [permanent secretary, Department for International Development (DFID)] gave quite a positive report on the humanitarian front. Lander said there was a worrying increase in talk of threats to the US and UK, while TB was also a current target. There was no real sign of fracture within the Taliban, and also we still had mixed messages about the Northern Alliance. Both CDS and Geoff Hoon said there was no real clarity of where it was going. Our special forces were obviously key but we needed far greater clarity about what they were required for. C was very helpful on the Arab–Muslim opinion front, and agreed one of his best people would come to my meetings on it.

We had a pre-meeting with TB re Arafat [visit]. It was tricky, in that in the current context, things that both of them had said hundreds of times, might resonate differently. We really didn't want Arafat just to go off on one on Israel. There had to be real substance coming out of this. Because TB was clear that getting the peace process going again was perhaps the single most important thing we could do. But it wasn't hard to see how you could go from that to a position that pushed the Israelis off the other end. Arafat arrived, with the usual large entourage, but they did most of it one-on-one, with David Manning in there taking notes, and TB seemed to have given him a pretty straightforward message. We had the extended meeting which was really just an opportunity to finalise the scripts, agree pretty forward language on Palestinian state but also be clear it should not be pitched as a change of policy, which is what Arafat really wanted. Arafat wasn't looking particularly well but as before, he managed to lift himself. The press conference went fine. TB had felt it wasn't a great idea for the media to see Michael Levy [Labour fundraiser and adviser on Middle East], as they would make it all about party funding.

So he wasn't very happy when Michael got himself into the departure shot. He just could not resist it. TB said he had only one thing to do – stay low profile – and he didn't do it. Michael had a real desire to be recognised for what he was doing on MEPP, and put funding behind him, which was understandable.

I had my meeting with the broadcasters. I went through the issues, pretty gently, not remotely bullying, absolved them of blame for most of the stuff I was talking about. I told them about our worries on the videos and emphasised that the security issues around TB were very real, and it wasn't on to report his movements in advance. Richard Sambrook [BBC director of news] said they would prefer I hadn't done this through the lobby. I said that was because we were exasperated by their continued reporting of his movements. I had a very good meeting with key FCO and SIS people on Arab–Muslim media. I said I wanted somebody monitoring this stuff for me full time, saying what we got right and what we got wrong. John Kerr had given me a very bright Arabic speaker called Gerard Russell who would be able to go out there on the Arabic TV and speak for us.

George Tenet [CIA director] was coming in to see TB with C, who brought him round to see me to discuss the notes I was sending through to Karen and enlist his help in persuading them of the need for much better communications. I told him we feared they were putting out messages that were very good and positive for the American audience, but not for the broader community, including here, but also above all in the Arab world. He said Richard [Dearlove] had talked to him about it, that Condi was the key to this, that I needed to get her on board to persuade Bush they needed to crack down on the mixed messages (the latest today, [Dick] Cheney [US Vice President] and the Health Secretary [Tommy Thompson] saying different things on bio-terrorism) and run a properly co-ordinated international structure. David Manning felt he and I should go there next Tuesday. Tenet said the US was totally fixated on the anthrax scare.[1] Tenet was bright, but had a slightly irritating habit of playing with a large cigar when he was listening. He said he totally bought what we were saying and he would feed it back. He agreed we needed more [Colin] Powell and less Department of Defense. Mum phoned later, saying Dad was going to have to get tests for a possible brain tumour.

[1] An outbreak of anthrax in the United States, intentionally spread via the postal system, caused five deaths and a total of twenty-two infections between September and November 2001.

Tuesday, October 16

There was a growing sense that things were not going brilliantly. TB was doing a speech on public services so I went up to the flat to work on that with him. He had pretty much done the draft himself. The Jo Moore thing was still big and we agreed she should do something to camera, which she did in the afternoon, apology then back to work. She did OK, looked fine but sounded very fed up. Colin Powell was going to Pakistan but the backdrop was the division between him and the Defense Department. David Manning spoke to Condi and said she was very excited at the idea of us both going out there and felt on the media side, I would be pushing at an open door. The aid agencies were calling for a pause in the bombing.

Wednesday, October 17

The general feeling was that Jo's public statement had backfired and made matters worse. Also, there was a real feeling media-wise that Afghanistan was not going according to plan. At the 8am meeting, CDS reported back from Tampa that they intended to carry on bombing at this intensity for a couple of days, then really push on for the fall of the Taliban. He said [General] Tommy Franks [commander-in-chief, US Central Command (CENTCOM)] was fine and strong but there was no clear political direction. Rumsfeld was felt to be very erratic. TB felt there were some critical decisions not being faced up to, e.g. on the Northern Alliance, we either get behind them or not. His view was we should go full steam ahead with them but at the same time put other groups alongside them. But it wasn't as simple as that, the Northern Alliance was not cohesive, there were eight or nine tribal chieftains in varying states of control. TB said the Northern Alliance must be sitting there thinking the Americans were just scared of suffering casualties.

TB said the Taliban will not fold unless there is someone moving in to drive them out. He also felt we were losing the battle on the humanitarian front, that somebody really strong had to be in charge of it. Chris Patten's name was floated. He also wanted more pressure on the Russians for the use of bases in Uzbekistan. David Manning pointed out that Ramadan began on November 17, which would be another complicating factor.

Karen Hughes called from Air Force One, said she had discussed my note with Bush and I should go out next week. TB spoke to Bush at 2pm. Bush said the anthrax there was weapons grade and probably given to OBL by Saddam. Later in the conversation he said he hoped

TB was in the loop about targets in other countries. TB made three main points: 1. we had to go for the Northern Alliance, let them do what they could, put them on a leash if need be and hold them back later. Bush said he agreed, that 'You are right as always', the Northern Alliance are the best people to help us but they have to be able to share power later. 2. get other countries involved, however small their commitment, e.g. Jordan, other friendly Arab nations. Bush said in fourteen days we would have Mazar-e-Sharif [city in north Afghanistan] and Kabul [capital of Afghanistan] in friendly hands. 3. on the humanitarian, TB said some truly awful pictures would start to come through and it was important people understood the bigger context first, otherwise there would be a bigger backlash against us.

They then discussed the propaganda side and Bush said he had heard that I was really discouraged after our visit to the Middle East and I had really got Karen and her people going. He switched between serious statesman and Texan redneck pretty quickly, e.g. when after a serious discussion on public opinion in the Arab world, he suddenly said 'We got the asshole on the run and we're gonna get the bearded one soon.' He also said 'I ain't got much credibility on this peacekeeping stuff so I want those Scandinavians involved.' I wasn't sure what Prince Charles wanted to do. His office having asked how he could help, now Stephen Lamport [private secretary to the Prince of Wales] wasn't clear what kind of visits he would do. TB called late after his call to Chirac and was plucking his guitar rather annoyingly. He was very pleased with himself that he had managed to fix a three-way meeting with Chirac and Schroeder before the Ghent [EU] summit.

Thursday, October 18
The *Mirror* was wall-to-wall offside, and other papers/chatterati were starting to get very flaky. Not even two weeks into the bombing and they were all very jumpy already. I did a briefing for the Arab–Muslim media, the first briefing I had done with three Special Branch in tow, though thankfully none of them seemed to notice. It went well and I enjoyed doing it, partly because I could feel that they realised there was a point. The questions were the obvious ones, MEPP, Iraq, protests. I promised them far greater access to ministers.

At the War Cabinet, Scarlett said the Americans seemed to be upping their support for the Northern Alliance and were starting to probe positions at Mazar-e-Sharif. CDS said CENTCOM had said they would give whatever support the NA needed. TB was back saying we needed to construct a leash to pull them back in. As he listened, I could see Blunkett getting more and more agitated.

Eventually he said it was incredible that we were all sitting around basically saying there was no clear strategy. He said I don't want to shoot the messenger but where is this all going? He said we were coming up to Ramadan and even bigger problems and if we weren't careful this would all turn against us. Kerr said [Lakhdar] Brahimi [UN special representative for Afghanistan] had to get his skates on. We went through the humanitarian side of things. Clare was up on the border today and doing OK. Lander reported on a specific threat to TB. TB was a bit irritated at Geoff and CDS who both seemed to have lost confidence and therefore weren't inspiring it. Afterwards, the full Cabinet in which they went over pretty much the same ground.

Then to TB's press conference where he was working from notes and we were trying to get up the line about the next two weeks being the most testing period. There was a bit of resistance from the Foreign Office that I was trying to take premises, people and resources, but John Kerr was being extremely helpful. We were starting to get the backlash following the announcement of the three-way trilateral with Chirac and Schroeder. Catherine Colonna called to say they were very keen to hold their press conference at 7, but Berlusconi in particular was throwing a total wobbly. There was a danger tomorrow's summit would be a total shambles. TB said to me he wanted me to try to take over the propaganda side of things because what it lacked at the moment was total single-mindedness.

Friday, October 19

Richard W came to see me, said there was a really bad feeling around the place re Jo Moore. I said it would get a lot better if civil servants weren't constantly briefing against her. At the morning War meeting, Scarlett said there was a clear sense of Taliban morale crumbling. The chief of the air force was among the Taliban waverers. A fair number of defections and confidence Mazar-e-Sharif would fall soon. The Northern Alliance were far more bullish. CDS reported that the Americans were getting a bit fed up with us for not agreeing to all the targets. TB said if there was any target that we believed should be hit and there were legal problems here, he wanted to know about it. He said if I was Bush, I would be going spare about this. Later he called [Lord] Goldsmith over. RW gave a word of caution in relation to the *Belgrano*[1] and TB said the problem there was not the legality,

[1] Argentine Navy light cruiser, controversially sunk in 1982 by a British nuclear submarine whilst outside the 200 nautical mile exclusion zone around the Falkland Islands. 323 Argentine sailors died.

it was the attempt to cover it up. I couldn't resist adding 'A failure of spin over a discredited Tory regime.' Richard smiled.

I did a conference call with Jack and all our ambassadors in the Arab world to get them bought into the need for a more proactive approach. Most of them seemed to get it, though there were one or two whingers who basically said there was nothing much we could do. But it was an OK call and I felt we were making progress. We left for Ghent on an RAF flight, the only real story the Big Three summit. TB seemed fairly relaxed about it. I was worried it would end up as a coalition fracture but TB felt the risk was outweighed by the benefit of Chirac wanting us involved in this way. We arrived and went straight to the meeting in the cellar room of a chapel. Chirac seemed a bit pissed off that it was TB plus three – DM, Jonathan and I – whilst he and [Lionel] Jospin were plus one. Schroeder was a bit late so Chirac kicked off going through what the French could offer, mainly AWACs [airborne warning and control planes] and special forces, reconnaissance and refuelling. He was clearly keen to get involved quickly. TB told him we had people working alongside the NA. Chirac felt pre winter and pre Ramadan we had to step up the pace. TB said at the moment we had no option but to work through the NA but we would need to bring them back in if they became too difficult. They were vital to taking Mazar-e-Sharif.

Schroeder's contribution was more about how they could help build a post-Taliban government. Jospin chipped in with a question about the post-Taliban regime and before he had even got the words out, Chirac interrupted and in the most patronising way imaginable said 'Can we finish on the military phase first please?' Chirac also asked Schroeder direct whether they would send special forces. Schroeder said if I was asked, I'd say yes, but I hope not to be asked. Germany was in a particularly difficult position and he pointed out that it would have to be put to parliament first as a fundamental change in their foreign policy. Even when he was onside though, Chirac would always make sure we knew his real opinions about the Yanks in particular, as in when he said that 'irrefutable proof' of anything was not necessarily proof if it came from the CIA.

It was a pretty odd meeting, not least because of the rather poky venue, the fact that there was not enough coffee, that the carpets were a bit thin and the noise from outside loud. TB said he felt there had been a shift in Israel's attitude to the UK and the US, and a big change in the US attitude to Israel. If Arafat made a positive move, e.g. handing over detainees . . . Chirac interrupted again, saying he would be assassinated. Schroeder said he had spoken to [Ariel] Sharon who referred to Arafat as 'my Taliban'. That is how they see them. It was by now like Babel's tower, with so many interpreters translating between three languages at once. TB still felt we had to construct a gesture from Arafat.

The rest of the day was by and large a waste of time for me. I had Tom Kelly to deal with the Ghent business and so instead I focused on planning the Saudi visit. Then a call from the *Mail* asking whether it was true that Prince Charles was to be a special envoy to the Saudis. It was frustrating. They clearly wanted to help, and to get a 'Charles joins war effort' story out there, but it was an odd way to go about it – briefing that we have asked them to do something when actually we'd talked about something else.

TB was bored with the summit deliberations and came out for a chat. As ever, they had not skimped on the food for all the under-worked hangers-on, with national dishes from each of the fifteen member states. We watched Louis Michel [Belgian foreign minister] stuffing his face. I reminded TB it was part of the deal that I didn't have to come to these wretched European summits any more. He said to see this as part of the Arab media brief. The main story was the Big Three summit upsetting everyone else but TB was unapologetic. The press conference was straightforward, they did the future of Europe over dinner, then off to the plane. TB said Chirac had been interesting because he so clearly wanted to be on the same page with us on this. TB recalled what [Margaret] Thatcher had told him – 'The Germans are big but they feel so guilty they don't use their power, you can't trust the French, the Italians are only good for clothes, the Dutch are the most like us but too close to the Germans. But I do like the Danes.'

Sunday, October 21
Up early and off to see Dad who was looking very frail. TB called as I drove up, still adamant we should stay robust on Jo Moore. I agreed it would be even worse to get rid of her now, but she must be miserable as hell. He was really worried about the Middle East, feared after his conversation with [Ariel] Sharon that after the seven-day mourning of the tourism minister [Rehavam Ze'evi, assassinated by Palestinian gunmen], the Israelis would go into real battle against the Palestinians. I got Godric to brief the Mondays that we were closer to seeing UK ground forces in action. I hadn't read the papers first thing, and I had a flick through when we got back home, a bit alarmed at how much 'spin' was back in the news because of Jo.

Monday, October 22

Godric's briefing went big, and alongside the Americans' weekend briefing on the [US Army] Rangers going in, there was a feeling of the temperature rising. However, the feeling of drift in the War Cabinet was grim. It must by now have become clear to John Scarlett, C etc. how different the mood was in the meetings with the broader group of ministers. John did his best to put over a sense of progress, with hints that Mullah Omar was worried, and reports on the sense of shock among the Taliban about how the attacks had intensified. CDS gave his usual very downbeat assessment, focusing mainly on problems. He said we were not advancing as fast as we should be, but we were looking at at least five more days for Mazar and that Kabul would not be taken before winter/Ramadan. John Vereker said we were still not talking catastrophe on the humanitarian front but we were just two and a half weeks from winter.

Afterwards, TB said he felt that the morning meeting was becoming too big, and he was worried about what might be leaked. He also said he felt Geoff and CDS were too negative, constantly saying what they couldn't do. 'I want my military to be straining at the leash, us having to hold them back.' He then told me to get a story planted somewhere that Boyce was doing a great job. He said my visit to the States tomorrow was vital, that I had to persuade them of the need for a central hub. It was like putting together a general election campaign, required that level of organisation and detail. I had to persuade the Americans how important it was to think beyond their own public opinion.

I was now working close to flat out on getting the Arab media unit up and running properly. Arab opinion was saying this unit would have no impact and was just propaganda. Julian Braithwaite's view was the SIS, or some of them, were feeling vulnerable, wanted to feel they were the only people who really got this stuff. It certainly read like something designed to deter us. John Kerr had been a fantastic support. I went over with him to meet the new team, who seemed pretty bright but I made clear we would need more still. Jo Moore was moving up the agenda again and my worry was that she would weaken in the face of all this. I got home fairly early as it was Rory's birthday tomorrow, but was dead tired again. The news was all [Gerry] Adams after he had called on the IRA to disarm which was a big moment.

Tuesday, October 23

BBC were getting more and more outrageous, Taliban claims were being treated pretty much the same as anything we said followed by endless Fergal Keane [journalist] emoting. At the 8am meeting, John Scarlett said all the terror camps had been demolished and I said why on earth haven't we done a big presentation on that? TB asked CDS at one point what size of an area was covered by 'the front line'. There was a long pause and he said quietly 'I don't really know I'm afraid.' TB asked him what kind of advice he should be giving to Bush. Boyce said it depends if they are prepared to go through Ramadan. TB said let's assume they are not. 'Mmm, mmm, it's very difficult.' If you were to sum up his contribution it was to say we couldn't take Mazar, the NA were impossible to deal with, the Americans were not being totally open. He had the top special forces guy there who sounded much more like he knew what he was on about, but who was also none too optimistic. The NA were finding it harder than we feared to take Mazar and we didn't necessarily have all the people there that we needed. On the military, the diplomatic, and the humanitarian, we just weren't where we needed to be.

Kerr felt Colin Powell's Middle East vision was wishful thinking unless they have a lot better intelligence than we do about the current state of Israeli thinking. TB asked David Manning and me to go through at the end of the meeting and said he was seized by how important our visit was. 'You have got to get a grip of the show.' I was tying up loose ends before getting ready to leave. Robin Cook came to see me before doing his first on-camera briefing for the Arab press. He was clearly a bit baleful about not being Foreign Secretary. I told him I was going to Washington with Jack and he said 'Don't jump on my grave.' He did one of his chirpy 'won't let you downs' and off he went.

I left for the Savoy where I was doing a 'turn the tables' interview with Jeremy Paxman [BBC *Newsnight* presenter] and had decided on a twin track – keep asking about his earnings and throw in general-knowledge questions about people from the smaller countries involved in the crisis. It seemed to go fine. Lots of nice charity types there. I teased him into whacking [John] Humphrys [BBC *Today* presenter] a bit, accepting the superficiality of TV as a medium, and he wasn't great on the general-knowledge stuff.

TB was at a session at the Commonwealth Club with all Cabinet ministers and their permanent secretaries in a kind of big bonding session. I went to meet up with Jack. He said TB had been excellent, really thought about it and the whole event had been a huge success. He then added that it had all been the idea of Alice [Perkins, Straw's wife, a civil servant]. In the car, and later on the flight, he and I had a series of really good conversations. He was very down on GB, felt that the mad streak had got worse and the combination of TB rising into a different league to the rest of them plus economic worries had put GB in a very bad frame of mind. Said he was loathed by many of his colleagues. On TB, he felt he didn't do enough in Parliament. A lot of our chat was about kids, football, stuff unrelated to politics and Jack was definitely still a fully paid-up member of the human race. He, I, David Manning, Simon McDonald [Straw's private secretary] and one of the coppers were up in first class when Alison [Blackshaw, AC's personal assistant] came down from club to do some work, some of the other passengers complained – tossers – so I went back with her to club.

I did a note to TB re his *Telegraph* interview and PMQs [Prime Minister's Questions] tomorrow in which I felt he needed to give a longer than usual update on overall strategy, the military, MEPP, thinking on the Taliban. For the bulk of the flight I was working on a note for the White House setting out ideas on a draft communications plan and structures. I said in terms the thinking needed to be on a par with the thinking applied to elections with many of the same functions. Jack and David read it through, made a few comments and were basically both happy with it. It was largely modelled on Kosovo with the Arab–Muslim angle meaning a different kind of response was required. Jack travelled with his own polish and made a big play of shining up my shoes.

We landed to be met by Tony Brenton [deputy head of mission, UK Embassy] and two pieces of news – the IRA had delivered, and Burnley had beaten Crystal Palace [1–0]. We went briefly to our ambassador's residence before I went out to a restaurant to meet Dan Bartlett [deputy to Karen Hughes] who with Karen and Ari [Fleischer, White House press secretary] was part of the press triumvirate during Bush's campaign. He seemed a bit nervy but seemed a nice enough guy. I had not really been aware of just how much the anthrax situation was convulsing the system and it meant Afghanistan was not nearly so much in the news as it was at home. I did feel though that I was pushing at a fairly open door. He said Bush was up for it, realised we had to make change. At one or two points he stated openly that they knew they were not up to their game, that they thought too much on American lines, not enough about opinion outside, and they were happy to take all the advice and help going. He was good at analysing problems – e.g. how the Arab media viewed us and why – but their solutions weren't that great. He gave me a paper from Karl Rove [senior adviser to Bush] that I think was meant to be their response to the brainstorm I had given to Karen, but it was not what

I expected. I think the basic problem was that they genuinely didn't understand anti-Americanism. They couldn't see how, given that in this instance they had been the victim, and given all the help they had tried to administer around the world, they were not more popular. So it made them more insular, and a lot of their ideas were actually about things that would simply strengthen their standing at home but do nothing for them overseas necessarily.

I was walking a fairly difficult line, because basically TB wanted me to try to take this over, but at the same time it was important not to give them the sense we thought they couldn't do this. I got a bit close to the mark when I showed him a polling presentation from Philip [Gould] which showed that quite a lot of Bush's statements had gone down really badly. He seemed surprised, even a little hurt. He said Condi was totally on board for trying to improve presentation and if I had her and Karen onside, I would get the president. I was in two minds about giving over the various papers I had done there and then but in the end did so and agreed they would form the basis of our discussions tomorrow. I got back to the residence, felt I had made a good opening. Stayed up for a long chat with Jack and [Sir Christopher] Meyer who said that the US military gave no clear sense of strategy. Sounded familiar. Alison came in with the cuttings from home, including some pretty big reviews of my session with Paxman, widely judged to be a straight win.

Wednesday, October 24

Washington. I couldn't sleep so I was up and about at 4.30 and chatted to TB in London before his *Telegraph* interview. The American papers underlined how totally obsessed they were with anthrax. It took up the first fifteen minutes of US bulletins. It confirmed me in the view that they were unlikely to have been thinking enough about the stuff I was trying to persuade them of. My first meeting was with Karen Hughes. I was accompanied by Bob Peirce [embassy press staff]. We arrived at the White House, a brief wait then up through the warren of steps and little offices and through to see her. It was a fairly small office, lots of pictures of her and GWB. She looked a bit shell-shocked, sounded it too. She said this was all very different to running a Texan political campaign. We went through the notes I had sent over, the importance of third parties, who their key communicators were, how to improve message co-ordination between the various bits of government, polling, Muslim outreach, the UN. I said why didn't GWB visit a few mosques? Who did they have in the US Muslim community who could be built up into being the kind of people

TV wanted to hear? Who were the right people to put on the Arab media and would they understand the need to use a slightly different language?

I went through the note done on the plane which she pretty much bought into but my heart sank a bit when she said Rumsfeld would in fact be agreeable to doing a lot of this. She said how can we set this up quickly? I said you just do, top down, all the way. Then to lunch with Condi Rice. She was already with DM and C, Dan Fried. Sebastian Wood from the embassy and Steve Hadley [US Deputy National Security Advisor] joined us later. Condi was a lot more relaxed than Karen and we started out laughing about the pictures of the Northern Alliance on horseback, suggesting we may have overestimated their military capabilities. She and DM had already gone over the problems caused by conflicting signals coming out of the different bits of government, the lack of a clear military plan. Condi had seen my paper and was pretty much signed up straight away. The concept I was pushing was a 24-hour cycle in which Washington, London and the region, probably Islamabad, were in permanent contact, and driving the news proactively in all the different time zones. There was some discussion about who and how to get into Islamabad. Condi said Bush believed the PR so far had been dreadful and had told her and Karen 'go fix it' and I was definitely pushing at an open door. Once or twice the conversation slipped into anthrax but it was important to keep that separate, not least because of the dire effect it had on their morale.

Condi was impressive, had the same kind of grasp of detail as DM did, good manners, pretty straight talking. I noticed no wine, just water on the table. She said she would give Karen the backing she needed to make this happen, and agreed Karen would chair a team here which liaised with me in London, and that we would send a Brit to them and get one of their best people to us. It was proving very straightforward to get them signed up to the kind of operation we needed. Then to the Pentagon, by now it was hot, and we had a fair old distance to walk before we finally reached [assistant secretary of defense for public affairs] Torie Clarke's office. She was nice, smart, also spoke in a very fast, clipped manner like Karen. She felt Rumsfeld was doing too much and agreed we weren't getting out enough pictures that showed progress. I also said it was important that she did what she could to stop the Pentagon/State Department public divisions and the best way to do that was to agree a very concerted 'White House in charge' strategy. She seemed up for that too though clearly one of her problems was the number of people who spoke to the press on background. I told her what Steve Hadley had said, that the State Department had a war room, the Pentagon had a war room. I said they seemed to be at war with each other. I started to push on the idea of maybe [UK General] John Reith [chief of Joint Operations at Permanent Joint HQ] getting involved in a cross-national way. She said Rumsfeld had committed himself to doing daily briefings with the bureau chiefs and could not get out of it. I suggested they could get out of anything if they were busy enough, but told her that in the European and our context, he scored last behind Powell and Bush in terms of the buttons he pressed.

Then to the State Department to see Charlotte Beers who had been hired as undersecretary of public diplomacy and whose background was advertising. I had been warned she was a lot older than she looked, maybe well into her sixties, and had picked up some opposition to her. She instinctively seemed to get what I was on about and also had some clever ideas for how to spend the money she had won for advertising. Her basic pitch was that the Arab world had a very narrow view of America based upon wealth, politics, films and music, and all the big companies. She showed me a portfolio of absolutely stunning photographs of mosques, most of which looked at first glance as though they were in the Arab world, but all of which were in the States. Then some wonderful pictures and stories from ordinary American Muslims. She was clearly going to be useful on the soft stuff in particular. I could see why she was getting up a few noses there, but I liked her style.

Then back to the White House to link up with Jack and have a meeting with Cheney. Jack told me my communications paper had gone down well with Rumsfeld and Powell. When Cheney came in with his people – Scooter Libby, his chief of staff, Mary Matalin, his press woman, and three military advisers – Mary and Cheney both had the note in their hands. On the military campaign, Cheney was bullish. Jack asked him outright what the strategy was. He said NA should take Mazar, then he went over some of the whys and hows and wherefores of what might follow vis-à-vis Taliban, al-Qaeda, Bin Laden, but it wasn't really an answer to the question what is the strategy. Jack said UK support was strong but could we hold the coalition together if this thing went on longer than expected? He said he thought so. They did the Middle East and Jack asked how difficult it was having such a strong pro-Israel lobby. Cheney said its influence is sometimes overstated and that at the moment they were pretty subdued. Jack said [Ariel] Sharon was doing things which were dangerous and could not be part of our strategy. I had always assumed that Cheney would be more open and forthcoming when he was in charge of meetings rather than, as when Bush was there, clearly comfortable playing second fiddle. But he was not one to speak too much for the sake of it. He had cold, slightly menacing body language, listened very intently without giving much away, and usually paused before giving a thought-through answer. I went through the concept I was trying to get him signed up to and he was fine about it, said we should just do it.

Mary said on the way out she was so pleased I had sent over the note and gone there because they had been pressing for this kind of approach for ages. She was a real bundle, as you'd expect from someone hitched up with James Carville [Democrat strategist]. I was fascinated how that all worked. I just could not imagine living with someone from the other party. She said it just about worked, but they were able to separate out different parts of their lives and they just got used to having good arguments. We definitely made progress though. Jack did a brief doorstep while David and I left from a side door and headed back to the residence. We had a couple of hours at the residence. I chatted with Meyer about things we would need to keep the pressure on over. I spent the first two or three hours of the flight back writing up notes with Alison [Blackshaw] out of the various meetings. We had got the cuttings through at the airport and Northern Ireland decommissioning was getting big play, but positive.

Thursday, October 25

I didn't sleep well. I drove in from the airport with Jack, mainly small talk, how hard it was getting the time you needed for kids and family. I had really enjoyed his company, and his manner. Sometimes, because of the nature of the job, there was just too much stuff going on around TB, whereas I felt in the last couple of days, we had clear and limited aims, and pretty much met them in full. He was very sound on schools, and the need for kids like ours to go to schools with a broad mix. We got back for the War Cabinet, which was all a bit grim, not really going anywhere, not really making the progress we needed, CDS as ever telling us what we couldn't do rather than what we could, weather bad, not enough agents alongside NA, not clear where key Taliban people were. TB said we must take Mazar before Ramadan. Boyce's understanding was that the Americans did intend to continue bombing after Ramadan. TB said we have to be absolutely single-minded in the next two weeks. He asked for a paper on how it would be taken if all available resources could be found. RC said we would lose support quickly without real progress. I filled them in on the media plans we had agreed with the Americans and TB was still banging on about the need to do more with Muslim opinion here. Scarlett said Al Jazeera had an OBL broadcast that had not been put out possibly because the interviewer had been asked to do certain questions, soft questions, and hadn't.

Full Cabinet was pretty much the same as the smaller group, and I sensed people beginning to get a little bit low and worried. I started phoning round and organising volunteers to go out to Pakistan and the US. Karen called me later with Dan Bartlett and a guy called Jim Wilkinson [White House deputy director of communications] on the line. Jim was going to run their war room. We went over what they needed there, and what we needed in Pakistan. I called Hilary Synnott, our high commissioner in Islamabad, and got him on board for trying to find premises. I called George Robertson [Secretary General] at NATO to get him signed up, then a few UK-based ambassadors. The German guy was helpful as ever. We had applied a catalyst and things were finally starting to move. When I did a meeting of GICS [Government Information and Communication Service] staff, I got more volunteers than we could initially handle. TB was pretty down about the military side of things. There were going to be redeployments of UK troops from Oman tomorrow which would be big news, but we had a problem with Rumsfeld saying something interpreted as an admission we would never get OBL. I got home to see the kids, and Fiona and I went out for dinner, and she was desperate for me to leave, and couldn't understand why now was not the moment.

Friday, October 26
I gave the morning meeting a miss and took Grace [AC's daughter] to school. TB said he wasn't sure he could cope with many more of these meetings where all he heard was things going wrong and things everyone agreed needed to be done but weren't being done. I spent most of the day working on setting up the new media operation. We were talking about whether we could use the spiked Al Jazeera interview [with Bin Laden], then a note to Karen. The need for what we were doing in Pakistan was shown up every time I turned on the news. The Taliban were getting far too easy a ride. I chatted to TB about the pressure I was under at home to leave. He said it was the worst possible time. He thought the problem was that I had an enormous job and Fiona felt undervalued by comparison. But she was extremely bright and able and we should try to build up what she did.

George Robertson called with some names. I went over to see John

Kerr who was trying to find me premises for our war room. He greeted me in a ludicrous plumed hat he was supposed to wear when he went to see the Queen. He was very funny, very friendly, despite everyone saying how devious he was, my experience so far was that when he promised something, he delivered it. I got Anne Shevas [Downing Street chief press officer] working on turning the offices he was offering into a proper war room. I called Will Farish, the US ambassador, to beg for Lee McLenny [press counselor, US Embassy]. I had Deborah Hermer [GICS] heading out to Washington and briefed her. Tessa [Jowell] was due out in New York for a ceremony and I fixed her to do some media before and after. I went to see Fiona in the office and tried to assure her things would get better, but she wasn't convinced. TB was obviously worried about what I had said about Fiona. But he said I had one of the best jobs in the world, I did it brilliantly and I would hate it if I was not involved. I was worried with all the trips coming up that Fiona would really decide she had had enough of it all.

Saturday, October 27

We had computers brought into the war room. Mary Matalin called and said Jim Wilkinson would be fine, that he was one of those people who 'walks through walls'. She said James sent his regards and was relieved that the Brits had finally kicked them into shape! I spoke to TB and agreed some lines for Tom [Kelly] to put out re moral fibre, this being a long-term battle. Boyce's briefing of yesterday was going big.[1] Boyce's interview and the gloomy photos of him played into the idea, gathering too much pace, that the war was 'going nowhere'.

TB was wondering whether I should take an upfront spokesman role either here or Pakistan and was worried 1. that we would lose sight even more of the domestic scene, and 2. that the media would not be able to resist turning it into the AC show. I felt we needed two different people to do it, one heavyweight, serious, big picture, maybe an ambassador, someone else doing the nitty-gritty. Paddy Feeny was out with Tessa and I persuaded her to let me redirect him to Washington to join the Jim Wilkinson effort. Boyce was still fretting about Guthrie's profile and about Rumsfeld criticising him. TB asked me to advise him to stop reading the press.

I had to leave for Chequers for TB's 9am meeting with him, David M, Jonathan, [General] Pigott plus two, C and the head of special

---

[1] Boyce had said that fighting the Taliban was not like fighting an army, but fighting an idea like communism, and may take fifty years.

forces. We met in the Hawtrey Room.[1] The message that came through from all of them was that the Americans were a bit all over the place. TB ended by saying that we had to become like an extra strategic mind for them, give them a real plan. Pigott said the Taliban obviously had to be attacked physically but we also had to attack their morale and attack the concept. For the moment their morale was quite high and the NA's was low. A lot of this was about changing mindsets there about how this was all going. He said if the Americans were here, they would explain their current thinking as follows: 1. assemble all the hardware they needed; 2. initial strikes and create conditions for the third phase – we are well into that; 3. march onwards to decisive action; 4. sustained effort, fall of the Taliban, humanitarian and post-Taliban really steps up.

TB said what would Tommy Franks say if I asked him what was going on. 'I'm building up, I'm looking to get the total picture by spring, I'm continuing air strikes, I'm giving sixty per cent support to NA at Mazar, twenty-five per cent Kabul, fifteen per cent Herat. I'm keeping the coalition engaged.' He said there was also confusion about Ramadan and it was important not to let the sense build that there would be an automatic pause. We should see Ramadan and winter as opportunities. There had been a very long conference at the Pentagon, the seventy top brains including five C.-in-C.s, and it was very frank. The main complaint was that there was no central plan, no real strategic clarity from the Pentagon. One had said 'We're still working to the president's speech on TV.' TB lightened the mood, by saying 'Christ, I hope you lot aren't following my party conference speech.' The special forces guy said they were.

Pigott went on, said the inter-agency machinery wasn't working, that there were constant arguments about who was in control, info ops not working, no clear understanding of how properly to use the coalition. He said there was a lot of praise in the American military for TB and the UK operation by comparison. TB said the Taliban would be feeling that they had a better chance than they thought as we go up to winter. He too did not like the idea of a pause because it indicated this was going on for a long time after and that would put pressure on the international coalition, including Pakistan who were getting worried that things were not going as they should.

He was still keen to step up the operations to take Mazar-e-Sharif. We kept being told it was about to fall. He said if nothing happens

[1] Named after an Elizabethan occupant of the house, William Hawtrey, whose family had owned the Chequers estate from the thirteenth century.

between now and the half-time whistle, and by the time they get back on the pitch, we will be in difficulty. Pigott said we should not encourage half-time thinking. We need to be thinking of more harrying, looking at this not just in terms of bombs and territory but total domination. TB said it would look like the Taliban were tougher than we thought and the NA more of a ragbag than we thought. He said if we were the NA we would be thinking 'Do these guys really know what they're doing and might I be better off watching my own back?' C said the US were using some pretty heavy power. That he had been at the CIA and seen live pictures of the C130 [gunship] attacks and that those big powerful drops had a big psychological impact. TB said he had used up a lot of political chips on Mazar-e-Sharif. Chirac and Schroeder both believed we would have taken it by now, but what were they using there? 2,000 horses! The SF guy said it was a mistake to think of the NA as an army in the conventional sense. He said it would take months to train them and even after that you wouldn't want to risk your lives on them.

I said we had to get away from the idea that progress was only measured in bombs and territory, that we had to do more to shape the perception of events inside and outside. TB said GWB would soon surely be getting the fear in the pit of his stomach 'that I've been having for the past two weeks'. The SF guy said Americans never lost a battle in Vietnam but they did lose a war. TB said again we had to strategise for the Americans. They were against using the Al Jazeera interview. It was classically the kind of thing that would give us a big media hit, and also unnerve them, but they were cautious.

TB was now more seized than ever that the information propaganda effort had become more important, not less. He summed up – first stage air superiority, better use of intelligence, reshape perception of progress, step up special forces operations and get alongside NA more, get them off the ground properly, start planning post-Taliban regime. He asked for a detailed list of everything these guys thought was needed to ensure success so that he could prepare another note for Bush. He and I went out for a walk in the garden. He said this was scary stuff but he couldn't understand why the Americans weren't focusing more on what needed to be done. Then the news came through that the US had hit an NA village. Another bloody mistake.

Sunday, October 28
Spoke to Jack several times before *Frost* and we agreed it was time to crank up the line that the media had very short memories and

next to no humility about their predictions that had been wrong. We had to be getting the focus on the long term. Charles Guthrie agreed he would speak to Musharraf about making sure that our media centre out there would be allowed to operate properly. Tanya Joseph [Downing Street press officer] had volunteered for Pakistan and I briefed her before she left. TB sent through a nine-page note based on the meeting yesterday, setting out where he thought every aspect of the operation should be improved and tightened. Jim Wilkinson called, said that he had premises and was setting up units to cover liaison with us, central desk, terrorist funding, humanitarian, Internet, Grid [diary mechanism to co-ordinate announcements], Muslim opinion, key opinion formers, writers. They were on the right lines and said they would take as many of our people as they could get. The Americans were saying they would reconsider on the Al Jazeera interview if we could give them a real reason, but he was not sure.

I drove up to Wolverhampton for the Burnley game. The phone hardly stopped on the way up and it was difficult to talk, TB on re matters in general, Tessa re some of her concerns about how the families of September 11 victims had been handled, C re Al Jazeera and personnel for Islamabad, Guthrie and Geoff H re the same. TB spoke to Bush later and started to talk through some of the points in his note. Bush mentioned twice how grateful they had been that I had gone out there and was sorting out the media. DM felt it was in some ways the best call yet, because GWB sounded more mellow, keener to listen, more on the same wavelength again. But Rumsfeld was still going on about Iraq the whole time. We lost 3–0. I got home to do a note for us and the Americans on why I thought we should use the Al Jazeera interview.

Monday, October 29

The press was wobbling even more. I told an 8.30 meeting that it was time for us to get more robust, challenge the fundamental flakiness of the media. TB was at Chequers, in full cry about the need for improved rebuttal. I had a good meeting with Jamie Shea [director of information and press] and Mark Laity [senior spokesman] from NATO and put together a note for George Robertson trying to persuade him to give us more people. Paddy Feeny and Peter Reid [press attaché, UK Embassy] were already installed in Washington. Jim Wilkinson had pretty much got the thing up and running and we had our first properly functioning conference call. Another round of calls on a regular basis was another big chunk out of the diary

October '01: GWB grateful to AC for sorting out media

alongside all the meetings already in there, added to which today I was trying to draft TB's Welsh Assembly speech for tomorrow. I had forty minutes on the phone with Piers Morgan [editor, *Daily Mirror*], who was basically driven by spite re what he saw as favoured treatment of the *Sun*. I had an hour with the South-East group of [Labour] MPs and was beginning to curse Robert Hill for having talked me into doing these groups, though the feedback was pretty good.

TB's note had further galvanised people, and was useful to me in making clear around the system that the demand for this new centre of operations was his, not mine. I fell in the road and ripped my suit and badly bruised my leg running back from a meeting at the FCO. I was also late home and walked into another huge row after I told Fiona I would probably have to go on the trip to Israel. TB, as was clear from the office meeting, was also frustrated about the public services stuff. He had seen GB for a meeting on tax credits, now costing £4 billion.

Tuesday, October 30
TB had left by the time I got in to go to Bristol, then Wales for the speech. He had married my draft to his and it worked fine. I did the usual morning meeting then took one separately for all the people in the new CIC [Coalition Information Centre]. I felt things were starting to motor. [Lee] McLenny had arrived. [Mark] Laity was starting, though there were one or two concerns about how much he seemed to want to be the front man. I spoke to the Australian high commissioner [Michael L'Estrange] to get some of his people. I was disappointed that Karen Hughes had not yet been on one of the conference calls. I got Phil Bassett [head of Number 10 Research and Information Unit] to agree to go over to the FCO war room. I wanted him to be circulating agreed lines to take on all the difficult running issues to the three centres and relevant capitals. It would take a bit longer before we had a real grip, but I felt it was coming. I went over and did a pep talk, felt they were a good bunch. I said it was almost impossible to imagine us losing the military battle but perfectly feasible that we could lose the battle for hearts and minds. There was definitely a mood in the media, who were talking up anything that went wrong. Nick Soames [Conservative MP, former Armed Forces minister] called and said TB should make another Commons statement before long. He felt we were doing well and said we should ignore the press who were just 'loathsome creeps'.

I was starting to motor again but was also agitated that actually getting the three centres moving was too slow. I was still pressing on the Al Jazeera [Bin Laden interview] front but Condi wanted to wait because the president was going to try to get the Qataris to make sure it wasn't screened. I was sure it would get out there at some point, and as we knew the content, and the Al Jazeera worries, far better we got it out there first. I spoke to Karen about the idea of generating big women's events to talk about how ghastly the Taliban were. Bush had written to TB today and amid the other stuff had said explicitly how grateful they were for what we had done to change the approach. So it was beginning to work through and hopefully within a day or two we would be properly up and running. Mark Laity wasn't getting on with some of the others and slightly driving people mad.

TB was out in Syria, and got a total banjaxing by President Assad, which was a bit of a problem.[1] Assad had basically said enough for it to be seen as lambasting our entire approach. TB was giving him the benefit of the doubt, he said it was as much a clash of media cultures as anything, which was the line we tried to push to the hacks when we saw them on the plane later. I wasn't wholly sure why we felt it worth him going there in the first place. TB was in danger of getting hooked on the international stuff, having at first promised to take it easy, though Jonathan was probably right in pointing out that he was as well placed as anyone to do this, and that a lot of people round the world would rather see TB doing it, even on Bush's behalf, than Bush himself.

We were starting to get press calls about the CIC, so I put together a line. [David] Yelland [editor, Sun] was pitching for an interview with Bush. I sent him a blind copy of the letter I sent to Karen making the case for it and he sent her the most over-the-top CV-type letter I have ever seen, but he was basically being helpful at the moment. Also the Mirror seemed to be a bit more positive on the domestic front. I was flying out to meet TB for the Jordan and Israel part of his trip and was hoping not to be noticed because they would want to use it as part of the Syria crisis jigsaw they were trying to put together after Assad's big whack at him. When I spoke to TB about it before leaving for the airport, he seemed OK about it, said it had

[1] After repeating Syrian condemnation of the September 11 attacks, Assad defended 'resistance fighters', saying 'Resistance to occupation is an international right. Nobody can deny we have many organisations, many people who support the resistance fighters who seek to liberate their land.'

actually been quite comic to stand there having been promised the guy was going to be supportive and then watch him deliver an attack totally lapped up by our lot.

On the flight out, I did a stack of notes with Alison [Blackshaw] on things we needed to do at the three centres, areas for brainstorming, note to Geoff H re helping the *News of the World* with a shock issue on the Taliban. We arrived in Jordan and were driven to the palace where we had last been for the king's funeral.[1] TB was now talking about going back via Rome because there was a trilateral planned for Sunday and he was keen to keep Berlusconi vaguely on board.

Thursday, November 1

Amman. TB got an absolute mauling in the press for the 'Syrian humiliation', 'Disaster in Damascus' etc., way over the top in some ways, but there we are. I went out for a run round some of the hills near the palace, and loved the sounds of the city starting to wake up, particularly the calls to prayer. TB once said if I was religious I would probably end up as an Islamic fundamentalist, and I think I know what he meant. TB was trying to put his best face on after yesterday, and was comical in his description of it – 'It could have been worse, he could have taken out a gun and shot me' – but we also had a long chat with Jonathan and Tom K, later with the ambassador, Edward Chaplin, re how to retrieve the situation. All we could do was emphasise his willingness to take risks, get his hands dirty, do whatever it took, to work up and see through a plan. There was clearly no point trying to make out Assad had been anything but unhelpful, though TB was still of the view it was as much a clash of political and media cultures as a deliberate act of hostility.

We left for breakfast with King Abdullah. In common with others we had spoken to, he was worried about the impact of Al Jazeera, which was developing real sway among the broader Muslim community. We talked about the need to get clerics out emphasising the un-Islamic nature of OBL's words and deeds, and the need to reframe the argument from Islam vs West to moderate vs extreme forms of Islam. He was in two minds about whether we should engage more fully with Al Jazeera. He felt we had to be careful not to be exploited, or get to a situation where the more we did, the more they felt they had to represent 'the street'. It was an interesting take. He said that looking at the latest unbroadcast OBL tape, the problem was he 'looked the part', and we should not underestimate his appeal. The original

---

[1] The funeral of King Hussein, February 1999. See *Power and the People*, pp 652–6.

plan had been not to do media but in the end we did, and got him to push the line about the need for moderate Muslims to defeat extremists in argument.

It was a useful and very friendly meeting, and he certainly seemed like someone who grasped what TB was trying to do and wanted to help. His father was a hard act to follow, but he cut it as king, even if he could come across as being quite nervous at times. I sensed he agonised a lot, and at points I saw similarities with Prince Charles, though Abdullah has raw power. We boarded the helicopters and set off for Jerusalem, on the way discussing with TB how to develop this argument about moderate vs extreme, and how to challenge the assumptions, how to win round those countries basically supporting extreme views even if not always extreme actions. While he was seeing Shimon Peres [Israeli foreign minister], the Al Jazeera OBL interview was already circulating amongst his supporters in Pakistan. So it was out. I got DM to call Condi, and I called Karen H. She was very stroppy about being woken, while George agreed with me that we should just go for it, just do it. I was furious because it was now twelve days since we first knew of this interview, we had had all this time to sort it, and it just didn't happen. Here we were discussing how we were going to react WHEN it came out. The Americans were negotiating with the Qataris to suppress it, which was crazy, as all that would happen was that it would get spread underground and in its own way have even more impact, whereas I was sure if we had got it out in our terms, we could neutralise it in the Middle East and turn it to our advantage in the West. I was particularly fed up with it because it meant in a way I had lost the first battle to mount a serious media job on a tricky issue, and I was worried they didn't really get it.

TB and Peres overran, then I travelled with him to the [Ariel] Sharon meeting, before during and after which I was struck just how much heavier the security was for him and TB, not just the number of bodies around, but the barriers and the closed roads. Even we had to go through a weird series of obstacles before arriving at a kind of back door and in to see him. Sharon was less belligerent than usual and the lunch in many ways went fine, but they really just wanted to whack the Palestinians the whole time. At the press conference he was very uncompromising and I could sense our press getting very excited, building up for 'rebuff for Blair' Day 2. In fact, set against what he often said and how he said it, it wasn't that bad, but it was enough to give them what they wanted. Even accepting how difficult the politics were and even remaining conscious, as I always tried to, of the reasons why Israel existed in the first place, it was very hard to warm to Sharon. And this was him in fairly mellow mode. TB felt there was a lot more to him than he showed and agreed these exchanges were difficult. But TB had his own mantra, commitment to the right of Israel to exist alongside a Palestinian state.

We left for another long helicopter flight and drive to Palestine, handover at the checkpoint and then on to see Arafat, struck as ever, as it was impossible not to be, by the immediate switch from First World to Third. We had the usual over-the-top welcome and guard of honour and then in to see Arafat and Co. TB was urging Arafat to be more constructive in his comments on the Israelis, but of course it was like dealing with a mirror – the things we'd heard Sharon attacking them for, now we got the reverse view, equally forcefully. I was tired and hungry by now, knew that if I started eating the selection of nuts laid out on the tables I wouldn't stop, and so it proved. We had another helicopter flight to get us to the airport later and we were running late, TB moaning about being away so often, yet he was the one who now wanted to go to Genoa to see Berlusconi.

Friday, November 2

I spoke to Wes Clark [retired US general, Supreme Allied Commander, Europe, during the Kosovo conflict] to suggest we stay in touch and that he did regular media. He felt he was excluded from some circles because he was close to Clinton but he felt he had a lot to offer. I saw the SpAds [special advisers] from all the departments, did the usual spiel, then a very long briefing with the foreign press. I felt totally on top of the issues and in command of the arguments but they were beginning to pick up on the gap in a strategy based on hammering the Taliban whilst not fully supporting the Northern Alliance. Guthrie called, said Musharraf was a bit alarmed about the use of the word 'war', felt there were better ways of describing the situation. I always enjoyed talking to Charles who had a grasp of the issues that went way beyond the military. I was also talking to the Americans about an agreed Grid format and process. TB called as I was on the way home, said he was sure he had the makings of a plan to take the Middle East peace process forward. I said we cannot get so focused on the international but then lose sight of the domestic.

Saturday, November 3

The main story of the weekend developed into a diplomatic fiasco. While we were in the Middle East, Chirac had suggested another Big Three meeting and TB had agreed. That was really why he had wanted to go to Genoa on the way back, to try to keep Berlusconi sweet. With the papers starting to talk of the Big Three again, Berlusconi called TB to protest, and TB relented. That meant asking the Spaniards too. So while we were busy briefing that there was to be a meeting between the five major European military contributors to the effort, the Belgians bullied their way into it too, leaning on the Germans to say they would not do it without the Belgians. So that was them plus [Javier] Solana [Secretary General of the EU Council] now involved. Then [Wim] Kok [Netherlands Prime Minister] called TB to say if the Belgians were there and he wasn't, it was a political disaster. It was a total shambles, and by tomorrow we would have problems with the rest and TB would be getting the blame for splitting Europe. He felt we could emphasise that it was a good thing they all wanted to come, which was pretty lame. Throw in Syria, [Ariel] Sharon and now this, and it wasn't a great diplomatic picture.

TB remained torn about whether I should go up front as one of the CIC on-camera spokesmen. He felt I was probably the best person to do it but it would make spin a problem again. And this time possibly not just with the media but with the public. It was probably a bad idea all round because with all the travelling, and the long hours, I was already walking on eggshells at home. I asked the conference call to get a figure from the Pentagon of the percentage of Afghanistan land space that was being bombed. It came back pretty quickly – 0.0002536. I got John Reid [Northern Ireland Secretary, former Armed Forces minister] up deploying it as a way of trying to counter the media impression of the blanket bombing of the whole country. John was very good at communicating strategy – lay the ground, go for the front line, then further options which we were not going to flag up. I was starting to get not great feedback from Peter Reid and Paddy Feeny about Jim Wilkinson's operation in Washington. They felt he kept stuff to himself, didn't delegate and didn't really appreciate what we were doing. Peter described him as a human dynamo, real bundle of energy, but not a manager and so people didn't really know what they were meant to be doing.

Sunday, November 4

There was still too much focus for my taste on the Taliban claims, and not enough scepticism about them. The dinner at Number 10 was growing more and more farcical and ridiculous as the day went on and the guest list grew. By the end of the day, some of the hacks were calling it a bring-a-bottle party. I spoke to TB and we agreed he shouldn't do any media, partly because he'd find it so hard to keep a straight face. He had given up on trying to pretend there was a way of saying it showed Britain strong in Europe. What it showed was a reality – namely that France, Germany and Britain were more powerful than the rest – that others didn't like the reality and that we didn't feel sufficiently comfortable with the French and Germans just to be able to tough it out. Most of the foreign leaders actively wanted to do media, which was fine, and even the big guys like Chirac I think liked doing stuff outside Number 10, but there was something very comic about the whole thing. I was working up a briefing on the CBI [Confederation of British Industry] speech. GB had done a pretty positive section on EMU [Economic and Monetary Union] but then the *FT* claimed the spin on it was anti euro. GB flatly denied to TB there had been an operation to do him in on the euro.

Monday, November 5

TB called, first asking whether we 'got away with the dinner' – just about, though Christ knows what the other leaders made of it – but also, and more seriously, worrying about where we were on the euro. I saw him as soon as I got in, and he was still going on about it. 'It's so obvious what is going on – he [GB] is trying to get the right-wing press behind him by seeming to be anti euro, and the left-wing press by being pro the poor. My problem is in not being able to trust what he's saying on the euro.' The problem when the two of them were mistrustful was that it spread down through the operation. I went over to the CIC and they were now pretty much clear about the different functions, and who was doing what. TB set off for the CBI in Birmingham and his speech seemed to go down OK.

The US conference call was better, more focused and confident. We collated all the different Arab leaders and voices criticising OBL and started placing them more widely. They were also starting to involve us more in working through GWB's basic messages. I was arguing for him to be closely involved in this argument about extremism vs moderate Muslims. Peter Reid said Bush had visited the Washington CIC this morning which gave them a real boost. Also, after the conference call today, they had had for the first time a proper follow-through meeting. But some, notably the NSC [White House National Security Council], were still a bit antsy about us being involved and sometimes telling them what to do.

Tuesday, November 6

TB got OK coverage for the CBI speech, but it was seen in part as a rebuff to GB on the euro. I went up to see him in the flat and he told me of his chat with GB yesterday when GB denied doing a spin job on the euro but then went into an elaborate thing about how it was TB's fault because he had got the *Telegraph* to do a story about Roger Liddle [special adviser, European affairs] saying we were going in at a certain date as though the tests were irrelevant. TB said what worried him was that their bizarre understanding of how we operated meant it was almost certainly how they operated. He said he didn't mind madness but he minded madness that had a policy read-across. He thought there was something almost comic about GB pumping out the line about TB being too presidential when he was the one arguing for decentralisation and GB was in practice the great centraliser. GB had been at him again, saying he promised to help him become leader to which TB said, I did, and I will, but only if you are going to help me do what I need to do while I am here. His worry now was so deep that he actually had moments wondering whether Gordon wanted him to succeed at all, e.g. on public services, or with the euro. 'He wants to be the prime minister that finally delivers excellent public services and the prime minister at the time we make the decision on the euro. What irritates him about the war is that it might just see me build a reputation too big for him to handle.' This was not good. The way each thought of the other was not healthy.

I asked Scarlett whether we could divulge some of the material they had on the Taliban running out of money and he came back later saying we could. The papers had calmed down again and I think we were beginning to see the benefits of a properly organised strategy. TB said 'My ass is right out there and we just have to pull this off.' Jack had done an interview on OBL in *The Times* and we tried to push on that. I was constantly toing and froing between Number 10 and the Foreign Office, had a quick meeting with TB before leaving for the airport with Alison [Blackshaw], Phil Bassett and Lee McLenny.

I was at the airport to do the conference call, the focus on Taliban lies, the need to do more re opinion in Pakistan, and generate more moderate Arab voices. On the plane, I worked on a draft script for TB for tomorrow. I was met by Peter Reid and drove in to the embassy. Chris Meyer had put together a good group for dinner – Dan Bartlett, Jim Wilkinson, Charlotte Beers, Richard Boucher from the State Department, Tucker Eskew [White House media affairs], who was going to be coming over to work in the CIC in London. It was a good discussion and I felt they were more or less buying into our approach. But there was still no sign of the Pakistan spokesman and the tension between the White House and State [Department] was pretty clear. I quite liked Charlotte because she was different and thought a bit laterally, but I sensed she was driving the traditionalists a little crazy. She left reasonably early, and once Richard left both Dan and Jim really tore into the State Department. We agreed to there effectively being one 24-hour Grid that we all operated to. Meyer raised the question of when Powell was going to make the MEPP speech that had already had a lot of build-up, even without a date. There was still no sign of a date. Dan said that my last visit had been a catalyst to get them going properly, and now we had to start producing results, and above all get the military plugged in better. That was the other big lesson from Kosovo.

Wednesday, November 7

Slept pretty well, out for a really good run in near perfect temperature, then back for breakfast with Meyer, Phil Bassett and Lee McLenny. What we had all picked up last night and again today, was the tension between the White House and State. It was clear this wasn't just about the Pentagon. I had a stack of meetings lined up, first with Victoria ['Torie'] Clarke at the Pentagon. We did the conference call from there. She was very easy to talk to, very open and receptive and agreed we had to find ways to help them off the hook Rumsfeld had landed them on of having to brief every day. We had to get the media to understand there was more to a media plan than media briefings, and that they couldn't expect to see the same people all the time.

Then to the CIC, which had been really well set up, with beautifully designed signs above desks saying what everyone did, the office well laid out, atmosphere OK, Jim Wilkinson very dynamic, a bit introspective. Then over to see Mary Matalin to discuss the *Sun* and BBC interviews we were hoping Cheney would do, and how best to project message from them. She was an interesting character, had a rich voice, an accent I couldn't place on the class scale. She was attractive in a very unclassical kind of way and could be very funny, e.g. about what life was like in the 'secure undisclosed location' they go to in times of crisis. I so couldn't get my head around how she, committed Republican working for one of the real hate figures of the Democrats, could live with James Carville, a committed Democrat even more driven and obsessive about politics than her. But she was adamant it worked. Of all of them, I felt she was the one who most shared my understanding of the difference between strategy and tactics.

Then over to see Karen, via Karl Rove. She had a bad cold. My main worry was the slowness with which we were going for the Pakistan operation, and the lack of a spokesman yet. I didn't feel

Karen was totally on top of things. She was obviously very focused on Bush, but probably not as plugged in across the system as I had hoped, and of course it was probably, almost certainly, a harder machine to drive. In between times, I was talking to Anji [Hunter] whose departure day was now set, and we talked over how to deal with any fallout. BP [Hunter's new employer] would be doing the basic announcement. She said she was relieved that she was finally going, but also upset at the way things had panned out. Then off to the State Department and the guy sent down to escort me up was clearly pretty disaffected. I was making small talk in the lift and before long he was saying he didn't like what we were doing, that it wasn't really diplomacy. Fair enough. I later told [Colin] Powell that we needed to see more of him and less of Rumsfeld in Europe.

I bumped into the [House of Commons] Foreign Affairs Select Committee who were on an official visit and chatted to some of them. Then back to the White House and over to meet TB. He, Jonathan, DM, Meyer and I went in to see Bush. They did most of the meeting one-on-one. [Retired US general] Wayne Downing [Deputy National Security Advisor for combating terrorism] said to me 'Ah, you are the infamous Alastair whose name I now see on everything.' I couldn't quite work out if he was being friendly or not. Jonathan and I were both talking to Powell to suggest he upped his profile a bit. He didn't do much to dispel the idea of pretty considerable divisions.

TB and Bush had pretty much done most of the heavy stuff by the time they called us in. They ran through things but in a fairly prosaic way. Bush cracked a joke about not being intelligent enough to meet the head of Pakistani intelligence, but apart from that there was not much of note beyond them both preparing lines for the media event. It went OK but Bush gave a really poor answer on the Middle East. TB by contrast was on form, as Powell told him as he came off. Over dinner, TB came close to being very irritating because he was in his full-on statesman mode, almost lecturing on the lessons from Northern Ireland, the advice he had given to Putin etc. Bush at one point was going on about going after OBL to kill him – 'I mean bring him to justice.' On the plane back, TB said he felt Bush had been a lot more focused, had thought more about the future of Afghanistan, relations with Russia. He had not been much impressed by his dealings so far with Europe.

Thursday, November 8

As we landed, Robert Hill called to say Henry McLeish [Scottish First Minister] was about to resign. This was what Peter MacMahon

[McLeish's spokesman] had called about last night when we were waiting to leave the White House, to say they believed the *Herald* had another story that was about to be a killer blow, which indeed it was.[1] I got TB to speak to him and he was very warm. We got in to Number 10. TB was a bit angst-ridden re Anji going. Cabinet was all Afghanistan and with GB at Treasury questions, the mood was a lot better than usual. The CIC was much more into its stride now. King Abdullah [of Jordan] was in for lunch and was pretty sound, privately and in the doorstep afterwards.

As during Kosovo, I was getting annoyed at the sense of moral equivalence [in the media] between what we said, in systems of democracy founded on the duty of politicians to tell the truth, and regimes like Milosevic and the Taliban who felt no such obligations, and yet whose word, even when proven to be false, was often given exactly the same weight. Musharraf came in and while he was talking to TB one-on-one, I had a long session with his finance minister [Shaukat Aziz] and press secretary [General Rashid Qureshi] who said they were supportive of the CIC in Islamabad and would help. The press guy and I were called in to see TB and Musharraf to go over basic arguments to push at the press event, again focusing on moderate vs extreme, and talking up the basic decency of the vast bulk of the Pakistani community in Britain. I was feeling the workload very heavy at the moment, because I was now more plugged into the American side, and had these three centres of operation, all of them producing their own paper flows, bad ideas amid the good, and personnel issues, some of them a screaming pain.

Friday, November 9

I felt bad at not having gone to Anji's farewell last night, but it would have been a step too far to have come back from yet another trip and then gone out, to Anji's farewell in particular. Kate [Garvey, events and visits team] came on in tears, said I was the only one of the old team who hadn't been there and it was terrible when people fell out. TB's big media event of the day would be a press conference with [José María] Aznar [Spanish Prime Minister], which would coincide with the news that Mazar-e-Sharif finally was about to fall after what sounded like some pretty heroic stuff from some of our guys out there. I was due to do a foreign press briefing at 12 and wanted to focus again on the unbroadcast Al Jazeera [Bin Laden] video. I got TB, DM and Scarlett

[1] McLeish resigned later the some day, saying he accepted full responsibility for mistakes in the subletting of his constituency office.

to agree to it and say we would use it to do a revised evidence document. I called Jim Wilkinson just before the briefing, said I was going to do it and he said hold on so he could speak to Karen H. The president had been against it before and that was a real reason not to do it. I said try to get clearance and let me know during the briefing. I left Julian [Braithwaite] outside to wait for the call while I started the briefing, largely on the MEPP discussions and TB's visits. Julian came in and said go with it provided I don't mention Al Jazeera, just that it's a video circulating, so that was fine. But because I did it in the middle of the briefing, it didn't fly as I hoped.

Before the press conference, TB said to Aznar 'What do you want me to say on Gibraltar?' to which I said 'Don't answer that.' Aznar was pretty strong on the war. Also the Dutch were preparing to send troops so I tried to organise the newly arrived Tucker [Eskew] to get some positive US reaction. The [*Evening*] *Standard* splashed on a picture of TB looking a bit tired under the headline 'Shattered', which at least communicated how much he had been doing. Geoff H was on the rampage because the *Mirror* had changed the words of an article he had done and totally misrepresented it. I gave the *News of the World* material on the Taliban running out of money and teed up the *Sunday Telegraph* to use the OBL video material to incriminate him more and highlight the stuff about him being genocidal vs the Jews and other races.

By the end of the day, [the capture of] Mazar-e-Sharif was a big story but I went ballistic about [BBC correspondent] Rageh Omaar's piece, called [Richard] Sambrook saying it was a fucking disgrace, really lost it with him.[1] TB was off to Chequers with Aznar. Cheney did his interview with Yelland which they planned to do over five pages. I was home by 8, tired, but feeling things were moving our way a bit.

Saturday, November 10

The main story was Mazar and an interview from OBL claiming he had nukes, but the best line from our perspective, which we got running in the US and Pakistan straight away, was the line that it was OK to kill thirteen-year-olds, and also that Afghanistan was the only truly Islamic country. One of the lines we had been trying to get up was that their basic desire was to 'Talibanise' every country, and this allowed us to do that. TB was due at the [Labour Party] National

[1] Campbell would fax a lengthy letter to Sambrook asking if he was satisfied that his reporters had not fallen 'foul of . . . [BBC] guidelines on scepticism, terrorist claims, speculation, staged events or the guideline which says reporters should make it clear when they have not been able to witness events themselves?' Sambrook defended their reporting.

Policy Forum and we agreed he should do a clip on that part of the interview, try to isolate OBL from more reasonable governments and opinions. I did a [Foreign Office] telegram to all posts saying they should generate reaction. TB said he felt for the first time things moving our way a bit, and the Americans deploying a strategy.

The White House/State problems had flared up a bit in the open, Karen Hughes reacting very angrily to an interview by Charlotte Beers in which she had spoken about Bush as a 'product'. We were still having trouble getting things off the ground in Pakistan. The Pakistanis were still asking for delay. I wasn't feeling terribly focused today, but a combination of Mazar, military momentum, and OBL's own remarks being used against him had us in a far better place. I managed a few hours off whereas TB, as well as the NPF, also had an Armistice event.

The *Sunday Telegraph* splashed on the OBL [Al Jazeera interview] words 'Yes I did it' which helped push it on into Sunday. I also had to get involved with the *Mail on Sunday* chasing Alastair Irvine.[1] Derry [Irvine, Lord Chancellor] had spoken to the paper and they were splashing on his words and that was that. I said to Derry, why didn't you phone me? He sounded very down. 'Don't persecute me, this is bad enough already.' Alison [Derry Irvine's wife] was very low, obviously because of Alastair and also because of all the coverage about them around the time of Donald's death [Donald Dewar, First Minister of Scotland and former husband of Alison Irvine]. 'I think we pay a heavy price for being in power. I sometimes wonder what is the point of being in power when we are powerless to do anything about the evil that the press bring into the lives of our families. When I say evil, I mean evil. They are Satan's people on earth, no compassion, no decency at all.' We agreed a tough line about this being despicable and their attempts to pretend it was a story about drugs policy as being utterly transparent. We had done an article for the *Mail on Sunday* by TB and I called them to pull it, saying I didn't want to see his name on an article that they would use to give credibility to a rag I viewed as being total scum.

Sunday, November 11
There appeared to be a bit of difference opening up. Bush saying to the Northern Alliance not to take Kabul, Hoon in the *Sunday Times* saying we were moving on to Kabul. I spent a lot of the day helping Derry

---

[1] The 24-year-old son of Lord Chancellor Derry Irvine had been exposed by the *Mail on Sunday* as a crack-cocaine addict seeking treatment in the US.

deal with the press trying to do stuff on Alastair. He called me at 8 to go over the letter he wanted to send to [Lord John] Wakeham [Press Complaints Commission chairman], who coincidentally was on *Frost* attacking a judge's decision to gag the *People* about a footballer's sex life. TB's basic take was that they were scum, but we had to deal with them, and he wasn't convinced that meant through legislation. Derry said he strongly believed there should be a privacy law and the requirement in law to strive for accuracy. He believed, and I shared his view, that they now actually do damage to the standing and reputation of the country, because serious people think there is something odd and a bit disturbing about a country with a press like ours. GH did *The World this Weekend* [BBC Radio 4] and said we had UK forces on the ground, which was bound to go big and would raise questions about why they were only mentioned now. I spent some time working on a letter to Sambrook. Catherine Rimmer and Chris McShane [Number 10 Research and Information Unit] had done some excellent work showing where specific reports broke their own guidelines. TB called after the Cenotaph, said he was surprised to see IDS wearing his medals. The Royals had been very friendly, especially the Queen Mum.

Monday, November 12

The news had turned right round because of Mazar-e-Sharif and there was a real impression of there being a strategy unfolding so there was a much better mood around the place. OBL saying Afghanistan was the only truly Islamic nation opened up a whole host of opportunities and we brainstormed on how to make sure it struck right round the Muslim world. At TB's office meeting, we tried to stay focused on the domestic and public services in particular. He was worrying that departments were slowing and slacking a bit whereas now, with so much media focus on the international, it was the time really to be driving forward. I sometimes wondered whether we weren't victims of what might be defined as success. For example, TB wanted a more centralised system, or at least one where Number 10 could pull levers more effectively in departments. But did it mean that when we weren't focusing so much, they were waiting for the levers to be pulled? Don't know. Also, had we to some extent been responsible for some ministers thinking things only mattered if there was profile attached to them? Again, not sure.

TB was also worried that Anji's departure would leave gaps – she did give him a particular Middle England kind of view, and she was particularly good at schmoozing those people that Jonathan and I didn't have much to do with, particularly some of the right-wing opinion formers. RW came to see me to say he was really angry at the dreadful press he was getting. I said I hadn't really noticed it. He said it was worse than anything I ever got. I said don't be ridiculous, I've been savaged so many times in the press I've given up even noticing. He said beneath the nastiness in the headlines, they sort of acknowledged I was brilliant whereas with him, they just wrote him off. I said this is what they do, try to undermine anyone who is doing a good professional job because they want to render us illegitimate. Papers like the *Mail* felt it was wrong for anyone to serve a Labour government. They had done it to Guthrie, and they will do it to him because he is doing a perfectly good job and he shouldn't let it get to him. I had to do the eleven o'clock because both Godric and Tom were late in. It went fine, and the main focus was the advance of the Northern Alliance and I got up the idea of Taliban morale crumbling. Vajpayee was in for lunch, mainly the two of them, then a doorstep.

As we began the 2.30 conference call a plane was crashing in Queens, New York, and it appeared to be on our television before theirs.[1] I could hear Mary Matalin calling James [Carville] to turn on the TV. But actually, considering, they were pretty calm and we discussed Ramadan and also how to build up the women's events we were planning. TB spoke to GWB around 4, reviewed military strategy, discussed Ramadan and how to use an evidence document. I called George Robertson and said Mark Laity was maybe too senior and was becoming a bit of a problem for some of the guys over there. I asked for someone more junior. Tucker [Eskew] was making a difference, hard-working, supportive, he seemed to be able to make things happen pretty well. I really wanted us to get up a humanitarian story now though, so it wasn't just about dropping bombs and fighting. The New York plane crash was pretty huge. Ari Fleischer was doing fine on it, but not a nice thing to have to deal with. The general feeling was that it was an accident but who knows?

Tuesday, November 13
I woke to the news that Kabul had fallen, with John Simpson [BBC world affairs editor] seeming to claim that he had liberated it.[2] All

---

[1] American Airlines Flight 587 crashed shortly after take-off, killing all 260 people on board and five people on the ground. Though al-Qaeda claimed responsibility, a subsequent investigation found that the crash had been accidental, caused by overuse of rudder controls during turbulence.

[2] Simpson, one of the first journalists to enter Afghanistan, having disguised himself as a woman in a burqa, declared on entering Kabul 'It was only BBC people who liberated this city. We got in ahead of Northern Alliance troops.'

the armchair generals now moved on from saying the military strategy hadn't worked to saying that we had fucked up the diplomatic channels. And that was what was worrying TB when I got in. He looked tired, had not slept much. I told him that GB was meeting all the church leaders downstairs and he just rolled his eyes. TB called a meeting of the inner War Cabinet. CDS was still pretty gloomy though he did at least have detailed plans for going in. TB wanted ideas on how the military plan should now be taken forward and extended and how we get the diplomatic channels moving faster. He also wanted specific ideas on the humanitarian side of things and he wanted to put forward military, political/diplomatic and the humanitarian plans to Bush by lunchtime. He wasn't sure they would listen but he said this was the time to build out with a real plan of action. I saw the Scottish group of [Labour] MPs where Tam Dalyell went off on one re TB being presidential and I really got stuck in. There were amazing pictures from Kabul, and now it was on to Kandahar and also get in a better position on the humanitarian front. Burnley beat Watford 1–0.

Wednesday, November 14

The news overnight was our troops on standby. I complained first thing about today's poll from the Muslim community.[1] The *Mirror* and the *Mail* led on a picture of the Northern Alliance butchery of a Taliban solider and it was obvious we were going to cop it for any brutality on the way in. There was plenty of 'What now?' stuff. Polly Toynbee [*Guardian*] did an excellent piece about our media culture. TB called as I was driving in and agreed that he should do a statement. He shared my amazement at the ability of our press to turn yesterday into a problem. I said to Tucker at the morning meeting 'Hey, great news, we lost.' He had been genuinely shocked by the desire of most of our media, or so it felt to him, to fail. TB spoke to Bush and then Schroeder then worked on the statement. The top line was that the Taliban was defeated. TB was still pushing to go faster and further on the political front but it was so difficult mobilising international action on the back of fast-moving events. The coverage out of Kabul was extraordinary though and there was a sense of people's lives changing instantly. PMQs was OK. The statement was fine content-wise but TB was really tired and not really on form. I think both of us felt a bit that you work your guts

[1] A BBC poll suggested eighty per cent of UK Muslims were opposed to military action in Afghanistan.

November '01: Kabul – the Taliban has been defeated

out, you strive with everything you've got to make something happen, every step of the way people are saying you can't do it and then when it happens, they are just straight on to saying you can't do the next thing. It wasn't even about a desire for recognition of achievement. It was just the feeling of grind that went with the situation that our media made everything feel like swimming through treacle.

There was going to be a UN presence by Friday and the UK diplomatic presence by the weekend. There was a fantastic story to be told about the role played by a small number of our spooks and special forces, if C and Co. were up for it. John Scarlett had also been superb, calm, clear, always meticulous about the material he assembled and put forward to the PM, but just as willing to give bad news as good. I had a meeting with David Puttnam [Labour peer, former film producer], who I like and think is one of the rare cases of people adapting from success in one world at a very high level to success at a different level in politics. He told me both the BBC and *Guardian* had said to him they were genuinely worried about their relations with us. He also wanted to say that Estelle [Morris] was a real star but she needed boosting and she needed help that she would never ask for herself. I got Tucker in to say hello to TB. He told me afterwards he had never seen a politician who thought so quickly on his feet, who could assimilate big arguments quickly and make them simple.

Thursday, November 15

The news was dominated by [eight Western] aid workers being released [after three months held captive by the Taliban]. Mullah Omar did the BBC World Service. At the War Cabinet, there was a bad scene with Clare because she was totally opposed to putting in a senior humanitarian figure in overall charge. The obvious assumption was her worry of being overshadowed or outperformed but her argument was that there were enough tensions between the various agencies and organisations and this would make it worse. Cabinet was obviously largely dominated by the events in Afghanistan and the diplomatic follow-through. Then I had a session briefing Clare before she did the press conference on the humanitarian side of things. She really was ghastly to deal with. She would give every impression of agreeing with you, and then do or say something different; or she would just have an argument for the hell of it, but in that whiney 'everyone but me is wrong' voice that made me want to seal my ears with hot wax.

Friday, November 16

We had to hope that the real story of yesterday didn't come out, namely that our our guys had landed but the FCO had forgotten to ask the Northern Alliance for authority and protection so that Abdullah Abdullah [soon to become foreign minister, Afghan government-in-exile] went crazy and at one point they were even asking our guys at Baghram [airbase, Kabul] to leave. The Americans had finally settled on a spokesman for Islamabad, former ambassador Kenton Keith, and he came in for a meeting. Nice guy, fairly quiet but intelligent and he seemed to be on the right track. I then had a meeting with David Manning and the NATO experts while David and I did a very good briefing on the new moves to bring Russia closer to NATO, which was very much a product of TB's thinking and DM's detail and drive. He was such a nice guy, and so absolutely professional. Often at these briefings, with a Foreign Office policy expert, I would just have at the back of my mind a worry that they would say something that would give us a problem. But with David I had absolute confidence.

Conference call was largely about the women's events, plus I was pushing for the *News of the World* to get a piece from Rumsfeld. The Americans were still focused almost totally on the military campaign. Rumsfeld did a briefing showing pictures of Northern Alliance forces with American special forces on horseback. Rumsfeld had definitely emerged as one of the characters of the campaign, was much more popular in the States than here but in his own way had been more impressive than Colin Powell who had come over as a bit weak and dithery. Then, from left field, Mo [Mowlam, former Cabinet minister] had done a [Michael] Cockerell film [BBC political documentary, *Cabinet Confidential*] and said TB was presidential, had killed Cabinet government and the TB/GB relationship was unhappy. JP was asked about it in front of cameras and used the line 'She's daft.' He called me afterwards. I felt he wasn't far wrong.

Saturday, November 17

The *FT* second lead, part inspired by Mo and part by the usual chat around the place, talked of an 'all-time low' between TB and GB, included the stuff about him doing in Byers, messing around on the euro, generally very anti GB. TB was exercised about it, said it was bad anyway, but also that the party really wouldn't like it if they felt TB was going for GB. It was one thing for the guy at the top to be under attack but it would look bad for TB if it was reciprocated. I spoke to Ian Austin [Brown's spokesman] who did his usual ludicrous 'we never brief the press' routine and descended into a lot of inarticulate rambling. The problem was there was a reality fault-line problem and it had to be addressed. But the thing was that other ministers were starting to take a lead, starting to think this was the way to get on.

TB felt Afghanistan was going better so far as we and the Americans were concerned but he couldn't understand why Brahimi was not more proactive. There was also a Reuters report of the Northern Alliance asking our troops to leave Baghram, so we had to deal with that. I went to Coventry vs Burnley with Calum, and did the conference call in the car park, regularly interrupted by supporters coming over to shout down the phone. Laura Bush was doing the broadcast out there as part of the build-up to the women's event. The Sundays were wall to wall and not much to worry about, though there was far too much TB/GB stuff. We were obviously heading for another wave of it.

Sunday, November 18

John Scarlett had been to the US and said they were more hopeful of finding OBL. He said it would be easier if he stayed in Afghanistan, so I suggested we have a plan to brief round the place that as Afghanistan is 'the only Islamic country on earth' it would be a terrible defeat and loss of face for him to go elsewhere. John felt that departure to Pakistan via the North-West was his only possible option for leaving but even that, it wasn't clear he could do. I had a long run, then took the kids to see Harry Potter [and the Philosopher's Stone, the first film in the series]. I couldn't quite understand the ballyhoo, and I slept through the second half. The GB stuff was running big again. There was no science to this but sometimes a mood just developed and a combination of Mo and the FT, then fuelled by others off the record, got us in a bad place. GB came out of it badly but so did the whole government. It felt dangerous.

Monday, November 19

I was really tired, and emotionally drained after a weekend split evenly between working, time with the kids, and arguing with Fiona. The news was ragged and there seemed to be real confusion over what our troops were doing. The American focus seemed to be almost entirely getting OBL, with the future of Afghanistan barely getting a look-in. So it looked like our troops were sitting there for no purpose, with neither the NA nor the Americans really wanting them there, so it was a bit messy. I probably underestimated how hard the last few weeks had been and maybe I was going in for a crash period. I had to find some energy from somewhere. TB said we had to stop any attacks on GB. He didn't think I was doing it directly, but the mood music he and I generated gave others licence, and we had to do everything we could to stop it. I spoke firmly to my lot while Jeremy [Heywood, principal private secretary] sent round an email saying the markets would react badly if this stuff went on. Later he, GB, Balls and Simon Virley [private secretary, economic affairs] had a PBR meeting with TB. TB said Balls was 'unbelievably rude' to all the Number 10 people, including him.

I had lunch with Andrew Marr at Christopher's [restaurant]. He said the problem was the reality – we could talk all we want about how well they work together, but they all knew GB was angry and smouldering because he was consumed with ambition for the top job. TB was back to his point about the danger of 'policy read-across' in what was essentially a personality thing. He had asked GB what he called a few polite questions about the tax credits and he was met with a bombardment. I had quite a nice time with Marr who, though self-obsessed, at least thought about things and I think appreciated how hard government was, and how comparatively well we did it. The Pakistan CIC was due finally to open tomorrow and the planning on that dominated the conference call. I saw Pat McFadden [former Number 10 deputy chief of staff] and persuaded him to go to Pakistan.

Tuesday, November 20
I didn't feel great and stayed in bed till 10. I wouldn't have gone in at all but I had a couple of meetings it was difficult to move. Clare gave us a bit of a problem when she told a select committee that the US record on aid wasn't good.[1] TB called re Clare and said 'Just try to finesse it.' I said finessing Clare Short was beyond anyone.

Wednesday, November 21
We were still communicating a sense of split with us wanting to put more troops in and the US not, us wanting the focus to shift to the future of Afghanistan, and the US not. Added to which Clare's comments to the DFID select committee gave us a continuing problem which was on the conference call, the Yanks clearly a bit agitato. Dan said to me later, how much money do we have to spend overseas before people start to recognise who the biggest donor in the world is? Jack Straw came through for the morning meeting to go over his press

[1] Short told the House of Commons International Development Select Committee of communications between aid agencies and the US military 'not being taken seriously enough at a high level'.

conference in the [Downing Street] Pillared Room re his trip to Iran and Pakistan and a bit more on the humanitarian push. The Taliban did a press conference with a 'No surrender' top line, also saying they didn't have contact with OBL. Rumsfeld's basic position was that they didn't want anything that detracted from the hunt for OBL, so having had out troops on 48-hour standby, they had to be let down again.

Halfway through the main PMQs meeting at lunchtime, Godric came through to say Clare had done *The World at One* [BBC Radio 4] and had another whack at the US, saying the UK and France were ready to go in but they were holding things back.[1] TB rolled his eyes, shook his head, muttered 'She's just not serious' but the truth was every time she did it and got away with it, she knew she was able to get away with it next time. She had been indulged too much for too long. I reminded him how virtually everyone, including Neil [Kinnock], who had ever worked with her, had said she should be one of the earliest casualties. [David] Yelland came to see me prior to his meeting with GB and I did my best to persuade him the TB/GB relationship was OK.

Thursday, November 22

I could feel myself going down with flu and losing my voice. GB had done an interview in *The Times* about how great the Cabinet was. It was all a bit much, protesting too much, and the general take around the place was that it was embarrassing. TB/GB was without doubt the government fault line, as well as part of its strength. But we had to do something about it. We couldn't allow it just to become a given, another Number 10/11 relationship going wrong because of personal rivalries. Prior to the War Cabinet, GH and CDS briefed TB on the operations going on in the south. CDS was looking tired and grey, and I didn't feel got any real satisfaction out of his job. He and Geoff were not in the same place about what to do with the troops who had been on 48-hour standby. John Scarlett said at the War Cabinet the Americans were putting massive effort into the hunt for OBL, and we had to be careful not to take our eye off other parts of this that needed very careful attention. I did a briefing for the foreign press on tomorrow's Europe speech and Afghanistan, using the line from the Taliban yesterday that it was 'time to forget' as a way of getting up facts about the nature of the regime. I had agreed with Tim Livesey

---

[1] After Short told the BBC radio programme of the 'regrettable' delay in deploying US troops to protect aid convoys, Downing Street commented 'Clare Short speaks for herself.'

[press officer, foreign affairs] we should use it to do a big number on the EMU section of the speech tomorrow. I had to persuade TB first though. I was rapidly losing my voice, and by the time I had done an interview with the 'Mind Out' mental health campaign [to raise awareness of mental health problems], I was washed up and went home.

Friday, November 23

Felt dreadful, and stayed in all day. My briefing of yesterday went big, leading several papers and the radio, the BBC doing the 'most pro EMU yet', usual bollocks. TB was happy enough with it, and did want to press on, but was pissed off at the *Sun*, which splashed on the line that we would have a euro referendum to coincide with a general election in 2005. Trevor [Kavanagh, *Sun* political editor] called early, claiming he had written it based on something I had said to Yelland, which was bollocks. The big problem with Europe was that most of the papers had a line and no real interest in setting things out as we said them. Despite feeling crap, I did the conference call but they were lacking energy and at the moment had just become glorified 'lines to take' discussions. The new common line coming out of the media re Afghanistan was 'bloodbath fears'. I turned on the telly to watch TB's speech, the start of which was delayed because a member of the audience collapsed, and TB called afterwards and said the poor guy had 'lost his bowels', said it had taken a while to clear the place up and it was the first time he had rushed through a speech because of the smell. The speech went fine, good mood music without anyone really going for it as a change of policy.[1]

Saturday, November 24

I took Rory to do his cross-country race. TB called and said we were still discovering things they [Brown's Treasury team] were trying to sneak by us in the Pre-Budget Report. It really was unacceptable the way they operated on these big Treasury moments. He was fine about the way the Europe speech panned out, worried about the PBR, and not sure where the war stuff was all going. He was also still anxious about the briefing going on re Anji. I was really fed up with all the soap-opera stuff. The conference call was all about the difficult questions re the siege [of Kunduz in northern Afghanistan, where the Taliban were besieged by the

[1] In the speech to the European Research Institute in Birmingham, Blair criticised the 'embarrassingly long history of Euroscepticism' in the UK, saying that whilst the economic tests for entry into the euro should first be met, it was time to recognise that Britain's future was 'inextricably linked with Europe'.

Northern Alliance] and whether we were responsible for prisoners. We agreed we must not make ourselves so in anything we said, whilst it was legally checked out.

Sunday, November 25

The war coverage in the Sundays wasn't so bad. Stewart Steven [*Mail on Sunday*] was apparently saying I should go. Crap stuff on public services clearly coming down the rails. Charles Clarke did the *Westminster Hour* and said some parts of the NHS were worse than before, which would go a bit.

Monday, November 26

Pat [McFadden] and Tanya [Joseph] both called me to say the briefing in Pakistan had been poor, because Kenton had been unable to say anything much about the Marines and Kandahar.[1] We were clearly going to have a problem getting all bits of the American machine to see the CIC operations, particularly the one in Islamabad, as a place where anything and everything could be briefed. I spoke to Jim Wilkinson [in Washington], and we agreed we had to be more punchy about the message, faster in prising information out of the military, and more disciplined in the deployment of lines to take. I took up the same theme in the conference call, said that the point of these was to set communications strategy, not just discuss the issues of the day. The other theme coming up, as well as the division in troop deployment, was 'where next?' I wasn't on good form. I felt that after a good start, we were no longer making the weather. The processes were the right ones but not being followed rigorously enough, and the calls were too unstructured and meandering. We went to the launch of the book on Neil [*Kinnock*, by Martin Westlake and Ian St John] with Calum and Grace. Neil got very emotional in his speech, and it was a nice enough do.

Tuesday, November 27

It was the start of the Bonn [inter-Afghanistan] talks under [Lakhdar] Brahimi, and also the battle of the Mazar-e-Sharif fort [Qala-i-Jangi prison] was still going on.[2] The main focus of the day was the PBR.

[1] The first of a major deployment of US Marines had landed by helicopter south of the Taliban stronghold of Kandahar.
[2] At the end of the prison revolt, eighty-six Taliban prisoners would be alive, out of an original 300–500, after seven days of fierce fighting with Northern Alliance and American and British special forces. The Taliban prisoners had surrendered at Mazar-e-Sharif believing they would be set free.

TB came down from the flat, having finally got GB to deliver more for health. It was ridiculous that we had to go through this rigmarole the whole time. We probably ended up pretty much where GB expected us to in the first place, maybe with a bit more on top, but surely we could have got there without what had been a very difficult process. It had been crazy. What's more, there was only one story that was going to dominate, namely that taxes would have to rise to pay for a better NHS. Possibly the biggest strategic decision we would take this parliament, and though we had all known it was coming, we were catching up late in terms of the strategic discussions that we should have had ages ago. But again, it was a result of having conceded too much to him early on. After the PBR Cabinet, I had a meeting with Ed Balls, who came in with all the published documents. I asked him when they went to the printers, and he said he didn't know. I said one thing's for sure, that GB was still getting his ear bent by TB about what was in it after it had gone.

At Cabinet, GB did his usual stuff, plenty of big message, plenty of figures and it went down OK, though this was an easier audience than the public would be. Taxes up for a better NHS was a pretty strong Labour line, and most Labour people would like it, but we were going to have to engage in a pretty big argument, not least around value for money, to win it with the public. If we did though, it would be a significant shift and an important win. Pat seemed to be making a difference in Pakistan and was pretty much in charge of Kenton's words. I had been hoping that once we got the CICs up and running, they would go on autopilot, but I was having to do a lot of hours every day re all three.

The PBR went OK, albeit surrounded by too much tax and spend. TB said GB's problem was that he sometimes lacked subtlety and everything was so obviously political. He had announced [Sir Derek] Wanless [banker] to conduct a review of future NHS funding but most people would see him as a stooge there to do what GB wanted done. I quite liked that, but there was a danger the only message was tax and spend.

DTLR put out minutes of the Byers Railtrack meeting but only four pages.[1] Crazy. I told Byers I thought it was a bad plan and they should never have hired Martin Sixsmith [DTLR director of communications]. Byers thought I had given my approval. It turned out he had asked his office to check what 'Alastair' thought of Sixsmith, and they had

[1] The government had decided in October to put Railtrack in administration.

asked Alistair Darling [Work and Pensions Secretary], who seemingly said he thought he was fine.

Wednesday, November 28

TB/GB relations were so bad that it was currently almost impossible to get either of them to say anything good about the other. TB felt there was a personal/political motivation to pretty much anything GB did. He was 'diddling' the whole time. TB said maybe he had always been like that, but when we did less important jobs, and when so much of what we did was about campaigning, it didn't seem to matter so much. He said we had to try to harness his ambition with the national interest. A lot of the time, it coincided, but not always. We had a meeting with GB re PMQs and how to handle the PBR fallout. The tax and spend argument was the obvious one for the Tories to go on, but we could take it easily to investment vs cuts. PMQs went fine, and style-wise, TB was getting more relaxed, less reliant on notes, getting the big arguments in his head and then finding ways of pushing them out there. I ran home, first proper run for almost a week.

Thursday, November 29

PBR coverage was going a bit awry. After a pretty low-key War Cabinet, TB saw GB and Alan Milburn, who was livid, said that basically GB was trying to use his position to take over NHS policy [via Brown's Wanless review], and he wasn't having it. He was not alone in feeling departments had not been properly involved in the PBR preparations. TB said we had to get an agreed strategy going forward and asked me to do a meeting with the Treasury and Health, which I did, and tried to make a start but there was no doubt Number 10, the Treasury and the Health department were not all in the same place, nothing like it. It did sometimes feel like there were two governments, and when TB had so much of his time and energy focused on foreign affairs, that feeling was maybe stronger. CDS was really steamed up about the arguments they had had to get involved in yesterday re SAS identification [an injunction had been taken out against the *Sun*]. For him, he was quite emotional, really felt that newspapers that couldn't see why it was important that these principles were adhered to were beyond the pale.

The mood at Cabinet wasn't good. TB was a bit late, GB was not communicating, the departmental ministers were largely pissed off because of the PBR. Robin [Cook] got rolled over on his paper [White Paper on reform of the House of Lords] and ended up looking a bit bruised. There was a discussion of sorts on health but it was a bad atmosphere and I was glad when they all trooped out. The *Mirror* came in for lunch, Piers Morgan behaving like a child. TB let it go for a while but then put him down heavily once Morgan started to get on his high horse about the *Sun* and his claims we gave them the election date. He went on and on until eventually TB said that he had better not be calling him a liar. Chirac was in later but I missed a lot of it because I was doing the conference call, which was mainly Bonn [Afghanistan talks]. We were slightly losing our way strategically. I had to motivate myself to get going again.

Friday, November 30

GB's latest thing was an interview with the *Sun* yesterday, done to try to show the PBR was not the end of New Labour, but he ended up going contrary to the strategy we had agreed yesterday and playing into their line that we had done nothing and that the NHS was all crap. TB told him it was a direct result of him doing his own thing, seeing everything through his own political prism rather than agreeing a strategy and seeing it through. Milburn, unsurprisingly, was incandescent. He said he knew how he worked, because he had seen him when he had been at the Treasury. He saw it as his right to trample on everyone else's territory. 'Can I go out now and make a speech saying that the economy ought to be doing a lot better?' Yesterday at Cabinet Geoff Hoon had dared to suggest we would have to look at NHS charges and GB had carried on the conversation afterwards and ended up jabbing him in the chest.

JP called from [a ministerial visit to] New Zealand to discuss *Frost* and I filled him in on how things were going – not well. He said he had always told GB he would be willing to support him as next leader but only when TB decided to go, never at a challenge. He felt there was an arrogance about him in feeling he could say when TB should go. JP believed that TB and GB effectively did come to some kind of deal way back, but TB denies it now and feels guilty, while GB remembers it only on his terms and feels betrayed. But he said the party will suffer, and will not wear it, if they fall out badly. He also agreed with TB's analysis that a lot of the time the personality differences didn't matter but when they affected the policies and the direction of the government, it became very dangerous. I spoke to Byers about Jo [Moore]. She was away with her husband, but [Number 10 Grid co-ordinator] Paul Brown's email expressing frustration with the department [DTLR] had leaked and it was all a bit of a mess. I told Godric to shut it down as best he could. I said to Steve he had to get out there and deal with Railtrack, try and close down this other agenda.

Pat McFadden called and said Islamabad CIC reminded him of a 1980s by-election campaign, no real resources, no real drive. We were giving them OK material and decent scripts, e.g. today on Bonn, but then the Americans would worry, think we shouldn't be straying beyond the region. Pat said the Pakistan-based press were getting a bit fed up with it all. He said we had to be more aggressive, not least in rebuttal and forcing the media to take the agenda. GB's *Sun* article was running on, *The World at One* doing a big number. It had definitely been a mistake.

Saturday, December 1

George Harrison's death [the ex-Beatle had died of lung cancer] was massive across the media. Politically though, there was a bad, febrile atmosphere. TB had a long conversation with GB, called me afterwards and said it was very difficult. He said the post-PBR problems were the direct result of lack of proper planning between us, the fact that we weren't working together well. GB's argument was that it was a direct result of him being briefed against and of us not having a grip of the government machine. His evidence for the second point was an admittedly silly interview by Charles Clarke in *The Times* giving the impression we should go for a euro referendum even if the economic conditions weren't met. So the Treasury, never slow to overreact or find out what exactly was said, went off on one on that. What they did, and seemed to believe, was to present themselves as victims, saying they bent over backwards to be helpful to colleagues, but were constantly attacked in return.

Milburn's rage had not abated with the passage of twenty-four hours. He told TB direct that if he went to the *Sun* and slagged off the work of another department, he would expect to be sacked, so why was GB allowed to slag off his department? I told both Ian Austin and Ed Balls that this arose both because of their propensity for acting in secrecy and also because they overreacted and overcomplicated things. They overdid the tax message, then worried about it, so ran off to the *Sun* but overdid the reform message in a way that allowed the *Sun* to ally GB to their own 'tax-funded NHS crap' agenda. Milburn was strongly of the view that we should whack back and at one point said if we didn't, he would. But TB was adamant that would be a mistake. He said when I make a move, I'll make a move but it has to be me that decides, nobody else. I went to [Crystal] Palace vs

Burnley with Calum, Gavin [Millar, Fiona's brother] and [David] Bradshaw [special adviser, Strategic Communications Unit]. 2–1 [to Burnley], and for once hardly any calls.

Sunday, December 2

The papers were full of TB/GB/health. GB was on *Frost* doing OK on health, but then a very odd answer when asked whether they had a deal about when TB would go. 'I'm not going to talk about a private conversation' was his basic line. He said it twice, and even though he said good things about TB, it was clearly going to be the story out of it. I was watching with Fiona and both of us felt it was deliberate. TB hadn't watched it and when I told him, he said 'What on earth does he want to do that for? Even by his own lights, it's pointless.' I could only think that he was trying to take the rather weird moral high ground from TB, give the impression that there was a deal, that TB reneged on it, but he had better things to worry about, like running the economy and helping the poor. TB again said though that it was important we didn't react, and did what we could to close it down. But I'd be very surprised if ministers weren't out and about. Milburn was calling regularly, fed up with the whole thing, feeling excluded from decisions with material effect on his department. I was pretty sick of the whole thing, told Ian Austin he could get on and brief what the hell he wanted. He did the usual victim act, how they were always being asked to respond because they were being briefed against the whole time and they were very restrained. I said if GB involved other ministers, and you covered bases properly with departments, you wouldn't have these problems with people like Milburn and Clarke. They need to be brought in, not kicked out.

He obviously got straight on to Balls who came on ten minutes later, and we went round the same block. As ever, he was blaming others – notably Peter M [Mandelson, former Cabinet minister] of course, who they always put close to the root of all evil, Milburn, Clarke, Blunkett – for trying to split TB and GB, and we had to close it down. I said they hadn't done enough to get colleagues in the right place, and to get the politics in the right place. He claimed he tried to call me five times on the day of the *Sun* interview but I was too busy. I said that was bollocks, that I was assiduous in returning phone calls. The problem was GB was in a different place, and actively wanted to be. And his anger was so great that it did have an impact on direction and policy. The TB/GB fault line had hurt us recently on the euro, on the NHS and the tax and spend argument. He realised

December '01: GB is in a different place – and wants to be

that, he also said, 'To lose your Chancellor is like putting two balls in the back of your own net.'

I had sent JP a digest of some of the press and he was pretty appalled. I filled him in on GB on *Frost* and said I really felt at the moment it wasn't TB vs GB but very much GB vs TB, that though Tony was pretty fed up with him, he was adamant we did nothing to undermine him and was trying the whole time to get things on a better keel. JP said it was one man's guilt meeting another man's betrayal and they had to sort it out themselves. He agreed he would speak to GB on his return and tell him to get his act together, and speak to Alan to tell him to keep his cool. JP said he knew I had my ups and downs with GB but accepted my main interest was the same as his, which was ensuring the third term and if we didn't stop this nonsense pretty soon, there would be a risk it never happened.

Monday, December 3

I used the day to take stock re Pakistan [CIC]. It just wasn't working in the way it should. I felt the structures were right but we were weak on output. At the morning meeting, I skipped over TB/GB and health and instead suggested in briefings we just bulldozed through it. The coverage of *Frost* was predictable enough but we just had to play it down, say GB was just refusing to get into all the personality stuff. We also had a problem re TB's stuff on the EU average [pledging to raise NHS spending to the EU average by 2005], though as TB said to GB 'Look, I made a mistake, now let's talk about how we can get it right.' I think sometimes GB and his people totally underestimated how many issues TB had to be on top of at any one time, and how infrequently we actually screwed up. But whenever we did, he went on about it as though it had all been planned. Things were looking pretty poor and confused. We needed greater unity and focus on the domestic front, greater unity, purpose and imagination on the international. Alan Milburn was still really pissed off with GB and needed to calm down a bit.

I was feeling tired, feeling that life was yet another problem, yet another meeting, yet another plan to deal with the problem, then on to the next one. I felt like I had been doing it too long. Iraq was still featuring too much in American thinking, they were still going on about December 11 [marking three months since 9/11] and the idea of a major event with national anthems and the full works. I know it affected them more deeply than anyone, but they were in a different place to everyone else on this, and we couldn't keep having memorial after memorial.

Tuesday, December 4

People as varied as Fiona, Pat [McFadden], Sally [Morgan] and [David] Bradshaw were all pointing out that I was bored and looking for something new and different to do. Although I didn't miss the grind of the briefings at all, and certainly didn't miss the press, I probably had lost something of my edge by not having that actual need to be on top of everything all the time. The conference call was all about December 11 memorials again and the idea of every country in the world playing national anthems, which I felt was all a bit much, but they were very keen. I went up to see TB in the flat and he said maybe we just had to resign ourselves to GB putting himself in a slightly different place, and operating differently.

Wednesday, December 5

A deal was being struck today in Bonn which would be a pretty amazing achievement. We were also getting reports of defections from the Taliban which we agreed on the conference call we should try to push. I had a meeting with [BBC] Radio 5 bosses, feeling we should be doing more with them, rather than everyone thinking the world listens to the wretched *Today* programme and the other Radio 4 news programmes. Fiona and Sally were seeing Yelland but I don't think either of them really had their hearts in humouring the commentators from the right-wing papers as Anji did. TB did fine at PMQs though IDS was a bit better. TB's preparations were certainly easier. We got a new poll in showing pretty good figures on the parties, but not great on public services. Paul Marsden [Labour MP] attacked 'Labour thugs'.[1]

Thursday, December 6

There was more and more intelligence suggesting pretty high-level defections around Mullah Omar, including some of his closest people, and also an account of three al-Qaeda advance scouts killed trying to work out an escape route from Afghanistan. GB was in a rage early on because Milburn was going further than agreed on the 'choice' argument with his proposals on patients being promised a choice of going to another hospital. Alan was doing a GB-style bounce and then trying to row it back a bit, and probably enjoying giving GB some of his own treatment. I had a session with TB pre Cabinet to make sure he was OK with the general thrust of what I was trying to get sorted re health. Cabinet was mainly a discussion on health

---

[1] An opponent of the Afghanistan war and Labour's anti-terrorism legislation, Marsden claimed several Labour MPs had physically and verbally threatened him.

which broadened to the public services more generally, and an update on Afghanistan.

At the War Cabinet, Scarlett was excellent, really clear exposition of what was going on, without being over-optimistic or over-pessimistic. Lander was warning in a rather less relaxed way of real fears of more attacks, including here. Boyce was almost becalmed and though he was nice to him, TB had become a pretty fierce opponent of the service rotating 'Buggins' turn' system of appointment. TB asked him about how something had gone and CDS gave all the reasons why it had been a bad idea and difficult, and a soldier had had his leg blown off yesterday. His worry, not unreasonably, was the idea that you had Brits in one part of Afghanistan killing Taliban, whilst in another we were like a police force. He said it was dangerous, not at all benign. Clare said the Americans didn't really want troops involved in the humanitarian effort at all. There was a difficult issue looming quickly, re whether Mullah Omar could get amnesty [on condition of renunciation of terrorism and disassociation with al-Qaeda]. The Americans were saying no, whilst we were a bit more equivocal. A difficult one. I had fallen behind with paperwork, hoovered through it. Philip [Gould] and Stan [Greenberg, US pollster] had a new poll. TB doing OK, the Tories absolutely nowhere, public services not as bad as we feared, apart from transport which was a total disaster.

Friday, December 7
I spoke to TB re counter-terrorism and agreed that we needed to get more political. I got Blunkett to do a letter to IDS asking how he could square his claim that they were shoulder to shoulder with us with the fact that they let their troops go through the lobbies in the Lords to do us in. The general sense re Afghanistan was that it was going pretty well for us, what with the fall of Kandahar, but the press were now looking for us to 'lose the peace'. The continuing hunt for OBL and confusion over what we would do with Mullah Omar were getting just as much attention.

The conference call was partly how to counter that, also about December 11, whilst I was now pushing for a big hit out of the football match in Kabul, trying to get some names out there to really make it fly.[1] I also made sure the Yanks knew, and that it got through to Bush, of the political problems the Tories were trying to give us.

[1] On December 15, the first post-Taliban football match would be played in the Kabul football stadium, once the scene of public executions. Kabul Red Crescent played Pamir, the latter team wearing West Bromwich Albion kit donated by BBC Radio 5 presenter Adrian Chiles. Red Crescent won 2–1.

I was pushing for publication of another al-Qaeda tape that was doing the rounds, which had yet more admissions re September 11. They said it was going to be discussed at a meeting with the president on Monday. I was amazed that something like that went to him. I would have thought it was a middle-ranking handling issue. [Paul] Marsden [anti-war Labour MP] was on an inexorable path to the Lib Dems, which was obviously the best place for him. We had a session with TB and Hilary Armstrong [chief whip] earlier in the week trying to get to a position where there was no fuss when he finally went.

Saturday, December 8

TB was worried that Alan Milburn was beginning to brief against GB as a matter of course. And whilst he understood how angry he was, didn't think it was sensible. I was pushing the Blunkett counter-terrorism attack on the Tories. Out with Fiona to [*Express* proprietor] Richard Desmond's party at the Roundhouse [North London performing arts venue]. It was handy enough, though neither of us really wanted to go and in truth were only going because TB couldn't. It was all a bit over the top, everyone photographed with *OK!* magazine photographers and backdrops. I had a long chat with Jonno Coleman [radio presenter], who was totally on board and who I reckoned we could use in the run-up to the campaign. I was chatting to Ulrika Jonsson [TV presenter] and Melanie Cantor [her agent] and Ulrika was all over me like a rash, which was all very well but Fiona was a few yards away and looking a bit askance. Sven [Göran Eriksson, England football manager] walked in, and I assumed she would know him. I asked her if she had met 'Britain's other famous Swede'. She said no, and I got him over and introduced them. He was pretty robotic when the four of us were talking in English, but then the two of them got going in real hurdy-gurdy [Swedish] and he was altogether more animated. Fiona and I were next to the Ronsons [Gerald, businessman, and Gail, charity fund-raiser] at dinner, and we were both surprised by how much we liked them. Gail was really lively, clearly big on family but also seemed to have a real heart. Gerald was totally open, quite interesting about his jail experience,[1] but also quite knowledgeable on the political front, very pro Israel, not keen on politicians generally but liked TB. I had an interesting chat with Tony Ball [BSkyB chief executive] and his absolutely gorgeous wife Gabriela.

---

[1] Ronson had served six months of a one-year prison sentence in 1990, for his part in the Guinness share-trading fraud of the 1980s.

He was another one who had a good feel for politics, and thought the TB/GB situation would become a problem for us. Desmond got up on stage. Though clearly a bit of a wide boy, he did have a certain charm and there was clearly part of him that just liked having loads of money to spend on his friends. They had Jim Davidson [Conservative-supporting 'comic'] as the comedian. Really bad choice. He completely, totally bombed, and deserved to. It was pretty vile and once the grave opened, he couldn't stop digging. It took Tony Blackburn [veteran disc jockey] of all people to rescue things by getting up and being DJ for the night.

Sunday, December 9

I did next to no work all day. Geoff Hoon had ballsed up on *Frost* when he said that if UK forces landed OBL, we would have to have assurances about the death penalty not being used before handing him over. It shouldn't have been difficult to have danced around it, and was a case of GH thinking legally rather than politically. TB was exercised about it, and made clear he didn't want it running as a problem. Of course, if we were too heavy it would become a TB/GH bad scene so we did a gentle ring-round trying to calm it without making it a calming story. I called Dan Bartlett to alert him and he told me the *Washington Post* had revealed, via the CIA he thought, the existence of the new OBL video and said that Bush would decide tomorrow whether to release it or not. I called Trevor Kavanagh, knowing the *Sun* were planning to do Hoon quite big, and gave him the story of OBL boasting about September 11 in the video, and the fact that only one hijacker per plane knew what they were going to be doing when they got on those planes. Blunkett called, a bit worried about the way his 'debate' on race was going after he told the *Independent on Sunday* that races had to become more integrated by being more British. These were tricky waters, and I wasn't sure we were sensible diving into them right now.

Monday, December 10

The OBL hunt was still going big, the DB race row likewise. The *Sun* splashed on the video and there was continuing coverage about the UK to provide troops for a security force etc. The [Paul] Marsden strategy was going OK. It was becoming a given that he would defect [to the Liberal Democrats], and though there was a fair bit of press coverage about our so-called thugs, people didn't really buy it as the reason. We had been talking over the weekend of defection as a fait accompli, and when it came, we all felt relief and the pretty certain knowledge that he would be forgotten within a week. I went up to see TB in the flat. He was totally relaxed re DB and race, felt that David had thought through his position. On Afghanistan, he wanted to get the MoD in the same place as us, then agree with the US a force to go there later and hand over to Muslim troops. Nigel Griffiths was the other story in town, another expenses/fees so-called scandal and TB said get the facts before we make a decision.[1] Good meeting with Charles Clarke and David Triesman [Labour Party general secretary]. The party was £8 million in debt. David said he was confident he could get the finances sorted but it would be tough. We also had a good session with TB on membership, message, ideology, etc. TB was encouraging Charles to generate more political and ideological debate. Charles and I both felt we should be making more of the way our media culture damaged debate but TB remained resistant. I went briefly to the *Guardian* [Christmas] party but I really couldn't be bothered with it and left after a few minutes and went for a run. The football match in Kabul had become my latest obsession. I really wanted it to go big. I was also very keen to push on the OBL video. I thought it was unbelievable that Bush himself would take the decision on that. We had put a lot of planning into tomorrow's 'We refuse to forget' [9/11] event which would get a lift with [Colin] Powell coming through.

Tuesday, December 11

Boyce did a speech at RUSI [Royal United Services Institute] yesterday, which was going pretty big today, where he basically said that the US were in a different position, that we had to choose between being part of a stabilisation force, and taking part in the wider war on terrorism. I raised it with TB, who just shrugged his shoulders and rolled his eyes as if to say 'not much we can do about it'. Later I raised it with CDS. I said it was good to see that we cleared the speech, an ironic reference to the fact the *Telegraph* reported that we had done so. 'Did I?' he asked. And I said 'No, you didn't.' 'Should I have done?' 'Well it is the normal practice that we see speeches likely to make news, which a speech by the Chief of the Defence Staff at a time like this might well do.' I couldn't tell whether he was

[1] The Small Business minister had been claiming rent through the House of Commons Fees Office on the Edinburgh South constituency office he owned, without declaration in the Register of Members' Interests. He insisted that monies paid were used to benefit his autistic sister. A 2002 Standards and Privileges Committee investigation would rule that although Griffiths had made 'technically defective' claims, he would face no further action.

irritated, worried or indifferent. He wasn't the easiest guy to work with, but he probably felt the same about us. TB raised the speech with GH who said he had tried to tone it down but the MoD was so leaky there was a limit to what he could do without it becoming an issue.

Then Colin Powell gave us a problem. In Paris, he did a doorstep saying he was pleased that the UK had volunteered to lead a security force. Given that Tom Kelly had been pushing the line that no decision had been taken and discussions were still going on, which all sent Adam Boulton [Sky political editor] into an absolute bilious frenzy in which he said it was extraordinary that the British public learnt of this kind of thing from a US politician and that Powell was coming for a 'bizarre event' to remember September 11. I sometimes wondered if Adam didn't let a lot of his own anger about whatever come through on issues like this. I got him in after his report in the street, and said it was outrageous that he editorialised like that. He held his ground and after a pretty robust exchange, went off in a huff.

Powell arrived and as they came in [William] Farish asked Straw to tell me that Powell didn't want press people in the meeting. We were called in at the end to make sure lines were in the same place before the press conference. TB was on pretty good form, bounced away the CDS stuff and put over a general message well. I felt that our event to commemorate September 11 struck the right note, dignified and respectful, not over the top. The US school band I thought was better than the New York trumpeter and I thought GWB's people made a mistake in having him in front of an Israeli flag. Not many would notice that it was an alphabetic point, as the flag was between the Irish and the Italian, but I suspected it would give them problems. I did a local Labour Party meeting, and got a fair amount of grief, particularly on faith schools.

Wednesday, December 12

The Yanks were still dithering on the OBL tapes, saying they were worried about quality, about translations, worried about the impact on relatives of victims at seeing him gloat. We had already got third parties lined up on reaction, but I was beginning to wonder whether they would ever see the light of day. We were also still in the same position on troops and the security force. TB was going through the terrorism bill in detail and said there were some real holes in it and it needed a lot of work. I took him over to the CIC, which was a real boost for them all. There was still a real impact on people when he walked into a room just to say hello, even if he did slightly give the impression of not having a clue what they did. We thought IDS would do war, sleaze and public services at PMQs. He did health and transport but the nervous cough was getting really bad, and he just lacked impact, even if he made a strong point. TB said afterwards he would be amazed if he survived the term. I ran into GB at Number 11 who was having one of his receptions. There were lots of other people around so he did one of his big, friendly 'How you doing?' greetings. I found it odd that he could paint it on like that, whereas if there had been nobody else there, it would have been the usual growl or heavy discussion, depending on mood.

Thursday, December 13

[Bill] Clinton was over making a speech and was up in the flat with TB. He was losing his voice so we sent out for some medicine and I chatted to him and Chelsea Clinton in the kitchen while TB got changed. He was clearly a bit worried re Bush, not convinced he was doing the right things, but even with us, he was pretty discreet. He had time to kill and TB had work to do. I took him for a little wander round the building to see some of the people these big cheeses wouldn't normally see, like the switchboard and the messengers, and of course he was brilliant with them. The War Cabinet was gathering outside the Cabinet Room and Dearlove and Scarlett were clearly pleased to see him. I took him round to see the press office and the Grid team and he made a total beeline for Harriet Quinlan [Strategic Communications Unit]. As I took him out, he said 'Gee, you got some great women.' Later Doug Band [Clinton aide] called in a bit of state because Bill had referred to 'Prime Minister Brown' in his speech on AIDS at the QE2 [Queen Elizabeth II Conference Centre in Westminster]. I assured him TB wouldn't mind.

I got back for the War Cabinet. There was discussion about whether OBL was now in Pakistan, but it was clear nobody on our side really knew. Our bottom lines were that any operation had to be under CENTCOM, the US had to provide lift and extraction if necessary, but it was already becoming clear that the French didn't want to be formally under CENTCOM. The Germans didn't want to be under CENTCOM for different reasons, namely it would suggest we were going to fight rather than keep peace. TB later met Jospin when we arrived in Laeken [European Council summit in Belgium], and he was very clear that the French couldn't operate like this. TB was clear that if there were no French or German forces, that politically and presentationally it was difficult. He felt we might have to call their bluff, say we would go ahead without them.

Cabinet was pretty short, John Reid on Sinn Fein offices in the Commons, DB on the fallout from the Sarah Payne case,[1] TB briefing them on the war situation, then a political Cabinet. TB did his usual script, at some length. Maintaining economic strength and stability, investment and reform, what type of society we want to live in, international strength, pro-European, strong on defence. In all of them, emphasising we had broken free from traditional positions, we can manage the economy but also attack poverty. We can invest in public services but also do difficult reform. Strong on people's rights but demanding responsibility. Tough on defence but proud of helping others in the world. All this matters for giving the party a sense of what we believe in, confidence in what we are for. He felt the Tories were in real trouble, and that the Lib Dems were becoming ridiculous, saying to anyone what they wanted to hear.

JP was basically defending himself on delivery, speaking almost exclusively about transport. GB said we were doing some difficult things and we had to get the party behind us on them. The press and Opposition were trying to demoralise people, make them think what we call progress was all spin. Jack was worried about cynicism, declining faith in politics. DB made a similar point, said the Tories were deliberately trying to erode confidence in politics. He said the papers were constantly trying to set us at each other, but in fact this was the most unified Cabinet ever in political terms. Tessa talked about a generation becoming disengaged. Alan felt the right wing were still better in some ways at conducting ideological battle. He felt we had been overly cautious about the country's desire for change and fairness. On public services, we have to be careful we don't revert to old-style command and control, that we have confidence in our own programme for change. And he argued strongly for under-promising and over-delivering. Darling was worried about the Libs. He said we all know they are wankers but out there it is not considered a bad thing to vote for them. Estelle echoed something Alan said, said we still have a language of caution when people are desperate for us to be more radical. Clare said this was a good government. She thought the Labour bit was good but the New bit wasn't. She felt the policies were good but the presentation was useless. She said everywhere she went she was getting this stuff

[1] Child sex offender Roy Whiting was convicted and sentenced to life imprisonment for the murder of eight-year-old Sarah Payne, who had been found dead near Pulborough, West Sussex, in July 2000 after disappearing from a field close to the home of her paternal grandparents. The case prompted a campaign, led by the *News of the World*, for the government to allow controlled access to the sex offenders register, which in 2010 resulted in the adoption of 'Sarah's Law'.

about Tony and Gordon, that it was stupid and dangerous and it had to stop, that we had to pull together politically. Charles spoke well, particularly on the need for more debate within the party, better relations with the media, and with academia. We need to get more out of the Civil Service.

TB said it was important to understand why the media was like it was. A lot of them believe we are omnipotent, that the Opposition is useless, that they have to do the job for them. They don't conduct a policy debate, drowning out the policy debate through scandal and controversy. It makes it hard to get definition. They deliberately breed cynicism. But New Labour, a modernised centre-left party, is strong enough to defeat that. Centre-left parties lose when they move out of touch from where people are on the basic economic and social issues. If we remain rooted in the instincts of people, we can defeat cynicism. It is not the left that is in retreat. He said we could be confident that we were in the right position, that the Tories had not yet learnt how to adapt, and that the Lib Dems, driven by opportunism, were storing up real problems for themselves in the future. Sally had worked on people, even on Alan and Charles, to be nice about GB. But, as TB said, 'Was he gracious? Was he hell.' Eventually, by 4pm our time, the OBL video was being played out and we got a good hit on it and had the third parties really going for it. We were into ping pong on the counter-terrorism measures [Anti-terrorism, Crime and Security Bill, which would receive Royal Assent the next day], dropped the religious hatred bit but finally got it through.

On the plane [to Laeken], TB, Jack and I carried on the discussion about cynicism in the media. I felt that unless the press bought into the idea that they have at least some responsibility, it was not going to be easy. The conference call was largely how to take forward the material in the video. Tucker [Eskew] had the idea of making a direct appeal to al-Qaeda people to realise they were working for someone who mocked their suicides. I watched [Sir] Ronnie Flanagan [Northern Ireland chief constable] on *Newsnight* when he was given a really hard time [Flanagan had been accused of 'flawed judgement' over the Omagh bomb inquiry], a really unpleasant interview. I felt so strongly about it that I wrote to him, said I thought he had handled it incredibly well and that the public would have ended up respecting him far more than the interviewer.

Friday, December 14

The OBL video was a massive hit, though there were still doubts being spread in the Arab world about its veracity. We were now

December '01: TB: 'Was GB gracious? Was he hell.'

co-ordinating third-party responses from around the world to show that opinion was changing. CDS was chairing a contribution conference in London but the problem was the French and the Germans not wanting to be under CENTCOM command, the French because they are French, the Germans because their parliament would only support peacekeeping forces. It was tricky, because our red line was CENTCOM in charge because it meant they would have to stay involved and make sure our troops were got out if things got really tricky. In fact it was clear from the overnight telegram from Washington that the Americans didn't mind as much as we did. After TB spoke to Chirac, who was adamant that the French could not be under CENTCOM, David M and Co. negotiated with the French and then TB personally negotiated a text, which they felt was OK, namely saying the UK would be in charge but working with CENTCOM. DM then spent much of the afternoon speaking to people in the MoD, eventually including GH, to emphasise it was what the prime minister wanted. He was getting quite stressed up and angry about it. I was even beginning to wonder whether CDS was looking for a reason to quit. Even though TB was very careful with him, and always polite, he probably knew the relationship was not as strong as with Guthrie, and he probably didn't much like us either.

TB and Chirac spoke again and TB said, to laughter at the other end, that he was having trouble with his military. Chirac was in good form, and was retelling the story about when a microphone picked him up saying he loved Scotland but the haggis looked like shit and tasted worse. There was a lot of talk about who we would get to chair the [Future of] Europe convention, Giscard [former French President Valéry Giscard d'Estaing] or [Wim] Kok. TB was planning not to waste too much capital on it. Kok would be an obvious choice for us, but TB wondered whether Giscard might not be better because he was from a big country, and though he liked Kok, he would be more minded to put the interests of the small countries first.

The discussion in the morning was Afghanistan, and at the lunch the ludicrous Louis Michel briefed the historic decision that there was to be an EU army of 3,000–4,000 people in fifteen different countries, massive development, blah blah blah, what a lot of nonsense. I was at lunch with Peter Hain [Europe minister] who was about to do *The World at One* so I briefed him to go very hard for it, as did Jack at the press conference. However, Jack had also had a private chat with Hugo Young and said we would go into the euro by 2003. They turned it into a splash, so we had GB on the rampage again. TB came out for a chat at one point. He said he thought GB's problems were deep and it was a shame because he was brilliant in many ways but in the end maybe he didn't have the breadth. So perhaps he was a great Chancellor and that was that.

I left TB etc. to meet up with the family at Neil and Glenys' [the Kinnocks] in Brussels. Neil had a real downer on most of the Cabinet, including GB. He also felt Charles was overdoing the 'openness and honesty' bit, because it was being done at the expense of others. They were both reasonably OK re TB, but very down on Hoon, Clare, Milburn. Neil was on his best form for ages though. But he felt GB was in danger of blowing it and that Balls was a bad influence on him. Ronnie Flanagan called me while we were having dinner and said that my letter to him 'meant more to me than you'll ever know. That someone like you could be bothered to say that with all the other things you have to deal with.' He sounded very emotional, and was clearly feeling a lot of the pressure, but I thought he was basically a very decent bloke.

Saturday, December 15

I managed to avoid going back to the summit, and stayed in touch by phone with Godric. TB did the press conference early and it was all a bit of a non-event, though he was doing well on the substance. He had settled on the view that Giscard was best for the convention because we would be able to influence it more. I got a very different take from Glenys and Helle [Thorning-Schmidt, Stephen Kinnock's wife, Danish MEP] who were really steamed up about it.

Rory and I went for a run then down to the Grand-Place. Carole Walker [BBC] was there filming and couldn't believe her luck at bumping into us there. She interviewed both Neil and Glenys before we had lunch. We went for a wander and I was sad to discover that the Stock Exchange pub where I based myself when I was a busker here had gone. Godric was calling pretty regularly to keep me abreast of the endless rubbish from the summit. They had meant to agree the sites of the planned new agencies, but had to defer it to the Barcelona summit. Berlusconi was arguing that the food agency should go to Parma because of the cuisine there. TB said he really did seem to believe that it was a food agency, like a kind of glorified restaurant. The favourite was in Finland and Chirac had asked TB 'Why do we want to send the food agency to a country that only eats reindeer?' TB said somehow Europe seems to work, but if we are being frank, a lot of it is haggling, deals and people missing the point.

Sunday, December 16

Someone was at it in the *Sunday Times*, with a headline 'Generals warn glory-hunting Blair'. There were clearly people at the MoD briefing against us the whole time. TB wasn't happy about it at all. We travelled back on Eurostar after what had turned out to be a really nice weekend. I went for dinner with the Goulds and David Triesman. We had a lot of problems in the party, but I felt David was a genuinely nice man who would make a difference.

Monday, December 17

Yesterday's *Mail on Sunday* had some crap about a so-called bugging scandal involving Lord [Nazir] Ahmed [the Labour peer, opposed to the Afghanistan war, alleged that his phone had been tapped during conversations with Foreign Office minister Denis MacShane]. I called Denis MacShane to say I thought he should go up and deal with it. By the time I got to the office Jack Straw was on in a real fury. They are my ministers, not yours, and I'm not having it. He said he was 'fucking angry'. I said he knew I directed ministerial traffic in the media, this was a situation when we had to move fast to kill it. And when I heard the *Today* programme was still doing it, I knew it had to be dealt with. He said they had agreed at the FCO last night to put nobody up and I should have called him. He said the first he knew Denis was going on was listening to it on the news. I apologised to him, though it would have been avoided if they had communicated yesterday on their decision not to go up.

TB was working on the [Laeken] statement for the Commons. He was very pissed off with the briefing against him [in the *Sunday Times*] from the MoD, which was clearly born out of their being in a slightly different place. Friday had been very difficult for David M [re CENTCOM], and later for TB with Geoff Hoon. As a result of their calls, the MoD agreed to speak direct to the DoD [Department of Defense] to try to agree what was going to happen. TB had negotiated the words direct with Chirac but every time the MoD came back with a new objection, their line was CENTCOM would not put up with it. TB was suspicious that our own people were winding up [General Tommy] Franks. Also, at the end of the morning war meeting, CDS said to me that if Laeken was as bad as everyone said 'That's the end of ESDI' [European Strategic Defence Initiative]. Another revealing statement. TB said he was giving us the impression that troops would not want to do this 'and I just don't accept that'. He felt it would be wrong if the UK was not properly involved in this. The Franco-German problem was a real one though.

Russia was also wanting to be involved, and winding up [General Mohammed] Fahim Khan [leader of the Tajik Jamiat-e-Islami party within the Northern Alliance] to say not many troops should go in. CDS took delight in saying he had witnessed a video conference in which Bush briefed Franks on the force and said 'I've spoken to the PM and I've made no promises at all.' CDS was really doing nothing but give TB headaches at the moment. He defended Franks by saying that Chris Meyer spotted immediately that the US would not buy the language TB agreed with Chirac. I suggested to TB that he had a private word with Boyce. After the Laeken statement he got him in with Geoff Hoon and 'cleared the air' and said we needed more questions to be answered than we were asking.

If ever we needed evidence of TB not focusing on the domestic, it came in a meeting with Hilary [Armstrong] and Charles [Clarke] when he asked whether we could get a piece of legislation through to be told it went through on Thursday night because our MPs stayed up all night. It was amazing he didn't know that and I could feel him thinking he was getting out of touch. He also wanted to get out of a dinner on Africa with ministers tonight but we pushed him into it by saying he was in danger of not being taken seriously on it. He agreed reluctantly but when it came to it, it was Bono and Bob Geldof [rock stars campaigning to write off Third World debt] who got the invitation up to the flat. He was happy enough with the outcome of Laeken and Giscard's appointment and felt he was far less federalist than people imagined.

On the conference call, we discussed plans for a 'one hundred days on' paper of some sort. Torie Clarke was on, warning after Rumsfeld's visit to Kabul that we should be very much in the 'this is far from over' territory. I was still having to deal with personality and personnel issues in the various CICs.

Tuesday, December 18

TB was back arguing for a big New Labour kick, feeling we had lost a bit of momentum on all the main domestic areas and needed it back. He was quizzing me about whether the operation missed Anji and what to do with Peter M. He said he wanted to bring him back if he could but his fatal weakness was the press and his belief that if his profile was low he would get nothing and nowhere. He was worrying about the Americans, felt that they liked our support but in the end felt they could do what they wanted. He felt Rumsfeld and the right were in the ascendancy. TB was fretting as ever re holiday cover, who would make things happen while he was away.

I went to Grace's school play and then for a long run on the Heath. Then out for dinner with Tucker Eskew and his wife [Lisa]. He felt that apart from NMD [National Missile Defense] and Kyoto [climate change protocol, 1997], there was a lot shared between the two countries' agendas and TB had more influence than maybe we thought. He thought our media was mad but that we dealt with it pretty well. I still felt the second-phase questions hadn't really been dealt with and also that 'where next?' was far too prevalent in Americans' thinking.

Wednesday, December 19

TB had dinner last night with GB and said he had been on best behaviour but it was still difficult. TB had given him a pretty frank assessment of why he (TB) was generally thought to be an OK PM – because he had breadth, could deal with a stack of different things at once, and get on with a range of people. He felt GB had breadth but was too narrow in the field of people he related to. He told him he still believed he was easily the best person to follow him but he was not going to support him in circumstances where he felt he was being forced out. They had also discussed the euro, where he felt GB was more open-minded but that Balls was pouring opposition into his head the whole time. TB was looking a bit downcast again, probably worrying that a basically bad set-up with GB was something of a reality.

The US conference call was largely about one hundred days on. I needed to talk to Karen [Hughes] about where the whole CIC operation went now. The *Sun* had a story that Byers was to be sacked so I called Steve to say it was balls. There were continuing problems re ISAF [the UN's International Security Assistance Force, agreed in Bonn that month] before Geoff's statement and we were busy getting all the words sorted with the Americans and the French. The Germans seemed to have an even bigger problem than the French with the idea of serving under CENTCOM. There was a lot of briefing against us going on. Meanwhile the Wembley [national stadium] issue was flaring up again. The FA [Football Association] were going to announce that Wembley was their favoured option and they didn't want to refer to the James report.[1] Called Tessa [Jowell] to warn her to be very careful in her choice of words, that she could end up having to resign if she allied herself to someone else's version of events that didn't

[1] The investigation and report by consultant David James into the viability of the Wembley Stadium rebuild and the legality of the procurement process.

turn out to be right. In the event she was even tougher than I would have been. I had both Adam Crozier [FA chief executive] and David Davies [FA executive director] on the phone trying to get me to persuade her to spin the James stuff as dealing with Wembley. Out for dinner with Tessa and family. She was in quite good form considering how badly Wembley was playing out. Earlier I had a pretty tough meeting with the BBC over their plans for their 'Your NHS' day [a day of programmes, 20 February 2002], which they said was meant to be a fair, balanced look at the NHS, but everything we heard around the place suggested that they were just looking for the bad the whole time. I left them with a clear impression we were thinking of not co-operating at all.

Thursday, December 20

I was due to have lunch with Peter M, which had been my suggestion after he emailed me re an article he was doing. I asked Hilary C to find somewhere discreet and she had booked La Trouvaille in Newburgh Street. I arrived first, Peter a few minutes later and we were put in the window. Who should walk by, just seconds after we sat down, but Andrew Marr, but he was so busy window shopping on the other side of the passageway that he didn't see us. Peter did most of the talking early on, re what he had now taken to calling his 'defenestration'. He was very calm and friendly, said he wasn't blaming me directly but described the whole episode leading to his resignation as a 'road accident' in which everyone accidentally conspired. I said if it had been anyone else, we would probably have survived but he had baggage that weighed us down. On the whole Geoffrey [Robinson, former Paymaster General] loan episode, he felt it was a case of the circumstances of one period being different to those of another. When he took out the loan, Geoffrey was not *persona non grata*, was not a media bogeyman, was a friend who had always taken an interest in helping Peter. Peter said he had always wanted a nice home and to find someone to live with. He hated [his former flat in] Wilmington Square [Bloomsbury] because it didn't feel like a home. The themes of his loneliness, and his sexuality making him more lonely, or certainly more secretive, came through. He hated being away from Reinaldo [da Silva, his partner]. His private life was happy, but why because he was a politician should there have to be comment about it at all, why? It was he who was the politician. Nobody ever disputed he was a good minister and he felt he had to get back to top-level politics. I said it was true, he rarely got criticised on ability grounds. He accepted a return to the Cabinet was difficult, so the options were probably Europe or the UN and he was intending to develop his international profile.

I discussed the lunch with TB in advance. He said he didn't rule out Peter coming back but he had to lower the personal profile. He was a phenomenal talent but flawed and the heart of the flaw was his relationship with the press. When I relayed that, Peter did the usual thing of saying he hardly ever spoke to the press, only read the *FT*, it was the media that had created the persona, not the other way round. He clearly couldn't accept he had done much wrong, certainly felt wronged and tried to come to terms with it every day, and said he found it difficult. He said he knew I thought his problem was the profile but it wasn't. His problem was that others, including me and TB, couldn't make the shift from seeing him as 'Bobby'.[1] He felt he never recovered from that, that he could never be seen as a legitimate politician, that it was cruel that even as a minister, TB and I often saw him more as a behind-the-scenes person. Add in his worries about the media constantly probing re his sexuality, add in GB 'always there, as a presence intent on destroying me', and it wasn't a happy mix. He felt the rift with GB, contrary to legend, was not when he supported TB. It was at Chewton Glen [country house hotel in the New Forest], when he, TB and GB had had a meeting before the dinner and GB, to everyone's astonishment, produced a blueprint of everything to be done, including personnel issues in the party. TB was visibly taken aback and asked Peter his view. Peter stalled and said we needed to think about it.

After TB went to bed, Peter asked Gordon 'Why on earth did you do that?' GB said between them they could control TB and all the big decisions. Peter said again, why did you try to bounce him like that without warning? GB asked if Peter supported him on the substance of the proposals he had made, which were a mix of policy and personnel. Peter said he needed to think about it and discuss it with TB. GB replied 'You've made your choice,' and stormed off. He said it was a pretty blatant attempt to use him in undermining TB early on. He felt one of GB's weaknesses was that he underestimated TB's steel. He saw me and Peter as the two strong people and had always felt if he could get us over to him, he could deal with TB. He under-estimated our loyalty, but also TB's steel.

[1] Mandelson's 'code name' during the 1994 Labour leadership election, a name often revived by those seeking to paint him as a Machiavellian figure. See *Prelude to Power*, pp 42–3.

By now, there were more guests in the restaurant who had noticed us and we were virtually whispering across the table. Peter told me of a meeting he had had whilst the Hammond Inquiry was going on.[1] He wanted to explain to GB why he was fighting so hard for his story to be heard. They met in Gordon's office at the Commons. GB put him at ease straight away, asking with seeming sincerity how he was. Peter said bruised and hurt and really trying to come back. He said he told him the story as dispassionately as he could, his role, Jack's role, my role, Mike O'Brien, TB, the Civil Service, 'I was as dispassionate as I could be, tried not to blame, no individual's fault, just a terrible set of circumstances ending in a road crash.' GB listened and said the problem was that I had created the context on the Monday by saying that was the only contact between you and the Home Office (via his private office) and it meant an elephant trap was laid. 'Then you fell into it. The only way out is for Alastair to say he misbriefed and apologise but he won't do that.' He said TB had always been a weak personality and he needed strong personalities to support him. First, it had been Peter/GB and then it became Peter/AC. But AC wanted to be the main voice 'so he conspired to push you out, it's obvious.'

Peter was in full flow, vivid, and I sometimes felt he had a photographic memory for these key moments and his key relationships. He said he told GB he didn't believe it was like that, pointed out 'You have to remember Alastair is different to us, he would happily walk away from politics, he has a different life he can lead, family, money to make beyond our dreams, he never chose this path, he was pursued, we poached him and a large part of him didn't want it.' Then Peter spoke as GB again. 'Yes, but once he chose it, he wanted to be number one and he's done it by getting rid of you at a time TB and I are seen as rivals.' Even aiming off for possible exaggeration, and I'm not sure there was that much, I was mildly shocked. Peter claimed he had remained supportive of me and said it was all too obvious that GB was just trying to use the circumstances of the time to get Peter to move in his favour. He said that TB was in a different class as a

---

[1] In January it had been claimed that Mandelson had helped wealthy businessman Srichand Hinduja's application for a British passport, and Mandelson resigned as Secretary of State for Business, Innovation and Skills. An inquiry headed by Sir Anthony Hammond QC was asked to establish what approaches were made to the Home Office in 1998 in connection with an application for naturalisation by Hinduja and the full circumstances surrounding the approaches and the later grant of the application. The inquiry found that neither Mandelson nor Home Office minister Mike O'Brien had acted with impropriety of any sort.

politician 'I love his deviousness, his selfishness, the way he is able to turn everything to his own advantage. His genius as a politician is his understanding of people, but also the fact that he is totally selfish and people either don't see it or if they do, they don't seem to mind because of what he brings to them and the job.'

I reminded him of the time TB had told us that Labour governments always foundered on issues of ego and personality, and that we had to be different. I agreed with his car-crash analysis, felt that if it hadn't been him, we would have handled it differently, felt that we both made mistakes. I felt sad that he was out of things, and sad that I had played a part in that. He was right that I could probably walk away. He wasn't able to, yet had had to. Despite it all, we were still able to talk openly and I still considered him to be a friend whose judgement I value. We went out, and stood there, in the middle of Carnaby Street, with a couple of bodyguards, passers-by shooting the occasional odd look and Peter said 'Happy Christmas. I had better do some shopping.' And off he went.

The conference call was all one hundred days, then we did a selective briefing for the broadsheets and the BBC, really greasing up Putin. Then a meeting with Crozier and Davies from the FA after yesterday's fiasco. They wanted assurances we were still up for it and they wanted me to persuade Tessa to put out something more supportive. I pointed out that politically we had to be very careful to cover our backs re the James report and anything else that may emerge. They also had to understand the political considerations concerning Birmingham missing out on a major national project. Crozier seemed a nice enough bloke, a bit looking after number one maybe, a bit pushy. I reported to Tessa that they felt there were senior people in DCMS [Department of Culture, Media and Sport] really trying to kill off the project. Tessa seemed keen on the idea of the stadium, but not keen on the FA, and she wasn't keen on pushing the boat out.

Peter had given me a lot of food for thought. It was, as he said, crazy that he wasn't in government. We weren't exactly blessed with A-league ministers. He pointed out that he may have made mistakes on the personal front, but he never fucked up on policy and he always gave real direction to whatever department he was in. It was true. All the departments he worked in said the same. He could make decisions, and he could run things. I tried to work out whether he had gone second time around because it was him, or because of what our media operation and media relations had become, and his role in that. In a way, the strength he had brought to the modernisation of our media relations was what made him the bogey figure he was, and that status plus baggage was what made us turn a mistake into something far bigger. It was the same reason so many in the media felt about me as they did. He also seemed more resigned to things. He believed that the new papers he had discovered for Hammond to look at showed that he was done in. But he had no desire to push it, felt it would only be worth it if it led to a change of attitude by the public and that would only come about if TB and I said that it changed things materially. And neither of us would want to do that because the world had moved on.

I was struck by how much he, and from his reported comments GB, believed I meant to TB, far more than I felt myself. He had said that both he and GB felt I was by far the closest, that he felt hurt because we had been such close friends, not so close any more, whilst GB just hated me and feared me in equal measure and saw me as someone that had to be dealt with. He really enjoyed the story of my row with GB during the election with Bob Shrum [Brown's polling adviser] trying to calm things. He was making enough money and travelling a lot but when he listed the countries he was due to be visiting, he said 'I'm busy, but it's no life.' He also wanted to dispute my line, which he had heard me say more than once, that he had dumped his old friends for a new rich set. He said he found his life very lonely at times and people like Carla Powell [socialite, wife of former Thatcher adviser Charles] gave him friendship and support and also a lot of fun that was missing a lot of the time.

I watched him wander off before going to do a bit of shopping of my own. In some ways, we'd grown apart, but I felt that between us we'd given something to TB, and the party, that really mattered, and that meant there would always be a bond there. I talked to Philip, and Grace [Gould], who was listening to the conversation, said she thought we would always be working together in some shape or form.

Friday, December 21

[Vladimir] Putin was coming over. TB was up north and flew back. I went down [to Chequers] to meet him so that we could prepare a proper script before Putin arrived. The only real announcement was a bilateral working group on terrorism, and the main interest anyway was Afghanistan. The trail for OBL seemed to have gone cold and that was casting a cloud over the whole scene. But we had the inauguration of a new administration in Kabul to look forward to tomorrow, and today the first Marines arriving there, so the media backdrop of the TB/VP press conference was OK. The MMR issue [questions over whether the Blairs had chosen the measles, mumps and rubella vaccination for baby Leo] was going from bad to worse, and in addition Fiona, Hilary [Coffman] and Magi [Cleaver] were trying to work out how to handle the Egypt holiday. Fiona had done a brilliant job getting CB in the right place with the public, and could see it being undone. She feared a combination of yet another fancy holiday, with questions over who pays, and MMR, could produce a bit of a tipping point.

The Putin meeting was largely Afghanistan, also Russia/NATO, a lot of it just the two of them. We were definitely more confident. Tucker [Eskew] had given me a baseball cap for Christmas with the words 'Media scum' on it, which I showed to Putin. TB said 'Don't encourage him' I think talking to VP about me rather than the other way around. The press conference at RAF Halton was fine, pretty low-key, but it looked good and the co-operation and warmth was strong. There was some interest in the terrorism issue. I went back for the office [Christmas] dinner but Hilary and I were still dealing with MMR. I did a little speech thanking them all, saying they were the best possible team, but afterwards admitted to Godric I felt we were coasting a bit and needed to up our game in the New Year, especially on story development and narrative.

Saturday, December 22

Up early to head for Burnley vs Millwall. The new administration in Kabul was leading the news all day. But I spent a lot of the journey dealing with MMR. We had got ourselves into a bit of a mess on this. We had had to hold a privacy line, and I did feel that it was the thin end of the wedge, that every time they had to do something like this with the kids, it became a big media thing. But the reality was that the doubt was being used to fuel doubt about the safety of the vaccine, with potential serious knock-on effects, which would be a lot worse if it emerged Leo hadn't had it. I spoke to TB, and we agreed that we should emphasise both of them supported the policy one hundred per cent but they didn't see why they had to talk about their children. I went a bit further with some of them, dropping a very strong hint in the hope they wrote it as fact without attribution.

Through the day, this took up the time and energies of Fiona, Hilary, Tom [Kelly], John Shields [press officer] and me, all dealing with it because of Cherie's views, and TB's disengagement. He was just angry, said it was monstrous that the press could get into the family like this, and it was, but we had to deal with it. I said to Tom we should put out a statement from TB making it clear he was pro MMR vaccine but if he commented on whether his child had taken part in one government medical campaign, he would be expected to do them all. It was all running pretty big by the time we finally got the words out. I spent the whole of half-time dealing with [Lord] Wakeham, and after a crap match [o–o], most of the journey home trying to get the press in a better place on it. Once it also came out they were spending $10,000 on a few days' holiday in Egypt, we would be in major out-of-touch land.

Sunday, December 23

TB's statement was being seen as a hint that Leo had the jab, though they were still saying we would neither confirm nor deny. Frank Dobson [former Health Secretary] called, and agreed, which was good of him, to take up the bids he was getting, and was on the robust end of the market re their privacy, also saying TB and CB clearly backed the policy. This was beginning to do us quite a bit of damage. The big story was a Brit caught on a US plane with explosives in his shoes.[1] I went for a massage and bumped into Rachel Stevens of S Club 7 [pop group], so got Grace to come over and she was incredibly nice to her, called us in while she was having a pedicure, her jeans rolled up and her tiny feet in a bowl of weird-looking stuff. She was so nice to Grace.

Wednesday, December 26

I worked on TB's New Year message, euro, public services, commentary on the war. TB called as he left for the airport en route to Egypt. He said he knew he would take a hit, he was desperate for a break and said he intended to come back firing on all cylinders. I had been approached by a TV company asking me to make a film on a year in the life of Burnley if we got promoted. Fiona was really pressing me to go for it. It was tempting but only as a halfway exit, not a real alternative.

Thursday, December 27

Jeremy [Heywood] sent through some good suggestions and additions [to the New Year message] on public services. TB changed the euro section, but otherwise it was fine. We agreed to get it out for the 30th,

[1] Richard Reid, a radicalised convert to Islam with links to al-Qaeda, had been discovered on an American Airlines flight from Paris to Miami attempting to detonate explosives hidden in his shoes. Pleading guilty to eight charges, in 2002 he would be given a life sentence without parole.

ahead of the honours briefing. The problem with the MMR issue was that it was such an obvious and easy talking point and people sensed the vulnerability.

Friday, December 28

I went up with Calum and Rory to Mum and Dad's. Fiona called saying Cherie had been on to say she had got a message that GB and Sarah [his wife] had had a baby [Jennifer Jane, born seven weeks early, weighing 2 lb 4 oz]. We had known nothing about it so I had to get Anne Shevas to track down Ian Austin so that we had a line ready when all the calls started. There's no doubt it would give GB an added positive dimension. There was already around the place a feeling that he was the real character of the government, and this would show that in a way.

Saturday, December 29

GB did a doorstep, looking pretty happy and human. TB's New Year message went fine, the odd splash, a few page leads, not massive. I wasn't convinced these New Year messages were worth the effort.

Sunday, December 30

I took Rory to Man U vs Fulham. Saw Alex [Ferguson, Manchester United manager] beforehand. Clearly thinking about staying another year. JP was on, pissed off, felt he wasn't getting proper support, e.g. before his *Today* programme interview. I sometimes wished politics could just all shut down during these holiday periods. I put in a couple of calls to get him where he needed to be. We went for dinner at the Milibands [David and Louise]. Lots of chat re GB. The baby would hopefully do him some good. I gave them a cut-down version of Peter M's account [see December 20]. David seemed pretty shocked too.

Monday, December 31

TB called to wish us a happy New Year, and also tell us what a great time he was having. I did my best to tell him it was cold and miserable and the country was falling apart. It seemed from the way he was talking about [Egyptian President Hosni] Mubarak, his sons, Egypt generally that he assumed he was being bugged. He was relieved the NHS annual crisis had not materialised, though I told him rail [safety] was running as a pretty big problem. He said he felt ready for the fray, public services and Europe were what really mattered and there had to be absolute focus on them. Kenton Keith was in town and came to see me at home at 3pm. Kenton was a lovely guy, but I think his way of dealing with the obvious tensions between the different parts of the US operation, and the scale of some of the issues we were talking about, was to retreat a little bit. He was due to leave, said he had enjoyed it, felt they had made a difference, in large part thanks to the people we sent. He felt the White House never really understood the need for Islamabad [CIC], and he was pretty scathing about Karen [Hughes]. He was intending to write a book and it would make clear she was only really interested in Bush's re-election, that there was no real understanding of the need for a broader approach on foreign policy and public diplomacy. The tensions between Pakistan and India [military standoff including movement of troops and missiles to borders] were dominating the serious news, and getting very difficult.

Tuesday, January 1, 2002

We saw in the New Year at Terry's [Tavner, friend] and had a perfectly nice time though I was feeling tired a lot of the time. It was also difficult to be open with anyone really. I was taken aback a bit by the bitchiness re GB, and the idea he was deliberately having a baby to soften his profile. It is the kind of thing people say joking, but here were people not centrally involved in politics who seemed actually to believe it. I spent most of today with Calum, football, cinema, just hanging around, and had a nice time. Mentally I was trying to crank up a couple of gears into work mode but was wishing I was somewhere else.

Wednesday, January 2

Fiona seemed genuinely happy with all her birthday presents and the way I and the kids were treating her, though I could sense her feeling that I had been more engaged over the holiday but was about to disappear again before the day was over. We had all her family around during the day and I managed to avoid doing too much on the work front. I'd written some half-decent lines for Tom Kelly to brief out re the visit to Bangladesh, India and Pakistan but Jack Straw called to say he was worried we were raising expectations too high and that we would not be able to meet them. Jack was a real team player at the moment, genuinely wanting to help and not making points like this unless he really felt he had to. But I sensed he worried TB was overreaching himself. I encouraged him to do a note to TB, which he did, saying we had to be careful not to let the Pakistanis get away with too much, that they did at times get too close to terrorists, and that we had to be fairly tough with them. We went out for dinner then I headed to Heathrow.

I tried to sleep all the way to Cairo, where it was 3am UK time when we picked up TB and CB. They were full of their usual post-holiday bonhomie and we were all feeling like shit after a sleepless flight and body clocks a bit screwed. TB seemed to have got a lot of his energy back. He knew not to push too hard on how marvellous a time he had, but clearly they had been looked after well. He read the voluminous briefs, then we did a briefing and afterwards a series of taped interviews. We had agreed that for the first leg we should be aiming news-wise for the agreement of the Bangladeshis to send troops as part of the ISAF. But the press were more interested in the euro and TB/GB and after pushing him several times on whether they had spoken while he had been away, his answers were evasive enough for them to realise they hadn't and that was good enough for some of them to run away with it.

TB told me afterwards he had tried to speak to GB three times about the euro in recent days. He felt that the baby, contrary to the general feeling, was unlikely to change him at all. I relayed to him Peter M's view that GB had somehow managed to alienate every single one of the people who might be able to persuade TB to move over at some point. TB felt Gordon just had too much time on his hands, and he had always over-calculated. He relied on calculation not instinct and feel, and he assumed others operated in the same way. On the euro, he did not feel GB was totally opposed as such, but a combination of natural caution and over-calculation took him to the wrong conclusion. It was a pretty grim start to the year though, if even a baby could become a source of tension.

TB said he was very clear where we needed to be focusing in the year ahead – Europe and public service reform, but on both he had ceded too much power to GB already and every step forward was going to be difficult. He said he wasn't overly worried, but I sensed he was. We then sat down to work out day by day what we were doing and what we were hoping for on the visit. The FCO briefs on the Kashmir background were fascinating. How one issue came to dominate the political and diplomatic relations of two major countries [India and Pakistan], one of them a future superpower, was a great lesson in how not to do diplomacy, but what the solution was heaven knows. TB's NI experience led him to be tempted to think he could sort it, but if anything it was even more intractable than NI. We finally arrived in Bangladesh around early evening their time.

Thursday, January 3
Bangladesh. The visit got off to a potentially embarrassing start. TB's suit was badly crumpled after his car journey in Egypt and not nearly

smart enough to wear as he left the plane. But all the other suits were in the hold and it would take a while to find them. So Magi [Cleaver] was despatched off the plane first to find someone wearing a smart suit that would fit TB. We watched her through the windows walking up and down the lines of people eyeing them up and down. None of them were suitable. Then she spotted a young man at the back of the crowd and went over to him. His face was a picture. I think he thought it was some kind of spoof but then Magi was doing her best 'this is fucking serious' look and seconds later the two of them were coming up the stairs. 'Ah, the body double,' I said. He was a DFID official and gobsmacked to be on the plane with TB, CB and the rest of us. TB said 'Sorry about this but as you can see my suit is not in good shape.' So then this poor guy is stripping off so that TB can try on his suit. It wasn't perfect but it wasn't far off. The swap was done and then we were ready to disembark.

There was a full-on welcome and then straight to the president's residence. There were some pretty overwhelming scenes of poverty on the way and once we got into town the open sewers took some getting used to. But the people were by and large friendly and welcoming. Also, whereas the leadership of some countries lived in inverse proportion to the poverty of the people, with the president [Professor Badruddoza Chowdhury] and PM [Khaleda Zia] too, you were always aware of this being the Third World. They did not overdo their own luxury. The president's trousers barely reached his feet. Yet the brief had talked of this being a deeply divided and corrupt country. The divisions were clear enough at the broader ministerial meeting where various ministers had a series of arguments right in front of us, constantly interrupting each other and point scoring.

The PM was good, she was just about able to calm them down and she was up for the idea of Bangladesh being part of the ISAF in the future so that was fine. They were all pretty upfront about pitching for money for bridges and roads and the like. We had a brief and very chaotic doorstep before the official dinner, which was like a low-budget wedding reception. The room was a bit dingy and with huge spaces around the edges. The food was OK but not your usual official dinner extravagance, and the cheap tablecloths and paper napkins were a world away from some of the fineries we saw in other parts of the world. I was sitting with our rather loud high commissioner [Dr David Carter], who I quite liked because he was out of the usual cut, though it was odd he spoke no Bengali. I watched Man U vs Newcastle on Bangladeshi TV, which was more than Rory was able to do because it wasn't the live match at home.

OK coverage out of yesterday but Gus O'Donnell [Treasury permanent secretary, former press secretary to John Major] had given us a bit of a problem. He had done a meeting with students and the papers were mangling it to say that he said effectively that EMU was a political decision and the economics were never likely to be clear and unambiguous. TB was pissed off not just at GB's general behaviour and modus operandi but also that Gus should be saying this kind of thing and talking about this kind of an issue in a way that gets to the media. I felt, to be fair to Gus, that it was just a statement of the obvious, in that ultimately politicians would have to make a political judgement based on the economic analysis, but TB felt it was where GB was currently parked, namely in a position to say, whatever the economic analysis was, that it was not clear and unambiguous.

The guy from DFID had another clothing mission to perform because I suddenly discovered a hole in my shoe, and he got a shoemaker to bring in a stack of different shoes, none of them terribly nice. Events in Kashmir were the backdrop to the next stage of the visit. TB, David Manning and I met to discuss how we choreograph a sense of TB playing a part in trying to get the immediate problem solved. DM had a paper, making clear our belief that the Pakistanis would 'go nuclear' and if they did, that they wouldn't be averse to unleashing them on a big scale. TB was genuinely alarmed by it and said to David 'They wouldn't really be prepared to go for nuclear weapons over Kashmir would they?' DM said the problem was there wasn't a clear understanding of strategy and so situations tended to develop and escalate quickly, and you couldn't really rule anything out. The Kathmandu Asian summit should at least be a chance to calm things down, but the tensions were pretty strong.

After dealing with all that, we then went from the sublime to the ridiculous, with a long discussion about whether TB should wear his Nehru suit. I was marginally in favour provided it didn't look too ridiculous, partly because hopefully it would be seen as showing respect, but also because if we could generate pictures, we were more likely to generate coverage. We got to the [Windsor] hotel [Bangalore] and he put it on. It looked fine. We went for dinner at the governor of Karnataka's residence [Raj Bhavan, residence of V. S. Ramadevi], terrific food, and I enjoyed talking to our high commissioner [to India], [Sir] Rob Young, about the enormity of their democracy, the four million electoral officers for example involved in the actual logistical running of an election.

Saturday, January 5

Bangalore. I went out for a run, partly through the affluent upper-middle-class parts, also through some of the new industrial bit, and then through some of the poorer parts, and the feel you got in all three was a real sense of energy and dynamism. There was a phenomenal amount of building work going on, and the high-tech centres were as high-tech as anything back home. I got back for a final run through the speech with TB. He was now beginning to worry whether it was a bit over the top to describe the UK as 'pivotal' even though he had said it before. The central argument, that a combination of Britain's history, current strengths within all the major international institutions, and vision for the future, made us uniquely placed in some of the big international arguments was right. We set off on the long drive out to the university campus in an old Raj-era car, which gave us both backache by the time we got there. The setting was good, though there were too many introductory speeches including one from a minister that was taken as a bit of a go at TB, but his speech went down fine.[1] At lunch, I was with some of the people in the big international financial institutions. It really brought home how the scale of development here was going to impact on First World economies.

There was a discussion about TB going to Baghram for a brief visit. Magi wanted to drop the ceremonial part of the Indian visit but David [Manning] and Rob [Young] were both worried about it. MoD security were advising against going there in daylight, so we settled on a rather grim set-up that would mean a long flight back overnight. Magi was really in Magi mode, very tough with both David and Rob, partly out of revenge against the Indians who had cut Cherie out of the [forthcoming] Vajpayee dinner. DM said it was not the same. TB not going to see their president because he wanted to go to Kabul was like Vajpayee cancelling the Queen because he wanted to go to Dublin.

On the way back to the hotel, TB was chatting away about how quickly India's power was going to grow. He had been quite impressed by some of the British business guys who were down here in Bangalore. We also talked about who was going to fill the gap Anji

[1] Blair told the audience of politicians and business leaders 'Today, inevitably, I speak against the background of September 11 and the tension here in this subcontinent. But I want to set even these events in a wider context: how Britain and India work together, with others, to confront terrorism; but also how we build support for the policies and values that promote peace and justice and mitigate against extremism and terror, in all nations everywhere.'

had left in relation to what he called 'personal care and attention', the problem about the suit on the plane being a classic example. There were obviously difficulties with GB's baby and TB spoke to him briefly after the baby was transferred to a special care unit.

Sunday, January 6

Gordon's baby was clearly dying. TB and CB were both genuinely upset. So was Alison [Blackshaw]. Fiona called a couple of times from home to say we had to be careful on the various visits not to look too happy, because the media were obviously trying to set up shots of TB not seeming to care about this developing tragedy at home. Through the day, it was announced that the baby was deteriorating and had had a brain haemorrhage. After Fiona's second call, we put out a line re TB and CB thinking of them. The Sundays were even more ridiculous than usual, most of them taking as the nose to their stories the throwaway remark by an Indian minister [Pramod Mahajan, parliamentary affairs minister] yesterday that 'We are cool enough' as a great snub, India saying fuck off as a response to him re his Nehru suit.

I was more convinced than ever that we had to articulate this business of us having a press that actively wanted failure. The Indian press had been overwhelmingly positive about the speech, about him and CB, about our role. I went to the gym, where the little guy in there insisted on giving me a workout on the weights, and I was in agony by the time I got back to see TB. We went out on the rooftop of the hotel for a chat and he was clearly a bit down. He was putting enormous effort into trying to get progress on various fronts at home and abroad and all the time we had this media shit to swim through.

We flew to Hyderabad. Vajpayee and Musharraf had met yesterday but every account we had underlined how difficult any progress would be. TB was trying to get the focus on to two key principles, that Pakistan restate and more importantly show their seriousness in renouncing terrorism, and then India say yes to dialogue. TB was taken straight off by helicopter to look at some education projects while DM and I headed for the hotel to work up a proper script for TB to use post Vajpayee. David said he was shocked, even knowing what he did about our media, at the way they seemed to want us to fail, when we were actually dealing with political/diplomatic issues that were literally life and death. TB came back and, as often happened, his mood had improved by going out and about and talking to people outside the usual mix.

We flew up to Delhi where TB did Indian TV, some European

January '02: Sadness at serious illness of Brown baby

media. We got to the hotel, then a pre-meeting before Jaswant Singh [foreign affairs minister] arrived. He was pretty much signed up to TB's general approach and agreed to try and get Vajpayee on that two-principles pitch. Several times he said we needed to know where the Taliban leadership were, implying that they were in Pakistan and the Pakistanis knew where they were. He said that Musharraf had implied to Vajpayee that they could turn the terrorist taps on and off. It was so like listening to the sides in Northern Ireland.

TB told him the Indians were on strong ground and provided they said they would have meaningful dialogue, they could use us to pressure Musharraf to take the first steps. He said the Americans had to hear loud and clear that India was prepared to have a dialogue and then the pressure on Pakistan over terrorism would grow. We left for the Hyderabad palace for the talks. TB pushed hard but got very little change out of Vajpayee. He was holding out for a lot more from the Pakistanis. He was pretty shrewd, and his total lack of embarrassment at long silences was a real strength. It meant others had to go running for him. He said he would only do a brief opening statement and then say in answer to questions that he was happy to go for dialogue but by the time it came to it he was so quiet and meandering that there was no clarity.

People were more interested in the huge contrast between his near-mystical manner and TB's boyish enthusiasm. Also, bizarrely, he wore interpretation headphones the whole time even though the entire proceedings were conducted in English. He did in fact explicitly say that he would go for dialogue if the Pakistanis renounced terrorism in word and deed but it wasn't done with the force and clarity required for our dunderheads to see it as a story, so it didn't really fly. Tom [Kelly] and I did our best to push it as him giving TB a message to Musharraf, but it wasn't easy.

At the official dinner, I was for some reason seated next to Vajpayee. He was an attentive host, but so quiet. I asked him whether it was a strength or a disadvantage to have such a quiet voice, and whether he used silence as a political weapon. He said he liked to think his authority came from within, as well as from the position he held. When he spoke in his native tongue, he could raise his voice to great levels and had regularly addressed crowds of half a million during the election. But words were precious, and there was little point speaking when nothing was to be said. He said Gandhi fasted to preserve his strength, and he too had learned the value of rest and peacefulness. TB was across the table talking to [Lal Krishna] Advani, the interior minister, and George Fernandes [defence minister]. At one point he joked across the table to

Vajpayee re me, 'Be careful, he's a bad man,' and Vajpayee said 'I don't think so.' Fiona called several times to keep me up to date with GB and the baby, which was obviously desperately sad.

Monday, January 7

Really, really heavy day. Breakfast with TB in Delhi. Both he and CB sensed that the GB situation re the baby was heading for disaster, and he said it will change GB, but he didn't know whether for the better or the worse. It might give him a different sense of priorities, but it might also feed the dark side of his character. We were starting to get more criticism re TB focusing so much on foreign affairs. He felt the answer was to build the logical argument re why these issues mattered at home. We set off for the airport and boarded the C130 for Islamabad. TB and CB were up on the top deck sitting just behind the pilot who had a paper cup fixed by a rubber band to his head and 'I am a Sunderland fan' written on the cup. TB was worrying about how to get Musharraf on to a tougher line on terrorism. The flight was uncomfortable and it wasn't easy to work. We landed, similar huge security, then left for the CIC.

I was travelling with David M and [Sir] Hilary Synnott, who knew his stuff. We got to the CIC, a nice, modern set-up but it did, as Pat [McFadden] had told me, feel more like a library than a communications hub. TB had a meeting with a group of Afghan women while I met Kenton Keith to discuss who should stay and who should go. Tanya [Joseph] had been winding me up about the American guy who called himself 'the hawk' and now I could see for myself why he had driven her so bonkers. He was the archetypal over-the-top US patriot. When TB thanked them all for the work they were doing, the hawk piped up 'It's easy, sir, when your children are at risk.' They were a pretty good bunch though, just hadn't gelled to make the difference I had hoped they would.

TB was on good form at the press conference. We were being lobbied by the American ambassador, Wendy Chamberlain, for the UK to become a mediator re Kashmir. TB was attracted, I could tell, but resisted nonetheless. I was worried about TB taking on yet another huge international commitment. She was adamant that only TB could sort this out. We went to the hotel and down to the pool to discuss how to handle the meetings. TB felt step one had to be Musharraf getting tougher with the terror groups, use that to press the Indians to engage. There had to be an absolute break with the Taliban and any of the groups they supported. But Pakistan also had to know there were benefits out of that.

We left for Musharraf's place and most of the talks were one-on-one, afterwards described by TB as 'very, very hard going'. I talked to [Shaukat] Aziz, the finance minister, who was very urbane and very charming, really trying to convince me that Musharraf wanted to break the terror groups. There was clearly a concerted effort going on as David M was getting the same message just as hard, hearing Musharraf had said before the December 13 attack on the Indian parliament that they would crack down on them. We were called in after a while and went over familiar ground on Afghanistan, then some bilateral stuff, and TB, clearly feeling the meeting was getting a bit rambling, suggested the two of them plus their press people should go through the difficult questions for the press conference. Musharraf went through what he intended to say, which was pretty much OK, then TB did the same and Musharraf clearly baulked at him saying 'Support for terrorism must stop for talks to begin.' He said he didn't like it because it suggested that Pakistan and its government supported terrorism. We persuaded him that the best thing to do then was for him to say right at the top that he opposed terrorism in all its forms. We also persuaded him not to talk about Kashmir as a 'freedom struggle' because that would not be understood by our and by US opinion. Better to say it was an indigenous struggle. We spent an awful lot of time toing and froing on it but eventually he agreed.

It was a pretty tortuous exchange, indicative of how deep-rooted the problems were, but it did mean we got what we wanted in terms of a tough anti-terrorism statement and even our media took it as a bit of a breakthrough for TB. The media event was strong. Then drinks, then dinner. I was next to General [Muhammad] Aziz Khan [chairman of Joint Chiefs of Staff, Pakistan] and the finance minister. Their general feeling was that India was in a box and didn't know how to get out of it. It was funny too how both sides seemed to talk of the other as equals, even though India was so much bigger and more powerful.

We had done pretty well though on both legs, then to the airport and back on the C130 for the flight to Baghram. The troops were loving it and the press were genuinely excited about the trip. We flew in total darkness to Baghram, with only the occasional flash of green from night sights. As we arrived, it was pitch black. TB and CB went out to a red carpet, [Hamid] Karzai [chairman of the Transitional Administration], the band playing the barely discernible tune of welcome, and general chaos to which I added, stepping down from the plane, when my briefcase, even though the combination lock was on, suddenly opened and papers were flying all over the place.

Thankfully, the hacks were all being taken off the other end and didn't notice as David [Manning], Anna [Wechsberg] and I scrabbled around using hands, feet and anything else to trap the paper and get, hopefully, all of it back. TB was now standing with an Afghan shouting into his face in what seemed to be part of the welcome. We were then taken to a line of armoured vehicles and the Special Branch advance guy introduced David and me to the special forces who were going to be looking after us.

The drive was slow, over endless tank traps, eventually reaching the old Russian barracks. TB had a one-on-one with Karzai, said he was very upbeat, probably too much, but he was clearly pleased that TB had come, particularly given the genuine security risks, and there was a good atmosphere between them. As we came out of the meeting, into the darkened corridor, Keith Lowe [protection officer] took me to one side and said 'You should probably tell the PM that the Chancellor's baby has died.' There is something about a baby's death. Even the cops, who can turn pretty much anything into a source of laughter, seemed really saddened, and were explaining to the Afghans what had happened. I told TB in between meetings. I said I'm afraid there's bad news, and he knew straight away what it was, and asked us to try to fix a call.

We had to move to a bigger room for a meeting with eight of the ministers from the interim government. One look around the room was enough to tell you what a nightmare job Karzai had trying to hold things together. TB and Karzai said a few words of welcome and then opened things up. They were a pretty aggressive bunch. One of them was the double of Orson Welles [heavyweight actor] and said they needed long-term help. His tone of voice suggested he didn't think we would deliver it. There was another guy who looked like something out of the Taliban and who spent most of the meeting trying to stare us out. One or two were dressed in Western-style suits but they said little. Karzai was definitely a cut above but he really had his work cut out. They had cobbled together from somewhere a collection of chairs and tables, and laid out a rather sad collection of sweets that nobody touched. TB said Britain would stay with them for the long term, and work to make sure that the reconstruction conference in Tokyo [January 21–22, to be co-chaired by Japan, US, EU and Saudi Arabia] went well.

Karzai said Afghanistan was well rid of the terrible leadership that went before. Abdullah said they were effectively reconstructing a country from scratch. Karzai obviously picked up on the somewhat negative tone of some of the ministerial contributions and concluded the meeting by saying they were all 'so glad that such a distinguished person has come to see us, taken the risk, you have demonstrated such goodwill. When the Afghan people get to hear that you visited us, they will be proud and thrilled.' One of the special forces guys said to me 'Welcome to bandit country.' We drove, as slowly and painfully as before, to the special forces HQ, to put a phone call through to Sue Nye [GB's personal aide]. She confirmed that the baby was dead and that it had now been announced publicly. TB was genuinely cut up, said it was a horrible thing to have to go through, and even worse with all the attention on it. He was having to talk quite loudly to be heard. I could sense that this collection of real hard nuts from the SAS and the SBS were a bit bemused to have their prime minister in there having a near-weepy phone call. He was due to be doing the press, so we went over how to respond to the baby's death whilst also covering the substance of the visit. He was pretty discombobulated and wanted further confirmation and assurance that it had been announced. Karzai arrived and we filled him in on what was happening, explaining why he would have to address it. Karzai showed a deft touch, taking his hat off when TB spoke later re GB.

We were taken to meet some of the real heroes from both SAS and SBS. The first presentation was from a guy who had been part of a team following a tip that OBL was in a certain cave. They had ended up living for days without supplies, having to make do with what they found, including a thirty-hour period in which the only consumption between four of them, apart from stuff off trees, was a small bottle of water. They had been calling on bombers and fighting their way, hand to hand, towards where they were going. But he had gone by the time they got there. Then a Geordie who had been at the fort at Mazar, buried under rubble after an American bomb went astray, got out, involved in all sorts of fighting, got out the body of the American guy who had been killed there, eventually flushing out the al-Qaeda people by pumping in freezing water. He told it all with a mix of real pride and deadpan humour. These guys were genuinely impressive people. Their living quarters here, let alone when they were out and about, were incredibly basic and yet there was an enthusiasm there that was incredible. None of them seemed boastful, or demanding of credit or praise. They just explained very factually what they did. One of the most impressive was the smallest, a Scottish guy so small I was surprised he was even allowed in the Armed Forces. We were then given a presentation by [Major General John] McColl on ISAF [of which McColl, a UK soldier, was leader]. He too was impressive, not least the way he worked out the details of the military technical agreements and the way he was establishing authority in Kabul, e.g. by troops being visible at DFID projects, being seen to do good infrastructure work. Once again, we were confronted by the ingenuity and the resilience of our troops. TB said he needed a pee and we were taken out, up a field, to a series of upturned tubes into the ground.

Back on the C130, I met the SIS guy who had actually been the first person into Kabul, even if John Simpson had never met him. He too combined modesty with a very matter-of-fact ability to describe astonishing events. We flew out in total darkness, with a flare going by every now and then. Eventually, I managed to sleep. We landed in Oman and were glad to be transferred to the million times more comfortable 777. I called Ian Austin, and later wrote a letter to GB, as did TB and Cherie. TB briefed us on the one-on-one parts of his various meetings over dinner. He felt we had achieved things in India and Pakistan that actually made conflict less likely. But he was beginning to take seriously the stuff about him being more abroad than home, and talking about pulling out of his Africa tour. I felt that would be a mistake because it would look weak and defensive.

Wednesday, January 9

We landed, straight into the office, and back to all the crap. TB had told Jonathan he wanted to pull the Africa trip. Liz Lloyd [policy adviser] said the four leaders [of Ghana, Nigeria, Senegal and Sierra Leone] had cancelled a dinner with Chirac in Paris to be there for him, so he couldn't. My first morning meeting of the year, as we went through the media brief, was like swimming through shit. Virtually every paper over every story in knocking mode. TB, the great man abroad as seen overseas, was being whacked at home over absolutely everything. It was easy to dismiss as the usual media frenzy, but it must be causing us political problems.

I went up to the flat to discuss PMQs. He said we had to resist the *Groundhog Day*[1] feeling, that it was the greatest danger we got bored or started to let these bastards get us down. It had always been a struggle, always would be, and we had to stick at it and really get going. PMQs was OK if not brilliant. Transport was going big and then it emerged [Peter] Hain had said we had the worst railways in Europe, which went straight to the top of the news. Very annoying and stupid. JP livid, said what is it with people like that? TB had spoken to GB who wanted him to go to the funeral on Friday.

---

[1] 1993 Hollywood comedy, in which the same day repeats ad nauseam.

At the morning meeting, I made sure the Foreign Office knew how pissed off everyone was at Hain, which was still getting a fair bit of play. War Cabinet was largely India/Pakistan, where is OBL, and some domestic stuff. CDS said if India and Pakistan go to war, we will be up the creek without a paddle. Geoff said there may have to be limited compulsory call-up of Territorial Army reserves. TB gave a pretty gloomy assessment re India/Pakistan, said Vajpayee was really upset at the way Musharraf treated him. Military dispositions remained the same, with more than a million troops there [Kashmir]. He assessed that the Indians believed that they could absorb 500,000 deaths. Pakistani capability was far greater than the Indians believed.

Cabinet was mainly a discussion re public services, and lots of people defending Byers. TB said the media were determined to give us a rough ride and would focus not on things we had done but on things we hadn't done. We shouldn't pretend everything is perfect but we shouldn't let them get away with the impression nothing is being achieved. We should be confident. Byers said the attacks over rail were an attack on the whole reform agenda, we had to be robust, emphasise the decades of underinvestment and failed privatisation and stick to the ten-year plan. He said he was delighted to have given colleagues a bit of a break from media heat. Both Reid and Jack Straw said the attacks on Steve were attacks on all of us and it was important we didn't allow these issues to be personalised but stuck together. Milburn echoed that, said it was railways today, could be any other service tomorrow because this was about an ideological assault on public services. Blunkett felt the Tories were beginning to get their act together and IDS was deliberately undermining confidence in the public services as a way of showing us as out of date. He felt they had hit on something and that disillusion went quite deep. It was a good discussion. And people were very supportive of Steve.

TB felt we had two years of struggle and provided improvements were clear at the end of that, we would win this argument. Their desire is to say the public services are hopeless and therefore we should return to the agenda of the 80s. Our argument is that through investment and reform we can build them up. In the afternoon, we had a four-hour strategy meeting with my main people plus other heads of department, but I felt just as I kept doing the groundhog stuff, so did they. TB chaired. We did agree TB should chair four new informal ministerial groups, on Europe, public services, rights and responsibilities, and also what someone called an 'ism' group, the need to knit everything we are doing together round a coherent set of beliefs. People kept arguing on the need to be more radical without being specific or clear as to what they meant.

TB felt that in health Milburn had come out clearly as a reformer and that had changed things within the department. He felt there was a danger Estelle [Morris] was opting for a quiet life. He was tempted to go back to a big speech on the lines of the one he had planned to make last September 11 [to the Trades Union Congress], about why [public service] reform was so important. Fiona and I both said afterwards it was the same people making the same points they had been making for years. We needed new people and we needed new ways of working. A lot of it was about the way TB worked with Cabinet colleagues. He was collegiate in some ways, and they would all say pretty easy to work with, but he didn't really let go. The meeting drifted into a discussion of specific areas like [banning fox] hunting and Lords reform. On both, TB was worried about buggering up the whole of our programme if we weren't careful.

Jeremy [Heywood] did a fascinating presentation showing that we were actually spending less of our GDP on public spending than [Margaret] Thatcher, if you looked at the figures in a certain way. Andrew Adonis [head of the Policy Unit] said we were wasting billions on GB's pet projects. Peter Hyman [policy adviser and speech-writer] felt we were deluding ourselves if we thought that TB would change his ways. He was wedded to his informal style, he let colleagues roam free only provided they were roaming in the direction he wanted, he would never go full frontal on the media, and he would always be as interested in positioning as in policy or people. He was what he was, and he would never change.

TB spoke to GB a couple of times, said he sounded devastated. He said it would change him fundamentally, but nobody could be sure how. Alistair Darling told me that GB had spent the whole time she was alive talking to the baby. He too felt this would change GB. Fiona and I were not so sure, felt it would increase his anger, his belief that TB got everything easy and he was a victim. Chris Meyer came to see me, lobbying for a seven-day trip to the US with lots of big events, speeches, TB being showered with prizes. It all sounded totally OTT, and not necessary.

Friday, January 11

TB called me on his way back from the baby's funeral to say it had been a nice service but with a very odd audience. He had been quite shocked to see how many journalists were there, including [Paul]

Dacre [*Mail* editor]. I said I couldn't imagine why they would have wanted anyone but really close friends there, and TB said different people react differently in grief. He said he went back to the house after the service and GB had been very warm, and that it almost reminded him of the days when they had been genuinely close.

Saturday, January 12
To the Goulds' for dinner. Gail [Rebuck, publisher and wife of Philip Gould] asked whether Philip and I had ever had a discussion that did not cover TB, GB, Peter M and their varying relationships. The answer is probably not, at least none that lasted more than a minute or two.

Sunday, January 13
In for the *Frost* interview, chatting to TB on the way, but we lacked a real hard story and I felt we were tired in our communications. Partly it was because [Sir] David Frost [interviewer] didn't really push him hard, but also both of us lacked the energy that we used to put into this sort of thing automatically. I felt that I was playing the old tunes but to a lesser effect. TB felt it was just that the press were in the mood to give no quarter.

Monday, January 14
The papers were dire and TB wanted to go on a blitz. I said I was not so sure, felt they would just say it looked like panic and this was maybe one of those periods we just had to take. What was clear was we needed to fight back better on public services. I called Piers Morgan who said to me that the *Mirror* was 'no longer a Labour paper', which not long ago would have been a big statement that would have made real waves. He also argued that we ought to raise income tax. I pointed out that we had made clear in the manifesto that we wouldn't. 'Nobody will mind if you break a promise like that.'

I had dinner with Blunkett at Simply Nico [Westminster restaurant]. He made pretty clear he felt he should be the next Chancellor. He said TB should stay as long as possible, and he should stay at home more. He felt both TB and I should do more to talk up the rest of the Cabinet. He understood why we had to keep GB sweet, but he doubted he was ever going to change, whereas the rest of them by and large responded well to being treated well. He was very down on his department. Something had to be done, he said, about the quality of people going into the Civil Service, because a lot of them were absolutely useless. He was very onside with TB but worried about the impact of the clear decision made by most of the media to turn against him. Someone in his constituency had said that if TB found a cure for cancer, the press would all ask why has Blair done nothing for meningitis? I put to him TB's notion that what the press were reflecting was that the public wanted to see us tested and survive, but he shared my view that public opinion was bound to be affected by the incessant media denigration.

David also said Jack was totally obsessed with the idea that he was dumping on him when in fact he was just putting through necessary policy changes. We had a nice evening, and David was reasonably relaxed for him, but it was sometimes worrying how much of the talk focused on the personal divisions. I had also noticed this morning that Charles [Clarke] had gone from being very engaged to being really pissed off quite quickly. TB had noticed the same thing and took him aside afterwards. Charles was feeling he just had a party management job without a real say in the politics. We clearly needed to involve him more.

Tuesday, January 15

There was growing disquiet about the Americans' treatment of al-Qaeda/Taliban 'prisoners' and Tom's eleven o'clock was pretty grim on the subject. I chatted to a number of commentators like Polly Toynbee, David Aaronovitch [*Independent*], Alice Miles [*Times*] trying to engage them in argument about defending the NHS. We were lacking strategy at the moment but we were also lacking freshness. The same people were coming up with the same solutions to the same old problems. Milburn was doing well today on his NHS reform stuff, and how to deal with failing hospitals. Dobbo [Frank Dobson, Milburn's predecessor] looked pretty bitter in his attack. TB felt basic message and policies were right but the media mood had changed again and we had to just think through how to deal with that.

Wednesday, January 16

The Rumsfeld interview last night was giving us problems because he basically made clear he couldn't care less about the condition of al-Qaeda/Taliban people in Cuba [Guantanamo Bay].[1] I wasn't sure whether this was a problem or not as a general issue, but I was pretty sure talking about it the way Rumsfeld did was not sensible. On the

[1] Donald Rumsfeld has been reported as saying 'I do not feel even the slightest concern about their treatment. They are being treated vastly better than they treated anybody else over the last several years.'

conference call, I was asking whether it wasn't possible to give a proper explanation of real conditions there, but Torie Clarke pointed out the questions they were getting were why any money was being wasted on these people at all. The story out of the PLP meeting was lots of critics rounding on TB and it was also clear the media were desperate to give IDS a lift to even things up a bit. I also felt, e.g. at PMQs meetings, that we lacked the obvious themes that tended to be clear when we were strategically strong. TB did OK on Guantanamo, but IDS had enough good lines for the press to give him the write-up they wanted to.

TB said afterwards he knew he hadn't been brilliant but he said he wasn't yet ready to go for IDS big time, that he wanted to wait and be sure he was going on the right line of attack. I was probably a bit harsh on him but felt he had been complacent. We weren't motoring at the moment. I felt I hadn't yet knitted together the various parts of the communications operation. We had been going through a bad phase and it was bound to show up in the polls soon. People were making comparisons with the Tories in their second term but there were big differences – the Tories basically had a supportive press, their people were less prone to panic and more up for a fight.

Thursday, January 17

The mood in the media was now pretty nasty. TB told Cabinet that while it was difficult, it gave us the opportunity to get up definition for reform. There were a number of interesting contributions, not least JP, who made clear that if we pushed too far on private sector involvement in health, we wouldn't be able to take the party with us. TB did at least steady nerves a bit. People were asking for a core script and I was clearly going to have to get back to doing the weekly strategy notes.[1] Charles Clarke felt he was being blamed for the lack of coherent strategy, but it was largely my fault, because I had been so demotivated. DB raised the need to stage prison pay. TB was emphasising that we were not going to improve public services without real change. We should be pointing to education as the area where reforms had most obviously yielded benefits. But in health now, virtually every indicator was moving in the right direction. So do not be apologetic or defensive.

There was a comic moment when TB started a sentence: 'If JP had come to me in '97 and said renationalise the railways, it would have been a short conversation.' 'It was a short conversation,' JP interrupted.

---

[1] 'The Week in Strategic Context', a strategic communications note drawn from the Grid, addressed to John Prescott but copied to all ministers.

Byers pointed out, and he was right, that since September 11 we had lost political definition on the domestic agenda. But it doesn't mean we don't have the right arguments. Jack said we were caught in a spiral of rising expectations. People's point of reference was not always their own experience but the national media. TB said that post '97 we were perceived to be on a massive burst of activity but actually to a large extent we were feeling our way. He felt that this term we had a clearer agenda and we just had to stick to it. Ed Balls called and later came to see me. He said GB had been pretty badly affected but was intending to come back to London next Monday.

We were still getting hit on Guantanamo with the ICRC [International Committee of the Red Cross] going today, and a UK team, including spooks, going tomorrow. I was frankly taken aback at the scale of the media opposition there seemed to be. On the conference call, Torie [Clarke] said it was time to get some steel in our spines re Cuba. We won the PCC case re Euan/Oxford, but Neil Wallis [editor, the *People*] told me a lot of key people at the PCC weren't happy.[1] The *Mail* were really gunning for CB at the moment and TB was worried about it, felt they were trying to do her in on a grand scale. I had a meeting with Byers, Jo Moore, Darren Murphy [Milburn's special adviser] and Sian Jarvis [head of communications, Health Department] re Tuesday's debate and the idea of a Byers/Milburn briefing for Monday showing the modernisers were still in charge. Byers was taking a hit at the moment but Milburn's stock was still high. I had a long chat with Mark Malloch-Brown [United Nations Development Programme] to try to co-ordinate Tokyo [Afghanistan reconstruction summit].

[Rupert] Murdoch [head of News Corp] was coming in for dinner, and along with Les Hinton [News International executive chairman] brought James and Lachlan [Murdoch's sons]. They arrived a bit early, and I took Murdoch upstairs because TB wanted fifteen minutes with him, then entertained the others in my office before we went up. I was interested to see how Murdoch related to his kids. Lachlan seemed a bit shy of expressing his views whereas James was anything but. Murdoch was at one point putting the traditional very right-wing view on Israel and the Middle East peace process and James said that he was 'talking fucking nonsense'. Murdoch said he didn't see what the Palestinians' problem was and James said it was that they were kicked out of their fucking homes and had nowhere to fucking live. Murdoch

---

[1] The Blairs had complained to the Press Complaints Commission about reports in the *Daily Telegraph* and *Daily Mail* about Euan Blair applying for a place at Oxford University. The complaint was upheld.

was very pro Israel, very pro Reagan. He finally said to James that he didn't think he should talk like that in the prime minister's house and James got very apologetic with TB who said not to worry, I hear far worse all the time. Most of the discussion was a run round the main foreign policy blocks, Israel, Saudi, Iran, Indo-Pak, a little bit of why does Britain have to bother so much? We didn't get into Europe at all, which was a bit of a waste. TB said afterwards he was quite impressed with the way Murdoch let his sons do so much of the talking. Murdoch pointed out that his were the only papers that gave us support when the going got tough. 'I've noticed,' said TB. I gave them my culture-of-denigration argument and was probably a bit over the top but I felt frustrated that we had to pander so much.

Friday, January 18
I took the morning off to go on Grace's school trip to a museum, which was a real reminder that it's not just people in jobs like ours that live in permanent stress. God knows how teachers do it. The kids were a handful, albeit very good fun. The teachers at least had a laugh when a teacher from one of the other schools at the museum pointed over to me and said 'That teacher is the spitting image of Alastair Campbell.' I did the conference call, after which the news moved on with a number of al-Qaeda related arrests in the UK [eight suspects had been arrested in Leicester].

Saturday, January 19
I took the boys to play football in Regent's Park, and TB called, emphasising again we just had to keep going because we had the right arguments and the right policies. But media-wise we had the *Mirror/Guardian* on one end of the spectrum doing us in from the left and the *Mail/Telegraph* doing us in from the right, and we weren't very good at fighting back. The *Mail on Sunday* had a Pentagon picture from Guantanamo Bay which they put beneath the headline 'Torture'. The issue had been bubbling up for days now and I suspected this could be the tipping point. Our problem was the Americans didn't seem to get how bad it was for them. We were in danger of losing the moral high ground, though of course they didn't seem to see it like that. They only ever looked at the US audience, which was a big mistake.

Sunday, January 20
Dad had another turn, and broke his shoulder falling, so I set off with Grace. I asked Tom Kelly to stay on top of the Guantanamo situation as best he could. Sebastian Wood [UK Embassy, Washington]

and his security service people were only there yesterday and only able to do interviews today, so it was going to be tricky. Tom called me on the train, said Jack S wanted to put out a statement calling on the US to clarify. I said to Tom to get TB to speak to him. They spoke, then Jack called me saying TB had agreed to him putting out a statement. I was a bit dubious but didn't think it was worth a great fight and instead toned it down a bit, taking out any reference to TB having raised it with GWB.

Jack said that Colin Powell had said to him on an open line from Kathmandu that he was beside himself at the way Rumsfeld and the Department of Defense were handling the issue because it was giving him so many knock-on problems. The statement went out and needless to say within minutes it was US–UK rift. TB denied to me that he had given JS the go-ahead to put it out. Jack said it was important because it was right in principle to push for the basic human rights of any UK citizens to be protected, and we had to watch out for TB being made to look weak by being complicit through neglect in bad things the Americans did. Tom did a ring-round of the lobby and managed to lower the heat on it.

Dad was a lot less sure on his feet than before and Grace a bit taken aback by how much weaker he was, but he was pleased we went up. Grace was playing cards with Mum and when Dad fell asleep in his chair, I sat down and worked through a response to TB's note re strategy, which I felt was a bit tired and weak. I set out a note based on four phases, Opposition/term one/term two/legacy; taking the same fundamentals to all – economy, society, public services, international – but trying to revive each for the different phases. I also felt TB's language was becoming a bit distant again.

Monday, January 21

Guantanamo was running big and bad, and we were not in shape to deal with it. At the TB office meeting, we were discussing his strategy paper and my response to it. It was the first one with Charles C present, one of the responses to his pissed-off mood last week, but he was constantly putting up objections to things being done, saying why things couldn't happen, e.g. lack of resources, or we didn't have an agreed core script or strategy, or ministers would not let him perform the cross-cutting role we asked him to do. He was slowly moving into my area too which funnily enough didn't bother me too much because I was conscious of not doing the job as well as I should be at the moment, and also I'd felt since he got the job that if I raised my game a bit Charles and I could do a good double act on the media. It was clear TB was talking to Peter M more and not happy with me that we had not filled the post-Anji gap re taking care of the right-wing media.

At my morning meeting, I said we had to start pushing back on Guantanamo. Once we got the Sebastian Wood report [on Guantanamo Bay], I got Ben Bradshaw [FCO minister] to do one [on detainees]. The draft done for him by his office was so poor that I found myself at 3.20pm, ten minutes before he was due on his feet in the House, rewriting it with him by phone. He did fine though and looked and sounded confident and on top of things.

I had lunch with Peter Kellner [political commentator and pollster] who wanted to help us more. He felt the [Evening] Standard would stay where it was politically under Veronica Wadley [editor]. He volunteered the view that we lacked the coherent narrative of the past, and he was right. I had a meeting with [Sir] Michael Jay [former ambassador to France] who was taking over from [Sir] John Kerr as permanent secretary at the FCO and I think persuaded him of the need for new structures ready to be properly activated in the event of a genuine international crisis. We had done fine re Kosovo and Afghanistan but we lost so much ground early on when actually setting up the structures from scratch. There ought to be a structure in place, ready to be manned fully if needed. I was spending a fair bit of time fixing things for the football match in Kabul.[1]

Tuesday, January 22

At the morning meeting I read the riot act re DTLR, and gave the same message at a meeting re the Tube later, re whoever was doing in [Stephen] Byers. It was clearly coming from inside the department. I was trying to sort out timing of teachers' pay before leaving for a very nice lunch with David Frost at Le Caprice. Whatever was going on, he seemed to give us the benefit of the doubt, and he felt TB was just in a different league to most of the politicians he dealt with.

More evidence of the Yanks' uselessness and lack of touch when DoD [Department of Defense] said on the 2.30 conference call they intended to announce today they [Guantanamo detainees] were 'unlawful combatants' and release another picture. They were clearly being driven by the insight that US opinion would just about take

[1] A 'unity' football match would be played on 15 February at the Afghan national stadium between Kabul Olympic Football Club and troops of the International Security Assistance Force, the latter including players from the UK, Denmark, Norway, France, Italy, Spain, Holland and Germany.

their word for it, and also the feeling that there was no reason why they should be treated properly, but they didn't seem to see through the implications elsewhere. Jim Wilkinson, who at least seemed to get that part, joined me in talking them out of doing the picture, and that then led to them suffering a hiccup on the other part of the plan. Rumsfeld then went off on another one re Guantanamo. He just lacked subtlety.

TB called an internal meeting re the domestic situation. He felt the key was the CSR [Comprehensive Spending Review] and the Budget and he and GB working together closely. PG said the Tories were nowhere but that had led to expectations on us being higher and we were really expected to fulfil them. He felt we had the basic script right but we needed a better communications plan. At the Tube meeting, I was arguing for Steve [Byers] to go head to head with Ken Livingstone. [London mayor]. The DTLR crew were a pretty hopeless and unconfident lot.

I did the East Midlands group of [Labour] MPs, who were the best yet in terms of engagement. Dennis Skinner was on good form. I got home for Man U vs Liverpool, where I'd fixed for the ball for the match in Kabul to be handed over. Karen Hughes called during the match. She apologised for having been a bit out of touch, agreed we should scale down London and Washington, put Tucker Eskew in charge over there, leave Islamabad to please Musharraf, then use three or four others as a roving team going at short notice to different parts of the world where we felt we needed a presence. But the longer we talked the clearer it was she was really just focused on the US audience.

Fiona was close to the end of her tether, fed up with me, fed up with the pressures I brought into the house all the time. She thought I had changed, that I cared more about the job than her. She said I never seemed to take her feelings and concerns into account as I went about the job in the way I did. She accepted I was good with the kids, but after the job and them, there was nothing left, and it made her unhappy. I tried to do my usual, say that this was not going to go on forever, that I had to do it this way, that we should be proud of the difference we made, but it cut no ice. She said it was all about me, she was only there as an appendage.

Wednesday, January 23

I slept badly and when I did had all manner of awful dreams, including one where a pack of lions and hyenas were hunting me down in the corner of a field. I woke up, my whole body in a sweat. The mood in the house was bad as I left for the morning meeting. I got a call from one of the hacks saying IDS was going to do health at PMQs, the *Standard* having done a big number of the treatment of a woman called Rose Addis.[1] TB was up for really going at him. IDS used the line from the woman's daughter that she had been treated 'worse than a dog'. TB stayed calm, just presented the hospital's denials, but it was their toughest exchange so far and the manner in which IDS put it meant it was going big. TB felt it was a mistake, that the public would instinctively see the difference between the role of a relative and the role of a politician putting them in the spotlight deliberately, but I was not so sure. The press would now do IDS' work for him, and if we were not careful we would be into a new season of personal case histories presented as the big picture. TB said he felt real heat in there. Equally it did allow us to get up definition of what we were doing, the idea of a struggle for the very future of public services. Some in the media were arguing the Tories can never win on health, but they can hurt us if all the public hear are bad case histories like this.

Milburn came into TB's room at the Commons and we agreed we had to get the doctors at the Whittington Hospital out there. They did the *PM* programme [BBC Radio 4] and were excellent. It then turned out the main one was a Labour Party member – so what, in a sane world, why shouldn't he be? – but we got him pulled for later media. Unfortunately at the four o'clock, Tom gave out personal details of the people covered in the *Standard*, material which had been prepared for TB's PMQs brief, and although it was already all in the public domain, either from the hospital or the family, it was a tactical error because it allowed the Tory papers to make it a 'Labour dirty tricks' story, rather than being about IDS getting his facts wrong. I felt provided we held our nerve, this would be OK for us, because it allowed us to get up dividing lines rooted in values. Tucker had an interesting take – said that it was the best example yet of our crazy media and political system. The idea that one elderly woman's care was the big political story for the entire country was ridiculous.

Thursday, January 24
The papers were full of the health row, with the doctors pushing back. I briefed Hazel Blears [junior health minister] for the 8.10 slot on the

---

[1] Addis, a 94-year-old, had allegedly been neglected in the Whittington Hospital in North London. Her daughter made a complaint to her MP – Conservative leader Iain Duncan Smith.

Today programme. She was calm and rational and did well. Up to see TB who felt even by our standards the press had been ridiculous over this, us being put in the dock over the so-called leaking of details when the family went to the press and the Tory leader raised it on the floor of the House. But the press loathed us at the moment and were just desperate to give IDS a lift. I wrote to Piers Morgan whacking him for taking the Tory line on health. Probably just frustration at TB refusing to take them on more vigorously.

Cabinet was interesting, in that it was clear the exchanges with IDS yesterday had really got them up for a political battle on the NHS. But there were some worries expressed, not least by TB, at the idea IDS could somehow set himself up as the friend of the patient. There was a brief discussion of the Lords where JP railed at the idea of an elected chamber, said it was only of interest to 'Charter 88 or Charter 99 or whatever they call it'. TB gave a very strong message on public services and the dividing lines and they clearly felt better afterwards, speaking to one or two outside. The BMA [British Medical Association] put out a rather unhelpful statement on the back of the Rose Addis case. TB and Alan agreed we needed white coats rather than politicians out there at the moment pushing back. We went to do the *Jimmy Young Programme* [BBC Radio 2 talk show], Jimmy complaining to us before the interview at the way he was treated by the Beeb. He was still pretty good and they got through a fair bit of ground. TB was good on overall message and was clearly feeling in his stride.

On the train to Darlington, TB was working on the speech [to health workers in Newcastle], did a very good section on the current row and set it in the context of the debate going to the heart of the parliament. We got to Myrobella [Blair's constituency home], worked some more on the speech, then I went for a run. We had dinner at Myrobella after a brief trip to the [Trimdon] Labour Club and I pointed out to TB that virtually everyone we had met today, including on the train, had complained about the way the media covered the country and then political debate. It was an issue waiting to be tapped. He didn't feel we were the people to do it though. TB asked how things were with Fiona, and I said not good. He said I had to involve her more but also be nicer to her. He said he had realised with Cherie that it was really hard for her. We were blokes, he said, and we were doing big difficult jobs and taking a lot of heat all the time. So we felt CB and FM ought to realise that, because they lived with us, and be totally supportive and understanding. But it was hard for them too, and we had to do better at understanding that too.

The NHS row was probably a messy draw, but the TB speech was at least reasonably well set up. I was sleeping in the room next to his and he woke me up at 6, asking if I wanted a cup of tea, meaning he wanted me up to work on the speech with him downstairs. He felt we just had to shut down the Rose Addis row as best we could so we removed the lines that would most obviously be taken as a reference. With the opinion formers, we were running the argument that IDS scored a tactical hit but it was a strategic blunder because it got him back to an arch-Thatcherite position. I had worked up some good lines on my run yesterday re what being on the side of the patient meant, including being on the side of the staff, who in the Addis case felt really angry. TB was in very jokey mood, saying what kind of political victim will the dirty tricks operatives go for next – nuns, Sunday school teachers, war heroes?

Tom was a bit worried about the briefing he did but I told him not to worry and it was one of the good parts of TB's leadership that if staff screwed up, he encouraged them not to let it fester. We set off for Newcastle, and though it was a bit flat, the speech went fine.[1] The medics and the managers both seemed to feel IDS had made a bit of a blunder, but of course it was always hard to tell at these kinds of gatherings how much was politeness and how much was real. At Darlington, we met up with Neil Wallis and Nigel Nelson from the *People*. TB did a crap interview, just didn't get engaged, and we didn't have a top line. He said to me afterwards when I pointed out how crap he had been that he assumed I would cook something up with them so he wasn't really concentrating. He said he was bored and irritated at the way they used anecdote to make what they thought were serious judgements, e.g. going on about what 'Mrs Wallis' would want to know. We talked about the press again. He said he was the one person who hates the press more than I do, but 'I should not be the person who takes them on the whole time.' He said we don't have a [Norman] Tebbit [Margaret Thatcher's Cabinet 'attack dog'] figure, which is a problem, but even if we did, he was not convinced it was the right way to go. Where I agreed with him was that they matter more to Oppositions than governments, but they are really up for damaging us at the moment.

[1] After telling the audience that each negative media story about the health service was 'tomorrow's fish and chip wrapper', Blair said 'This is the decade when we look to public service professionals as the new byword for can-do innovation and dynamism. For shaking things up and getting things done.'

Saturday, January 26

TB was off to Paris with CB and called for a brief chat re the NHS before he left. He felt we could win the argument and had moved to a position, as it was clearly going into the Sundays, of saying it was in our interest to keep this whole thing going. I took Calum to Regent's Park to play football but Neil Wallis was pressing me re TB's NHS words and wanted them harder and harder, basically to run the line that if we didn't fix the NHS we wouldn't deserve to win again.

Sunday, January 27

PG called to say he felt we needed a new sense of drive and strategy, that it all felt a bit stale. He was right. He didn't feel Charles Clarke spoke the same language and strategy as us, was too conceptual, not hard-edged enough, felt he was deliberately placing himself off centre as a way of building up a 'not TB' positioning. I was pissed off with myself re the *People* which as I expected went on a very hard line re the NHS and TB was concerned that it made it seem that unless we met any and every expectation re the NHS we would be admitting to failure.[1] Not surprisingly, he was not one hundred per cent happy that it came from something he didn't say, but that I said for him. He agreed that as it was the *People* it was unlikely to fly, but we prepared lines on it in case. The worry was that it became one of those statements that stuck and which the Tories could ram down our throats at the next election, exactly the argument I had used with Wallis before I got fed up and gave up.

Monday, January 28

Health had died down but the *People* interview was worrying both of us. I apologised to TB for pushing it too far. He was fine about that, just wanted to make sure it did not become an enormous hostage. It had the feel of something that could become big at a later date, and I was amazed the Tories weren't pushing it. If they had any sense they would keep it running till PMQs. My hope was it just went away but it nagged away at me because it was a mistake and I was angry with myself. TB wanted a transcript to see what he actually said but of course we were talking about 'add-on words' agreed between me and Wallis.

[1] Blair was quoted as saying 'If the NHS is not basically fixed by the next election, then I am quite happy to suffer the consequences. I am quite willing to be held to account by the voters if we fail.'

At his Monday office meeting, TB said so much depended on how he and GB operated together and that depended on GB. He said he was willing to co-operate in every which way, but Jeremy said the current vibes the other way were not good. We talked about Charles [Clarke], me saying we really lacked a politician attack dog who did not mind putting the boot in big style. I could only do it up to a point. I was constrained by the position and by the fact I didn't go on camera. Peter [Hyman] was very down on Charles, said he sometimes felt we had a party chairman who was against party campaigning. The Tories were vulnerable. They were just going negative negative negative, talking the country down, willing everything to fail, and without real policy prescriptions, and that was not a great position for them, but we didn't have the firepower to hurt them for it.

I had a visit from one of Crown Prince Abdullah's right-hand men, wanting advice on how to improve the Saudi image in the West (not knowing at this stage the *Guardian* were on to a story of Brits being tortured there). I was as frank as I could be within the confines, even at a meeting like this, of diplomacy. But I said they would need more than a few ad campaigns to win people over. They needed the reality to change. The look in his eye suggested that was not certain. I had a stack of meetings planning the Africa trip, then Peter Hill and Hugh Whittow [editor and deputy editor of the *Daily Star*] came in to see TB. They were very straightforward, said they didn't want much politics in the paper, but they were up for stories if we thought of them once in a while. As to what kind of story, Peter said what people really wanted was fame and if they couldn't have fame they wanted to feel close to it. He suggested we try to get the spirit of *Pop Idol* [TV talent contest] into politics. TB asked me afterwards if they were for real. I said they were. I had been trying to persuade them to draw *Mirror* readers over by starting to be more pro Labour.

I was also working on my speech on public diplomacy for tomorrow, which I had been getting ideas and comments on from around the place. On the conference call, I told them the Powell/ Rumsfeld splits were bad for everyone, and asked if they couldn't do more to contain them. I also felt they should be getting a lot more out of the [Hamid] Karzai visit [to Washington]. I felt the calls were becoming a bit vague and waffly, not least because the top Americans were not always on them. Jim Poston [FCO] was doing a good job progress-chasing in the London CIC though, was really making a difference.

The *Mail* splashed on Enron, totally overlooking the fact that the Tories took money from them.[1] This was clearly the latest smear zone for the scummy end of the media. When I went up to see TB, he said maybe there is a case for resurrecting 'Mailwatch'. He really hated them, he said. It didn't feel like a scandal to me and I was confident the public would see through it but you couldn't be sure. DB was struggling to get up his ASBOs [antisocial behaviour orders]. I went over to Lancaster House [government building] to speak to the conference of all our ambassadors from Arab and Muslim countries. I was arguing for a deeper engagement and urging them to badger us for more, not just leave it to Gerard Russell [Islamic Media Unit, FCO] and Co. I said TB took this seriously. I argued that we should stop thinking purely in country-to-country terms but see the need to put the case pan Arab. There was actually a case for some of these guys becoming spokesmen across the piece, not just in their own posts. Some of them had gone totally native, others felt we were wasting our time, but some of them seemed to get it and wanted to engage more. Julian said as we left, the problem is the clever ones realise you are taking over a chunk of their jobs, and the really clever ones realise that might help them take a chunk of their colleagues' jobs.

I was trying to get on top of Bush's State of the Union address and eventually Peter Reid got hold of an advance copy. It named Iran, Iraq and North Korea in the context, or so it would be taken, as possible targets of attack.[2] Karzai was doing well out there. I got hold of his draft itinerary for his visit here and it was ludicrous – forty minutes with TB and lunch with Robert Cooper [UK special representative in Afghanistan] for heaven's sake. I put a note round saying it was being revised and we went for Karzai coming to the end of Cabinet, proper meeting with TB, joint Al Jazeera interview kind of thing. Also we should get Afghan exiles in to see them.

GB was back in action again and TB said they had one or two nice conversations, almost like the old days, but that he was currently totally paranoid re Milburn, Clarke and Hain, felt they were all positioning as rivals. I asked TB if he felt he had come back a changed

---

[1] Allegations that collapsed energy company Enron had offered financial support to Labour in return for a change of policy on gas-fired power stations. The allegations were denied.

[2] In what would become known as his 'axis of evil' speech, Bush specifically homed in on three nations he claimed were developing weapons of mass destruction.

man. He shook his head. Ed Richards [senior policy adviser on media business issues] came to see me re the media ownership policy discussions. He said in the end it boiled down to a decision about whether we were prepared to see Murdoch become more powerful. He felt that we shouldn't. I got a crazy letter from [Piers] Morgan in response to mine, saying I had misquoted him on saying the *Mirror* was no longer a Labour paper, but I could always rely on [Neil] Wallis to 'squeeze in Blair press releases in between Jordan's tits and kinky sex spreads'.

Wednesday, January 30

We assumed IDS would do health at PMQs but without an individual case, though the *Sun* had a story about a baby that got lost in the laundry. IDS majored on rail and was a lot better. He had definitely improved, and TB didn't really think on his feet. I was working on the speech for [the Labour Party spring] conference, trying to turn the strategy paper into a speech that could be used to disseminate strategy. After PMQs I went with Geoff Hoon to the MoD to meet the air commodore and his deputy in charge of the team responsible for the Mull of Kintyre Chinook [helicopter] crash [in 1994].[1] They realised this would come our way and they wanted to persuade me of their case that the two pilots, whatever their supporters said, had been guilty of gross negligence. There was a Lords committee report coming up so it was going to be back up in lights and they felt they had to make their case better than before. GH let them do pretty much all the talking. I listened, asking questions as we went, for about ninety minutes, at the end of which I was pretty well convinced, though the unanswered question remained why they made the error they did. Their theory was that the pilots believed they were in a different place, above water, and also that they realised too late that they should not have been flying in those conditions [too low, in heavy fog]. I got back to work on the speech, then up to see TB to tell him I thought he had been poor at PMQs, and we had a bit of a post-mortem.

Thursday, January 31

Before Cabinet I went round to see TB who was in with GB. It was the first time I had really seen Gordon since he came back. I said

[1] The helicopter was carrying twenty-five British intelligence experts from Belfast to a conference in Fort George, Scotland. A 1995 RAF board of inquiry ruled that the crash was caused by gross negligence, a judgement challenged by families of special forces pilots Jonathan Tapper and Rick Cook.

hello. He kind of grunted. Not 'Thanks for your letter', but a grunt. Fiona had also sent them a present which I know must be really difficult for them now, having all these kids' clothes and other presents, but I found it odd he couldn't be civil at a time like this. TB said at the earlier ministerial meeting, he had sat there scribbling notes, refusing to engage even though the others were trying to bring him in. At Cabinet itself, his presence transformed the mood from Cabinets where he had been absent. There just wasn't the engagement from others when he was in this kind of mood, and TB looked disengaged and distant. They were going through the motions, and then at 11.15 TB had to leave early to meet Karzai.

As we walked down the corridor to the front door, TB said 'I'm afraid he hasn't changed. If anything, he has changed for the worse.' He said people were feeling sorry for GB, and trying to express it, but he was just pushing back the whole time. Karzai was in one of his long capes, and when I told him he was getting as much coverage for his fashionability as his politics, he said he had started wearing it one day because it was cold, and he just kept wearing it. Now it was part of his make-up. In Afghanistan, he said it was a very conservative form of dress. TB had a tête-à-tête with Karzai. I was chatting to [Ahmad] Wali Massoud [Afghan ambassador] who was very shrewd, pushing the line we needed more ISAF forces there. As they met Afghan exiles, Tom warned me the big talking point was Karzai saying Sharia law had a place in Afghanistan. I raised it with him and he said he had said no such thing. Welcome to our press, said TB.

They both did fine at the press conference, though the story was Karzai asking for more troops and TB saying there had to be a limit. They did a joint [BBC] World Service interview, where they were asked about GWB's axis of evil. At the lunch, you could see them trying hard to adapt to this new way of life. Karzai had his wits about him, and looked and sounded the part, if a bit forced at times. But [General Mohammed] Fahim Khan [new leader of the Northern Alliance], a real brute with enormous hands and a big growly face, could barely hold a knife and fork. It was an interesting lunch, Karzai now moving on to drugs, and explaining the help they would need to change crop production patterns. They were virtually rebuilding a country and its infrastructure from scratch, as when he said they would be grateful for advice on how to establish a new central bank. Khan was even more straightforward, said we had been giving a lot of help to the regional warlords but now we had to start giving more help to the centre – i.e. him.

On the conference call with the White House, I told them there had been an overwhelmingly negative reaction round Europe to the GWB ['axis of evil'] speech. They seemed surprised. It wasn't a good call. TB and I had another session re the press. I said I was convinced we needed to make them part of the debate much more than they were. He said he was in two minds but in the end he would decide. I said fine but there may come a point where I can't do it this way. He said we had to be clear that if we were effectively declaring war on them, that was a big decision to take. I said three-quarters of them had declared war on us and too much of the time we just took it. TB said remember Machiavelli, kill or hug, but don't wound.[1] He felt I was landing the odd blow and leaving a few wounds. I said maybe I wanted to kill and I could no longer pretend with papers like the *Mail*, and some of the chatterati, that that is exactly how I felt. He said when we were at media dinners together, e.g. with Murdoch recently, it was clear to everyone how I felt and I needed to be cautious. I said I hated having to pander to these people, and that they took it as weakness not strength. I had said the same to Blunkett re his greasing up to Dacre. TB gave me a look that suggested he was fed up hearing the same old song. I said it is no good just being fed up. I'm fed up too, fed up with the fact we are in power and doing nothing to change the poisonous media culture which is actually damaging the country now. I said I couldn't stand the *Mail*, most of the *Telegraph*, a fair few of the broadcasters, most of the Sundays, and now Piers [Morgan] was on my list of barely worth talking to. Fiona was back on at me to quit if I felt strongly, and disagreed on a fundamental strategic point. Fiona and Sally [Morgan] both felt he was still talking to Anji the whole time and she was winding him up re us not doing enough with the right-wing media. Fiona said she just could not do what Anji did, grease up to all these people and pretend we liked them. In Kabul, they were talking of tens of thousands for the football match, which cheered me up a bit.

Friday, February 1

TB was at Chequers and I spent most of the day working on the upcoming speeches. TB asked why I was so low. I said I felt I was doing the same old stuff the whole time, and I was frustrated we were not really changing things as I thought we would. I took Calum

---

[1] Blair paraphrased a line in *The Prince* (1532) by Niccolò Machiavelli: 'Men ought either to be indulged or utterly destroyed, for if you merely offend them they take vengeance.'

to tennis, and TB called again. He said he knew how frustrating it was, but we had to keep going on the things that really mattered.

Saturday, February 2

TB still felt we were not winning the basic arguments on public services, or shifting the dividing lines to where we needed them. He did not like the mood in Cabinet on Thursday, felt there was a grumpiness and a grunginess that could not be allowed to fester. It wasn't just about GB, though his mood did not help. I spoke to JP about it too, and he felt there was just a bit of unease around at where we were going, and also people getting used to the media being so much more hostile. He was trying to do a bit of work as a go-between between TB and GB, to get them engaging and working together better, but it wasn't easy. He too felt GB had come back worse not better after his baby's death. There is a lot of distrust there and he is not the kind of guy just to get over it. Andy Grice [*Independent*] wrote definitively that Leo had had the MMR jab and there was a strong feeling we must have put it out there deliberately. I certainly hadn't but I wondered if someone else had done it for TB. It ran as a main broadcast story most of the day, alongside the measles outbreak in a London nursery.

Sunday, February 3

Down to Chequers, TB ranting against the media. We finished the speech and the main line was meant to be this being a fight between wreckers and reformers. There was a political problem though, Jo Moore calling me to say Byers had used the same line and indicated at the time he meant the unions when he referred to wreckers. It meant that despite our efforts, that was where the story was heading. It was clearly going to be tricky. We had an OK line re small-c conservatism but of course that too was likely just to get played straight into the tricky political angle they would all want. We flew down to Cardiff [Labour spring conference] by helicopter and the speech went down really well with the audience.[1]

Halfway through, I always try to find time to pick out half a dozen or so average-looking people and see 1. whether they are really listening, and 2. whether they seem to be going along with it. They were all pretty rapt, and as the argument developed, the head-nodding

[1] Blair told delegates 'Forget the nonsense about privatising public services . . . if we are to win the argument for collective provision, defeat the wreckers and secure the future of our public services, then we must be prepared to use all available means to make the improvements that patients and pupils and passengers demand. And we will.'

became more pronounced. TB went off script towards the end and did a good section on how at every stage of reform – expelling Militant, policy and party changes under Neil [Kinnock], the difficult changes we had made in Opposition and government, there were always voices saying don't do it and others crying betrayal. But only through change do we advance, etc. But even though it was pretty obvious he had the Tories in his sights when he talked about wreckers, the unions couldn't resist doing the victim thing and making it seem as though he meant them. I did a quick briefing, reminding myself how glad I was I didn't do them all the time.

Helicopter back and then home. Later, I was really hacked off with Fiona when TB called to speak to me about something, she answered the phone and was nice as pie to him, said none of the things she was constantly saying to me, and I thought at least I tell him when I'm pissed off and I tell him why. It made me think that actually a lot of the attacks on him made to me were surrogate attacks on me for doing the bloody job in the first place. I was also back in a depressive mode, I was sure of that, which didn't help. She felt I just didn't want her to take on a bigger job because it threatened me somehow. I didn't buy that but I did feel it wasn't on for both of us to be full-on working the whole time, and that we both should be spending more time at home whenever possible. He called back later and said what was I on about, telling him Fiona was pissed off, she seemed fine! I told him I was totally hacked off. He said I was frustrated because I spent so much time clearing up after other people, but never lose sight of the things we were getting done, and in the end they were the things that were important and would be remembered. TB did the [*Evening*] *Standard* drama awards and was amazed that Natascha McElhone [actor] went up to him and asked him to ask me to give her a call. 'She is gorgeous,' he said.

Monday, February 4
The public services speech was all in the wrong place, thanks to the dunderheaded unions taking the whole speech as an attack on them. Then John Monks [TUC general secretary] was wound up by the unions and the media and he was leading the news with comments re TB making 'juvenile remarks'. DB did pretty well whacking back but our overall message was a bit confused. TB insisted we had to hold absolutely firm, that we were doing the right things for the long term and we would hold firm. He seemed a bit down, worried we could not actually get our own people properly to understand what was needed.

I raised MMR with TB. We both felt it was yet another case of the media stirring to try to make the story even worse, because that was then an even better story. The problem was if this did become a huge public health issue, there was a real danger he would get the blame and it would stick and inflict real damage. CB was adamant she wanted to take the *Independent* to the PCC for the Leo-had-the-jab story and I was adamant that was crazy, even though she had a case. TB had been telling all sorts of people he'd had the jab and was probably in some ways, maybe one removed, the source and he seemed relieved it was out there. I felt we were going to need a really strong MMR campaign to get over the benefits and the risks if people did not have it.

I met Tessa [Jowell] who wanted a bit of advice on her image/profile. Her great strength was her niceness and her enthusiasm but I said sometimes the Florence Nightingale touch could grate a bit. She needed to be more wedded to policy issues linked into real people. I bumped into GB as I took her out. Another monosyllabic grunt. Peter M called from South Africa, denied he had got up the Hammond [Inquiry reopening] story, said on the contrary he had not wanted it to happen. He could tell I was unconvinced. He said originally he had pressed for it then TB said he didn't think that would help him. Peter then agreed but by then TB had changed his mind and RW told Peter the new inquiry was going ahead. He sounded OK but he was clearly very fed up with his lot. Condi Rice slapped down Jack over his remarks that Bush's axis of evil speech was about electoral US politics. Not a great day, but I had a long chat with Natascha McElhone which cheered me up.

Tuesday, February 5

TB's 'wreckers' [speech] was still running big and bad. The GMB and UNISON [unions] took out full-page ads attacking us. There was now no sense anywhere of it having been about the Tories, but there was also a feeling that it was just a phoney row. I was really down again, struggling to get out of bed, struggling to get through the front door, feeling demotivated all day. TB later asked me if I was fed up. Very, I said. Why? A mix of things – grind, GB making life more difficult than it should be, being expected to do too much, including work others should be doing, the media, feeling that so far as my particular skills were concerned I had done my bit and we were now in a different phase requiring different skills. 'You're not thinking of leaving are you?' he asked and I said maybe I was. He said he felt I had a massive contribution to make and also that I would miss it more than I thought. Nothing else will ever replace this professionally, he said. But the grind gets me down. The media were a screaming pain in the backside and I had such contempt for most of them, I couldn't hide it and maybe he was damaged by that.

He said you are not just a media person, you do far more for me than that, don't worry about them, let the others take care of them. He said he had a lot to do and he couldn't do it without a strong team to help him pull the horses. The GB problem was graphically on display again this morning. He did *The Times* on his Commonwealth Education Fund [overseas education advocacy project], which was fine in that it was on two of TB's areas – education and Africa – but GB did it without any consultation and without any reference to TB or the broader Africa agenda at all. I told TB that in both the *Today* and *GMTV* interviews, GB did not even mention him and he seemed taken aback. He said the one thing capable of destabilising me is the lurking presence waiting to do me down when the opportunity arises. The truth was if these two worked together, this government would be fifteen per cent better than it is. That was a margin worth worrying about.

What was clear from any reading of the media was that GB's people poured poison vs TB the whole time – how they were the real radicals, how TB didn't care about the real issues in the way GB did, how GB was the substance and TB the style. There was clearly a plan to get him up on development issues to ensure TB did not get too much out of Africa. If they worked together on this, they would be unstoppable. But it wasn't happening. MMR was running big. As for 10,000 extra nurses – no fucking coverage at all. Milburn was ballistic about it. I went with TB to a young people's event at Westminster Hall organised by the Lib Dems. TB was OK but a bit passionless. [Liberal Democrat leader Charles] Kennedy was predictable and his speech a bit dull. IDS surprised a lot of them by being pretty good and was well received.

The top story politically was the Chinook inquiry [see January 30] on which we just had to hold firm, though the Lords was coming out pretty hard against us. It all looked nakedly political and maybe people saw that. I had lunch at Wiltons with [Field Marshal Lord] Peter Inge and [Air Marshal Sir] Erik Bennett [adviser to the Sultan of Oman] which was good fun. Both were lively and engaging, and pretty gossipy. [Nicholas] Soames was at the next table and when he got up to leave I made a point of saying, very loudly, 'Can you get the car round, I'll be there in five minutes.' Inge [a former CDS] said he hoped I was being nice to Boyce. I said I was. He said I should tell him we valued him because he tended to get down on himself.

Both he and Bennett felt the US would become a real problem for us and that TB was really the only person who could hold things together. They seemed to feel he had real influence and that he had to use it.

Wednesday, February 6

The *Sun* yesterday did a front-page campaign pitch on giving everyone the choice of three [individualised MMR] jabs not one, and today led on a story that TB was wobbling, and had ordered a review of the costs of three in one. Because [David] Yelland had been in yesterday to see FM/SM and briefly seen TB the buzz went round that it came directly from us. We denied it last night but then the Tories jumped on the bandwagon and by this morning it was leading the news. The media were really whipping this into a frenzy but it was one with potentially serious consequences now, and the Tories ought to get hammered, but they wouldn't be, at least not the way we would have been in Opposition for something of this kind. We had some good facts to get over, like there were ninety countries using the vaccine, like the fact that in the US you had to have it to be able to go to local schools. I warned Yelland we were going to dump hard on their story. Both the *Sun* and the *Express* agreed to take rebuttal articles on it.

Dacre said he would only do so if it was TB or CB writing re Leo. I wrote telling him I thought their coverage on MMR was irresponsible and dishonest. I bumped into Piers [Morgan] coming out of a meeting with GB. We said hello and later he called, said he wanted to be more supportive re MMR, but we ended up having another argument about the nature of their war coverage. TB left for the airport [for Africa], called from the car to go over how much media he should do on the way and once he got there. He kicked off by dropping another hint Leo had had the jab. I left early, collected the boys and off to Watford for a fantastic match, which we won in the last minute, Marlon [Beresford, Burnley goalkeeper] having saved a penalty at 1–0. It was one of those wonderful matches that makes all the crap ones seem worthwhile.

Thursday, February 7

I felt a bit odd, both good and bad, that I wasn't on the Africa trip. Good because hopefully it would show to Fiona I was serious about trying to do things differently; also because I could have a bit of time to sort some of the personnel issues; bad because I would be worrying whether things were being handled properly, and whether in fact I ought to be there. TB was getting good if low-key coverage for the speech [to the joint national assembly] in Nigeria and it was definitely the right thing to do to stick to our guns and go. JP was standing in for TB at Cabinet, and as when he did PMQs, the massive differences came over – TB who would want the minimum of fuss and preparation pre Cabinet, JP who wanted to over-prepare, almost rehearsing what he would say and how he would handle things. As well as Joan Hammell [Prescott's special adviser], Jonathan and Richard W were brought in. JP stumbled over a few words and I suggested he just take the agenda and see how things go, as there were no real big decisions to be made.

There was a seemingly endless conversation in Cabinet itself re [reform of] the Lords. JP said he intended to be clear outside that the party did not want an elected second chamber as a rival to the Commons. He told me earlier he was fed up with 'the little red gnome' (RC) briefing the press about some of his moves re Parliament and then expecting the Cabinet to be bounced and I think the Lords gambit – out of nowhere – was his warning shot. Cabinet lasted far longer than usual, again reflecting an earlier comment by JP that TB did not let discussions flow enough, but you would be hard pushed to refer to any decision or new point that was made. They also got into a discussion re the Speaker [of the Commons, Michael Martin]. They were worried re MM saying the Tories couldn't attack TB over his role as leader of a party, because ultimately that would constrain us more than them. John Reid was the only one really to speak up for Michael, saying he felt there was a lot of snobbery around re the fact a working-class Glaswegian got the job but we should support him. I noticed GB muttering under his breath to himself. We got a letter from Sarah [Brown] re our letters and gift today, so I was trying hard to be understanding of GB's situation but he really didn't help himself.

DB was doing his immigration White Paper, which was going OK, but was a bit too pitched to the right-wing media for my taste. I had just concluded the highly vituperative exchanges with Dacre. I went home early to collect Grace from school, then Fiona and I went out for dinner at Les and Mary Hinton's, a fair old crowd there. I was sitting next to Zeinab Badawi [Sudanese-born BBC newscaster] who was nice enough, and interesting on Islam. Rebekah [Wade, *News of the World* editor] and Ross [Kemp, her actor fiancé] were there but fairly quiet for them. Jeff Randall [BBC business editor] was anything but, full of right-wing views dressed up as fact and wisdom. I liked Mary Hinton, a real good old working-class type who struck me as someone who saw through the lot of them. Les told me he had been shocked by Rupert's tolerance of James [Murdoch] swearing so much in front of TB. I said TB rather liked it of him. He said afterwards they had gone to a pub for a drink, James had started up again and the barman told him to shut up and stop swearing.

Friday, February 8

Alex [Ferguson] came in and he and I went for lunch at the National Portrait Gallery. It was always good to get his take on things because he followed politics closely, but with a very outside-the-beltway view. He felt we were doing OK, but he thought immigration really picking up as an issue. I told him re my current doubts about the job, and he still felt I would regret it massively if I went. He wondered if the press were getting to me more than I realised, but it was more the stuff at home and the feeling at the office I was doing too much of the stuff I had now done for years. He was glad he had stayed, said it was as much Cathy [his wife] as he who had made up his mind on it, because she realised just how much he would miss it. He was still fit and relatively young and he just would not be fulfilled without it. We both had fish and chips, the most amazing chips I've had in yonks, identically shaped. He said [David] Beckham [Manchester United footballer] was becoming more and more difficult to deal with. He now had four different agents who came in last time with forty-nine different demands related to his new contract. He [Beckham] was also beginning to commute a lot more between north and south, flying up for training, which was OK once or twice, but ludicrous as a long-term thing.

I did a conference call to plan next week's football match in Kabul. They were reckoning on 30,000 people turning up for it. TB called from Ghana, said he was enjoying it and glad he had gone. He said the president of Ghana [John Kufuor] had introduced his press officer as 'my Alastair' to which the press guy [Kwabena Agyepong] said 'I wish.' 'Your notoriety has spread to the continent of Africa,' he said. He seemed in relaxed mood, at one point asking me 'What are the Sundays up to?' then before I could answer 'Aw, who cares?'

Saturday, February 9

Nick Matthews [senior duty clerk] called before 8 to say that Princess Margaret had died. TB was currently being told and it would be announced by the Palace shortly. There was no need for him to come back, but he would need to say something so I might want to start thinking about that. I reminded Nick that he was the one who called me re [Princess] Diana's death. 'That was a bit more dramatic than this one,' he said. TB called as he waited to leave for Sierra Leone.

Tanya [Joseph] had done a draft statement that was OK so things were basically under control. I said it was important he didn't try too hard, or appear emotional, just say she was basically a good thing, thoughts with the Queen, Queen Mum, rest of family, etc. [Sir] Robin Janvrin [the Queen's private secretary] called to go through the statement they were putting out. He said the Queen actually saw it all as a bit of a release and a mercy because she had been in a good deal of pain. Her instincts were to carry on with her (fairly light) duties next week, and to make the funeral private. He said the Queen would probably want to speak to TB later.

TB set off for Sierra Leone, met the troops and the government welcoming party and then did his doorstep on Margaret. It was a bit actorish for my liking, but OK I guess. We had to watch any sense of this being anything like Diana. Janvrin was thinking the same thing though perhaps for different reasons when he called pre TB's call with the Queen. He said she wanted advice on how to avoid the comparisons with Diana in terms of tributes, flowers, mood etc. I felt the simplest thing was to say it, to make clear this was different in part because it was expected. I also felt people would respond to the fact the Queen and Queen Mother would take this differently and there was a case for them being seen fairly soon, showing she was still up and about and doing her duty, but also showing some emotion at the loss of a younger sister. She would clearly be thinking of her own mortality, not to mention her mother's. [Prince] Charles went to Sandringham 'to comfort the Queen Mother' and also did a broadcast, which was OK but he was not a natural presenter and he shifted around too much, creating constant distractions from what he was saying.

I spoke to TB again after his press conference in Senegal. I suggested he advise the Queen that she needs to be seen, because that would attract support and also crowds, albeit nothing like on the scale of Diana's death. 'How can I advise her to do that?' I said just say the country needs to see she's OK and bearing up. They want to find a way of expressing sympathy for her. He also needed to make sure they were aggressive in dealing with any media attempts to make Diana comparisons as a way of reflecting on the Queen. Burnley 1, Barnsley 1.

Sunday, February 10
The only political story running out of the Sundays was the *Sunday Telegraph* reheat of the *Western Mail*/Plaid [Cymru] story on [Indian industrialist Lakshmi Mittal's donation [£125,000] to the Labour Party. The donation seemingly came a few weeks before TB wrote to the

PM of Romania [Adrian Năstase] to welcome a deal with a Mittal company, which was basically Dutch rather than UK. Our line was that this was something done following a request by our ambassador, but it was clear this was going to be the next media frenzy to deal with. I took Rory to his mini-marathon heats, which he won easily, then to Charlton vs Man U. We met up with Alex F pre match. Rory was loving it, down the tunnel as the players warmed up, Alex talking to him about why he was picking the team he did. There was a minute's silence for Margaret, well observed. Janvrin called to get my take on how I thought things were. I felt fine, but still thought there should be more focus on the Queen if she was up to it at all. Rory Bremner [TV satirist and impressionist] had a sketch on 'me' telling 'TB' why I wasn't going to Africa.

Monday, February 11

The Mittal situation was tricky.[1] Jonathan had been through all the papers and realised that he (Jonathan) had advised against doing anything on the grounds that Mittal was a known Labour donor and supporter. For some reason that did not appear to have been communicated to TB and the letter as prepared was put in his correspondence folder. It meant we could stick to the line that he had merely done something as asked by our ambassador for sound reasons to do with his assessment of Anglo-Romanian relations, no big deal unless people were determined to make it so in retrospect. TB was totally dismissive of the whole thing, saw nothing wrong with it at all. I said it was a bit odd that he was writing letters to the Romanian PM about what was in the end a Dutch deal, even if Mittal ran the company. He found it bizarre, as did Jonathan and I, that he did not see the point made by Jonathan – rightly in my view – but even so he was clear we just had to ride it out and tell them to get stuffed.

I went over to the DTI for a meeting re the Post Office. Pat [Hewitt, Trade and Industry Secretary] didn't seem totally on top of it. We had allowed the debate to develop in a way that suggested the Post Office was a public service on a par with health and education, so the idea the country was ready for what would be seen as privatisation by a Labour government was self-kidology. The timing was tough and the Dutch were going to be the bigger party. Weird that the two tricky

[1] The situation, which Blair would dismiss at PMQs as 'garbage', became known as the 'Garbagegate' affair. Mittal, a substantial donor to the Labour Party, had been seeking control of Romania's state steel industry, and despite one per cent of his company's workforce being based in the UK, Blair's intervention was seen as decisive.

issues I was dealing with involved the Dutch. Back for a meeting with TB and Alan M on health communications. TB felt we just were not getting over the reality of the progress being made and we were not getting over the scale of reform planned or required. There was a conflict though between a message that said 'things going well' and one which said 'lots more to do'. The *Guardian* splashed on how GB was going to 'stand up to Europe' on the Stability Pact [safeguarding fiscal discipline of EMU], and warn they would not get in the way of our plans for investment in public services. It was a classic piece of GB spinology, a phoney row if ever there was one, launched without our knowledge, but one we would have to row in behind.

Tuesday, February 12

Brian Groom [FT] called to ask whether it was true that there had been an earlier draft of TB's Mittal letter which referred to 'my friend', and that the reference to 'friend' had been deleted. It transpired that there had, and that Michael Tatham [private secretary, foreign affairs] had – again, rightly – deleted it. This was getting a bit weird and was obviously being briefed out by someone. So our line that TB had not changed the draft was true. But it wasn't true to say that 'we' had not changed it. TB was adamant we should not engage, not get into drafts, simply say TB signed the letter as requested, end of story. I suggested we get our man in Bucharest [UK ambassador Richard Ralph] to write a letter to *The Times* explaining why he had wanted to get the TB letter but though he was keen Jack and, even more so, Michael Jay were less so. I had a meeting with the Northern group of [Labour] MPs at 5, and there was something really sad in seeing Peter M there as just another back-bench MP [for Hartlepool] listening to me blather on about the message and the machinery. David M [Miliband, Labour MP for South Shields] was there too, and seemed to be getting on fine with the real Northerners.

I then got back to learn Jonathan had spoken to Jack in Istanbul, and then to Michael Jay, who were adamant it would be bad for the diplomatic service if an ambassador was personally placed at the centre of a diplomatic controversy. I called Michael and said, jokily at first, that he mustn't feel got at by the right-wing campaigning elements in the press, and whatever happened to the great FCO, scared of nobody? He said he was totally against doing this, because it put an ambassador right at the heart of it. I said he was already, and there were plenty of situations down the years where others had been. I said it would help him and it would help us. He was adamant though. I was impressed at the way he stood up to me, if unpersuaded by the reasons. I suspected they just felt a bit beleaguered and said as much to Jack when he called. He said no, it wasn't that. It was simply that they felt they should protect a member of the service.

As TB came back from the Palace [Royal Audience], I told him the *Guardian* were on to the fact Mittal had been at [Labour fund-raiser] Michael Levy's party for high-value donors on June 24. Again, he was totally dismissive, and said I needed to stop giving off worried vibes about it. His mix of bluster and head in the sand was really irritating. He was irritated when I said so, said he was not prepared to take this seriously, it was a fuss over nothing and we should not be getting our knickers in a twist. I said my knickers were not in a twist but it was a frenzy and we had to have answers to questions even if we thought the questions were ludicrous. He would not be able to dismiss it in the House. He would have to answer questions on it.

Wednesday, February 13

I was in early, and up to see TB in the flat. It was dark up there and he seemed a bit down. He asked me if I was depressed. I said yes. Clinically I mean, he said. I said I think so. He said my problem was I was agonising – stay or go. He felt I would hate it if I went, no matter how much I sometimes hated it now. I needed to see the press as the inevitable downside of a job that had a huge upside, namely doing an important job and being part of a huge process of change for the country. He came back to the theme over at the House pre PMQs, said I should remember what Leon Brittan [former Conservative Cabinet minister] said about leaving power, leaving powerful jobs – for a year you feel better, eased of pressure, able to do normal things, but then you realise what you miss, the ability to make change. He said 'If I die tomorrow, they would say he was the guy who modernised the Labour Party, made it electable, won two landslides, sorted the economy, improved public services, Bank of England, Kosovo, Northern Ireland. They would barely mention the frenzies we have survived, so always remember the big things, the big reasons why we're doing it.'

He accepted Mittal was a problem for us, the focus moving to Jonathan's role as gatekeeper to TB and how that fits with any political or party role. The ticking timebomb that worried me was Mittal's letter to Levy, and Jonathan's notes. I was angry with Jack and Jay for their refusal to let Ambassador Ralph set out the case, because I felt it was what our current argument lacked – the reason why it mattered to him. TB looked tired, Jonathan looked nervous. They both hated this kind of thing. We had to decide how heavy TB should get [at PMQs], and we agreed – heavy. PMQs was not as bad as we feared, because the Tories were not forensic enough, and TB really went for IDS and we avoided the question about whether he or Jonathan knew Mittal was a donor. Back to a press event with [Rudolph] Giuliani [mayor of New York] where TB managed to avoid any Mittal questions. TB spoke to Jack to emphasise we needed the ambassador's reasoning out there. He was also worried after his meeting with Eddie George [governor of the Bank of England]. He had not liked what he heard re the euro, where Eddie seemed less and less keen. TB felt if we didn't go for it this parliament, we would lose out a lot more in the long run.

Thursday, February 14

The *Mirror* and *Express* had stories that Jo Moore had suggested that DTLR put out railway indicators on the day of Princess Margaret's funeral – another 'bury bad news' situation. They denied it last night. I missed the 8.30 meeting because I was at a *Guardian* breakfast with TB. Godric was agitated when I got back. Martin Sixsmith had said at the meeting that Jo had indeed said something like that and though the email referred to in the *Mirror* did not exist, there was another one – which he gave to Godric. It was an email FROM Sixsmith TO Byers and which suggested Steve HAD suggested using the cover of Margaret's funeral to get out bad news. I smelled a very large rat. It was already known – because Byers had announced it – that we were planning to do the railway indicators. It was hard to get a full picture, not having been at the meeting, but both Godric and Tom felt there were some really funny games going on. It looked like Jo was being totally done in. Given what they had been through, politically and media-wise re Jo's 9/11 'bury bad news' email, it was pretty much unthinkable that they'd have done a version of the same thing again, so I didn't buy the idea Byers would have done this. Tom and Godric both thought it odd that Sixsmith had brought the email to the meeting, and on reading it they saw it was not clear that Steve had suggested doing this. It was Sixsmith suggesting he had.

We got back from the *Guardian*, where TB did fine on the war, despite them pushing the whole time re Iraq and a bit on party funding. I told Godric that at the 11.30 he should make clear what balls the stuff on Jo Moore was. But Godric was really concerned something odd was going on. He, Tom and I met with Byers before Cabinet, and agreed we should say the email in the *Mirror* was a total fabrication, but point out there had been an e mail exchange between Sixsmith and Byers pointing out that as Friday was the day of

Margaret's funeral, there was no question of doing railway indicators then. It was another load of old balls really, but with the potential to do real damage. I got the feeling that if ever there had been any trust between Byers and Sixsmith, there was none now.

At lunchtime Anne Shevas took a call from Jon Smith at PA who said he'd had a call from someone claiming to be a press officer from DTLR who said Sixsmith wanted it known that Godric had got it wrong at the morning briefing, that there was indeed an email that had the words 'Margaret, burial etc.' in. It was hard to disagree with Godric's analysis that something very odd was going on. Byers had been complaining that he had parts of his department out of control and Richard Mottram [permanent secretary, DTLR] seemed unaware how to resolve it. I called Mike Granatt [Head of the Government Information and Communication Service], said clearly things were going on there which were inexcusable and he had to get involved. He drafted a letter making clear officials simply could not brief against ministers. Godric went off to the four o'clock and came back to say they were going crazy, and based on the weird call to Jon Smith had accused him of lying, having yesterday accused us of lying over Mittal.

I had to leave for a Q&A with permanent secretaries and a few business people at Chevening [in Kent, official country residence of the Foreign Secretary], which I could really have done without. It was basically about crisis management communications. When I worked on the speech, I found myself trying to work out how many genuine, genuine crises we had had and it was probably fewer than half a dozen. Yet we had hundreds described as crises and dozens that felt like it from time to time. But most of these guys had never actually been involved in a real full-blown crisis, and yet felt they were in one every time they were in the papers.

I got back to find Mittal on the news and the Jo Moore situation back running big. Godric was really angry that his honesty was being questioned. I spoke to Byers again and said it was obvious he couldn't work with his own press team, but I also felt this was heading towards Jo's departure. It was totally unfair on Jo who though she had made a dreadful mistake on September 11, was basically loyal and a good person. My sense was that Jo was fed up with the whole thing anyway.

Friday, February 15

Godric texted me just before 7 to say he felt we should put the Sixsmith email out to set the context. I talked to Byers who agreed. He had felt strongly yesterday that I should stay out of this but it had to be gripped. Godric spoke to Sixsmith who agreed that Jo had never suggested using the funeral. Godric said he was given a different impression yesterday. TB was heading to Italy and had finally agreed this was damaging us. I told Steve it had to be brought to a head quickly. I talked the whole thing through with Richard Wilson who was seeing Mottram at 9.45. Richard was pretty good on this. He knew that there was funny stuff going on inside the department and he didn't much like it. I took Calum to tennis and RW called to say he had been 'very heavy' with Mottram, had told him there were only three routes – muddle on (not acceptable), lose one of Jo or Sixsmith, or lose both, or possibly suspend them while it was sorted out. I was trying to play tennis with Calum but got call after call on this bollocks.

Sixsmith saw Mottram at lunchtime and seemed to be in agreement to go, provided he got money, Jo went too, and we did not dump on him. So by the time I got in – around 2.30 – we seemed to be ready to go with it. Jo wanted to get her kids home from school so the plan was then to go for 5pm. Then Byers called to say Mottram was now not so clear that Sixsmith had actually resigned. He had seemingly gone out for treatment on his eyes, and come back to say he was still thinking about it. This was being so badly handled. It seemed Mottram had not actually got a bloody resignation. So we now had a situation where we thought both had resigned, Byers had now said so on TV, Jo had gone, but Sixsmith hadn't and was, like as not, liable to pop up and say this was like Soviet Russia, where his resignation was announced when in fact he had never resigned. TB called from Italy and said that whilst this was all crap, it was dangerous crap and we had to be careful. I said I was fed up with the whole thing. Byers, to be fair, was amazingly resilient and had a bit of the Zen about him, but he was damaged.

The Kabul soccer match had been an amazing success, spoiled by crowd trouble among the thousands who couldn't get in. There were about 42,000 inside to witness a stupendous goal, thousands more outside. Lawrie McMenemy [Football Association special ambassador] did fantastic interviews in his trad Afghan cap. Simon Wren [MoD] called me, said it was the most exhilarating thing he had ever been involved in.

Saturday, February 16
Another crazy day. TB called as I was going out of the house to take the kids to Regent's Park. We had talked briefly last night but now I filled him in on the whole madness of yesterday. He said he would

speak to RW and they agreed we should play it a bit long. I said it would be too much for Byers and probably for Godric too if Sixsmith was allowed to stay in the GICS, just move on to another job. The trust issue was a problem. Steve [Byers] was quite clear an agreement was reached on the basis both Sixsmith and Jo would go. Then Granatt called me to say TB/RW seemed to think Sixsmith could stay. This was getting ridiculous. Mottram then spoke to Sixsmith to work out a deal.

I spoke to Sixsmith, the call taped by Martin Sheehan [press officer], and played along with him, just tried to get a sense of where he was. I said both Godric and Tom felt they had been misled by him. He was apologetic for the mess, but said he had not deliberately done anything wrong. Of yesterday, he said he had had an assurance from Mottram he would not be 'sacked' while he was out at the eye doctor. Byers called to say Jo had gone on the basis they were both going, and he was not prepared to let Jo go and him stay. TB was pretty fucked off with the whole thing, as was I, and felt there were real problems at the top of the department. Mottram had been clear with me he [Sixsmith] would go if the money was right, Jo went and he got a testimonial. Now he was apparently in a position where Jo had gone, he was staying and he was getting a glowing tribute from Mottram.

I spoke to Alistair Darling, who knew Sixsmith better than I did and who had spoken to him earlier. He said Sixsmith seemed to think he was being offered gardening leave [instructions to stay at home] and let's see what turned up. Mottram called around half five to 'pick my brains'. I said I felt we should let it calm for a bit and see where it went. Sixsmith was going to be seen as a hero in the press, because they love the damage being done to Byers in all this, and he may want to go back to the media. It was ridiculous TB even had to be bothered with this. Byers was livid we were even thinking about Sixsmith staying. I said let's sleep on it and see where we are tomorrow. He said if he stays it means 'they have won'. He felt that the whole episode risked sending the worst possible signal: that ministers and special advisers can be done in by anyone with an agenda. I was now way beyond the end of my tether and thinking fuck the lot of them. Godric was the one I felt for, because he really cared about his integrity, and he felt he had been dropped in it.

Sunday, February 17

Byers called again late last night, after having told TB he would have no option but to resign if Sixsmith was allowed to stay in the Civil Service. TB told him it was simply not worth resigning over.

TB felt Mottram had clearly not handled things well, but that Byers also had to take responsibility for relationships between key people in the department. He said part of the job is building an *esprit de corps* and he clearly failed to do that. But what do you do if people inside are doing you in? TB's view was you don't let it get to that. Easier said than done. Byers felt if Sixsmith stayed, then because of the way this was playing out, it would be felt within as a great victory for the right of civil servants to undermine ministers and they would just move on to the next one they don't much fancy. Sixsmith called, claimed Byers was not taking Mottram's calls. I had now reached the point where I was very cagey in what I said, assumed he would be taking his own legal advice, so said little, advised him to bide his time and not do anything too rash. He said he had been offered thousands by the papers to tell his story, which I guess was a way of saying he had other options if he didn't get a decent deal. I told him Byers was hostile to any kind of deal but we just had to wait and see whether once he got a new team in there he was less bothered.

On the media, TB felt there may be a case for a new ethics commissioner, tougher rules for MPs alongside a statutory watchdog for the press, including re accuracy. He felt we should go for the liberalised view on media ownership, and encourage European companies to get involved in taking over parts of our press. I said when he told me he had been thinking re the press, I was hoping he was going for PCC on statutory footing with fines for inaccuracy, VAT on newspapers, privacy laws, really put it to them. He felt it wasn't worth all the aggro. Godric was still very steamed up re Sixsmith, sent me a five-page note setting out why he believed he had been misled, and how.

Monday, February 18

At TB's morning meeting, he was mainly focused on the war again, feeling he was going to have to get back in the saddle more. Byers came in to see TB and we just about persuaded him Sixsmith wasn't worth resigning over. We had to bide time then move on and we were better leaving RW to manage the process. Byers was adamant we would regret it big time if Sixsmith was allowed to stay in the system. I met [Mike] Granatt and Sue Jenkins [GICS] to put together a hit team to go to DTLR. The best part of the day was when Rory came in and we went for a run through Hyde Park. Stan [Greenberg] and Philip [Gould] came in with a new poll. Not brilliant. Down on state of the parties and on right/wrong direction. Trust and openness bad. TB felt it could have been worse given recent events and the tone of the media debate. Stan felt we had endured a lot worse but I didn't like the feel of it.

We went in for a meeting with the *Observer*. Mary Riddell [columnist] making a big thing of saying to TB 'Of course nobody is saying yoooooou are corrupt' when [Andrew] Rawnsley [*Observer* political commentator] had done just that and had his piece bought up by the fucking *Mail*. I saw the BBC team re NHS Day and finally agreed we would co-operate as best we could. I had a meeting with TB/CB re the US trip. I thought it a bit odd she wanted to be on holiday in the States when Euan was doing his A levels. TB said there was no way in the world he could have a holiday at the moment. CB was pissed off but adamant she was going. I even felt TB going out early for a couple of days was not a good idea, but she just felt I was being too puritanical and worried re the press. I said I wasn't bothered about the press, I was worried about the public. She said we should not let the press run our lives. TB said we have to apply common sense and at the moment it is not on for me to be seen taking a holiday.

Tuesday, February 19

Godric was getting a small taste of the media shit I endured most of the time, and I felt it was getting to him a bit. TB had a 'Phase 2' war meeting with David Manning, C, Peter Ricketts [FCO], Tom McKane [Cabinet Office], Jonathan and me. TB was not sure if the Americans had taken all the decisions. He wanted to be in a position to influence their strategy, which we would project as being about fighting poverty and taking aid, but which they would see as fighting for their values. He also wanted to commission papers on Iraq, Libya, North Korea and the European trade in WMD. He wanted work done on how to rejuvenate the MEPP. He assumed by the time of our visit to the States in April, there was a chance the Americans would be casting around wider, and he wanted all the facts at his fingertips. He felt that the political situation would be different and internationally a lot harder for the Americans than things were post September 11, if they were thinking of going for any of these other countries.

I had a meeting with Tucker [Eskew] and Jim Poston. Tucker was due to go back [to Washington] on March 13 to replace Jim Wilkinson and set up a new Office of Global Communications. He said he was phenomenally grateful for the opportunity he had had to work with us. I was still having to deal with the Byers/Sixsmith fallout. Byers adamant Sixsmith had to leave. Sixsmith telling me that SB had cut a deal with Mottram – a new job and a mild testimonial. Byers read to me what he called a 'threatening letter' from Sixsmith, still describing himself as his director of communications, saying he didn't want to damage him, saying AC didn't want 'collateral damage'. Sixsmith was constantly dropping hints to me about how he was being offered money to 'tell all' in a way that would damage the government. TB had clearly led SB to believe he would be sacked, RW that he could ease him out. RW was telling Mottram to play it long. Byers was sure Sixsmith was taping all calls, possibly with a view to doing a big thing about it all afterwards. Piers Morgan was adamant they'd been within their rights to run the story they did, not least because they ran it by the department's press office. TB told me Peter M had said to him it would be a disaster for the TB operation if I left. TB felt I just had to rise above the day-to-day.

Wednesday, February 20

NHS Day was in fact nothing like the stitch-up we feared. Jack S came over for a chat. He was strongly of the view that TB should do something that would symbolise a greater respect for Parliament, maybe appear at the PASC [Public Administration Select Committee]. He asked how I was, and I said pretty fed up. Why? Because I spend so much time clearing up the shit, and I don't always feel I get the support in return. Number 10 is seen by departments as interfering, and yet they are on to us the whole time to sort things that go wrong. Jack felt we had made Number 10 more powerful but not necessarily more effective across government. He felt there were too many of our people who called departments and said they were 'Number 10'. If it was me or Jonathan, people knew that mattered, and in any event we would deal with ministers. But departments had any number of people calling up and saying what TB wanted, or what Number 10 wanted.

Sixsmith was calling me all day, but I decided not to engage. The *FT* were on to the story again and I suspected he was trying to bounce us into a deal. The phone logs apparently showed both Sixsmith and Ian Jones [DTLR head of news and Sixsmith's deputy] called the *Mirror* and *Express*. Hardly earth-shattering. It would be very odd if they didn't call them pretty regularly. Sixsmith was not wanting to say he was talking about the terms of his departure. He wanted the line to be he was going to another department without a stain on his character. Byers, Mottram and I did a call at 6, and we agreed Mottram would say to Sixsmith that he had clearly resigned on the Friday and we were now working out the terms of his departure, and this is what we would be saying. But after they spoke, Mottram backtracked on that as well. Philip was doing [focus] groups tonight specifically re the press and called after the first one to say maybe I was right, that they really didn't like the press, and they liked TB when he was strong. They wanted more not less leadership. The RCN [Royal College of Nursing], King's Fund [health think tank] and others, including [Sir] John Stevens from the Met [Police], had written an open letter to TB which was going to be seen as a big attack re public services, low morale, pay and conditions etc. I spoke to TB who agreed we would do an 'open reply', full of praise for them and setting out some of the things we were doing. TB was alarmed that DB had bitten off more than he could chew re the cops. He had always seen the police as something of a touchstone. If you have them offside, that is not a good place to be.

Thursday, February 21
We were about to leave Number 10 [for TB's constituency] and as I walked to the foyer with Helena [Hopkins, duty clerk], Sixsmith literally charged through the front door. He didn't see me but headed to my office. I was determined to leave Mottram to sort this out, so I went to the car to avoid him and left Anne Shevas to deal with him and try to calm him down. She said he was clearly on the edge, that she had just let him talk and didn't engage much at all. He was saying our line in the *FT* that he had resigned from DTLR was wrong and we had to correct it. If not, he would, or he would have to get the deal agreed. I spoke to Richard Wilson and said we should not be having to deal with this. Mottram should be dealing with it. RW called later, said Mottram had made clear if he didn't resign he was sacked and they started to talk about a deal. The *FT* story didn't go too big. It was going away and Mottram was finally getting the message to Sixsmith that he was not on very strong ground.

We got a small plane up north. TB then did a series of visits around Sedgefield while I worked with Anne-Marie [O'Brien] from the Garden Rooms [offices of the Downing Street secretarial support] on the speech [for the Scottish Labour Party conference in Perth], working up the public services sections, and the interdependence theme. I felt we had got things back on a proper agenda. Philip said people were crying out for a plan and a proper sense of direction and would be relieved simply to hear us talking about issues they understood and cared about, not all the bollocks from inside the Westminster village. TB went out for dinner with John Burton [constituency agent] while I worked on the speech, and tried to make sense of the clashing drafts we now had. I got TB to do a Good Luck letter to the UK curling team at the Winter Olympics in Salt Lake and then stayed up to watch. It was brilliant, really exciting, and we won gold. Myrobella was the usual chaos but we just about managed to get the speech for tomorrow sorted.

The speech was just about finished. Felt a bit flat and uninspiring, though it was OK for the job of getting up investment and reform again. We signed it off on the flight up to Perth. Nice hotel, but he was in real witter mode re what the line was, and did we have the argument right? The *Record* ran a quote from TB saying 'If the unions want a fight, they can have one', which he never said. I asked for, and got, a correction and apology. They said it was a 'production error'! TB finally spoke to GB who was livid at what we had done re NHS Day. He argued that it was totally counter to HIS strategy. Even by their standards, it was a grim conversation. Basically, so far as GB was concerned, TB was only the PM and he should not be talking about tax, NHS spending, any spending really.

We did a visit to a science company and then to the conference. TB tried to ad lib but it didn't really work. In his peroration he talked about winning a third term and how we should dominate the next hundred years like the Tories did the last hundred, so most of them had a headline out of that. It was probably a mistake. We flew back, I did a box in the car then out to Rachel's [Kinnock] for dinner. My lot were late but Neil and Glenys were there, and I had a chat with Neil re TB/GB. TB had been down on GB today, said he was currently impossible; that the way he tried to present the [EU] Stability Pact as a public spending defence of our schools and hospitals was 'pathetic'. Neil agreed, also said he noticed how TB always talked up GB but it was never reciprocated. Both he and Glenys were also incredulous that [Paul] Dacre had been at the funeral of the baby.

Saturday, February 23

We went to see *The Lion King* [Disney stage musical]. Halfway through the play Anne Shevas texted me to say the *Sunday Times* were splashing on 'Sixsmith not resigned' and they had a massive write-through, clearly well briefed from the Sixsmith perspective. I went out at the interval, spoke to Anne then to Mottram, said there had to be a statement out from him making clear Sixsmith resigned TO HIM on the Friday. It was ridiculous that so much time and energy was going into this. He couldn't possibly stay as a departmental spokesman after all this. It was clearly going to be the start of another great blah but we just had to get through it.

Sunday, February 24

TB called, said the Sixsmith stuff looked like a spin doctor using spin to complain about spin. He felt we should stay out of it. I called RW to say he should get Mottram to deal with it. Mittal was still running too. We had lost the agenda again to a heap of crap. I briefed Helen Liddell [Scottish Secretary] who was on the media rounds, to be totally dismissive of the lot of it. I spoke to Byers before his [Jonathan] *Dimbleby* [ITV] interview to make sure we were saying the same thing. During it he appeared to suggest he had no role in personnel issues and denied he had blocked a deal to allow Sixsmith to get another job. That wasn't a hundred per cent true and would cause us real problems. Godric and Tom were dealing with the lobby on it, but the media were determined to see Sixsmith as a creature of probity and honesty and anyone who disagreed with him was a liar. Godric was in a total rage about it. Byers called me a couple of times for reassurance. It was difficult now, he having suggested he had no say in whether a deal could be done to move Sixsmith to another department.

Monday, February 25

TB called me early re Byers' statement he had nothing to do with personnel, and Sixsmith's position. 'Isn't this a bit of a problem?' Both he and RW said it was simply untrue. TB felt the only person who could put this right was Mottram and he would speak to RW to get Mottram to put out a statement. Mottram was reluctant but agreed and set to work on a draft. TB had now reached a judgement there was a problem at the top of the department, ministerial and civil servant. He was clearly moving to the view Byers would have to go. I still felt he had been victim not villain. He had been done in by civil servants operating from within, and screwed up his handling of it.

At the morning meeting I just skipped through the Sixsmith situation, didn't allow discussion, though Ian Austin couldn't resist a dig at [Ian] Jones over Mottram's 'We're all fucked' line in the *Sunday Times*.[1] Phil Bassett [Number 10 Research and Information Unit] made a crack about Sixsmith's homes, and within hours something was running on PA, friends of Sixsmith saying he was being smeared over his 'property portfolio'. Sixsmith was meanwhile doing little photo-calls with 'Liar Byers' headlines draped over his arm as he went home carrying a pack of bacon.

TB and I had lunch with the *Express* lot. TB was really motoring on crime. [Richard] Desmond was indicating he wanted more favourable coverage of the NHS. TB said to me afterwards I had to do

[1] Sir Richard Mottram reportedly told Sixsmith 'We're all fucked. I'm fucked. You're fucked. The whole department is fucked. It's the biggest cock-up ever. We're all completely fucked.'

better in curbing my contempt for the media. He said it was hard to charm them when your main press man sat there radiating a clear desire to wipe them off the face of the earth. I got back to the office to see the Mottram letter which needed strengthening. As drafted, it made matters worse for Byers. He needed to be clear that Sixsmith had agreed to go in the meeting last week, and also something that left open the possibility that Sixsmith was negotiating with Mottram and so Byers could not actually veto a deal any more than he could deliver one. This was clearly the point of vulnerability though. RW got the Mottram letter strengthened, removed some of the earlier ambiguity. TB agreed it could go, but I could tell he was mulling over whether SB could or should survive. He had failed to grip the department. He had failed to pin down events on Friday. True, he was only dealing with a difficult situation because people who were supposed to be working for him had created the difficulties, but TB felt the basic failure to grip the department was the problem. Steve was clearly worried, raised the situation with me several times through the day and all I could say was that his statement yesterday was the most difficult thing. I was now getting anonymous text messages saying things like 'You're losing 8–0.' The press was also in total kill mode and though things seemed relatively calm when I left for home around half seven, I still had very bad vibes. Martin Sheehan had taped my call with Sixsmith but the tape was wiped, so I asked for a note as detailed as possible. TB was the usual mix of exasperation, irritation and determination. He had had dinner with JP and GB last night and said it went well, though I would believe any progress when I saw it.

Tuesday, February 26

Papers grim. The *FT* had been briefed that Byers did indeed block the deal and Sixsmith was about to do the rounds playing the victim. TB called at 7.15 and said 'How difficult is this?' I said very, but if SB went it would be totally unfair because he had been done in from within. What was also clear was that there would be some who would try to move on to me/Jonathan straight away. The problem was it was not possible to square what Steve said on *Dimbleby* re not being involved. It was a big problem. TB was clearly thinking he should go. Sally, Jonathan and I were pushing hard for SB, and Peter [Hyman] was manic about it, saying he had only been put in the position he was in because he was done in from inside.

TB took a long meeting where everyone, including Jeremy, Tom and Godric, agreed it was unfair for Steve to go but TB kept saying he could not answer the question about how he came to say something that was not true. Steve called and I suggested the only way round this was for him to apologise for giving the impression he did. RW came in for the end of the meeting pushing for Steve to go. Also both Charlie [Falconer, former Solicitor General, now housing minister] and Derry [Irvine] had been sent the papers and transcripts and both called me to say they thought he would have to go. I still felt if he apologised, possibly in the House, and we went on the offensive against the internal operation against him, we could get through it provided the PLP remained supportive. As Jonathan said, we were going to have to throw him into the gladiators' ring and see if he survived. It was not the best way to deal with it, but there was a reluctance to toss him overboard given the background.

We watched him do the statement in the Commons and as Peter Kilfoyle, Tam Dalyell [senior Labour backbenchers] and others got up to back him, there was at last the feeling that we could fight back. The main thing was that SB was thought by MPs to have done well. I was impressed by his Zen-like qualities today. He didn't panic. It could so easily have gone the other way. TB was just about OK with the way things went, but clearly felt there was something odd, which of course there was, about the *Dimbleby* interview. What was clear was that without today's statement, TB could not have got through PMQs tomorrow defending what Byers said on Sunday. We had to get back on the big picture pretty soon.

Wednesday, February 27

TB called and I said though the press were in full cry, the party was fine and the issue was subsiding. TB was still worried about forensic questioning. The key problem remained why Byers said what he did and the extent of his or his office's involvement. If IDS did a proper forensic six-question job, it would be difficult. In the end he didn't and he was as hopeless as Theresa May [Shadow Transport Secretary]. Andy Grice got hold of Sixsmith's 18,000-word dossier but people were bored with it now.[1] One or two said it would only fly if they could somehow move it towards me. TB had said at PMQs that the hunting [ban] vote would happen shortly, which led the BBC *Ten O'Clock News*. Inevitable suspicion that we put it out because we wanted a diversion. Would that we were that well organised.

---

[1] Sixsmith had kept detailed contemporaneous notes and verbatim accounts of conversations with Campbell and others.

TB did OK out of yesterday but though the mood was calmer, you could still feel the anger in the media. Loads more pieces on me, notably a big one in the *Mail* about my so-called army of spin doctors. TB was doing an interview for ABC in the States, very forward on Iraq and pro GWB. He had decided that was the best position to adopt to gain influence. At Cabinet, he said it was important to emphasise that nothing re Iraq was planned and that we were a long way off taking decisions. Blunkett referred to the unsettling speculation and said a lot of people had difficulties with Rumsfeld. TB said Bush was in charge, not Rumsfeld, and David said, to some laughter, 'That's mildly reassuring.' There was a lot of support for Byers. TB said there were two agendas, the policy agenda we were trying to address and a media-only interest in the scandal and sensation, with the Tories preferring that agenda as a way of avoiding questions about policy. They had been on a tour of Europe to look at public services and come back with no great insights.

Byers said he was grateful for the support of colleagues, said the PLP had been superb. Also, we shouldn't forget there were a lot of dedicated, hard-working civil servants. John Reid said the media will want revenge. What was interesting about most contributions, e.g. Margaret [Beckett, Secretary of State for Environment, Food and Rural Affairs], was that the press and media were as much the Opposition as the Tories. This had been a media-driven frenzy, with the Tories playing shotgun. TB said we were more spinned against than spinning. They cannot find a full frontal policy assault so this is the substitute for it. It makes it all the more important to stay on a proper policy agenda. DB said the role of special advisers had to be properly understood and defended. He said at the Home Office there were serial leakers. Without his SpAds, he wouldn't have got a White Paper finished. He said he was lucky to have good press secretary who got on with the SpAds but it wasn't the same story everywhere.

The Peter M situation was also back with us. I ran a line past him re our response to the second Hammond report.[1] It didn't go far enough for him. He said why can't you just be honest and straight-forward and say that if we had known everything then that we know

---

[1] Anthony Hammond had reopened his investigation into the Hinduja passports affair after Peter Mandelson submitted correspondence between himself and his private secretary, Mark Langdale. Hammond conceded that though the correspondence offered 'some support' for Mandelson's account of his conduct, 'it is still not possible to reach any firm conclusions about the contacts which took place between Mr Mandelson and Mr O'Brien'. Hammond's main findings, and Mandelson's situation, were unchanged.

now, he wouldn't have left his job. I said we couldn't have a situation where we were saying TB got it wrong. He said we could say we all got into a muddle. He was calm but firm, said he wasn't prepared to haggle or beg for us to do the decent thing. TB spoke to him later and said that 1. he didn't believe the new papers necessarily helped him because they showed he had been more involved not less, and 2. he didn't accept he did the wrong thing because Peter had misled us and therefore allowed us to mislead the public.

We had an office meeting about how to frame this and TB redrafted the statement to take it closer to what Peter M wanted, namely that things, including his resignation, could have been different. The other problem, as Peter Hyman pointed out, was the clear contrast to draw between Peter M being sacked when we were saying he hadn't lied, and Byers not being sacked when people were saying that he had. I left early for Rory's parents evening then afterwards to [outgoing *Times* editor] Peter Stothard's party where GB was pretty much monopolising the new editor [Robert Thomson]. I had a nice chat with Ken Baker [former Conservative Cabinet minister], who advised me to get out at least a year before TB.

Friday, March 1

The Peter M report, Hammond Mark 2, was the main political story and we bent over backwards to be nice about Peter, to the extent that the story effectively became TB apologising for him being sacked. I felt sorry for him. The reality was if it had been another minister, he or she probably wouldn't have paid with their job. Also, though we could present it in the way we did, it wasn't the case that the report fully exonerated him.

Saturday, March 2

TB was phoning fairly regularly from CHOGM [Commonwealth Heads of Government Meeting in Australia] and was pretty fed up – first, because it was raining and second, because they just weren't serious about dealing with Zimbabwe [impending presidential election]. It was coming over as black vs white. He said he was thinking a lot about the press. No to jihad, yes to a tougher stance. But the note he sent through was the usual mix of pandering and using different groups of people to deal with them. I was a bit alarmed by it. We needed a big message that blasted through to the public. Calum and I set off for Burnley vs Norwich, crap match [1–1]. Home by half nine. The *Sunday Times* had another 4,000 words of Sixsmith, used as 'evidence' that Byers had misled the Commons. IDS weighed in re TB, me and trust. Not good. The *Mail on Sunday* did a big number on pictures of nude women allegedly inside TB's cuff on his shirt.[1]

Sunday, March 3

TB was doing interviews pushing a very hard line on Zimbabwe [human rights], whilst on Iraq, he was making supportive statements for Bush and hotting up the rhetoric for action.

Monday, March 4

I spent part of the day working on a note responding to TB's note on the press. We had to break the herd instinct. I had lunch with Richard Wilson. He clearly believed I had been briefing against him during the Peter M affair, which I hadn't, and we cleared the air on that. He seemed pretty down, said he had just about had enough of the job and really hated recent events, as had I. I felt he had done pretty well and that TB was probably right, that we should have involved him more, but Jonathan basically felt he was hostile. He said he felt I was exceptionally good at the job but perhaps the GICS had withered a bit under my weight. He liked Tony, felt he was an extraordinary character and the way he used the impact he made on people was a real gift. But he wished he could have done more to help him.

He thought maybe it was a generational thing, but he never felt that he got into the inner circle. He felt Jonathan despised him. He said permanent secretaries felt real respect for GB. He sometimes thought Tony believed he could live with GB on the back benches, but he didn't think so. He gave me the impression of someone who felt he hadn't succeeded. He was keen for a Civil Service Act but didn't seem sure what he would want to do with it. There was something very sad about him today. It was in its own way an enjoyable discussion in that for once we had been very frank, cut through some of the crap that sometimes surrounded us. He talked a lot about his kids and in particular how proud they were of their deaf son, and what perspective his deafness gave them. The nonsense about TB's shirts was getting out of hand. He was now getting more coverage for his bloody clothes than we were for policy.

Tuesday, March 5

We were doing an article for the *Express* on Iraq, which TB had toned down, though one paragraph he had written was totally

[1] At the Commonwealth summit, Blair revealed Paul Smith-designed shirt sleeves featuring a naked, kneeling woman holding a telephone on each cuff.

incomprehensible. I took in some changes from DB, the FCO and John Scarlett and then got it signed off by TB. TB was disappointed about CHOGM, both the outcome and the lack of real commitment there had been re Zimbabwe. Sally was worried about the Iraq article, felt that we were in danger of getting into a real mess with the party on this. Jack was also cautious, said he felt TB was more vulnerable than he had ever been and had to be really careful. Jonathan, though totally supportive on the substance, made an interesting observation. He said he couldn't put his finger on it but he felt we could be at the point of the beginning of the end. The big problem domestically was GB looming large, difficulties in driving through the changes in the public services, and the international agenda developing in a way none of us had planned or predicted.

Wednesday, March 6

It still felt like we were swimming through treacle. TB called just before 7, having landed at 6.15 after a 24-hour flight via Singapore. I was down on him at the moment, annoyed about all the stuff about his clothes. He felt we were far too defensive about it and I thought in its own way it was damaging, suggested out of touch. He believed our problem was one of communication. I believed there was also a problem with reality and that currently we lacked purpose and direction and when that happened, the trivia and the shit took its place. Clinton had told him that the press and the Tories were doing exactly what his opponents had done to him – drown out policy debate, attack integrity and persuade the public that we spent all our time dealing with all the shit, not worrying about the things people cared about. TB believed we did have a real strategy, and it was the right strategy, but the press were just trying to distort it the whole time. I felt we weren't disciplined enough at agreeing to a strategy, sticking to it and driving it through.

We had a good meeting with Charles Clarke, David Triesman, Douglas [Alexander, DTI minister], Ed Miliband [special adviser to GB] etc. going through Philip's latest groups. They were neither bad nor good, just indifferent. We agreed on 'Investing in strong communities' as a basic local election message and agreed TB would have to go out campaigning to show we meant business. We had to get back to values-based politics, which meant handling better the frenzies when they came and using them to emphasise the two agendas. TB was tired at the PMQs preparation meeting and very pissed off that we were all so pissed off at all the coverage of his clothes. We were finding each other irritating at the moment. I ran home, then to Rory's GCSE options evening. TB had a stack of different meetings but he didn't seem to be up for anything at the moment. He was a bit spooked by GB.

Thursday, March 7

I drove in with Philip who felt we needed a plan to deal with spin and sleaze. He said switchers had been getting jittery, no sense of delivery, nothing going on in the debate that they identified with. TB leadership and the economy, commitment to public services and the Tories were what kept us going but we weren't in good shape. TB felt this was the effect of the press drowning the real agenda. I felt he was a bit head-in-sand, couldn't see, or didn't want to see there were reality as well as perception problems and they couldn't all be addressed by a communications plan. Blunkett was in a foul mood because someone had briefed the *Guardian* against his spending bid. TB felt David was slightly losing the plot with the police.

Cabinet was mainly about Iraq. Not exactly division, but a lot of concern, where is it going? DB saying he didn't feel there was much support. Several saying the real concern was the Middle East peace process. Charles [Clarke] said the party would support provided the case was real and properly made. Jack pointed out it was untrue to say sanctions had stopped food going to Iraq. Geoff H said that if action was taken it would be because of UNSCRs [UN Security Council resolutions]. DB raised the international and legal basis for action. He said that support for Kosovo and Afghanistan had been pretty overwhelming. He felt a military assault on Iraq would carry less weight. It would depend on the role of the UN. Robin started off by saying that Saddam was a shit, a psychopath, who resolved their prison overcrowding problem by shooting 15,000 people with the longest sentences and who gassed the Kurds. On military action, he said there was a fine balance to strike. Saddam will not listen to Kofi Annan [UN Secretary General] unless he believes there might be military action. He said he wasn't convinced that action three years ago had been productive. He doubted whether it would be worth taking action if he was still standing at the end, and said he will be much cleverer than the Taliban. He said the best way of isolating Saddam from the rest of public opinion there was progress in the MEPP. He also warned that Britain could end up isolated, with a number of EU governments sounding sympathetic but on past form would not sign up. Charles C felt the judgement that would be applied would be one of success or failure. He felt people understood TB's position of support in exchange for influence.

TB said people's concerns were justified. 'I do want to assure you that the management has not gone crazy.' What are the dangers? US unilateralism. Bush doing it for the wrong reasons. Lack of progress in the Middle East. Taking action which proves to be ineffective. He said post September 11 there was a huge dialogue over a new UNSCR. Russia is owed a lot of money by Iraq. Egypt said Iraq had the most dangerous leader we have ever come across. [Hosni] Mubarak saw him as a real and present threat. He said we had to try to influence and shape US strategy. But we have to try to put ourselves in the right position. Get the weapons inspectors back in. He said the only thing Saddam responds to was real fear. If we had regime change it would make a huge difference to the whole region. It wasn't a row as such, but it was immediately briefed to the [*Evening*] *Standard* as such and that would frame it for the rest. It was a good discussion. TB said nothing decided.

Later we saw Milburn who said the problem was we were still behaving like a first-term government. We were too timid. We should be bolder, risk more arguments, more enemies. John Monks had written a bad letter to TB, saying we were in danger of losing our roots. Alan felt GB was the problem, that he spooked TB and we were paralysed on the economy, euro, public services.

Friday, March 8

Cabinet awayday at Chequers. Mood not great. The papers were full of division, threats of resignations over Iraq which even though untrue was clearly being flammed up from somewhere. TB and I were not getting on at the moment. I was fed up with the whole business, and he knew it. He was probably going elsewhere for advice, notably Peter M and to be fair, I could see why because I was giving him very little by way of ideas and support at the moment. I was down on him and down on the job. TB emphasised the need to get through this difficult phase with direction focused on values and delivery. He was still on the basic message mantra focused on the economy, society, public services, the international agenda. He felt the crime agenda was the most important at the moment. People needed to know we got it.

GB was looking odd, his face often contorted, his lips pushed out like he was blowing the whole time, his hands often clasped together over his eyes. He couldn't bring himself to look at TB when he spoke. TB said we were currently facing a test of mettle and maturity and had to hold our nerve. He was worried about yesterday's briefings out of the meeting. But after three months of sustained onslaught, we were still in a pretty strong position in the polls. The strategy against us was to assault our integrity because that goes to trust. Then it was to say that public services were crap and it makes no difference spending more money.

On the Civil Service, be careful not to be in a state of war with it. Win them over for reform. He said the fundamental positions we took were right, the specific programmes were right and the values were right, and though government is tough, what we've been through is nothing like as tough as other governments have, so we need to exude a sense of leadership and confidence, hold firm, take the tough decisions, drive the programme through. JP said whoever briefed yesterday's discussion on Iraq had behaved appallingly, that we worked hard to unite on policy and we should protect that unity. He said yesterday was a good discussion but then loose talk, nonsense about hawks and doves and threats of resignation had damaged us. Blunkett said it was rare he disagreed with TB but he disagreed with him about the Civil Service. They put SpAds on the back foot. They were in the strongest position they had been in for ages. There needs to be more Civil Service reform. Clare said the Cabinet was not ideologically divided. The '45 government achieved a lot but there was a real bitterness there. Of course there are differences here, but there is no big ideological divide. Our values are different to Tory values that have dominated in the last century. Our kind of values can become the norm, she said, which will be phenomenal.

Margaret B warned that though IDS was hopeless, we shouldn't underestimate because he may have a certain appeal. She said the mood in the party was terrible, they think we are growing out of touch. She also felt we needed to do a better job of challenging cynicism. The press are more poisonous than ever before, churn out all sorts of stuff that's untrue, unchallenged. Byers felt the Cabinet was too pessimistic. Strong economy, good record on jobs, inflation and interest rates. Robin lightened things a bit, started off by saying if JP was blaming him for briefing on Iraq 'he can step outside'. He said he totally supported TB in saying we needed to use Parliament more. We were not using Parliament enough to set the agenda. He said the problem with disengagement was one affecting the whole of Europe. Politics is now seen as a matter for politicians not people. We must convey a sense that we are not an elite constantly rubbing shoulders with the rich and famous. He said GB has been a very distributionist Chancellor but we never talk about it. We don't talk enough about the changes we are making.

John Reid said he could remember a time when the press was more poisonous, when Neil was leader. It will get worse than this. But what they prey on above all is division, and we should do nothing to feed it. He said we needed to be more political, less managerial, emphasise values, struggle, change, then delivery. GB said we had a historic opportunity to dominate for a generation, and deliver full employment. He felt we should worry less about the media, get the strategy right and shape long-term expectations. He said the Budget would further establish a strong economy, fairness agenda, solid foundations for the public services with the stress on reform as much as money. Alan M said values-based politics, being politicians not managers, was what was needed. When we were doing difficult things, explaining why according to our values, that was when we are strong. We had allowed ourselves to be projected as being on the side of the wealthy as well as the poor and sometimes the people in the middle didn't feel we were on their side.

TB summed up at some length. He said that after yesterday's Cabinet Richard Wilson had said to him he had never known a Cabinet with less malice in it and it was important we stuck together. When colleagues are in trouble, we support them. There was no doubt the press was in a different mode to the public, who wanted to see us with our sleeves rolled up, getting on with the job, doing the things they elected us to do. Our opponents remain frustrated because we have a strong coalition of traditional Labour and aspirational Labour, and we have to hold that together. He said the reason centre-left parties have lost in Europe is partly because they allow different parts of their coalition to erode. They don't get the importance of the anti-social behaviour agenda, rights and responsibilities. He spoke well, and the mood at the end was better than at the beginning.

Saturday, March 9
Middle East, Zimbabwe and Iraq the main issues at the moment. I took Rory to a race at Chelmsford where one of the coaches came over with some kids and said they were studying me at school.

Sunday, March 10
TB called re the [Dick] Cheney [US Vice President] visit, not sure what we were meant to get out of it. On the domestic front, he was worried we were losing the tough-on-crime bit. We went out for dinner with Tucker [Eskew], Lisa [his wife] and their son Thompson. He said basically we had been responsible for his new lease of life.

Monday, March 11
We had a meeting with Julian Miller [Cabinet Office intelligence and security official] on the idea of a WMD document. Cheney arrived for talks with JP, then a tête-à-tête with TB during which they went

over Iraq. So far as Cheney's mood music was concerned, he was when not if, and though they hoped for a lot of support, he didn't consider it to be essential. The Americans claimed to be conscious of the importance of the MEPP but we were not sure they really got it. At the lunch, Cheney had a quiet manner, was pretty calm and although he had gravitas, somehow the whole wasn't as impressive as it ought to be. They started on Afghanistan. It was clear the Americans wanted out as soon as possible. He said if we were still there in a year then questions would be asked. The aim was try to help the Afghans get themselves a proper army and security force. TB was clear we had to be in it for the long term. Cheney felt building the new regime could be tougher than taking down the old one and that the poppy crop remained a real problem. He was worried about Saudi and its fundamentalists and felt the regime's deal with the fundamentalists made it harder for them than for Pakistan to keep control. On the MEPP, TB went through the similarities with Northern Ireland. Cheney was very down on [Yasser] Arafat [Palestinian leader]

They discussed NATO expansion and TB said re Putin that the key to understanding him is that he is a Russian patriot. At least Communism got them noticed. He's not a Communist, far from it, but that colours his thinking. He wants to be at the top table. He raised steel tariffs and got very little response. Cheney was one of those politicians not embarrassed to say nothing. After lunch we took Cheney over to the CIC where he said a few words. After he left, I went for a run but had bad asthma and cut it short.

Up to the flat for dinner – TB, Peter M, PG, Sally, Jonathan, Robert Hill [Blair's political secretary] and I. Peter M was on better form and we had constant references to his own demise, and my/TB's roles in it. His analysis was that we came in after a pretty unedifying election, had a bad start, lacked clarity on the agenda, then Afghanistan drowned out domestic issues. Now there was a different mood where anything we did was being turned against us. TB insisted the problems were perception not real. Peter, Philip and I argued that some of the problems had been real. We had lacked clarity. We had lost the clearer sense of purpose we had before. Jo Moore staying was a mistake. So was the Mittal letter but TB always defended our basic position. I said there was a real problem, not just one of perception, even if it was a succession of different perceptions that created the problem. He said no, this is dangerous thinking which has to be resisted because what they want is to stop us being effective.

Peter felt TB had certain blind spots. He should do more in Parliament. He should do more in Cabinet. We should try to generate an intelligent debate within the media about the media and its relations with politics. Philip felt that in some ways perception had become reality, but it was reality that had to be dealt with. I said just because our opponents said we had lost direction or that we were out of touch, didn't automatically mean it was untrue. And then there was GB. I said the reason TB was so confident and commanding on foreign policy was that he didn't have GB getting in the way the whole time as he did on public services and Europe. Philip asked him direct whether he enjoyed dealing with foreign policy more than domestic, because that's what he felt. TB felt, particularly post September 11, they couldn't be separated in the same way as before, but his main focus was always domestic and at the moment specifically crime. He agreed on the need to do more in Parliament and develop a better media strategy. TB no longer really bothered to hide the way GB was affecting his thinking, e.g. when Philip said it had to be a Budget for crime, TB said he won't get that because GB won't want Blunkett to come out well. Jonathan's view was that the media were just bored with us. Mine was that we lacked clarity and conviction. Peter's that we lacked the bigger narrative, so the drip-drip had to some extent worked and people no longer believed us in the same way as before or respected us in the same way.

Tuesday, March 12

We decided not to brief the speech in advance. The result was there was nothing in the papers and the result of that was the broadcasters concluded it couldn't be newsworthy and didn't do much with it.[1] It was extraordinary the extent to which they let the papers decide the agenda for them. TB was up at 5 to work on the speech. Though he didn't change it much, he did enough to make it less values-based. He was strangely lacking in confidence at the moment.

Wednesday, March 13

Crap press for the speech. Not trailing it hadn't worked at all. Up to see TB early. We had a cup of tea in the kitchen and as he made it, he said he was alarmed at the damage GB had been doing recently. Tube, Post Office and Railtrack were all 'disasters waiting to happen' and he felt they were disasters made in the Treasury. Yet he felt we

[1] In the speech, delivered at the London School of Economics and entitled 'Next Steps for New Labour', Blair said 'Remember ten years ago: we were on our knees, out of office and out of hope. Now look forward ten years and imagine what could be possible . . . imagine too what we could achieve pulling together if we show our determination, stick to the values we believe are right, stick to our plans and see them through.'

should be involving GB more in strategy. This was real groundhog-a-go-go. He felt there was a shape to every parliament and we were just going through a bad patch. We would come out of it. Murdoch was in for breakfast, friendly but still very anti euro. Philip had a session with GB and said he was pretty pro euro at the moment. He felt that we were useless on strategy and that we should stop talking about public service delivery and just do it. Philip pointed out to him that was the opposite of TB's approach, and that we wanted the two running alongside each other and said 'Why on earth don't you talk about it? If you work together properly, we would be unstoppable.'

Thursday, March 14

Stan came in with a polling presentation that showed things shifting towards the euro. But better public services and higher living standards were what people wanted now. Cabinet was nearly all foreign, mainly Zimbabwe[1] and MEPP. GB sat there the whole time looking phenomenally pissed off and at one point appearing to be asleep. Jack was a lot more confident than before. I had a meeting on media ownership with Ed Richards. TB was keen for total liberalisation as a way of getting more Europeans into our market but it could lead to Murdoch getting ITV news. TB's general view was that we got nothing worse out of Murdoch than we did from anyone else. Ed was with me in bemoaning the lack of focus on the cultural impact, the fact that content regulation was virtually non-existent and these people had too much unchecked power. He said that Pat [Hewitt] and Tessa [Jowell] were also opposed to TB's view. They wanted controls on it. Then to a meeting with TB and DB re the blitz on street crime we had been pressing for. DB was using it to push for more money. TB wanted something that was visible, that worked, and that sent out the right signals. He set off for Barcelona [EU summit] and said he wanted me to focus totally on crime and the Blunkett package.

Friday, March 15

The riots in Barcelona were taking off as the main story there.[2] I was working with the Home Office to get up some decent crime stories

[1] Following Robert Mugabe being returned as president in the election of March 9–11, the Commonwealth Observer Group's preliminary report on the way it was conducted claimed 'a high level of politically motivated violence and intimidation' by supporters of the ruling party, Zanu-PF, had marred and influenced the poll.
[2] The EU leaders' summit was disrupted by anti-globalisation protesters in Las Ramblas.

pre DB on *Frost*, but they weren't motoring. TB was clear he wanted a proper blitz on this but even DB was now irritated by it all, the feeling that Number 10 was intervening the whole time. Natascha McElhone came in for a cup of tea and it was nice to hear her say the kind of thing I said the whole time, so often I was never quite sure whether I believed it or whether it was just a line to get me through, namely that by the time we were gone all the press frenzy would be forgotten and people would see we had delivered real things that mattered. John Monks was leading the news with an interview in *The Times* attacking TB over being too close to [José María] Aznar [Spanish Prime Minister] and [Silvio] Berlusconi. TB, GB and JS all went up and hit back on it. It was the main story out of Barcelona. TB's basic line was that the press were going through a mad phase and we just had to wait till normal politics could be resumed. He was quite chipper but the mood was bad.

Saturday, March 16
West Ham vs Man U. I saw Alex F beforehand who, a bit like Natascha yesterday, felt things were not nearly as bad as we seemed to think. Astonishing match, 5–3 to United, with a stunning goal by Beckham. I was amazed how many people from overseas there were in the crowd, seemingly just over for the day.

Sunday, March 17
TB had been on several times yesterday and today re Blunkett on *Frost*. He was OK without being brilliant and later did a lobby briefing. I worked on a note to put round the party on the public services argument. Then to Gavin's [Fiona's brother] for Burnley vs Preston on TV, with Paul Gascoigne [former top-flight midfielder] having signed for us. We went to the Hodges' [Margaret, minister for universities and husband Henry] for dinner with DB, who was a bit down. I said he shouldn't have referred to TB talking about the management losing their marbles re Iraq. Margaret H was pretty down as well, felt that GB had got himself into a much stronger position and TB was slightly losing the plot. I said I could easily see circumstances where GB never became leader. David claimed that he would never work under GB other than as Chancellor and in any event GB would be his own Chancellor. It was a very jolly dinner, as they always are with Margaret and Henry. But the backdrop was TB in a bit of trouble, GB and Co. at it more than ever and DB feeling he was a contender too. TB had said to me earlier that there was too much knicker-wetting going on in the Cabinet. They had to get

tougher. He said he'd had Clare on talking about what her 'bottom lines' were on Iraq.

Monday, March 18

Heavy news day. SRA [Strategic Rail Authority] bad figures, hunting[1] and an 'out of the blue' Geoff Hoon statement on 1,700 fighting troops going to Afghanistan. The DB interview plus briefing led to some pretty grim headlines, e.g. Blunkett saying our streets are not safe. Up to the flat on arrival. He seemed about as up as I was down. He said we came out of the election with the press trying to do us down, they wanted to give the Tories a lift but have given up on IDS so are now trying to build up GB. TB said all that mattered was that we delivered. He was frustrated at lack of delivery, at departmental slowness and the poor quality of cross-cutting work. He wanted to set up Cobra-style groups to tackle pinch points in the public services like bed blocking, Internet crime, weaknesses in the transport system.

The morning meeting was more meandering than ever, tired and lacking in drive. Ian Austin was pissed off that our crime meeting was going to get in the way news-wise of GB's speech on the NHS. I made little effort to dispel the impression that it had been deliberate. TB also had a difficult meeting with Tessa and Patricia [Hewitt] on media ownership. Their approach was fairly liberalising but he wanted to go the whole hog and said again Murdoch was no better or worse than any of the others, and what the media needed was real competition, takeovers galore. Patricia said this would go down badly with the party, the media and the public. TB said he didn't think the public obsessed about it. Jack called me to say he was worried about our direction on WMD. If WMD alone was the issue, Iraq was not as bad as Iran and Korea.

Tuesday, March 19

The Treasury was still gibbing at the crime meeting tomorrow because it would hit GB's speech coverage. Hunting was going big and so was the follow-up to military deployment and the growing political row about our failure to brief in advance. We had taken our eyes off the ball and not covered the bases. TB was not feeling great. I went with him to the stocktake on health with Alan. Then a communications meeting with DB and team. DB was clearly pretty beleaguered at the

[1] MPs voted for a complete ban on hunting with dogs when asked to choose between three options: a complete ban on fox hunting; the preservation of the status quo, and the compromise of licensed hunting.

moment. TB was far too nice about the Home Office being dictated by events. Yes, they had to deal with a lot of stuff that just happened, but it didn't mean they couldn't be more strategic.

[David] Yelland was in to see TB. Quite interesting, because Yelland was very down on the press, saying something had to give, the negativity had to stop somewhere. Then out to do Zimbabwe's suspension by the Commonwealth, at last. [John] Howard [Australian Prime Minister], [Thabo] Mbeki [South African President] and [Olusegun] Obasanjo [Nigerian President] did their thing. TB wanted to do a Cobra-style meeting for tomorrow's effort on crime, which I thought was a bit silly but there we are. TB had a one-on-one with GB and said afterwards he now felt he was operating the whole time, positioning himself in slightly different places all the time.

Wednesday, March 20

A row between GB and DB re who was doing what today. GB's NHS speech was fine but DB's crime summit, as planned, was going to get far more coverage. DB agreed not to do the *Today* programme as a sort of peace offering to GB, but he did breakfast telly and it was pretty much leading the news. GB's 'tough choices' message was seen as a hit at other ministers. I had a very frank discussion with TB after the crime meeting. He said GB was operating the whole time. It is nothing new in politics but at the moment it is particularly bad. He was setting himself up as Mr NHS now, trying to divide and rule e.g. between Alan M and the other ministers. The worry too was the idea that education was no longer number one priority. Ian Austin was in a major strop and at the end of the day we had a real row, me saying at the end I couldn't care less what they thought; that this was payback for years of them treating people like shit, including GB's Cabinet colleagues. He said it simply wasn't true that they were 'at it' and I had to believe that. I replied then all the journalists who said they were at it were liars?

TB was good at the crime meeting, closed it really well, drew in the centre of gravity of the comments. He felt DB was too emotional about it, saw it too much in personal terms. We had good ideas but we needed to know we had the systems and people to put them into practice. [Sir John] Stevens was pleased and did clips with DB that went fine. TB was raving about the crime meeting, felt it had been a really useful exchange and that if we listened to the cops more, we could get more done. On the hunting vote, Hilary [Armstrong] called and said TB was in some bother on this. TB wanted to push on and was in real 'fuck off' mode. All a bit grim at the moment.

TB/GB relations getting worse. Then an extraordinary thing later when George Pascoe-Watson [*Sun*] read to me the opening sentences of the draft of TB's [planned education] speech, accurately. It had gone to the Treasury and DfES [Department for Education and Skills] private offices earlier. Ian Austin, Ed Miliband and others denied it was them, claiming it must have been Education. All very odd. After Cabinet, TB had a meeting with GB, Margaret Hodge re student finance. GB was arguing strongly for a graduate tax, TB for top-up fees and it all ended a bit ugly when TB seemed to put his foot down, said eventually we have to make a decision and this is the decision we are making. GB said nothing after that and walked out as soon as it was convenient.

Our immediate problem for the day was [Labour MP] Alun Michael's hunting statement. TB was in a rage at not having followed his instincts, having voted for when he hadn't really wanted to. Deep down, he wished he had never let this thing on the agenda. Alun's draft was long, rambling, a bit unclear. But when he came in to discuss it at 9 and we went through it, the more you pressed for clarity, the more obvious it was the only way to get it was to come down on the side of the ban. The solution was a new bill. TB didn't really want that. He wanted more delay, more consultation and was in a foul mood on it. [Margaret] Beckett and [Alun] Michael were perfectly calm but getting a little bit exasperated. Before the statement, Gerald Kaufman [veteran Labour MP and chairman of the Culture, Media and Sport Select Committee] called me to say he would never see himself as a loyal TB supporter again if we backtracked on this. I said I never realised he was so passionate about it and he said he was, adding 'If the Tony who stood up to Milosevic and Bin Laden can't stand up to the Countryside Alliance, I can't support him.'

The mood with GB was poisonous. At the start of Cabinet, when TB read out the absences, he said in a perfectly friendly way 'It says here you're in Monterey, Gordon.' GB didn't even look up, let alone smile. TB said later he found his behaviour at times weird. I said we just had to accept there was a counter-strategy. Cabinet was largely foreign affairs, a bit on CSR/Budget. Milburn was good, emphasising the need for a more collegiate approach. TB saw Clare earlier and told her to watch this stuff about her being offside on Iraq. He said she had been very disarming, saying she had been done in on it and would not be a problem, but then at Cabinet whacked Geoff on Afghanistan. Then to Northolt and the flight up to Manchester with Tessa. TB wasn't sure what to push in the speech but we worked up education still the number one priority, tough on truancy. We visited the Commonwealth Games stadium which looked great, fantastic atmosphere, then to Bolton Arena, where he did an OK Q&A. There was a group of councillors from Burnley lobbying me to be their MP.

Overnight at the Lowry hotel in Manchester. Another discussion re strategy over dinner. He had had dinner with Clinton last night who had suggested I pick his brains on how to deal with this changed media mood. He had said the danger was doing the wrong thing instead of the right thing. Keep listening to your instincts that got you there in the first place, not the press who want you out. Keep getting out with people. TB and I were still disagreeing about the extent to which this was a reality or communications problem. What I did agree was that we needed more imagination in our communications. TB said there was a danger he, TB, was just becoming boring because people were so familiar with him. Bill's great appeal, or part of it, was his celebrity. He felt we had become too defensive about TB the phenomenon. He said this isn't your fault because everyone says you're the best in the world at what you do but we need new thinking, new ideas. I said it was about reality, lack of texture and enrichment. It's about you, drawing on real interests, real passion, real experience. I said we could do all manner of new interview ideas, pictures, talking points, but in the end it was about how he spoke about what he really felt. It became quite a tough exchange but we both felt better after it. After the others left, he filled me in on his earlier conversation with GB. He said Gordon's view has always been that when the going gets tough, I [TB] should disappear in a puff of smoke and he'll come in. He doesn't really get me. I do this job better than he thinks.

Friday, March 22

IDS had done a local paper interview in which he said TB ruthlessly exploited his children. I filled in TB who said IDS would regret this. If he had any sense he would apologise, but probably he wouldn't. Yelland called and, bizarrely, IDS had called him to say he didn't recall using those exact words, he felt really bad and he wouldn't do it again. I said to David that that was more about the desire to stop the papers whacking him and if he meant it he should call TB. Off to Abraham Moss High School. Good speech but limited coverage.[1]

---

[1] In a speech focusing on secondary schools, Blair said 'We should be proud of our education system, our teachers and staff. There is, however, a lot more to do. We want to be the best. And we can be. The challenge is to educate not just the top twenty or thirty per cent well but all our children.'

We flew back, and I met up with Fiona and the kids on the M4 and headed for Devon.

We were staying in an area where the mobiles didn't work, so I had limited contact with the office to a couple of calls a day, and did very little work. When I bothered collecting any papers, the theme of TB in trouble was developing pretty fast. I felt we had a clear difference in how to deal with it, which meant I felt I wasn't really offering solutions at the moment. He had been clear he didn't see the current situation as my fault, but I found his obsessive belief that it was about communications rather than policy or overall positioning a bit odd. We were staying in a house near Totnes and the local pub was run by a couple of party members who were generally OK about things, though there was nevertheless a sense that we weren't on top of things like we used to be. We went back to Tavistock a couple of times including a visit to the *Tavistock Times* office.[1] As often happened when we were away, usual suspects and others were lining up to whack us on various policy areas – Iraq, Post Office, tax and spend, TB's relations with Berlusconi. We got into a routine fairly quickly. There were some great hills around and I ran every day as well as playing tennis with Calum and swimming. We had a couple of days on the beach. The kids were an absolute joy at the moment.

Saturday, March 30
Jeremy [Heywood] called to tell me, in total confidence, that the Queen Mother had died. Although she had been frail, the actual death came as a surprise. The Queen was there [Windsor] now and they were trying to tell Charles who was in Klosters [ski resort]. They hoped to announce it soon. They were aiming for around 6. TB came on the line and we went over what to do. Unlike with Diana's death, there were well-laid plans which swung into action pretty quickly. But it was evident from the call I took from Robin Janvrin early evening that they were a bit worried, unsure that there would be crowds to justify three days' lying in state, or that there would be the level of interest necessary to fill nine days of news. I felt that it would develop a strong momentum of its own and that they were worrying unduly, though I could see why. TB, Jeremy and I agreed that we should go

[1] Campbell and Fiona Millar had met as junior reporters on the Mirror Group training scheme, and worked together on the weekly paper.

for a recall of Parliament before people started to call for it, and got Hilary Armstrong on the case.

TB worked on his words and as soon as it was announced formally, we got a crew to Chequers. He spoke well, and all the better for it being all his own words. The atmosphere was very different to Diana's death. It was not a Diana moment. TB felt there would be quite an outpouring of grief but I felt more that it would become one of those moments where people simply reviewed the past. Cherie was out in the States on her holiday and we had to make a decision about whether she came back or not. She clearly didn't want to. TB spoke to the Queen around 7 and told me afterwards she was 'very sad but dignified'. I spoke to Janvrin again, who agreed we should go to the US as planned and Jeremy H successfully pushed them for a Tuesday funeral so we could get to the US and back. I spoke to JP, who agreed to do the media on the Queen Mum tomorrow. Jeremy was doing a fantastic job with the Palace.

Sunday, March 31

TB called re the fact that cameras were still hanging around. He was volunteering to do more extended interviews today but we took the judgement it would look like he was muscling. Maybe another time. We did a couple of conference calls to agree what we should be saying about the visit to the US going ahead, recall of Parliament, receiving the body to Westminster Hall. TB, Jeremy and I went through the draft guidance on national mourning and took out a reference to businesses closing down on the day of the funeral, instead putting in the idea that schools do something to respect it, also give guidance on how practically people went to see the body. Our input was fairly minimal compared to Diana's death, but there was nonetheless a steady traffic between us and the Palace. I felt Charles should do something public fairly soon, the Queen maybe later in the week. JP did fine on the lunchtimes. Once all the amendments were put into the guidance, and some of the more antiquated language was taken out, we put it out. There were the beginnings of chat about the Royals coming under more scrutiny, how long would the Queen stay, would she abdicate kind of thing, but it was still pretty low-key.

Monday, April 1

Philip [Gould] gave a hilarious account of TB's behaviour last week at the various strategy meetings, that whenever he was challenged or under attack he just curled up into a foetal position. He said he was wearing the most extraordinary collection of brightly coloured shirts and ties whilst GB was always in a plain white shirt and red tie. 'It was a classic style meets substance moment.' He said GB hadn't really engaged. TB finished his note and as I had told him we were at Philip's, he sent it through there. The fax ran out of ink after page three, which ended 'Here is what we should do.' There then came through seven blank pieces of paper. When I finally got it, it was fine, but the kind of note I had seen so many times and we never really fully delivered on them.

Tuesday, April 2

Chequers. I was working on a response to TB's notes. He asked me what I thought of his note when we got there. I said good in parts. He said I really had to read it carefully, because it meant a lot of change from him, and he was serious about making that change. We both felt we needed new blood around the place. I said he could only get new blood if he got rid of the old blood and if he was looking for volunteers, I'd be happy enough to go. He asked if I actually wanted to go. I said I'd stay if he really wanted me to but I wasn't enjoying it and therefore wasn't doing it as well as I could, or possibly vice versa. I felt I was stuck in my own tram lines and so were others. He asked who could replace me and said he couldn't just take a chance. At one point we thought of Adam Boulton [Sky political editor] but coincidentally today we had the TV political editors in for lunch at Chequers and he thought Adam lacked judgement. I said people may emerge if they knew there was a vacancy. Most of the hacks would be amazed we were having this discussion. He said so was he, that I was too important to the operation and gave it strength which would be impossible to replace. I said all I was saying was that if he was looking for space for new blood he should feel free to look for a replacement. Later we were talking about Manchester United. He said that I was his [Roy] Keane[1] and he was very loath to lose me.

On Iraq, the meeting started at 10 up in the Long Gallery. It was a repeat of the smaller meeting we'd had on Afghanistan. Boyce was looking very tanned and smartly dressed and mainly set out why it was hard to do anything. He even talked up the Middle East peace process as a problem, as if TB had never thought of that. TB wanted to be in a position to give GWB a strategy and influence it. He believed Bush was in the same position as him, that it would be great to get rid of Saddam and could it be done without terrible unforeseen

---

[1] Aggressive and highly competitive central-midfielder, hugely successful captain of Manchester United.

circumstances. We were given an account of the state of Iraqi forces, OK if not brilliant, the opposition – hopeless – and Saddam's ways – truly dreadful. CDS appeared to be trying to shape the meeting towards inaction, constantly pointing out the problems, the nature of the administration, only Rumsfeld and a few others knew what was being planned, TB may speak to Bush or Condi but did they really know what was going on? TB said in the end Bush would take the decisions. CDS said so far he had followed the Rumsfeld (he always pronounced it Rumsfield) advice. He said apart from Rumsfeld, there were only four or five people who were really on the inside track.

There was also a different understanding on UNSCRs, the US thinking they have existing cover, us believing we need a new one for foolproof legal cover. Both C and John Scarlett kept saying co-operation was better, e.g. on intelligence, but CDS would keep coming back to the problems. I recalled his dire warnings about the Taliban skinning people alive. Now he was saying this would not be as easy as the Taliban. General Tony Pigott did an OK presentation which went through the problems realistically but concluded that a full-scale invasion would be possible, ending up with fighting in Baghdad. But it would be bloody, could take a long time. Also, it was not impossible that Saddam would keep all his forces back. He said post-conflict had to be part of conflict preparation. The Americans believed we could replicate Afghanistan but it was very, very different. There was a guy there called [Lieutenant General] Cedric [Delves], our military man based in Tampa, working with the US inside CENTCOM. He was sunburned, wearing American lace-up boots, and said Tommy Franks was difficult to read because he believed they were planning something for later in the year, maybe New Year. He basically believed in air power plus special forces. CDS said if they want us to be involved in providing force, we have to be involved in all the planning, which seemed fair enough. TB said it was the usual conundrum – do I support totally in public and help deliver our strategy, or do I put distance between us and lose influence? We discussed whether the central aim was WMD or regime change. Pigott's view was that it was WMD. TB felt it was regime change in part because of WMD but more broadly because of the threat to the region and the world. On WMD, people will say that we have known about WMD for a long time. He said what was sure was that this would not be a popular war, and in the States, fighting an unpopular war and losing is not an option.

C said that the presidential finding, based on an NSC paper, made clear it was regime change that they wanted. Pigott kept coming back to the point that Saddam could pull forces back to the cities, put them among civilians, meanwhile reinforce the CBRN [chemical, biological, radiological and nuclear] sites. There was a discussion about who would replace Saddam and how could we guarantee it would be better. Scarlett said it couldn't be worse. There was a discussion re Kabul which CDS said was getting more and more dangerous, and Turkey, who, CDS said, were taking over ISAF but basically leaving us to do the work. The Beeb was in the news because of a row about Peter Sissons [BBC news anchor] not wearing a black tie during the Queen Mum death coverage.

Wednesday, April 3

Amazingly, the row about Peter Sissons' tie was still raging. Of course it was a mistake, but in the end so what, but the *Mail* et al. were in total fulmination mode. Peter M had responded to TB's note in not dissimilar terms to mine. TB had obviously been talking to him about my state of mind. He said he felt he knew how I could regain happiness through work: 1. be nicer to TB, 2. get new blood around me, and 3. manage my time better. The lack of cohesion with the Treasury was really bothering me. TB was anxious that we get the focus for the meeting at Crawford [Texas] off Iraq simply and on to the Middle East. Second, how do we get the Americans to do more re the Middle East peace process without it looking like we are criticising them for not doing enough? He had told Bush a year ago that he should get more involved now because he would have to and he would eventually be playing catch-up.

The [pre-US trip NBC] interview was fine, pretty straight, Middle East, Iraq, Afghanistan, about thirty-five minutes in total. TB was thinking hard about the visit, said his job was to give Bush a strategy, and to get the political processes up and running. It was clear both from David M and Chris Meyer that the US government was in a divided state, bordering on chaos. Cheney and Rumsfeld vs Powell, with Condi trying to get Bush engaged more, possibly with Powell. Bruce [Lord Grocott, Blair's former parliamentary private secretary] did some good lines for TB's [Commons] statement on the Queen Mum and between us we got some half-decent anecdotes. TB just about caught the moment.

Thursday, April 4

I ran in, thirty-six minutes, up to see TB to go over Crawford/Middle East. DM wanted him to speak to Bush who coincidentally came through later in the day and they had a pretty good conversation. Bush was about to do a speech attacking both sides and saying he was sending Powell to the region. That gave us plenty to brief around. TB had an hour with GB on the Budget but Gordon was still on his kick that we shouldn't be talking too much about public services, a view TB described as absurd given that was the platform we were elected on. GB said you never heard the Tories talking about unemployment. They never said they would sort it, said TB. It's like saying we should never talk about asylum. If it's a problem, people know it's a problem, and we have to deal with it. I saw what Philip meant about their clothes. GB was wearing a dark suit, a white shirt, a red tie, shoes that weren't cleaned properly and socks that fell down round his ankles. TB was wearing Nicole Farhi shoes, ludicrous-looking lilac-coloured pyjama-style trousers and a blue smock. After GB left, I said he looked like [spoof 1960s spy] Austin Powers. He said you are the second person who's said that. Gordon wasn't the first. Probably one of the kids.

He was clearly not hopeful we could get GB any closer onside at the moment. But he still wanted me to try to work with him on strategy. I was in with him when he spoke to Bush and he was happy after the call, felt Bush was far more engaged and on the detail than we had been led to believe. I left to take Calum to a tennis match but then had to deal with a little flurry about TB/CB's Egyptian holiday last Christmas. TB's entry in the Register of Members' Interests said it had been paid for by the Egyptian government and that he had made a donation to charity. But it seemed the money never went, partly because the Egyptians never said what charity it should go to. This would be the next crapola to deal with.

Friday, April 5

It was the day of the procession of the Queen Mother's body to the lying-in-state. A beautiful sunny day, wall-to-wall coverage for the Royals, OK crowds, nice atmosphere. Up to see TB in the flat. Another Austin Powers moment. Yellow/green underpants and that was it. I said what a prat he looked. He said I was just jealous – how many prime ministers have got a body like this? Re the Egyptian holiday, he thought they had paid, but it seemed there was a mix-up at the Egyptian end and the cheque never went. Fiona spoke to John Sawers [UK ambassador to Egypt, Blair's former foreign policy adviser] who was out in the desert and we told him it had to be sorted and we would get the cheque sent off today. Just before we took off for the States I did a conference call with Fiona, Anne Shevas and Martin Sheehan. We wanted to rectify the inaccurate Register [of Interests] points. I reminded TB that Henry McLeish [former Scottish First

April '02: Flurry over TB's Egyptian Christmas holiday

Minister] ended up resigning over an inaccurate statement in the Register.

TB was seeing Jack later who suggested walking over to Westminster Hall. TB agreed and asked Gordon to go too. I said I thought it was a bad idea because it would look like they were trying to get attention. In the end they went by car. They went off as the procession came through. The crowds were far bigger than expected.

On the plane, we worked on the speech for tomorrow, pretty much wrote it himself, having decided he wanted to be totally supportive but also push for more US engagement. He would make clear we would support them on Iraq but also make the point about UN inspectors effectively as an ultimatum. We chatted around it for ages. I was worried it was too sugary re the Yanks but he insisted we had to do that to get them engaged in other ways. For example, he thought it was fair to say Bush's speech on the Middle East yesterday was, at least in part, influenced by us. For the first time I could recall, he did his own written checklist for the meeting with Bush. He wanted to do Iraq and MEPP first so that he knew where he was. We arrived and TB was met by Condi and flown off to the ranch. We were taken to our hotel. TB was having a one-on-one dinner and we went out for dinner with Condi, Andy Card [chief of staff], Karen [Hughes], Anna Perez [press secretary to Barbara Bush], Karl Rove [senior adviser]. A lot of it was small talk, and Karl Rove trying to persuade us to get fitted up with big Texan boots. Meyer was the only one who did. We were eating in a steak house which served obscenely large steaks. They seemed a bit more tense than the last time and it might be they were just starting to feel the pressure more, or more likely that they knew this was a bit trickier.

Saturday, April 6

Crawford, Texas. I went down to the gym in the hotel. There was an enormous woman on the only treadmill. Robin Oakley [CNN European political editor] called and she heard me speak and then, as she padded at the slowest possible pace, asked me if I was English, then if I knew Tony Blair. I said I did. She said she was so happy that the world was run by two God-fearing young men, Bush and Blair. She asked if I was his bodyguard and I said no. She said she prayed for Tony every day and she prayed for his bodyguards, for him to keep the world safe and for his bodyguards to keep him safe. She asked if I believed in God and I said no. She gave me a rather pitying look and then told me she was a member of the George W. Bush email prayer group and she was happy for me to be added to their list. Eventually she got off the treadmill. I ran for half an hour but then got called up because TB had asked for me to go out to the ranch with David and Jonathan. I set off with Magi [Cleaver] for a 45-minute drive down dull roads through pretty dull scenery. The rain started. The security checks were fairly light and we were driven down to the guesthouse where TB, CB, Leo [Blair], Kathryn [Blair], Gail [Booth, Cherie's mother] and Jackie the nanny were due to stay. It was a nice enough place but not exceptional. A flat bungalow with three bedrooms was the main residence. I hung around for a while in TB's room. TB and Bush had talked mainly about Iraq last night and today had been more focused on the Middle East peace process, about how to deal with [Ariel] Sharon [Israeli Prime Minister] and Arafat. Bush felt they were tired and old and with no new vision. He thought Arafat was weak and useless. They were turning their minds to the press conference and Bush was someone who liked to prepare for these events carefully.

We were doing the press conference at a school in Crawford and the toughest questions were why had there been no response from Israel and did TB agree Saddam had to go. Bush's posture and delivery were a lot better, more confident. We talked about it at the ranch before dinner. He said in the early days he got really knocked by the way they took the mickey out of the way he mangled words, and it made him hesitant, like when he said infitada instead of intifada and got mauled for it. Now he had given up caring what they think and it had made him more confident. He said the truth is I have a limited vocabulary, I'm not great with words, I have to think about what I say carefully. They had both been pretty heavy on Iraq and that was the story for most of them. The atmospherics were pretty good though. As we left the school, TB and I were walking to his car, GWB waiting and he shouted over 'too late for fine tuning now'. I said I hear you didn't like Trevor McDonald [ITN journalist who had recently interviewed Bush]. He said it just maddens him the way they all ask the same questions, so it's a pain.

When we arrived back at the ranch, we chatted in a little group outside the bungalow. Barney his dog came over and he said 'This is my Leo.' I said hold on, Leo's not a dog. Yes, he said, but Barney's the substitute for the little boy I never had. They went back to talking about the Middle East, David [Manning] and Condi having spoken earlier to Colin Powell to try to get him to the Middle East earlier. TB was setting out steps that could be taken. He was convinced that Bush valued our input on this at least. I left with David and Jonathan. We went for lunch at the coffee station in Crawford with some of the

White House staff including Andy Card. They were certainly doing their best for us.

We were driven back out to the ranch for a drinks reception and dinner. It was very relaxed, a three-piece band playing in the corner, waiters and waitresses in jeans and work shirts, no starters, tournedos and a selection of puddings. GWB and Cherie were at one table with a set of guests and TB and Laura were at another and then other tables all around. Bush was wearing Texan boots and jeans. I was with Condi, Karen, a very right-wing former ambassador [Anne Armstrong, first female US ambassador to the UK] who was going to the Queen Mum's funeral and one of the Bush daughters' boyfriends.

Over drinks before and after dinner, I had a couple of long chats with GWB. He asked me why I wasn't drinking and I said I was a recovering drunk. Me too, he said. I asked him how much he drank. He said two or three beers a day, a bit of wine, some bourbon. He gave up in August '86, a few months after me. I went through the kind of quantities I was drinking at the end and said they dwarfed his efforts. I said that having a breakdown and not drinking had been the best thing that ever happened to me. It was like seeing the light. But you still don't believe in God? he asked. No I don't. We talked about his axis of evil speech. Karen had said to me earlier they had had no idea it would impact quite as hard as it did. He said that was bullshit – he knew, and he was serious. We talked about running. He could still do between 6.45 and 7.15 a mile and was thinking of doing his own race for charity. He was also a member of a club, qualification for which rested on the ability to run a sub-seven-minute mile when it was a hundred degrees in the shade. He had dragged TB out for a run and said he had had to hold back a bit. TB said it was the first run that far since he left university. After a couple of toasts, Bush then just got up and said everyone could leave because he wanted to go to bed. Everyone signed the menus. They were always extremely respectful in front of him. I couldn't see any of them suggesting he had a touch of the Austin Powers about him. TB thought that was why he seemed to enjoy the banter with us, because he didn't seem to have anyone there who really stood up to him and just had a laugh. On Iraq, it was clear they genuinely hadn't decided what to do, or even whether to do anything at all.

Sunday, April 7
TB called early to give me a few final changes for the speech. I could hear Bush rushing him in the background. They went off to church, which was a three-hour round trip. We both reckoned Bush had been

quite a lad in his youth, both on the booze and the birds front. But they got on, there was no doubt about that, and they were both people not afraid to face down critics. They both seemed to view Iraq and Saddam as an issue of conviction. We finished the speech, which was now strong, putting in a few final changes strengthening the references to the UN and also strengthening the use of the word 'justified' when talking about regime change. Most of the world's media was on the Middle East, but our lot would be on Iraq because that was the better political story.

The big thing was trying to get the peace process going again but Bush was very down on both Arafat and [Ariel] Sharon, who he had bollocked in a phone call yesterday. The drive down to the speech venue was much more scenic, including past some of the most incredible wild flowers any of us had ever seen. TB was speaking at the [George] Bush Library [at College Station, Texas]. While we waited for everyone to gather, I did a note to him on the advisability of doing a statement to the Commons on Wednesday. He was concerned it was setting a precedent that he would do one every time he went abroad and we were being pushed to do things no other prime minister would do. But I tried to push the positive reasons. He was the only leader really plugged into Bush and able to exert influence. He was far better than Bush at empathy and explanation. And it was important that we set this out as British foreign policy not theirs, and Parliament was the best place to do that.

George Bush Sr [former President] came through to say hello and ask us if we wanted to change his introductory remarks. Maybe it was just age, but he seemed a lot more comfortable in his own skin than Bush Jr, though less jokey. The only change I made was to delete England for Britain when he talked about us losing the Queen Mum. TB and I went through the speech one last time. He got a very warm reception, the speech went well[1] and although he got some tricky questions in the two separate Q&As, he was on form. I heard Bush Sr say to the people he was with how impressive he was. He had definitely made an impact. The argument was clear, he set up difficult questions, and answered them. JP called and said he really liked the speech.

On the plane I had dinner with TB and Jonathan and we discussed where we were going to find new blood for the office. I suggested a minister or senior MP getting involved in managing and motivating.

[1] Blair said 'Leaving Iraq to develop WMD, in flagrant breach of no less than nine separate UN Security Council resolutions, refusing still to allow weapons inspectors back to do their work properly, is not an option.'

Neither of them seemed keen. The reality was Jonathan wasn't a traditional chief of staff, in that he didn't manage a lot that went on, and I wasn't a traditional communications director. What we did was largely driven by what TB wanted us to do and what our personalities best allowed us to do. But it meant gaps that sometimes led to lack of clarity. Also the Policy Unit was badly managed and not properly integrated. TB was clear he wanted it sorted and wanted the game raised.

We debriefed him on the private sessions with Bush. He had been surprised how relatively positive he was about the idea for a big push on Africa. He had not enjoyed his contact so far with Europe. He liked Schroeder, loathed Arafat and had a total reversal of view of Putin. He now liked him. Bush had told him he had learned a lot from talking to his dad about success and failure. Bush Sr had told him he had not been nearly ruthless enough with his appointments and the people around him. He was trying to learn from that. He was also trying to learn the lesson that no matter what you did, you had to be out talking to the people that elected you. We got a few hours' sleep, landed and straight to the office. He had agreed to a [Commons] statement on Wednesday.

Monday, April 8
I called [Sir Robin] Janvrin to say I thought they had handled events incredibly well and today's broadcast by the Queen was the crowning glory of a very good PR campaign. They had done well every single day. Today, as well as the broadcast, they had the [Westminster Hall] vigil of the four grandsons. I spent a lot of the day working on Wednesday's statement with David Manning and Matthew Rycroft [private secretary, foreign affairs] Peter Hyman was nagging me to set up a Budget strategy meeting every day from now on in. Fat chance. GB just wasn't engaging. He was clearly trying to position himself as the saviour of public services whilst TB was fighting hard for more money for defence.

Tuesday, April 9
The Queen Mum's funeral would be a media wipeout so the morning meeting was brief, though I did relentlessly take the piss out of Ian Austin who had said a few days ago that nobody would be interested in the Queen Mum's funeral. I went upstairs to watch the cortège go through Horse Guards and towards the Mall. Big crowds, real solemnity and the BBC did a good job on it. I went to TBWA [advertising agency] who did a terrific presentation on the idea of

segmentation, targeting campaigns to specific groups of people. They were very good on overall branding but their basic take was that we needed to isolate groups and direct our communications to them through policy that impacts upon them rather than through the media they consume. Trevor Beattie [chairman of TBWA] gave me a copy of *PR Week* which had said that New Labour, New Britain was the best consumer PR campaign of all time.

Wednesday, April 10

GB had got hold of a tape of Liam Fox [Shadow Health Secretary] making very unwise comments on the NHS. GB got the *Mirror* to splash on it. Philip felt opinion was moving back to us a bit, with health improving, education not as good as it should be, crime worse. We worked on the Middle East statement which was fine, and it was right to go for Israel and the Palestinian Authority equally. The statement on the Middle East had definitely been the right thing to do. The right-wing press were trying to cause trouble. The *Telegraph* were trying to link the success of the Queen Mum's funeral with hostility to New Labour. The *Telegraph* were also saying we tried to change the arrangements for the funeral, and Peter Oborne [columnist] was saying the same thing in the *Spectator*. I got Jeremy to write to them to complain. I had a meeting with Ed Balls on the Budget. He was happy where expectations were. I was less happy. We worked out what message TB should do in setting it up. They didn't want too much focus on health yet but we did need to start a campaign to stand up for the NHS. We were going to be putting up taxes but it was vital that a New Labour message runs through it all. PMQs was fine, the Middle East statement OK, the PLP not too dreadful.

We had a reception for [former Labour Prime Minister] Jim Callaghan's ninetieth birthday at Number 10. He made a really warm speech, terrific about his wife in particular, Audrey suffering from Alzheimer's, and he said how he sat with her and talked to her every day and sometimes she said a few words that made sense and it was magical. Michael Foot [Callaghan's successor as Labour leader] and I talked endlessly about Burnley and Plymouth [Argyle, supported by Foot]. Tony Benn [former Labour Cabinet minister] was filming the whole thing. Betty Boothroyd [former Speaker of the House of Commons] was there to call everyone to order. There was a good turnout of ministers though JP was angry he hadn't been invited. Denis Healey [former Labour Chancellor of the Exchequer] and I nattered about Keighley [where AC and Healey grew up]. Merlyn Rees [former Labour Home Secretary], Bernard Donoughue [head of former Labour Prime Minister Harold Wilson's Policy Unit, 1974–76], Tom McCaffrey [Callaghan's former press secretary], [Roy] Hattersley [former Labour deputy leader], Margaret and Peter Jay [Callaghan's daughter and former son-in-law]. TB said afterwards they were a good bunch of people but in the end they had failed to stay together.

Thursday, April 11

We were due to have a meeting on Budget strategy. TB was delayed at an NHS seminar. GB arrived on time but because TB wasn't there, he buggered off for ten minutes, came back and said 'What's this meeting about?' What became clear was that he didn't intend to expand on what was in the Budget. He said I wish we could do a presentation based on delivery but we don't have any. Puzzled looks all round. He told us about a campaign to be fronted by [Sir] Magdi Yacoub [pioneering heart surgeon] that was about getting up third-party support for the NHS. We would involve doctors and nurses in a fight for the future of the health service. I said that's all fine, but are we clear that taxes up to pay for health is going to be the main line out of the Budget? He was, but felt we needed this bigger campaign to lay the ground.

GB also wanted enterprise talked up and investment dividing lines laid down. As ever, he was a mix of strategically clever and clear – as in keep the Tories out of the centre, stop them becoming New Conservatives – selfish and exclusive – as in clearly not wanting TB too closely involved – and unrealistic, as in imagining that tens of thousands of doctors and nurses would come out to make the case for us. TB was weak at the meeting, looked tired and fed up. After half an hour GB just upped and left. Ed Balls treated TB with a bit more respect, but not much.

Then Cabinet. TB started with a contextualisation of the Budget, with a focus on enterprise, the need for a big battle on investment and tax, the need to get up delivery and reform. He said these are the areas where political battle will be joined, that this is far more important to the PLP than Iraq. He spoke for a few minutes, then said 'Anything you want to add, Gordon?' No, he said. So there was no discussion at all. I slipped a note to JP saying that they would all be very pissed off if there was no discussion at all on Budget strategy, saying why didn't you come back in the context of the local election launch today, but by the time he did GB said he had to leave for Treasury questions. TB had also slipped a note to GB saying he should say something. He said nothing. Absolutely ridiculous.

Later GB, Charles C, Alan M and I met to discuss the strategy for the Budget. GB set great store by his 'Say yes to the NHS' campaign, though I remained to be convinced we would get all the professionals properly involved. Likewise, Charles seemed nervous about how readily the party would get involved. GB was claiming he didn't want to rewrite the local election campaign but clearly wanted this to be a big part of it. I left with TB for Northolt [en route to Sedgefield]. I said GB could be a total pain but he still had amazing strategic energy and drive, that nobody but him or us could have motored on the NHS Fox story like that. TB did the *Northern Echo* when we got to Myrobella, then to the Labour Club for a Q&A where he was excellent. Don Macintyre and Andy Grice [*Independent* journalists interviewing Blair] stayed for it, and it ought to give them plenty of decent colour. We took them for dinner at the Dun Cow pub and TB talked about how much he enjoyed the Callaghan event but also how sad it was that this group of people seemed the best of friends now, but how they had split apart and how history might have been different if they had stayed together and the left of the party hadn't made the right feel that they had to leave.

Friday, April 12
We left for a business Q&A, which was pretty dull, and then to a much more interesting Q&A with leaders and others working in the public services. The cops seemed the most onside, health and education less so, but the basic message was that things were getting better but money was tight. Then to Darlington Memorial Hospital, where again the mood was OK but they said they needed more [investment]. We flew back and I got in for a meeting with Number 10 and the Treasury re GB's NHS campaign. My worry was that they didn't have the infrastructure to mount a campaign and also that they lacked anything to campaign against. I was ready to go to war with the *[Evening] Standard* over Oborne refusing to accept we didn't interfere in the lying-in-state arrangements. I had a meeting with Clare Sumner and Simon Virley [private secretaries], who had handled arrangements with the Palace, to go over it all. I sent a letter off after talking to TB and Guy Black [director of the Press Complaints Commission], to the PCC, who said if everyone is going to be clear that the report was wrong, it's fine and we should go for it.

Saturday, April 13
[Policy adviser] Liz Lloyd's wedding, TB came to the church service and briefly to the reception where he did a nice little speech, referring to the ghastly process of conference speech-writing and also to our

'dysfunctional relationship'. Tim Allan [AC's former deputy] and James Purnell [Labour MP, former Blair adviser] did a very funny song about Liz's past and Tim said that the new people he worked for [in public relations] were all totally indifferent to the fact he used to work for TB, but dead impressed that he worked for me. Most of the old office were there, and Ed Miliband turned up late for a while. Work-wise, fairly quiet though later on a rash of calls about Mo [Mowlam] in the *Observer*, extracts from her interview for a documentary to go with a book which was the usual over-the-top bollocks about her being smeared.

Sunday, April 14

We went out for dinner with the Goulds and Bob Shrum [Brown's polling adviser], who had probably worked on the Budget speech far more than we had. He said he would really like to get a better relationship between me and GB because he felt our politics were actually quite similar. I said I feared it was pretty hopeless.

Monday, April 15

TB was in pretty much constant dialogue with GB. The papers were full of Budget trailers. There was very little left and they had not done much by way of holding things back. The basic problem was no acceptance of a minimum delivery, not least because GB didn't talk about delivery, possibly preferring for him to get credit for the economy and TB none on delivery. His latest line was that we had delivered nothing, despite the strong economy. On sleaze, TB was moving towards an ethics adviser. I was chasing the *Standard* and the *Spectator* re the Queen Mum lying-in-state. I spoke to Boris Johnson [*Spectator* editor] who tried to be all jokey saying he would consider correcting it if I did a piece on the Blair/Bush relationship. TB wasn't feeling well and had picked up the bug that Leo had. The Tories had done a health document and Alan M and Darren Murphy put together a very good response on it. The *Guardian* was running a two-part series on the Treasury, its power and how it was built. Real self-aggrandisement with the help of two of their fans, Larry Elliot and Kevin Maguire [*Guardian* journalists]. Cherie and Fiona visited Holloway jail, which Fiona said was about as depressing as it gets.

Tuesday, April 16

Met Ed Miliband to go over the Budget broadcast script which was OK but lacking in a reform message. TB and GB were going through the final meetings both on policy and the tone of the statement. Magdi Yacoub finally got his article in the *Mail* but I didn't feel the 'Yes to the NHS' campaign was properly cooked at all. All the bulletins were leading on our troops fighting in Afghanistan. Some of the squaddies gave tremendous interviews. The pre-Budget coverage was cranking up, GB out with young kids. TB saw Hugo Young [*Guardian*] and then Peter Riddell [*Times*] trying to win the argument for tax for the NHS. I had altogether more difficult conversations with the *Sun* lot.

TB called a discussion on the ethics adviser idea. The worry was it was merely a response to a spasm of 'something must be done' which in fact would give us nothing but problems. TB felt that we needed something that gave us a bit of distance and a bit of time. He felt that for example with Peter M we might not have lost a very good minister if there had been a process one removed from us. But what both the Americans and [John] Major's government had shown is that just about every time they set up new bodies and structures to look at these kind of issues, they seem to make matters worse not better for themselves. We had an internal meeting to work out how best TB could take forward the Budget message in the coming months. TB was happy enough with the Budget and GB clearly did not want to be seen as Old Labour.

Wednesday, April 17

The Budget was reasonably well set up but the dominant story was clearly going to be tax for a better health service. TB was clearly a bit nervous, said we were doing something very few people in politics ever did successfully, openly advocating tax rises. I felt it could be the thing that gave us the definition we needed. At Cabinet, GB did a very good presentation. TB looked really tired and a bit out of it. Jack slipped me a note saying he thought TB looked ghastly and we needed to get him in better shape before this afternoon. GB did his usual mix of big message and factual rat-tat-tat. On the big message, what I liked about it was it was all the same arguments coming through, and the spending figures were fine.

TB said it was a crucial moment for the government. There were three things to get across. Strong economy the basis of everything we do. Continuing determination to get people off benefit and into work. Strong economy plus more people in work means more investment in public services. He said that there should now be a critical argument on the NHS. The issue is not whether we spend more but how. We have to win the argument that our system is better and more efficient than the French or German social insurance systems or the

Americans' way of doing things. This issue about whether more money in this way delivers better services will dominate this parliament. There was an odd moment in GB's summing-up when he referred to the NHS campaign and said 'I think' it's called 'Yes to the NHS', as though it had nothing to do with him. But he did a good job, and it went down well with colleagues.

TB was on great form at PMQs, GB did well, IDS was crap. The immediate business reaction wasn't great. The PLP was fine. A lot of the vox pops of families were positive, though there was quite a lot of 'broken promises' re tax. I did a ring-round and certainly they saw it as pretty epoch-making that we were openly going for a tax rise as the top line. We had a strategy meeting, TB plus the internal team. He agreed finally to appear at select committees and agreed also that we should move to cut down on briefings. I was arguing for a real shake-up in the way we communicated. Peter M felt we needed to change things gradually, both in terms of policy substance and presentation, a lot of it just do unannounced and build towards people realising that there was such a thing as New New Labour developing.

Thursday, April 18

Press as expected. The *Mail* a total parody. The *Sun* grim, *Guardian* OK, *Mirror* not great. GB came over at 9.15 to leave for a visit with TB, complaining that there was not enough reform in Milburn's follow-through statement. TB said that the thing to watch was people thinking this is a return to Old Labour. GB up in arms. 'God almighty, you can't say we didn't deliver on the message yesterday.' 'No, but . . . ?' The line was running a bit that it was an own goal because as the NHS was such a huge employer, the NICs [National Insurance contributions] rise would have a disproportionate impact there. The press were pretty determined to make the general Budget story a problem for us, but the Tories were hopeless. TB told Cabinet that as he saw it, the two big areas for us in the next phase were health and dealing with antisocial behaviour. Reform was every bit as important as money. He said if we can't feel confident about these arguments, we don't deserve to be in business.

As GB arrived, TB said it was a brilliant Budget, brilliantly delivered and these arguments would dominate politics for some time. DB said we again had the opportunity to emphasise values, our belief in mutuality, the belief that we have obligations to others. TB felt the media could have been worse and on the TB/GB stuff, building up GB at his expense, he said to us it didn't matter, they are going to do that. He felt the public took the view that GB was good at what he did but they also wanted me here checking him. He also felt it was good to have a range of big figures around the place.

Sally [Morgan] and I went to see TB to say we were worried, that he looked ill, wan and grey. He said he was tired, feeling stressed and more than usually discombobulated re GB. I was working on a letter to the PCC, Clare Sumner having worked out what happened. It was clear that in her dealings with Black Rod[1] [Lieutenant General Sir Michael Willcocks] she had set out what she thought the guidance for the PM and the government was, and Black Rod had taken that as us complaining about it, which was then passed on in distorted form. Black Rod was clearly tricky. Both Clare and Simon Virley were adamant they had done nothing more than get clarification on what TB was meant to do.[2]

Friday, April 19

Business was attacking the Budget a lot now, and when TB did a round of TV interviews there was a lot of stuff about trust, whether we should have been more up front at the election that we would need to raise taxes. The *Mirror* led on Sven's [Göran Eriksson] affair with Ulrika [Jonsson], which was truly gobsmacking for all sorts of reasons. I told a few people in the office that I had introduced them [see December 8, 2001] and not long after Tom Baldwin [*Times*] called to ask if it was true. I had told only a handful of people so it was extraordinary that he knew. I stalled and spoke to Melanie Cantor [Ulrika's agent] who confirmed that the [Richard] Desmond party was the first time they met, when I had been talking to Ulrika. She said it was amazing but true. The *News of the World* was going to do something and the *Mirror* was basically a spoiler, her role having been essentially just not denying it. She said she had been amazed when Sven called her for Ulrika's number. The dreadful thing was that the FA was pressing him to put out a statement, but it seemed Nancy [Dell'Olio, Eriksson's partner] hadn't known. I just could not fathom who would have told Baldwin. I tried really hard to work out who told him, but he was giving away nothing. The only

[1] The Gentleman Usher of the Black Rod, the sovereign's parliamentary attendant, sergeant-at-arms and Keeper of the Doors in the House of Lords.
[2] The *Spectator* having claimed that Blair had tried to 'muscle in' on plans for the Queen Mother's lying-in-state, the *Mail on Sunday* asserted that a Downing Street aide had telephoned Black Rod to ask if the Prime Minister would be able to greet the Queen and the coffin as it arrived at Westminster Hall. Downing Street confirmed the call, but maintained it was only to clarify the Prime Minister's role. A complaint to the Press Complaints Commission resulted in the regulator finding there was no evidence that the Prime Minister had done anything wrong, but Number 10 dropped the case.

(*Right*) The moment that changed the world: the al-Qaeda attack on the Twin Towers.

(*Above*) George Bush is told the news by his chief of staff Andy Card whilst listening to schoolchildren reading; (*above, right*) Tony Blair is about to tell the TUC that he must return to London; and (*right*) Bush speaks to Blair by phone the following day as Condoleezza Rice stares out through the Oval Office window.

(*Right*) Bush waves the Stars and Stripes and shows solidarity with rescue workers at Ground Zero.

The Blairs in the US: (*left*) Tony Blair, Laura Bush and New York Mayor Rudolph Giuliani applaud President Bush's speech to Congress; Cherie (*below*, *left*) looks at the helmets representing some of the firemen who lost their lives; and (*below*) Tony and Cherie Blair, Kofi Annan, Hillary and Bill Clinton join in singing a hymn at a memorial service in New York.

(*Right*) Osama Bin Laden is one of the FBI's twenty-two 'most wanted' members of al-Qaeda; (*below*, *left*) Saddam Hussein, President of Iraq; (*below*, *right*) a headline greeting Bush's labelling of Iraq, Iran and North Korea as 'the axis of evil'.

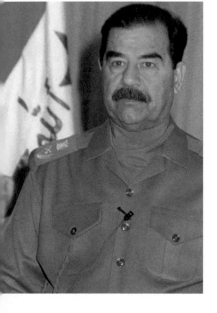

TB and his two GBs: (*right*) together in Washington on the day Bush hailed Blair 'a true friend'; (*below*) a cartoonist's take on Gordon Brown's troubled relationship with Blair, which at times (*bottom*) could not be hidden from the cameras.

(*Above*, *left*) Transport secretary Stephen Byers and (*right*) his political adviser Jo Moore, whose political career came to be defined by one email about 'burying bad news'.

(*Below*) The Queen with five of her prime ministers: Tony Blair, Margaret Thatcher, Ted Heath, Jim Callaghan and John Major.

(*Above*) US actor Kevin Spacey adds a bit of showbiz sparkle to Labour's 2002 conference, here with Tony and Cherie Blair and Bill Clinton.
(*Below*) The former US president and his actor friend later enjoyed a night out in Blackpool's McDonald's.
(*Right*) Tony Blair with weapons inspector Hans Blix.

(*Left*) Carole Caplin and Peter Foster, the Australian fraudster who sparked a crisis over two flats bought by Cherie Blair, and strained relations further between the Blairs, AC and his partner Fiona Millar (*below*, with Cherie Blair).

(*Right*) Strategists together: Peter Mandelson, Philip Gould and Campbell at a meeting with the German ambassador.

Me and my shadow: (*above*) Campbell and Blair in a lift in Brussels, before a very difficult conversation over Iraq with Jacques Chirac (*left*). And another difficult conversation, this time with President Putin (*below*).

person I had phoned on seeing the *Mirror* was Fiona, so it must have been one of the handful of people in the office.

I spent part of the day finishing the letter to the PCC. I had sensed from the earlier conversations with Clare that maybe Black Rod was playing games here. She called him again and had the exact same feeling. He told Clare he felt we were just keeping it going, that it was a mistake, and he clearly didn't want it to go to the PCC. As far as TB was concerned, even if someone had said it, it was one hundred per cent wrong and if the PCC couldn't deal with something like this, what on earth was it for? I also had another chat with TB re Gordon. He felt there was a real problem of temperament. He felt it may just be the case that he's a great Chancellor but that doesn't necessarily mean he could do the job of prime minister.

TB had clearly taken to heart our strictures about him needing to do more spontaneous stuff with people. I was talking to Jonathan in the private office. The door opens, TB comes out and says 'Hey, this guy doing the marathon in a diving suit, he's about to finish.[1] Shouldn't I go there, or get him in for a cup of tea or something?' Peter Hyman fell about at this sudden conversion.

Saturday, April 20

The Times page 1 and the *Mirror* splash were on me supposedly playing cupid between Sven and Ulrika. Talk about being in a fucking soap. I spent the morning working on a note for TB who was doing *Frost* tomorrow, on the need to get back into big message and the big promises kept, notably stability, jobs, constitutional programme, the specific tax pledges. I wrote it in the car on the way to Stamford Bridge [Chelsea football ground]. Philip had spooked me a bit, saying that after the Budget GB had definitely moved up a few notches at TB's expense, and we had to get the focus back on TB being the guy leading the big driving agenda. We met Alex before the Chelsea–Man U match [0–3], he and just about everyone passing by mercilessly taking the piss re Sven and Ulrika. Thank God he got us tickets with the fans because then I discovered Sven and Ulrika were both there, separately.

Sunday, April 21

The *Mail on Sunday* ran something about GB being against a full-scale war in Iraq, followed up by the *Mirror* despite GB office denials. [Sir

---

1 Lloyd Scott completed the London Marathon route in five days and eight hours, wearing a deep sea diving suit weighing 110 lb. He and Blair would appear on *Breakfast with Frost* on April 21, though not together.

David] Frost wasn't on form, TB didn't really get going but it was OK as a post-Budget message interview.

Sven was massive in the tabloids but thankfully I was fading out of the story. Sunday's coverage on the Budget wasn't as bad as I thought it might be, though there was a bit too much 'GB the Colossus'. Calum and I set off for Burnley vs Coventry [1–0], on the phone most of the time.

As we drove home, Jonathan called. John Holmes [UK ambassador to France, former foreign policy adviser to Blair] had been on, saying it was [Jean-Marie] Le Pen [National Front candidate] second and [Lionel] Jospin third in the French elections [determining a run-off election between Le Pen and Chirac]. Political earthquake time. I chatted to John Holmes about how we should react and then briefed Jon Sopel [BBC] who was covering it, to make sure he got over the message that it was unlikely for the hard right to rise like this here because we did take crime and other issues on the respect agenda seriously. TB felt we should stay out of it as far as possible but there were definitely going to be spillover problems from this.

Monday, April 22

TB's interview came out OK but Le Pen was dominant. TB's worry was that it gave the BNP [far right British National Party] a boost by allowing them to be seen as the British equivalent of Le Pen. Sven/ Ulrika was still massive and Sven did a press conference, pretty Zen-like, refusing to say much, did OK, but I guess it all depended what was happening behind closed doors both with him and Nancy, and him and the FA. Melanie told me it was real love as far as Ulrika was concerned. The PCC situation was dragging on. Jeremy sent my letter to Janvrin who was happy to say that the *Mail on Sunday* story as it referred to the Queen was rubbish. TB was due to do an interview with the *Guardian* tomorrow, focused on more personal stuff. He showed we were still able to have a laugh. As when he said he thought he'd say that the people he really related to now after a few years in the job were the Royal Family, that Prince Charles was really his kind of guy, and that both of them were much misunderstood and took great solace from each other. 'Think that should satisfy the *Guardian*, now what's next?'

Tuesday, April 23

Some of the right wing were trying to present the Le Pen outcome as a sign of the left across Europe under attack. But there was a general understanding that New Labour was different and that we had taken the right course on crime and immigration. With so much focus on Europe now, because of the French elections, there was also an opportunity in the fact that e.g. the Dutch and the Germans were desperate for a TB-type figure. I finished the PCC draft that Clare [Sumner] took to see Black Rod at 2. She came back and said he had said to her that there had been other calls, suggested there was something to it and he had had no problems with the *Mail on Sunday* story where it referred to him. We were clear that the only calls had been from Clare and Simon and that Jeremy had dealt with Janvrin. Godric was asked about it at the four o'clock so having got the draft statement to Guy Black (who by 4 knew that Black Rod had seen Number 10), put out a line that we were lodging the complaint. There was a line developing that this was the Establishment against us. Yet we had cleared the whole thing with the Palace.

The morning meeting was mainly a discussion of the BNP. I spoke to Charles Clarke who was visiting Burnley and felt they might win one seat on the council and wanted TB to stick to his Blackburn programme. The PCC story took off on the *Ten O'Clock News*. TB watched it, for once, and said we seemed to have lit the blue touch-paper and we had better win this. He still thought it was the right thing to do, but thought Black Rod was going to be a real problem. [Peter] Oborne was moving the goalposts to this being about us and the press rather than the facts of what happened. I had a meeting on Iraq with John Scarlett, Tom McKane [Cabinet Office] and Martin Howard [MoD] to go through what we needed to do communications-wise to set the scene for Iraq, e.g. a WMD paper and other papers about Saddam. Scarlett a very good bloke.

Wednesday, April 24

The PCC stuff was running straight. Guy Black called to say he thought my statement was masterful, that he felt we had a strong case anyway but it was even stronger when it was laid out like that. I met with Jeremy, Jonathan and Martin Hurst [Number 10 adviser on agriculture] re the FMD [Foot and Mouth Disease: Lessons Learned] inquiry to get me ready for when I gave evidence. Re PMQs, I was worried about people going for us on David Blunkett talking about schools being swamped with asylum seekers' children at schools near reception centres. I thought it was a stupid thing to say and called to say we needed to let the heat out of this, but David was very high horse, said he was not going to apologise and he believed in calling a spade a spade. PMQs went fine, TB setting a new cat among pigeons saying that we would get on top of street crime by September.

Guy Black called again to say he had advised Black Rod not to talk to the press now that it was all under investigation. Back for a meeting, me, Peter M, Philip G and Peter H re TB. Peter M thought our problems were 1. sleaze, so-called; 2. the charge he was hollow; 3. the feeling that he wasn't in charge. I said we had to get back to TB being seen as strong, on people's side, in charge, delivering, the same TB that they elected. PG felt we had to decide what we would do, almost as if it was a leadership election, what were the things we would emphasise, experience, tested in a crisis, rounded, gets people's lives, capable of leading a team. GB had his issues and never tired of hounding them. TB had become too managerial again.

Thursday, April 25

There was quite a good discussion at Cabinet on the Le Pen situation. Robin [Cook] said there had been a genuine miscalculation re the two rounds of voting. Jack said Jospin had fought a terrible campaign. What it showed was that post the collapse of the Berlin Wall, asylum and immigration were big problems for a lot of countries, and governments would get judged on how they handled them. He said there was a lot of racism in France and there was a problem with Muslim youth feeling disconnected. Then, in a very Jackish kind of way, he referred to an article he had written for *The Times* in 1985 in which he said PR [proportional representation] would lead to the rise of Le Pen. John Reid, warming to the anti-PR mood, pointed out that Hitler was elected by PR. TB summed up, saying asylum was a problem to be dealt with, not exploited. People want to know there is a fair system, rules with integrity. He said up to now, EU colleagues had been reluctant on this and we had been something of a lone voice but now they would realise more. GB was at UNISON, and it was noticeable how much lighter the mood was.

To Windsor for the Queen's Golden Jubilee media reception. It was a beautiful evening, about 700 journalists there. Oborne and [Simon] Walters [*Mail on Sunday*] both tried to engage me in conversation but I pushed them off. The general feeling among most of the hacks was that we shouldn't have gone to the PCC but that's because they were self-serving. I had a chat with Janvrin who said he really hoped Black Rod would deliver for us, but he didn't think we should put our house on him. The event was a huge success for the Queen. There was something truly pathetic about these so-called hardened hacks, many of them self-proclaimed republicans, bowing and scraping the whole time. She moved effortlessly between them and left grown men in little puddles of excitement as she moved on to form the next one.

She was such an old pro but there was something mildly sick-making about the way they fell about in front of her.

Friday, April 26

TB did the PEB [party election broadcast] last night in the margins of a visit to Dudley, and today was off to Blackburn [local elections to be held on May 2], allowing me to complain all day that he had never ever been to Burnley. Jack was in his usual Blackburn–Burnley wind-up mode, and sent me a message that the road into Burnley had been blocked by a broken-down banana lorry taking in the food for the natives. The visit went OK without too much focus on the BNP. TB was back mid pm, had enjoyed getting out, and felt the mood out there was better than we thought. Boris Johnson wrote to say would I do a letter next week setting out our position re the lying-in-state, which suggested they were looking for a way out.

Saturday, April 27

Someone had briefed, or possibly the Sundays just picked it up from Mary Ann Sieghart's column in *The Times*, the possibility of child benefit withdrawal from parents with persistent truants who veer towards crime. The problem was that whoever was briefing was doing so by saying it was TB against GB and others. Amazingly, TB had been asked about it when filming for the PEB in Dudley on Thursday, but there was no way it could have been briefed out of that. It was possibly a sensible idea to look at, though at first blush I didn't think so, but in any event there was no point getting it out in a time or in a manner that would send the party neuralgic. Once the papers came in and we basically said it was being looked at, we were facing an ill-discipline problem – ill discipline of those who briefed it with a particular slant, then the ill discipline of not standing up for it properly so that in the end it looked like a gimmick.

Sunday, April 28

JP was doing interviews and I briefed him to hold firm on the child benefit issue, but he was clearly uncomfortable and didn't. GB called TB and complained both about the policy but also, and this made me suspicious, said that it was being deliberately fuelled to do him in, totally overlooking the fact that it had been pitched as a hit on TB. Jeremy, listening in, said it was a truly dreadful call. Even when TB said he wasn't prepared to put up with this any longer, GB was unmoved, kept at him. TB was also struck by something Charlie Falconer had said, namely that Balls had briefed DTLR officials to bid over the odds on housing because 'Number 10 are not interested in housing'. It was beginning to feel a bit too warlike. During the day I briefed variously TB, JP and Estelle [Morris] who would all be expected in their various media appearances to say something on the child benefit row. Estelle was fine, JP wasn't. TB was angry and frustrated, said it only became a problem when we sounded like we were in retreat. GB was currently working on Cabinet, party, press, the voluntary sector, the lot, just getting himself in a slightly different position.

Monday, April 29

Child benefit story was still raging on, with lots of split-ery around the place. The take generally was that the Cabinet was against it. TB was a bit head-in-hands mode. We put it round that the story was clearly put there by someone who wanted to kill the policy, which was probably true. I suspected GB's people were responsible for the *FT* story saying that [Rupert] Murdoch would be shafted by the media ownership bill. So I called Les Hinton simply to say don't believe everything you read in the papers.

TB's big concern re the GB situation was the feeling that ministers were unsure what their instincts were meant to be, because though we were the present, they realised GB was the future. TB needed to be clear that they were answerable to him. I said there was a case for sacking one or two Brownite ministers like Nick Brown [minister for work], tell them it was unfair but it was needed to shake things up a bit. He was more up for it than I thought he would be. I told the morning meeting that the real story here was not [child benefit] policy but ill discipline. TB intended to go up and defend it big time on his local election visit, which is exactly what he did.

I had a few meetings then up to 9 Whitehall to give evidence to the FMD inquiry. Quite tough, and maybe I didn't prepare enough for it. I gave them a paper on the media and how hard it had been to put over what we were trying to do. He [Dr Iain Anderson, chairman] clearly felt that we had ballsed the first stages and never really got over it. He suggested that maybe in future we should bring journalists in as part of our team, which was an interesting idea.

Back to get changed for the Number 10 dinner for the Queen, which was being attended by all her PMs or, in the case of those who'd died, by family reps. Terry O'Neill [photographer] in to do pictures. Ted Heath [former Conservative Prime Minister] complaining about the seating plan. A bit of a problem re Stockton [the 2nd Earl Stockton, former Conservative Prime Minister Harold Macmillan's grandson] taking the place of Macmillan's daughter [Lady Caroline Faber]. But it went well enough, nice pictures of her with all her surviving prime ministers which we got out by 8.45. TB's kids were downstairs to meet her when she arrived then up for drinks. The Queen said 'Isn't it wonderful not to have to be introduced to anyone?' [John] Major and I had a very civilised conversation, re Chelsea, cricket, small talk. But there was always a tension there and Norma [Major] was very distant. Thatcher was complaining loudly about the decor and the paintings, how some of the carpets and furnishings looked worn, and the colours in the Green Room weren't properly co-ordinated, tut-tutting, not exactly saying 'wouldn't have happened in my day' but not far off it.

The Queen, the PMs and their descendants went into the State Dining Room whilst Robin Janvrin, Jeremy, Fiona and I had a very nice dinner in the White Room. Robin was a thoroughly decent bloke. There was another drinks do at the end and I had a long chat with Mary Wilson and Robin [widow and son of Harold Wilson]. At one point Ted [Heath] was sitting on one sofa, Jim [Callaghan] on another, just having an old man to old man conversation about how things used to be. Ted could barely bring himself to look at Thatcher but she teased him a bit, tried to make him laugh, without any apparent success. Prince Philip was deep in conversation with TB, the Countess of Avon [widow of former Conservative Prime Minister Anthony Eden], Macmillan's and [former Conservative Prime Minister Alec] Douglas-Home's families, and there was lots of reminiscing about life in Number 10. It was interesting to see the difference between the Queen's demeanour at the do at Windsor, when she had been doing her professional small-talk thing, and here, where she seemed genuinely happy.

I said to Fiona that nobody else had really had the kind of access and contact that she had had and yet while everybody thought they knew what she thought of them, nobody could be sure. But I don't think I've ever seen her smiling so much. TB occupied pretty much a back seat, wanted the others to be talking to her and enjoying it. I also knew he was worrying about the question he had asked earlier, whether he had already ceded too much power to GB, and whether it was too late to get it back.

Tuesday, April 30

The *Mirror* splashed on a poll, figures bent and twisted against TB. He was almost minded to scrap the interview with them but we went ahead and it was OK, Brian Reade [columnist] basically onside but there was little point dealing with Piers at the moment. I called Byers who said there was an agreed statement going out today effectively exonerating Sixsmith. He had delegated to mediators and the lawyers had totally caved in. We got RW to stop it going out today because it would look like we were burying it under the Queen's address to both Houses of Parliament. I couldn't believe this was still dragging on.

We had a long-term diary meeting based on the plan Peter H, Philip and I had put together. They all basically disagreed with it and it turned ugly and I said I was fed up with being surrounded by commentators who were great at criticising other ideas but didn't deliver their own. Then to a meeting with GB and the Eds [Balls and Miliband], which was better than usual because TB was much firmer. There was a big disagreement though, TB and I strongly believing we had not only to deal with crime and antisocial behaviour, but be seen to deal with it because in part the signals you sent out were important actually to dealing with it. Their basic take was that to talk about crime was to alarm the public that it wasn't being dealt with. Ed Balls felt we had lost the 'causes of crime' part of the argument. TB said that we always had to do both. GB thought the Tory strategy was to say they were moving to the centre now but they would become more right wing later. TB not sure, though at least on that there was a civilised and sensible discussion.

Sixsmith was clearly threatening to go to the press if things were held up any longer. TB kept going on about how incompetently it all had been handled. Godric was more wound up than ever. I told Richard W we were fed up having to cover up the incompetence of people who should have sorted this out. He looked really hurt, said the senior Civil Service really tried to work with us. I said a lot of them used the SpAd issue to hide behind. He got really angry at that, said that he was happy to resign if we thought it would make it better. I said nobody was talking about that, or even thinking about it. I calmed down a bit, said I was sorry that he and I had ended up shouting at each other. The truth was with the combination of the *Mirror*, the whingeing at the diary meeting, still having to deal with Byers and the ludicrous discussion with GB about crime, I had just about had enough.

Wednesday, May 1

I was in a foul mood with everyone. The *Mirror* interview was fine but there was a big factual error about TB's kids which we got a correction for. I spent most of the day locked away, and most people knew to avoid me. Yesterday's diary meeting sparked a flurry of emails, Sally M and Robert [Hill] in particular feeling I had just dumped a long-term plan on them without consultation and was trying to bounce them. It was more that I was just trying to get some proper direction and movement and was fed up of the endless circular conversations without agreement. Creativity was dead, had been for some time, and there had to be change.

Thursday, May 2

Up to see TB. He said the row he had had with GB at the weekend was as bad as it got. He was effectively fighting a campaign of attrition, wants me out and thinks he has to wear me out to get me out. In the end 'I'm quite stubborn.' He said he had called back to apologise and GB had been nicer since. I said that's how he works. It's the banging-head-against-wall theory. He forces you to lose your rag, you feel bad, he feels a bit more empowered. Interestingly, though, the undertone for a lot of the five-year coverage was that GB might not be rounded enough for the top job. Things would be so much better if they could work together. GB had been a bit better but when I bumped into him this morning getting a coffee pre Cabinet it was the usual total non-communicado.

Cabinet was mainly Middle East and Afghanistan. Charles C was looking for reassurance on his recent whacks on the media. I advised he keep going, but get himself some cover by making clear there was a lot of good amid the bad, and engage other ministers on it too. Then we got ourselves into a bit of a mess re changes to the lobby. I had floated the idea at the meeting with the BBC and then Tom Baldwin called to tell Godric that Simon Walters was planning to present it as a great attack on the media, so I decided to go upfront on it now. I called James Hardy [*Mirror* political editor], the chairman of the lobby, and suggested he get together a group of people to do a meeting with me, Godric and Tom [Kelly]. I told them we were going to change things. TB would be doing more in Parliament. He and other ministers would be doing far more press conferences and on days they did, we would cut down on lobby briefings. We also intended to open the briefings to others, including more foreign media. They were suspicious but some, like Patrick Wintour [*Guardian*] and to a lesser extent Trevor Kavanagh [*Sun* political editor], seemed OK on it.

Meanwhile Andy Marr [BBC] had been on broadcasting that we were scrapping the lobby which put them all into a total tizz, and they were disappearing into real media wank. They couldn't quite work it out. The meeting went on for about an hour, some genuine concerns, which we could work out, few real complaints but by and large I think it was OK. I called JP to talk it through, he having earlier complained to me that we didn't seem to be in touch as often as we used to be, when changes were happening. TB called later from Ireland and asked if I had sparked a meltdown. I left early for Calum's parents evening. Tom and Godric were having to deal with the immediate fallout and Godric was a bit stressed out that the briefings would if anything become even tougher in the short term. Our aim had to be to make the briefings themselves less newsworthy and also extend the range of people there. Ludicrously, it was the second item on the *Ten O'Clock News*.

The local election results started coming in and it was clear we were not going to do as badly as some of the predictions.[1] But the BNP won three seats in Burnley, including in a beautiful leafy village, so that was going to take a lot of the attention, and was pretty grim. Most people seemed to think though that the big picture was us OK, Lib Dems OK, Tories pretty poor, plus embarrassment over elected mayors re the monkey in Hartlepool and Robocop in Middlesbrough.[2] Good news in that turnout was better than expected where there was full postal voting.

Friday, May 3

RW came to see me, said was I sure I knew what I was taking on with the changes to the lobby? He said lots of people had tried this. The scale of the coverage on it was ludicrous, a further sign of their self-obsession and their obsession with me, which in part was what we were trying to address. Once we talked it through, he was pretty supportive, and said he would help to find premises so that we could do the bigger briefings with the foreign media included, and any other accredited journalists who wanted to turn up. JP called, said that he had premises in his office, in the room that used to be [former Conservative Prime Minster Winston] Churchill's cinema. The general feeling on the local elections was pretty good for us. TB was at Chequers, pretty chipper. We were under pressure on elected mayors, farce thereof, but TB was adamant we just hold firm.

[Bill] Clinton called me at 1am to go through some changes in the article he was doing for us re all the attacks on TB. He didn't want

[1] Labour: 2,402 council seats and control of sixty-three councils. Conservatives: 2,005 council seats and forty-two councils. Liberal Democrats: 1,263 council seats and fifteen councils.
[2] Stuart Drummond, who played the local football club's mascot monkey, was elected mayor of Hartlepool, while former 'zero tolerance' chief superintendent of Cleveland Police, Ray Mallon, won the mayoralty in Middlesbrough.

to attack the motives of our critics, just attack the attacks. It was a good piece though, and worth the effort. He was always good to talk to, because he had such a good feel for our politics, and for how best to position TB. He felt we were just going through one of those phases where people wanted to see us tested and pressured and coming through. TB must have said something, or his instincts told him something, about me going a bit offside, because he said that in these top jobs like president and prime minister, you really need people close by that you can trust and rely on one hundred per cent. He said it was important that I hung in and kept helping TB through.

Saturday, May 4
I chatted to a few columnists and the general take was that a combination of the local elections and people taking stock in a measured way five years on was pretty good for us, bad for the Tories. The conference call was mainly Middle East and the lead-up to the French election second round. Papers arrived.

Sunday, May 5
French elections were dominating the news and it was pretty clear as the results came through that Chirac had won. We put together a line fairly straightforwardly and got that out. I had a nice day out with the kids, tennis with Calum. Went to see *About a Boy* [film], lunch, then Rory won his race.

Monday, May 6
Bank Holiday. Pretty quiet until later with news of [right-wing Dutch politician] Pim Fortuyn's assassination [in Hilversum, Netherlands]. Conference call with TB, Jonathan, [Sir] Stephen Wall [EU adviser]. We agreed to cancel the planned visit tomorrow and put out a short statement. We were already getting a bit alarmed by all the focus post elections on the politics of the far right, and this wasn't going to help.

Tuesday, May 7
Up to see TB in the flat. He was clearly thinking about bringing back [Ken] Livingstone [into the Labour Party]. Also wanting to get back into the antisocial behaviour agenda. TB set off for Scotland for the Donald Dewar [former First Minister of Scotland] memorial event. The Sixsmith pay-off deal was an absolute outrage – big pay-off, Byers in deep shit. I did an interview with [Tom] Baldwin for *The Times* re our relations with the press.

Wednesday, May 8

Massive suicide bomb in Israel. TB said the problem now was that Israelis were stating as a fact that [Yasser] Arafat was behind the latest bombings and even though there was no direct evidence it was very difficult to counter and it would push the US into a much harder-line position. We spent some time working on the right response. TB wanted to keep the balance but felt that basically we had to tilt towards pro-Palestinian. He was really worried about the impact in the States – another bomb, another massacre, [Ariel] Sharon back from the US successfully able to make it look like it was impossible to negotiate with Arafat.

Thursday, May 9

The *Times* interview went quite big and got too much pick-up in later editions and on the broadcasts. I was a bit concerned about the stuff at the end re not being sure about staying. TB called me at 7.10. Said he felt that Byers was pretty shot. He said he was going to give him a chance to step down of his own volition before a reshuffle which he planned for the next few weeks but wanted total radio silence for now. He felt it was monstrous the way Steve had been treated internally but ultimately ministers have to be responsible for their own departments, and he would have to go fairly soon. TB said GB had asked him if it was true that I was going to leave and TB had said no. I said his boorishness yesterday, not just with me but with Vera [Doyle, Number 10 messenger] when she was trying to pour him coffee, was Olympian.

TB took a strategy meeting with the internal team to go through the big strategic overview paper I'd done. It had caused a lot of anger, people feeling I'd bounced it on them, but Peter M was totally supportive, which was important, and would help with TB. TB's meeting with JP didn't get off to a great start. As we walked in, TB didn't realise JP was right behind us as he said to me 'What on earth are we going to talk about in here?' JP was pressing him on the need for greater involvement of Cabinet committees. Cabinet was largely a row about select committees, and Clare going on about every issue she could think of. Later meeting of [departmental] heads of information to go over the lobby changes, which was more productive than usual. TB off on a visit to South London and back for a visit to Number 10 by Sven, [David] Beckham, Gareth Southgate, David Seaman [England footballers] and the suits from the FA plus some kids from Southwark. Big media turnout in the street with kids having a great time though CB was monopolising Beckham, or possibly vice versa.

May '02: GB asks if AC is leaving

Friday, May 10

TB at Chequers working through a stack of boxes. Called a couple of times to discuss German TV and *Newsnight* [BBC] interviews planned for next week. I was putting together a series of briefs re *Newsnight* when news came in of a bad train crash at Potters Bar. The early indication was that it was a points failure, seven dead. TB wanted us to rebut some of the coverage of last night's David Beckham event, and in particular the widespread regurgitation of the story of him claiming to have seen [former Newcastle United footballer] Jackie Milburn, which was one of those annoying urban myths.

Saturday, May 11

We were dealing with the train crash aftermath, then up pops another sleaze situation. This time re [Richard] Desmond offering free ads, which we then said should be a financial donation which we could use to buy the ads. The claim was that this was all agreed at a meeting of me, TB, Margaret McDonagh [former Labour general secretary] and Desmond. One thing we knew for sure was that no such meeting ever took place. But it was the usual Saturday problem of getting all the facts together. The direct allegation seemed to be that the donation was made as some kind of thank you for nodding through the *Express* takeover. In fact, there was no need for ministerial reference because the OFT [Office of Fair Trading] would do it and he had no other newspaper interests so reference up didn't apply. But it was one of those stories that whatever the facts would be made to look bad. I spoke to Desmond who confirmed he had never discussed funding with TB.

The Express group put out a statement confirming a donation but it fell in the period before the Electoral Commission rules on disclosure came in. The *Mail*, *Observer*, *Sunday Times* all going big, so needless to say the BBC followed it up big. We got John Reid straight on to Radio 5 as the papers dropped and he was excellent. Another Saturday taken up dealing with nonsense. These funding stories were actually born of the fact we were more open, but got no credit for it at all. This one was not a scandal at all but they could make anything look like a scandal. I was really impressed with Reid today. He could assimilate facts quickly, get the point quickly, and express it on the media having thought it through rather than simply parroting a line.

Sunday, May 12

The fightback re [Richard] Desmond had gone OK. We had success-fully shut down the allegations re a meeting. So it was basically a question of whether we should take money from someone who made money from pornography and the Beeb found a few MPs, after a lot of trying, to say no it wasn't. Gerald Kaufman called to say he had been asked for his view and as soon as he made clear he didn't intend to be critical, they made clear they didn't want him on. I called Desmond from Northolt. 'I wouldn't have your job for all the money in the world,' he said. I was a bit pissed off that so much of this was again focusing on me, because I was a so-called 'friend' of Desmond's when all I had done was go to his birthday party because TB couldn't. The *Mail* of course had two interests here, do us in and do him in.

On the flight to Germany, we went over the interview TB was to do with Sabine Christiansen [German television talk-show host], which Schroeder had asked him to do, but which had the feel of something a bit eccentric. On arrival, we went to meet Schroeder. He looked tired, said that he was doing OK but his party was not and it was tough to change it. He and TB went out for a quick chat on the balcony and then back in for the broader meeting – Europe, world economy, Afghanistan, Middle East, on which Schroeder said 'You know more than I do,' and TB said 'What I know is that it's bad.' He said he was trying to persuade the US to keep on engaging. They both agreed nothing could happen without the Americans, but their opinion was in a very different position to ours. Democrats as well as Republicans are lined up behind [Ariel] Sharon so Bush was in quite a difficult position. Schroeder said the Jewish people in Germany tended to present any criticism of Israel as anti-Semitism, which was a dangerous route. He said they were fairly lucky in avoiding a big debate about right-wing extremism in their election, 'which given our history is a good thing'.

We had a long and pretty tedious session with bureau chiefs and then the Christiansen show. The German translation was played over speakers above the audience's heads as TB spoke so it became quite hard for him, but he did pretty well. We flew back late in one of the smaller RAF planes, wondering whether the visit had been worth the effort. What was absolutely clear was that the Europeans saw TB as the number one star of European politics at the moment.

Monday, May 13
Spoke to [Richard] Desmond again. He said he had paid 'only' £75k for the Beckham party [publishing rights]. Some of our MPs were going on about him not being a fit person. Godric was feeling pretty jaded at the moment as well and was needing more than usual support. I

decided we should not do a four o'clock, which produced the expected tantrums. Fuck 'em. Desmond still running as a big negative for us.

Tuesday, May 14

Sally M sent a note to TB of a conversation with Frank Dobson, who was seriously offside. He said our current difficulties were being made worse because 'TB and AC have lost the plot'. The main news running today was the three new asylum centres, with lots of attendant nimbyism ['not-in-my-backyard']. Media-wise, our main focus was the extended *Newsnight* interview which he had agreed to do as part of our strategy of doing more sustained and serious interviews, which *Newsnight* have agreed to run over three nights. TB looked pretty knackered first thing, then had [Thabo] Mbeki at 7.30, [Jean] Chrétien [Canadian Prime Minister] at 8.30, before we got down to briefing for the interview. He was sure [Jeremy] Paxman [interviewer] would want to do lots on [Richard] Desmond, but they pretty much stuck to the deal – three sections, public services, foreign policy, society and belief. Paxman was tough but fair and TB held his own. As an exercise, it definitely worked. TB said he thought it was odd that Paxman was always lumped in with [John] Humphrys [BBC *Today* programme presenter]. He thought the big difference was that Paxman was actually interested in the answers.

Wednesday, May 15

The general view of *Newsnight* was that it was a strong interview. Good coverage. We thought the Tories might come on [Richard] Desmond at PMQs, but IDS did NHS and crime and TB was able to hit him hard on investment. TB was OK, though he didn't think it was one of his best. Also, Robin [Cook] seemed to be asleep on the front bench. I had a meeting with the whips and went through the lobby changes, the determination to do more in Parliament and the need for them to be fully engaged in what we were doing re message and strategic communications. Charles C was also focused on the need to work up a 'new politics plan' basically an end to top-down command and control message work, more about how we develop MPs as local ambassadors, and how we make a link between politics and liveability issues. Charles was really enthusiastic, really wanted to motor. I was in favour but worried that a lot of the MPs wouldn't be as enthusiastic as he was.

Thursday, May 16

Newsnight getting lots of coverage, euro the lead in several papers, big coverage in the Middle East for what he said about that. There was a bit of a flurry when the BBC put out the transcript of the stuff being broadcast tonight which seemed to show he was saying he would stay for a full third term, which he actually hadn't meant that way. Cabinet, without JP, and also without Clare, which in her case made a big difference for the better. Nepal, Dutch elections, rail, bits and bobs. The *New Statesman* had a line claiming Charles C and David Triesman wanted an inquiry into the Desmond donation.

Guy Black called through the morning and said there was a snag. He came to see me at 1.30. He had been to see Black Rod and asked him for a draft of what he would say. He said he would prefer it if nobody knew that he had been to see me, and he showed me the draft statement. It was dreadful. It backed the *Mail on Sunday* story. Guy said 'We have to stop that letter going to the PCC.' I think Guy was trying to be helpful. I said all I wanted was acknowledgement that TB had done nothing wrong or disrespectful. Then came news Byers had done a lunch with the women's lobby [of parliamentary journalists] and talked about a paving bill [allowing for further reforms in the next parliament] on the euro being planned and saying fifty-one per cent was enough in a referendum. He was wrong on the paving bill and I'm afraid we had to say he was plain wrong. What a prattish thing to do, as if he didn't have enough problems. Phil Webster [*Times*] called to say the Tories were putting it around that Byers was about to be sacked, so we had to deal with that, say it wasn't the case.

Friday, May 17

Up very early, in to meet Robert Thomson [*Times* editor] and Bronwen Maddox [*Times* foreign editor] who were coming to Spain with us to do a TB interview. Re Byers, in the car out to the plane, TB said Steve was becoming accident-prone and would probably have to go. I said what about splitting the department, as we had discussed before, and leaving him with one part of it. TB shook his head. The *Newsnight* interview was still producing positive coverage elsewhere, though the Beeb had 'accidentally' sent the full tape to the *Telegraph*, including at the start where I interrupted TB and got them to refilm which unleashed the latest storm of bollocks. It was interesting spending the day with Robert Thomson, who was not really immersed in the UK media culture. The interview was serious and fair, whereas most interviews these days are purely designed to get a story. He struck me as being a quirky but decent character. We were in Spain purely as a favour to Aznar who had really wanted TB to go to the EU–Latin America summit. While he went off to that, I went with Robert and Bronwen to a cafe in Madrid. I don't think he was clear yet what he

May '02: Snag with PCC complaint

wanted to do for the paper, but he was definitely an interesting addition to the media scene.

Saturday, May 18

Very depressed. One of my major glooms. Went for a run but lost the will after half an hour and came back. Work-wise, trying to get Aznar meeting on Monday focused on asylum rather than Gibraltar [sovereignty]. I never felt less like working.

Sunday, May 19

The *Sunday Telegraph* splash said GB was supporting TB's push for an early [euro] referendum, which they went into overdrive to rubbish, prompting me to wonder if they had set the whole thing up. Some of the papers got hold of John Birt's [former BBC director general, now Blair's 'blue skies thinking' adviser] report suggesting massive new toll roads which ran. I took Rory to Basildon where he was racing and had a long run myself round the town centre and some of the estates. I went into a shop to buy some water and the guy behind the counter said he couldn't believe I was in there, at which point TB rang and I got him to speak to the shopkeeper, who practically fainted. I said you now have to promise me you'll vote Labour for the rest of your life. He said he would. Rory ran well, won the 800 metres, second in the 1,500. The news was dominated by Afghanistan and another suicide bomb in Israel. The Sundays had loads of *Newsnight* follow-through and though they were contaminated by the thing about me interrupting TB, the overall impression was good. JP called from China to agree a statement confirming he had diabetes, which the *Mail on Sunday* had run.

Monday, May 20

We were hoping to get the Aznar focus on asylum, along the lines of the letter Stephen Wall had done for TB on the need for the Seville summit to address the issues. But Gibraltar was running pretty hard. Charles C seemed very het up at the office meeting. He tended to go from being superconfident, quite strategic and clear one day, to being a bit hyper and all over the place the next. TB was emphasising that all that mattered was policy, making the right decisions for the longer term. Aznar arrived for lunch, first just re Gibraltar, which was really difficult and on which zero progress was made. Jack S had said on the radio that if the Gibraltarians rejected a deal that would be the end of it, which the Spaniards felt was a shift. They were very suspicious, a bit paranoid, and so didn't really accept the truth, which was that it was a bit of a cock-up. Aznar was fine at the lunch, said he was over for a speech at Oxford and said he intended to say that there should be a president of the European Council, elected by the members of the council, who should be a former PM. 'That's why I'm putting you forward,' he said to TB, who replied 'I'm putting you forward as well.' A short press conference, half Gibraltar, half asylum and off they went. Meeting with Mark Bennett [Labour press officer], trying to get him in for a while to help out.

Tuesday, May 21

The CBI speech was in OK shape but he wanted to do a lot of it from notes, so all I did was draft a few clips and put together a release based on extracts. The best line was probably the straight passionate defence of the Budget, especially as we heard Iain Vallance [CBI president] was intending to go for the Budget tax rises and say we were on a yellow card re the economy. Stupidly, despite having an enormous blister on my foot, I ran in and later in the day was unable to walk. IDS was making a speech on equality and opportunity and how he would stand up for the poor and vulnerable so I got Fraser Kemp [Labour MP] out motoring re his kids going to Eton.

I spoke to Guy Black and then sent over the latest letters on the case. Charlie Falconer's view was that if Black Rod was being this difficult we should just get out of it. We now just have to get shot of the whole thing. I went to the Gay Hussar [Soho restaurant favoured by politicians and journalists] with Fiona and Fraser Kemp and had a very nice lunch at which I was being drawn for a cartoon to go in a book of cartoons of regular Gay Hussar customers. Martin Rowson's cartoon was pretty good, though I looked alarmingly like Jeremy Paxman. He had Fraser peeping out of the corner of the page. I got back for a series of meetings, including the main TB/GB strategy meeting. GB and the two Eds arrived late, walked in surly and it was as bad as it gets.

They seemed genuinely to think that the more we talked about crime, the worse it was politically. TB was convinced, and I was sure he was right, that we had to be seen to address crime, antisocial behaviour, respect, order, the basic-values issues that flowed from them. He said to GB that he had a point but he was totally exaggerating it. Of course we shouldn't be going on about crime the whole time but it was ridiculous to say that we shouldn't talk about it. People have to know that we get it. GB said it was far better to do things first, do them properly, then say they had been done, rather than announce what we were going to do, then do it, then have everyone say it wasn't working. He was obviously referring to the child benefit situation. But it was a totally unrealistic approach.

The combination of TB's lack of focus, GB's combination of sulking and aggression, Ed Balls' near contempt for TB, my and Philip's near exasperation at the whole thing made it a particularly bad meeting. You would also have thought we were in an election campaign. GB said why are we fighting the election on crime? Sally M pointed out we weren't fighting an election at all. TB said don't see it as crime, see it as respect, community, values. I asked GB to explain what he meant by doing things without getting coverage for them. He gave me the death stare, said nothing. I said you got up a big message on the economy by making difficult decisions, announcing them, arguing for them, then seeing the benefits through. We had to do the same in every other area. He said the economy was different. I said we had a big agenda on public services and on the state of society, and they required a similar political strategy. TB was pretty gloomy as the meeting ended and he set off for the CBI. The speech was strong and went down fine.[1]

Wednesday, May 22

Not much out of the CBI speech, mainly TB vs Vallance et al. The *Mail* really getting stuck in re Carole [Caplin] as personal trainer to CB, TB etc. Party funding went as well as it could, though [David] Triesman wasn't too great when asked about [Richard] Desmond, who would now get a bit jumpy. My foot was now in a really bad way. Alison [Blackshaw, AC's PA] suggested the NHS walk-in centre at Soho which was absolutely brilliant. Another Labour success. They drained off some pretty ghastly looking liquid inside the blister, patched it up and I could walk pretty well straight away. I had a nice chat with the nurses who showed me round. Fantastic facility. Back for a PMQs meeting, not clear what IDS would do but we were set for possibly TB's worst ever with a real cock-up when he got a factual answer wrong re which department was responsible for elections and referenda. Fall-about time for the Tories, though it wouldn't get through to the public much.[2]

---

[1] In a speech reported as Blair taking on business critics, he told the CBI dinner 'Nobody likes paying taxes. Even after the Budget we remain a relatively low-taxed economy and one of the best of the world to do business. But I was elected to fix our public services, schools and hospitals first, and that is what I intend to do.'
[2] Asked by Iain Duncan Smith which Cabinet minister was responsible for referenda, Blair indicated the Home Secretary. However, responsibility for referenda had been passed from the Home Office to Stephen Byers' department (DTLR) a year earlier.

TB had Jonathan, Sally and I in for a chat afterwards, said he didn't really know how to take things forward with GB at the moment. I was now having regular weekly meetings with Peter M, Peter H and Philip, which were useful, proper strategy discussions not always getting sucked down into what was going on day to day. Home via the gym, and TB called, joking about the earlier disaster at PMQs, agreeing that next week if the Tories had any sense, they would turn it into a general knowledge quiz.

He was worried about the way they [the *Mail*] were going for their connections with Carole. He said the problem is you are under such scrutiny that you become a kind of prisoner and you can't actually do a lot of the things you want to. He said I know there are lifestyle issues that are a problem but I can't stop Cherie having a life and there are things I ought to be able to do without everything being an issue for the press. I said maybe, but there are plenty of upsides, e.g. running the country, being involved in all the major decisions affecting the country, the kind of people you meet and the places you go to, people at your beck and call. I was trying to persuade him that we needed to be much more forward thinking about new communications, use of the Internet, direct mail, more genuine interaction. He felt it would take a long time before we were in a position where the press was not setting the agenda for the rest of the media.

Thursday, May 23

Asylum took up a lot of the day, and the French so-called deal re Sangatte [refugee camp] and the *Guardian* getting a leak of the paper written by Olivia McLeod [policy adviser] on 'radical' asylum measures. Everyone assumed Clare Short had been responsible. The story made clear she was opposed to some of the plans, as indeed she later made clear on *Question Time* [BBC TV programme]. Cabinet was mainly Kashmir with a feeling sometimes that we had five Foreign Secretaries – TB, JS, Geoff H, Robin C and Clare. GB as ever saying nothing unless he had to. Afterwards I had a long chat with [Alan] Milburn who felt we had to move to a different sort of political discussion, get definition less according to events than arguments and values. Philip had been to see him and was pretty down about public opinion, trust.

On the way home I had a row with Michael Levy, who, with Charles C's and the party's backing, had decided to do an interview with Rachel Sylvester [*Times*] tomorrow. I said I thought it was a mistake, we had just about managed to park the issue of funding and we should let it lie down. He got very emotional, said he had been put in a box for eight years, done everything asked of him, yet was treated like a leper. I said the Lords was not a conventional home for lepers. He said he was determined to have his say and defend the line that we had to keep on raising funds. I had pretty much the blue mists both with him and with Charles, who also thought he should do it, and my mood got worse watching Short on *Question Time* making clear she wouldn't have taken the [Richard] Desmond money and attacking us over asylum.

Friday, May 24

The SPD [Social Democratic Party] team came in from Germany for a series of meetings with me, Jonathan, PM, PG, SM, RH [Robert Hill], DA. They were similar to us but also very different. They didn't really have a clear strategy or message. When you asked them what it was, a huge great jumble came out, and when you implored them to get the focus on the economy and less on the cultural issues that they seemed drawn to, they sort of said they agreed but I don't think they did. TB joined us at the end of the lunch and when we filled him in on the discussion so far, he said it was obviously, keep the focus on the economy, and in relation to the straight Schroeder vs [Edmund] Stoiber [Chancellor candidate] battle, try not to go too head-to-head and do it almost indirectly and through policy. They seemed a bit beleaguered, also said that because Stoiber was successfully 'hiding' from some policy areas, they couldn't really get the political debate going. I said it was always possible to get the debate going, it's how you frame the debate and then generate the arguments.

Philip got very aggressive, saying it had to be economy first, social second, cultural issues third. It seemed so obvious to us and yet ask them what their strategy was and it was thin, clearly designed for the party, words like innovation and justice, rather than the public. TB was going to have to speak to Schroeder if these were his top campaign people. They wanted TB to go to Germany for two days' campaigning, which would pretty much kill any relationship with Stoiber at birth if he won.

Saturday, May 25

Birthday. Forty-five today. The herald for a weekend of gloom. Feeling really down again. Best thing was that Rory was running in the South of England qualifiers, so he and I went out to Watford. Fiona had bought me a pedometer and I ran for over an hour to get it working. The Roy Keane/Mick McCarthy drama was for some reason really draining me too, even though I knew neither of them well.[1] I felt a real sense of empathy with Keane, felt he was driven but also haunted by demons, depression, violence, an inability to share all the same emotions as everyone seemed to have around the big moments. TB, coincidentally, said he had had friends over for dinner, one of whom asked what I was like. TB said he is the Roy Keane in the operation, driven, doesn't suffer fools, expects everyone to match his own standards, flawed but brilliant.

Sunday, May 26

I ran for an hour then had a heart-to-heart with Fiona, who was finding my depressions harder and harder to deal with, which I completely understood but it didn't exactly help. At the heart of it was probably stuff that had always been there, and also a feeling at the moment that I hated the job but I couldn't work out how much of that was because of the pressure she put me under to leave, and the pressure TB put me under to stay. Charlie [Falconer] called me about the Dome because they were close to a deal that was being presented as giving it away. So another hour trying to help deal with that.

Monday, May 27

Up to see TB early. He had been thinking over the weekend about a reshuffle, perhaps on Wednesday, with Steve [Byers] out. He didn't want a major reshuffle but he knew Steve had to go. There were others he would like to get rid of, notably Clare and Nick Brown, to a lesser extent Robin, but he knew he couldn't, certainly not all at once. He was thinking of AD for transport. TB agreed with me that Steve had been the victim, but he did feel a lot of it was his own fault. But I think we both felt sorry for him where it was ending. He was totally fed up with Clare and intended to see her to make clear she understood she was far from being indispensable. These reshuffles, like pregnancy, dentistry and exams, were further proof that pain has no memory. I didn't know how many we have done now, but until a new one starts, you forget how awful the process is.

First the usual and occasionally random discussion of who could go where. Then the unstructured remembering by different people at different times of reasons why such and such a move was unwise or

---

[1] A public row between Republic of Ireland football captain Keane and manager Mick McCarthy during preparations for the World Cup in Japan resulted in Keane leaving the squad. The Irish team was defeated by Spain in the second round.

even impossible. With each reshuffle also came the realisation that the PM's power and room for manoeuvre is more limited than people might think. In an ideal world, there was no way people like Short, Nick Brown, Michael Meacher [environment minister] would survive. But there were balances to be considered, and you couldn't make all the personnel changes at the same time. We also knew with absolute certainty that today's broadly loyal minister was tomorrow's bitter and backbiting backbencher, their only hope of salvation in their mind turning against the government, giving the impression it was out of principle rather than bitterness. We had seen some already, and there would be more after tomorrow. He was pretty clear he couldn't get rid of Nick Brown. He thought of making him chief secretary [to the Treasury] but it was interesting that GB rarely wanted in his own team the people whose claims he pressed hardest with TB.

Then a couple of quite extraordinary serendipitous moments. JP came in, and TB told him he was thinking of making a few structural changes, and JP said he shouldn't rule out hiving off parts of DTLR. Then Byers came in and said to TB that he wanted to go, if TB felt that was the right thing to do. Steve said he had had enough, and he knew it was the right thing for him. We agreed to separate the Byers announcement from the rest of the reshuffle so that we could genuinely say it was his decision. He was still extraordinarily Zen-like, very calm, only very rare flashes of emotion. He said he passionately believed in what we were trying to do as a government and now felt he was a liability and that was something he didn't want to live with. We chatted with TB for twenty minutes or so and Steve and I walked round to my office to sort the detail. I got Godric in, who was really angry. We agreed the best thing to do would be a short statement to camera in Number 10, which would show he was not being forced out, no questions. I said I was astonished how calm he was. He said politics is a rough trade, but we love it, and I found myself replying 'Do you know, I'm not sure that I do any more.' Yeah, he said, maybe not. He said he had spent so many years working for a Labour government, had been proud of what we had done, but he knew this was the right time to go. He asked me if I thought he should have gone earlier. I said probably, yes. But I was like him, I really didn't want those fuckers to get a scalp. I was worried even now that TB would look weak out of this because in the end it was Steve deciding to go, basically driven out.

We agreed that Milburn and Blunkett should do the rounds for him, speak up for him. What he needed to get out of this was a bit of dignity and self-respect. He went off, and I think the people in the outer office could tell from the body language what was going on. I joined a TB office meeting plus Hilary Armstrong to go over the rest of the reshuffle. I was still pressing for Clare to go, but TB really felt it wasn't possible yet. There was a bit of pressure for Paul Boateng [financial secretary to the Treasury] for chief secretary. Hilary agreed that if he sacked Nick Brown, he was just setting up a rival GB whips operation. We made a bit of progress, and then TB said we should prepare a list to send to him in Rome tomorrow so he could work on it on the flight back, by which time we would be announcing Byers. I saw Michael Levy who said he had been really upset at our conversation the other day, that I'd been thuggish towards him, that nobody ever spoke to him like that. His interview went fine and he would never do anything to harm TB.

Tuesday, May 28

TB left for the NATO summit in Rome, which was genuinely historic on one level but when he called in, it was to tell me inter alia about Berlusconi getting some dolly bird to hand out watches to all the leaders while Chirac made a speech attacking him over his pronouncements that NATO was the key to our defence. We had an internal meeting plus Hilary A to go over the reshuffle options for TB. We persuaded ourselves that [David] Miliband could go straight in as a Minister of State because he was nice enough and popular enough for the inevitable jealousies to be contained. Just how big a twat Sixsmith was became apparent when he appeared at the gates after Steve went, wanting to be let in, saying he was still his director of communications.

Steve was more nervous than I had ever seen him now that the moment was coming, Jan [Cookson, his partner] was fine, relaxed about it, happy even. His mother felt he was doing the wrong thing. With Mark Bennett working at my computer we finished the statement. Steve read through it a few times, kept in 'friends who knew me know I am not a liar and try to behave honourably'. I got the office to call round the media to tell them to come to a briefing without telling them what it was about. We thoroughly enjoyed the spectacle of [Adam] Boulton blathering from Rome for ten minutes about all the things it might be – referendum on the euro, declaration of war, TB illness. Others were speculating it would be me resigning, one or two that he was going back on some of the decisions in the reshuffle.

Nobody mentioned Steve. He was still fairly calm but not quite so Zen-like. I left him for a while to compose his thoughts and he asked for a glass of water. I went back in, asking him if he was ready, then took him up the long route through the basement so that nobody would bump into him. We got to the side door, he took a deep breath, said 'Here goes then', and in he went. He did well, held it together but as he came out he was a bit choked. I took him back to my office where Boulton was still blathering away, now saying it was evidence of how few friends he had that the news didn't leak. What total scum these people are. Couldn't bring himself to admit he hadn't heard a whisper, and all his speculation had been for the birds. We sat around chatting with Hilary Armstrong and Sally M while Mark B tracked down Mike White and Lucy Ward to do the *Guardian* interview. Again, he was pretty good. He seemed happier in himself already. He looked grey as he started but the colour came back as the interview went on. We knew the press would be pretty merciless about both him and TB, but we just had to get through it.

I joined the TB meeting on the reshuffle, the usual agony. JP was worried it would look like he was losing part of his job rather than gaining. Hilary A and Robert Hill said his reputation in local government was not good, but TB saw no way of changing what he had agreed with him. Jeremy gave TB a long list of what JP wanted. Fiona and I went out for dinner at the Mannings' [David and Catherine] but I was in and out the whole time. Estelle [Morris] was worried she was being heaved because she had a call that TB wanted to speak to her first thing. I called David Miliband to tell him to be in London. Milburn called to get briefed on Byers for the *Today* programme. The whole thing was a bit draining and I didn't much enjoy dinner despite David and Catherine being very good hosts, the Master of the Rolls [Lord Phillips] interesting and a Frenchwoman there [Christylle Rouffiac, wife of Lord Phillips] who had a good take on our media culture. At one point I looked out of the window and saw a druggie breaking open a pay and display box where the car was parked.

Wednesday, May 29

The press was vile about Steve. 'Liar for hire' in the *Star*. The *Mirror* was merciless. It's like they get a corpse, but then are disappointed there is nothing left to try and kill, so they kill the dead body too. TB had to get on with the reshuffle. [David] Miliband could scarcely believe he was going to be a minister let alone in charge of schools as Minister of State. Estelle not totally happy and had wanted Margaret Hodge out, but TB resisted on that. He had a number of difficult conversations with GB. TB wanted to move Yvette [Cooper, junior health minister, wife of Ed Balls] but GB was resistant. 'You can't do that. She won't accept it.' To which TB said she would get very short shrift. GB described the LCD [Lord Chancellor's Department], where TB was planning to send her, as a graveyard, which was rubbish. She had also gone AWOL but eventually came through and was clearly expecting a big job. When he told her she said straight out 'What do I have to do to become a Minister of State?' He should have said 'Not talk to me like that for a start', but instead said these reshuffles were very difficult. Doubtless helped by Ed, they were out spinning straight away that she was going to be the minister in charge of referendum administration.

We now had the ever-changing grid of all the ministerial changes, Jonathan trying to keep a grip of the master copy. He started the calls to ministers. He was certainly tougher than in the past, usually saying 'There is no easy way to say this but I need your job to make space for changes. It doesn't mean you haven't done well or can't come back.' Seven sackings in all. We got it all done in time for Tom to do a briefing at 3. Alistair Darling and I had a chat about how to grip his department [Transport], and also how to avoid becoming a pawn between TB and GB. Alistair was pleased TB had entrusted him with a pretty big challenge, said he intended to get on top of the detail, worry more about doing than talking about it. [Paul] Boateng [as chief secretary to the Treasury, becoming the UK's first black Cabinet minister] came in and I warned him against getting trapped by the GB machine.

There was a fair bit of 'blow to GB cronies' around the place, so I got Tom and Godric to call round and get that in a better place. TB and I went upstairs and Peter M was there, playing with Leo. He was clearly annoyed for three reasons – first he was not back in government and nobody had called him to say so. Second, he had been brought back from Korea for another meandering meeting. Third, Douglas [Alexander] was there for the strategy part of the meeting. He was very snappy, ate very little and was the first to leave, though as ever made some sensible and telling contributions amid the histrionics. TB was very solicitous of Douglas, and clearly wanted him to feel he was part of the inner team. He failed to persuade TB that he should do more to deal with some of our negatives, like Parliament, greater interaction. Then another argument about how to deal with the press who were in total kill mode most of the time. TB was looking a bit frail, physically and politically. I ran home around 10.

Thursday, May 30

TB called first thing after reading my note on the PCC which warned him how Black Rod was behaving, and we had to look for a way out of this. He asked me to send all the papers to Derry [Irvine], who quickly came to the view that we should try to get the papers involved to write to me around a deal that we would drop it on the basis they accepted TB had not been involved, which had always been our concern. TB was torn, as was I. On the one hand TB didn't particularly want a great row with a senior official of the House, but nor did he want to back down. I went in to see him first thing to go over the options, then had to leave because I was having breakfast with C at SIS HQ. I liked Richard [Dearlove] a lot. He was witty and engaging, and also had a real strategic understanding on the big foreign policy issues. Kashmir, it was a disaster waiting to happen. He was really worried about the Americans' lack of proper engagement in the Middle East. Lots of small talk re Cornwall, where he had a house, as well as big talk on the foreign policy stuff.

Some of the papers, most adamantly David Yelland at the *Sun*, were saying that Sixsmith was lining himself up to do a deal on his story. Yelland was really steamed up about it, said he held no candle for Byers but he didn't like this. I did a note to RW, Jonathan and Mottram, setting out what was being said, which, if true, would seem to be a breach of the agreement I thought Mottram struck.

TB called a few times from his visit to East Anglia, pretty perked up at the reception he was getting. He was pretty exercised re the PCC. I had a good chat with Douglas. I was very frank re GB, said he had been a nightmare to deal with of late and I was reaching the point where I couldn't be bothered with it. He agreed to be a conduit if it was helpful. On the TB/GB front, he felt it would only work if Philip and I were properly involved. I said I thought the Eds were a problem too because they were constantly pushing GB in a different direction. He said he hoped he could help there too.

Guy Black came in. I went through his various Black Rod meetings. The *Spectator* and the *Mail on Sunday*, post Guy's meeting with Black Rod, had gone from wanting mediation to wanting adjudication. Guy had told him he didn't want to receive his letter. Black Rod said he wanted the truth to come out. As Guy said, it was inconsistent, and a lot of it irrelevant and it would lead to a massive public row. Both RW and Jeremy said they totally believed Clare Sumner on this. I left it with Guy that we would either go to adjudication or settle through an exchange of letters. I had a quick lunch with Andy Marr at Orso's [Italian restaurant, Covent Garden] and back to work on Sixsmith. The cheque was stopped for now though he would almost certainly get his money in the end. Godric was in an absolute rage about it.

Friday, May 31

Start of the World Cup. Mottram had a 10am deadline for paying the cheque to Sixsmith. But on the back of a story in *The Times*, he got counsel's advice that there would appear to be a breach of agreement if the story was true and therefore we had good reason not to pay it. Sixsmith had obviously been told that I was trying to stop the cheque. He started to put stuff out over the weekend about me running a smear campaign against him. I was also trying to work through the PCC situation. Guy Black called and I said I would try to get TB to a position of an agreed exchange of letters. It was going to be messy but the sooner we were out of it the better. TB was in a real fury about it. The idea that Clare [Sumner] would get on to him [Black Rod] and try and get us a bigger role – it just doesn't merit a moment's thought.

Later, TB called to say he had agreed Michael Wills [Labour MP and GB adviser] should be minister in charge of the criminal justice service IT systems! I really couldn't be bothered with it but I eventually spoke to Michael at 6 to agree a line to put out on PA [Press Association], but it transpired that PA didn't think it was a story and then Joe Murphy [*Evening Standard*] got on to it and turned it into a TB/GB row splash.

Saturday, June 1
Dominated by England vs Sweden – good first half, dreadful second half. A short letter came through on the fax from Sixsmith – 'Alastair, we haven't spoken since February 21. Perhaps we should.'

Sunday, June 2
Michael Wills came on to say the *Mail on Sunday* story re him and a row between TB and GB must have come from Number 10. I thought he'd been wound up by GB and I gave him very short shrift. GB's other claim, that Peter M was behind it, was ludicrous. Sixsmith sent a long letter to Mottram, copied to me, with all manner of claims about us smearing him. I dictated a response to Mottram which stuck to the facts. Darling had an interview in the *Telegraph* which was taken as a hit on [John] Birt, who went into a really precious tantrum. Jeremy called to say we needed to be very nice about Birt, which we were, and could I get AD to speak to Birt. I was helping David Miliband with his first big [ministerial] speech for Thursday.

Monday, June 3
Darling called me after speaking to Birt, said it was the most extraordinary call he had ever made. 'I said I wanted to have a discussion with him about transport policy and he said it was very important that I built a bridge to him. He was unbelievably difficult.' I did a note for TB suggesting how we take forward the PCC case

and talked it through with Guy Black. Then, with all the family and the neighbours out to St James's Park to watch the Golden Jubilee concert on the big screen. There was a fantastic atmosphere and the Royals had handled the whole week brilliantly. It was interesting to see how much more enthusiastic older and middle-aged people were compared to the kids. Certainly for our lot, the Jubilee meant pretty much nothing compared to the World Cup.

Tuesday, June 4

Another bank holiday, so a quiet day, and I felt sorry for TB having to go to St Paul's for the Jubilee service. Then back to the Guildhall where he had to make a speech about the Queen. Not easy, getting the balance right, trying to say something significant whilst also trying to avoid just sounding like a creep. He had written a passage comparing her commitment to that of a cleaner or a doctor, which didn't ring true. He asked me to work on a passage about the reception she got at the concert when she walked on, which had certainly been impressive. Fiona and I were both worried, having been there, that there would be a lot of comment on the reception for him which had been cool by comparison, especially when the cameras panned to him as Ben Elton [comedian and author] made a joke about the NHS and transport being no better than when she first became Queen. What a tit. TB had said to Prince Andrew we could have done without the Ben Elton jokes and Andrew said surely politicians just have to live with that kind of thing. It was clear every time he talked about it, though, that TB liked the Queen, rated and respected her but he felt that Charles' speech, the way he framed the argument about traditional, the un-pc second verse of the national anthem, was meant to be a dig at us.[1]

Wednesday, June 5

TB was seeing [Hosni] Mubarak and Rumsfeld at Number 10, and I wanted to get up to see my dad in this relatively quiet period. I took the boys up and watched Ireland draw with Germany with him. Also working on [David] Miliband's speech.

Thursday, June 6

The *Independent* led on an email which was misrepresented as an attempt to dig dirt on Pam Warren [survivor of the 1999 Paddington

---

[1] In his speech at the Jubilee party, the Prince of Wales had referred to the 'politically incorrect second verse' of 'God Save the Queen', which asks God to 'Confound their politics, frustrate their knavish tricks', etc.

rail crash]. AD wanted to put out an apology from Dan Corry [former special adviser to Stephen Byers] and from Byers straight away, as a way of showing this had nothing to do with him and he condemned it.[1] He also wanted to publish the emails which in fact showed something different to what had been reported. I was a bit worried we would set a precedent, and also reluctant to be issuing apologies for things that had not been done. Why shouldn't political parties try to check if there are any political affiliations of people who suddenly become part of public debate? I consulted TB at Chequers and he felt that AD should do what he wanted and it was probably right. The facts were actually on our side but that didn't stop the papers going into total blah overdrive. Mike White pointed out to me that we had now definitely passed the point where newspapers allowed facts to get in the way of a desire to hit the government.

Friday, June 7

I had pretty much finalised an exchange of letters with the PCC. TB added two points – first, an even more staunch defence of Clare Sumner, and second, we reserve the right to come back on this if any of the papers suggested that he had tried to muscle in on the arrangements. I took a very chatty call from JP but he was pretty menacing as well about the planned Third Way event [policy discussion organised by Peter Mandelson] coming up tomorrow, saying that 'If it's a beautiful people, New Labour, pointy head, Mekon kind of thing, there'll be a backlash and TB should know that.' He said there were people in Number 10 who never bothered to think about him or the party in this and he wasn't happy. Trying to play down its importance, I said I wasn't even going to it and it was a Peter M, Andrew Adonis [head of the Policy Unit] thing, which got him going even more, divisive and stupid, chickens would come home to roost, etc.

Dan Corry was tracked down at the World Cup in Tokyo and we agreed a statement for him to put out as an apology. The *Independent* had a partial account of our dealings with AD yesterday, presenting them as Number 10 not happy with an over-the-top apology.

[1] Corry had emailed the Labour Party asking for information on the political affiliation of the Paddington Survivors Group, which Pam Warren co-founded. The email was sent the day after Mrs Warren had publicly accused Stephen Byers of misleading Parliament over the decision to take Railtrack into administration.

Saturday, June 8

I was trying to get the Sundays focused on TB's welfare speech next week. The Corry email died down pretty quickly with a few pieces saying it was actually an OK thing to do. I had dreadful hay fever and was feeling a bit ground down again. I was reaching the point when I really couldn't be bothered listening to the news, reading the papers or talking to journalists. TB was at the Third Way conference with Clinton et al. and seemed to think it was worthwhile. I think he was surprised I didn't go.

Sunday, June 9

I briefed John Reid for *Frost*. He had been at the Clinton/Peter M wonkathon and said he had had a terrific conversation with Clinton re Ireland. JR was totally up for going for the press, so we had now reached a stage where all communication was dismissed as spin, all funding was sleaze, all attacks were smears. Gwyneth Dunwoody [Labour MP] did an interview saying she had been smeared. IDS was on the broadcasts really going for us. There was a real nastiness and poison about where we were at the moment and I wasn't quite sure how we dealt with it.

TB came back from his weekend policy wonking seeming very up and energised. Clinton had been through something similar to the attacks we were getting. His view was that they went on character because they couldn't win on policy. The challenge was to use that to build a position of confidence and strength. The challenge for modern politicians was understanding change, developing and implementing policy but also shaping and winning arguments. He said we were seen around the world as probably the best and most successful modern left-of-centre party in terms of winning and doing, but we rarely came over as being confident in our own position. TB felt too there was definitely something about people on the left, that sometimes power scared them, or troubled them, and they started to believe the message from the right, that actually they were the people best able to handle power.

Monday, June 10

The welfare speech wasn't badly set up. A couple of pieces of spin by media. First my letter to the *Indy* was used on page 1 for a 'We will learn lessons' headline, burying the fact that it was about their story being wrong. Also, the *Sunday Express* made-up spin on TB's speech was described by the broadcasters, without any knowledge at all, as our handiwork. I finalised the exchanges with the PCC, toned them down a bit at their request, and then, after Guy Black told Black Rod that it was on, the rumour mill started. Then a truly pathetic meeting with Mavis MacDonald [permanent secretary, Cabinet Office], Jeremy and Godric to agree what to do re Sixsmith. TB told us not to go against the legal advice. We should seek to establish what we could legitimately do to get the assurances we sought and if the QC thought we were not within our rights we should not go beyond that. It was pretty clear everyone just wanted shot of it. We left it that we would see what he was prepared to do by way of assurances but the reality was if the answer was nothing, they were going to shell out anyway. As I said to TB, he would get his cheque and then there would be nothing to stop him building a career attacking a government that paid it to him. The message to everyone in government would be fall out with elected ministers and you can make a lot of money out of it. TB said it may be unjust, but it was time to leave it.

I told the Monday morning meeting there was more departmental leaking than ever, there was a culture of acceptance of it and it meant we looked weak. On the press generally, Charles C wanted to campaign in defence of politics. Everyone agreed we were being damaged by all of this, as Clare Short so kindly pointed out on the *Westminster Hour* last night, and none of us were really clear how to get out of it.

TB went off for the welfare speech wearing his glasses for the first time delivering a speech. On his return, he said that whenever he was talking about policy, he felt strong and confident. It was dealing with all the shit that ground us down. The key to re-engagement was as much about policy as anything – particularly public services but also red tape, crime, causes of crime. Godric was also feeling worn out, ground down. Philip was worried that TB and GB were in very different places and we had to get them closer together. The new media environment was definitely something in which we had to agree and implement the strategy. Their view was pretty much now that a story about the government was only really a story when it was a bad story, and that even when the facts didn't fit the bad story, they were made to. It was a cultural shift, born of the impact of 24-hour news and the press, which had forced them to change their role. It required a strategic response but we spent hours over months talking about it without agreeing what that response was. Mine was to make them part of the debate, confront them with the reality that they are players as well as spectators. It was risky, it might make them worse, though it's hard to see how much worse it could get. TB still seemed to think we could muddle along, charm and cajole a few from time to time, divide and rule. We were miles apart on this.

Tuesday, June 11

[Roy] Greenslade [journalist and former editor] had a piece on page 1 of the *Guardian* re the PCC, which was about as good as we could get in terms of where it was pitched. I knew the next few days were going to be grim. TB called as I was running through Green Park on the way in. He said if the press were going to say this was a climbdown, they would give the sense that the original stories were true, in which case we might as well have gone for a full PCC judgement. We released the letters, then Tom did the 11 and they were on the rampage. What was clearer than ever was that the *Mail* and the *Telegraph* were going to crank up into an even bigger gear in terms of going for me personally.

We had a dreadful TB/GB plus key people strategy meeting in which we were trying to sign him up to the six-month strategy paper. Every time we put forward a specific idea or thought, GB would say something slightly different. When he read Philip's analysis, which was not new to him and with which he basically agreed, he feigned shock and said he would now have to rethink the CSR strategy. His basic line was that going on about crime had been short-termist and we needed long-termism. If TB said responsibility was a key theme, GB would say what about opportunity? If TB had said opportunity, he would have said what about responsibility? This was hopeless. Thankfully I was called out to take a call and afterwards went back to my office. Douglas called me afterwards and said he couldn't believe how bad that had been. The truth was GB was winning the ghastly war of attrition.

Earlier, even before that meeting, TB had called in Jonathan, Sally M and me and asked if we thought it was possible for him to announce publicly that he wouldn't fight the next election and tell Cabinet that if ministers wanted to fight a leadership election, they would have to do it outside. Sally feared it would make him a lame duck straight away, though Aznar had seemed to survive a second fixed term pretty well. I said he had to decide whether it was the right thing to do, and that if it wasn't, he was simply caving in to psychological warfare. Did he really want to go? And was it really the right thing? He said that's exactly what Cherie would say. What he'd like to do was win an election, win a referendum, then go after getting the new leader in place or, if a referendum were possible this side of the election, win that, stay to the election and get a new leader in place.

He said all GB ever asked him these days was when was he going. There was a real sense around that GB was at it the whole time. Sally said disgruntled former ministers and disappointed backbenchers were being given strong hints of jobs. He was courting JP the whole time. He was going more and more sceptic in his dealings with Murdoch and his papers. TB had devolved too much power in the areas he really cared about like public services and the euro. Godric felt that on the press front, the new level of nastiness was a direct response to the changes to the lobby. They really did believe we were trying to do them in the whole time. There was no doubt that now with Byers gone, and with TB still pretty impregnable, I was the next best target. Charles Clarke did a piece for *The Times* attacking parts of the press, which would fly a bit.

Wednesday, June 12

The *Mail* and *Telegraph* absolutely vile about me, the others a bit more balanced. Charles' attack was going big and I admired his guts in doing it but GB and Co. were straight out saying it was a mistake to attack the press. TB was still in an absolute fury about Black Rod. We had agreed to try to close it down but it was clear we would not have long to wait before more Black Rod-ery came pouring out. I was managing just about to hang in there but I was going through a mega down phase, worried I wasn't being terribly effective, worried about being strung out by sustained attacks. Even Fiona was adamant I couldn't leave now because it would so weaken TB. Peter M said if I went GB would be home and dry and the Tories would be jubilant, so I just had to hang in there. He said TB relied on me as a brute force able to drive the machine. He said he too was worried about the extent to which they wanted to go for me, but still felt I had no choice but to stay.

At PMQs, TB thought IDS might do the PCC business. In the end, nobody raised it. IDS did Pam Warren then welfare but didn't land a blow. TB had a good tone. Our side better. Weekly meeting with Peter M, PH [Peter Hyman] and PG. On the euro, we went over the various scenarios. Don't go for it, and TB is weakened. Go for it and win, and TB could successfully bow out, though GB would be likely to think TB would use it as an excuse to stay longer and so might block. So option three, do a deal, but GB is unlikely to trust. Option four, do the euro and lose, then GB is home and dry. PH felt that just going for it would show courage and conviction, but I was sure it would be the end of him, if he went for it and lost. Peter M was a real strength at these meetings, seemed to worry less about status or how he was perceived by us, and was most of the time giving very clear and concise strategic advice.

Starting to get calls from journalists who were picking up on Black

Rod's evidence. TB said if Black Rod had had a genuine complaint, why had he not come straight to him or RW? He said he was totally satisfied civil servants did nothing wrong. He said things were going to get very tough and we had to be strong. Tessa [Jowell] called, asked if I was thinking of going, said I mustn't.

Thursday, June 13

[Roy] Hattersley and [Trevor] Kavanagh were both saying I had to go, Kavanagh in quite a friendly way. Piers [Morgan] had actually been pretty good about me on Channel 4 last night so I dropped him a friendly line. Alex F called, said it must be serious because he even had people phoning him to say how hard I was getting it at the moment. He said don't let other people think for you, because they'll all have their own motives. If there is doubt, he said, then there is no doubt. He said it was an old Irish saying. I thought about it through the day. When it came to it, I didn't just want to run away. I still had a job to do. It was pretty heavy though, evidenced by the kind of people sending in letters of support. Not just people I'd expect to like Bruce [Grocott], but also Alice Mahon, Ann Clwyd, David Clark [Labour MPs]. I even had Gwyneth Dunwoody defending me on the radio. Jonathan at his weekly meeting tried to be chirpy as ever, said it was a 'Save AC Campaign' meeting. People looked a bit shot, particularly Sally.

David Manning was genuinely shocked by Black Rod's behaviour. The *Spectator* cover had me and TB getting spanked by the little fucker. We were of course building up to the *Mail on Sunday* who would no doubt publish the memo from Black Rod to the PCC so we had to decide whether to put our version out, with our own dossier of evidence. I felt we had to because Sunday was in danger of being a massive event with only one side of the story there. Tom had forty-five minutes of it with the lobby. This thing took up hours through the day. Meanwhile, perhaps the most dramatic Cabinet yet. TB meandered through the Grid in the usual way, bit of chat, bit of Middle East and Afghanistan, then GB came in about the Tories doing an opposition day debate on world poverty. He said it was strategically important because they were trying to become New Conservatives, position themselves in the centre through mood music but we should be wary because in policy they would be very right wing. He said their weakest point is health. The unspoken message was that TB does Grid, spin and foreign whereas GB does substance and strategy.

But then JP came in with a virtual declaration of war on TB. He said he knew we had to do the press stuff and he wasn't knocking that but it was interesting that the Tories were trying to echo New Labour and avoid substance. But he said we have a very good compromise between Old and New. He said we all have to be involved in future policymaking but 'I'm bound to say if we're going to have weekend retreats for some at Hartwell House [Buckinghamshire hotel, venue of Peter Mandelson's Third Way event], and Mandelson giving interviews saying we're all Thatcherites now, then we're going to have some very serious discussions in here.' He said the compromise between Old and New means we're Labour again and there will be real division if we try to replace policy structures.

TB was looking at him with a mix of steel and humour whereas others in the room clearly sensed it was quite a moment. GB had the beginnings of a smile on his face which was as broad as I've seen it in years by the time he left. JP said the Labour Party has always been lousy on the back foot. There needs to be more forward strategy and it has to be discussed right here. TB hit back pretty hard, said it was time for a little reality check, time to stop believing everything people read in newspapers. He said we are on our sixth year in government and sometimes government gets difficult. The way not to deal with it is to wet our knickers every time it gets difficult. We are in a strong position. The economy is good, we have the right agenda on public services, the right approach on social exclusion. The Tories were coming at us on character because they had nothing else to go on. They had lost on policy. We have to stick on policy, not get distracted or irritated. He said we had been uniquely blessed as a government, to a large extent free of many of the problems other Labour governments had faced. Our mettle was being tested and it's at times like these that we had to hang together, not fall apart.

The history of Labour governments, he said, is that they make themselves fail rather than others make them fail. We are winning all the arguments, so let's get a sense of perspective. He then looked around, smiled, said 'I've got the Indonesian president coming in now, so that's the end of that.' JP put on his real sour look and walked straight out. GB smiled. The rest were blank. It was Paul Boateng's first Cabinet and Bruce's [Grocott] first actually at the Cabinet table. Paul looked really shocked. RW came to see me later. He said that was a big, bad moment. TB was pretty calm afterwards, convinced it needed saying. He had had a pretty heavy session with JP earlier, who was going on about the Hartwell business. It was now an open thing around the world that GB was doing in TB. Yesterday he had spoken to Chrétien, who referred to having a Brown problem, namely that his Treasury minister was after his job and he had told him to fight for it from the outside. But the message out of Cabinet had been pretty clear – from JP, I've had enough and I'm going to throw my weight around, and from GB, I'm moving in. From TB, I'm staying. From the Cabinet, confusion and concern.

Alan Milburn was worried enough to wander over later, bring in some sandwiches, said TB had to face up to the fact that GB was killing him, and if he didn't stand up to it, his supporters would get very demoralised. He said there was no way I could think about going and if anything I should go back to doing the briefings. But TB had to get back rooted in more substance and politics, cut the crap. He was very calm, clear and strong and I was grateful that he came over like he did. Meeting then with TB, Derry [Irvine], Charlie [Falconer] , RW etc. to go through PCC/Black Rod again. Agreed to a strategy with TB, covering note plus evidence dossier to put out pre Sunday. Fraser [Kemp] was fantastic, organising support for me in the PLP.

I collected Fiona from Sarah Brown's book launch [*Magic: New Stories*] and we went to a very nice Robert Thomson dinner with the Scardinos [Marjorie, chief executive of Pearson plc, and Albert, her journalist husband], James Baker III [former US Secretary of State] and his wife [Susan], Ian McEwan [author] and his wife [Annalena McAfee], who was literary editor of the *Guardian*. Baker was impressive, particularly on the Middle East. He felt that Bush was moving in the right direction but had made a huge mistake in giving DoD an equal seat at the foreign policy table. It meant Powell and Rumsfeld were at odds the whole time whilst Condi was less a full-time National Security Advisor to the president but a mediator between the two. His view was that one day there would be a land-for-peace deal but he felt it likely it would only happen under a Labor government [in Israel]. Baker had picked up on the scale of coverage and the level of nastiness around me and once we got through all the jokes was very supportive, said I should take it as a compliment. I liked Ian McEwan too once he opened up a bit, while Marjorie Scardino's husband shared a devotion to a struggling league club [Notts County]. Marjorie said this is a good government, I was doing a great job and I had to keep at it. TB called late for a chat. He said JP would be reflecting and would come back a bit now. He hadn't liked the mood today, which was why he had really gone for it.

Friday, June 14
Most of the papers had some sort of editorial comment about me. The *Guardian* – I should go. [Richard] Littlejohn [*Sun* columnist] snide.

Telegraph snide. *Independent* not so bad. *Mirror* bad. TB said 'That's it for Piers with me.' I wrote a short statement for TB to go on the front of the dossier. I got the staff together after the morning meeting to explain what was happening. Jeremy then called, said there was a real problem. [Lieutenant Colonel] Malcolm Ross, comptroller of the Royal Household, had told Charles Moore [*Telegraph* editor] yesterday that they too had been told TB wanted to walk [through crowds from Downing Street to the Queen Mother's lying-in-state] and they had said it was a bad idea. If true, it was dreadful. But it was not true that Number 10 had said to the Palace that he wanted to walk. I had put in TB's statement that nobody from Black Rod's office had complained to TB or Richard W. RW didn't want to be in there. He told Clare he was fed up of being a human shield, to which she had said, 'You are supposed to be a human shield, protecting and defending me.' She was really upset about the whole thing. But I took out the reference to RW and instead put 'me or anyone on my behalf'.

Richard came to see me. I offered him tea but he said he wouldn't stay. He then said 'I just want to say two things. The first, you are probably not fully aware of how stressful and traumatic this has all been for you personally. Second, I don't think there's much support for you around the Cabinet table.' I said I think I'm a better judge of those at the Cabinet table than you are and apart from GB from time to time, and Clare who doesn't matter much, I have no real problems with any of them, and I'm one of the few people who gets on equally well with TB and JP. So what are you saying? That because the Tories and the press are after my blood, I should get out? No, no, no, he said. But just be very careful. There was a hint of menace there. He stayed for a matter of minutes and unlike previous such visits, my antennae told me the intention had been to unsettle me. If so, it didn't work. On the contrary, I felt strengthened because I drew a contrast between those who were calling and writing to express support, and those who were going on the airwaves to say they wanted me out. What sort of people were calling? RC, Jack S, Margaret B, Brian Wilson [energy minister], Kim Howells [culture minister]. Lots of backbenchers. Family, Fiona's family, Alex F, people at Burnley. PR people like Matthew Freud or Melanie Cantor. At one point Alison [Blackshaw] was just coming in with lists of names. My team was totally solid too. TB did a clip on the whole business from Jersey which was strong, and Godric did the briefing, followed by the honours briefing and we were in a much better position. We briefed ministers and MPs going up on it and I felt the machine starting to roll, but even better Oborne was out saying that he had never said TB did anything wrong.

The other big drama was JP. He called me at lunchtime. I said 'That was pretty dramatic yesterday.' 'What?' 'What you said in Cabinet.' 'Well, you've created camps and you're in one of them and you've pushed me to the other. There you go.' 'Oh well. I just wanted to say I was taken aback. Me, not him.' He told me that just before Cabinet TB had accused him of messing around with GB and said he wasn't having it. JP said he wasn't prepared to be excluded from strategy and he wasn't having all this Third Way/Mandelson policy stuff bypassing the party. He let off steam, said he had warned him again and again and he thinks if he strokes my arm I'll be fine, but it goes much deeper. He has to do things through the Cabinet and his ministers and not his own little Loya Jirga [Afghan Grand Council]. He then said 'You've withdrawn from all this anyway.' I said that I'd tried to pull back because of the attention I was getting, but it hasn't worked, has it? He said no, you've got your own problems. I've never had a problem with you but we've grown distant again. I'm loyal to TB and you both need to understand that. I always will be, I'm not going over to GB, but Tony has got to start treating people better than he does. I know he has a lot to deal with, a lot of problems, a lot of difficult people, a lot of big decisions. But he knows he can do it better. We chatted for close to an hour and I think both felt better at the end of it. We agreed to have dinner at our house tomorrow night. TB called later and said JP had been transformed, which showed I should keep close to him.

As ever, JP then started to worry about tomorrow, about taking up all our time at the weekend, said he would get a takeaway. I said 'Aw, aren't you sweet?' TB spoke to GB who was on his way to Canada. GB said he was thinking of him and if there was anything he could do to help either of us, he would. I was almost minded to write to him to thank him for all the support he had given and to say if he ever ran into difficulties, his support would be reciprocated in full. TB was pretty feisty about things but at the end of the day it was all pretty tough. He got back from the BIC [British–Irish Council] in Jersey. He said Northern Ireland was a mess and we may lose [David] Trimble [Ulster Unionist Party leader and First Minister of Northern Ireland].

Fiona took Grace to the ballet and I had a great chat with Rory and Calum who were developing similar views to my own about the press. Calum said something really sweet, that I'll still be standing after all these people are gone. Richard Desmond called and asked if there was anything he could do to help. I suggested a piece from Jack Straw defending me. Desmond came back saying Jack's office had said he didn't want to do it. I called Jack, who said he hadn't even been told about it and was more than happy to do it.

Saturday, June 15

We agreed re the *Mail on Sunday* that the best line would be to point out the inconsistency with the statement at the time. Once the papers dropped, we had a quick conference call to agree the lines and Martin Sheehan put out a statement. Most felt the whole thing was overblown bollocks, Black Rod says AC must go. Nothing much to it.

JP and Pauline [his wife] arrived about 8. After all the small talk, JP with some anecdotes on his trips, taking the mick out of Pauline's hats, then we got down to it. He liked TB, felt he was the right guy at the right time and a good leader. But he wanted to be properly involved in decision-making. He only felt he was in the areas for which he had direct responsibility but if he was going to be a proper deputy, he had to know a lot more about what he was up to and where we were going. He said he sometimes felt TB stroked his arm, patted his head, that it was about managing him rather than using him properly as a DPM [Deputy Prime Minister]. He had used the line on Thursday about 'the snake leaving the skin behind', that TB seemed to have this ability to lose people but not necessarily lose his strength. He said that he felt I had pulled back and that meant people in Number 10 didn't always feel there was a proper understanding of JP's views. I said that was true, but it wasn't personal. The personality clashes did my head in. GB was in TB's head the whole time messing it up.

He said TB had directly accused him of playing around with GB, building an alliance to isolate him, but that misunderstood things. He had told GB he would support him to take over but he would not be part of any plan to force out TB. He agreed with me that it was almost like a failed marriage, they had fallen out but they knew they had to live together. He felt there was a deep belief inside GB that they did have a deal, that GB had done his bit and he felt TB was doing the dirty on him. He felt TB was still popular in the party and the country and he couldn't see any pressure for him to go. He also felt that on the policy front, and again he felt my partial disengagement had something to do with this, the balance had tilted too far towards [Andrew] Adonis and what JP saw as a very right-wing agenda. We both agreed how much we missed David Miliband there [i.e. as Adonis' predecessor in charge of the Policy Unit].

I tried to give him a sense of what it was like for TB getting his head pummelled every day by GB. I tried to explain too why sometimes TB didn't want JP at some meetings. I said when TB is making a big decision, he prefers an endless series of circular conversations with different people rather than full-blown confrontational sessions that are supposed to reach conclusions. It's just his style. I suggested a weekly meeting of TB, JP, Charles C and I to keep JP more involved with political strategy. It was a really good evening, because we both laid things out very frankly, both also knew we needed both of us to raise our game again, and in a bizarre sort of way we needed each other to do that.

JP warmed up as the evening wore on and was in full flow by the end, totally open about himself, his background, his chippiness, why he felt as proud as he did of where he had got to, why he was so desperate to play a role getting TB and GB to work together better than they did. He said he would do nothing to damage the party and even though they had different views about lots of things, he felt TB was in the same place on that. He said between us all, we have put Labour in the strongest position ever and a lot of that has been down to TB and GB hanging together. I said don't underestimate the impact GB is having on him for the worse at the moment. I said he had not exchanged a single civil word with me since the election. They stayed till close to midnight.

Sunday, June 16

TB called, even more outraged and angry about Black Rod than ever. I filled him in on the JP dinner. He said the only question is whether an open and admitted two-term strategy weakens me or gives me more space. He said that even though GB had behaved abominably towards him in many ways, it was really important that leaders did not try to get successors in their own image, but go for the best on offer. He said it was important to his own legacy that the party does well after he's gone. So if GB was the best option for delivering a third-term Labour government, it's the right thing to do. But he admitted he had doubts about him temperamentally, that he worried what he would actually be like. He thought that perhaps two full terms is pretty close to the limit for jobs like this. But what really mattered was what we did policy-wise. He felt if he could get GB working with him properly on policy, we would be unstoppable. He said JP was key because he was the one politician that GB feared and the idea of a black spot being put on him, JP saying he wasn't fit for the job, he would really worry about that.

The *Mail on Sunday* stuff didn't go very far, and though there was reams of it in the papers, nothing deadly. I briefed Margaret Beckett for *The World at One* and she was absolutely brilliant. Haughty and dismissive. Reid was excellent on *On the Record* against Tim Collins [Conservative Party vice chairman], whom God preserve. The story was going nowhere but it didn't stop the BBC leading on it most of the day. We went out for dinner with the Goulds and the Milibands, all very supportive though Gail [Rebuck, publisher and wife of Philip Gould] said, probably rightly, that it was worth me trying for a concerted period of being nice to the media and then getting out.

Monday, June 17

Only the *Mail* with 'the smearing of Black Rod' led on it, but the mood was definitely different now. I agreed with TB we should just shut up shop, say we had said all there was to say. There was an excellent story in *The Times*, saying the Palace were worried Black Rod was dragging them into a political row, but it was dropping down the agenda. At the Monday morning meeting, TB was worrying about how we get back on the front foot. He was very nice to Clare Sumner. She was so manifestly nice, and professional, and mortified to have been accused in the way she had been. I saw TB on his own later and he was clearly thinking a lot about this two-term plan, moving to the view that if he did it soon it might give him more freedom. His only worry was his fear that GB would not change, and continue not co-operating properly. He said it was extraordinary to think that GB discusses the euro more openly with Murdoch than he does with him.

Tuesday, June 18

The Black Rod story was dying, yesterday's *Times* pretty much the turning point. David Davies [Football Association executive director] called as I was in a cab to the Eurostar, asking if TB would go out for later rounds of the World Cup. We agreed he would certainly come out if England got to the final, possibly before, and we also had to think about receptions etc. afterwards. He said they were having a fantastic time. What was clear was that if Japan went out, most of the Japanese would swing behind England. I explained some of the recent madness re the Queen Mum, so it was important it was clear the invitation came from them to TB, rather than TB 'muscling in'. We agreed both to speak to the Palace to find out their plans, which looked like [Prince] Andrew for the semi, Charles and Andrew for the final.

I left for Brussels with Danny Pruce [press officer, foreign affairs]. We went to [Ambassador Nigel] Sheinwald's residence where I briefed the Brussels hacks on the summit, pushing hard on asylum and immigration. The mood was fine and it was definitely worth doing. Then to the EPLP [European Parliamentary Labour Party] where I pushed the line that the Tories had moved out of policy, were trying to turn politics into a policy-free zone and make character the issue, which required a fresh approach to communications again.

Godric called to say Cherie had given us a bit of a problem. Without knowing there had been nineteen deaths in the morning in the Jerusalem suicide bombing, she said something that was taken as a defence of suicide bombers.[1] She was with Queen Rania of Jordan to launch a charity. And after Rania said something fairly balanced, Cherie said something that appeared to offer justification for suicide bombers and off we went on the next great frenzy. We needed a statement out from CB, plus Rania's words to give the context, plus getting Labour MPs attacking Michael Ancram [Conservative deputy leader and Shadow Foreign Secretary] for making a big issue of it, plus we needed prominent Jews out defending her and putting a more balanced message. After the Black Rod/AC spin row, this was the next one and it wouldn't be very nice for CB.

Wednesday, June 19

CB row died down quickly, more support for her than I expected. All the country really cared about was the World Cup, which was great. We were starting to think about going to Japan if they got through. David Blunkett did a pretty heavy attack on the press which though it was fairly light-hearted would probably prolong the Black Rod/AC/CB stuff. TB was off to Paris for dinner with Chirac, called afterwards, said he had been good on beef, Sangatte and the general need for more co-operation before summits, so he was pretty pleased with himself.

Thursday, June 20

Ran in, thirty-five minutes, 4.4 miles. Whizzed through the morning meeting, need to get the focus totally on TB's [televised] press conference. He was over at a Cobra meeting, back really late, eating into preparation time. I had worked up the script pre Seville [EU summit] but it was all going to be about his demeanour and body language under questions. The only strategic decision was whether he engaged in all the current debate about the press and the nature

[1] Mrs Blair said young Palestinians felt they had 'no hope but to blow themselves up'.

of the debate. He was minded not to and I didn't particularly want the Black Rod business reopened so we agreed just say he wanted to be judged on substance, that he was prime minister, not commentator. The backdrop for the media was a *Telegraph* poll saying fifty per cent didn't trust him. Cabinet, better mood than last week but a bit meandering. They discussed foot and mouth, the Tube, a lot of foreign affairs stuff. Clare made even by her standards a ridiculous intervention, saying could he make sure that if Bush sent in Saddam death squads, there was a proper discussion here in Cabinet before they went. He and several others flashed identical looks of disbelief.

He went up [to the press conference], with only Saeed [Khan, Number 10 press office] for company, and we stayed back to watch it on TV in his office. It was very long, he was solid and serious, with a few really good moments but it was definitely worth doing, though the coverage was as much about the wretched hacks and what didn't happen as about what he had said.

Friday, June 21

Good coverage for the press conference, even in some of the hostile press. He was good at them, but we needed more colour and texture. TB was off to Seville via Scotland. England vs Brazil was all anybody cared about. One up, then lost 1–2 and the whole country was deflated. TB called afterwards and sounded pretty down about it. I was also feeling a lot more disappointed than I thought I would. Godric had spent three days working up a proper communications plan on asylum and we now discovered we had been holed by Clare Short doing a pre-recorded *GMTV* interview, recorded after the meeting at which we had agreed we would not tie aid to asylum. It was a mad idea which we had somehow allowed to get away from us.

Saturday, June 22

TB in Seville, going OK but he was a bit bored and in any event the media was wall-to-wall World Cup. I watched a lot of soccer, slept, then we went out with Philip G and Gail to Chequers for dinner to raise money for a Roald Dahl museum. I had an interesting chat with Jackie Stewart [former world champion racing driver] on how useless the civil servant he had dealt with re Formula One had been.

Sunday, June 23

DB called Fiona for what turned out to be a very difficult chat. She had said to Tessa she was really angry about a line in the *Mail* that Blunkett didn't rate me. He was adamant he had never said it, and

I was perfectly prepared to believe him, but it was clear Fiona didn't believe him at all, and made sure he knew. She said whenever ministers were in trouble, they came to me for help, so it would be nice if it was reciprocated. I spent most of the day at various sporting events with the kids, which is what I like doing most at the moment.

Monday, June 24

Coverage of Seville crap. Lots more GB-ery around the place. At his morning meeting, TB was tired, vacant, had nothing to say. At one point he asked Charles [Clarke] if he had anything to say and Charles said 'Yes, cheer up a bit.' It was mainly a discussion about G8 [forthcoming summit in Canada], but with no real focus. Peter H and I left pretty appalled and later had a long session to go over it. We just weren't professional enough. We had slack in the system. We didn't prepare him properly. There was no sense of grip. The real problem, as I'd said to JP, was that TB was spooked by GB at the moment. Even when he wasn't pummelling, there was a part of TB's mind given over to worrying about him. Bad start to the week. Calum came down to the office and I took him to Wimbledon [tennis championship] and we had a great time. Bush's speech on the Middle East was going big. It was taken as 'Arafat must go' and it was going to be quite hard to work out a proper response.

Tuesday, June 25

The Bush Middle East speech was making big waves right round the world but it didn't seem terribly thought through. It seemed the White House was too consumed with the squabbles and struggles within the government, particularly Powell vs Cheney/Rumsfeld, than in really thinking through a plan on the Middle East. Also, truth be told, Bush had a surer touch on domestic than international. I pointed out that Bush calling for the Palestinians to reject Arafat was the surest way to ensure a boost for Arafat. TB didn't really want to end up in a US–UK rift situation, but we said it was up to the Palestinian people to elect their leaders, which was taken as an attack on Bush so we were heading for the rift headlines, even though TB was really in agreement that Arafat was weak, and that there had to be more sympathy for the Israelis.

We had an office planning meeting re September, at which Fiona said they were thinking about going to the Strozzis [Prince Girolamo and his wife Irina] again and also going to Aznar's daughter's wedding. He knew my views on holiday with the Strozzis, but I thought the wedding was equally ridiculous given he didn't know the daughter. Aznar really wanted him to go, but this was behaving like royal families. If I raised it with him he said, OK but I do need to have some kind of life as well. Going to a politician's daughter's wedding in Spain did not strike me as being life.

GB called, said he wanted to come over and go over the Mansion House speech which was a very sceptical speech, lots and lots of focus on the tests, the combined weight of which would ensure very sceptical headlines. He came over and was also trying to go back on the idea of the £1 billion commitment for Africa which we had agreed yesterday and which had been leaked to the *Guardian*. TB wanted it changed to tone down the scepticism, a discussion that continued in the car on the way to the airport [en route to Canada]. GB said he thought it was quite positive. TB said it most certainly was not. Godric did a briefing on the Middle East but it was hard to answer the direct question: if Arafat was re-elected did we expect the US to deal with him? The answer was yes, but what we didn't know was if they would. We landed, got taken by helicopter to Kananaskis, up in the mountains where you could feel the thinness of the air as soon as you arrived. It was perhaps an indication of how unfocused I currently was that my immediate thought was to call Brendan Foster [former Olympic runner and friend of AC] and get some tips on altitude training. We went straight to the [Jean] Chrétien bilateral where he was clear he wanted to make sure Africa remained the main focus. He had seen Bush and said he would need pressure putting on him. He wasn't keen on the extent of commitment we were trying to get. He was good on the detail both of what was happening in Africa but also realistically what we could expect from the other countries. But it was clear his worry was that the Middle East stuff would just keep raging away. I went out for a run along a mountain road through some fantastic scenery, but it was pretty tough going because of the air.

Wednesday, June 26

G8 summit at Kananaskis. TB had bumped into GWB at the gym and they had forty minutes in there, mainly just the two of them. TB felt that they could tolerate Arafat as a titular head but not as the man who led the negotiations. They just didn't trust him. Bush wanted to do media at the start of their bilateral, not least because there was another fraud-related company crash [WorldCom]. But I was worried that if it went to the Middle East, which it would, TB would get put into the poodle position. TB said we must not change the line, and instead should let them move to us a bit. But Bush was basically someone who said what he thought. It's a quality people always say they want in a politician but when the politicians are in the really big jobs, I think it's sometimes the reason they turn against them. In Arafat's case, he thought the man was a terrorist. Listening to him later, I felt sometimes he imagined he could just say things away, just as he had said to us he thought Bin Laden was dead but he daren't say it in case Bin Laden popped up again. We worked through and thought we got to the right position, namely the Palestinians should elect their own leaders but they should elect leaders who could be relied upon to negotiate.

Then off to a very dull [Junichiro] Koizumi [Japanese Prime Minister] bilateral, lots of football talk, Koizumi saying everyone in Japan thought England would win. He did a big tribute to TB's leadership post September 11, said he had read biographies of Churchill and applauded his and TB's efforts to get the Americans properly involved in world peace. TB was equally flattering about Koizumi's reform programme. They went over debt, aid, Afghanistan. Then off to see GWB. The little doorstep they did was OK. I got the feeling that Condi was a bit put out that I was there as well as David Manning. She was pretty status-conscious and I don't think had got the point that I was more to TB than Ari Fleischer [White House press secretary] was to Bush. Bush was on good form, but you did worry whether he had thought things through. He said the problem with Israeli politics is that they tend to unite around the toughest lines. As to why he was so hard on Arafat, he felt he had lied about the money he gave to families organising terrorism. He did seem to have the outlines of a possible step-by-step process, but nobody seemed terribly confident. He felt neither Arafat nor [Ariel] Sharon were capable of delivering peace. TB felt there had to be improved security structures, otherwise they were at the mercy of suicide bombers. GWB said 'I think I've stopped Sharon from killing Arafat – I don't know if that's a good thing or not.'

Bush was pretty scathing on some of the Africa stuff. He said he liked the plan, but then through the discussion came out with hard lines on corruption, conflict. He said 'I'm enthusiastic about Africa. What pisses me off about Africa is that for every good intention there appear to be more bad actions.' TB felt the issue was leadership. He strongly felt the debt issue wasn't just moral, but ultimately we had to get these countries on their feet for sound political and economic reasons too. Bush said he was putting up half a billion dollars for AIDS in Africa but he wanted to know there was strategy. GWB was a weird mix, much wittier than people would imagine, quite self-deprecating, very open for someone in his position. At times too, you felt he had a real grasp of issues, but then he would just go off on one like 'If Chirac pushes me on trade, I'm going to crawl over his chilli' – a new one on all of us. He couldn't pronounce 'Yemenis', when he was telling a story about how Yemenis were taking out lots of US thermos flasks filled with honey. Then he'd give a clever and broad-ranging analysis of the dangers to America of reliance on Saudi oil, how to get out of that. TB and GWB went off to the heads-only session and later Putin arrived and scuppered the $20 billion deal to sort the issue of Soviet WMD, because he had decided at the last minute he wanted something different to what we thought was agreed. Inside the summit, there were a couple of massive bust-ups, first Chirac claiming the US didn't really care about Africa, and Bush hitting back hard. He was being exposed to the kind of anti-Americanism they didn't really understand. TB played a bit of tennis with Schroeder. I had a drink with Schroeder's interpreters and got the very strong feeling they thought he was going to lose the election.

Thursday, June 27

The summit was going fine and the Africa plan resolved better than expected. TB and Chirac were also getting on better. A number of the African leaders were in for part of the summit and although there was an inevitable feeling of poor men coming to the rich men's table, the Africans were pretty positive and TB started his own press conference with a quote from Obasanjo [Nigerian President] that it was a historic turning point for Africa. TB's press event was a bit weird, one camera, one reporter, the pictures being beamed back to the hacks miles away in Calgary. Tom felt it was fine. TB wanted another discussion about his future, or 'La Grande Stratégie' as he now called it. The only question that mattered was whether it strengthened or weakened him. I veered to the lame-duck side of the argument, putting GB in an even more powerful position on the euro, but TB felt it would allow him to be himself more. I was worried that all that had happened was that GB had effectively worn him down to force him out ahead of his time. It was true that he had always imagined only doing two terms, but I wasn't convinced it was remotely time for him to go yet. I also shared his worries about the GB temperament question. TB still felt that two terms was about all you get in the modern world. But if it took a couple of years to do the euro, he would be happy to hang around for that. I asked him what Cherie thought. The same, he said. But I have to resolve the question whether it weakens or strengthens me.

The more he talked about it, the more I feared it was one of those things that had a certain immediate appeal but which would go in the box marked 'things I wish I hadn't done'. He said it wasn't a case of being fed up, but eight years was roughly what you got, and if we couldn't see the sort of progress we wanted in public services in that time, there was a bit of a problem. We started to talk about the conference speech, and I got the sense he was thinking about using it to indicate departure. I felt the conference speech should be about explaining change and communicating change, answering the question 'Was the country really changing for the better?' We believed it was, and if we were right, then we could communicate the vision of a better country out there in the future, nobody left behind.

He talked about Cherie, said she was very hardy, tough, could endure the rough-and-tumble and was certainly not pushing him out. He said nice things about Fiona and what she had been doing, said she was important to the operation and it was important I kept her happy. We spent what seemed like hours driving to the plane because there were demonstrators clogging the motorways which pissed him off. But overall it was a good visit, we got in the right place on the Middle East despite Bush, Africa was OK and in our private conversations we had got back some of the old working relationship and warmth. But I was a bit worried that mentally he was moving towards the exit door with only the euro to hold him back. As we arrived at the airport, he got even more pissed off to hear Oxfam said the deal was peanuts so I got the office working out how many peanuts you could buy with all the millions that had been pledged. The flight home was fairly uneventful apart from when I lost my credit card down the side of the seat and they had to take the thing apart to get it out.

Friday, June 28

Jackie Stewart came in to see me about the Silverstone Grand Prix situation, genuinely concerned we were going to lose it. It was a long, convoluted story of how the British Racing Drivers Association, of which he was chair, lost the rights to Bernie Ecclestone [Formula One supremo], how Bernie had built and accumulated power. He controlled all the TV, advertising, corporate revenues and he and Max Mosley [President of the Fédération Internationale de l'Automobile] just took an aggressive view that in all sorts of ways the BGP [British Grand Prix] wasn't good enough. Jackie's big worry was that we would lose the centrality of the UK to the whole motorsports industry if we lost grip of the grand prix. He was an interesting bloke and I enjoyed talking to him about his career. He said he thought TB looked really tired and was losing his sparkle. He said it was really important we didn't push him too hard and also he should think about having a personal trainer with a daily regime.

Saturday, June 29

The whole weekend ruined by hay fever. Not much on the work front, the usual Sunday newspaper shite, the *Sunday Times* on some fiction re Number 10 refurbishments, *Mail on Sunday* rather hopelessly trying to link CB's Palestine charity [Medical Aid for Palestinians] to Hamas [Islamist political party with military wing]. Part of the day taken up dealing with Steve [Byers] in Greece. I tried three or four times to talk Rebekah [Wade, *News of the World* editor] out of doing the Byers story [about a relationship with a woman in a hotel] on the front but in the end she did and it was pretty grim reading, though she said it was a lot worse and tackier before they spoke. I fixed up for Steve to have a chat with her. Rebekah said she felt sorry for him. He sounds really nice and I wish we weren't doing the story. 'Well don't then. Just dump it, bin it.' She said they couldn't, but they were taking the woman to France for a week to stop her talking to anyone else so hopefully it would die down fairly quickly. I did a call with JP to go over everything pre *Frost* tomorrow. He was a lot more onside after our dinner.

Sunday, 30 June

JP on *Frost*, followed by a conference call, but with the World Cup final on [Germany 0, Brazil 2], I wasn't keen on working too hard today. The Byers story didn't really run so I think we had handled it reasonably well. TB sent over a note on forward strategy. He emphasised yet again that getting the policy right was what mattered above all. On political positioning, he was worried that the 'Nobody left behind' slogan was too exclusive, not New Labour enough. It suggested we were only concerned with the people at the bottom of the pile, not everyone else.

Monday, July 1

TB used his Monday morning meeting to hammer home his determination to keep the focus on policy. He felt there was a danger that because of all the noises off the whole time we became a bit timid. He had a meeting with Charles C, David Triesman and Hilary Armstrong about the trade unions. TB felt they were becoming an even bigger nightmare than ever. Hilary felt the problem was that GB was running a counter-strategy with them. TB agreed reluctantly to do another dinner for them but felt we needed to divide and rule a bit. The leaders of the big unions were indulged by the media because they attacked us, and they were capable of talking the most meaningless drivel. Simon Heffer [*Daily Mail* columnist] came in to see me for lunch. It was the usual jolly chat but he also said that 'as a friend' he would advise me to leave fairly soon because the *Mail* was really going to go for me personally from now on in. I told him to 'take a message back to your leader [editor Paul Dacre] that I gave up long ago worrying where his bile was poured'. We were still trying to find a venue for the press briefings out of Number 10. The QE2 [conference centre] was the best option but it would cost four grand a day. Ten-mile run.

Tuesday, July 2

Ran in. TB called me up as soon as I arrived, in a stew. GB had done an interview in *The Times* suggesting massive investment in EMAs [education maintenance allowances], on the day that we were pushing the antisocial behaviour strategy. He said it was complete news to him, and typical of the way GB did his own thing without regard to others. GB was complaining the whole time that we didn't have a strategy. But the problem was we did have a strategy but he had a counter-strategy as a counterpoint to TB's profile. TB was now of the view that GB was just doing him in the whole time. What would it do to the country if he took over? He felt that the tragedy for GB was that they were both actually in the right jobs for them. TB was now going through the CSR bids from different departments, then saw GB who complained we were operating on a different set of figures. In fact the figures had been agreed between Jeremy, Ed Balls and 'Mr Adonis' as GB called Andrew. But GB said these were different figures to the ones they had been working on. The EMA move was a classic exercise to get up a big GB story to counter TB doing something different. TB then did the *TES* [*Times Educational Supplement*], for which he was pretty good, much better than Channel 4 later.

With the *Sunday Telegraph* in for lunch, he was back on pander mode, and I felt a bit queasy at some of the things he was saying, particularly about public services. I also felt he talked too much about focus groups and what they said. Later off to Channel 4, which we had agreed to do on the basis of real interchange with viewers but it wasn't great. He didn't really drive the message about this being a CSR for schools as he had done with the *TES*.

Wednesday, July 3

PG called, said that for the first time there was polling, bad for TB, that had the idea in there that GB would be better. I felt this had been a media thing but clearly it had got through, because GB was fortunate that people didn't focus on him in the same way. Philip was worried about it. Yet when I had a meeting with Jim Naughtie [BBC *Today* programme] I was quite taken aback by just how negative he was about GB, felt he wasn't a serious option, that he was 'so strange, humourless, simmering with such resentment that I couldn't see him being a good leader'. He said he found it incredible that the second most powerful person in the country felt such a compelling need to have people think he was able to duff up Estelle Morris. Jim was on good form, very lively, said that he felt our recent problems were partly because people felt we, particularly TB and I, were too big for our boots, a bit arrogant, always thought we knew best. He felt, and funnily enough it was one of the points I made in the notes done last weekend, that we needed to take the lead in generating more honest and realistic debates, because the media wouldn't do it for us.

After PMQs, I saw TB to agree a line to give to the *Spectator* who had some story about TB and CB using private-school tutors for Euan and Nicky. It was odd how virtually every bad argument we ever had tended to be in the area where public life and private life collide, and often related to education. He said most normal parents would sympathise. I said you are not a normal parent, you are the prime minister, and if you are that you have to think through the politics of everything you do. Out of school lessons, fine, but given how many decent teachers there are what was the point in sticking your chin out to say 'Hit me, I'm getting private school teachers'? He said if Rory and Calum were struggling, we would get them help. I said I sure as hell wouldn't go to a private school for it. I had a long meeting with Peter M and Peter H. Peter M felt that the real damage was being done below the surface, that we were not in as good shape as we wanted or needed to be.

Thursday, July 4

Philip had briefed TB on the latest poll which showed the trust problem growing. TB felt the lack of a clear strategy driven through in communications was the central problem. I felt it was more that GB was running a counter-strategy which meant we were being presented negatively from the left and the right. And the party was picking up the idea that on policy substance, we had moved to the right. As John Reid said to me before Cabinet, Number 10 had lost Pat [McFadden, former Number 10 deputy chief of staff], [David] Miliband, Jon Cruddas [Labour MP, Blair's former deputy political secretary for union liaison], and 'the only person left who would bleed a hundred per cent red blood if you cut him is you'. He said TB was losing his networks in government, Parliament and party. He also felt JP was not as powerful as he was, GB basically hostile, RC on his own kick in Parliament, plus he had people like Clare offside anyway, so TB was becoming more and more isolated. TB looked a bit wandering at Cabinet, which was mainly GB going through general state of the economy, said the spending review would be the week after next. He said our underlying position was sound and he was cautiously optimistic about growth, industrial production rising, the job situation pretty good.

I had lunch with Jonathan Dimbleby to discuss TB doing a solo *Any Questions* [BBC Radio 4]. Dimbleby said he was struck by how TB always looked tired. Back for a brainstorm with Philip, Douglas, PH, Michael Barber [head of the Prime Minister's Delivery Unit], Andrew Adonis and some of the key policy people. How to address specific issues of delivery on the public services in London. Some of the best and worst was in London, but the fact that the national media was based here tended to skew things towards the worst, added to which virtually none of the senior media people used state schools or the NHS and so had a vested interest in running them down to justify their own decisions to themselves. Douglas and I were both a bit worried about the idea of specifically identifying London in terms of its special problems. But we agreed to do a region-by-region report on the public services setting out good and bad.

Phil Bassett [Number 10 special adviser] had been over briefing JP for *Question Time* and he had gone mad at the *Spectator* story on private tutors. He said I ought to call JP to try and calm him down. He was in a total rage, said it wasn't about tough choices for parents, because we all had tough choices. Pauline was always telling me we should use better schools and I felt we had to use the local school. So does virtually every Labour MP. He said Cherie does all that Liverpool stuff and her poor background, but when it comes to schooling for her own kids, there's this snobbery about the best schools and now private-school tutors. JP called after the programme and said he hadn't done well, so I made a point of watching it and he was fine. Called him to say so and he said he just felt tired and jaded at the moment.

Off to the US ambassador's residence for their July 4th do. Usual mix of politicians, media, great and the good. The best moment of the evening was when I was chatting to [Sir] Roger Bannister [first athlete to run a mile in under four minutes] about Rory's running, introduced him to Fiona as 'the former athlete', and she asked him what his distance was. 'Lots really, but I was probably best known as a miler,' he said without a hint of embarrassment, while she blushed when she realised what a daft question it was.

Saturday, July 6
Another quiet day. Only work-related thing was the *Observer* getting hold of the fact we were selling HUDs [eye-level 'head-up' displays for F16 combat aircraft] to the US, knowing they would go on to Israel. Had a series of calls with Jack S to agree what to say in the morning interviews – not a new policy, but addressing a new reality of multinational assembly lines. The vice president of Afghanistan [Haji Abdul Qadir] was assassinated [shot in the head in Kabul], so we were scrabbling around a bit on that too.

Sunday, July 7
Patricia [Hewitt] was on *Frost*. She was fine but was not even asked about arms [sales], which surprisingly didn't take off. There were a few GB/CSR stories around, but all a bit incoherent. We lacked a strategic theme that was drawing policy together at the moment. Out for dinner with the Goulds. Philip was worried TB didn't really get what our weaknesses were at the moment.

Monday, July 8
At TB's Monday meeting, TB was baulking again at 'Nobody left behind' as a theme for conference. He felt reform was the most important focus, that conference should be about the remodelling of the welfare state around the themes of rights and responsibilities. I felt we needed to be bigger than that, that we were going through a bad time and we lacked clarity about how to get through it. TB also wanted to go into another round of persuasion with the right-wing media, and we just disagreed on this. I felt that if we isolated the *Mail*, we would gain leverage with the press on the left, one of whose main angsts was the feeling we had courted the right too much. There was also something so putrid about these papers that culturally it was right to challenge them rather than keep trying to win them round, which in the *Mail*'s case was an utterly lost cause. But the key to everything was to get up a bigger message about where we were going. Thatcher always had a sense of direction, even when the shit was flying. Often we had it, but at the moment we didn't. Charles C was in very grumpy mood at the meeting and later told me he hated the job.

I listened in to a couple of bad TB/GB calls. First, with lots of dicking around on the date of the CSR, TB feeling he was trying to bounce us into the 15th. TB made clear he was not signing it all off until he was happy with the Home Office budget. It had not even been taken to Blunkett yet. I pointed out that again, important detail was being held back from him. He said he was so used to being abused and mistreated by him that he had almost stopped caring, and just wanted to make sure the final package was OK. We had all sorts of CSR follow-up planned, e.g. visits, but we still didn't have a date. I had a meeting with Afghan journalists, which was interesting not least for the way that they saw Britain's role, namely far more positively than our media did.

Tuesday, July 9

TB called an internal meeting to run through the final difficult bits of the CSR. He was playing far tougher with GB than before. TB said he was pressing for yet more for education and we would get it. The Home Office settlement still needed to be improved but he was confident we would get there in the end. The process was crazy. Jeremy [Heywood] and Ed Balls would agree, only for TB and GB then to reopen and disagree. To get where we needed to be on education, we were going to have to take something out of JP's and Milburn's budgets. The outstanding issues were becoming small in number but very difficult and the TB/GB bilateral this afternoon was the most difficult yet. Nothing was really agreed. They both had to leave for the Barbara Castle [former Labour Cabinet minister who had died in May] memorial, and even that had its own TB/GB-related problem. The initial suggestion had been that TB and GB do readings but GB had seemingly insisted on doing a big speech and in the current climate, it would look odd for him to do a big number and TB a little reading. So quickly we had to work up a speech for TB who until this point was not even aware he was doing it.

I went to retirement parties for Geoffrey Goodman [*British Journalism Review*] and Michael Jones [*Sunday Times*]. I got TB to come to Geoffrey's and make a nice little speech about integrity in journalism. Betty Boothroyd was at Michael Jones' and told me there was quite a lot of disillusion out there now. Charlie F was in to see TB re the Home Office and popped round for a chat. I made the argument that it was possible, and at times I felt probable, and very occasionally felt certain, that GB would never be leader. Charlie was not convinced, felt there was nobody else really emerging. Mike White called to say Stephen Bates [*Guardian* religious affairs correspondent] was doing a story that TB had rejected several names for the new Archbishop [of

Canterbury]. In trying to rebut it, I helped confirm it would be [Dr] Rowan Williams [Archbishop of Wales].

Wednesday, July 10

Ran in, up to see TB in the flat, who was hugely seized of the importance of IDS and [Michael] Howard [Shadow Chancellor] making clear they didn't intend to match our spending plans. It was classic Hague-ism.[1] He [IDS] had tried compassionate conservatism but now he had moved back to where his instincts were, on the right, a hard-line cuts agenda. It was a defining moment for Parliament and we had to pin it on them big time. But the big government story of the day was DB reclassifying cannabis [from Class B to C]. Keith Hellawell [government drugs adviser, or 'drugs czar'] went on *Today* and 'announced' he had resigned in protest. I had always tried hard with Hellawell, tried to boost him re his communication skills, but he had never quite cut it within the government machinery. I had to calm Blunkett down, say the most important thing was getting cops to back us and by and large they did. But I felt a bit uncomfortable both with the policy – but also the clear mixed messages of saying it was OK to take it but dealers could get fourteen years.

TB and GB met, and it was a collector's item. GB constantly complaining there was no strategy. Why did we do a crime initiative on the day he had done his NHS speech [see March 20]? TB saying 'I cannot believe you are still going on about it.' GB blaming TB for the *Telegraph* attacking him and when I pointed out that the *Telegraph* tended to attack TB a lot harder, he was having none of it. After he had left, TB said we just had to keep managing him. It's a pain, but he is still the best politician in the government, 'with the possible exception of me'. He said 'I've thought long and hard about whether I could put him out, and I don't believe I can. I feel a sense of duty to leave the Labour Party in good shape and the two of us as avowed enemies would be too bad to contemplate. I've thought about it but it's just not realistic, because whatever his faults, which are many, he is still the best qualified to take over.'

He said one of his weaknesses was that he forced others to adopt his own failings. He said Nick Brown would probably get hit hard in the FMD [inquiry] report [he had been agriculture minister during the 2001 foot and month crisis] and why? Because he didn't go to the centre for help when he most needed it because GB, as we knew, was

[1] Labour had attacked former Tory Leader William Hague for tacking to the right under pressure.

urging him to ignore all the presidential bullshit, so-called. I felt GB was trying to force him out by wearing him down. There was no doubt in GB's own mind that TB had reneged on a deal of some sort, but perhaps more significant than that, TB was moving to the view that GB was not temperamentally suited to a bigger job.

Fiona had a meeting with Jan Taylor [Number 10 Correspondence Unit] who had noticed a lot more disaffected mail coming through, the feeling that TB wasn't trustworthy. It chimed with what Philip was saying. PMQs was OK, and TB managed to get up the Tory cuts plan. IDS not great. I got Godric to say at the four o'clock that TB had to cancel his regional visit tomorrow because he had more CSR meetings. The Treasury went bonkers about it and I told them that was their problem. If they worked to a proper agreed strategy, there wouldn't be a problem.

Thursday, July 11

TB called me through and we went out for a chat on the terrace. Philip had briefed him on how his trust ratings had really dipped. He said 'In truth I've never really wanted to do more than two full terms. I could fight a third election *in extremis*, but it would have to be *in extremis*, namely that my worries about GB were such that I feel it would be wrong.' It was pretty clear to me that he had just about settled his view, that he would sometime announce it, say that he was going to stay for the full term, but not go into the election as leader. The big question was the same as before – does it give him an authority of sorts, or does it erode that authority, and do people just move automatically towards GB? He felt it was possible that it would strengthen him because he would be able to move people without anyone saying it was because he feared a rival. I had noticed, and he did it again today, that he had started to think about legacy, and how his premiership would be viewed, another indicator that he was moving psychologically to the exit door. He said 'I think even if I went now, it would be pretty good. Clinton-plus, certainly Clinton without the baggage.'

He felt in terms of transforming the party, winning, and the big policy changes we had made, there was a lot to point to. 'But the euro does matter a lot to me. Not because of a place in history but because I think it is the right thing for the country. The only question is whether it would just be seen as a deal with GB, that we do it, I go, he takes over. If I said I was going, sometime in the run-up to the next election, it would actually give me more power over him. I could move him. The question is whether politics would just want to move on to the next story. Maybe, but it would release me to do all the things I want to do. Really drive the public services agenda, really go for Europe and other foreign policy issues.'

He had mentioned the idea to Peter M, thinking he would be totally hostile, but he wasn't, because he could see the logic. It seemed to me he was definitely moving towards it. We walked in from the terrace to the Cabinet Room, and I asked him whether he really thought this was the right thing to do, or whether in fact he was being intimidated into doing it, and thinking it was the right thing, by a mix of GB and the press. He said, I don't think so. 'You have to know when to go. I also think the history of leaders trying to choose their successors is a very bad one.' So far as I was aware, only Jonathan, Sally, Cherie and I, and now Peter, were aware he was even thinking about this. As we walked back to his office, I said 'Christ, how much could I get from the press for this one?' He smiled, then stopped again and said 'Is it the right thing or the wrong thing? I want your best brain on it.'

At Cabinet, TB asked GB to speak on the economy pre CSR again and he warned it was going to get tougher and that there would be a need to reshape perceptions and expectations re pensions and house prices in particular. He said that problems in the American economy were going to have a big impact here and we would be 'severely tested'. TB spoke briefly about pensions and asked for a note. GB, very deliberately as part of the current style vs substance line they were running, said he would be happy to provide a note on this for Cabinet but 'It's very important that we focus on next year not next week.' In other words M was long term, TB was short term.

DB briefed the White Paper on criminal justice reform. Derry showed once more why he is not the most natural of politicians when he followed DB's presentation by saying 'I counsel caution about rebalancing the system in favour of the victim. This needs a more balanced approach.' Everyone knew what he meant, but it was the sort of statement that if made publicly would be a pretty full-scale disaster area. Joan Hammell [Prescott's special adviser] came to see me, said we really needed to watch JP, that he was very pissed off again, the bilaterals were not really serious. He was talking about not doing the visit with TB next week. GB had shown him the *Mail*, said that we cancelled the regional visit for CSR meetings and he said to Joan 'I'm just a pawn in their game.' TB, JP and GB were due to have dinner next week and I told her JP just had to understand how grim GB makes it for him from time to time.

Friday, July 12

Up at 5 to head off to Nottingham to see Rory running in the English Schools [athletic championships]. He had to stay with the rest of the team so I had hours to kill and worked up a speech for TB to set the tone for the CSR. It worked well as a newspaper story. Over to see Mum and Dad, and he was looking really ill.

Saturday, July 13

Back to the stadium for the finals. Really hot, nice atmosphere, but considering these were meant to be the best young runners in the country, the facilities were dreadful. Tom was doing a ring-round re the CSR briefing I had done and I was topping up with a couple of them to push education. The other situation we were having to deal with was Anji [Hunter] and Adam Boulton [in a relationship]. Anji called me about it last night, and Adam this morning and we agreed it was probably best that they let the *Mail on Sunday* do their worst and just say nothing. Sky wanted Adam to put out a statement and I called Nick Pollard [head of news] and said it was best not to. If they did, everyone would feel they had to run it. It was quite a turn-up for the books. Adam was very apologetic at the fact we were having to advise him on how to deal with it. TB called about the leak of the criminal justice White Paper to the *Mirror*, the *Independent* and *The Times*. Blunkett was livid, and demanding a leak inquiry which TB agreed to.

Sunday, July 14

We were getting into a much better place on the CSR, but why had it been so difficult? Peter M had noticed a shift, called to say 'For once the Treasury seems to be in the right place.' He was calling about a story in the *Observer* that he might become ambassador to the US. 'Please kill this at birth because it has clearly been put there to damage me.' We still didn't have agreement on DB's budget. Tessa called to say that she and other ministers were appalled at the letters being sent to them by the Treasury which were essentially telling them not just how much they were getting, but what to do with it.

Monday, July 15

Ran in, 31.03 minutes, personal best. TB had spent a lot of the weekend trying to influence GB's CSR statement to the House, felt it was too much focused on 'spend, spend, spend', not enough on reform. But we definitely had it set up in a better place, and GB was working for a good parliamentary and media response and by and large he did it. He delivered it fine, if a bit monotone, and he was effective in dealing with [Michael] Howard's not brilliant response. Education was running big out of it, but though there was reform in there, it didn't come through strongly. The CSR pretty much took care of itself so we had plenty of time to prepare for TB's meeting with the [Commons select committee chairs] Liaison Committee tomorrow. It would be like PMQs but without the noise and with more than just the Opposition party leader able to follow up forensically. So TB was mainly focusing on fact whereas I wanted a discussion of message and texture. We had the annual Labour Party reception in the garden but TB had to leave to take a call from Bush. Nothing much of substance, Bush saying he understood TB was taking a fair bit of stick for being supportive, and he was grateful.

Tuesday, July 16

Press OK for GB. Up to see TB in the flat, another chat about his future. You only get two terms, not sensible to choose a successor, usual stuff. I said what I couldn't work out was whether he really thought this was the right thing, or whether he had been pushed into it by bullying. He felt not, but though GB could be very difficult, he always tried to put that to one side when he worked out what to do. His big worry was still whether GB was suited for the job. We went through the Liaison Committee briefing, maybe an hour or so on that before he said he now wanted to prepare on his own and we left him. It was getting a big build-up from the media but he was pretty much on top of things by the time we left for the Commons. He was a bit nervy and faltering at first, and the interchange with the MPs wasn't terribly relaxed, but he picked up when they got on to serious policy, particularly foreign policy. They didn't really go for him, though there was far too much focus on the centre. It was definitely worth doing, was getting big play and good reviews both for him and for the MPs.

I went as [*News of the World* columnist] Chris Buckland's guest to the IDS press gallery lunch. I got a good look at IDS. He was much more personable than I thought, also more presentable. He told a couple of OK jokes at the start of his speech, mentioned me four or five times, which was far too often, because it suggested they were the ones obsessed with communication not us, and his main point was to attack the BBC over scrapping political programmes. Also said he would reverse our lobby reforms. It was OK without being brilliant. What I didn't feel was a big political or intellectual challenge to us.

I got back for a meeting with Tom McKane, David Manning and Jonathan re Iraq and when to do the documents. TB had raised the temperature another gear by making clear publicly we intended to do something and also saying that Saddam had to be dealt with. We agreed not to go for it yet, because it would look like we were going to go to war if we did, TB having made it clear that it would be the start of another phase. TB was pretty pleased with the way the Liaison Committee went, felt it had been worth doing because it was possible to engage in depth. The main news running out of it was Iraq. Philip called after the recent groups, which were grim. GB's CSR was just seen as more promises and the real problem was they didn't really feel there had been proper delivery yet. So the trust problem was real and deep. We really had to watch it now. The general judgement, fair or not, seemed to be not good enough, too many promises, not enough delivery.

Wednesday, July 17

Ran in, bang on thirty-one minutes. Union strikes [council and public transport workers] and the criminal justice White Paper were running big. TB was fine at PMQs, but frustrated that they didn't really go on the CSR. We agreed 'Schools and hospitals first' as the slogan for conference. I had a very interesting meeting with Carol Fisher [Central Office of Information] who felt there was a system of apartheid in the Civil Service, that people who came in from outside were tolerated but not welcome, and though she felt she had had some success in making change, her life had been something of a misery there. She clearly couldn't stand the old-style directors of information. It was quite an interesting take on things.

I read the FMD [inquiry] report which was pretty devastating, basically said every major decision was wrong. Although he [Dr Iain Anderson, chairman] was by and large OK about TB, it was clear he felt we should have done more early, should have called in the army and set up Cobra earlier. It was well written, well argued and all the better for that. It was a considered piece of work and I felt the sustained impact was pretty awful. Jeremy and I reacted pretty much identically. We showed it to TB without comment, and he felt pretty much the same. TB got a good press at the Liaison Committee but of course the apology from the IRA yesterday was a massive story and took over.[1]

To the Roof Gardens in Kensington for Ross [Kemp] and Rebekah [Wade]'s marriage party. Anji and Adam [Boulton] there together,

[1] The IRA issued an unprecedented apology to the families of those 'non-combatants' it killed during the thirty-year campaign of violence in Northern Ireland.

which was all a bit weird. GB and Sarah. Mo [Mowlam], Chris Smith [former Cabinet minister], DB came later. I enjoyed talking to Mark Bolland [press secretary to the Prince of Wales] who was incredibly indiscreet, not least in the way he talked about Prince Charles. He was scathing about the Palace establishment, said they hated him and they distrusted Charles' whole operation because they felt he was a threat to the Queen. He was pressing me re TB and GB, and also re what TB thought of matters royal, but I was rather more circumspect than he was.

Thursday, July 18

Fiona spotted a photographer in the street when she came back from swimming. He was from the [Evening] Standard trying to get a picture of me running. Up to the flat to see TB. He had not seen the Spectator interview with Piers [Morgan] which was a total diatribe against him and CB and had called for GB to be leader.

Went through to Cabinet with JP. He had had a couple of differences with GB over policy. As we walked through, he told me he was going to get rid of the RMT flat because it wasn't appropriate to have his own house becoming a story while he was doing a lot of difficult stuff on that front.[1] JP talked about the housing issue at Cabinet. TB did a bit of general spiel, but what was interesting was that he didn't really do what we discussed beforehand, instead went off on one on ministers' failure to deal with red tape and bureaucracy. He said if the Tories had any sense they would latch on to this, create a political narrative around the fact that we are demanding more in the centre whilst at the same time pursuing policies of devolution, and sometimes businesses feeling we have tied them in knots.

GB didn't speak, which again was a bit odd a few days after the CSR. Fiona had given a lift in to Ed Miliband and just as we felt GB and Co. were doing us in the whole time, they felt we were. GB didn't like the drift of policy but Ed said he felt powerless to do anything about it. Fiona felt GB now feared he was running out of time and the question was no longer whether he would take over but what there would be to do when he did, would he just come in on the back of failure re public services? Fiona had told Ed that if TB and GB worked together as a team, TB would be far more likely to be happy to let him take over, but the more it looked like GB was trying to

---

[1] Prescott was paying rent of £220 a month under a protected tenancy for a flat subsidised by the Rail, Maritime and Transport Workers' Union.

force him out, the more TB would dig in, and the more his people would be loyal to him even if they disagreed with some of what he did. She said Ed presented GB as a victim. But he had to use his power to be part of a team. She said why not just do the job, be nice, work with everyone else, and wait in the near-certain knowledge that before too long he would be prime minister? She said Ed had said it would be great if I worked with GB, but Fiona told him GB had barely acknowledged us for months now.

I went for lunch with David Frost at Le Caprice. He felt TB could pretty much stay as long as he wanted because he was in a different league, could probably win four elections if he put his mind to it, could certainly beat Thatcher's record. Then in for a meeting with TB, Margaret Beckett, RW and all the FMD people. TB had read the [inquiry report] introduction thoroughly, skimmed through the rest and felt it was pretty damning. But neither he nor Margaret were really up for saying someone should go for it. I said the overall sense as you read through it was of chaos, near panic, all the big decisions badly taken and there was bound to be a real drive for resignations and if we felt that was the case, and that's where we would end, we should do it now. Margaret felt that wasn't right, that Nick Brown was popular in the House and there would not be a real demand. I felt if the Tories got their act together, and really went for this, then we would be in difficulty. We would either lose people, or it would become a real symbol of arrogance. Billions wasted. Total fuck-up all round. But nobody says sorry and nobody resigns.

Margaret was pretty clear, said the Tories didn't resign over BSE. I felt if we were serious about the new politics, there had to be heads rolling, but Margaret was totally opposed and TB was a bit flaky about it. Margaret was very robust about the need to tough it out, felt it would be wrong for there to be sackings out of this. I totally disagreed but in the end if TB wasn't going to push it, there wasn't much we could do. I said if we are complacent or unapologetic we will be killed on this, and if the Tories or the Countryside Alliance can't put together a decent summertime campaign on it, they are totally useless.

Friday, July 19

Got in and TB called me up to the flat. He was wearing the most extraordinary collection – a white collarless Nicole Farhi shirt, plain blue trousers and England football slippers with the three lions on them. I said I find it very hard to take him seriously wearing kids' slippers and that shirt. He said I had a bias against style. He asked if I had thought any further about his *'grand projet'*. He felt it was nonsense that the Cabinet was moving towards GB and he really thought this could give him strength. He would announce it in the autumn, pre conference, make clear to the Cabinet that if anyone sought to exploit it or organise a leadership campaign, he would sack them. He felt it would actually allow him to move GB e.g. to the Foreign Office, because the charge could not be levelled that he was doing it to damage a rival. It would allow him to do what he thought was right without people saying he was simply interested in staying in power. Bill Clinton had said to him 'Whatever you do, go when they're still asking for more. Don't go like Thatcher.' TB said if she'd gone in '88, it would have been very different for her. Her last two years were just a downward path.

He had also decided that GB would not like it. It would mean the curtain on him would open more widely and the spotlight would fall upon him more. Deep down, he felt GB probably was flawed, not right for the top job but it was not a good idea for leaders to pick their successors and the party and the country had to discover these things for themselves. I had quietly discussed what he was saying both with Fiona and Sally and both were adamant it would make him a lame duck overnight, but he was persuading himself it would give him extra authority. There was also the possibility of space opening for another successor to emerge. I wasn't sure about that but for now he seemed set on it, constantly saying to me 'You only get two terms in this job.' I told him what Frost had said, namely that he could easily go into the record books for longevity. He said the great difference between him and other politicians was that he could walk away from it.

He then walked over to the wall, leant against it, laughed and said 'There's another complication I need to tell you about.' He said 'I think Cherie is pregnant.' He said they were both absolutely gobsmacked by the whole thing. But it did mean it was forcing him to think about the future. 'I've effectively got two families with the same woman.' He had known she might be pregnant for a few days and it had clearly had an impact on his thinking about the *grand projet*. I felt a big weight carrying two pretty major secrets from the same conversation, his apparent decision to go before the election, and Cherie pregnant again.

Saturday, July 20

I slept really badly, lots of different worries just floating around, couldn't decide whether TB was right with his *grand projet*, was trying to separate out my own feelings about my own position, which would probably welcome it. As for CB being pregnant again, it was mind-blowing. It was a nice morning and I went out into the garden to dictate some notes to the office, and was stung by a bee, much to the Garden Room's amusement.

Sunday, July 21

Conference call re FMD. Jeremy and I both felt that the FMD draft statement from Defra [Department for Environment, Food and Rural Affairs] was poor and both of us made various efforts through the day to get it improved but the department was very resistant. There was something of an irony in it, as one of the subtexts of the whole report was that they had been slow to exploit necessary help from the centre. It was only when I spoke to Margaret B herself that we started to make some progress. Jeremy and I still believed TB was slightly head-in-the-sand about the potential impact, but TB felt it might not be the total disaster we feared. I found myself beginning to wind down and think about the holiday.

Monday, July 22

Ran through the parks, six miles in just over forty-two minutes. I bumped into Michael Martin [Speaker of the Commons] in Green Park, where he was out walking, and had a really nice chat with him, about bagpipes and about Scotland. Through the day, a series of meetings with the policy people on the pamphlet we were planning for September. The balance to strike was between reform and values. I wanted the focus on values, as a way of saying we were New Labour delivering Old Labour goals. TB was on reform for a purpose. I was really impressed with Douglas [Alexander] at the moment. Of all the GB people, he was the one least wrapped up in the whole TB/GB thing.

TB had a conversation with Iain Anderson [FMD report author], then spoke to Margaret B, then to Nick Brown to tell him that he was not going to have to resign and we would tough it out. He went [to the Commons] for the [FMD] statement, which was just about OK. He filled in Sally and me on last night's dinner with JP and GB. He said it was pretty awful, GB doing his usual complaining that there was no strategy, what was going on, who does what, with the unions his latest area for complaint. TB told him to calm down, said we had a problem and we had to deal with it but let's not get our knickers in a twist. He said it was quite useful for JP to see so clearly the extent to which GB failed to hide the fact he could hardly bear to be in TB's company. JP had said at the end that a lot of the attacks had been personal dressed up as political.

TB and I went for lunch at the *Guardian* and he was on good form, but Iraq was clearly going to be a major problem with everyone, though helpfully Mike White reminded us that TB had talked about WMD, and his worries about the link with Iraq, when he last went for lunch there last September. Later I had a meeting with SIS re Iraq. C had just come back from the US and had reported from his discussions with Condi and George Tenet [CIA director] that as far as they were concerned it was when not if, with or without us, and they did not feel the need for a new UNSCR. TB was right out there and was going to be very exposed. Then to the farewell dinner for Richard Wilson, which was a nice enough do. TB was fulsome in his praise and though Richard and I had had a few ups and downs, he was actually not a bad guy, and I liked his kids. You can tell a lot about people from the way they react to their children and the way their children react to them, and I was really impressed by their relationship with Tom, their deaf son. I sat next to him at the dinner and really liked him.

Tuesday, July 23

TB chaired a big Iraq meeting, JS, GH, CDS, C, Francis Richards [director of GCHQ], Peter Goldsmith [Attorney General], plus the key Number 10 people. C reported his strong feeling that the US had pretty much made up their minds. Steve Hadley [US Deputy National Security Advisor] was saying there was no need for another resolution, and how many more times do we hang around watching the Iraqis stiff Kofi? Condi was a bit better but not much. TB was asking whether the Iraqis would welcome an invasion or not. Jack felt the regime would appear to be popular until it tips, but when it tips, it will happen quickly. All the signs out of Washington were that their thinking had moved forward, as per Bush's remarks about taking the battle to the enemy, taking him on before he takes us on. Boyce set out military options. These would vary from provision of bases, maritime support and special forces, right up to the provision of thousands of troops. Geoff felt the preparations either for a generated start or a running start were well advanced. Kuwait was essential to the plan, so is the UK because of Diego Garcia and Cyprus [airbases].

On the heavy side of things, we could be looking at two armoured brigades entering via Turkey. Jack set out the political difficulties. He said it was all being driven by DoD and NSC, and Powell and the State Department were not fully involved. Apparently Powell would not be at the August 4 meeting at which all this was being thrashed out. Boyce thought CENTCOM would be briefed on August 1 or 2, Rumsfeld on August 3, Bush on August 4. TB said he did not want any discussions with any other departments at this stage and did not want any of this 'swimming round the system'. He meant the Treasury, because Boyce had been talking about the need for new money, e.g. for tank desertification. Jack said that of the four powers posing a potential threat with WMD – Iran, Korea, Libya and Iraq – Iraq would be the fourth. He does not have nukes, he has some offensive WMD capability. The tough question is whether this is just regime change or is the issue WMD? TB was pretty clear that we had to be with the Americans. He said at one point 'It's worse than you think, I actually believe in doing this.' He was acutely conscious of how difficult it would be both with the PLP and the public, but when Jack raised the prospect of not going in with the US, TB said that would be the biggest shift in foreign policy for fifty years and I'm not sure it's very wise.

On the tactical level, he felt maximum closeness publicly was the way to maximise influence privately. Geoff pointed out the Americans' clear view that they already had legal justification. They had a different take to Goldsmith, who did not see regime change alone as having a legal base for force, and also that self-defence/humanitarian were not current overwhelming arguments, which leaves UNSC. TB said he needed to be convinced first of the workability of a military plan, and second of an equally workable political strategy. Jack said we could probably get the votes for a UN ultimatum, but the Americans may not want to go down that route. TB saw regime change as the route to dealing with WMD.

As if to go from the sublime to the ridiculous, TB, having spent much of the morning dealing with Iraq, spent part of the afternoon doing an interview with readers of *Chat* magazine, including a ventriloquist and a fortune-teller. There were some days I wondered how he kept going with all the different things he had to do, because sandwiched in was a meeting on euro preparations plus a stack of different policy issues. On the euro, TB was keen that we crank up but Roger Liddle [special adviser, European affairs] said that most of Europe thought we were not going to do it because GB was blocking him.

Wednesday, July 24
TB at the PLP, PMQs and the Northern Ireland statement at which we were raising the bar on a ceasefire judgement [amid renewed violence in Belfast]. He did well at the PLP and at PMQs and we

were ending pretty well. IDS had not covered himself in glory with his reshuffle and as he came back from PMQs TB said 'That is a dead man walking. We should be thinking when, not if, and who's next.' TB had chatted with JP about his own future and had said that if he went at the election, JP should go too so they could let in a new broom, and he was pretty much up for that.

We were picking up signs that Clare was at it over Iraq. TB called her in to say he did not want her messing around on Iraq. She said she would be supportive and that she was not out to cause trouble. Yeah, sure. At Richard [Wilson]'s main farewell, he [RW] told a story about Leo pulling on his trouser leg and saying 'Alastair'. It was a nice enough do and I was tired. I also noticed there was not a single black face apart from his old driver. This was the never-changing Establishment.

Thursday, July 25

Today the second of TB's new monthly press conferences. He called me up to go over tricky areas, mainly Iraq, Ireland, unions. We had got Michael Barber lined up to do the press conference with TB to try to get some focus on public service delivery. On Iraq, he said he didn't really want a big fight on this unless he has to have it. TB ran up the stairs for the press conference so started out of breath. Michael Barber did well and it was interesting enough. Questions mainly Iraq and Ireland. Hopeless on the personal stuff, e.g. would the 21-year-old TB approve of the TB of today, and he just muttered about being less radical. Then he was off to Manchester [for the opening of the Commonwealth Games].

I had a long session with JP re August [recess] but we mainly talked about GB. I said TB was at the end of his tether and really didn't know what to do about him. JP said he could see that and after Sunday's dinner he understood better what I meant. GB just raged at him, at one point asked him the same question ten times. JP asked him afterwards why he behaved like that. He said he just got an outpouring of bitterness and anger and mistrust. 'It really is like a lover spurned.' JP said he saw his job as trying to make sure the party held together and came out stronger. He had told GB he would support him but not if he took on TB, and nor would the party, so he had to bide his time. He shared our view that GB was in part using the euro to do in Tony. He said if it was true that he spoke more to [Rupert] Murdoch about his thinking on the euro than he did to TB, it was an outrage. He told GB it was make your mind up time.

His assessment was that TB wanted to do the euro and get out. He didn't really want a third term for himself but he did want it for the party, and that's what JP wanted too. If TB and GB split the party they will not be forgiven and that's why we have to do all we can to keep them together. But it was going to be difficult. I said I was glad that he had seen for himself what TB had to contend with in the face of this hatred. TB was growing almost immune to it. JP said I have to keep TB onside for an approach based on working together, and he had to work on GB. He said obviously some of these things are too sensitive for wider discussion, but he intended to get his own assessment of the two of them on their own intentions. Also, TB had to involve him and GB more on discussions of strategy.

I asked him about his own intentions. I said TB felt that if he went before the election maybe they should step down together and maybe that would make transition easier. He said that was probably right. He said he had been very angry when TB directly accused him of siding with GB. He said he will always be loyal to the leader because 'that's my job'. GB had said he would keep him on but 'I'll have to make a judgement. I can see how a clean break might be best.' He said if GB waffled on about the fourth quartile of the economic tests then he would know he was messing about and he would say no. He intended to get to the bottom of GB's euro intentions. He agreed with me that GB was probably panicking, that he was running out of time, but also he was worrying about the economy. 'He took all the credit when credit was going, so now he worries that he gets the blame,' he said. It was a good, friendly discussion and I think we both knew we would have to work together pretty well to keep the two of them in some kind of partnership.

TB called a couple of times from his visit to the Commonwealth Games. I watched the opening ceremony, which was excellent, and after all the bollocks in the media that Manchester would be a disaster, it was looking pretty good. TB raised his *grand projet* again. I said I don't know why you keep asking me, because you've basically made up your mind. He said no, depends on a lot of things, and I really want you to think over the holiday about whether there is a way I can use it to strengthen myself.

Friday, July 26 – Wednesday, August 28 (holiday)
We had a great start to the holiday, driving to Paris for the last day of the Tour de France and staying with John and Penny Holmes. It was a beautiful hot day and Grace was having a fantastic time in the garden with Bonny the dog, and just looked as happy as I had ever seen her. The cycling itself was less exciting than the stages, just a

procession, but there was a nice atmosphere. The first time I was really bothered was when we got to Pizay for our second overnight stop. The *Mail* were on to the story that Alastair Irvine [son of Derry Irvine] was in jail [for drugs offences in the US]. It had been hard enough for Derry just to deal with the fact of what had happened, but having to deal with these fuckers could make it worse. I did a conference call with Godric and Alan Percival [Lord Chancellor's Department] and put together a statement and an outline strategy. Derry agreed to it. He said things had been pretty unbearable recently. I said I thought people would think it odd that they hadn't gone out and he said he didn't want to create a UK media circus around him. He was pretty clear that the only real route to rehabilitation was to stop taking drugs. The *Mail* did it big a couple of days later but the follow-up was relatively limited.

Philip and Georgia [Gould] joined us in Paris and on the drive down Philip typically left his passport at a service station. TB called as I was driving down to discuss Iraq. It was clearly going to be a problem and we were not on the pitch. We agreed that we should start to push out some of the Saddam material. He and CB went on their mini-break in Cumbria and she had a miscarriage. By now we were down in Puyméras, from where Fiona and I sorted out with the detectives how to get them in and out of hospital without anyone knowing. Keith Lowe and Charles Lindsay [detectives] did a great job, got them in, got them out the next day and as when Leo went in, the hospital didn't leak.

TB sounded pretty down about it though he was philosophical. He said Cherie was feeling very low and sad. They were also worried that it would crank up the media interest in their holiday. We decided against actually putting something out and instead waited for calls from the press once they noticed what was going on, which they did when the kids went to France without TB and CB. We had a statement ready with the bare facts plus an appeal for them to be allowed a quiet holiday. Coverage was big, fairly sympathetic and once they got away the next day, they were basically just doing captions stories. The local French paper said that Britons had been '*stupéfaits*' at the news of the pregnancy. The main news back home was two young girls who had gone missing.[1]

The Commonwealth Games had become a real success story but

[1] Two ten-year-olds, Holly Wells and Jessica Chapman, had gone missing in Soham, Cambridgeshire. After a search lasting two weeks, their bodies were found and school caretaker Ian Huntley was arrested and subsequently convicted of murder.

Brendan [Foster] called me to say people would go apeshit when we ripped up the track at the end. The boys and I were pretty hooked to the European athletics. I was playing tennis most days with Calum but just as Rory was now way ahead of me on running, so he was way ahead of me on tennis. We had a little running drama for the holiday when Anne Messelink [holiday agent] called to say that a friend of hers had been approached by a *Sunday Times* journalist trying to find me. The next day, he appeared at the bar in the village and Eva, the bar owner, called me to warn me. She then set up a little network of people round the village who kept tabs on him and for the next two or three days I was able to dodge him. On the Friday morning, when I was out in Marseilles collecting Gail [Rebuck], the reporter arrived outside the house and later came back with a photographer. Fiona told them we did not want to be disturbed. I called [John] Witherow [*Sunday Times* editor] to ask what was going on and he said it was a piece about how New Labour was taking over the area and turning it into the new Tuscany. 'It's the price of fame. You do know you're a bit of a fashion icon don't you?' I said I reckoned Murdoch was a lot more famous than I am and I bet they are not doorstepping his holiday.

TB was due to do a meeting and photocall with [Jean-Pierre] Raffarin [new French Prime Minister] after their lunch in Cahors on the 12th. The French wanted a real big-licks press conference but TB and I were worried we would simply end up with totally different positions on Iraq. Totally counterproductive. Neil [Kinnock] was very down on GB at the moment. He had told him that he was the only person in history who could say with almost total certainty that he would be the next PM and the only person who could stop him was himself. If people felt he was trying to shoehorn Tony out, there would be a real reaction against him. Neil had his own problems through the summer, namely a woman in Brussels from the court of auditors attacking him, making all sorts of allegations, which he was pushing back on.

I had a series of conversations with TB re the US. Bush had suggested that he go there for the September 11 commemorations and they have a discussion about Iraq around that. I was worried about it, felt that people would see through it and also it ran totally counter to the strategy we planned for September. We agreed to keep it on hold for now. There had been stories about how Robin was leading Cabinet moves against our position and when I told him TB said 'Well, they can just calm down.' I had to get a bit involved sorting the French re his meeting with Raffarin, which they wanted to do bigger than we did. He felt that working with the French was a bit easier now that it was clear who was in charge, without the uncertainty of cohabitation.

I was running most days and one day Richard Eyre [theatre director], who was staying nearby, wanted to come out with me and we did about eight or ten miles, and at one point I thought he was going to pass out, and suggested we stop. Eventually, I ran ahead. We spent a lot of time with the Kinnocks as well as the Goulds and did a better job at avoiding political talk. Philip was very excited about a Milburn article in the *Spectator* which he felt took him into a higher league and showed some of the qualities that had got TB to the top, notably guts. Philip's general view at the moment was that TB could come back really strong but he had to resist being spooked by GB. Neil felt GB was capable of throwing it all away, but did anyone really think Milburn was the answer? I doubted it. Hugh Hudson [film director] came over for a night and it seemed so, so long ago that he, Neil and I had worked on that election broadcast.[1]

Cherie called Fiona on the 17th and said TB's dinner with Alan Milburn recently had had a profound effect on him. It was one thing to hear from me and Sally that GB was at it, but Milburn, given his experience as chief secretary, was another thing. He had given an assessment of how he [GB] operated in the Treasury – the secrecy, the divide and rule, the briefings. He felt TB needed to strengthen his team and he wanted to help him do it. Jack Straw was on a few times towards the end of the holiday as he was due to visit Powell in the US and we discussed whether to announce it, given it would be seen as a big Iraq thing. After a bit of toing and froing we decided not to. Jack was keen that we push the Yanks towards accepting that there had to be a UN mandate re Iraq but the noises from Cheney and Rumsfeld were very much focused on 'do it whatever'. There were a number of articles in the States, e.g. from Jim Baker and Richard Holbrooke [senior US diplomat], voicing real caution. Philip came home a couple of days before us to do some groups on his first night back, which were dreadful, particularly on delivery. The end of the holiday was hit by some pretty bad weather which washed out the village fair, and although we had a nice time, I had not been sleeping that well.

[1] The 1987 broadcast, popularly known as 'Kinnock: The Movie', mixed footage of Kinnock's speeches with shots of the Kinnocks walking on a coastal path in Llandudno, Wales. As part of Labour's highly professional, but ultimately unsuccessful election campaign, the broadcast strengthened and broadened Kinnock's leadership profile.

Thursday, August 29

First day back. Didn't feel like going in. JP called from South Africa, wanting reassurance about how he had handled the summer, also saying I had to get some more passion into TB's speech for the [Johannesburg] summit [on sustainable development] and only I could do it, and he was really worried that we wouldn't get a proper agreement without TB doing the real hard negotiations towards the end. TB spoke to Bush. He had sent him a long note in late July and David Manning had been to see Condi. The next day he had been called in to see Bush himself. He had been pretty frank and made clear that this was very difficult for us. Equally TB's note said we would have real public and party problems and things would be even worse in Europe. David's worry was that there seemed to be no thought-through political or public information strategy and too many difficult unanswered questions. He also felt Condi was far too optimistic about the Middle East and prospects for progress. Their meeting had been earlier and David had said we needed to exhaust the UN route but in the ensuing weeks Rumsfeld and Cheney had both made what were seen as fairly belligerent speeches. David had put the case forcefully that they had to understand the difficulties of other countries. He believed that on the idea of an ultimatum the Russians, Chinese and even the French would support or acquiesce. David's strong sense was that though they might go it alone, they didn't want to. They valued TB's advice. They needed to be persuaded on UN/ultimatum and on the need to do more re the Middle East. Bush felt that it was possible to see a quick collapse of the Iraqis. He had also talked up evidence of links with al-Qaeda, which our and US intelligence were not convinced of. We were pushing the idea of a tough, time-bound ultimatum. Bush had said he was 'evangelical' re getting rid of Saddam and was a 'good vs evil guy'. He felt equally strongly about Korea. But David felt it was not a lost cause to push him down the UN ultimatum route. TB's note had made clear our basic support but also said we had to be blunt about the difficulties. His note went through the need for an agreed strategy on six fronts – UN ultimatum route/evidence/MEPP/post-Saddam/Arab Muslim worlds/Afghanistan. Finally and fairly briefly he addressed the military plan and of the running start vs generated start, he preferred the latter.

When they spoke, TB sensed Bush was a bit nervous about the UN route but equally he wasn't happy about the Cheney/Rumsfeld comments, which he tried to justify by saying they had been reacting to [Brent] Scowcroft [former US National Security Advisor] and Jim

Baker. Later though I spoke to Mary Matalin [Cheney's press secretary] who was adamant that Cheney had not 'gone freelance', by which I assumed she meant he had been speaking with Bush's knowledge and approval. David was not so sure. TB was now clear he should see Bush as soon as possible and felt that we had to get at it before he was making his UNGA [UN General Assembly] speech, and preferably whilst Bush was still having his 'Council of War'. He was clearly getting a lot of competing advice.

TB still felt confident we could turn the argument. He felt the left had got itself into a ridiculous position by appearing to be standing up and protecting Saddam. The reality was people had let him get away with it for too long. Everyone felt that if we could get the UN route it would be a lot easier. TB, when I first saw him today, was wearing the full Rio Ferdinand [footballer] look – shorts, his FA slip-ons and the trendy vest. He said he had been thinking a lot and the most important thing now was that he did what he thought was right, on foreign and domestic regardless of what the focus groups or anyone else thought.

Friday, August 30

TB had decided he wanted to delay the EMU referendum to 2004 so we had lots of time to make the case. He wanted to calm Iraq and we spent some time working out what he should say to the press on the plane tomorrow. He had done an exceptionally long note on the general position, the need to get a big political argument re the individual and the state, the need for much greater radicalism re reform in the public services. It contained a few barbed criticisms about what was coming out of the Policy Unit and his continuing frustration at the lack of strategic capability in the main departments came out of virtually every note he wrote. I think we both felt frustrated that so much fell upon the centre, whilst departments complained that it was because we took things away from them. If they were more competent and capable, I think everyone would be happy.

TB also said, though we had heard it after holidays before, that he wanted to change the way we worked, so that we became more formal, with a proper approach modelled on a company board. We went through his note page by page, general direction, radical reform the answer not the problem, discussion about the pamphlet. Jonathan was pushing even harder than TB on the radicalism front, re diversity, choice of provider [in public services], Civil Service reform. He thought the Tories would come in and take a big-state argument against us.

TB had also proposed trying to establish a cross-party commission on pensions and transport. He felt both were issues that would require several terms to sort and we should try to build support across the board. But why, we all thought, would the Tories go for it, taking away two of the most potentially difficult areas for us?

TB was also banging on even louder than ever about crime and asylum. Felt that if we weren't careful asylum would become the next fuel-protest situation, and for obvious reasons have the potential to be even worse. There were more bad figures out today and he felt that the Home Office just weren't on top of it. Nor did they get the need for the message on this to be so widely understood that it had an impact on behaviour. On Ireland, he was more not less worried than when he went away. On Europe, he had really gone through the detail of the IGC [EU Intergovernmental Conference] negotiations, and said that whilst on the big message we were standing up against the superstate ideas, it was in the detail that these arguments were won and lost. The one big surprise out of his holiday was him saying he didn't want to do the [euro] referendum before 2004. On GB, he felt we had to keep trying for an agreed strategy but at the same time broaden his efforts with the rest of the Cabinet. He was worried about the party but totally dismissive of the unions, felt they were just misreading what was happening in the country. Finally on the office, he said he wanted fresh people but didn't go beyond that. I got David Manning to tell Condi that we would like to announce the TB visit on Tuesday but it would be difficult to pin down re dates. I was also concerned that the mood music going out from us about the need for a UN resolution was being picked up by the US as evidence of us diddling them.

Saturday, August 31

Up at the crack of dawn to go to Number 10 and meet the TB convoy. The *FT* splash said TB pressed Bush for a UN mandate, which could be a problem with the Yanks, while the others were saying TB would break his silence on Iraq on the plane to Mozambique. We both wanted to avoid talking about Iraq, but it would be difficult and we agreed we would have to say he was not letting it overshadow the [Johannesburg] summit. If pushed, he'd say that doing nothing was not an option but he didn't particularly want to go beyond that. Privately, he was growing more and more dismissive of the critics. He found it unfathomable that even the [Church of England] bishops almost appeared to be defending Saddam as if he was some great liberal. Equally, he was clear that the Yanks had not handled it well over the holiday. Condi had admitted as much to David, that they had allowed the game to run ahead of them, and Cheney and Rumsfeld had just made it worse.

We spent ages on the plane working on the three speeches he would be making on the trip, including one in which he intended to be very forward on Kyoto [climate change protocol, 1997]. He was clear that he wanted to be more and more himself, but also that we did need fewer papers and fewer journalists who were basically out to kill him. He was a lot steelier than when he went on holiday. Clear that getting Saddam was the right thing to do. Barely mentioned GB. Very strong language on climate change in the speech. He saw the press and it was going to be hard for them not to make Iraq the story. We arrived [in Maputo] and a somewhat chaotic and noisy motorcade took us to the hotel. Clare Short arrived and TB was pretty chilly with her.

We drove out to the presidential palace where they [TB and President Joaquim Chissano] had a tête-à-tête and I talked with the finance minister [Luísa Días Diogo], the daughter of a nurse. The dinner was pretty ghastly, cold soup that was meant to be hot, cold prawns that were meant to be hot, a strange-tasting turkey and a fruit salad out of a tin. I'd love to know if Chirac, should he ever be here, would do his usual over-the-top 'look at all this wonderful food' routine. I liked the politicians. They had a directness that was appealing. There was a lot of talk about Maria Mutola [800 m runner, nicknamed 'the Maputo Express'] and the president told us she was so good at football that the boys demanded she was sex-tested to see if she was a girl. She was a major national heroine though.

David had got Condi to get GWB to offer TB next Saturday for a meeting in the margins of his so-called war counsel. I think they realised they had messed up the presentation and had to get into a better position, so it seemed clear Bush did want TB there, but heaven knows what Cheney and Rumsfeld would make of it. TB was up for it. JP was in total summit mode and calling the whole time from Johannesburg.

Sunday, September 1

Iraq was becoming a frenzy again. TB was becoming more and more belligerent, saying he knew it was the right thing to do. He said the US had to be managed. Obviously the best thing to do would be to avoid war, get the UN inspectors in and all the weapons out. It was obvious too that the US had to be managed into a better position.

That is what we have to do, he said. But we won't be able to do it if we come out against the US the whole time. He was developing the line that the UN route was fine if it was clearly a means to resolve the issue, but not if it's a means to duck the issue. Equally, it was clear that public opinion had moved against us during August. I worked on the speech while he went to church. He came back to sign off the speech, including the very strong line on Kyoto.[1]

I went out for a run, first through the diplomatic compound then drifted into what looked like the middle-class area of town, and eventually into a shanty town, where the kids were surprised to see someone like me running through, and joined in for a bit. They were incredibly friendly, and parts of the countryside were lush and rich. But the signs of extreme poverty were everywhere amid sporadic signs of wealth. Later we flew to Beira [second city of Mozambique]. We had *Marie Claire* magazine with us and I got them to interview the finance minister. We visited the hospital. The kids' malarial ward was pretty depressing, several kids to a bed, helpless-looking parents. One of the little girls was called Grace so I phoned home and told her about it. Then to a town called Dondo, TB pretty much mobbed going round the market. Watched a children's show, then a school visit before flying back to Maputo. The hotel seemed obscenely nice after some of the things we had seen. Up to see TB and finalise the speech. Spoke to Fiona who had received an email from Cherie about discussions she had been having with Cate Haste [author, wife of broadcaster Melvyn Bragg] about a book she was planning to do on PM's spouses.[2] Fiona sounded very fed up about the whole thing.

Monday, September 2

Flew down to Johannesburg, finished the speech on the way. It was one of these difficult little five-minute jobs, where everyone was trotting out the same clichés and we decided to concentrate on the big-vision message. TB had a chat with Clare at the hotel. She said that if she had a problem with Iraq, she would tell him. She said too that she was very surprised when TB had said GB did not always work closely with him. I had an example, the *Mirror* doing a story re

[1] 'Kyoto is right and it should be ratified by all of us . . . the facts remain, the consequences of inaction on these issues are not unknown, they are calculable. Poverty and environmental degradation, if unchecked, spell catastrophe for our world, that is clear.'

[2] *The Goldfish Bowl: Married to the Prime Minister 1955–1997* would be published in 2004.

GB warning against the cost of an Iraq war. We reached Johannesburg and set off for the usual summit bollocks, I could tell TB was a bit nervous about the speech because it was one of those where he and a small group of others were expected to make the biggest impact, but it was a pretty tough audience. He was also livid at all the stuff appearing in the media about the UN and now, the *Mail* splash on TB going out there to see Bush. He spoke to David [Manning] and Jonathan, saying he wanted a message round the system that all this loose talk had to stop. And he wanted the Americans to know how angry he was. He thought it might be Sally thinking she was protecting his internal position, saying he was pushing Bush, but TB knew it would be damaging with the US. Condi had said it looked like we were trying to push them, and they didn't like it.

Iraq scene was a bit grim and all building up to the press conference. Condi liked the argument that the UN was the route to dealing with it, not the route to avoiding it. TB's speech got a pretty good reception but the Namibians whacked him [Namibian President Sam Nujoma demanding sanctions on Zimbabwe be lifted] and when [Robert] Mugabe [President of Zimbabwe] had a go as well, that was the news for the day. We had a bilateral with Zhu Rongji [Premier of China], who agreed we had to deal with Iraq but said he felt strikes would be bad and dangerous. He said 'wisdom and patience' were required. Then Chirac, and we agreed to get the focus not too much on Iraq, had a short press event, which was a bit chaotic. TB had a warmer conversation with him than usual, sensed that Chirac was worried about a Schroeder victory because it would mean bad relations after his backing for Stoiber.

We left for Alexandra township, where we had been before. Plenty of progress to see, lots of change amid all the problems. They had set up a huge marquee with music playing, dancing, nice food, where TB planted a tree and made a little speech about how steadily this place was changing for the better. He was good at this type of event and it came over well on the media here but by now Mugabe was the main story at home, at least as far as the main papers were concerned, though Fiona said he was coming over really well on TV. He did clips on the tour of the township saying Mugabe etc. did not represent the true voice of Africa and he was worried that other leaders would look at these comments and say why should we help them? On the edge of the township, new homes had been built which were being shown to us as evidence of the great progress, though in reality homes housing large families were of a size a modestly well-off single person would expect at home.

We got back for a reception hosted by the British delegation to the summit, I spent most of the time chatting to Jack McConnell [First Minister of Scotland]. TB had a stack of bilaterals with Kofi [Annan], [Thabo] Mbeki who was very weak on Zimbabwe, [Jean] Chrétien and Helen Clark [New Zealand Prime Minister]. Although a lot of the talk was about the summit business, most conversation turned to Iraq at some point and TB was clearer by the end of the day that we had to get the Americans down the UN route. President [Abdelaziz] Bouteflika of Algeria told TB he wanted Algeria to be able to join the Commonwealth. TB was so taken aback that he said yes, I'm sure that's fine. He felt that all the angst that was coming our way about Iraq would strengthen our hand as it was clear that a lot of them would come with us down the UN route and we'd set that up with the Bush speech to UNGA. On the way back, we went over the lines for the press conference tomorrow. TB said he intended to be on the tough end of the market as we ran through some of the questions. I went to bed and slept almost till we landed. The summit outcome was OK but the general take was that it hadn't delivered all that was promised or hoped for.

Tuesday, September 3

Landed 7.15 at Teesside, and drove to Myrobella with TB. Press working themselves into a lather re press conference. I finished the script and TB decided in the end to do very brief opening remarks on the North-East, Johannesburg outcome and then Iraq, but the bulk of the argument was going to be made during questions. He came back and we went through some of the hard questions on Iraq. The hardest was 'Why now? What was it that we knew now that we didn't before that made us believe we had to do it now?' It was not going to be at all easy to sell the policy in the next few months, especially because GWB was so unpopular in the UK. TB, Tom Kelly and I went through it all again in the garden. He said several times he was going to be on the tough end of the market, and he was. He kept going for ninety minutes, really hitting the ball in the middle of the bat, top lines very clear – dealing with Saddam was the right thing to do and we would stand by the US. Major bulletin coverage. The *Sun* thought he was brilliant. Even critics said he was on top, committed and passionate about it. Definitely worth doing.

He then did a call with GWB who was planning to tell Congress leaders TB was going to Camp David, so I got an operational note ready to go. The toughest question was what new evidence was there. He said the debate had got ahead of us, so we were going to do the dossier earlier, in the next few weeks.[1] The problem was this was going to raise expectations massively. Today was about beginning to turn the tide of public opinion and it was going to be very tough indeed. We went to Trimdon Labour Club for a reception mainly for the foreign media. Then Tom and I headed back to the airport. Good trip overall, strong press conference but a long way to go.

Wednesday, September 4

Generally positive press for TB. The problem, as shown by [now FCO minister] Mike O'Brien's dreadful interview on the radio, was the dossier and the massive expectations. TB felt we could make the case. The story today was going to be Bush saying he would consult widely and go to the UN. Meeting on September 11 [anniversary], agreed we should be low-key, no minute's silence other than at St Paul's. Then I left for home and had a conference call with Condi and the White House team. Not brilliant. We agreed we needed a way of telling the whole story from the word go, maybe year by year. They were making fairly small presentational points. But we agreed we had to get CIC structures back up soon, and that there must be much better co-ordination of message than in August. We then discussed what message they wanted from Bush's speech [to US Congress representatives at the White House] e.g. challenge to UN, bad stuff on Saddam, make clear he was going down the UN route, but it could not obstruct and divert. It was an OK call but I didn't really feel we were at the races yet and it wasn't clear how we were going to get there. The Commons would be important, but it was not going to be easy. Robin Cook called because he was doing press tomorrow re Commons modernisation and was clearly up for causing problems on Iraq. He said he would 'try to stay on message' but then said 'I hope Tony and you don't want a shooting war.' He said Bush and Co. had screwed it up and we should not be held responsible for that.

Thursday, September 5

The Bush [White House] speech went down OK. At the office meeting, out on the terrace, ostensibly to talk about follow-up to TB's note, we

[1] Blair also undertook to publish a dossier on Iraq's WMD development, saying 'Originally I had the intention that we wouldn't get round to publishing the dossier until we had actually taken the key decisions, but I think it is probably a better idea to bring that forward . . . a lot of the work has already been done. There needs to be some more work and some more checking done, but I think probably the best thing to do is publish that within the next few weeks.'

just talked about Iraq. All of us were pressing TB to go with the flow on the demands for a recall of Parliament, but he was very resistant. We were saying it would let off steam and show he was serious in our Parliament strategy. But he said there were too many questions that we could not really answer, added to which there was not really much to say at the moment. The press conference had settled things but the media were determined to keep a sense of frenzy going on this. Agreed to put out the line that there was no question of troops being sent without Parliament being consulted. But the idea of a 'Council of War' had taken hold. Added to which [Michael] Cockerell [BBC political documentary maker] was today screening his special-relationship documentary [*Hotline to the President*] in which TB's answer to a question about 'blood price' was the big story.[1] TB said we had to get the UN route but could not do it too much. We were pushing him on dossier timing.

JP was very loyal, said he was totally supportive. There was a lot of angst around. I called Robin C to give him the line on recall of Parliament and he said I hope you are not going to go down the road of war because I believe it could mean the end of the government. Meeting with John Scarlett, Tom McKane, Des Bowen [MoD], Edward Chaplin [FCO], Julian Miller [Cabinet Office intelligence and security official] to go over 'the dossier'. It had to be revelatory and we needed to show that it was new and informative and part of a bigger case. John Williams [FCO director of public and press affairs] was offering to write it full-time. John Scarlett was clearly aware of the responsibility, he was so serious. I felt he was very human. He warned us that there was very little re nuclear. JS called to say he had seen C who had agreed to go through all the relevant material.

Friday, September 6

In late. TB meeting with Hans Blix [head of UN Monitoring, Verification and Inspection Commission, UNMOVIC], plus David Manning, Jonathan, AC. He went through what they had to do, said that WE were the military threat and there was no movement by Iraq. But also, said that if the Iraqis felt the US had decided to do the military

---

[1] Asked if Britain was prepared to 'send troops . . . to pay the blood price', Blair replied 'Yes. What is important though is that at moments of crisis they [the USA] . . . need to know, are you prepared to commit, are you prepared to be there when the shooting starts?' He added 'We are not at the stage of decision on Iraq, and there are all sorts of different ways in which we might decide to deal with this Iraqi problem in the end.'

option come what may, they would not move. DM spoke to Condi and got the sense they were going to be sensible re UNSCR. TB talked to Putin and Chirac who were OK.

Saturday, September 7

In to chase TB up to be ready to leave by 11, CB fretting over his clothes and hair. Cherie said she felt we were fine on Iraq provided we could go down the international route. TB said he believed we had materially influenced GWB and that DM was worth his weight in gold for the way he framed the argument. Despite the negative public line put out by the Russians, both he and GWB were encouraged by the Putin calls. Felt that he was saying the UN had to deal with it, though he was not keen on war. On the flight out, TB meeting DM, SM, Jonathan, Matthew Rycroft [private secretary, foreign affairs] and [General] Tony Pigott. TB did his usual thing, of going through things with a pad and pen and then calling us round. He set out what we should get into a UNSCR. Query over whether there should be a specific timeline. And the toughest question was whether we would have to go back to the UN for a second resolution if the first one was rebuffed. DM's view, which TB came round to after a long discussion, was that it was probably best to get a tough first mandate by promising to go back to the UN, but make clear the UN had to face up to this. About half an hour or so going through all the tactical considerations, what the French and Russians would live with, how to get the US not to put in things that they would see as unreasonable, e.g. elections.

TB was clearly trying to get GWB in a more doveish position, all the more necessary when we heard that Cheney would also be at Camp David. When we did the media, TB pushed the IAEA [International Atomic Energy Agency] report on potential activity at nuclear sites and we briefed the Sundays re threat to UK, dodging questions re the UN. On the plane, after the diplomatic run-through, Tony Pigott went through the US military thinking. There was a build-up going on now. The timelines were quite short because once we got to the really hot season it was impossible to fight. He said the Saudis would not give their territory so they had to go through the Gulf and Kuwait. But they also wanted to go in from the north, with our and Turkey's help. He said there was a plan for a fifteen-day air build-up, followed by a massive ground force, which would be the moment of maximum danger because that would be the point at which he might use chemical/biological weapons. Tony Pigott said there were three packages on offer for the UK. One, weakening

Iraq's ability to fire off at Israel. That was the most strategic. Two, a bigger land and air package. Three, a huge – possibly 15,000 troops – force as part of the northern advance. It would mean calling up reservists soon as well as doing something visible eg movement of warships. TB was clear that the threat of the build-up had to be real for the Iraqis to respond at all, though they may respond with madness.

Pigott was clear that the US were gearing up for it but didn't want to do it alone. They would probably get a few others, e.g. Australia. TB was keen that we emphasise the Dutch had come out for it. He was clear the UN route was the best route but equally clear that if that was used for delay, we should not tolerate it. TB got changed at Andrews Airbase and we got on to the Marine 1 helicopter with Will Farish [US ambassador to London], Chris Meyer [UK ambassador to Washington], [John] Negroponte [US ambassador to the UN] and Bush's main protocol guy. Forty-minute flight, going over what TB should say at the arrival doorstep with GWB. We landed, TB out the front, us out the back. They walked through a line of soldiers to where the doorstep was set up. Bush was his usual rather faltering self. TB OK, both talking up the threat. We went up to the main building and TB, Bush, Cheney, Condi and David had an initial session. TB felt that his job was to sell the case for the UN route to Cheney. Jonathan and I met with Karen Hughes [AC's opposite number in the White House], Dan Bartlett [her deputy], Andy Card [chief of staff], Steve Hadley and Farish and went over the communications issues. I told the Bush advisers there was a lot of scepticism about motive, including people feeling it was about avenging Dad [Bush Sr]. I also said the sole superpower status of the US raised anti-Americanism and they didn't understand that. Karen was pressing the usual stuff re visuals, Dan [Bartlett] saying we had to get Saddam's story up, the abuses, etc. We gave them an honest assessment of where EU/Arab opinion was. I said our domestic problem was 'poodle' but also why now? Why only Saddam? What about the Middle East? On why now, the case had to be built on evidence. On why only Saddam because he was a unique threat.

On Middle East, TB was clear to GWB he really had to engage on that. Karen was asking if we could help the Middle East peace process by dealing with Iraq. [Steve] Hadley was pretty hard over, talking about the importance of promoting democracy and freedom, and I said we had to be careful we were not talking about Americanisation. After some of us were called in to the TB/GWB meeting, and asked to brief on our own discussions, I said to GWB I felt they had to GET this anti-Americanism. A lot of it was jealousy and some of it resentment that they felt obliged to feel sympathy and solidarity post September 11. But some of it was just fear of their power. When I said we were worried about some of the language they used, Cheney looked pissed off and said 'You mean we shouldn't talk about democracy?' I said not if what people take out of it is not a message about democracy but a message about Americanisation. GWB seemed to get it. At one point we had a break and Bush shouted out across the room 'Hey, big guy' to me. TB was not there at the time but I went over and Bush said 'I'll say this, and I don't want it on the record, and with apology to the mixed audience, but your guy's got balls. But it's the right thing to do and future generations will surely thank us. I really believe that. I really believe the world has to get rid of Saddam and I really appreciate y'all coming over.'

When TB came back in, GWB said he'd decided to go to the UN and put down a new UNSCR, challenge the UN to deal with the problems for its own sake. He could not stand by. He would say OK, what will you do? Earlier, not too convincingly, Karen had claimed GWB was always going to go down the UN route. Cheney looked very sour throughout, and after dinner, when TB and Bush walked alone to the chopper, Bush was open with him that Cheney was in a different position. Earlier, when we had said that the international community was pressing for some direction but that in the US there would be people saying 'Why are you going to the UN, why aren't you doing it now?' Cheney smiled across the table, making it pretty clear that was where he was. The mood was good. As we left, Bush joked to me 'I suppose you can tell the story of how Tony flew in and pulled the crazed unilateralist back from the brink.' He said he was going to make clear that if the UN didn't deal with it – no hesitation. He said he didn't commit troops lightly, nobody would. Said TB totally understands link between WMD/Iraq and terrorism. Condi said the Cold War was about our values winning and we should push that. I said it was important they didn't come over as ideologues.

DM said the TB/GWB/Cheney meeting was quite extraordinary, a US president using a UK prime minister to persuade an American vice president. Cheney had not looked happy but it was clear Bush had made his mind up. He was very clear on the threat, and the need of the UN to deal with it. He said he would get something on the Middle East. 'That's a promise.' He was, as Sally said, far more impressive close up. At the dinner, a lot of politics having been done, there was a fair bit of small talk. He was quizzing TB about what Balmoral was like. Also filling us in on the row at Augusta golf club [in Georgia] where women were trying to win entry against the rednecks. He said they would have to let them in so the sooner the better. He and I discussed our running. He had done one marathon and his mum and dad had come out to cheer him at nineteen miles and his mother had shouted out 'There are three fat ladies ahead of you.' Cheney said next to nothing over dinner, ditto Hadley. TB got very bad stomach cramps. On the helicopter, TB and I agreed the top lines for the media waiting at Andrews Airbase. Shared strategy, shared determination to deal with it. The press conference went fine, TB feeling a job well done. I slept right through the flight to Aberdeen [where TB was visiting Balmoral]. First thing, TB, Godric and I discussed the line from the [forthcoming TUC] speech to push. The argument that the UN was the route provided it was dealt with was perfectly strong. Briefed on that. Maybe went a bit far for the Yanks, but TB and DM had done a bloody good job.

Monday, September 9

The press on the trip was OK and there was a sense we were in a different position but we were still facing a lot of press and public hostility. I did the morning meeting, then chatted to TB up at Balmoral re the speech. He was a bit alarmed that the story on Leo singing the national anthem to the Queen had been leaked to the *Sun*. He remained of the view that we would get there in the end, and also that it was still possible to avoid war.

Meeting with John Scarlett on dossier before being joined by three senior SIS people. They were all pissed off at reports in the *Telegraph* and *FT* that MI6 were unhappy at being asked to do the report and put intelligence material in it. They said that was not the case, and they believed it was the FCO setting them up for the blame if the report was not good enough. We agreed a process for writing the report. Scarlett agreed with me that the FCO was trying to take it over and I said I will chair a group looking at it from the presentational point of view. Jack Straw called me about it and I said John Williams should be part of the team, not the writer. John Scarlett felt there was an ownership issue. He said he must feel he will have ownership of it. He and the SIS guys were really helpful. Went over some of the issues, Arab media, links with CIC, agreed there should be a permanent plug-in. Good meeting and felt they were basically OK to deal with. Then did a note to JS [Scarlett], copied very widely, setting out the process. JS to own. AC to help.

Left for the train to Preston. Had to drop out of the US conference call. I worked on an overnight script on TB's [TUC] speech, which

Tom briefed, main focus on Iraq but also the hostile atmosphere with assorted union leaders getting on the news with real criticism over Iraq and much else besides. TB was in no real mood to be nice to them. We drove to Blackpool, then up to see a very downcast John Monks [TUC general secretary] with a very downcast Brendan Barber [his deputy]. I think they were worried that their modernising legacy was vanishing amid the noise of the dinosaurs. TB was definitely going to get a hostile reception tomorrow. He spoke by phone to Chirac who really went off at the Americans again, said they didn't understand the Middle East, or how they brought anti-Americanism upon themselves.

Tuesday, September 10

The overnight briefing went pretty big on the line that he intended to be very robust. It was being built up as real lion's den stuff. The speech was in three parts – Iraq, which would improve by being clearer about the balance between UN and determination to deal with it. It was measured, calm, serious. Second, public services, which was all a bit samey and listy, and third, partnership with the unions. We were a bit worried that some of the lines were so hostile – e.g. indulgence or influence – that he might get booed but he wanted to do it and felt it would strike a chord with the public. Monks wanted him to tone it down, which he did but I still felt it lacked clarity. TB got a much better reception than we feared, was even applauded for the attack on indulgence, and a fair few got up for a standing ovation, so he was pretty pleased with himself as we went back to the hotel for meetings.[1]

Alex F called, really worried about Iraq, said he thought it was a very dangerous situation for TB. I said TB had a real sense of certainty about this one. He was really on the rampage about the press as well, said we had to do something, they were out of control. We had very little time before [Labour Party] conference and we hadn't done a lot of the planning we normally do. The Tories were clearly going to reposition as being more interested in domestic policy than Europe, and they were going to try to get up compassionate conservatism. They would try to do us as being distracted by foreign policy, and divided on Iraq. There was a bit of a flurry later on when Charles C

---

[1] After telling union leaders that his door was open to any of them, Blair told TUC delegates 'Partnership doesn't make headlines. But the vast majority of trade union leaders and members know that it does far more good than a lot of self-indulgent rhetoric from a few that belongs in the history books. Indulgence or influence. It's a very simple choice.'

said the recall of Parliament was under review. TB was still not keen, but I was sure we were going to have to do it. Got Iraq dossier draft, read it at home.

Wednesday, September 11

Good press for the TUC speech. TB was with Robin C, even more puffed up than usual. Robin said we had to recall Parliament and better we do it sooner rather than later. We were behind the curve. He was making clear he felt we had to avoid military action, saying he didn't want to serve twenty years under a Gordon Brown premiership. He even mentioned Suez. This is not Suez, said TB. That was not thought through and the US were not there. I'm not going to let the US go unilateral. It would be wrong and this way I get to influence them. RC spelled it out, said the US didn't understand the Middle East peace process. They were doing Iraq for the wrong reasons and they were hugely unpopular. He welcomed the fact TB had been able to restrain Bush, but they were clearly determined to go to war. 'I'll put you down as an unenthusiastic then,' said TB. RC said he feared it would be the end of the government. TB really was isolated at the moment and yet he kept going on this. We agreed that I would draft the letter from TB to Michael Martin setting out our thinking, saying it would be connected to the dossier and unrelated to UN thinking. Then we had to square MM. David Hanson [Blair's parliamentary private secretary] got him in New York, read him the letter. Later Jack S called me from NY, he was with MM, who said maybe we should think of a two-day debate instead, because lots would want to speak.

Meanwhile I was working on the Iraq dossier. Long chat with John Scarlett. I said the drier the better, cut the rhetoric. The more intelligence-based it was the better. There was a need to separate IISS [International Institute for Strategic Studies report] from what was new in this one. I gave some suggestions later re a different structure. We had the basic story and now had to fill it out. TB looked at it and felt it was pretty compelling stuff. He was in a bit of a strop re recall of Parliament, said that it was a new precedent. He also didn't want Cabinet until after a recall. Ridiculous. No wonder Betty Boothroyd said it was becoming more presidential. I watched the St Paul's [anniversary of September 11] service, to which I was invited but couldn't go, while reading the Iraq dossier. Then meeting with TB to sort lines on the recall of Parliament, and briefing. Philip had now done ten groups since the holiday and the pessimism was dreadful. They were close to a turning point, and really angry about Iraq. Robin put out a line effectively claiming he persuaded TB to do the recall.

GWB speech to the UN [General Assembly] was leading news all day, up to delivery at 3.30 NY time. They sent a draft through yesterday but though good in tone, it lacked the crucial point that they would go for another UNSCR first. It just wasn't there. This was what Cheney/Rumsfeld wanted. They felt that more 'UN-ery' was just a way to give Saddam the chance to mess them around. So David Manning sent through a passage from TB and spoke a couple of times to Condi. But it was only at the last moment that we heard he WAS going to include reference to UNSCR and in the end he delivered it in plural. That meant that others would be able hopefully to welcome it more than they would have done. RC was on the *Today* programme, diddling like crazy both re his alleged influence persuading TB to recall, and also on the issue of whether there would be a vote. Nobody pointed out there was no vote when he was Foreign Secretary re Kosovo, Gulf, and the attack on Iraq a few years back.

I had a long chat with Alan Milburn. JP had had the same conversation with him as he had had with me, namely saying he would support GB but not if he went for TB. 'There can only be one prime minister, and we have already got one.' But Alan said TB was very isolated and Iraq was going to be very difficult for him. He said he and John Reid would be there totally. He put down DB as 'cautiously supportive'. We were hoping to get Margaret B fully on board. But he felt there was quite a lot of dicking around. TB, at the political strategy meeting, was beginning to focus on his conference speech. Douglas and Peter M both made the point that we lacked a narrative for this phase of New Labour. TB wanted to make 'reform the route to social justice' a big theme.

Meeting with TB, Jonathan, DM, AC, C and an SIS colleague re chemical and biological weapons, and what Blix would be looking for if the inspectors went in. It showed what was going on was really bad and getting worse, that he was determined to keep WMD for reasons of regional power. They were strategically vital and he was going to keep them come what may. C said we could use some of the material through assertion.

They were confident this stuff was real, not being run against us. SIS believed the regime would collapse and there would be lots of defections etc. Very interesting meeting. TB saw Charles Kennedy and then IDS who immediately went out and said we were publishing the dossier before the debate. IDS was basically just diddling about with it. GWB speech going OK. David Davies came in and asked if I wanted to be chief executive of the Football League. He thought they would definitely go for it and I would enjoy it.

Friday, September 13

Meeting with Julian Miller on the dossier to go through the new structure. I was worried that it was going to have to rely too much on assertion. We also had a flurry with an overnight telegram re Scarlett's US trip, because he'd been told the US were going to publish their own dossier using US material and we worried it would undercut ours. I raised it on the conference call. There were also persistent reports of problems re Cheney and Rumsfeld pushing for much more robust, less UN-related lines. GWB speech had gone down well and seemed to shift opinion around the place but they were arguing for such a tough UNSCR that it would not be acceptable to anyone.

Geoff Hoon called me last night before *Question Time* and said it was going to be tough, not least, as he first intimated and later confirmed, the US were on the point of asking us to upgrade [RAF] Fylingdales [radar base] for National Missile Defense. Otherwise we were working out how to 'park' Iraq pre Parliament recall. I was worried that the dossier was going to be too assertive and that even though the agencies presented it as their work, it would be seen as us trying to spin them a line. GB did an *FT* interview saying he supported TB on Iraq. I called JP in Thailand and said it would be good to get him out there in similar vein. He agreed I could brief out his support whenever I wanted. I briefed Phil Webster [*Times*] who got it on to page 1, and we got a bit of broadcast play too.

Saturday, September 14

Burnley vs Stoke. Good win, 2–1 after going one down. TB called after his visit to Peter M's Progress [New Labour policy pressure group] event. Philip said TB was on great form. Lots of Iraq in the Sunday papers, but a bit of a lull. We killed the story in the *Sunday Telegraph* re TB demanding from each Cabinet member what their view was on Iraq.

Sunday, September 15

Up at Mum and Dad's, eight-mile run, lunch, then back with Calum. Göran Persson [Swedish Social Democratic Party] won the Swedish election. TB had given him Clinton's advice about looking hungry to the end, even if you already know they want you to win.

Monday, September 16

Chat with Scarlett re dossier. He was still worried the US were going to do their own version first. It came up on the conference call again, and I had to pin down Dan Bartlett afterwards to try to get it back out. We were really needing to get some focus back on the domestic agenda but it was going to be hard. At his Monday meeting, TB was going on about parking Iraq, and then getting proper focus on Home Office and asylum. This was real groundhog day, him just railing and railing at their inability to grip these issues properly. Yet again, he said he wished we could get out of hunting. Today was the tenth anniversary of the ERM.[1] We were blessed with the current Tory lot being so useless, but he really felt that on some of the toughest issues, departments just weren't delivering. They lacked cutting policy edge.

Tuesday, September 17

I was in bed after midnight and Dan Bartlett called. Kofi had announced a letter from Iraq saying they'd let the inspectors back in. Dan wanted us to share a sceptical line, making clear the issue was disarmament. That was fine. We put out a fairly tough line. Needless to say our media was on the case straight away saying how that clever Saddam had done us in. I commissioned the CIC to do a paper on his past dicking about. TB wanted to be on the very tough end, saying we needed a tough new UNSCR and that had to be about maximum inspections, etc.

Meeting about Iraq's 'offer' of inspections, as on conference call later. I agreed with Jack he'd do a doorstep on it. I bumped into RC who said 'great development and we should claim it as TB's success'. Jack said to me he felt Robin was on an exit strategy and he was going to cause us real problems. I got the new dossier draft and did detailed comments on that. TB also read it and made some comments. Nuclear was the most difficult part. Scarlett and I chatted away re that. Then a meeting with Jack and [Sir Jeremy] Greenstock [UK ambassador to the UN] to go over tactics on the UN negotiations. Greenstock was very good on the detail. TB felt the US hawks would be trying to say to GWB we should never have gone the UN route and now it becomes a mush and we had to be really hard over on them. Debate meeting with Hilary Armstrong, who said there were massive expectations re the dossier. On hunting, she

---

[1] Black Wednesday, when the then Conservative government withdrew the collapsing pound from the European Exchange Rate Mechanism at a cost of £3.3 billion.

September '02: Iraq agrees to let inspectors back in

said it simply wasn't possible to get out of it. TB said he would rather be humiliated for doing a massive U-turn than stay in a position he believed to be wrong.

Wednesday, September 18

Iraqi move being seen as blow to us. The overnight briefing on TB's [poverty] speech and the commitment to 'redistribute power, wealth and opportunity' was seen e.g. in the *Mail* splash as a hint at more tax rises and a sop to Old Labour. TB called at 7am. 'What on earth is this?' I said we just had to stick to the same message that we had agreed yesterday, that we were back on the domestic agenda, doing the things we have to do and being open about it. He was not overly pleased. The Treasury were in a real flap about it. TB's speech went OK,[1] then he did some clips on Iraq which were seen as keeping up the pressure, then did five minutes for BBC crime day. I was still working on the dossier. I got Jo Nadin [Number 10 special adviser] to read it with a fresh eye. She felt it was very convincing, apart from nuclear. I made a few more suggested changes to John Scarlett and went through the nuclear section with Julian Miller, which was OK. JS was keen to keep in the very downbeat assessment. Got TB foreword signed off, then to meetings re dossier production. Charles Clarke came to see me to say he was worried there had been friction between us at recent meetings. I said no, but we had a basic disagreement re ways to attack the Tories. I felt also he had been too focused on so-called attacks on him. He said he didn't see politics as his sole job. His job was to get the politics done by others. On the dossier, the Tories were making clear they felt we should have something on the link to terrorism.

Thursday, September 19

TB was down at Chequers hoping to get going on the conference speech. The A-level exam row was in danger of getting out of control.[2] Estelle Morris decided on an independent inquiry. TB spoke to her at length and sensed a bit of panic around the department. After the criminal records [vetting of education employees] issue post Soham

[1] Speaking at an East London school, Blair said 'Our goal is a Britain in which nobody is left behind, in which people can go as far as they have the talent to go . . . in which we continue to redistribute power, wealth and opportunity to the many not the few, to combat poverty and social exclusion, to deliver public services people can trust and take down the barriers that hold people back.'
[2] A new two-level exam system, filtering out less able students at the halfway stage, led to accusations that exam boards had fixed grades to avoid much higher pass rates.

[child murders], a decision allegedly taken by officials, and now this, she was in danger of becoming tainted goods, not reforming fully, not competent. We were also getting bad coverage at the moment on crime, asylum and transport. As I said to the Yanks on the conference call 'Joy to be back on the foreign agenda.' Most of my work at the moment was on the dossier. Nuclear timelines just about sorted. Jo Nadin had one or two good thoughts and I put them through. I agreed to drop the conclusion. Some people reasonably convinced, others not. We'd end up convincing those who wanted to be and not those who didn't.

TB spoke to GWB yesterday and got him on to the same strategy. TB said we had to hang tough. He later spoke to Putin who was very wary re a UNSCR. Blix was at UN saying he could be in there soon but being quite conciliatory with them. The Iraqi foreign minister [Naji Saberi Ahmed] was at the UN saying, via letter from Saddam, they had no WMD programmes. I signed off on the dossier before John S' final meeting on it. DB came round for dinner. He was getting whacked by the *Express* in particular at the moment and it had made him a bit paranoid re the press in general. He was also defending his relationship with the *Mail*. I could see no purpose for the government as a whole in his courting of Dacre. He was interesting on his visit to GB's house in Fife at the weekend. He said neither had really acknowledged any difficulty between them. TB was barely ever mentioned. GB had not really engaged on the euro, on Iraq, or on the future. On the Sunday they had asked him to go to church. DB said TB had to stay for the next term because there was currently no one else ready to challenge GB. He said I had to stay too.

Friday, September 20

The French food standards authority said UK beef was OK [and the unilateral ban should be lifted in France], which ran quite big for the whole day. On Iraq, the US were making it clear they would go it alone whatever. They also published their new security strategy document, full of the theory of pre-emption and their determination to make sure they are never again rivalled as the world's foremost military power. Tricky. I did a final meeting re how to do the dossier arrangements. I spoke to Jack Straw and said I was really worried about him briefing foreign governments in advance. Jack had promised it, and said he was a bit hacked off because he'd had Number 10 backing for it when he suggested it. I was worried that they would leak and there would be a Parliament problem. So we agreed a compromise: that our ambassadors would brief host governments from a speaking note. We agreed no media briefing in advance. John Williams not very happy with it. I was sure it was better that it was written by spooks not spin doctors.

Saturday, September 21

We went to the cinema to see *My Big Fat Greek Wedding*, but I couldn't get into it at all. Lots of A-level stuff around, plus Iraq, and the massive build-up for the countryside [pro-hunting] march. We then learned that Prince Charles' letter to TB re hunting was being leaked to the *Mail on Sunday*. It could have been really bad but thankfully they didn't have the text, just a briefing on it, and the line that if we banned hunting he might as well go skiing all year round. Then we learned that Clare Short had pre-recorded *GMTV* and there was plenty in it to make news – no second Gulf War, protect Iraqi children, so on and so on. What a self-indulgent bitch. I didn't bother TB with it. What with her, the march, and Schroeder expected to lose the elections, it was shaping up to be a big and bad news day tomorrow.

Sunday, September 22

TB called after church. He was praying for Schroeder to win, not least because Stoiber had communicated to us how angry he was at TB's pro-Schroeder *Tagesspiegel* interview. The exit polls suggested Stoiber winning, which he found a bit alarming. He said Clare was a pain in the arse but it was still better off keeping her inside 'So I'm afraid we just have to bear it.' But what with Robin as well, there was certainly a sense of ill discipline on Iraq. On Prince Charles, he thought it damaged him more than us. He had said to Robin Janvrin at Balmoral that he has to learn the difference between short and long term. He felt it was OK for him to give us a bit of a kicking now and then but that if he started to get too political, eventually the next generation will think who elected you to talk about all this stuff? The [Countryside Alliance] march was big [estimated 400,000 people]. We went to Jamie Rubin [former US State Department chief spokesman] and [CNN journalist] Christiane Amanpour's house. They were very down on GWB. Jamie felt that TB was basically the articulate voice of the Western world, but that the right in the US was bad and dangerous and we should be very, very careful getting too involved with them. TB had done a near complete [conference] speech draft, which was good news.

Monday, September 23

Massive coverage for the march, and TB adamant that we should be trying to find a way out of this. Schroeder had a narrow win

[Bundestag elections], which cheered us up and by the end of the day, they had been on saying he wanted to come for dinner tomorrow night, which was one in the eye for Chirac. On Iraq, post Clare's interview there was a lot of focus on division and before Cabinet TB got her in for a little chat, though again was not as tough as he should have been. Meeting with Jack re UNSCR and also votes. We agreed we should make UNSCR the focus of HoC [House of Commons] vote. TB was working on his statement for the Commons.

DM said over the weekend TB had to work on GWB in a thirty-minute call because the US was going down an impossible road again, basically a route that was unsellable. We were worried that Rumsfeld and Cheney were pushing for the idea that we get in conditions that we know Iraq could not meet. Chris Meyer popped in and said 'Beware these right-wing people in the US government. They are bad news for us. They see TB as a bit of an irritant, a complicating factor, and though they like the articulate support if they felt the need to hang us out to dry, they would do it.' He said he had recently seen Scooter Libby, Cheney's chief of staff, who was virtually dismissive of the whole UN route. Geoff Hoon came in to go through all the military options with TB.

TB had just seen GB. 'He was totally ridiculous. Even Balls looked shocked. He was basically just saying we could not afford a military conflict and making clear he had to be consulted on every piece of spending.' TB felt he was getting worse, in part because he didn't react much other than by making clear he thought these outbursts were ridiculous. At Cabinet, TB did the intro, went through what the dossier was based on, emphasised the need to put over the history of UN resolutions and also the nature of the regime. The dossier brought together accumulated evidence about Iraq's attempts to build WMD, part historical, part intelligence-based. We were not saying he was about to launch an attack on London but we were saying there was an attempt to build a WMD programme in a significant way. He made clear we were still focused on the UNSCR route and if he doesn't comply there will have to be international military action. He will not comply unless he thinks the threat is real. Meanwhile, we have to redouble efforts on Afghanistan and MEPP.

Jack Straw went through where we were on resolutions, then JP came in with quite a hit on Robin and Clare, said we could all do our bit of positioning to make our own views heard, and get a few plaudits, but we were in this together. He said TB had done a brilliant job moving the US down the UN route and we should stick with him and stick together. He said it's easy to do, a briefing here, a word there, and it's not on. Go down that road and we're in real trouble. One or two do it and it's indulgent. He said Tony had an incredibly difficult job at times like this and we should support him. He said he had been asked by the BBC if he agreed with Clare about killing innocent children and 'I said I'm not very keen on killing innocent children either.' Clare sat looking out of the window with a face like thunder, but didn't interrupt him.

GB came in with a few long-term points for the US, the need to think through post-Saddam, the importance of MEPP. Patricia Hewitt suggested the Attorney General came to Cabinet to explain the legal position. Robin was pretty creepy. Both Jack and JR had a bit of a dig at him. Even after her performance yesterday, and even after JP, Clare was still full of herself. She said if we are going to have collective responsibility we should have a collective decision. There was no doubt Saddam was dedicated to possessing WMD but re the UN, there's a double standard vis-à-vis Israel. She said she admired TB for the way he had got the US to go to the UN, but then she went off about Afghanistan being a mess. JR said 'I think we can all make our points without giving the impression that some of us have a monopoly on caring and humanity.' Most of them said what we would expect them to say, though I was quite impressed by [Paul] Boateng's speech, during which Clare spilled tea over Andrew Turnbull [new Cabinet Secretary and head of the Civil Service].

It was a pretty good discussion, though focused as much as anything on the idea that we were having to deal with a mad America and TB keeping them on the straight and narrow. JP referred to the idea that TB would have sleepless nights, that we knew it could go to a difficult choice between the US and the UN. TB said he believed it would be folly for Britain to go against the US on a fundamental policy, and he really believed in getting rid of bad people like Saddam. The discussion was serious and sober and hard-headed and TB was in control of all the arguments. Several of them praised him and his leadership without it sounding sycophantic. Milburn had one or two interesting observations about anti-Americanism. He too felt there was a problem re double standards, and the lack of drive on MEPP. Charles C said the mood in the party was apprehensive. GH said the ultimate objective was disarmament and that weapons inspectors are a means to an end. The clearer we are that we would use force, the likelier it may be that we don't have to. On the question 'Why now?' he said his record, his use of them, and his continued development.

TB said if he fell, the people who would rejoice most would be the Iraqis. It is basically a wealthy country whose people live in poverty. He said the US can go one of two ways. It can go unilateralist, and there may be some who want that, but he was sure Bush was not one of them. Or they can be part of a broader agenda on Africa, MEPP, Afghanistan. Funnily enough, I think TB won the Cabinet over more easily than the public. A poll tonight showed us below forty for the first time since the fuel protests [in 2000]. After Cabinet, Jack did clips on the idea that we were not talking about leftovers from when the [UN weapons] inspectors were in but an ongoing programme. I put out TB words which led the bulletins, but as I briefed [Andrew] Marr and others I realised once more it was not going to be easy.

Tuesday, September 24

Dossier day after months of waiting. Adam Boulton was good all day. [Andrew] Gilligan [defence and diplomatic correspondent, BBC *Today* programme] and [Tim] Marshall [Sky News foreign affairs correspondent] and the so-called experts went on about nothing new, but a combination of TB's Commons statement[1] and the gradual serious build-up re the dossier got us into a better position. TB had to go to the NEC [National Executive Committee of the Labour Party] but had done the statement pretty much himself, gone through most of the difficult questions and was OK on it all. The only really tough question was, if the UN did not sanction war, would the US and UK go along with it? The Iraqis put up their culture minister [Hamed Youssef Hamadi] to deal with it, and he was crap, his main line that it was all a Zionist plot. TB did well. He came back from the NEC laughing because Mark Seddon [NEC member and editor of left-wing magazine *Tribune*] said he had been to see Tariq Aziz [Iraqi Deputy

---

[1] Blair told MPs 'As the dossier sets out, we estimate on the basis of the UN's work that [in 1997] there were: up to 360 tonnes of bulk chemical warfare agents, including one and a half tonnes of VX nerve agent; up to 3,000 tonnes of precursor chemicals; growth media sufficient to produce 26,000 litres of anthrax spores; and over 30,000 special munitions for delivery of chemical and biological agents. All of this was missing or unaccounted for.' Blair concluded the statement saying 'Look at Kosovo and Afghanistan. We proceeded with care, with full debate in this House and when we took military action, did so as a last resort. We shall act in the same way now. But I hope we can do so, secure in the knowledge that should Saddam continue to defy the will of the international community, this House, as it has in our history so many times before, will not shrink from doing what is necessary and right.'

Prime Minister], that he was a nice man and it was easier to get in to see him than it was to see TB!

Couple of Q&A sessions before statement, but he was so good on this now. The general feeling re the dossier was pretty good. Massive around the world. Leading almost every bulletin in the world at lunchtime. TB's statement was really strong and I felt Jack did OK yesterday after Cabinet and again today. I called John Scarlett a few times and he was OK too. The conference call was largely about the dossier. Chirac, Bush, lots of others responding to it going well. TB saw Piers Morgan but Sally sat in because, as TB said, it would be like a red rag to a bull if I had been there. Sally said he was reasonably tough, saying it simply wasn't true when they said they supported us on the domestic agenda, and he had a real thing about Cherie. Meanwhile Fiona had a meeting with Cherie and Cate Haste re this ridiculous book project. I felt it was just wrong that she was getting money out of this and we shouldn't do it. Schroeder arrived at 6.15. It was quite a thing for him to come to see TB rather than Chirac after his election and it was playing big in all our countries.

Wednesday, September 25

Massive coverage round the world and, apart from the *Mirror*, doing pretty well in UK media. Really big hit but still pretty difficult. TB/ Schroeder meeting went OK and he was very much trying to get into a better position re the US. The *Mail* did something on letters from Prince Charles to Derry [on the legal system encouraging a US-style compensation culture]. The LCD were clear that they hadn't leaked them. But it was a very difficult situation, à la Black Rod, and they were clearly fighting back. I got Godric to speak to Colleen Harris in Charles' office and she said they were clear it had not been leaked by government, as alleged by the *Mail*. But through the day lots of Charles surrogates were up saying he was being attacked by us.

TB and I had several conversations on it through the day. He felt Charles had been captured by a few very right-wing people. TB felt the only line we could take was to make clear it was not government who leaked it and express total respect for Charles' right to speak on these issues. Some of our MPs were wading in but there had to be a worry he would come over as the man speaking up for 'ordinary people' against an over-mighty government. The *Mail* was revolting even by its own standards. It led the bulletins most of the day until Estelle [Morris] came under attack for undermining, allegedly, the [Sir Michael] Tomlinson inquiry [into A-level standards]. TB said it was all very unfair but if this thing becomes the fiasco it risked becoming, Estelle may well lose her job. She just wasn't gripping it and was getting bad advice. Jeremy [Heywood] saw David Normington [Department for Education and Skills permanent secretary] to find out what was going on and Bill Stubbs [Sir William Stubbs, chairman of the Qualifications and Curriculum Authority] took that as us interfering with the inquiry.

Conference was really looming now. I had a long session with Philip to go over our difficulties, ended with me saying I wanted out and him saying I would never have such a great job and that maybe if I needed a new challenge, I needed to grip the party stuff as I had the government. JP was on the rampage, he had clearly been wound up by GB over foundation hospitals. TB was clear it was the right thing to do but GB was almost ideological about it.

Thursday, September 26

Stayed in all day with Peter H to work on the speech, namely re optimism/boldness and the forward vision section. Sent a vile letter to Dacre, and got one back, re their continuing to suggest that we were involved in the leaking of the Charles letters. Philip called, urging me to get involved in stopping Britain in Europe [pro-European pressure group] from publishing a pamphlet that was going to be 'Labour's case for the euro'. Also pulled an idea from the party that we get Clinton sticks of rock made.[1] TB was at Chequers, called a couple of times to say he was struggling with the argument for the [conference] speech. He also felt a dark cloud of GB over him the whole time. He said GB was getting desperate and now was acting as a destructive force much of the time.

Later Andrew Adonis called to say GB had sent a 44-page letter to all Cabinet ministers attacking foundation hospitals, under-delivery by the Department of Health, as well as some of the proposals [on NHS funding and structures] coming from Adair Turner [former CBI director general] and Simon Stevens [health policy adviser]. Earlier, Alan Milburn had said to me that GB was positioning himself as reforming re PFI [Private Finance Initiative] but totally against anything that looked like private sector provision of public services. Not surprisingly, Alan was pretty ballistic about the letter, and said what it showed was GB's determination to kill any real progress. When I told TB about it, he paused for a long time and then said 'He's brilliant and ambitious but he's also bonkers and I just can't be bothered with it.' I spoke to Balls and asked him what plans they had to ensure this letter, written

[1] The former US president was to attend part of Labour's conference in Blackpool.

September '02: GB's letter attacking foundation hospitals . . .

for leaking, didn't leak. JP was also of the view that if Cabinet ministers suddenly found themselves hit with fifty-page letters about another department's work, when he had not even gone through it with the minister, they would think he was mad. But JP also felt TB had brought this upon himself by hitting the reform buttons so hard and by not having proper discussions. I said he avoids it because he has GB sitting there absorbing anything he can use to do him in. He said that debilitates all of them. He was friendly, basically sympathetic but did repeatedly make the point that a lot of it was TB's making.

Friday, September 27

The GB situation was really serious now. On close reading, GB's letter to ministers was, as both Jonathan and Sally said, a declaration of war. TB spoke to him when he got up in the States [Washington DC, where Brown was meeting fellow governors of the International Monetary Fund]. TB said I view this as really very serious, to which GB said 'It is very serious,' and he made clear it was deliberate too. Alan [Milburn] was on the *Today* programme, and when asked re GB's opposition to foundation hospitals, said that TB backed it in the Fabian pamphlet [*The Courage of Our Convictions: Why Reform of Public Services is the Route to Social Justice*] today. It was a bad scene. TB felt GB had reached the point where he felt TB was not going to move over so he had to do what he could to bring it about. JP came to see me, and said he felt this could end with GB going, that TB could not back down on foundation hospitals. Alan said that TB had to establish command, that GB was looking for a fight and we needed to understand this was a fight with TB, using him as a surrogate.

TB was still working on the speech at Chequers and felt it was kind of getting there. The QCA [Qualifications and Curriculum Authority] report on A-level results came out, which cleared everyone, but then Estelle sacked [Sir William] Stubbs. Conference was going to be tricky and tomorrow we had the massive march against the war in Iraq. I had a series of exchanges with Ian Austin [Brown's spokesman] to establish an agreed line to take on the policy issues in GB's letter, in which he just sent back the Treasury line. I sent back some changes and he said the line said nothing about the NHS being free at the point of use. They were now being puerile about the whole thing.

Saturday, September 28

Woke up to one of those rare and totally gobsmacking revelations that newspapers very occasionally produce, namely that John Major had a four-year affair with Edwina Currie [former Conservative minister]. It was one of those 'cor, fuck me' jaw-dropping moments. How on earth did he get away with it? I had never heard so much as a whisper. I went in to discuss the *Observer* interview with TB. We had worked up a pretty good message note, but he wasn't on form. We wanted the story to be a mix of confidence plus reform but it didn't really work. Bill Morris [general secretary, Transport and General Workers' Union] had done a big attack on foundation hospitals in the *Observer*. The anti-war march was big and the coverage enormous. TB was in no doubt what we were up against. He was still exercised re GB. 'My worry is that he is so ambitious, and so keen to bring me down, that he might bring the whole show down.'

In recent weeks, he had found him impossible to deal with. He was sure GB had effectively decided to stop us doing the euro, even if it was the right thing. He felt he had nobody close in giving sensible advice. He said he had said to GB after the election that he was happy to help him become leader but he had to work with him. But TB stopped short of thinking he had to strike against him. What works, we have to keep it working. What doesn't, we have to manage it. He had told GB that if the foundation hospitals memo leaked he would hold him personally responsible. He said he had tried all reason with GB, but it was hopeless.

He'd seen Prince Charles who was raising concerns about the equalities legislation for the disabled and what it meant for the armed forces. Later we flew north to Blackpool and TB went off to do a visit in Manchester while Peter Hyman and I went to the hotel to work on the speech.

Sunday, September 29

The papers were quoting Prince Charles re a letter of apology to TB over the leaked letters but we hadn't got one and they told Jeremy that none were sent. TB was pretty supportive of Charles though, and said it was really important we should not let them think they fazed us.

I stayed in the hotel all day apart from a run out on the beach. Speech meetings on and off all day, honing lines with Bruce [Grocott], David Miliband, Peter H. At 10pm, I said I felt the structure had gone backwards and TB went into a major rewrite mode, working for a couple of hours on his own. He had said after the holiday he wanted to be more his own man, and of all of the speeches, this had the most of him in it, on Iraq – worried but clear – on EMU – keen to get out there – and on public services – resolute and determined on reform. There was a narrow dividing line between confidence and arrogance and I think we were just about on the right side. He wrote a very clear and passionate attack on anti-Americanism. GB was on his way back from the States and we didn't even see a copy of his speech through the day. Foundation hospitals wasn't really taking off, and I was amazed the letter from GB hadn't leaked. TB did a Q&A in Blackpool, and was on really good form, though he nearly let out a couple of the best lines from the speech.

Monday, September 30

We were pretty much there now, though TB still wanted better lines, more colour and texture, and we also needed to take out about 1,000 words. It was a bit meandering in places, and the public services section wasn't hanging together. But he was determined to do it his way, much more than usual, was far more resistant to making changes, unless the case was absolutely overwhelming. GB's speech was OK without being great. It played too much to the party, wasn't modernising or challenging enough. It was GB's attempt to cover the waterfront but it lacked boldness and was not memorable. TB read it after the event, said it wasn't a great speech. Lots of people were noticing that GB just looked a little diminished at the moment.

Clinton called me from Number 10, having gone there with Magi [Cleaver, press officer], having flown in early, and was clearly enjoying himself. He read me a very funny spoof draft, said he was going to do a 'never give in to Tony' speech. He said the US press were giving the Bush people an easy ride. 'Our press is either right wing or Establishment so they don't care too much about the economy, jobs, health care, because they are all OK. They know that the Democrats want to be on the economy and Bush wants to be on the war.' A Karl Rove [senior adviser to Bush] memo was leaked saying that 'war is the only issue that excites our base'. He said if Labour or the Democrats had ever done something like that, there would have been a total outcry. He was worried that TB was being used. I told him what TB had said a while back about 'really believing this'. He said a lot of Democrats were up there asking 'Why is Blair helping Bush so much?' We talked over how his speech might fit into the general pattern of conference, and help lift the mood. He was clear about how he could help, and looking forward to it. I told TB later what he had said about the view of Democrats. 'But what do I do about it?' He believed we were doing the right thing, and also that Britain basically had to be with America at these really difficult moments.

Tuesday, October 1

Philip, Liz [Lloyd, policy adviser] and I had been up till 3am going through the speech line by line and trying to get in more colour and texture. It was in good shape. TB was up around 6, and I went in to see him at 7, and he was pretty happy with it. He felt it was the most rounded intellectual speech of the lot. The overnight briefing had not gone particularly well, it didn't matter much. We did the read-through and it felt pretty good. We made the right cuts and it was fairly lean. The big argument that we were trying to recast the 1945 welfare state settlement came through clearly. There was the usual last-minute cutting, minor chopping and changing, the running up and down the corridor with last-minute changes for the typists, and also a very annoying last-minute fuss over his shirt, most of us thinking after the sweat pictures [wearing a blue shirt for the conference speech in 2000] he should wear a white shirt. Cherie for some reason was desperate for him to wear blue or purple, and even got Carole [Caplin] to call. Total waste of time. At least ten minutes wasted on it. Then off we went. TB was less nervous than usual going on, and the audience was pretty much with him the whole way.[1] GB's body language was unbelievable. At times his face and his body seemed to contort in pain, and he found it virtually impossible either to laugh or applaud in the same way his colleagues were. The briefing afterwards pretty much took care of itself and people seemed to think it was strong and confident and very much himself. It was a hot day outside, bit too humid but I walked back to the hotel feeling we had done pretty well.

I got Robin C to meet Clinton on arrival, which seemed to chuff him up no end. Bill arrived to a great scrum. He was just what we needed to take us through the next twenty-four hours. I took him up to see TB. On Iraq, he said the Republicans were really hitting the Democrats hard and using TB. He said TB had to keep the US going down the UN route. Clinton was pretty bitter about [Al] Gore, felt he should have won convincingly. He had been a great vice president but ran a poor campaign. In politics, you are dealing with a mix of reality and rhetoric. What we did was speak to our base through our values and have policies that went to the centre. Al did the opposite. He had right-wing policies but left-wing rhetoric and it was a mistake.

Clinton was still at his best when defining the big political sweep, the strategic big picture, and his analysis of our situation was pretty good too. He was also brilliant at talking in big geopolitical themes, but then bringing them down to stories and pictures of people in their lives. We got him down to the gala dinner where he made a good little

---

[1] After paying tribute to 'the brilliance and vision' of Gordon Brown, Blair told Labour conference delegates 'We are at a crossroads: party, government, country . . . I believe that we are at our best when at our boldest. So far we made a good start but frankly we have not been bold enough.'

October '02: Megastar Clinton arrives in Blackpool . . .

off-the-cuff speech, then down to Northern Night [regional reception] with TB. Clinton was loving it now, big crowds gagging to see him and get near him and he was turning on the full charm, really hit the buttons when he spoke about TB, about the UK, how important we were, how the world looked to us, blah blah. TB got a bit carried away, said something in his speech about the world needing the philosophy and leadership of Clinton right now, which could easily be turned into a big hit on Bush. I could tell as soon as he said it that he was worried. On the way out, he asked me if I thought it was a problem. I said it partly depended who was in there, but I would put in a call to the Yanks.

Of all the visitors we had had to conference, Clinton was the one with the most star quality, up there with Mandela. As we were heading back to his suite, BC said he fancied going for a walk. It was windy, a bit cold and it was starting to rain, but he was like a big kid enjoying the lights. 'I love this place. I love Blackpool.' The security guys were clearly used to these kinds of eccentric excursions. We passed a big bingo hall, which advertised itself as the biggest amusement arcade in the world. 'Hey, I wanna go in there. Let's go play the machines.' We got to the door and it looked a lot less inviting close up, so we walked on. We were trying to find somewhere to eat. He said he wanted some fast food, nothing fancy, but we walked past two or three places that were closed. By now the rain was getting a bit heavier. Kevin Spacey [actor and friend of Clinton] was with us, having been on a trip with BC. We must have walked on for a couple of miles. Eventually we found a McDonald's that was open. Bill was now on the phone to Hillary, a mix of heavy politics and small talk, going on with her too about how great this Blackpool seafront was. He made quite an interesting point when he came off the phone. All the delegates and the conference people are inside the security bubble, but more of them should get out here with the real people. The tighter the bubble, the more you should try and get out of it.

The staff were gobsmacked when we trooped in. There was a young kid behind the counter who was shocked enough to clock Kevin Spacey, but then saw Clinton and went a funny shade of pink, before getting everybody out of the kitchens to come and see. Doug Band [Clinton aide] ordered massive amounts of burgers, chicken nuggets and fries while Bill went round saying hello to the small number of customers in there. There was a fringe event going on at a pub or hotel over the road and word went round there. [Former Labour minister] Margaret Jay's daughter Tamsin came back with a few journalists including Matthew d'Ancona [deputy editor, *Sunday Telegraph*] but they just sort of gawked, pretended they had just been going out for a night at McDonald's. I got them over to say hello a bit later on. Meanwhile a crowd was building outside, some of them classic Blackpool landladies out of the postcards, looking and pointing and then when he occasionally turned round and waved at them, they were waving back in a state of high excitement.

So there we were, sitting in a Blackpool McDonald's, drinking Diet Coke and eating chicken nuggets as he poured forth on the theme of interdependence, the role of the Third Way in progressive politics. He was also quizzing me about GB, and could sense that GB didn't really want to acknowledge TB's peculiar skills and talents, just as Gore hadn't used him properly in the campaign. He spent a while talking to the crowd on the way out, then we got driven back in a little van. He was like a man replenished, not because of the food but because he had been out with real people, and got something out of it. It was probably the single biggest difference between him and TB. They both loved political ideas, wrestling with policy problems and the rest of it, but of the two, Bill was the one who most saw politics in terms of its outcome in people's lives.

We got back to see TB who had been doing the rounds of receptions and was on a bit of a high, chilling out after the speech, which seemed to have gone down really well. They talked about Bush and it was pretty clear that though Clinton didn't go for him in public, he didn't rate him much and thought he stole the election. 'The problem was that we let them,' he said, and then gave another pretty negative analysis of the Gore campaign.

Wednesday, October 2

I went to the office meeting, then did a few bits and pieces for Bill's speech, including the suggestion he kick off with 'Clinton, Bill, Arkansas CLP, New Labour'. He needed assurance that it would work. He also asked me to work on a few lines on Northern Ireland, and on the Third Way. Hans Blix seemed to be making progress and looked like he was trying to do a deal which would not necessarily include palaces. It wasn't good enough for the US but the UN were pushing it and suggested that we didn't need another UNSCR. Powell was very hard line that there could be no new inspections without a new UNSCR. We were saying the same but TB and Jack had a very difficult meeting early on, Jack explaining that the US were getting very jittery re the UN route. As Bill said, Rumsfeld and Cheney didn't want to go the UN route, Powell did, and Bush was not so sure. Jack said the French were simply making clear they would not support war at all. The Chinese didn't care, the Russians were playing hardball.

TB was also conscious that he had told Bush that Blix was a good guy who knew what he was doing and he was worried Bush would doubt his judgement. TB would speak to Bush later, after Clinton's conference speech, and it became quite fraught because the Americans wanted one resolution that would allow them to hit Iraq at the first sign of Saddam lying or causing trouble. TB came off the phone around 4pm and said 'That was difficult. He is beginning to wonder whether we are going down the right road.' The Americans basically felt that Saddam was fucking them around and they were getting more and more impatient.

TB and I had the *Mirror* lunch to endure, which considering recent events was reasonably friendly. [Sir] Victor [Blank, Trinity Mirror chairman] made his usual spiel about the *Mirror* being a constructive friend. TB did his usual stuff, Piers [Morgan] being cocky, then we left so that I could hurry up Bill. He had put a fair bit of work into the speech and it went down a storm. He was very good on TB, the best exposition of the Third Way I had heard, awesome on the purpose of politics and on the big geopolitical questions. He did a terrific denunciation of so-called compassionate conservatism, got very close to the mark on the Republicans' domestic agenda and was fairly heavy on them on the international stuff too. Some of our press were seeing it as a big attack on Bush's policy, whereas we wanted it pitched much more as his expression of support for us.

The real line Clinton was pushing was that we should appreciate the fact that TB was in a position to influence US policy vis-à-vis the UN route, and get Bush to side with Powell versus Cheney and Rumsfeld. Earlier, when we had been running through the speech in his room, he was scathing about the American press, and the corporate corruption they didn't pursue, the laziness of their coverage. Jonathan and I both felt there were likely to be reverberations from Washington, and TB made sure he was the one who briefed Bush on it on the call. He got fantastic coverage on our news, and the top line running was that he was backing TB to keep going down the UN track. But it was becoming more and more difficult. TB was less confident we could get the tough resolution we wanted. Peter H suggested earlier that we get TB to do a press conference before leaving Blackpool and we got TB up for it, so then we had to sort a venue, backdrop etc. Word had got out about the McDonald's trip, which was also running big. Jack and Powell had talked five times and Powell was worried that Bush was struggling to keep on the right side of the line. Bush himself had told TB that 'I'm having trouble holding on to my horse' but what was clear was that GWB was trying to get TB to agree that if Saddam was found to be lying that was *'casus belli'* [case for war]. David Manning and Condi spoke to try to get things back on track, then TB spoke to GWB again. Bush was clearly being assailed by his right wing at the moment. TB felt his problem was that his rhetoric was aimed at the Republican right wing but it would stop him getting to the right policy positions. Perhaps it was the Clinton influence, but he seemed to be moving to the view that this was a government which was ruthless about its own power and position. Jack had told him, and we assumed this was in part based on American intelligence, that Chirac was basically intent on avoiding military action come what may.

The GB situation was no better. TB and I both noted that Clare Short had looked like death warmed up after Bill's speech, presumably because it had been so fulsome about TB and his unique position. Ditto GB. While TB said Ed Balls had brushed shoulders with him when he walked by, like kids in a schoolyard do. Fiona and I went out for dinner with the *Independent*. They were all swooning re Bill and felt TB had done really well yesterday. But there was still resistance there and one or two of them were really pushing for GB. Then a flurry of calls, including from James Blitz at the *FT*, re foundation hospitals. He had been told that GB had seen TB and the policy had been sorted in GB's favour. In fact it hadn't and I told James so, which led to the *FT* splash 'Blair and Brown at loggerheads over foundation hospitals'. TB was neither angry nor upset, just said he really had to sort it. He agreed with me that GB or Balls must have set Blitz up to try to bounce us. He felt Gordon was now so bitter and jealous that it was hitting his judgement. GB was worrying he was running out of time. If it was going to be resolved, then maybe TB ought to press the advantage now, the week definitely having strengthened him.

Thursday, October 3

Awesome coverage for Bill. Not least the *Mirror* front page – the *Mirror* salutes you, sir, an American leader who says everything we have been waiting to hear. Up early and in to see TB pre the *Today* programme interview. The hard question was whether the conference vote meant that we could only take military action with a specific UN mandate. TB felt we just had to dance around it for now and point to the UN process. He was actually more worried about the A-levels issue. He could not find the rationale as to why, if it was an accident waiting to happen, and then it happened, no minister carried the can. He felt that nobody had really thought through it all and gripped it. For the press conference, I drafted very brief opening remarks on reform, Iraq and the French beef ban being lifted. On Iraq, the Americans were saying today they were putting out a dossier on [Saddam's] palaces, which they never did. But we used the line that it was no good going for ninety-nine per cent of Iraq being inspected if the WMD were in the other one per cent.

TB was OK on foundation hospitals, said there was agreement on principle but technical details needed to be worked out, Milburn was right to want greater autonomy, GB right to press for value for money. The truth is that both had cocked it up by overzealous briefing which we had allowed to get out of hand in the crazy conference atmosphere. He was good on *Today* and [James] Naughtie said he looked like he had got his second wind. TB said he had never been clearer about the direction of the government, a theme picked up by *The World at One*. A lot of the journos were pissed off at having to stay in Blackpool for his press conference but he was on a roll. He was amazingly bouncy for the end of such a heavy week. On Iraq, he said Saddam would be disarmed come what may, but we must have a new UNSCR before inspections go ahead. Then lots of regional questions for those stations that didn't get full interviews. And though it wasn't chart-topping stuff, it was definitely another win for us, 4–0 I would say. We went down to the conference centre and I watched John Reid who had real presence on the podium, could deliver a joke and a message. Good mood at the end. I listened to Reid on *The World at One*. He was absolutely superb.

I spoke to a number of columnists on the drive out to the airport and they all seemed to think TB had had a particularly good week. GB could win the lesser races but he wasn't in the same league. We were in a great position. The Iraq row never really took off. TB had been commanding and strong. GB had put himself around everywhere but had not been brilliant. And the Tories were gathering against a backdrop of worries about Jeffrey Archer,[1] Major shagging Currie, and growing concern over IDS.

Friday, October 4

Iraq still really tricky. TB just wished the Americans would do more to put over a proper message to the world and worry less about their own right wing. First, a meeting in the garden, TB, AC, Jonathan, Andrew Adonis, later joined by David Manning. First we had to work out how to respond to the breaking news that Sinn Fein members

---

[1] Lord Archer, former Conservative deputy chairman and London mayoral candidate, was serving a four-year sentence for perjury and perverting the course of justice. Despite being imprisoned, he was continuing to attract a lot of media coverage.

were being arrested for arms offences and the obvious worry the ceasefire was breaking. Just had to play it along. Then foundation hospitals. There was a plan for a major presentation on this to ministers on Monday but Andrew said the Health department and the Treasury just could not agree on the facts. It was clearly going to have to be sorted at political level and I suggested a TB/GB/JP/AM meeting with no officials at all. TB said he was worried GB was just looking the whole time to position himself slightly to the left on everything. He felt Balls was a real problem, clever but often giving him wrong strategic advice.

Then A levels, on which he was persistently worried, saying we had to find some good people to put round Estelle. On student finance, again a GB problem, with AA saying the Treasury were preparing to undermine it as 'the university poll tax'. TB said 'I'm afraid there does rather appear to be a pattern here. It could be he is getting desperate and maybe preparing to bring the show down.' David Manning joined us, said we were in a much better position with Blix having said yesterday he was keen to get a tougher resolution with no inspections till then. TB felt there was a case for trying to get Putin more firmly on board and then get him to work on Chirac. He felt the Americans simply had no strategy for the French because, as Bill [Clinton] had said, it was all being driven by his [Bush's] own domestic politics.

David Manning felt that Saddam was probably going to make positive noises about inspections and try to drag things to February because then the 'window of war' would close because he couldn't expect troops to fight in fifty-degree heat. I got a message from Godric that Charles Reiss [*Evening Standard*] was picking up on a line from Mary Ann Sieghart's [*Times*] column that GB was 'insanely jealous' of TB. TB wanted us to put out a very pro-GB line and make clear he would never sanction such a statement being made. But it was worrying, given he had said those very words, and I wondered to whom as well as to me.

In the conference call with the Americans I stressed the worries from here that Bush needed to get out a message to the world, not just the US. Tucker Eskew [White House media affairs] said Bush had said that war was his last choice not his first choice. Then spoke to Blunkett to get him signed up to do the first of the planned new briefings to be done by ministers rather than officials. Jeremy did a note to TB on EMU, saying that even Gus O'Donnell [Treasury permanent secretary] did not know what GB was really thinking but Jeremy's guess was that GB would come to us in the next six months and say that four out of the five tests were met or being met but that one, sustainable convergence, was not. TB said that on everything, even these vital national interest issues, he was just using them to position himself in a different place to TB. However, surely the lesson of the week had been that the party had changed and it was GB who was not properly adapting to it. TB remained adamant that we should not go after GB and his people through the press, because the party would not like it and would get confused. But the GB fog was clouding everything.

I called Doug Band in Germany to fill him in on the coverage of Bill's speech, and Bill came on the line and said 'Hey man, what is going on in Northern Ireland?' I explained how some of the SF people were stuck in the arms game. He said if there was anything he could do, he wanted to do it, and he would go there at the drop of a hat. He asked if Bush's people had reacted to his speech. I said not officially, but my sense from Dan Bartlett and Tucker was they weren't terribly happy about it.

Saturday, October 5

Ran a half marathon around the Heath. Papers moving on to the Tories. Iraq fairly low-key, focus on trying to get the UNSCR. I took Grace and her friends to the cinema but was called out by TB, really obsessing at the moment about GB and what he was up to. He feared it was coming to a head.

Sunday, October 6

Philip called, said it was obvious that Jonathan did a lot for TB, particularly foreign and Northern Ireland, but that I basically held it together and I could not possibly leave. Also, he said, what else would I do? He felt TB was moving to a different phase, developing in an interesting way and I should be part of that history. Silly briefings on foundation hospitals still going on over the weekend by Treasury and Health. As a policy problem, it was one easily sortable behind closed doors but they were at it.

Monday, October 7

The Tories were in pretty dire straits. They had had a dreadful press over the weekend, were now trying to get up the idea of twenty-five policies being announced in the week, but IDS was looking vulnerable. They briefed overnight that he was going to go for the Thatcher mantle on public services, which totally played into our hands, allowed us to attack on lurch to the right and cuts. Quite a big news day with

Northern Ireland still very difficult, Blunkett up with some tough new asylum measures.[1] At the morning meeting, I told everyone we say absolutely nothing on foundation hospitals other than that the principles were agreed and the details being worked out.

TB saw JP to get him on board. JP was pretty much onside at the moment. TB told him that he felt GB not only wants him out of the job, but was also trying to make sure we don't succeed while he's doing it. It makes him even madder when people say that TB's doing well. He was genuinely concerned GB would bring the whole show down. At TB's morning meeting, he said we needed a strategy to build up the better union leaders. 'I can't believe I find myself saying this, but [John] Edmonds [GMB union general secretary] is about the best we've got.' Peter H was saying that for once we had the chance to drive real momentum forward from the conference and the key was the Queen's Speech. Philip had done an excellent note pointing out that on four fronts we faced the toughest battles – Iraq, EMU, public services and economy – none were easy but TB had strengthened his position on all of them. TB wanted a big, bold Queen's Speech but that was not what was going through the system at the moment. We just didn't have the big theme and it was all too piecemeal.

I did a staff meeting to explain how we should now be more focused on strategy and less on day-to-day news, and what that meant in practice. TB was still on about seeing [Viscount] Rothermere [chairman of Associated Newspapers] to try to get the *Mail* neutralised a bit. I felt they were a total waste of time and we should go for them harder. On Iraq, we still felt that Bush was looking to TB to move Chirac, but TB was sure he could only be moved by Bush, if at all. I saw Alan Milburn to discuss foundation hospitals. Alan was very down, and I tried to persuade him it wasn't as bad as it seemed, that all that mattered was the policy that was agreed in the end and he should ignore the rest of it. He felt we underestimated the negative impact GB had on progress. I said we didn't, but we had to try and make things work. I felt GB had made a mistake in allowing himself to be presented on a par with Alan because it was clear where TB needed the policy to go. I went to a meeting on asylum where DB and Derry had a few rather lively exchanges, Derry accusing Blunkett of taking cheap shots at judges for the sake of a few headlines.

[1] Blunkett proposed denying support to asylum seekers unless they claimed asylum at a port or airport and declared how they entered the UK. He also proposed that failed claimants should be less likely to be granted exceptional leave to remain.

The Treasury couldn't resist doing a bit of briefing on foundation hospitals. Basically TB supported GB in that he felt Alan was using this to try to get more money for his CSR settlement. But he supported Alan in that he wanted foundation hospitals with the ability to borrow, within overall Treasury controls. TB was happy enough with the policy outcome but of course GB had to insist that he had won.

Bush's speech [in Cincinnati] of late last night was leading in the news and was a bit more aimed at the international community, so maybe they were listening a bit more.[1] I had a meeting with Dickie Stagg and Asif [Ahmad] in the Foreign Office, and then all the CIC staff, to get a bit more direction into their operation. Asif was going to the US tomorrow so we needed him to keep going at the Americans to be more international in their message. I had a conference call with Peter Reid [press attaché] at our embassy in Washington re the same.

TB did a brief doorstep on Ireland after his meeting with the Bulgarian president but wasn't happy with it. Then [David] Trimble came in for a shouting match. TB was going to have to go over there soon. We had a long-term diary meeting, desperately fighting to get more domestic stuff back in the diary but it wasn't easy with all the foreign commitments in there already. There was a lot of dithering internally and with the FA over whether we should have cameras in for the World Cup reception. Eventually we agreed to have a pool [media sharing]. They [England players] arrived by coach, most of them with wives and girlfriends, though Beckham was solo because she [Victoria Beckham] was at a birthday party for one of [their son] Brooklyn's friends. Of all the people who had been into the building in our time here, these were the ones getting the most rubbernecking, particularly him. I spent a lot of the time chatting to Emile Heskey as we had both gone to the same school [City of Leicester], also trying to make Paul Scholes and Nicky Butt feel more at ease than they looked. Nancy [Dell'Olio, partner of Sven-Göran Eriksson] pretty much stole the show from all of them when she arrived in an amazing red outfit that was bound to be all over the front pages and very much seen in the context of sending a message to Ulrika [Jonsson] that she was history. TB did a little speech and then off he went.

[1] Bush laid out in detail, for the first time, his case for disarming Iraq, saying 'If we know Saddam Hussein has dangerous weapons today – and we do – does it make any sense for the world to wait to confront him as he grows even stronger and develops even more dangerous weapons?'

Wednesday, October 9

I ran in, a bit sluggish. Nancy totally stole the show last night with the plunging neckline on her scarlet trouser suit. David Davies [FA] called to say he was really sorry that that was about all anybody knew from last night. I said it was fine, I thought she was a real character. Lots of people in the office were saying how unimpressive they had found most of the players. TB, JP, GB and Alan M were due to meet to resolve the foundation hospitals policy. Andrew Turnbull had been asked to try to draft a compromise. As of last night, it was far too close to the Treasury view but had been improved overnight. Simon Stevens had drawn up a press release making clear we were going ahead with foundation hospitals in the Queen's Speech and they would enjoy substantial freedoms, which was OK for Alan. But, with TB's support, it was going to be 'on balance sheet' which was enough for GB to claim victory. We should never have got to this at all. At the start of the meeting, GB indicated how he intended to carry on by saying the previous minutes didn't accurately reflect the last meeting. Rolling eyes all round. TB was clear he wanted to support GB in not letting Alan use this to reopen negotiations but he did want to be able to press all the reform buttons. Once the meeting finished, we decided to put the press release out straight away and do the briefing speaking for everyone. But because it didn't suggest GB had 'won' he went mad that the press release had gone out. Also Balls was going berserk because he had not been in on the process.

Meanwhile Northern Ireland was going bad. TB saw Mark Durkan [Social Democratic and Labour Party] and later Bertie Ahern [Taoiseach of Ireland] and it was pretty clear that we were going to have to suspend the Executive. Philip called having done some groups on the Tories last night. They were beginning to break through a bit. They were getting somewhere with the idea of modern Thatcherism. Major was basically out of the political script, but the idea of a softened and modernised Thatcher had appeal. Philip and I both felt that TB was being too complacent about the Tories. Both he and Peter M felt the public would not be impressed with anything they had seen, but I sensed the media still trying to give them a lift. The big problem for IDS was an incoherent economic policy – where was the money coming from? – and silence on Europe.

Thursday, October 10

Foundation hospitals worked out as a bit of a score draw but it was perfectly obvious GB was going to keep at it and cause more trouble. I felt though that he had really messed up the handling of it. It hardly helped with their presentation of him as lord of the domestic manor while TB and JP had to sort it out, with Alan and GB seeming to be equals. TB saw [Gerry] Adams, [Martin] McGuinness and Bairbre [de Brún, Sinn Fein]. I went in at the end of the meeting and GA was giving TB the usual rather patronising history lesson. TB did though believe that Adams and McGuinness were genuinely trying to move towards non-violence and there was little chance of the IRA going back, but they had real issues in dealing with their own people. McGuinness and I had a long chat about football while TB and Adams had a little session in the corner of the room. Adams did a big number in the street.

Then we left for the airport and I listened to IDS' speech, which I thought was really poor, no real argument and very negative about Britain. I did a quick conference call with the party people to agree lines on it. TB had a brief session with the hacks on the plane to Moscow and they were winding up the line that he accepted Russia had legitimate financial interests in Iraq. Over dinner, he and I had another little argument about how to handle the Tories. He denied being complacent but felt IDS was just useless and that the Tories had not faced up to the change they needed to make. I agreed it was hard to take IDS seriously but felt that some of the strategic moves they were making might have appeal. The Tories were pushing IDS' line about 'the determination of a quiet man' but it was pretty woeful.

TB felt the press conference with Putin tomorrow could be tricky because we were in such different positions and there was little point pretending otherwise. We flew out in a crappy little airbus, then TB, CB, David Manning, Tony Bishop [interpreter], cops and I were flown by helicopter to the hunting lodge [at Zavidovo] forty-five minutes away. Pretty bleak landscape on the way, and the odd ramshackle home in the middle of nowhere. TB and CB were taken straight away to see Putin for dinner. I went for a run around the lake inside the grounds. TB came back a bit more confident that Putin would be in the right position re the UNSCR but there were other problems to come. On the way out to their dacha for dinner, Putin had taken them on a diversion to go and look at wild boar.

Friday, October 11

TB spent several hours one-on-one with Putin, so David and I were hanging around a lot of the time. They seemed to be getting on fine, though at the press conference, Putin took a bit of a pop at our dossier.[1]

---

[1] Putin remarked that the dossier 'could be seen as a propagandistic step' to influence public opinion.

Earlier we checked what he would say about a UNSCR, namely that he might consider one, but on the dossier there had been no prior discussion, so the perfectly avoidable problem became a story for some of our lot. I was kicking myself, thinking maybe I wasn't as alert as I used to be, not to have spotted that one coming. TB was less bothered about it than he was about actually sorting the UNSCR situation. Putin took me aside at the end and said he hoped they realised he had just announced a change of position in saying he would consider going for the UNSCR.

But the press were happy for the wrong reasons and we were slightly on the back foot. The one thing we lacked, during the brief time we had the hacks in the compound, was a picture so [press secretary Alexey] Gromov and I agreed TB and Putin would do a little walk through the trees by the lake. We went over to meet TB and VP who had just been having breakfast with their wives. TB was wearing what I can only call an Afghan hippie coat. I said there was no way he could wear that. Mohni Bahra [protection officer] had a fairly ordinary-looking sheepskin and I suggested they swap. This is ridiculous, Cherie said. Just ignore him. I said my job was to stop him looking ridiculous and try to get the press focused on real issues and not his bloody clothes. I said if he walked out in that, they would fall about and we'd have endless blather about his coat rather than the substance. Putin was looking on a bit bemused and TB, a bit embarrassed, said 'He doesn't like my coat very much.' Putin smiled and nodded in a way that made me think he thought I was right not to. He then tried on Mohni's coat, which just about fitted and looked fine and unremark-able, at which point Cherie said to me 'You are a total fascist.' I said I think that's a bit over the top but he would look a complete clown going out in that. Mohni meanwhile was trying on TB's coat and launched into an impersonation of Elvis Presley. Godric, Magi and the cops were all totally on my side, really felt it was over the top but it was all a bit bloody. The walk-by went fine. They had another meeting, then off on a boat trip, stopping at a field for lunch where a marquee had been set up and they served barbecued wild boar.

TB liked him. I got the sense he was still a bit isolated. Putin told him he was pretty much alone in the leadership re pursuing a very pro-Western policy, and he felt he was getting very little in return from the US. TB told him he thought Bush got it but he wasn't sure about some of the others. As the day wore on, TB seemed to buy more into the Putin charge. He said he would have to talk to Bush about it. Putin said that if there was something the Americans were worried about, they expect the whole world to share their concerns and drop everything, but if it's something that the rest of the world are interested in, like the Middle East peace process, they don't get the urgency. He was clearly pretty pissed off and the rhetoric cranked up through the day. But he was making an impact on TB, who was even saying to us by the end of it we had to get the Americans on a more multilateral track. On Iraq, VP said to TB 'Do you really think Iraq is more dangerous than this fundamentalism? Course not'. His bottom line was the oil price. The Iraqi debts were one thing, but if the oil price went too low, he was in trouble with his electorate. We had to remember he was putting through big reform and he was not always going to be popular. But he felt the US didn't sufficiently understand the problems other countries had. I think TB was beginning to feel the same, for example on missile defence.

On the flight back, we discussed it further. They were about to go public with the demand re [RAF] Fylingdales and we had a discussion about whether to go on the front foot. I felt we had to. TB said he was more confident than ever that the Tories didn't have a thought-through strategy. He said that before we went snap on New Labour, we had gone through a thorough intellectual examination of values, policies and the means. The presentation came at the end of all that. They had gone for presentation first. If they really wanted to signal change, they would go for Europe as the issue. It had definitely been good for him to have had as much time as he had with Putin on his own, away from some of the more conservative elements. Putin had also suggested setting up a secure line between the two of them. TB and VP had been swapping notes about other leaders and both confessed to a great fondness for Vajpayee [Indian Prime Minister]. Putin said that he sometimes felt that if he asked a question on Wednesday, he had to wait till Friday for the answer.

Saturday, October 12
Quiet work-wise. I settled down to watch the England game [European Championship qualifier, England 2, Slovakia 1]. The car bombings in Bali were totally dominating the news agenda.[1]

Sunday, October 13
Jack seemed to be handling Bali fine, it was apparent early on that there were quite a lot of Brits involved. I put out TB words after he

[1] Three bombs detonated in the tourist district of Kuta killed 202 people from twenty-one countries, including eighty-eight Australians and twenty-six Britons. Various members of Jemaah Islamiyah, a violent Islamist group, were later convicted and three sentenced to death.

spoke by phone to John Howard. I was working on a speech for the media correspondents lunch tomorrow.

Monday, October 14

Bali still absolutely dominant. Today was the first of our new-style lobby briefings, with Blunkett on street crime. The lobby was still very pissed off. The venue, a room upstairs in the Foreign Press Association [Carlton House Terrace], seemed fine and the mechanics seemed to work but to our annoyance, Jack Straw did a doorstep on the Bali figures just before DB was on, which took away the point of the whole thing. The morning meeting was largely Bali, A levels and Northern Ireland, with JR about to suspend the devolved institutions, so it was a pretty big news day.

At TB's meeting, he was pretty dismissive about some of the policy ideas being put forward by AA and others. He felt they weren't being radical enough, not motoring, going along in the comfort zone. But as we went through the various problems, it was clear that the common link was still GB, and on the euro, TB was in no doubt now it was being sacrificed to their internal difficulties. We had a meeting on the Queen's Speech and TB was still not happy about the radical edge. The big things seemed to be fines for child truancy, foundation hospitals, housing benefit, student finance. Hunting was still a problem. If there was one thing he could just wish himself out of, this was it. I was pushing for a statement on Bali tomorrow, which he eventually agreed to. The basic line coming over was that you could not do the war on terror and Iraq. He however said it all showed up the dangers of the modern world.

I went off to Christopher's restaurant to do a speech and Q&A with academics, opinion formers and media correspondents, the bulk of whom actually seemed broadly to agree with my analysis of media/politics and the questioning was far more supportive than I expected. I felt I had a proper argument to put to them, also accepted our share of the blame and said that the press had to face up to their responsibilities too. Even Stephen Glover [columnist], for all the bile he pours out in print, asked a very tame question. Charlie Burgess [*Guardian*] wanted me to do a piece for them based on what I had said. I felt what it showed overall was that I was at my best when defending and promoting politics in general, strategy and policy, and not when getting down into the areas for a dogfight.

The lobby meanwhile were whingeing and whining about the changes. What a bunch of tossers. Blunkett was a bit pissed off because he felt he had had to take the heat. We just had to persevere with this.

It was right to try to broaden the range. It was right to try to involve ministers, and it was right to try and do it outside Number 10.

Ran in, thirty-two minutes. Home in 31.37.82, a homeward personal best. During the day I formally signed up for the [London] marathon. Up to see TB in the flat. Anna Wechsberg [private secretary, foreign affairs] had done a good draft of the Bali statement. I did a new ending, then he did his own with a couple of over-the-top lines, e.g. a reference to 'satanic struggles' then a tacit comparison with the Second World War. He was meant to speak to President Megawati [Sukarnoputri, of Indonesia] but she was on answering machine, and the ambassador in Jakarta [Richard Gozney] couldn't find her! He seemed to be fretting a lot about it when it was actually quite straightforward. But the question was growing how can we do terrorism and Iraq and TB was keen to build the argument that they were part of the same coin. TB had lunch with the Danish PM [Anders Fogh Rasmussen] then over to the House, no real problems out of the statement.

Back to meet Jeremy and Sally and go for a meeting on the honours list with [Andrew] Turnbull, Hayden Phillips [permanent secretary, Lord Chancellor's Department] and people from the [Cabinet Office] Ceremonial Branch. It was a really dull list and we were creeping back towards more Establishment dominance. We wanted more head teachers in there. We fought for George Best [former footballer].[1] OBE for Anthony Buckeridge [children's author]. The thing had actually gone backwards and though we had lots of ideas, it was too late for most of them, and it just felt like one of those fights not really worth having.

Jeremy said the TB/GB meeting today had been absolutely disastrous. They had gone through the most difficult issues – euro, pensions, child and housing benefits, university finance. He said the atmosphere was dreadful, that he had never seen a more difficult TB/GB session. On the euro, GB effectively refused to discuss what was happening inside the Treasury. He ended by saying that TB was not the only minister in the government and he didn't have a veto. It was very hard to see how we could sustain this position much longer. Relations were if anything getting worse.

---

[1] Belfast-born Best, a world-renowned winger who succumbed to alcoholism, would die in 2005 without receiving an honour. He has been honoured by a saying in Northern Ireland, 'Maradona good; Pelé better; George Best.'

Fiona was losing patience with Cherie, over the Cate Haste book, but also the trip to Bermuda next week where she was staying with the governor [Sir John Vereker].

Wednesday, October 16

One or two potential problems developing out of Bali. It emerged that we did put out local warnings about the danger of visiting night clubs, but didn't put it in our [FCO] travel advice. I spoke to JP re doing the briefing tomorrow and he was clearly a bit nervous. I said don't rise to the bait if they try to wind you up. He said they would probably succeed because 'I bloody hate them'. We assumed IDS would come on A levels, which he did, and when he said they weren't worth the paper they were written on, TB really picked it up and went for it as an insult to people who passed exams. The press felt it had been a huge mistake and TB came back convinced IDS was a goner. I had quite a good meeting with Charles C on the Tories, tried to get him signed up to a big push on the Tories so that we could get dividing lines in place so the election was not a battle between us and perfection, but between us and them.

Philip's groups were very down on IDS at the moment and up on TB. Philip's new thing was that Theresa May [chairman of the Conservative Party] was a great hope for them, which was ridiculous. The TV news [re Bali] was dreadful, and I sent a message through to the FCO that all we could get in these situations was empathy and competence. We should have put Tessa [Jowell] on the case. We were also getting into a muddle on Bali intelligence, with the Americans and the Australians indicating that they did get specific threats, but of course it was always very easy after the event. I was worried this was not being gripped. Saddam won his elections with one hundred per cent.[1]

Thursday, October 17

I made contact with Leukaemia Research [charity] re the marathon and they sounded very up for it. I spoke to [Andrew] Turnbull and Jeremy about generating sponsorship and they were fine providing I wasn't using government facilities. At the 8.30 meeting, I read the riot act re the general lack of grip re intelligence warnings, especially now as the Australians were saying all Aussies should leave Indonesia. Later saw TB and asked if there was any point thinking of TV [election]

[1] Of 11,445,638 eligible voters, it was reported that every one of them voted for Saddam Hussein, the sole candidate.

debates. He said no, that it was totally one of those that just placed you on the at-risk register. On the Tories, we all agreed IDS was probably dead meat, we had to stay focused on the character and ungovernability of the Tories as a whole. We also needed to get up delivery through definition rather than through lists of statistical claims, e.g. 'I'm not prepared to put at risk the smaller class sizes we have delivered by accepting a Tory approach based on . . .'. Douglas [Alexander] was really impressing me with his strategic mind at the moment. Philip said the Tories were nowhere and IDS was just the worst message carrier they could possibly have.

Then a meeting with TB, Jack S, Geoff Hoon and CDS. First Jack went over where we were re the UNSCR, with TB feeling he was too close to caving in on the two-resolution route. Then GH and CDS re the military options, which included substantial numbers of 'boots on the ground'. CDS said he would have a real problem with his army if they were not properly involved and also TB would have far greater influence with the US if we were there on the ground. Sally was totally against. I was probably for, but the costs, around £1 billion for Package 2, and £2 billion for Package 3, alongside the far greater risks, were pretty horrific. The question to resolve was really whether we went in for the whole hog.

CDS said that [US General] Tommy Franks was going to a meeting in Ankara with the Turks next week and really needed to know what our answers may be. TB said it was not no, but it was not yet yes, and he wanted more work done analysing the cost. Then to Cabinet. The discussions were almost all foreign, with incessant interruption from Clare including a real display of rudeness to TB on the Middle East. She said Palestine was getting worse and worse and what was he going to do to make good what he had said to conference? TB said he was continually pressing the US and she said 'Is that it?' with real disdain and contempt. She and Jack then had another little spat re India and Pakistan. Then a discussion on Bali, then where we were on Iraq, then JP on fire, then GB re the need to be very firm on the pay awards. The atmosphere wasn't great. We briefed hard out of it. TB's warning that there could well be more attacks.

Hilary Armstrong said to me afterwards that Clare was angling to become deputy leader under GB. She was a totally ridiculous figure. Today had been like listening to someone on a bus, chipping in comments about other people's conversations, totally unable to see why people wouldn't see that she was right about every-thing. I saw JP before he went over to the briefing, told him not to say that there was no Bali warning, and not to rise to the press bait. He did fine and later we had a bit of a post-mortem on the week.

Adam Crozier and David Davies came in to see me, said that the FA was moving towards a position of support for a regulator to bring order to football. They wanted to sound me out. I said I felt there were fundamental design flaws in the game, with the FA in charge of the national team and the grass roots, but not the bits in between, and it really made for chaos. TB was off to Northern Ireland and his speech went really big, and we were pleased that Sinn Fein were not too dismissive.[1] The French were winning the day at the UN and watering down resolutions.

Friday, October 18

TB, now in Sedgefield, got very good coverage out of Belfast. The main story today was the Fire Brigades Union strike ballot [over pay], Bali, and the UN with the French claiming they were pushing things to a different position. Adam Boulton called, said he was doing *The Week in Westminster* [BBC Radio 4], and why didn't I do it with him on the lobby changes. I decided to do it to put over the points of principle – more access to ministers, more access for more media, expert briefers. On the US conference call, I was still pushing for more CIC reform. The [Fire Brigades] ballot came out nine to one in favour of strike action, so that was going to be the main focus domestically for the coming period. Alex [Ferguson], Mark and Jason [his sons] came round for dinner. We'd all done pretty well sorting things out when a couple of lowlifes had tried to set him up in South Africa last week. Mark was saying Alex owed these journalists nothing, that he kept some of their careers afloat by talking to them. He said he felt Alex should cut himself off from them, that he was the best club manager ever, a historic figure in football, and he should be rising above them all the time. They were very nice kids, clearly adored their dad but were worried for him. Jason said that when he had been in trouble last week, 'the people at this table, not journalists he might think he could trust, sorted it'. Alex said 'That's what friends are for. They are the people who walk into the room when everyone else is thinking of walking out.'

[1] In the Belfast speech, Blair asked Northern Ireland politicians 'Do we have the courage as politicians to do what the people want us to do? Do we trust each other enough to make the acts of completion happen? I can only tell you as British prime minister that I have that trust in all the parties I have worked with. We must implement the [Good Friday] Agreement in full, because it is the choice of the people; the people here, the people in the South and the people of the United Kingdom as a whole.'

October '02: Fire Brigades Union votes to strike

Saturday, October 19

Calum and I left early for Leicester. I had a long chat with Estelle [Morris], trying to persuade her to do the ministerial briefing on Tuesday, partly because she had something to say, but also because it would show she had guts and was prepared to fight back. But she said her confidence was low, one more mistake and she would be in real trouble, and she didn't feel up to doing it. We got to Leicester fairly early and I took Calum to see where we lived and went to school. Both the house and the school looked very different to how I remembered them, and the street seemed wider and the whole area seemed more prosperous than I imagined them to be. Then to the Aylestone Leisure Centre where I was doing an anti-racism event and a couple of interviews. I had lunch at the ground, then over to the away end for the match itself [Leicester 0, Burnley 1]. Our lot were generally OK, but when the anti-racism stuff was mentioned, there was a minority started singing 'You're just a town full of Pakis', indicating how far there was still to go.

Sunday, October 20

I was trying to persuade TB to make the speech to midwives part of the general strategy on public services staff, trying to bind them in. I got Godric to do a very tough line on the FBU, no going back to bad old days. TB was still worried we needed the Queen's Speech to be stronger, particularly on [higher education] top-up fees and child benefit conditionality. He was worried about the intelligence issue and the handling post Bali, so when I heard Jack wanted to make a statement tomorrow, I felt it was an opportunity to put out the broader picture re intelligence and warnings, drafted a section for Jack making clear that there had been no warning, that we had to assess this stuff the whole time. And to overreact to every warning, every piece of intelligence, would be to do the terrorists' job for them. TB said we had to be very wary of the French, watch they didn't do us in on the UNSCR, maintain the position of broker. Jack, a pretty rare thing this for ministers, called later simply to thank me for it.

Monday, October 21

Someone had briefed the Cobra meeting on fire [strikes], so the media coverage was giving a sense almost of national emergency. It was all a bit chaotic, and [Nick] Raynsford [minister] gave us a bit of a problem by saying that the army would not cross picket lines. There was just no need to get into that yet. My day was rather overshadowed by illness. After a few days of low-level colitis, it was back with a vengeance. By the evening, I was back on the steroids. [Professor] Michael Farthing [gastroenterologist] thought it was a mix of stress, lifestyle, plus maybe a bug from Russia. He was sceptical about me doing the marathon though he conceded I looked fitter and better than before. TB's other worry was the [EU] Stability Pact. He and JP had both been putting pressure on GB at least to discuss the euro properly, and JP had warned him he was thinking of making a speech about the Stability Pact. It led to GB then briefing the *FT* that he was looking into the issues. JP came to see me to discuss fire and whether he should meet [Andy] Gilchrist [Fire Brigades Union general secretary]. We agreed that for now it should be left to Raynsford.

TB asked me, David Manning and Jonathan to think through a strategy to avoid Chirac being credited with sorting Bush. It was TB who had persuaded them of the UN route, got it up and running. At TB's weekly office meeting, his big worry as ever was public service delivery. We had a bit of an up-and-downer on schools when he said he wanted to replace the word comprehensive with specialist. What on earth was the point of that? Post Bali, he felt that on issues of intelligence, we should take the public much more into our trust and explain how we make these judgements, set out the difficulties we face in doing so. There were calls for an inquiry but our feeling was best to let the ISC [Intelligence and Security Committee of parliamentarians, appointed by the Prime Minister] look at it. As if to underline how difficult all this was, a new JIC [Joint Intelligence Committee] paper came in showing there were lots of different areas considered liable for attack – British schools abroad, airports and airline desks, bars. We were tightening security on official buildings and more vulnerable soft targets, but if we actually put up warnings about every target that might be considered vulnerable, should the terrorists be able to do it, the whole place would shut down. They also thought Bin Laden wanted to do a few high-profile assassinations.

Tuesday, October 22

David Miliband called late last night to say Estelle had pulled out of the 8.10 *Today* programme slot because the Tories had dug up her pledge to resign if Key Stage 2 targets were not met. It was pretty black and white and DM and I discussed a line to help them through it, which was not brilliant but would have to do. But as she had a press conference later it was going to be pretty tough for her. Estelle asked to see TB and having been with him for a while, he asked me and Sally to pop round. She was basically saying she felt that her integrity and honesty was what made us value her and if TB felt she should go, either because of this, or because of the cumulative effect of recent events, she felt that they should have that conversation. TB said he didn't think this latest thing on the 'pledge to resign' was serious enough. I said it all depended deep down on whether she felt she was up to doing the job. She was clearly stressed, fiddling aggressively with her hands, her neck was bright red and at times she seemed close to tears. Sally felt that the team around her wasn't strong enough. It seemed to me that deep down she maybe felt she wasn't up to it. TB said we should all think about it. I had a couple of long conversations with her later in the day, during which I felt she was moving towards leaving, and I started to draft an exchange of letters. If it was going to happen, it was best to do it before a head of steam built up, and for her to say what appeared to be the case, namely that she found the pressure and realities of modern politics very difficult. We had the *Times* team in for lunch, during which I wrote the [exchange of resignation] letters, Alice Miles [columnist] constantly asking me what I was writing, was it newsworthy, and at one point, is it a reshuffle?

I spoke to Estelle around 6pm, having said I would take TB's mind on things. He basically didn't think she should go, but that only she could know if she was really up for it. She said to me that she just was not capable of coping with the nasty personal stuff in the media, like her nieces at school being approached, or a boyfriend of fifteen years ago being looked into. The growing sense I had was of someone who was looking around for reasons to go, but didn't want to say that actually she was just finding it very difficult. When I next spoke to TB, he felt she probably would have to go and the only question was when. We didn't particularly want tomorrow because of PMQs. In any event it was worth her sleeping on it again, thinking about it for a day or two, so maybe Thursday. She sounded pretty confused, very down, kept asking the same question – what do you really think? What does Tony really think? TB called when we were having a party for Rory's birthday, and he was already thinking about a reshuffle. I felt maybe Tessa [Jowell] or Pat [Hewitt], not Charles [Clarke] because I felt he was beginning to get the hang of the chairman's job, and also was it a good precedent in a sense to reward the fact that he had spent most of the time doing the job making clear he didn't want it. TB felt he might be the right person for now. Peter H was particularly down on Charles, felt he was all problem, no solution. And he found his meeting style, which was basically get everyone to make random points, deeply irritating. JP's statement on fire [describing threatened strikes as 'completely unnecessary and completely unjustified'] went fine.

Wednesday, October 23

Fire dispute really picking up strong. The FBU was seeing the TUC but we were in a much better position than we might have been. The first meeting of the day was a rather alarming security meeting with Jack S, GH, CDS, DB, John Scarlett and the agency chiefs. There was a lot of specific threat stuff around, particularly re Heathrow. We agreed that there should be visible stepping up of security at airports. Then to a fire meeting, TB being ultra nice to JP, who was glad not just to be involved, but that TB seemed to be trusting him fully with the negotiations. He was so on board that in the Commons office after PMQs, when TB was doing his usual whisky-bottle and photo-signing session, JP was organising the bottles. We agreed it was far better for now we stay very calm and reasonable, lots of public information stuff.

At the pre-PMQs meetings, for obvious reasons TB and I were more worried than the others about questions on Estelle. After the meeting I went to my office and called her. She had just made a speech in Birmingham [to secondary-school heads]. She said she had slept on things, and now she had made up her mind and was clear that she was going to go. I had suggested yesterday that she might think about going back to being schools minister, and she said she would think about that. She said she had worked out what she was good at and what she was less good at. She was good with people, and she was good on policy but she couldn't run a big department strategically and she just couldn't cope with the modern media and its intrusiveness and nastiness. She said there was something I had said yesterday which had made a real impression on her, when I pointed out that compared to others, she hadn't really had a hard time in the media and I had said 'Maybe Tony and I are just so used to it that we have grown immune.' She said 'I don't want to be immune, because it would mean I would stop feeling.' She asked me repeatedly if I thought she was doing the right thing, and what TB really thought. I said he basically worried that she had lost her nerve, and that if she didn't feel up for it, there was no point hanging around. He also felt she was an asset and he wouldn't want to lose her, but if she had decided, he would respect that. She said she yearned for her old job in a way, but maybe it was difficult going back. I filled in TB who was still keen we did nothing pre PMQs but felt he should see her later, go ahead with it tonight, reshuffle tomorrow. Sally, Jeremy and I were arguing for Alan Milburn. TB was concerned because he had promised Ian McCartney [minister for pensions] the next Cabinet job. He called Peter M for views and he said we would be made to let her go.

TB was on great form at PMQs, hit IDS hard both on fire and on health, but was also strong on Northern Ireland. He didn't like having to defend the line about the army not crossing picket lines. I arranged for Estelle to come in just after 6. TB's view was that if she had decided to go, she should go now, which was also JP's opinion when I spoke to him after PMQs. I was honing the resignation letters but also beginning to sink in a sea of unread paper, re the GICS review, Queen's Speech. It always seemed to happen when I was drawn into the day-to-day again. TB had a call with Bush. It was clear the Americans were getting more and more impatient about the UN and at the way the French in particular were slowing things down. TB made clear he really felt we were best to stay on that course, and he would talk to Chirac again tomorrow. Estelle arrived and Sally and I had a long session with her in my office. She said she felt she was really good with teachers and she could do that part of the job great. She was hopeless with budgets and figures and there was too much of the department for her to stay on top of it all the time. She said it was the right thing to go but if we wanted her to stay to Christmas, that was fine, or if we wanted her to go back to the old job under David M – who she clearly thought was going to get the job – that was fine too.

I showed her the letters I had drafted, she read hers first, and said yes, that's right, it sums it up fine. When she looked at the one I had done for Tony, she started crying. Sally went over to her and hugged her and after a minute or so she regained her composure, but she looked broken. She said it was just very tough for her and she hated the media side of things and she never felt able to cope with it. By the time we took her round to see TB, she was fine, very strong now, clear she was doing the right thing. TB was not sure it would be possible to put her back to the old job straight away, but maybe later when he moved David [Miliband] on. We finished the letters, TB changing the draft of his to be much warmer and making it clear that he was keen to have her back. We got Sue Littlemore [social affairs correspondent] in from the BBC to do an interview in Sally's office.

We finally got the letters sorted and out by 7.45 after Estelle had called her parents and her permanent secretary. Her private secretary came in and was crying. I briefed Tessa [Jowell] to get her round and about on the interviews tomorrow. I sat in on Estelle's [BBC] interview and she was excellent, really open and candid, saying she had decided she was not doing as well as she wanted to. It was a really strong, quite moving interview that would do her and politics some good. Afterwards she came over and gave me a big hug, said she had always enjoyed working with me and hoped we would again in the future. Chris Woodhead [former Chief Inspector of Schools] was out dancing on the grave straight away. TB was going out for a dinner and came to see me before he left. He said it was important that I moved Estelle away from the idea she was coming straight back, because he would probably leave David M where he was. He wanted to take time on this and get it right. How many resignation letters have I now written? It's a bit alarming how easily they flow from the pen. Estelle didn't change a single word, TB just inserted a little bit of extra support. He felt people would find it odd that she went but it was 'for the best'. It sounded pretty ruthless and probably was. I had said to Estelle 'Sometimes I feel like the executioner. I always seem to be there at the death of a ministerial career and I find it unbelievably draining.'

Thursday, October 24

Estelle got a good press. David Puttnam [Lord Puttnam, friend of Morris] sent me a message saying that she had been really grateful for all the support I had given her. I was in early, did a note to JP on his fire interviews and also a message note on the Queen's Speech [November 18]. Sally M and I went up to the flat. She had spoken to Alan who was adamant he should should stay at Health, but after speaking to Darren Murphy [Milburn's special adviser] and others, came back to say he could see the merit of a move to a big challenge that was behind the curve on modernisation. TB was moving towards Charles Clarke. I had doubts about how modernising he was on education and whether he would work properly with the centre. Peter Hyman said that Charles was constantly decrying the [Prime Minister's] Delivery Unit and was also opposed to targets. John Reid was up for the chairmanship, so once the main decision was taken, the rest should flow quite easily. But TB wanted to take his time. He said there were four possible names – Milburn, Hewitt, Clarke, Jowell. He got Hilary A and Andrew Turnbull to join us. Andrew said he felt Milburn was the most proven, was more respected than liked by officials. TB wanted to speak to JP, then see Charles. We arranged for Charles to come through 70 Whitehall in case he said no. JP was OK re Charles, if not terribly enthusiastic, but not OK re John Reid [becoming party chairman], largely because TB had made a promise to Ian [McCartney]. TB didn't even tell him what he was planning to do with [Peter] Hain [Europe minister], namely Welsh Secretary. He didn't consult GB at all, largely because he couldn't face the usual nonsense of GB trying to promote his own people way beyond their abilities. He did consult JP, Blunkett and Jack, who said yes to Charles

October '02: GB not consulted over reshuffle . . .

provided he got a warning about being more disciplined. The general feeling was that Charles had not done the last job particularly well and it was a risk. TB accepted Charles had not been a great party chairman but education was a job he really wanted, he was a big personality and he thought he could do it. He felt Alan needed a year to get critical mass on [NHS reform] delivery. So we got JP in to agree, then Charles, then Paul Murphy [replacing John Reid as Northern Ireland Secretary] then the Cabinet meeting. TB saw Charles privately and said he had given him a real warning about the need for reform, the need to work better with other people. Charles looked shell-shocked on the way out, as if congratulations were falling on deaf ears.

It was education questions at 11.30. We had to decide if Charles went to the House for questions. David M and I put together a script but once TB got into Cabinet, he wasn't keen for us to announce the names. But with the lobby waiting, and all but Peter Hain now announced, what was the point? In Cabinet, GB, rarely, spoke several times, first on the need to stand up against the French attack on the [British EU] rebate. He also chipped in on Lords reform and on Iraq. With Charles due to leave any moment for questions, I slipped a note to TB saying he needed to announce the first three changes, otherwise they would all hear it first on the media. GB went virtually white. While others were nodding approval, he looked around with something close to hatred. He puffed his cheeks out, his eyes narrowed and he just scanned the room. He knew he had been hit. He went to see TB afterwards and as we waited outside in the private office, GB's raised voice, and TB's attempts to calm him down, could be heard.

As GB left, thunderstruck, he said nothing to any of us, just stormed out. I asked TB what he had been saying. 'He was mad. The whole thing was a conspiracy against him. Every single one of them is a disastrous appointment. All designed to damage him.' He said he had also railed against me [AC] and my diary and said he wanted to raise it in Cabinet! He had railed at Cherie, said that she hated him and wanted to do him down. He told TB that his office was full of Tories. Later, I was talking to Tessa in the foyer when GB came by, still storming. 'That man is fucking insane,' she said. I told her she had been in the frame for education, which cheered her up. Neil called, thrilled at the appointments. All very Kinnockite. He was also supporting my push for Kim Howells [culture minister] to get Europe. TB got to Brussels and was immediately upstaged by Chirac and Schroeder doing a deal on [EU] enlargement/CAP [Common

Agricultural Policy] and saying that the UK rebate would have to be looked at. This was payback time for Schroeder going to see TB rather than Chirac after winning. The French were gunning for us again.

Friday, October 25

Ran in in the pouring rain. Really like running in the rain. Good press re reshuffle. John Reid had been excellent on *Newsnight* last night and I called to tell him so. I called Andrew Turnbull re whether we could use John for briefings and he was clear we could provided we didn't make them party political. He felt the reshuffle was strong too, that we had good people in the toughest departments. JR said he would take his time to build a proper relationship with JP, but he saw little point trying to build bridges with GB at the moment as he seemed to be in a total rage the whole time. Did the 11 and was being pushed on why Robin said Estelle was 'hounded out' of the job. TB spoke to Putin to offer our support after Chechen gunmen took the audience in a Russian theatre hostage.[1] He called from the [Brussels] summit. Said that Schroeder had been taken in by the usual Gallic swagger. He said after the bilateral between the French and German, Chirac had called him in, totally patronised him, tried to say the whole thing was sorted because France and Germany had decided and that was that. 'I'm not having this,' he said.

In the discussions through today there was a lot of angst about taking radical CAP reform, as per Berlin, off the agenda. Chirac waded in and said that was exactly what was happening. Jack gave TB the passage from the Berlin outcome that committed them to further CAP reform and TB made clear that they had to get on with it. Chirac said this was a personal attack that in all honour and all morality should not happen. TB said 'I've been very polite' and insisted. Others then backed him. Chirac later walked up to him and said that was an all-out attack, he would not tolerate it and maybe we should call off the Anglo-French summit. TB said fine, no problem, but there will be CAP reform and we are not going back on the rebate. He said he had stayed really calm, as he always tried to when people are losing their temper, but what it means is that they will really come at us on the rebate. They had also had some pretty fiery exchanges on Iraq, TB telling him the US were going to do it so it depended if he wanted to be part of the equation or not.

---

[1] Armed Chechens claiming allegiance to Islamist separatism had taken 850 hostages in a Moscow theatre and demanded the withdrawal of Russian forces from Chechnya.

Schroeder's interpreter had said to TB afterwards, 'Wow, what was all that about?' as Chirac stormed off, and TB said he didn't care about him losing it. The French had to accept that they should treat the UK as an equal in Europe. 'He can present me as an American poodle if he wants, but we're not putting up with his shit any more. We do it on our terms now.' Sounded like it had been fun. I agreed with Godric we should brief a couple of the Sundays that Chirac's real anger had been Schroeder coming to the UK first after his election, that this was all about that, and he had to get the message that the UK should be treated as an equal. On the Europe job, TB was moving towards Denis MacShane [junior FCO minister]. Had a bit of a comic moment on the fire front when a Green Goddess [auxiliary fire engine] crashed and had to be rescued by the fire brigade.

Saturday, October 26

TB was a bit pissed off at the way it came out in the media that somehow the French had 'won'. All the more reason to get out what had actually happened, and the fact that this was Chirac's revenge for Schroeder coming here after the election. TB strongly felt the real significance of the last couple of days was that the Franco-German gambit had not worked. The Russian [theatre] siege ended, all the Brits were safe, and TB spoke to Vlad. I spoke to JP and suggested we had radio silence on the fire dispute. [Andy] Gilchrist was beginning to make mistakes. JP agreed, felt he was beginning to behave like an old-fashioned general secretary. JP offered four per cent back on the table with talks on modernisation. He called me around 5 to say it seemed to have worked and the FBU executive had agreed to call off the first two strikes. He had done a good job on this. TB called, still angry about Chirac, said that once they started speaking again, it would be to have strong words, that we were not going to be 'treated like a dog' in the way he had tried on Friday. 'I love Jacques, but he can be fucking arrogant and needs to be taught a lesson.' The Sundays had loads of write-throughs on Estelle, and maybe I should have talked to them more, because they were all just the usual clichéd stuff about the fact that women couldn't survive. Education were also briefing stupidly, that it was actually all about top-up fees and that I had asked her to stay.

Sunday, October 27

Conference call re the post-summit fallout. For some reason, our media just did not want to acknowledge that TB had actually stopped the French gambit from working. The weather was dire. Mum had been staying and her train north was cancelled so I drove her up, briefing a bit on the way. Charles Clarke called re the Sundays. We agreed he should use his first speech on Wednesday to set the full strategic picture.

Monday, October 28

TB working on the statement, including re Russia, though the Russians were causing a bit of concern by refusing to say what gas was used in the attack to free the Moscow theatre hostages.[1] The death toll was now a lot higher than first thought, but TB was instinctively sympathetic to Putin. It was one of those damned if you do, damned if you don't situations where whatever the outcome some would find grounds to criticise. At TB's office meeting, we went over the merits and demerits of the various contenders for Europe minister, and ended up going for Denis MacShane. TB did not want a lasting stand-off with Chirac, and though he was glad we'd stood up to him and seen the strategy through, he did not want to see Chirac go through with cancelling the Anglo-French summit.

Then a meeting re the FBU and how we get them off the sixteen per cent [phased pay increase] figure. At some point this was going to become a big communications job. For the time being, JP was handling fine behind the scenes but he said too at some point it would take off in the wrong direction, and we would have to be ready. I had a stack of meetings, including re top-up fees, which David Miliband was warning me had the potential to be political disasterville. A good Queen's Speech meeting, which I felt was beginning to hang together better, then another pretty dire meeting on the euro. I felt a bit for Douglas [Alexander] because people were looking at him almost as the GB presence but he knew, as we knew, that he could not really speak for him, and we all knew that this thing was undoable without TB and GB playing on the same pitch in the same way.

Interesting meeting with the French ambassador [Gérard Errera] who wanted to explain to me why Chirac was like he was, and why we should not let these bust-ups affect us too deeply. He said Chirac felt he always had to stand up for the French national interest. I said why should anyone imagine TB does not always have to stand up for the UK national interest? Yes, he said, but sometimes we seem to think they are the same. I wasn't quite sure what he was on about. 'And then there is Iraq,' he said. Yes there is, and TB again thinks he

[1] Russian special forces pumped an unknown chemical agent into the theatre and raided it, killing thirty-nine of the attackers and upwards of 130 hostages.

is standing up for what is right, and for the UK national interest. Unconvinced grimace. Then there was ESDP [European Security and Defence Policy], he said, where Chirac felt we were not European enough . . . then there was Kosovo . . . then there was Macedonia. I said at least it was best to be open about the differences, and try to sort them, but I made sure he knew TB really did not think a cancelled summit was a good idea.

Then to a meeting with Cathy Gilman of Leukaemia Research, who was very jolly and seemed to know what she was on about, and was really keen on the idea of the marathon, with Amanda Delew [campaign director, the Giving Campaign] who agreed to help out with ideas on the fund-raising side. Fiona joined us for a while and when Amanda suggested a whole load of 'meet AC' sponsorship ideas, Fiona said she couldn't quite see why anyone would want to pay to meet me. I pointed out that she does not always share the high view of me that others seem to at times. But I was convinced we could raise at least half a million. Then to the opening of the new party offices [16–18 Old Queen Street] across the park where TB made a very funny little speech, watched by an unsmiling let alone laughing GB, followed by an even funnier little speech by Richard Wilson [actor and Labour supporter].

Then to dinner at the German ambassador's [Thomas Matussek] residence, with Peter M and PG the other guests. The ambassador's wife [Ulla] took pictures of the three of us and I think it was the first time we had ever been photographed together, having always tried to avoid it when the media were asking. I liked the ambassador, though I suspect he was a bit less of an Anglophile than the last guy [Hans-Friedrich von Ploetz], and he had certainly done his research on us lot. Peter was on very good form, very funny, taking the mick out of the ambassador and me in a way that nobody could find offensive, talking as though it was a matter of fact that I had gone out of my way to destroy him. He was also pretty caustic re Schroeder and the way the German left had responded to modernisation here.

We also had some pretty heavy exchanges on Iraq. We knew the Germans had pretty much the same intelligence as we did, but were pursuing a very different line. We felt that Schroeder's stance during the campaign had been so crass that he would have a real job getting back in with the US at all. The ambassador took it all in good spirits, but also took a serious message from it. Towards the end, Peter said what should he say in the speech he was due to make in Berlin? The ambassador said you should say Germany should show more leadership, carry out far greater reforms and do a lot more to co-operate with Russia. He was pro TB but also believed he was at his zenith and the only way now was down. He thought the Tories were hopeless. As we left, PG said to me we had to find Peter M a job. He was a wasting talent. He had so much more to offer than most members of the Cabinet and we had to find him something proper to do. It was true that someone like the ambassadors would listen more to Peter than to most ministers, and he did cut a sad figure at times, because he knew he had a certain authority, but no express power to deliver anything.

Tuesday, October 29

The French row was in danger of escalating out of control. TB called as I was running in. On the one hand, he wanted to be on good terms but equally Chirac had to know his recent behaviour was intolerable. The line from the French was now that this had all come out the way it did because of our briefing. TB wanted the message fed back that we had to be treated as equals, and would not accept anything less, but also that he wanted to calm things. I spoke to Peter Hain before he did *Today*, and agreed the basic line that we fight our corner as aggressively as any other country. David Manning, Jeremy and I had all spoken to the ambassador in the last twenty-four hours, so he knew this was serious. He also knew we didn't want to inflame further. But he knew that to us there had been a cumulative effect building over time.

I spoke to Catherine Colonna [Chirac's spokeswoman] at 11.10. I always liked dealing with Catherine. She was very French in her style and elegance but there was something Anglo-Saxon about her directness and I was always able to have frank conversations with her. Jesus, I said, we left them for ten minutes on their own and they started a riot! She said she felt Chirac had lacked '*politesse*' with TB and now, probably because he knew it, he was '*têtu*' [stubborn]. We agreed to try to calm. But then ninety minutes later up it popped on AFP [Agence France-Presse], that the Anglo-French summit was cancelled. David Manning and [Sir] Stephen Wall [EU adviser] were both up for a big counter-attack, but TB was more of the view he go up to do media and try to settle it down. I was not sure about that.

It rather dominated the Tuesday strategy meeting, but we did manage a decent discussion re the euro, and convinced TB that there were some very live questions that had to be addressed. But we couldn't get going until we had some sense of direction from him and GB, but all GB was doing was saying he would do nothing to compromise the tests. TB said again that he believed we could win a referendum, but Peter M, PG and I all felt we needed to know the shape of a plan sooner not later, e.g. could we have a positive assessment pre election and a referendum after? Did we envisage the assessment and referendum close together? How did we put together a campaign? What are the rules? It was all a bit high-wire and yet I did not feel we knew where GB really was, other than probably not in the same place as TB.

On the Queen's Speech, the focus on crime, rights and responsibilities was strong. We then discussed the politics of tuition fees, which seemed to be getting worse not better. It was almost without doubt the right thing to do, and there was a perfectly good argument for it in terms of the long-term benefit to the country, but it was not easy to persuade people that education was anything other than a right that should come free. I felt we needed a much bigger communications strategy around the bigger arguments. We also had to ensure there was not a diminution of access, and we were not yet convinced the work on that had been done either.

After I got home, JP called re a visit on Thursday, and also to go over the Fire Service situation. I asked how things were with GB. He said he was at a crossroads. He didn't much like some of what TB wanted for health and education. He felt he had been bounced to some extent on foundation hospitals. Also he was not going to get himself into a position where because he was being used to shift GB on the euro, that was used to say he was anti GB on big domestic issues too. I sensed JP was back to a 'plague on both houses' mood and he sounded a bit more menacing than usual, though we did end with a laugh when he heard the doorbell going in the background and he said 'Go on, that'll be Tony popping round for a nightcap.' Catherine Colonna called late, said she was trying to calm things but suggesting there were *'d'autres dans la forêt'* [others in the forest] who were still stirring things.

Wednesday, October 30

TB called at 7, said though the French row was calming a bit part of him felt it had been good to have it. He had been trying to get into a proper position with the French for five years and maybe this was the only way to have done it, now we can work out what we really agree on and what we don't. He felt he understood Chirac's position on most things but Chirac did not understand his, or really try to. He wanted to fix a proper summit meeting for February now and work through a really substantial joint programme. He felt there was a lot more we could do on defence. He felt even on Iraq it was possible to get to a closer position. He was growing a bit disappointed with Schroeder and saw Anglo-French relations as important in part because the Germans were a bit flaky. I spoke to Catherine a couple of times to try to pin down a date for a proper meeting but we didn't get there in the end. Things won't have been helped by [Labour MP] Tony Wright's question at PMQs.[1]

Because we pretty much all felt now IDS was a goner, and because we all would prefer he stayed, the PMQs meeting was full of black humour about how good he was, but TB was finding it harder to get up for these encounters because he just didn't feel IDS had it. The papers were full of stories that there were now enough people up for a challenge. In the end IDS and [Charles] Kennedy both went on tuition fees trying to pin TB on the manifesto commitment not to introduce them. This was going to be difficult, because TB had pretty much decided this was the right thing for the country, and the right thing for the universities, but politically it could be as difficult as anything we had yet done, especially as GB had now pretty much admitted he was putting together a slightly-to-the-left platform and this would be part of it. At PMQs TB effectively had to stand by the manifesto whilst making the case for a different position.

After PMQs I told TB and Sally M re my conversation with JP last night, his general offsideness. 'This is all pressure from GB,' TB said. Yesterday's GB meeting had been dreadful. 'I said to him at one point, sorry but I'm not listening to this any more. You've lost it.' In the pensions meeting, GB did the old trick of identifying the position of others, misrepresenting it and then having a non-argument so that the real positions were not addressed. I said to TB he had a limited period of maximum strength and he had to use it. He knew what I meant but said 'If he walks, or if I push him, we have to be very careful because the party will not like it and blame will not just fall to one side.' GB was making mistakes though, because he was growing desperate his time would never come. TB said he had no idea if it was all going to end in divorce but we had to be on the right side of the arguments if it did.

John Reid's first meeting re party issues, and he was good, if a bit loquacious. The thing I liked about him was his ability to think things through quickly and articulate them clearly. Philip gave the

[1] Wright said 'Could I ask the prime minister to tell us exactly how rude he was to Monsieur Chirac? Did he perhaps remind him that if the French president was not in the Élysée he would almost certainly be in jail?' Blair responded 'No, I didn't say that.'

October '02: Duncan Smith looks like a goner

most positive polling readout for a while, and some of the deeper strategies – e.g. anti spin, focus on long term – were getting through and making a difference. Pat McFadden came in halfway through, having finally decided to take Robert Hill's job [as Blair's political secretary, Hill having been appointed special adviser to Charles Clarke]. Pat had to decide if he was going to pursue a serious political career now or meander into middle age. I had an hour with David Wilkinson [Cabinet Office] for his GICS review and was perhaps too frank. I said I felt the GICS was to a large extent a barrier to good communications and that leading people were obstructive to change.

I had a good meeting with Peter M, who was pro John Reid and up for a more political role at some point, and PG. I was working on a fund-raising letter for Leukaemia Research and read through all the old cuttings and speeches re John [Merritt, Campbell's late best friend who died of the disease]. TB called a couple of times later, really turning over top-up fees in his mind. He knew this was going to set the next phase of the domestic context. He was up for being 'at our best when at our boldest' and up for a debate taking off in that direction. He agreed to do a press conference on Monday to get up pre-Queen's Speech messaging on crime and antisocial behaviour.

Thursday, October 31

The day didn't start very well, Fiona repeating her view that she didn't see why people would pay money to talk to me at sponsored events, which was her way of saying she didn't really want the pressure of the marathon adding to the pressures of the job. But I was sure I wanted to do it, could do it, and needed a new challenge like this. I left in a pretty foul mood though. First meeting re European defence where Jonathan and I both thought TB was kidding himself if he thought we were going to get a decent deal with the French any time soon. Another meeting re top-up fees. Surely, I said, there must be another way of doing this. TB said ultimately not. You could fiddle at the edges, rename and repackage but ultimately it was a top-up fees system we were proposing and it was right. In which case, there was a big job to be done in winning the argument, and we were going to need the universities to carry a lot of the load. If this was genuinely the only way they could keep developing in the way they needed to in order to remain high quality and compete with universities around the world, then they had to be making that case too.

John Reid was at the political strategy meeting and was a bit more focused and less anecdotal than Charles. He had a good line re the Tories playing the man not the ball, going for TB personally because they were scared of the policy debate. The general view was IDS was a goner and we went over the various [Conservative leadership] contenders and worked out the outlines of a strategy for each. It was an excellent meeting. JR was clear, and very, very political, and Douglas was developing a real grasp of what was needed for the mechanics of the euro campaign. We also agreed to go for a much simpler, clearer Queen's Speech message so I spent part of the day working on that, as well as TB's press conference script for Monday.

GB was being pretty difficult re the ASB [antisocial behaviour] agenda, trying to run the line that the more we focused on it, the more people felt we were failing on it. TB tried to explain that he needed to stop seeing it as a political issue. It was a REAL issue, about people's lives, and they wanted us to GET it. Milburn came in to discuss the [NHS] consultants' contracts with TB who told him GB was now deliberately winding up JP to see all difficult reform as being essentially driven by Tories in Number 10. AM said JP had been at him the whole time re foundation hospitals, but he was determined we had to press on.

A TB meeting with JS, GH and CDS who said the Americans seemed to be cutting us out of some of the military decision-making because we had gone for Package 2 not Package 3, and also reporting that some inside our army were pissed off not to be more involved. God, he was hard to read, sometimes giving the impression none of them wanted anything to do with this, then at others giving the impression they all wanted to be off to the front line. Cabinet – discussion re Europe and the CAP, with Jack clearer than ever we had to mount and win an argument re CAP.

Clare's interruptions were even worse and more irritating than usual, because she was doing her serious questioning act rather than the holier-than-thou bit. At least with the holier-than-thou bit, people knew how to deal with it, which was basically ignore. At the end she came over to me, all smarmy, and said 'Well done for doing in Chirac,' then added 'I love him on Iraq but I hate him on Africa . . . We have to think about the world!' Really? I said we all think about the world and I for one would prefer a world in which Saddam does not have weapons and does not terrorise his own people. To be fair to her, she did a decent presentation to Cabinet on what was happening humanitarian-wise in Afghanistan. GB waded in pretty heavily on Europe. Alan was excellent on the consultants, really on top of it, and political, but I could see GB looking very darkly at him as well as TB.

I had a get-together with the staff from the media team and I was pretty heavy with them, said too many of them were operating in the comfort zone and we needed all-round game-raising. I think one of the reasons I was tired and down was because they all kind of felt I would come up with the creative stuff in the end, and they just had to deliver. But I wanted all of them to be thinking more creatively and strategically. Two or three of them looked a bit hurt, but I feel it needed saying. I showed TB my marathon fund-raising letter and he had reservations. He felt it would get me up in lights as a target again and I had to be careful about the donors. He also thought I should not state explicitly I was trying to raise a million, but maybe aim for £100k to start. It was all good advice but I wondered if he was also worrying that I was focusing on this as a substitute for work.

Friday, November 1

The [Paul] Burrell [former butler to Diana, Princess of Wales] trial was about to collapse, meaning a welcome news sponge for the weekend. Burrell had told the Queen after Diana's death that he'd taken some of her possessions for safe keeping, so the prosecution case that he never told anyone was debunked by Her Maj. TB had been told on Tuesday and then the Attorney General had to broker a prosecution statement between the CPS [Crown Prosecution Service], the police and the Palace, and which was due to be read in court this morning.[1] The AG had had to go to see the Queen yesterday, to alert her to some of the difficult questions that would flow, but in any event to alert her to the fact the case was being dropped. It was going to be seen as a total fiasco, though the Queen had been through far worse.

I was working on TB's words for Monday re the ASB bill for his press conference, the plan having gone a bit off track yesterday with a consultation paper containing the idea of £50 fines for dropping chewing gum in the street. It was total bollocks, and annoying, though I suppose it did at least get over the kind of issues we were talking about. I took the office through the plan for the Queen's Speech, then did a session with SpAds. I felt we were strong on message at the moment, and also that the changes re the media operation were beginning to bed down well. We were certainly hearing less about spin than for a while, and TB was finding his voice better.

[1] Burrell had been accused of stealing more than 300 items belonging to Diana, Prince Charles and Prince William. Late intervention by the Queen, who recalled a 1998 conversation with Burrell, raised questions as to whether the trial should have gone ahead in the first place.

Fiona was very down on Cherie at the moment, having discovered she had already signed a contract on the book [on Prime Ministers' spouses], TB having told us she hadn't. Cherie basically admitted to Fiona that she hadn't consulted us because she knew we were hostile to the project. Fiona said we were hostile to people coming in and potentially landing her in difficult circumstances through their own ambitions for the 'project'. I said to TB that I could not see the advantage to HIM of this happening, I could see plenty of possible downsides, and in the end it was him and his reputation we had to be focused on. He just had to accept Cherie was not going to get the same kid-gloves media treatment that Norma [Major] got. TB was at Chequers, pretty unbothered by it all.

Saturday, November 2

The *Telegraph* had the MoD saying GB was blocking cash needed for Iraq. Then I became worried that the government role in the Burrell trial would become an issue so did a conference call with [Lord] Goldsmith and his team to agree the best lines to take if it did, emphasising the AG was the only member of the government with any active role in this. The CPS took the decision to go with the prosecution. The Queen told [princes] Charles and Philip last Friday about her conversation, the prosecution then realised they'd had it, told the AG, who then told us. It had all been a bit classic Establishment for a while, running around rather than sorting quickly.

Goldsmith was very conscious of his position. When I said we should be saying this was in no way a government decision, he said we have to be careful not to imply he is not a member of the government. He is, albeit independent when it comes to legal advice. When I asked why he personally had had to see the Queen, he said 'Because I am HER Attorney General and HER senior lawyer.' We were all pretty clear he had done nothing wrong, but it was one of those with plenty of scope for media mischief around the edges and we just had to get the lines cleared. Frank Dobson [former Health Secretary] had a big go in the *Observer* and *Mail on Sunday* re 'elitist' policies on health and education, which would run on the broadcasts. There was something sad and a bit bitter about Frank, but in truth we had not done a good job at keeping him on board.

Sunday, November 3

Eight-mile run with Rory and some of his mates. Conference call to pin down the detail on tomorrow's press conference. I had a couple of long chats with Douglas and Gus O'Donnell re the GICS review, and both felt a proper outside review was needed. Gus felt we almost needed to start from scratch, get rid of the GICS and start all over again with an outsider in charge. An ex-Health permanent secretary was being suggested, but I called Alan who felt it was a bit old school, as did Godric. Gus was clear this was the one opportunity we would get to be radical and we needed to get [Andrew] Turnbull signed up for that too.

TB called when I was at tennis with Calum. He was unaware of the Dobbo attack, and when I said he had gone for Andrew [Adonis] in particular, he got pretty angry, said it was a way of attacking New Labour without saying so. 'If we followed the lead of people like Frank we would be straight out of power again. They do not get how the country has changed.' He felt that with David Miliband leaving [as head of the Policy Unit, to become an MP in 2001], we had lost a very deft political operator – which Andrew was not – but he felt he got more policy drive from Andrew, whilst we had to do the politics. He said David was a good Policy Unit head, but so is Andrew, in a different way. I said he cannot just ignore the political fallout though. Andrew lacks certain political skills and the Policy Unit has become too managerial, with the result that the party sees it as soulless and right wing. Fair or not, we have to deal with that. I said your friends as well as enemies think it is sending out conflicting messages and is not sufficiently political or Labour. I was worried he was just becoming stubborn about this, when with a few modifications we could deal with the problem. It was not as though anyone thought he was not constantly looking for the modernising options. But seen as it was, it was also giving the GB lot a good deal of licence to cause trouble in the PLP and the party.

TB said there were elements who wanted to slow down or stop the process of reform and we just could not let them. I said I am not arguing for that. I am arguing for a more political policy unit to help us make sure they cannot win that argument. Andrew is just a surrogate for attacks on you, I said, but don't get angry or stubborn about it, work out how we deal with it. The answer is better policy and better communication of the arguments. If it all sounds managerial, we lose. It has to be about values all the time, and that is where we are not as strong as we were. It is nobody's fault, it is just where we are. The GB point was brought home again when Darren Murphy picked up from some of the hacks that the Treasury were briefing fairly aggressively against top-up fees. I called [Ian] Austin to rail at him but he did his usual. He dropped in that [Ed] Balls was doing an interview with Jackie Ashley [*Guardian*].

I dropped in that GB had effectively told TB he was putting together a left-wing positioning strategy and we would be watching for the signs. I was never sure whether Ian was really at the top table so maybe I was wasting my breath, but I told him I was really sick of their modus operandi.

Monday, November 4

The *Guardian* splashed on the Balls interview and a not very uncoded attack on TB's policy direction, which all tied in with Dobbo. TB was furious but it was difficult to respond without provoking a TB/GB row publicly and there was just no point. He said the worst thing about all this is that 'I still try to help him and he basically treats me like shit.' He felt that they were now running a basic destabilisation strategy, though one without a clear outcome. Every time they did this, they tended to reinforce rather than weaken TB's resolve, though they definitely had an impact on morale and effectiveness. He said this was all about trying to portray TB as being in love with markets, and therefore effectively not Labour. TB said if people knew the truth about how GB treats him, they would be appalled. He felt that GB was trying to push him into trying to get rid of him, and he would then seek to mount a challenge. But it was impossible to be sure.

I pointed out that GB tended to back off whenever it looked like becoming too public that he was up to this kind of stuff. I felt the loss of the baby had also had a profound effect and in its own way added to GB's hatred of TB. It all added to the sense that everything came easy for TB and hard for GB. Leo was such a cute kid and added to the idea TB got everything. Austin fed back my comments re GB's left-wing platform because GB raised it later, trying to make a joke of it. TB was at a loss how to handle things at the moment. He said GB was operating as though he were part of a different operation, not the government. There were plenty of problem areas to go through at the press conference pre-meeting – Royals, Iraq, Chirac. TB wasn't brilliant, not as bouncy as usual, but OK.

Tuesday, November 5

Press conference coverage fairly low-key though TB was pleased that the *FT*, which most of Europe's leaders take a look at, led on the row with France. He was fairly big in most of the papers though on a mix of subjects and the original intention, of driving through a message on ASB, didn't really come off. The main political focus of the day was meltdown for IDS after the rebellion against his three-line whip on gay adoption [the Conservative whip being to oppose]. There was a swirl of rumour that he was about to quit.

There was very little interest in us today. We had the first of the new 'board meetings', part of TB's efforts to get a bit more managerial focus into the working of the office, but I didn't hold out much hope of this lasting. The style didn't suit him and some of the discussion was below his pay grade. Cast of thousands. The bulk of the discussion related to his continuing unhappiness about the lack of strategic and delivery capability, both at the centre but above all in driving progress in departments. He felt there was a big disconnect between radical policy thinking and front-line delivery. There was no strategic economic narrative. We went over the 'traffic lights' review, a [Michael] Barber innovation showing [red, amber, green] how well each department was doing on the main public service projects. It was a mixed picture, but not enough green for my liking. TB was also exasperated at the general failure on major IT projects. Several people said in their different ways that departments did not respond well to calls for change. [John] Birt ['blue skies thinking' adviser] said departments see the centre as something to be worked around. But I felt they now had so many different voices representing Number 10 that they were able to play us off against each other. The key had to be getting ministers signed up to a shared vision and then wanting to put it through with the same vigour as we did. But departments were complaining all they ever got was pressure from us without clarity or follow-through.

We had far better discussions on Europe and Iraq. TB was still worrying away about the French, said this was 'Macmillan–de Gaulle all over again, but we have to think our way through it very carefully.'[1] They basically think we are too close to the US and we think they are too old-fashioned and blindly anti-American. We needed to keep improving alliances with others, not just Germany. He felt there was also a personal element to Chirac's current stance, that he resented how TB was seen as the great white hope around the new EU.

I watched IDS [press conference] and his basic line – 'Unite or die' – was simply going to add to his problems. First, unite around what? Second, the unity call came very badly from someone who had helped do in [John] Major. There was a hypocrisy attached to it and also something absurd saying the fight was about modernisation, coming

[1] Then French president Charles de Gaulle vetoed the British application to join the European Economic Community in 1963 because he thought the UK, under the premiership of Harold Macmillan, lacked the necessary political will to be part of a strong Europe.

as this did on the back of what he did re gay adoption. I had lunch at the Savoy with John Witherow and David Cracknell [*Sunday Times*]. Witherow was starting to bid for my post-Number 10 book! He was pretty positive re TB, very up on Milburn, felt GB OK as Chancellor but not convinced beyond that. I drove back with Michael Jay [FCO permanent secretary] who was having lunch there. We discussed the UNSCR state of play and though we were still on course for tabling tomorrow he seemed pretty pessimistic. On the euro, I said TB was as keen as ever but GB was making it virtually impossible, and I didn't think it could happen unless TB moved him.

TB saw Fiona re CB. She felt we were totally hostile to the book idea which is why she hadn't involved us. He felt it was not about her making money but trying to do something useful. Fiona felt Cherie had not been open with any of us, including him, about the project. She was happy not to work for CB, and do something else, but needed to know the lie of the land. She had tried to rub along with Carole [Caplin] but she had no idea how involved she was. I met Nick Robinson who had been made ITN political editor, full of the usual stuff about wanting to do more serious in-depth analysis blah. I'll believe it when I see it. We were in OK shape at the moment. The reshuffle had worked out well. Charles Clarke was starting to motor on policy. John Reid was a breath of fresh air at the centre. GB's currency was a bit low, which had its upsides and downsides. As TB said, if only he could get that relationship back on some kind of keel, we would be in very good shape.

Wednesday, November 6

We were going to get the UNSCR tabled today. TB didn't quite know how to handle PMQs with IDS in the state he was in. He was very focused on the GB situation at the moment. He had a euro-specific meeting with him, and got Gus [O'Donnell] along too, but said it had been as grim as grim can be. I called Gus later who said the lack of GB communication was almost comical. We thought re PMQs that IDS would do top-up fees and Gibraltar, and indeed he did, but the mood around him was so bad at the moment, it was like a dead man walking. I was beginning to feel sorry for him.

We had a good political strategy meeting, working on how we get definition out of their current situation being a problem about the Tories as a party, rather than just IDS as a leader. John R said we had to watch out for the line that we were too powerful. There was an even greater mood around in the media at the moment that with the Tories so useless, they had to go even more into Opposition mode. I wanted to see and hear a big argument out there, possibly a JR speech, making clear that to a large extent we had created this turmoil, and we were very proud of it. After PMQs, weekly meeting with Peter M, PG and Peter H. Peter M was really motoring on the line that the City felt TB was being weakened at GB's expense, and also that they sensed GB was basically Old Labour. Later I bumped into GB, the Eds and Gus in Number 11. GB grunted a kind of greeting, but friendly it was not. The best thing that happened all day came later, Burnley 2, Spurs 1.

Thursday, November 7

UNSCR was the main news all day and we were building up Jack's role. TB had a long call with Bush yesterday, who had been celebrating his election win. TB said he was much clearer about what to do and more interested in trying to get better relations with Chirac and Schroeder. He couldn't deny that he had felt personally affronted by Schroeder, and he wasn't going to hide that, but he did want to build things up. Today TB spoke to Putin who said he would vote for or against, but would not abstain.

IDS was finished. TB was starting to think that [Michael] Portillo would be OK for us, that [Kenneth] Clarke [both former Conservative leadership candidates] would give them a lift but in many ways present an even bigger target. Today's Cabinet was straightforward – Iraq/UN and fire, which was getting difficult again, and asylum/ Sangatte [refugee camp], DB saying [Nicolas] Sarkozy [French interior minister] was being helpful. TB said Jack had done really well on the UN situation. Jack did a very Jackish explanation of the background. I went for lunch with Gus Macdonald [minister for the Cabinet Office], Barry Cox [deputy chairman, Channel 4 and government adviser on digital television] and Richard Tait [former editor-in-chief, ITN] to discuss a few ideas re elections. I started to feed in the idea that there would be none of the old battle-bus routine. I was also quite keen to move away from the expectation of a press conference every morning. The 24-hour media beast had been an absolute bastard to deal with last time, so much effort for so few viewers and it would be even worse next time.

I got back for a very alarming terrorism meeting. Eliza Manningham-Buller [new director general of the Security Service, MI5] gave an overview, then Julian Miller re some of the voluminous stuff out there, then a specific discussion re Heathrow airport and the London Underground. The top-level worries were chemical weapons in the Underground, a hijacked plane into Heathrow, suicide bombs on high-profile targets. Alistair Darling was pushing quite hard on it, asked if we were prepared for the kind of blind panic that would follow. He for one did not feel we were. TB said it was important to strike a balance. Milburn and Liam Donaldson [Chief Medical Officer] wanted to put out a lot of factual material on 'what if'. There was also clearly a need for more training re major incidents on the Tube. There was a fiasco later when the Home Office released the wrong version of Blunkett's statement which meant the media got the draft that had the section in about a dirty bomb that we thought better out.[1] I called Huw Evans [special adviser] to ask how on earth could that happen? But I suppose it did get up the focus on terror.

I chaired a two-hour meeting on Iraq communications. Went through a lot of different scenarios and planning. We agreed that the crunch was likely to come quickly. We needed communication plans ready for all the different scenarios. I went to meet Alex [Ferguson] at the Hilton and travelled with him to a charity dinner. GB was there with Gus O'Donnell and I took Alex and George Graham [former football player and manager] over to say hello. Even in those circumstances, GB and I barely acknowledged each other. I spoke to Gus and Sue Nye [GB's personal aide] and said they had to get their boss to stop treating TB like a hate figure. Gus said it takes two to tango. I said TB tangoes all day long with him. Alex coughed up five grand for my marathon. I shared a car home with George Graham who clearly wanted to be back in the game.

Friday, November 8

I didn't sleep well, but ran in, up to see TB to discuss political Cabinet. I filled him in on the encounter with GB and Co. last night, his inability even to look at me when I was taking over Alex and George Graham, and also the subsequent discussion with Gus and Sue. Alex noticed the vibes. Philip had spoken to GB last night and asked why all the communications channels had closed, and he simply said 'A lot has happened since last year.' TB was more open than ever, said he was thinking about the denouement on this, but it was important if it ended in a fissure that people genuinely understood he had tried

---

[1] Blunkett took responsibility for the error. The statement as released said: 'Maybe they [al-Qaeda] will try to develop a so-called dirty bomb, or some kind of poison gas; maybe they will try to use boats or trains rather than planes.' The revised statement, which Blunkett said had been amended to avoid creating panic, said: 'If al-Qaeda could mount an attack upon key economic targets, or upon our transport infrastructure, they would.'

everything. He felt he would at some point have to move him over or out, go out and say that he had been willing to stand aside before a third election, but even that had not been enough for him, that he would not work with me. The only other job he could realistically offer him was Foreign Secretary and he felt he would refuse that and walk.

TB said the reason 'psychological flaws' had been so damaging was because it rang so true with people who knew GB, and it rang true with GB himself. TB felt he was beyond repair. I said he had maximum power for a limited period, and it usually drained with time, and he had to use that power, not let more drain away before he decided and acted. I think the general feeling now, not just in Number 10 but around the Cabinet table too, was that GB was pretty hell-bent on TB's destruction. TB said he still felt we had to try to get it back together but he didn't hold out much hope. What was really important was that the upper echelons felt he had tried, and GB had refused to co-operate. JP was the key to this, and he was currently of the view that they were as bad as each other, even if GB had started to take the thing off the rails. TB felt it would be wrong to cave in to the kind of psychological and political pressure GB was piling on.

The main focus of the day was the UNSCR being agreed later in the day and I worked up a script for the UK on that. The morning meeting was largely about clearing up the dirty-bomb fiasco of yesterday. Political Cabinet was a good discussion. PG did a presentation which was realistic without being too downbeat, and on the fundamentals we were in a very strong position. TB did an overview – public services, antisocial behaviour, economy – and was very strong and clear on reform in particular. GB spent most of the time with his head down looking at his papers, but looked up a bit angrily when TB said there was a missing ingredient to the economic argument, its relation to the new economy and the developing economic giants, the whole science and research area. JP raised one or two concerns on the public services, and the fears of reforms leading to two-tier services, but he was OK generally. Hilary A spoke as well as I had ever heard her speak, said we had got into a rut on this two-tier thinking, said that a drive to uniformity had let millions of kids down. Schools and hospitals in the poorest areas were the ones that would benefit most from reform. Blunkett said two-tier exists now. In Hackney twenty per cent of parents send their kids private. People are opting out of the system and we have to attract them back. They won't come back to an unreformed system.

Reid, Milburn and Charles C were excellent on reform. The centre of gravity had definitely shifted to the reform end of things, which made GB's contribution a bit odd. It was a verbal version of Ed Balls' recent article, and he said the coming argument was about the limits of the market. It was reasonably politely put but the coded message was fairly clear. The impact was muted though because he did not put the case with his usual vigour, and he sounded a bit old-fashioned and out of touch. It was as though he had decided what he was going to say in advance and couldn't adapt to the discussion, and he didn't resonate as he had planned.

Milburn spoke at length and in detail on the health reforms and how they related to other reforms and he had a good line, that if independence was good enough for the Bank of England, it was good enough for schools and hospitals, which brought a thin smile to GB's lips. Margaret B said the message we put out on this was unclear, and there was a lot of confusion in the PLP about what we were actually saying. TB made clear that if we lost the ground on reform, we were giving the Tories the opening they needed and we must not give it to them. He said re markets that we would end up in an 'absurd situation' if we allowed our opponents to present this as an argument about privatisation. It is about choice and empowerment. If that wasn't a big enough hint to GB, he then said we needed to learn lessons from Al Gore's failure and defeat. Gore got himself into the wrong position on the role of the state. The Tories want to do us as the big-state party, holding the individual back and we must not let them. He was really on form today and a number of them commented on it during the break.

They came back for another good discussion, this time on ASB. Peter Hain said he had been told so many times that Cabinet meetings were boring, but he had felt this was a really strong discussion. 'Who told you?' snapped TB, joking, and they all laughed, with the usual exception. The mood generally was good. Even Clare was broadly on message on the ASB agenda. Only Alistair D came in on the GB point, saying that if we focused on excellence there could be a problem – the elitism point. JP said at the end that it had been a breath of fresh air to have a longer, broader-ranging discussion that went into themes rather than just policy. TB said he would look to do this more often.

The only bad note, as TB and JP discussed afterwards, was what he saw as GB's diddling on the markets argument. It had merely been an attempt to disrupt the flow. JP felt it wasn't that bad, but he came to see me before leaving and said though he was going to have one more go on Sunday at getting them working together, he felt things were as bad as ever. He said TB had guilt. GB had hatred. And though TB was a more generous spirit, there was wrong on both sides. But he felt TB was the more rounded and complete politician. He was brilliant at winning arguments and he should do it more with the whole Cabinet like that, rather than just let these things simmer. He should force a proper Cabinet discussion on the euro and the five tests, let's see where people really are, including Gordon.

JP said he had raised with GB why he had gone incommunicado with me and GB said he knew I was keeping a diary and he was sure I would publish it while he was still in power. I said why doesn't he fucking ask? It's not really that, said JP, it is all about the trust broken between them and he sees you as an extension of TB. I said if he spent more time building bridges and less time knocking them down, alienating people, treating them like dirt, he would find he had a lot more support than he thinks. JP felt TB should involve the Cabinet more, stop handling so many issues, particularly the euro, bilaterally with GB, and he would tell GB to stop demanding a date because it was counterproductive. He said both of us were important to getting them to the right place, and we should have one last go for peace. I said it was beginning to sound and feel like a peace process between enemies, like NI or the Middle East. JP laughed, said you're not far wrong, but these are the two giants of the Labour Party and if they do not work together, the party suffers.

Saturday, November 9

The best part of the day was [Burnley] getting Man United in the FA Cup draw. Also watching *Bend It Like Beckham* [comedy-drama film] with Fiona, Calum and Grace. Fantastic little film. I worked with TB on his *Observer* article [on rights, responsibilities and criminal justice] and did a conference call with JS, GH and DB who were doing media tomorrow. David didn't sound good and I think the terror fiasco had hit him a bit. He hated it when he was being blamed for cock-ups, even though this was clearly not his fault personally. The issue had subsided a little but there was still the mood in the media that we were hiding something. I was feeling back on form and worked on TB's Mansion House speech for Monday, using some of the lines and arguments that came out of yesterday's discussions, getting up arguments pre Queen's Speech as well as on the international agenda. TB was off at the Albert Hall [British Legion Festival of Remembrance] tonight but also working on the speech. Meanwhile the Royals story was going from bad to worse and TB was worried about it.[1] The idea of the Royal Family being run by a load of gays was taking hold. Did an eleven-mile run along Regent's Canal. Sundays full of Royals, Iraq and the Tories who were progressing steadily towards meltdown.

Sunday, November 10

TB called at 9 to go over where we were on the [Mansion House] speech. His basic message was that we could not defeat terrorism by security measures alone but we needed a coalition of common ideas and a shared agenda. He was really concerned re Chirac, felt that he was likely to be hostile for some time, and it would be difficult to rebuild. He felt JC was in the wrong on a lot of these issues, but he was sure we were heading for an extended bad time with him. On Iraq/WMD I said I felt we needed to be much more open and take people into our confidence much more about the information and arguments he was having to weigh up. He thought the Royals situation was damaging them. I felt what it was exposing was that the Queen was solid as a rock but beneath and around her things were a bit weak. He felt Charles should be staying above it all like the Queen if he wants to be seen in the same league.

TB was due to meet JP and GB later, ostensibly to discuss the fire dispute. I told him JP was pretty much in the 'both as bad as each other' camp at the moment. TB said deep down he knows that isn't true but he has to maintain that to be in a broker position. He thought GB will have gone away from Friday's Cabinet a bit worried, because it was so clear that the body of opinion wasn't with him. He thought he might come back to the idea of some kind of deal based on co-operation and departure. When TB told Jeremy he was still thinking he might go before the election, Jeremy said the senior Civil Service would be up in arms if they thought GB was taking over any time soon 'and for once they would be right'. Jack Straw was so horrified at GB's recent behaviour that he had asked TB 'Has he got something on you? How else do we explain to ourselves why you tolerate it?' TB's answer was the usual – that although he can be maddening, he has a brilliant side to him. TB was thought to be on such good form at the moment that his colleagues were clearly thinking GB could be moved. JP called re the fire situation. Gilchrist had heard [Professor Sir George] Bain [chairman of a government-funded independent

---

[1] During the Paul Burrell trial it had been revealed that Diana had secretly kept tape-recorded conversations in a locked box. These reportedly included details of an alleged rape in 1989 of a male member of Prince Charles' staff.

review of the Fire Service] would be publishing tomorrow, and he was worried that we were pushing it out. I said no way, and we would just keep radio silence on it.

Monday, November 11

We were well set up on the CJS [criminal justice system] reforms and on the speech, and on Iraq TB was at least getting some credit. There was still huge coverage for the post-Burrell Royals fallout. Bain put out his review, which the FBU rejected immediately needless to say. It was a good piece of work and I think serious people would wonder why on earth they could throw it out so quickly. We had a brief discussion on the Queen's Speech debate and also truancy, where it was clear TB was moving to the idea of fixed penalty notices with child benefit sanctions. David M, Jonathan and I went through the speech to work on the balance between warning and assurance. I think we just about got there, though it was one of those that could go either way.

We were also having to get the balance right re Bush. There was no point him [TB] just getting up there and putting the US line but he did not want to be seen as anything other than supportive. The question was how you weave in the argument about maximising influence without being explicit. The problem was, as he said to the morning meeting, that Bush did not really seem to take account of different concerns. President [Vicente] Fox [of Mexico, visiting Downing Street] felt the same. The speech came together OK though and he had done some strong stuff on MEPP and on the Muslim community. I had a ninety-minute meeting re the GICS review. Gus [O'Donnell] made it clear from the off he was on the radical-change end of the market, which was good news for me. He said he did not feel what was currently envisaged as change was nearly radical enough, and would not be seen as such. What was slightly depressing was that some of the people and arguments were exactly the same as those we had in '97.

Tuesday, November 12

[Andrew] Gilligan was doing a big number on security at Posts [UK embassies], clearly on the alarmist end of the market. Lots of 'intelligence says this, intelligence says that'. I called [Sir] David Omand [permanent secretary and security intelligence co-ordinator, Cabinet Office] who said there had been a warning in Australia re an attack on Posts, which had been checked out through Cobra and found to be nothing. We agreed a line that there was no general new threat to Posts and people should not change their plans. Then after I ran in, John Denham [Home Office minister] called, to say there had been a warning that went out via Transec, that part of the Department of Transport responsible for security, which did say there had been intelligence, though it did not say put out a new level of vigilance. The Gilligan report was outrageous and we used it to set out how difficult it was to make these judgements.

Up to see TB in the flat. He was more worried about fire and the FBU claim that we had been spoiling for a fight. Another discussion re GB. He said JP was the key and I really had to work on him. He knew deep down that we were in the right and he also knew he was in a powerful position and was using that. TB said 'The crazy thing about all this is that I never wanted to fight a third election but I may have to because I don't feel I can trust him to take over when he is as impossible as he is now. The only question is whether I can move him or get rid of him.' He said we were strong on policy substance but GB hung over everything like a shadow. I had a chat with C on the phone to take forward what we had been discussing about use of intelligence in the public diplomacy campaign. The Palace were setting up an inquiry into the post-Burrell issues, rape, gifts etc., which was a massive story. I had lunch with Jeremy Vine [BBC]. There was something very positive and likeable about him. He was desperate for an interview with TB on the whole God thing. Then to the Newspaper Press Fund at Australia House, lots of the old crowd from the *Mirror*. I went for a drink with Rebekah Wade [editor, *News of the World*], interrupted by a call from Gerard Russell [Islamic Media Unit, FCO] re an OBL audiotape where he seemed to be taking credit for the Bali and Russia attacks. We got Hoon up.

Wednesday, November 13

Queen's Speech was running fine, but drowned out by fire, Iraq and the Royals, particularly after last night's interview by [Sir] Michael Peat [private secretary to the Prince of Wales] on the so-called 'St James's Palace inquiry'.[1] Morning meeting largely on the OBL video. Then I met some of the Middle East experts who had been looking for the kind of thing that could be surfaced publicly, for example only one in three actually voted in the recent referendum. Also, the fact that Saddam seemingly listened to Radio Monte Carlo [Arabic service],

---

[1] The Prince of Wales had announced an internal inquiry to be headed by his private secretary. Sir Michael Peat had responded to criticism of the limited scope of the inquiry by saying it would be conducted 'without fear or favour'.

so we agreed it was worth trying to fix a TB interview for any direct messages we wanted. We agreed that the Middle East guys should come more regularly to our meetings. In between Queen's Speech meetings with TB, we had the first fire-strike meeting with JP, Nick Raynsford, Omand and Hoon. JP had done well and the next phase was going to get particularly tough. Omand and Jeremy were both pushing for a programme of training of new people or moving on anti-strike legislation but we were still in a position of saying that we didn't want to inflame. At the political strategy meeting, we were trying to hone the local elections message to get local parties motoring more on crime and community campaigns. I went over to Derry's rooms in the Lords for his Queen's Speech reception, where I came face to face for the first time with Black Rod, all dressed up in his finery, his face too pinkish for my liking, and a rather smug grin. 'We meet after all this time,' he said. I said that he had caused us a lot of grief. He said he had only been trying to help. I was pretty short with him. Derry was thoroughly enjoying himself, delighting in introducing me to all the men in tights as 'the prince of darkness'. He asked me if I had hit Black Rod. It was quite a jolly do, a mix of ministers from the Lords and Commons, officials, ambassadors. I asked Derry if he hated all this flummery and nonsense as much as I did. He made a jokey little speech about how he came into politics so that he could preside over ceremonials, walk backwards in front of the monarch, listen to a Labour legislative programme being delivered to rows of tiaras. David Hanson [Blair's parliamentary private secretary] was telling me around a hundred MPs would vote demanding a UNSCR second time around. Queen's Speech was going OK, but Iraq plus fire made sure it was surrounded more with a sense of problems than solutions.

Thursday, November 14

TB really tired. He didn't get a great press out of the Queen's Speech debate and in any event fire was getting much more attention. He said if we had a Tory government, they would not be getting attacked in the same way. Also the notion of industrial unrest was being taken to the Tube, with Mick Rix [general secretary of rail union ASLEF] out there. JP was doing a statement which I rewrote during Cabinet, giving him some cover by making clear that if we moved from a two-day to an eight-day strike, we were in a different ball game and some of the issues that had been kept off the table to suit them when we were trying to avert the strike would then be on the table. JP was up for doing the tough stuff if we had to. He was very on board at the moment, just took the changes, including a sound bite that said we had bent over backwards and been met with a response that was wrong, irresponsible and puts lives at risk.

The morning meeting was mainly Iraq to go over TB's interview and the response to the Saddam statement. We needed to get out as well the fact that only one in three voted in the 'election' for Saddam. I was very pissed off at the GICS FCC [fire co-ordination centre] and the lack of co-ordination in ministerial interviews. I got TB to say at Cabinet that we needed volunteers to go out around the regions. Cabinet was largely about fire, JP making clear that we would shift gear now, especially if they moved their position to an eight-day strike. I was outraged at the way they were using Fire Service buildings to plan the strikes, to protest, but then go inside when it rained. The employers were totally useless, the TUC not much better. Our MPs broadly OK. Cabinet also discussed Iraq, and TB was looking tired and fed up.

He did the Radio Monte Carlo interview, got up a few strong clear lines – not about oil, not going to push in an exiled government, only one in three voted. We had a meeting with Tessa on sports policy. The presentation was too long and TB wasn't really engaged. I said I had no real sense of a grass roots sports strategy. Then did a visit with other key Number 10 people to PINDAR, the three-storey underground bunker [below the MoD]. Very basic living quarters, internal TV station. A bit alarming in that before these kinds of emergency sites had always seemed a bit fanciful, but at the moment they didn't.

Friday, November 15

The tougher message on fire strikes was coming through but the press was so desperate for us to fail, that they couldn't resist trying to turn it into a story about mixed signals. To lunch at MI5. We discussed the US, these guys seeming as frustrated as SIS at the Americans' inability fully to understand why they needed to motor more on the Middle East. There was clearly a lot going on, much greater threat closer to home, and they said it was sometimes difficult for Western minds to come to terms with the added dimension of terrorists who in many ways didn't mind if they were disrupted because they didn't fear dying, but welcomed it. I said we had better relations at the centre of SIS than with them and we needed to keep more closely in touch because I was sure that as they spent so much of their time thinking strategically and thematically, there was a lot of their work that could dovetail with public communications. They were clearly worried that they were having to move resources from organised crime because of the growing need to keep tabs on Islamic fundamentalism, added to which for all the progress, Northern Ireland still took up a lot of resources, they clearly felt under pressure.

Then did a speech and Q&A for the staff. There were about 400 people there, generally a lot younger than I would have expected, pretty poor on the ethnic mix front, but very welcoming, good atmosphere, good reception. My main theme was the gap between messages being pumped out daily in the media, and the reality of most people's lives, and how that impacted upon the way governments operated and communicated. Quite a good range of questions, from the obvious – how did I assess the Security Service's profile, was spin our fault, how do you deal with 24-hour news – to the less obvious, e.g. on hunting. The last speaker had been the Archbishop of Canterbury who had managed to speak for a whole hour without mentioning God. I said I think I would find it impossible to go for an hour without mentioning TB, not that TB is God. TB had gone off to Warsaw and was due to do the *Mirror*. He called afterwards, said it was a crap interview. It had been arranged on an agreement to get the focus on crime, but he said crime was barely mentioned. On fire, he said if e.g. the RMT [rail union] went for secondary action, or the FBU went for eight days, we would have to go for them big time.

Saturday, November 16

TB at Chequers. [Sir George] Bain called to speak to him, to say in his view they [FBU] didn't deserve much at all, and he was worried JP just saw this as an old-fashioned split-the-middle negotiation. He felt it would be bad all round if we caved in at all. The other thing we had to track all day was the *Sunday Times* story on a plot to attack the Tube.[1] I did a conference call later on the Sunday broadcasts with JP, Hain, [Margaret] Hodge [minister for universities] plus the spooks to get lines squared, but it was going to be difficult to keep the press under control, not least because they would want to know if this was the reason we changed the 'poison gas or dirty bomb' warning by DB [see November 7]. The current game by the media was to get us into confusion stories, mixed messages whether on fire or terror. TB felt that for the next phase, basic competence was going to be the issue – on fire, asylum, PBR – plus of course we had Iraq to deal with. He was still saying that the US did understand the need to move on the Middle East peace process.

[1] Three men had been arrested in London on terror charges and the *Sunday Times* had speculated that they had planned to release cyanide gas on the London Underground.

Sunday, November 17

The *Sunday Times* story was going big all day and the broadcasters were taking it into mixed-signals territory. JP was OK on *Frost* but I was a bit worried that he said there was no threat to the Tube as reported. The papers as ever were being irresponsible and stupid.

Monday, November 18

Hans Blix going back to Baghdad. Fire difficult. On fire at least, the media were on to something re mixed signals, e.g. JP saying let's talk, TB focusing on money for modernisation, GB there's no more money for anything. TB's *Mirror* interview was crap, total waste of time. Fire was the most pressing issue. We still didn't have a grip of it. While the softly, softly approach was right in the early stages when trying to avoid the strike, we definitely needed a change of gear. What we had to watch was a sense of division, and the idea some would willingly put in lights that TB was being urged to take them on and defeat them. He and JP had to be in the same position, focusing on the need for long-term reform, but we weren't there at the moment.

Top-up fees was also a bit of a disaster area at the moment. AA said at TB's Monday meeting that we needed a while to sort it. Philip warned he thought it was a potential tipping-point issue. TB's weekend note had been largely devoted to a plan for dealing with the French, relations with Chirac still causing him a lot of concern. Media-wise, our main event of the day was the Trevor McDonald [ITN journalist] interview, and though we had managed to get a fair bit of preparation time in the diary, TB wasn't really fired up, didn't really engage or have edge, so on balance it was a negative. They had wanted a line on fire and on terror for their news coverage, but the exchanges on crime were pretty average. Planning meeting on the Prague [NATO] summit, then on the euro and Britain in Europe [pressure group], where yet again we agreed they had to do more work independent of us, but it was a pretty hopeless situation. The news coverage out of Trevor McDonald was a lot better than I thought it would be and the reactions to the interview as a whole pretty positive.

Tuesday, November 19

Called JP to discuss fire. I felt it was all a bit ragged, that we had GB tough on public spending, TB tough on modernisation, JP basically just wanting a settlement. We also had word through the *Mirror* on the elitism front that GB was against top-up fees. We then got filled in on GB's breakfast meeting at the *Guardian* where it seems he had been off-centre on EMU, top-up fees, and Iraq. Peter M called, said he felt the ground was moving somewhat. There was a distancing strategy going on.

JP said his basic approach had been to try to stop the fire dispute whilst preparing for one anyway, then get very tough if it came to an eight-day strike. I drafted him a few sections for his speech in the [Commons] debate, which broadly he was happy with. Later the employers offered sixteen per cent with modernisation. The FBU rejected it, wanting twenty per cent without modernisation. TB had a speech on e-commerce, which was actually quite a good speech, though it was never going to fly and we put in a few lines on fire. I had a meeting with SIS on some of the anti-Saddam activity inside Iraq.

We had the *Express* lot in for lunch, which was a pretty weird event, largely Richard Desmond [proprietor] and Peter Hill [*Daily Star* editor] talking about the business of newspapers, as if we were supposed to find it as endlessly fascinating as they did. TB was OK, good on fire, but as with the Trevor McDonald interview yesterday, he wasn't really pushing out message in these media encounters. Peter Hyman felt we were a bit complacent and that we had slipped back from the [Labour] conference success on public service reform.

At our 6pm strategy meeting with TB, PG went through the recent groups and said the mood was uncertain, and with the potential to turn sour. We then got to an interesting discussion on TB/GB, Sally M feeling even more strongly than I did that Gordon was effectively running a daily strategy against TB, and we had no counter-strategy. TB said he admitted that he had moved on this, that he now accepted that GB was a largely malign force, but we had to understand that the party would make a judgement about who was responsible if there was a split which led to a schism. Also, he was in ability terms head and shoulders above the rest, and he really didn't want TB/GB to be THE story of this government. It will always be a story, but we should all do what we can to ensure it is not THE story. Peter M and Pat [McFadden] both said that the crux question was what was his plan for GB? TB said the ideal was to work with him on the programme we have got, but it's getting more not less difficult. 'It's almost like he pours concrete on top of the policy areas.' It even crossed his mind that he was trying to stop us reforming as a way of setting himself up as the reformer for the future. Peter M said it was absolutely clear from the recent briefings to the *Mirror* and the *Guardian* that he was up to no good.

I was arguing that we should get out there his modus operandi, the fact that he said different things to different audiences in a way that he wouldn't be able to if he had the top job. TB looked very down, and also said he still felt we should try to keep managing it. We have managed it successfully for several years and we needed to think very carefully before rushing into anything rash. Peter M said their game was deliberately to put TB into a box marked 'right wing' so that where progressive change was made, it was seen as theirs, whereas all the difficulties and controversies had been made to stick to TB. I felt that if TB really believed it was going to end in tears one day, better to get it dealt with now. Peter M sort of agreed, though his worry was whether it would be sufficiently clear that it was GB's doing that brought us to this, not ours. Jonathan said his concern was that GB was not beyond bringing the whole show down.

Wednesday, November 20

Kevin Maguire had a piece in the *Guardian* doing in TB on our handling of the fire strike, as did [Paul] Routledge in the *Mirror*. Jonathan Freedland [*Guardian*] had a big piece on how the fault line was now opening for sure, while Patrick Wintour's [*Guardian*] news story, also based on yesterday's breakfast, was GB coming out against top-up fees. It was pretty tricky stuff. When Jeremy spoke to Balls first thing, he denied GB had spoken against top-up fees and said the problem was in the current febrile atmosphere, anyone who was anything other than totally in favour of top-up fees was seen as anti TB. Classic Balls. The reality was there was a deliberate strategy going on to put us into a right-wing construct in the eyes of the left – foundation hospitals, top-up fees, pro US on Iraq.

Peter Riddell [*Times*] also had a piece saying it was time for GB to speak out re the limits of the market in the NHS. There was no doubt that there was a major operation going on. But TB, who called me up as soon as I got in, said his instinct remained to let it run, not to respond, just let them get on with it. But he accepted it was serious and that the most serious point was that policy issues were being blocked. My belief was that GB had been gifted a policy cover for what in reality was a personality battle and something of a vendetta against TB. TB was adamant that if it came to a split it had to be absolutely clear who was responsible. But I felt we had a strategy being run powerfully against us, and we were doing nothing in return. TB said I had to trust him on how to deal with this one. I said the problem was the party didn't see him coming out with enough that was seen definitively as Labour.

We got a bit of a problem out of the Hoon/CDS briefing, where

CDS said something pretty daft, making clear he felt it was bad for the Armed Forces to be involved in the fire dispute. We were getting ready for Prague but first had to endure a pretty useless political strategy meeting with John Reid, Douglas etc. where Spencer Livermore [special adviser, Treasury] was meant to do a Pre-Budget Report presentation, but pretty much said nothing that wasn't already known to a reasonably well-informed member of the public. Catherine Colonna called to say if TB asked Chirac for a summit date he would offer one probably. I said it was a pretty silly way to work. When we finally got there, TB said Chirac was so cold that there was no way he was going to risk humiliating himself, so they just had a cordial handshake and that was that. He said he was happy to hang tough for a while longer.

PMQs preparation was focused on fire and Tory calls for a director of homeland security, on which IDS did six questions, though not terribly well. TB did OK but missed the opportunity to do a values-based answer on top-up fees to Tony Wright [Labour MP]. I don't know why he won't do it. He said afterwards it wasn't the time, and he didn't want to look like he was making a U-turn. I felt the only way to win this argument was to make it about values and opportunity, whereas he was more on the idea that the status quo wasn't an option for the universities, as if they as institutions rather than people as individuals were more important.

I drove out to Northolt with TB. I had dinner with Dan Bartlett [now White House communications director] once we got to Prague. We went through why the US was so unpopular, the need to understand it and broaden the agenda. He was very down on the State Department, which of course outside America was the one part of the US government that was seen as vaguely bearable. The Americans currently thought it was seventy to thirty that there would be war, but that the thirty was genuine. We needed to set up a proper operation in Qatar, not least to have people able to make an impact on Al Jazeera. He was pretty down on the new [White House] Office of Global Communications, which of course the State Department were pretty much opposed to because it cut across much of what they did. He said the problem with State's communications was that some focused on long term, some on three metres at a time and there was not much in between. I said I strongly felt they should try to keep Rumsfeld off the international airwaves, and broaden their messages beyond America. He told me GWB intended to visit Africa, which I suggested was a great opportunity for a much broader repositioning of their global message.

I had agreed with Dan last night that TB and GWB would do a short media event together, so we went through key messages on Iraq and fire. GWB arrived for the summit, was met by a beaming GR [George Robertson, NATO Secretary General] and then through for a meeting. Bush had the most extraordinary pair of cowboy boots on, and was full of the usual hail fellow well met, how ya doing? They did an OK doorstep, including on the latest bombing in Jerusalem. But the press were all focused on Iraq, and on the line that the US had pretty much decided. Bush felt there was a need for real pressure to build through troop movements, international condemnation, really tough and unpredictable inspections, to get Saddam off balance.

He said that once we made that phone call that agrees Saddam's in breach, we had to do something militarily, and quickly. Quick sustainable bombing raid, and boots on the ground. He said if Blix gets dicked around, while a US or UK plane is shot down, we go for him. He was clearly not keen on Blix, said he was wringing his hands and talking war and peace but 'That is our judgement. He is not going to get between us and freedom. Once we strike we go for it, we don't wait for the world to sing "Kum ba yah", to hold hands and wait for Saddam to develop a better karma.' TB said he felt there was a twenty per cent chance Saddam would co-operate, but Bush said he didn't know what co-operation meant. TB believed the regime would crumble pretty quickly, and Bush said both our secret services needed to be put to work to help that. They were thinking of a list of the top ten most wanted as part of a divide-and-rule strategy, e.g. put some members of Saddam's family on there, not others. He felt Saddam was making Blix and the UN look like fools. He also felt that if we got rid of Saddam, we could make progress on the Middle East. He reported on some of his discussions with [Ariel] Sharon, and said he had been pretty tough with him. Sharon had said that if Iraq hit Israel, their response would 'escalate' which he took to mean go nuclear. Bush said he said to him 'You will not, you will not do that, it would be crazy.' He said he would keep them under control, adding 'A nuke on Baghdad, that could be pretty tricky.' He was also clearly worried about the stability of Saudi Arabia.

I then left for the airport. The fire scene was pretty bad. On the flight, I did a note on the dinner with Dan Bartlett and what we needed to do to take things forward. There was some interesting stuff around on deception programmes, for example [Iraqi] officials being forced to put papers and materials in their homes with the warning that they and their families would be harmed if they were lost. JP was doing a fire statement at 7 with the strikes due to start, making clear that there was no more money, and that pay must be matched to modernisation and that in the meantime, preparations go on. We had to start getting a bit tougher in our language on modernisation.

Friday, November 22
The unions and the employers did a deal in the early hours which they sent through to ODPM [Office of the Deputy Prime Minister], we said no and they got out to say we had scuppered it. The problem being exposed was that we weren't in control of the negotiations but we would get the blame. The FBU and the employers both came out to say we had scuppered the deal but the problem was we were being asked not just to bless a deal but to fund a deal. JP was doing the *Today* programme and I tried to get hold of him but was in the shower when he came through and missed the call. It was pretty grim. He was clearly tired and took everything too personally and the message was pretty mangled.

We agreed at the morning meeting to get more on the offensive and we put together some aggressive lines for Godric at the 11, that it beggared belief the employers had signed up to this, that the unions were determined to avoid modernisation. We had to get back on the front foot because the FBU were making all the running. JP though was still putting out different kinds of noise because he was saying ultimately we would have to do a deal. He was also wanting to get the TUC more involved though they had been pretty unhelpful and difficult. We did a conference call with TB in Prague who was wondering whether to do media on it. He felt it was best not to because JP would feel undermined, though we got JR on to the lunchtime bulletins, who was excellent. TB flew back later and was in one of his irritating 'all that matters here is the facts' moods. His basic argument was that we would have to foot the bill and yet the talks had led to all the modernisation measures being removed.

We had a meeting with JP and GB at which we agreed to publish a paper on the economic impact, the Treasury having done a paper on the figures with £4 billion for local authorities and £16 billion for the public sector, making clear that if this was applied across the economy, it [the settlement] would cost hundreds of millions without modernisation attached. GB's main point was that we had to get the local authorities to negotiate this, but it wasn't clear what we were meant to do to achieve that. TB and JP both said afterwards it was a very Gordonic point, focusing on something that wasn't actually central. JP had become more seized of the TB/GB problem, and we both agreed it was surprising that the media weren't currently making more of what GB had been up to recently. It was not a great meeting. JP wanted to do interviews. I suggested he did one-on-ones, but he got a bit ratty and wasn't clear enough. We were not in a very good position. TB was pretty clear there was no way we could give in on this.

Saturday, November 23

TB called at 9. He wanted to do a press conference on Monday to set out the whole case, make clear why we couldn't give in, make a direct appeal to the firefighters. He was worried JP would react badly to that, wouldn't want him to do it, and asked me to speak to him. JP and I chatted for an hour or so before I sensed the moment was right to raise it, and he was fine. He was really fed up though with some of the personal vitriol he was getting from some of the papers. He was scathing about [John] Monks, who was leading the news today saying the TUC 'supported the FBU'. I said we needed to use the next few days to set basic expectations, and he should see the TB press conference as part of that. He wanted to know if TB would let the TUC have a role in trying to sort this. The *Mirror* had been pretty vile, and he said he would like to have a go at [Piers] Morgan publicly re the DTI investigation [into share dealing by journalists at the *Mirror*]. I said that would be a mistake, and he mustn't let them think he was taking any of it personally. He said that's the way I am, I can't help it, what am I supposed to do, if someone whacks me unfairly, I want to whack 'em back. He did think I should be toning down the really heavy messages because in the end we would have to negotiate. We seemed to have a cast of thousands on the ministerial conference call. JP was down at Dorneywood [official country residence] and was clearly having dinner because at one point, as we were discussing Iraq, we could all hear him saying 'I'll have rhubarb on mine.' The main message was all about getting the talks back up and focused on the right issues.

Sunday, November 24

JP called several times pre *On the Record* [BBC]. Tried to get him on the broader economic message. TB was getting more focused on it, wanting greater clarity. The plan had been for JP to say in the interview that TB was doing his press conference tomorrow, so that nobody thought it was him being bounced out of the picture, but he forgot to mention it. He did very good clips that were used for the bulletins. We briefed out a pre-press conference message on today's pay rise being tomorrow's rise in interest rates and inflation. The press were picking up on GB and JP saying slightly different things re sixteen per cent [settlement]. The Sundays were cranking up the idea of the unions now being at war with the government and John Monks was not exactly covering himself in glory. I went out for a seventeen-mile run, stopped a few times to take calls.

We did at least now have a bit of process story re fire and I felt if we got through today and tomorrow properly, on the comms front we would be in better shape. The FBU and the Tories were both out on mixed signals with GB making clear there was no more money and JP saying the deal on the table last week was still worth talking about. JP had been fine yesterday about the press conference but he was now getting worried it looked like TB was taking over. JP called me at 7.15, really down. He said he was thinking about handing it all over. He thought the soft-cop routine would work, but it hadn't and maybe he should put out a statement or go up on how sixteen per cent was no longer a runner. He said he had always felt he could do a deal of some kind with [Andy] Gilchrist but maybe he was wrong, maybe we should just go hardball. I said there was no need to change his role, and we would make sure there was no question of tomorrow being seen as sidelining him. I said if he suddenly put out a clarifying statement, they really would have a field day. He agreed, but he was clearly very down. He said he felt it deeply, in his heart, and he absolutely hates it if people think he has fucked up.

Monday, November 25

News leading on press conference and the line that TB would speak direct to firefighters and their families. We needed a stronger process story. Pat McF was talking to [Sir] Jeremy Beecham [chairman, Local Government Association] to get a line on the streamlining of discussions. He also wanted TB to speak to Monks which he did just before the press conference. TB wanted to get up modernisation and the need for change in working practices as the issue. JP came over for a meeting and asked for a private word with TB and me. He said he felt dreadful. Because of his background, he really wanted to think he could handle these kinds of disputes, and thought he had got some kind of agreement worked out with Gilchrist but it couldn't happen. He felt like he wanted out of the whole thing. He wanted GB to make clear in his opening statement that he and GB were not at odds. TB was very good with him, said he had worked incredibly hard on it, and done the right things, and don't let the press play the game they are playing and unsettle him by attacking him. Put it behind him and don't worry.

We went through the draft script I had done yesterday, toning down some of the rhetoric. We had three aims. First an economic message about the potentially dire impact of the FBU winning; second, get up what we meant by modernisation, and third, process. TB was on pretty good form [at the press conference]. The economic message came over and for the first time we really got the modernisation proposals on the agenda. I called JP in the evening, after he had finished the [Labour] NEC awayday in North London. He had pretty much had it with Monks on this one, felt he had been gutless, but said he had found more support than he expected among the union guys on the NEC, including the RMT. I said we had started to turn things and we could turn things more quickly if we kept things focused on the modernisation agenda. He sounded happier, said he was thinking about doing the government evidence to Bain tomorrow to keep the modernisation message going and give a sense of what a modern Fire Service should look like. I had a meeting with Tessa on sport. On the [2012] Olympics bid, the sooner we made the decision the better. I also felt we should get Patrick Carter announced [as chairman of Sport England] soon.

Tuesday, November 26

Struggling to get a grip on Iraq co-ordination. There was definitely now something of a turf war between the FCO and the CIC operation, driven by John Williams' [FCO] genuine and loyal belief that Jack was a key communicator. TB had definitely got fire into a better place. Before he left for his education speech in Birmingham, we agreed to take out all the stuff on top-up fees, which in the current atmosphere would just set off a different neuralgia, and the speech didn't actually need it. I was taking a hands-on interest in story development on fire. We were starting to bank them up, e.g. a report on joint control rooms, as well as some of the specific modernisation issues, e.g. the shift system, second jobs. We got up more modernisation messages through the publication of our evidence to Bain. Anecdotally, we were being told support for the FBU was weakening. JP's statement was OK but in questions he pointed up that twenty per cent were due to retire, which led to headlines about 10,000 job losses. But we were still in a far better position than before. TB called a couple of times, and said that you couldn't keep dancing around the jobs issue forever but it was good in a way that JP blurted it out. Then to the FPA [Foreign Press Association] dinner. Clive Anderson [broadcaster and comedian] hosted it extremely well, though Jack's speech didn't quite hit the notes. We were shortlisted for press office of the year though thankfully didn't win. I quite enjoyed the event but I hate these late nights.

Wednesday, November 27
I was working pretty much full time on fire, trying to keep going on modernisation. PBR Cabinet was very dour, and I didn't get the sense ministers were terribly impressed. We had a whole series of fire meetings over lunch. I stayed over at the House afterwards for the PBR. [Shadow Chancellor Michael] Howard's response was pretty good. Fiona called to say that our cops had a piece of paper from Cheshire cops about someone who had gone to them warning that Carole Caplin's partner was a fraudster. Peter Foster, the boyfriend, was apparently once involved in a tea scam in which he used Samantha Fox [former topless model who had dated Foster]. We saw TB later and of course he was in denial about it, said that her mother was marvellous. If Carole was now in cahoots with someone trying to set themselves up on the back of them [the Blairs], things could get tricky. Fiona said she had felt increasingly frozen out by Cherie and Carole, whose choice of men was a bit worrying, and yet all we ever heard from TB and CB was that she was marvellous.

Thursday, November 28
Dreadful press for GB on the PBR. I wrote to Ed Balls, said we should have kept in much closer touch in the build-up and needed to keep in close touch re a strategy to improve on the very negative day one. We were winning back a lot of ground in the fire PR battle, but with the talks due tomorrow we needed a strong line. So after Cabinet, TB, JP and officials met and we agreed to a very tough line, namely no commitment for government cash, nothing to risk stability, money tied to modernisation. JP was still very sore, said that he would never forgive the way the TUC denounced him. We were worried that Bain was coming under a lot of TUC pressure and was heading closer to sixteen per cent over two years. TB told JP that we had to break them on this, not in a rub-your-face kind of way, but simply making clear they did not win anything for their strike action. He was still pissed off that that red fire engine issue was not being handled properly.[1] TB spoke to Bain and was a bit concerned at his tone. We agreed to put out a tough statement at 4. TB had also been working on the

[1] Rather than elderly Green Goddess auxiliary fire engines, in the event of industrial action by firefighters, a reserve of modern red fire engines should be available to military crews.

Europe speech, which was a big one, but lacked a fundamental driving point, was a bit too nerdy, and with everything else going on, unlikely to get much coverage. We were getting up the notion of joint [Fire Service] control rooms with JP doing a visit with Bob Ainsworth [Home Office minister] to Devizes.

The other thing taking up a fair bit of time through the day was the Peter Foster issue. TB had told Cherie that she and Carole had to go through it all with me and Fiona, but it was pretty clear they weren't keen. Cabinet was mainly fire, with the general sense we were in better shape, NHS pay deal, and the bombing in Mombasa [Kenya], on which there would be the usual post-event finger pointing about what we knew of any threat.[1] We then left for Cardiff with the speech almost done, and agreed we would get cameras in for the Welsh Labour Party fund-raiser. We flew down, got driven to the hotel, which was besieged by firefighters and supporters, making a phenomenal amount of noise with Klaxon horns. TB was worried he wouldn't be heard, and the police had turned the venue into an island site, about as heavy a policing presence as I'd seen outside conference and summits. We were feeling a bit besieged. The speech was an OK piece of work[2] but we ended up getting more coverage overseas than we did here, when we got more for TB's piece in *Paris Match* saying happy birthday to Chirac.

As TB was speaking, I took a call from Ian Monk [PR consultant]. Ian had always been perfectly friendly, but my guard was pretty much up from the word go. He said that Carole, Foster and a lawyer had been to see him to get advice re their protection. I took the call from the stone staircase going down from the floor where TB was speaking, and could hear the applause for his speech at various points. Yet here I was, talking to a former hack turned PR about what was clearly going to be the next self-inflicted frenzy.

I did a two-page note for TB saying the Foster story was clearly going to become public and that we had to have defensive lines ready making clear that he had never met him and that it was not true, as he was saying, that he was their financial adviser. I said we had to

[1] A vehicle drove into the Israeli-owned Paradise Hotel and exploded in the lobby, killing thirteen, and two surface-to-air missiles were fired at but missed an Israeli charter aircraft. A previously unknown group, the Army of Palestine, claimed responsibility.

[2] Blair referred to the fire dispute at the fund-raiser, which had been boycotted by up to seventy trade unionists, saying 'It's better to do the right thing even if it is the unpopular thing, than to do the wrong thing and have the country pay the consequences of it.'

November '02: Carole story about to become public

be very careful not to be thought to be, let alone seen to be, giving any advice to Foster. Monk had told me CB called Carole twice during his meeting with her. Fiona said Cherie had told her that she had not been able to get hold of her today and was really pissed off that we were being excluded, not least because neither of us trusted the people involved to grip it properly. TB called CB when we got back to the hotel and said it had to be gripped and Carole had to understand this was about us every bit as much as it was about her. As he understood it, the guy was a total conman, and dangerous. Monk had told me Foster [an Australian] had lost his deportation case and we had to hope he went. I could tell that after the initial insouciance of yesterday, TB was genuinely worried, though he was pretty soft with CB. Re GB, we agreed that if only we had a proper co-operative operation at every level, they would have got a far better media out of the PBR. On fire, the FBU were much more on the defensive, being forced to defend questionable working practices.

Friday, November 29

TB called before doing clips at a temporary fire station near Sedgefield. Richard Boucher [assistant secretary for public affairs, US State Department] was in town. On Iraq, even the State people were pretty clear they were going for it. On the Middle East, they were currently against a conference. Richard was clearly up for working together more closely, and it was almost as if he was trying to build alliances outside the government to improve the operations within it. I set out how I thought they could do quite simple things to do with Bush's profile abroad. In the end most questions came back to the need for a broader agenda, and a strategy that clearly went beyond merely American interests.

Chirac called TB to offer February 4 as a summit date. TB's birthday present and the *Paris Match* piece had obviously worked. Then a fire meeting to work out the next stage in communication terms, working up the idea of the MoD reviewing shift patrols, more public safety campaigns, more red fire engines. TB was angry because the squaddies were clear they needed more red fire engines. He was very clear that we had to get really heavy if they went for a second eight-day strike, that we would have to take the negotiations over, give them a take it or leave it deal, and if they left it, tough.

Had a very interesting discussion with TB about the nature of these jobs and friendship. He said he felt part of the problem of his life was that it's not possible to make real new friendships once you get to a position like his. It meant that if you are already close to people, you got even closer to them, both at work and outside work. So people like me, Sally, Anji [Hunter] and Kate [Garvey, events and visits team] he felt very, very close to, felt he could trust us. But even if he met new people that he liked, it was always difficult because in the end he was the prime minister, and that was bound to affect the way people think about him. Carole had come on the scene fairly early on, and they had both liked her. She was a bit wacky, fun and interesting. But don't worry, he said, I do realise how dangerous this is. I said it came to something that we were worrying about a professional conman close to the heart of the whole bloody operation.

Saturday, November 30

I was up through the night, vomiting several times. But I still had the Cobra paper on the fire dispute to finish, and took a couple of conference calls to get into really good shape. Then Gilchrist, who was not operating terribly well under pressure, made a big mistake, did a speech attacking us over Iraq and New Labour. I felt he was already losing a fair bit of support, and if the public thought he was actually out doing this as part of a general political kick, he would lose a lot of support across the spectrum. On Foster, the *Mail on Sunday* sent over more than twenty questions. We decided not to answer question by question and instead gave them a short statement making clear TB had never met Foster, he had never been to Number 10 or Chequers.

The real problem was over the flats.[1] TB admitted to me he was always against the idea of a flat on political grounds, but also that until today he had no idea they had bought two. I felt people would just about understand a mother wanting to get a decent place to live for their son, and might just about understand that she didn't trouble TB with all the detail, but they would find it a bit weird to think they had got two flats with the help of this guy Foster. He was still, however, very defensive about it all, said Carole was basically nice, and maybe this guy wasn't so bad after all. For crying out loud. Anyway we got through it and when the papers dropped, the others seemed to see it as much a story about Foster as about TB, though Cherie didn't come out of it too well. All very messy but in some ways could have been worse. In a way it was probably best that the *Mail on Sunday* had done it, because the other papers tended to think the *MoS* would have flammed it up as they were so oppositionalist. I was still feeling wretched by the evening and stayed in.

[1] Foster had assisted CB when she bought two flats in Bristol, where Euan Blair was at university.

November '02: TB 'no idea they'd bought two flats'

Sunday, December 1

I felt much better after twenty-four hours' illness. The Gilchrist overly critical speech gave us a big opening. But there was clearly a bit of briefing around on a strike ban, which, as TB said, made it look like we were lurching around again, just when we didn't need to, because Gilchrist was on the run. The *Mirror* was the only paper left on his side now. JP was being pretty tough while TB was making clear we should move towards taking over the FBU negotiations, making a final offer and if it was not accepted making clear they would be fired and new personnel hired. There was lots of GB in the press post PBR, and some pretty major diddling on the euro. TB still felt his strong card remains that the public wanted him, not GB, and he felt that even if he became unpopular, that would remain the case. The PBR had included a euro reference but was now being seen as blocking the euro and TB was in no doubt GB was trying to thwart it.

On the flats, he denied they had evaded stamp duty or that Foster had helped them get a mortgage, though he later did say Foster had been to the flat in Bristol with Carole, and sent Cherie an email about the building society and the mortgage, so TB accepted Foster was able to present himself as an adviser. He said he had formed the view that Carole was basically decent but naive. I said I felt she had pretty much got them where she wanted them. She also had very bad judgement about men and while this guy was around we had a potential problem the whole time. It had to be sorted. He said he had left her in no doubt what he thought and she was going to reflect on it. Carole had said to TB that maybe the best thing was if Foster got deported, but that was just another excuse to be a victim. How people like this got into the system was beyond me.

Monday, December 2

The Iraq human rights dossier [containing information from human rights groups, government sources and the United Nations] and the fire report were doing well on the bulletins. Only the *Mail* were really going at Carole. The other big story was TB/GB split on the euro with several following up the *FT* splash of Saturday suggesting that the PBR report on macroeconomic stability should be read as being clear we were not joining the euro. TB called me up to the flat, had toughened his mind on fire, felt we should get to the position where we put down an offer, that was it, and if they kept on striking we make clear they would be sacked and others hired. He said his real concern was GB. Maybe he had been too naive for too long but he realised we now had to have a real strategy for him. He had one big card, namely that he was the elected PM. He believed it would become more and more clear that GB was responsible for a lot of our problems. But he had the ability to hold us back on policy and he felt at every level he was going at us in a pretty big way. He wanted to play long.

He was making tea while I was leaning against the oven and Cherie came in wearing her nightdress to get herself a drink, not totally hostile, but we didn't discuss the issue in hand. I went off to my morning meeting and there was too much going on – fire, Iraq human rights, plus Blunkett and Sarkozy meeting on Sangatte. I was trying to get a line agreed with TB that Foster gave no help in getting the mortgage on the flats but TB admitted we couldn't really say that. There was a real problem re CB's judgement on Carole, who could do no wrong. TB was also a bit all over the place. I told Tom [Kelly] and Godric to be very careful because I wasn't confident in the robustness of the case we were putting, and feared the facts on Foster would come back on us at some point.

The FBU did a four-hour meeting at the end of which they said ACAS [Advisory, Conciliation and Arbitration Service] had asked to intervene. The press took it as the first sign of crumbling so we pushed hard on the line that our position was as before. TB saw Monks and [Brendan] Barber with JP, said he felt they [TUC] had behaved really badly on this, that if they kept pushing out all this stuff about the link with the unions broken, it would be self-fulfilling. Fiona spoke to Carole and said she was back to thinking Foster was victim not villain. Ian Monk was still on the case advising her.

Tuesday, December 3

TB/GB thing was messy, one or two reports suggesting GB would get chopped. TB felt GB had overreached again and was now trying to pull back. He felt he was moving to a different mode, and the problem was he did have real reach in the party and was doing it on policy issues of substance. I was amazed by the fact the press weren't going bigger on it. TB said I had to leave it to him to sort with GB. But he did accept that there was a reality problem. He said GB had raised me again, and my diary, and had asked TB to discipline me. TB had said to him that if you treat serious people like shit, don't be surprised if they are not exactly rushing to help. Also, [Ed] Balls was about to make a speech about the history of the euro. That would inflame further and risk things getting out of control. I did a few meetings on fire, top-up fees, sport strategy, then home to collect the boys and off to Burnley vs Man Utd. I did the US conference call on

December '02: GB raises question of AC's diaries

the way, which was poor. Saw Alex briefly before the match, which we lost 2–0, but it was a terrific night to see the ground [Turf Moor] full and humming.

Wednesday, December 4

Student march on top-up fees included Will Straw [son of Jack and President of the Oxford Student Union], and by the end of the day we were in a different position, TB ruling out 'upfront fees' during PMQs. Crap day. At the John Reid party meeting, I had a real pop at Spencer Livermore, who was resisting any message focus on ASB, saying schools and hospitals were all that mattered. TB was fairly relaxed after a not very good PMQs but top-up fees was going to be seen as a U-turn and a victory for GB. Pat [McFadden] had lunch with Sue Nye yesterday and said GB's lot were totally convinced we were doing him in the whole time, me in particular. They felt I was trying to disable him as a possible successor to TB. They denied having any strategy against TB at all.

There was a flurry before I left. The *Mail* called to say they had an exchange of emails between Foster and CB which totally debunked the idea that he was not an adviser. Even though I had half expected this, I was absolutely livid, and Godric was worried he had been put in a position of misleading people. TB and Cherie were at the theatre. Bloody hell. I told the *Mail* I couldn't find them and we would have to deal with it in the morning. We were being hit again because we didn't get the full facts out. I dictated a note to TB saying this was likely to be big and bad. He called me at ten to twelve, said it was ridiculous to say Foster was their financial adviser. He was still in denial about it. He said at the weekend he had said that Foster had sent Cherie an email but CB did not even reply, so it was ridiculous – one of his favourite words at the moment – that this was a big story. I said we had given, in his name, the clear impression that Peter Foster had had nothing to do with the whole thing, but these emails would show very clearly otherwise. I said this was a problem born of Cherie going to a different place getting bad advice. I also felt he was far too tolerant of the whole Carole scene. As we were speaking, I got a message that the *Mail* had done three pages, all pretty grim. I told him, and he said he was going to have to get to the bottom of it. He went off and got all the emails from Cherie and was up most of the night going through them and working up a response. I went to bed but was unable to sleep. Why the fuck should I spend so much of my life digging them out of shit of their own making?

Thursday, December 5

Carole had been a disaster waiting to happen, as I had said for years, and it was happening. I called TB who had been working on some kind of statement overnight. We both knew there was no point going over the old ground. This just had to be sorted. I got a cab in and was hugely cheered up by the driver who said the reason the media went at the government was because we were doing a good job on the main things, and the reason they went for me was because they hated people who stood up to them. I got in, up to the flat, where TB was sitting at the table in the window, a welter of emails spread out in front of him, having written a draft statement. There was no small talk, no banter. Cherie came in wearing her pyjamas, could barely look at me and we didn't speak. TB and I agreed that the problem was going to focus on the fact that we misled the press. They continued to insist that this guy was not their financial adviser, but based on these exchanges, they were deluding themselves if they thought we could persuade people of that. When it suited the media to treat Foster as a conman, they would. When it suited them to take things at face value, they would do that too. This problem arose, like others before, because TB and CB so often wanted to believe the best and ended up doing so. But we were going to get the blame for this.

I said there was a case for turning the draft into a CB statement and she agreed to that. We spent ages going over it. As the day wore on, I could see TB was becoming more and more worried. He and I went up to the little changing room by the bedroom and he said his instinct was to fight it out. I said if we gave nothing on this, we'd be dead. He said it was only because we lived in a world infested with this media scum that we had to get into any of this. Cherie joined us, looking very downcast. I then worked on a Number 10 statement followed by a CB statement which said she would have been more circumspect if she had known and that she regretted causing misunderstanding. TB saw the Danish PM while Jonathan, Sally, Tom and I went to CB's office in the flat with the latest version. We had to fill in some of the gaps with copper-bottomed facts. I read it out. At the end she looked to Sally and said 'Alastair hasn't looked me in the eye since the weekend. He thinks I'm a fraudster.' No I don't, I said, anything but, but I do think you can be a bit daft and have some odd friends, but we are where we are. We went through it, and Fiona joined us, Cherie didn't change much and then she had to leave for court. She was very emotional, bottom lip quivering when she spoke to me, but otherwise OK.

TB came back and was fine with it. He said we had to clear up the idea we had misled the press. He was worried we were going to end up with the worst of all worlds, which of course we were, but I felt we just had to get the facts out as best we could. We finally got it sorted, TB taking out the reference to the *Mail*'s 'vicious personal campaign' and agreed it before Cabinet. I left Cabinet early to put in an extra couple of lines and then spent some time with Tom before he did the eleven o'clock. He went off armed with the best answers we could muster but it was going to be pretty grim. He came back to say it had been particularly torrid, that they didn't really buy the idea that we didn't mislead them. The hacks were also moving to the idea that it was me and Fiona who were responsible for the misleading.

TB spoke to CB and she agreed we could make clear she alone was responsible for any misunderstanding. Through the day the story developed into one about Cherie's judgement re Carole and re them not telling us that Foster had indeed had a lot to do with these transactions. TB called Tom and me round and Tom filled him in very honestly on how hard the briefing had been, and said it was moving to a great row about us and the press, focused on me in particular. TB said he was sorry we had been dropped in it like this. Sally said he really had to sort her out, that he was far too tolerant. She should not be doing the book. She should take proper advice. Carole had to be off the scene. TB was clearly worried about the impact of all this on Cherie, said it was monstrous that she was being done in like this, that she is a far better person than all this suggests. I said he should worry less about Carole and more about his own position. Later he set off for Bristol where he was due to do a Q&A and see Euan. I worked the phones, mainly editors and columnists, all feeling pretty sore about it all, and we were heading for an orgy of stuff about the Number 10 media machine again. This was a massive setback to the new media strategy. Tom did the four o'clock, gave out the CB statement that she alone was responsible for misleading the press, which helped us. Foster did a little doorstep, protesting innocence. He was clearly going to be around for a while. We were going to take a real hit on this, and as I said to Godric, pretty much the whole day taken up with dealing with this bollocks.

Friday, December 6

The papers were dire for CB, while the *Mail* and the *Telegraph* were really going for me – Liar-in-Chief. The storm was probably at its height and would blow out before too long, but TB was really worried. Cherie had been very frosty with Fiona last night. I explained that Fiona had a lot of sympathy for CB, but there was no point disguising the fact we felt this was a problem of their own making, and in part the result of Cherie relying far more on Carole than Fiona for advice on things which ultimately could impinge on him. He said I was talking about his wife, whose character was being assassinated. He said they were trying to do to her what they had done to Diana. I said it was nowhere near as bad as that yet, but why give them ammunition? It doesn't mean you have to totally change your lives, but you just have to be more careful about who is around. It was not a warm conversation. These character issues, where the political and the personal collided, were always difficult, and it must at times have felt like they both had me and Fiona on their backs the whole time, trying to cut out what they would regard as any fun or escape out of their lives. I said we were trying to help navigate through shitty waters. He said I know, but we are talking about my wife here.

I asked how Euan was. Fine, he said, but he won't be fine when he sees what this is doing to his mother. He accepted she had not been totally open with us, and also that we should have been able to go through everything as soon as this issue emerged, but it was clear he still felt they were more victim than villain. I was feeling crap all day because Grace and I had a rare flare-up in the morning, the kids as ever picking up on the tensions from elsewhere. TB called from Bristol and said he was worried we had no line out to Carole. He wondered if Hilary [Coffman, special adviser] shouldn't speak to her, but Hilary felt Carole would just see her as my agent.

TB called again from the train and said of course there was one person – GB – who would be loving all this. I had a few ministers on saying they would happily go out and defend Cherie – Hilary A, Robin C for example – but in the end we settled on Paul Stinchcombe [Labour MP] who was a genuine friend and who did well in making the case for some perspective in all this, and saying her faults were excessive loyalty and protection of her children. TB called again to say he had now spoken to Carole, and he sounded a lot better. He was talking about her like a doctor talking about a patient – she was stable at the moment, but she would need attention. Foster and Monk were still with her, so the dangers were still there. He felt she knew Foster had to go. He said you have to trust me on Carole. I honestly believe she would never sell her story, she is a good person, just naive in many ways.

Today's broadcast story was to a large extent about me, which was a pain, and a total joke in the way I was being collared on this. Meanwhile, there were all sorts of ridiculous rumours swirling round the Sundays, the most outlandish of which was that Cherie, Anji and

Carole used to take showers together. It was beyond belief the way some of the Sundays operated, literally just made it up. TB said we had to get to a position where we were saying, and the public was believing, that there were two very different agendas, a press agenda and then the issues that really mattered to people. But we were not there yet. And my next worry in all this was [CB's] clothes and discounts.

Saturday, December 7

Went for a run, but couldn't get going. The media were kind of on hold waiting for the Sundays. The whole day was a series of conference calls as the various sets of questions came in, mainly from the *Mail on Sunday* and the *News of the World*, a few from the *Sunday Times* and the *Observer*. I was buggered if I was going to be tarnished any more with this nonsense. People knew that I had always been warning about this woman. TB said that we had to be professional and focused. But I feared there was a lack of professionalism and focus coming from his desire to believe the best not just of Cherie but also of Carole. He said that Cherie was the subject of a vicious character assassination. I said I thought a lot of this was self-inflicted. He said that was really unfair, Cherie didn't deserve this. I said I had been warning about Carole for years. He said that's not true, that I had stopped a few years back. I said that was because it became pointless, the more I tried the more difficult Cherie became, to the point where I was worried neither of us were wholly rational about it.

He said you have to understand the pressures I operate under. I said I do, probably better than anybody else, but you also have to understand how damaging this kind of thing can be. It's been building up, and you also need ways to defend the individual situations to do with lifestyle, and by and large that can be fine, people will tolerate it but then sometimes there's a tipping point and that's where we are now. In all we must have had ten conference calls through the day. He said he resented having to deal with all this nonsense when he was also having to worry about Iraq. I continued to say it was all avoidable. We got the *Mail* questions in the afternoon and they related mainly to Foster and Carole being invited to things with Cherie, plus the issue of a trust that bought the flats, plus Fiona's role. We were dismissive of the invite stuff, fairly detailed on the trust. Then the *News of the World* came in with various groups of questions, first the claim that CB definitely knew about Foster's past so her statement on that was false, second that Carole tried to do a deal on clothes as we had always suspected, and third the wacky stuff about them having mudbaths and showers together.

By now, we were at Catherine MacLeod's [political editor, the *Herald*] farm in Essex to get a Christmas tree, but I spent most of the time on the phone up in one of their boys' bedrooms, Fiona popping in and out. TB had Cherie with him though she wasn't on the call, and he was saying to her 'This has to be one hundred per cent accurate' and it was easy to hear she was on the edge of it all, crying and saying why do you believe him not me? What a fucking mess this was. The fact of the purchase was politically grim, the sense of a cover-up and misleading was disastrous for our media relations, and the whole image being created of CB was appalling. When the *News of the World* stuff came through, the lack of a direct channel to Carole became an issue and in the end TB had to speak to her himself. She was denying that Cherie misled anyone about Foster and also denying she did deals on the clothes, which I didn't believe. TB wanted Fiona to act for Carole and put out a statement for her, which we refused to do.

Catherine and her family all seemed to be of the view that our life was absolutely crazy. Even when we went out to the field to pick a Christmas tree in a howling wind, I was called by Switch [Downing Street switchboard] for yet another conference call. The *News of the World* stuff came from someone who used to work with Carole but helpfully she used a different name so we could be fairly dismissive. Again, I was struck by how blinkered TB could be re some of the central allegations. For example, Carole saying she didn't do deals on clothes was enough for him but there was no way we could become their defenders. I was also angry that the press office had been put in a position where this shit was taking up all their time.

I was also sick of so much of the flak flying my way. I didn't mind when it was over things that really mattered, or when it was things I'd done that people disagreed with, but I hated it when I was copping it for things I had always been against doing. TB said, when I pointed it out, 'This is not very nice for me either you know.' I said yes, but at least you have some control over your own life and how you spend your time. At one point during the day, CB came on the phone, thinking I was Tom. 'Oh, it's you,' she said, and gave the phone back to TB. She really was resentful of us at the moment. Fiona's theory was that TB was so tolerant with CB because he had fallen for some of the Carole stuff himself. We had the worst of all worlds at the moment. I got Stephen Pound [Labour MP] out publicly asking [Paul] Dacre if the *Mail* had paid Foster for the emails. There wasn't too much to worry about in the various Sunday stories but the compound effect of a great morass was difficult.

TB and I were both feeling the pressure, and finally snapped in the evening when I said the whole fucking thing was their fault. He came back pretty heavy and the call ended badly. He called a bit later to say he understood this was difficult for us too, but we always did best when we hung together. The low point though had been when he was calling me and then calling Carole in quick succession to get her responses. The idea of a prime minister talking to this ridiculous woman who was sitting next to some ghastly conman was absurd and degrading. We got through the day somehow but I felt bruised and fed up.

Sunday, December 8

I did a long conference call with Jack Straw and Alistair Darling last night but amazingly neither was asked about CB in their interviews. Jack was doing fine on Iraq. I went for a six-mile run, then a swim, then a few calls, the press basically focusing in on the trust and how could they buy a flat through a blind trust, whilst my fears about the clothes issue were not yet realised. TB didn't call me during the morning which was rare. Philip was worried about the *Sunday Telegraph* because it looked like I was dumping on TB and CB. It's true that in some quarters I had let my anger get away from me. But I felt entitled to be angry when our advice was ignored with this kind of effect, and we were now having to deal with it, something that should have no government significance at all. I also felt that if they didn't change their ways, there would be more of this kind of stuff to deal with and I had just about had enough of it.

TB was down at Chequers seeing [Bill] Clinton, and it was pretty obvious as the day wore on he was not in contact, presumably because he was feeling I had distanced myself and briefed against Cherie. Philip, Gail [Rebuck] and Peter M came round to discuss the whole picture. Peter M took out his yellow pad. Must be serious then, I said. Fiona and I were in a state of real anger about the situation, and we had to try and work out a way out of it. Peter M had no idea of the extent of the problems we potentially faced, e.g. clothes, discounts, all the New Age stuff. We agreed we needed 1. to get Foster out of Carole's life, and 2. to manage Carole out of theirs. Gail said it would mean us giving massive support to Tony and Cherie, and also embracing Carole. I said there was no way I could do that, or let any of my staff do it. Fiona said even they had no real idea what our lives were like having to deal with this for so long. I feared that a lot of the really positive side of TB's image was eroding.

It was a good discussion and at the end we agreed we needed a proper audit of clothes, freebies, Carole's access, any use of government facilities, and we needed to put the fear of God into TB and make him understand the political precariousness. TB was fed up of hearing all this from me and I agreed with Peter M he would go with a warning that this was a real disaster unless gripped, that CB had to be reined in, Carole managed out over a six- to twelve-month period, and meanwhile we had to be very supportive. Peter was horrified that I was even thinking of going, but I really did feel the time was coming. He then called TB and arranged to see him tomorrow. Philip and Gail felt this could be the beginning of the end if not gripped. Peter believed if we did grip it, we could then repair, rehabilitate and move on, but it was difficult while Foster was still there.

Sally M called to say that Cherie had called her to say that AC/FM were briefing against her. Sally believed there was real damage to be done to TB by all this. TB had said yesterday this was not why he came into politics. I felt exactly the same. Cherie later called Fiona, was very frosty, said it was very clear Fiona disapproved of her, and intimated that maybe it would be better if she didn't work for her. Pretty unpleasant, after all Fiona has done for her.

Monday, December 9

I said to Fiona I felt we could be out by Christmas. I sensed a denouement. I said I wasn't going to be in a position where I was defending the indefensible. I took enough blame without taking it for things that weren't of my making. At the morning meeting, we skipped over CB, Iraq the main focus, while at the TB meeting we were mainly on asylum, NHS and fire. TB saw Sally, Jonathan and me, later joined by Hilary [Coffman] and Fiona. We agreed we needed a full audit of the clothes situation, and we would probably have to register retrospectively any discounts. TB kept trying to persuade me that Carole was basically a decent person and would do nothing wrong, e.g. on clothes. I said this had to be copper-bottomed, and I'm not sure I believed it. He got very defensive and we had another row about it, saying that we had a real problem because he took what she said at face value and I didn't. It was not an easy conversation. All of us felt he was not being quizzical enough.

The main area of press interest was the blind trust, but Andrew Turnbull backed TB's view that it was in accordance with the ministerial code on blind trusts. He was also OK about the Number 10 press office being used because we were only being asked any of this because she was the PM's wife. TB did the *FT*, and was on very good form, really pushing the New Labour reform agenda, definitely worth doing. But there was only one political story in town. There was an awful lot of [broadcast journalists'] two-way chatter about me and Fiona, while [Trevor] Kavanagh [*Sun*] had a big piece re how TB couldn't afford to lose me. Hilary was up seeing CB, came back and said she was not exactly on the same page as TB. She had also spoken to Carole who said she had not kept receipts. He said he obviously understood Carole could not come into Number 10 but then Hilary discovered she was coming in to see Cherie at 4.30. We put a block on that.

I had several meetings with TB, who was looking more and more depressed about the whole thing. Then Tom got totally banjaxed at the four o'clock – Foster's solicitor put out a statement which showed that CB had taken part on a conference call with Carole and Foster's solicitor. It sent the media into a frenzy. I went to tell TB, who looked grey, angry and sick. Cherie was due to be turning on the Christmas tree lights outside, but TB called for her to come down to the office, told her the questions that had now been put to Tom and she said yes, she spoke to the lawyer because Carole was worried Foster's case wasn't being handled properly, and what was wrong with that? She had a look of injured innocence. TB looked really angry, was close to the end of his tether. This is the worst possible nightmare, he said. She talked us through it and we put together a line which said she didn't know his past and she had made a short phone call.

TB said the whole thing was ridiculous, the media just moved from one charge to another, and when one fell down, another came up. We had gone from stamp duty evasion via slimming pills and now this. The problem was he saw nothing wrong in her making such a call, and I did, because she was the PM's wife, a QC, a judge, and she should have better judgement. TB said OK, she's maybe been daft but does she really deserve this kind of treatment? TB didn't raise my briefing against CB but Hilary came to see me, said it was the right thing to do for the credibility of the office. IDS was now writing in about the blind trust, about my role.

I had a long chat with Peter M before we went to see TB. He felt we could fight back harder and I said the solicitor's statement was a tipping-point moment. The politics on this were getting worse and worse, elitism while top-up fees was the issue, a real sense of out-of-touch lifestyle. [Conservative deputy leader and Shadow Foreign Secretary Michael] Ancram was out and about on it. TB was keen for us to get people up so I briefed Stephen Pound and later Clare Short. She did a good job on *Newsnight* but it wasn't great having to ask people to do this. TB did at least apologise to my team, or at least tell me to tell them that he had, for what they were having to do. He came through later to say a milder version of the same thing. God knows how many hours and how many people this was taking up at the moment.

Tuesday, December 10

Ran in. Papers grim, and the news leading with the Tories calling for an inquiry. Up to see TB, and we did a conference call with Peter M who had seen both of them last night to go through the facts of it all and was confident that CB was OK on it and there were no real new problems to worry about. I argued there *was* a problem in CB making a call to a lawyer, because she was a QC and his wife. TB was getting very agitato. He said 'I'm not having my wife treated like this and we have to fight back on the basis we have done nothing wrong.' He wanted to go up and do a big defence of her, but I said if he went up and just stated nothing had been done wrong, he would be more tarnished by it. He was so angry that I felt it would backfire if he went out now. TB's anger was affecting his judgement on it. He really seemed unable to see anything wrong in it. I felt that unless we let some air out of the situation, this was just going to go on and on. We also had to divide and rule, isolate the *Mirror* and the *Mail* from the rest. Peter M was keen for CB to do something today. Fiona, who later also saw Carole, felt too that CB should do something. I wasn't so sure. I chaired the first Iraq Strategy Group meeting and we agreed to do an objectives document. It was an OK meeting but we needed to get to a position where we were far more in control of the agenda.

Fiona came back from her visit with Carole, who didn't want to say she was dumping Foster, and had moved towards thinking as I did, that Cherie should do something public. TB was off to see the Prince of Wales for lunch, and new questions came in from the *Mail*. They were now suggesting 'judge nobbling'. It was time to go for it. It was a tipping point and we were all now up for CB doing a big number. I put calls out to Peter M and Charlie [Falconer] to get them to come over and we went through things line by line, making sure that all the difficult questions were answered in there, why the flats, how Foster, what she knew, why Carole. Fiona was terrific today, so was Peter M, saw things really clearly, but we had to fight back and that meant changes in the dynamic. An interview would be no good, because then someone else would set the agenda with it. It had to be bigger to break through. We decided that in the end Cherie was going to have to go up on this, break through, let the public see it and judge for themselves. She was due to do an event [Partners in Excellence children's services awards] over at Millbank, with a ready-made audience, who would be sympathetic.

I called a few ministers to line them up to do supportive media on the back of a statement from Cherie. I think we all felt that though there was a risk in this, it was probably the best way to blow the storm out. Writing the statement, Fiona was sitting at my computer, while I dictated the draft, Tom chipping in, then we were joined by Peter M, Charlie F and Sally and we did a bit of writing by committee. The first draft was too long, but we had cut it by the time Cherie came down. She was a lot calmer than yesterday, though she and I were still finding it hard to engage. I gave her the draft and she had a few minor changes which she explained to Peter M and I put them in. We suggested she did a read-through to ensure she was happy with it and also so she would be aware of the points where emotional intensity might take over. Peter M said she should pick out people in the audience, look in their eyes and speak to them direct. She looked at me and said 'I certainly don't want to look at him.'

We all said good luck and off they went. She looked very pale, said she was worried about crying and went upstairs to compose herself. It was a minuscule drive to Millbank, but Fiona called to say they got stuck in traffic. She got through the scrum, she read the statement pretty well, looked very emotional, pretty close to tears.[1] After the event everyone felt a lot better. TB had been with the Queen when she did it and they hadn't watched it. He caught it on the news later and said he was really proud of the way she stood up to it. He really felt there was an opportunity to go for the *Mail* now, and to a lesser extent the *Mirror*, because there would be a market in the rest of the media to do so. He was finally angry about the state of the media and realised there was no way papers like the *Mail* were going to be anything other than hostile. TB did for once thank us for what we had done for him. As Peter M said, he had a real fright and we had to make sure he did not go back, and that Cherie didn't either. The news ran fine, and the centre of gravity of the story had moved, so that it now just looked like journalists with an agenda rather than

[1] Cherie Blair said 'My immediate instinct when faced with the questions from the *Mail on Sunday* ten days ago was to protect my family's privacy, and particularly my son in his first term at university, living away from home . . . I am sorry if I have embarrassed anyone, but the people who know me well know that I would never want to harm anyone, least of all Tony or the children or the Labour government.'

genuine important questions that needed to be answered. Everyone agreed today had just about paid off. The old team had got together and done it again, but it had been a very tough few days and the press would be reluctant to let go of it entirely.

Wednesday, December 11

The papers were much better, the *Mirror* the only really vicious one. Margaret Beckett went for the press in general and was wonderfully dismissive of [BBC *Today* programme presenter John] Humphrys. TB much happier. We had to decide whether to do a doorstep or wait for PMQs. We agreed he should do a doorstep, support CB, attack 'parts of the press' and say there were more important things to focus on. We were all feeling a bit battered but in stronger shape and there was definitely an appetite among some of the media to go for the *Mail*.

Then a meeting with TB, GH, CDS and C. C and David Manning were just back from the US and they reported the mood there was far tougher. They felt Saddam was just messing about and that Blix was hopeless and too soft. There was a hilarious headline in the *Süddeutsche Zeitung*: 'Rumsfeld promises patience as Blair threatens war'. We went over the various military options. It would be possible to do something fairly quickly but TB didn't believe GWB wanted 'an ugly start'. I presented my idea of a strategy document to clear objectives which they agreed, but later Jack and GH put out some signs against it. Geoff was very much on the Rumsfeld end of the market at the moment. CDS was a bit more engaged. David felt the US were in a very different position.

The news was still leading on CB but it had a very day-after feel to it. Fiona was in touch with Carole who claimed she was easing Foster out. TB's doorstep was running big. Then a meeting with Peter M and Peter H. Peter M felt TB would learn from this, that he had had a genuine scare. Fiona and I headed up for dinner with TB and CB and the Yellands [*Sun* editor David and wife Tania]. We had a nice enough time, mainly chit-chat, but I'd have preferred to have been at home with the kids. It was pretty clear there was no real change at the *Sun* re the euro. But Yelland was still broadly supportive, clearly liked them both personally. TB was out hard on Iraq/WMD. The other big story today was Yemen and Korea exporting WMD materials. Later I discussed with TB whether I needed to go to Denmark [EU summit]. Part of me wanted to, but a larger part didn't. A lot did depend on whether TB and CB really were going to learn from all this. The PLP had been terrific in the main. The *Mail* and the *Mirror* had been vile but some of the others pretty reasonable.

Thursday, December 12

If we thought it was all going away, we were wrong. Radio 4 was leading on a *Scotsman* story that CB had been more involved than admitted before in the Foster case, with lots of detail based on a fax that he had. It was running wild again. Tom [Kelly] called and we agreed we needed a line very quickly. Tom spoke to CB, FM spoke to Carole. Both said it was Foster who faxed pages to CB's flat at Carole's request, but with the current microscope on it, it was going to be difficult to explain as innocent. Really grim again. I ran in and did a quick conference call, including with TB. There was so much in the story that was wrong that we ought to be able to explain it away quite quickly. But the problem was because of recent events, the media had an excuse constantly to say our word could not be trusted. Very difficult to deal with. On the call, TB said that CB, who was due to leave for Warsaw at 9, was adamant she never saw these papers or Foster. Godric and I went up to see TB. Godric was confident these issues could be explained, but it was like there was an equivalence, a moral equivalence, between us and Foster. TB was getting exasperated. He looked tired and grey and could not work out where it would end. Fiona was talking to Carole, saying she needed to put out a statement, which she did, saying that she had initiated this, Cherie did nothing wrong and she was sorry. I was worried it was all getting to TB again. He was desperate to get closure on it.

In the margins of Cabinet I was trying to persuade Jack and Geoff of the need for a campaign objectives document as an important piece of strategy if and when things happened. Cabinet was mainly fire, and Turkey [US support for Turkey to join the EU]. TB thanked colleagues for their support. Clare for once shipped in with something supportive and sympathetic, said the whole thing must have been horrible for him and Cherie. The Turkey discussion was interesting and important and I wrote a script for GS to try to get it up at the 11. But he had yet another pretty torrid briefing and he and Tom were pretty pissed off about the whole thing. I did a fresh statement for him for the four o'clock, to try and shut it down, but it was probably too aggressive, and after a conference call with TB and Peter M, I toned it down. TB felt Cabinet had been supportive but jittery. He was looking wan.

TB popped in a couple of times, pleased when Foster's solicitor backed up our story. It was now beginning to feed into broader questions. Philip did groups later and said the link was lack of trust in institutions that were supposed to work. It hit authority to govern. Peter M sent over a note saying we needed these three things: 1. us clearly focused on real issues; 2. the sense of a media vendetta; 3. Carole had to dump Foster otherwise we were linked in through her to a conman.

Charlie [Falconer] came over and he and I went through it again from square one trying to work out a way through. The *Scotsman* story was pretty comprehensively knocked down but they were all still going with it and the *Sun* tape wasn't as exciting as it first seemed. TB did a brief doorstep in Copenhagen, and he looked pretty rough. I went to Rupert Murdoch's party, nice enough do, usual News International lot plus the likes of [Sir] Alan Sugar [businessman], [Paul] Dacre, Victor Blank. Dacre was at one point talking to IDS and I walked by and said to Iain 'How nice to see you talking to your leader.' Philip called and said that despite the *Sun*, the bulletins had been dire and it had definitely broken through to the public. What a fucking nightmare.

Friday, December 13

The *Sun* tapes story helped on one level in that it put more of the focus on Foster. The BBC led on Foster saying that Carole covered up for CB. The whole thing was absolutely ghastly. Andrew Neil [editor-in-chief, the *Scotsman*] was on the *Today* programme at 8.10 blathering away rubbish about Watergate. The frenzy was still raging, but both Tom in Denmark and Godric here were saying very little. I was exhausted and fed up with the whole thing. The *Mirror* was saying I was increasingly demented. I agreed with Tom and Godric we should not defend the *Sun* over its story but simply emphasise this was a story about a conman. I finished the Syria article we were doing to set up President [Bashar al-] Assad's visit. I went home early and was at the school when it came out that Foster was planning to make a statement on Monday.

I said to TB that we had to work out the worst possible stories that Foster could come out with. So long as there was that link to him through Carole, there was damage being done because we were being asked to defend the indefensible. Turkey and accession was the big issue for the meeting in Copenhagen and it was resolved OK for us, though the Turks weren't terribly happy.[1]

---

[1] It was resolved in Copenhagen that if political criteria were met two years later, negotiations for Turkey to join the European Union could begin 'without delay'.

Saturday, December 14

For the sixteenth day running, most of my time was taken up with Foster and Caplin. Peter M called, very Peterish, pretending nothing much was going on, asked how I was. Spitting tacks, I said. 'Do you like anyone?' he asked. I said Rory, Calum and Grace, and Fiona when she's not disagreeing with me. The rest can fuck off. TB called as I was out on a run, and said that we just had to shut it down, not answer any more questions, and tough it out, I said something that made both of us snap. I was at the top of Golders Hill, had just got my breath back and said to him the real problem was that whether you like it or not, you are linked to a conman. He said I resent that. 'You are. You're married to a woman who is determined to protect and keep a woman who is in love with a conman so you are linked to a conman.' He shouted at me down the line 'I am not linked to a conman.' You are, and until Cherie dumps Carole or Carole dumps Foster, or preferably both, that's the way it is. And every day it's like that it hits your authority more, both with the rest of the government and with the public.

TB was having none of it. 'We have a fundamental disagreement. You think Cherie has done something monstrous and I don't. You think Carole is monstrous, and I don't.' I said there was a difference between monstrous and wrong. 'Well, I disagree. She is not a bad person and I'm not going to dump on people just because the press tell me to.' I said it was time to do the right thing despite the press, not the wrong thing because of stubbornness about the press. 'Well, if you're going to take that attitude, we have a problem.' I agreed, and said I wasn't going to defend Carole or anything to do with her. 'Fine, don't then. Just say nothing about it.' Fine, I said, but if this goes on much longer I'm off, out of here, goodbye. There is only so much of this shit I'm prepared to deal with. 'Well that is hardly the best attitude at a time like this.' He then went into a spiel that our opponents were always trying to divide us, we had to stick together, that this would blow over soon and we would be back on a proper agenda again. It was a very difficult conversation, among the bloodiest we had had and devoid of the humour that usually laced difficult conversations between us. I was basically saying I felt their judgement on Carole was terrible.

TB called later and we had another half-hour on the phone, this time a lot more friendly. I explained that one of the building workers we had in recently had said 'Mr and Mrs B were floating off to a different world.' He said 'Look, I know how difficult this is for everyone, but in the end we have to hold together and get through it. We've actually done nothing wrong other than live in a country with a totally insane media. Without the media we have this would not be the madness it is, and we cannot let them drive us apart.' I said I agreed, but he knew I needed to let off steam now and then, and also we really did need to rethink his modus operandi. PG spoke to TB, told him the public was bemused and not really giving us the benefit of the doubt. Sunday paper write-throughs were OK-ish, but the whole impression left was of a total mess, not at all pretty.

Sunday, December 15
Neither of us spoke to TB or CB today. We had both had enough of dealing with it, and they had probably had enough of hearing our complaints about lifestyle and out-of-touchness. We went out for dinner with Philip and Gail. Philip was very down about things while I was just plain angry. He felt there was a problem of trust anyway and this made it worse. Even though the press was vile and ridiculous, people felt there was something in it all.

Monday, December 16
I felt a lot better running in. Foster fairly low-key. The *Mail* ran a story that TB called Carole's mum from Copenhagen. There were pictures in several of the papers of Foster driving Carole, her filming the media. Bits and pieces about me, generally negative of course, and lots about CB's judgement. The feeling was the heat was going out of it though. Assad's visit and Iraq were the main focus of the day. We were in an OK position on the Blix dossier but it was going to get more difficult. Good piece from Phil Stephens [*FT*] on the press destroying the political discourse.

The mood at TB's office meeting was a bit muted. Sally told him that people felt let down. We were going over his weekend note on public services and Iraq. You had to hand it to him, that even on weekends as bad as the one he must have had, he still found the time to set out the forward plan and the arguments on the public services. I felt on Iraq we ought to have a slightly different line to the US, not become an extension of them. TB wanted me to work more on Iraq, possibly go to the US. He spoke to Bush re the UN process. The Americans clearly felt Blix was a problem, his dossier was poor.

TB had a private chat with Assad and agreed lines on suicide bombers/Israel. The lunch was OK if a bit dull and the communications minister [Bashir al-Munajid] gave us a long lecture about their different IT systems. Assad was very odd-looking, tall but with quite a weak chin. TB was pushing on Iraq, making clear that if the US went for it, they wouldn't stop until the regime fell, also saying it was clear to us that Iraq was concealing and not being open. He said that David Manning was in constant touch with Condi Rice, 'who is Bush's American adviser'. 'As opposed to his French adviser . . .' I whispered to Jonathan. Assad said they believed any US attack in that region would strengthen the country under attack. He said a lot of people were against Saddam in Iraq, but all of them were against the USA. Jack said that it was 'five to midnight' and both of them were pretty clear about how serious Bush was about it. TB said Bush understood better than they thought about the impact on the Arab and Muslim world. Leo came in, which had the usual effect of warming things up and Assad was clearly up for a rather more friendly press conference than the last one [October 31, 2001]. It was actually a pretty good event. TB saw them off and then left for the House.

Foster had done his statement, said he was going to write an autobiography, had a bit of a go at me. We decided just to ignore it. Later TB called me in for a one-on-one chat. We gave each other the eye and he asked me what the problem was. I said I felt there was a reality problem. We had to change ways out of this. He said he didn't believe the damage was long term, that it would blow over and we would get back to a proper agenda soon. I said I know, but I sometimes worried that we didn't do enough to counter the out-of-touch problems. He was clearly angry I had been dumping on Carole and by implication CB in the press. 'Your great strength is that you feel things deeply and you think things clearly. You are the Roy Keane of the operation, but like him you sometimes stamp people on the head without meaning to. That's how Carole and her mum have felt and they are not like us, they are not used to it. I know that you and Fiona basically just want to protect the show. But you can come over as being unbelievably hard, Cherie needs support. She will listen to you and Fiona more than anyone, but only if she feels you are being supportive.' I said I never felt that he did not appreciate what I did for him and I sometimes felt Cherie should be far more appreciative of what Fiona does for her, that it's hard to feel warm towards someone you think is taking you for granted. As over the weekend, it was pretty frank stuff. He said he knew that if Carole stayed with Foster, they could have nothing to do with her. Also, even if she dumps him, he has to be more careful. 'I have been reckless and foolish and paid a price. So has Cherie, who had a terrible shock. But she is a good person not a bad person. And you have to take us as we are, strengths as well as weaknesses.'

I said what had been frustrating was that Fiona and I felt so clearly we were giving the right advice in these lifestyle issues and yet we were really just seen as irritants banging them round the head. Now we felt vindicated, but no satisfaction in that in any way, because we also felt let down. And there was a lot of that feeling round the building which he had to put right. He said we all had to learn from it, and never forget that the only people who want us divided are our opponents. The Tories, because they fear our professionalism. The press, and also GB who would love it if you and I were at odds, so we have to hang together.

Tuesday, December 17

Foster was down the agenda and we were getting back to proper domestic issues, e.g. pensions, GPs, transport plan update. Good press on Bain,[1] very good press for the Assad visit. So things felt better though we were all still bruised. We had the office strategy meeting up in the flat. TB said we had to have a strategy for rebuilding trust and connection. I said another foreign holiday is not the best start. Even though they were paying, it would not be billed like that. TB wanted the focus for the next stage on antisocial behaviour and public services, but the reality was Iraq and terrorism plus Northern Ireland meant we faced a tricky New Year. I felt we may as well play into that reality and put together a plan for TB on Iraq communications. It was the usual end-of-year feeling. What do we do for the New Year message, what have we got planned when we get back, who's around over the holiday, everyone feeling tired.

The MoD were doing a background briefing on Iraq military build-up which was going to move things up a gear. The American conference call was pretty hopeless, not very strategic if the big players were on it and not at all strategic if they weren't. TB was looking pretty grim. During the meeting, Peter M slipped me a note to say I had to be more supportive, that I had an ability to make him feel very low if I wasn't. Yet when Fiona called Cherie for a chat, she was curt and dismissive, even rude. TB had another bad meeting with GB who was arguing for a two-year delay on university [top-up] fees. NMD was running quite big, the US making the formal offer for the upgrading of [RAF] Fylingdales [radar base], and the PLP were a bit jumpy. JP came in for a chat, said that TB was too prone to letting

[1] The final Bain Inquiry report recommended an eleven per cent pay rise over two years, compared to the FBU's demand for a forty per cent immediate increase. It also proposed replacing an automatic wage mechanism, dictating the level of pay, with a new formula which would simply inform the bargaining process.

guilt run his whole life, that he was maybe too tolerant of some of the things CB did because of it, same as he was too tolerant with GB some of the time. He also feared TB and CB were both a bit too much into the celebrity bollocks and GB would use that against them.

Wednesday, December 18

The Cherie stuff was almost totally gone now, but Hilary [Coffman] was still pursuing the questions of the clothes. She called CB to discuss it, and CB said, to Hilary's utter amazement, 'Why don't you pop up, Carole's here, and you can talk to her direct.' This after TB assured us she would not be going back in. Of course Cherie was getting lots of letters of support and this made her feel that we had overreacted. She was still not speaking to me, nor I to her, every effort having been rebuffed, and I was making no secret of the fact I found the whole thing absurd. It seemed TB didn't know that she [Caplin] was coming in.

The MoD's briefing on Iraq had gone big and [Sir David] Omand was doing a terrorism briefing, with all manner of dire warnings, which would be leading the bulletins by the end of the day. At the political strategy meeting, David Triesman [Labour Party general secretary] told me that Piers Morgan had said to him 'The country is being run by two couples and I'm at war with both of them.' Spencer Livermore made the ludicrous statement that tax rises would be popular. Philip put his finger on the problem when he said we had two political strategies running against each other, opportunity versus security, and we should be wedding them together. But GB really saw his job almost as frustrating our political strategy. We had a whole succession of non-arguments. It was perfectly possible to link jobs and education to a strong society founded on values and respect, but we went round in circles on it.

I left for Grace's school concert then back home to work on the New Year message and the Iraq note to TB. The reports of chaos out of the various briefings were soon coming in. Geoff H having a statement on Iraq forced out of him, Jack S conflicting with TB on Iraq dossier response, plus the Omand briefing. As Mike White [*Guardian*] said, if that was all meant to calm things down, it didn't exactly work.

Thursday, December 19

I started the day in a rage because Omand's briefing was unplanned big news and [John] Williams' [FCO] briefings re Blix were a hardening of our position. Both had almost caught out TB in the House yesterday, so I did a major bollocking at the 8.30 meeting, said there was no point trying to co-ordinate if we had this kind of thing. Then to see TB re the *Guardian* interview where we wanted to get up the New Labour message again. He was OK, but not on sparkling form, as Polly Toynbee [journalist] noted. Interesting on Rowan Williams [Archbishop of Canterbury], who TB felt was intelligent Old Labour.

I chatted to Milburn and Charles Clarke who were both sympathetic but also said it was a real problem if I went offside on anything. TB mentioned to me later that three or four ministers had raised me with him, not in a critical way, just a bit worried. He asked 'Have you reassessed recent events?' 'What do you mean?' 'I think you slipped the reservation for a while. You went for Cherie and Carole. I know the reasons, you wanted to protect your people, but you should have discussed it with me. If this kind of thing ever happens again, we just have to have it out.' I said a lot of people, and Fiona and I are among them, felt we make pretty big sacrifices and get taken for granted. There is a lot of give and not much take. I didn't mind so much with him, because I knew the pressures he was under and basically supported what he was trying to do. But he always knew that I was not prepared to defend what I thought was indefensible. True, he said, but in the end we could discuss these things. But if he decided something, he had to be able to make those decisions from a position of leadership and we couldn't have a situation where his senior press person was briefing against his wife. He thought it all led to the impression that we had lost the plot. I held my own, saying the people around him weren't machines and he and CB had to take into account what they thought. They had asked an awful lot in the last few days, of Tom, Godric, Hilary. He said they were fine. I said not so. They might not say to you what they say to me. They are not happy about it. He disagreed, but I knew. I said I really felt they had to change their ways.

He said I was such a big personality and so forceful that if I was pissed off, everyone felt it and it dragged the whole show down. It's why he made the Roy Keane analogy. He said you lead by example which is great, but if you're pissed off, everyone around you gets pissed off. You wear your heart on your sleeve and give out very powerful vibes, and I'm just saying that in the last few days, that's not been a good thing. Now we have to put it together. I think both of us felt better afterwards but I really felt it was ridiculous that Cherie was still seeing Carole, and not protecting herself sufficiently on the freebie front. Milburn was sympathetic, said hold firm. Charles said you have to let Cherie be herself, whatever that is.

Cabinet was low-key, fire, Iraq, Clare as ever pointing up the need for more discussion. Jack on Blix. He was going to the UNSC today and we and the Americans were both going to be saying the process was holed. Bad political strategy meeting with John Reid, Douglas etc. at which TB said he felt we lacked real strategy at the moment and needed new structures. I said I felt he was looking for new structures as a way of avoiding dealing with the personal/political problem, namely that the TB/GB schism was growing. Things had got worse without Ed Miliband there.[1] Not only were we not on the same pitch most of the time now, but if we ever tried to get on the same pitch, one side would pretend that in fact we were apart. Douglas felt polling was the way to engage GB and then get some kind of agreed plan out of that. John R and Douglas both called me afterwards to say how grim they thought things were. John was beginning to realise what a difficult job it was. TB called on his way north and I briefed him re Blix who had been pretty negative on the Iraqi declaration.[2] Jack called again to agree a line and we agreed he should do a doorstep outside Number 10. He did fine. There was no doubt the mood music was clearly building up to war.

Friday, December 20

Guardian interview OK. Got TB up on a clip on Iraq when he was in Hartlepool. He was worried about Blix's comments that we had not been helping enough with the intelligence. Cleared my desk, shifted loads of paper, then left for the *What the Papers Say* awards at the Café Royal. I was sitting next to Jane Moore [*Sun* columnist], who said didn't I find it irritating that they kept panning the cameras on us? Some of the awards were ridiculous and I said to [Alan] Rusbridger [*Guardian* editor] 'Your profession is in trouble.' The 3am Girls [*Mirror* gossip writers] – columnists of the year. Picture of the year was a fake. The Paul Burrell reporter [Steve Dennis, *Mirror*] got reporter of the year. Dacre won 'scoop of the year' for 'Cheriegate' and he very sarcastically thanked me for all my attacks on the *Mail*. I told him I had only just started. I did manage to get a few marathon cheques, including from Annie Robinson [broadcaster, former *Mirror* colleague]. TB's interview for Forces Radio was now leading the bulletins as a warning of war.

Saturday, December 21

Eleven-mile run, averaging eight minutes ten. Drove down to Gillingham vs Burnley, lost 4–2. The big US build-up re Iraq was going

---

[1] Miliband had taken a year-long sabbatical to teach at Harvard University.
[2] A 12,000-page weapons inventory given to the United Nations by Iraq maintained it had no nuclear, chemical or biological weapons programmes.

on. The Egyptian press printed details of TB/CB's holiday [in Sharm el Sheikh] and the security committee decided to meet to reconsider. I felt the best outcome would be if they didn't go.

Sunday, December 22

The *Observer* splashed on TB saying no to the Olympic bid, which immediately became a broadcast story. We put out a line making clear no decision had been taken. We got Dick Caborn [sports minister] on to Radio 5. In saying he had barely discussed it with TB he was trying to say no decision taken, but it was taken as a signal of lack of interest and commitment. Sarah Hunter [policy adviser] had done a good note on it which made clear it was potentially winnable, though we lacked Brits in the right places on a lot of the international sporting bodies.

Monday, December 23

TB called and signed off the New Year message. I went into the office, cleared my desk and brought home a stack of paperwork. Patrick Diamond [policy adviser] had done a good paper on New Labour renewal. Stephen Wall had done a big note on Europe, which suggested to me we had far more problems than previously imagined. I felt in general that we were not in great shape. Iraq was building up pretty big now. The Iraqis shot down a US drone. There was no way they were not going to go to war now.

Friday, December 27

Thirty-five minutes on the treadmill, pretty fast. Kamal [Ahmed, *Observer* political editor] and a photographer here for four hours to do a piece on me doing the marathon. Saw an osteopath who said I had one leg slightly longer than the other and my right knee was inflamed. I had a really vivid dream about Dad dying. Mum and I were out in the field and then we went back into the house and Dad came through from his bedroom, sat down and said 'I'm absolutely buggered. I'm not sure I can go on much longer like this.' Small trickles of sweat and blood started to come down his face and I just hugged him and said he was a great father and I hoped I was too. Mum was crying.

Saturday, December 28

Took Grace to Brighton for her first solo Burnley match. On the way down, a call saying Clare [Short] had done Radio 5 and said it would be deplorable if England played [a cricket World Cup match] in

Zimbabwe, how she intended to press Tessa [Jowell], etc. More evidence of how Clare just stirs. It was a difficult line to tread this one, making clear what we would do if it was our decision, but also making clear that it's not. The difference between having a view and being able to make a decision. Jack S and Tessa both livid at Clare and her usual moral-conscience stuff, as though she was the only one who had one and the only one who says what she thinks. Tessa said we could all go out and say things to please certain constituencies but we don't because that is the deal on which a system of collective responsibility works. It was bloody cold. We went 2–0 up, then conceded two in the final two minutes. Dreadful.

To the Milibands for dinner. David had quite a detached view these days, felt the government was losing its way. We were both very frank about recent events and our belief that we were talking about rather ridiculous people who had somewhat left the planet. Fiona was feeling it much more than me at the moment and I was also finding it hard to get up much enthusiasm. And TB/GB was a total, probably irredeemable fault line. In the *Sunday Times*, the Olympic bid was the latest issue seemingly to be the focus of TB/GB division. It was all dispute and difficulty by proxy.

Sunday, December 29

Conference call with Jack Straw, Mike O'Brien [FCO minister] et cetera re Zimbabwe and we agreed that Mike should do clips making clear that the decision was for the cricket authorities but if it WAS our decision we would say do not go. It was a tricky one because on the one hand there was a clear political message to send, and on the other it wasn't the job of government to say where sportsmen should and shouldn't play. The problem with a compromise position was that it tended to land you in the worst of all worlds. Clare and now Nasser Hussain [England cricket captain] were saying that we should set up a body to decide on these things. IDS wrote to TB urging him to 'clear up the confusion' and take a lead. Jack though was very unkeen to move the line. I reminded him that the last time he, Mike, Tom Kelly and I were on a conference call it was followed not long after by a ministerial resignation, namely Peter's. Tessa was seething at Clare, felt she was just stirring on this and she intended to write to her rather than speak to her, so that the argument could not be misconstrued and spun against her. TB called for a general chat which seemed mainly to consist of telling me what a marvellous time he was having. 'How lovely,' Fiona said when I told her.

Monday, December 30

Zimbabwe ticking over. Finished the New Year message. It was pouring all day so Calum's tennis was off again. Instead, I went for a long run, 8.7 miles in one hour ten. The *Sun* had a two-page spread in 'Bizarre' [gossip column] on me allegedly dumping Britney [Spears, American singer] for Ms Dynamite [award-winning British singer], seemingly based on the fact that I listened to Ms Dynamite when running, though in actual fact I was mainly listening to the Lighthouse Family [British musical duo] on long runs. Godric was doing the honours briefing, plus Zimbabwe. Went to see the new James Bond film [*Die Another Day*], which was total crap.

Tuesday, December 31

Agreed with Anne Shevas [chief press officer] to put out the New Year's message for tomorrow. But no doubt that I was letting my own mood affect it and the overall impact was pretty downcast and gloomy.[1] Fiona and I both agreed we could not recall feeling less like the New Year mood you were meant to feel. It was largely because we knew that TB and CB had to change but saw little sign of it happening, and had very little belief that it would.

---

[1] In the message, Blair said 'With the world economy, Iraq, terrorism, the Middle East, Africa, the environment, Europe, the euro, this is a big and difficult agenda . . . the world economy will intimately be affected by world events on peace and security, for good or ill.' The *Daily Telegraph* described Blair's words as 'unusually grim and distinctly unfestive'.

December '02: Rain and crap film end the year

Wednesday, January 1, 2003

Very quiet on the work front. The New Year's message got big coverage, but there was no doubt I had allowed my own somewhat gloomy view of events to colour things, so the coverage was pretty much on the 'we're all doomed' lines. As Mike White said when he called me to discuss it, 'Don't jump.' Fiona and I were both pretty down about the thought of going back. Partly it was the weather, partly the thought that actually the tone of the message was pretty much where things were, and also the fact that TB, whenever he phoned, went on and on about what a marvellous time they were having, and how energising it all was for him. I said there was a time when I felt natural warmth to his irrepressible enthusiasm and zest for life. But it can sound unbelievably irritating and selfish when he's basking in sunshine and we are swimming through floods.

He was mulling over the various pressing problems and they were pretty much the same as a year ago, if a bit more advanced and a bit more difficult in some cases – US–UK, terrorism, MEPP, Northern Ireland, public services, Europe and the euro. We had to get through it as best we could, but within that list there were a lot of complicated and interacting problems. I felt out of sorts personally, not motivated by much other than the kids and the marathon training. I had stopped doing the weekly strategy notes, and in trying to analyse why, I feared it was largely because he and I were in slightly different strategic positions. I felt we needed to be more on reconnection with party and public whereas he was still pressing on all the controversial buttons, often with right-wing positions flying from them.

Thursday, January 2

Had a nice enough day for Fiona's birthday, got her plenty of decent presents, out for dinner and also had an OK session at the track. All quiet on the work front.

Friday, January 3

David Davies came round to sound me out about the FA chief executive job. He wanted to mark my card about the politics, and to go over why he thought it was a good idea for me. It was clearly a highly political organisation and very difficult to reform, but he felt even the non-modernisers would be impressed and flattered if I was interested and he reckoned I had a good chance of getting it. He felt the job would be as big as I wanted it to be, and that above all the organisation needed greater focus and clarity about priorities. It sounded tough but Fiona was very keen and at the end of a few hours mulling it over, I was quite keen as well. I liked David who was pretty straightforward, and a very good ally. I then headed north with Calum and on the way fixed David Hill [former Labour Party chief spokesman], Howell James [former political secretary to John Major] and Richard Tait for the GICS review team. Dad was a bit worse but still hanging in there. I went to the local gym, did seven miles on the treadmill.

Saturday, January 4

TB back, called on his way from the airport to Number 10, said he was really fit, full of energy and ready for the fray. He said he was clearer than ever about all the problems but we just had to hold firm. On GB, he said he had a plan. I asked if it was cautious or radical. Radical, he said. He added there was no point being in the job if you couldn't do it properly, so the situation has to be resolved. On the euro he was still of the view we should try to go for it. He was chirpy enough but keen for a realistic take on our problems.

I felt we had slipped back on Iraq, slipped back on Europe, enjoyed no real breakthrough on public services, crime and fear of crime were a bigger problem than the figures suggested, the GB relationship had become a fault line, and I felt we needed a fresh and discrete TB strategy too. Overall, I said I didn't think we were in great shape. Also, though it could be rectified, I felt our own relationship had changed as a result of the CB/Foster saga. Most of the time, I couldn't give a fuck when the press turned on me, but I really resented it over shit like that. Calum and I left for Grimsby vs Burnley. We were two up, then blew it and drew. It was freezing cold. Drove back, very little traffic from the press, the Sundays were full of crap, mainly on gun crime.

Sunday, January 5

Alice Miles called from *The Times* to say that [former Labour Cabinet minister and co-founder of the Social Democratic Party] Roy Jenkins' death had just been announced and would TB do a piece? I said maybe, but later spoke to TB and said I felt not, but maybe he should just do his own short tribute. He sent it through. It was very warm and personal, I felt the combined effect was over the top. I called TB to say so and he agreed to take out 'mentor' and instead talk of his support. I also pointed out he should at least say he disagreed with the formation of the [breakaway] SDP. 'But won't people think I'm just doing that for the Labour Party?' I said 'You are the leader of the Labour Party, and they did try to kill us.' 'Yes, but he was right in a lot of what he said, do you want me to say that?' Laughter. I said no. 'Surely the party is used to my little eccentricities by now.' Yes, but one day they might decide you have gone too far and rise up against you. I just feel it's a bit over the top. He said I thought you would but OK, take out the word mentor and put in something about me disagreeing with the formation of the SDP, but I do think he was a great figure and I am very sad about his death. At least he took the changes and agreed not to do *The Times*.

Andrew Adonis [Jenkins' biographer] called to get the go-ahead to do his own big tribute piece to Roy. *The World this Weekend* had yet another discussion of the New Year's message, which must be the first time it was still being covered five days after it was published. Mike Granatt [head of GICS] called from Scotland Yard to say there had been some arrests, possibly related to a ricin factory.[1] Out for dinner with the Goulds. Philip really not keen on the FA idea. Gail thought it was a useful bridge to a new phase. All of us felt that TB was not in a strong position and really needed a new approach. Philip felt I should make clear I would only stay if there was a real onslaught on spin, a real effort at rebuilding trust, a new modus operandi and with him leading by example, e.g. on the lifestyle issues. The only other people I discussed the FA with were Godric, who felt it would be a good way out, and Alex F, who was also very positive, felt it

---

[1] Six men were arrested after a police raid in Wood Green, North London, on suspicion of manufacturing ricin with the intention of attacking the London Underground by releasing the poison in airborne form. The only subsequent conviction was of Kamel Bourgass, who had already been sentenced to life imprisonment for the murder of Stephen Oake.

was a real job that I could do well. He felt [Adam] Crozier made too many enemies because he was too much of an empire builder. They were both very positive about the whole thing, and I respected their opinions. But both Fiona and I felt guilty at the idea of leaving just at a point when we knew things were going to get very rough.

Monday, January 6

Papers full of gun crime and Roy Jenkins. We got a bit of stick for the focus on crime looking like a response to recent events, which it wasn't. Derry was on the morning media re courts and sentencing, and Tam Dalyell [senior Labour backbencher] was on re Iraq. I called Jack S to discuss the best way to handle it. He was pretty much echoing [Colin] Powell's line that it was 40–60 [more likely that there would be a war]. He had called me a couple of times over the holiday and emphasised the importance of TB not positioning himself so that no war looked like failure. TB was pretty sure that there would be a war, or that in any event Saddam Hussein would go, and war remained the likeliest if not only way of that coming about. I chatted to him first thing, and then did a conference call to agree we would publish the Iraq policy objectives paper. John Williams rightly said it would get lost with all else that was going on but I felt it was important to have it out there at the moment. These strategy papers were as much about internal understanding as publicity.

TB's morning meeting with the office went on for two and a half hours as we worked our way through the twenty-page note he had sent to us at the weekend. Much of it could have been written for any other year ahead – prioritising public services, Europe, crime and asylum, delivery and trying to get the Civil Service to modernise more, relations with GB and the lack of proper economic narrative. So it went on, and we all had our usual position, all a bit stuck in tramlines. TB was not for giving an inch to the party, wanted to be even more modernising than ever, at the cutting edge of reform. I said he didn't need to keep winning modernising spurs, and I was worried that whilst he was identified so personally with all the controversies, it was being put together against us as being right wing, and he had to be careful. On Iraq, pretty much everyone was emphasising how little support there was, how little understanding there was of a real threat, but he was in pretty defiant mood on that too, said the threat was real and people would come round.

Later he called me in, was very friendly, and said he just wanted to know how I was. I said fine, up to a point. 'But only up to a point?' he asked. Yes. I couldn't deny that I felt pretty ground down by things.

I asked what he was going to do about his 'friend next door'. 'I'm going to sack him. I've come to a settled view that he has to go. There was a time when I could make the case that the tension was creative. But it has reached the point where it is destructive and it can't go on. I'm not prepared to be in a position where I have got the job, but I am not allowed to do it properly. It could be that it ends up with me being toppled but I would rather that than this situation. I remain of the view that the party will not get rid of a leader if they think the leader is doing basically what the country wants and needs.' He seemed fairly set on it, but doing it would be harder than saying it. He was also keen for Ken Clarke to become Tory leader, feeling it would waken up our lot and also help the country on Europe. The general feeling was that IDS was fucked.

Then we had a meeting with the political team in the flat. Hilary [Armstrong] said that John Healey [economic secretary to the Treasury], Jon Cruddas [Labour MP, Blair's former deputy political secretary for union liaison] and others were really organising now over the 'elitism' issue and trying to get TB on the wrong side of the divide. She was very fretful on Iraq and hunting. TB seemed much more relaxed after his break but in a way that just added to the sense that he was slightly losing the plot. Sally said she would go bonkers if she heard him say one more time that he was clearer than ever. It was all a bit groundhog day. Later we had pretty lengthy discussions on his speech tomorrow to the FCO heads of mission conference, where he wanted to say we were a unifying force around our vision of the world and that we had to get influence with the US and use it to broaden out our agenda. I asked him if he genuinely thought that our role was to keep them on the straight and narrow. Too damn right, he said, but if we say that's our role, we lose any influence. He said he only wanted to make speeches that really made a point, which meant we could strip out a few in the forward Grid.

Tuesday, January 7

I ran in the long route with Hugh Jones [former international marathon runner and first British man to win the London Marathon] but I was struggling. TB called me up to the flat just before 8. He was worried about the Palestinian reform conference. The Israelis' response to the latest suicide bombing was to prevent the Palestinians from coming to the London conference, so the conference was effectively scuppered. He was not happy with Jack's saying the chances of war were now 40–60, thinking we should not get into that type of running commentary. And he was livid that Derry gave us a batch of dreadful headlines from his *Today* interview on how we would let burglars go free, just as Blunkett was up doing his tough anti-gun crime stuff. We were a bit ragged generally, and he intended to make clear to Cabinet we couldn't tolerate some of the looseness we had been enduring of late.

I had an Iraq strategy meeting, and took them through what TB had said in his note and we discussed how we needed to do more on WMD education, e.g. the dossier, the need to communicate more what was happening on concealment. We had a good discussion about the basic distilled message, namely that the reason Iraq WMD was so important and linked to terror was because one day terrorists would get them. Then the John Reid/AC party meeting. Greg Cook [Labour polling expert] said we were at our lowest lead since TB became party leader and moving down on all issues and attributes. People seemed a bit down, but both JR and I made the point that we were in a remarkable position for a third term midterm. We had been defying gravity for too long. Then a discussion on the Lib Dems. I felt we were missing tricks in not going for them hard enough. JR still felt it best to leave them alone.

A lot of the day was taken up with the ricin issue. Since the arrests on Saturday, lots of tests had proved negative but there had been a Cobra meeting this morning which was told ricin had been found in Wood Green. Mike Granatt came to see me to say they had agreed to do a joint Met/Department of Health briefing while DB wanted to do a written statement to the House. I was fine with that, provided it was mainly all operational, police security story with some health backup. That was all agreed, but Mike called back two hours later to say DB had really gone against the idea of a police press conference because he worried they always went over the top. Instead he had agreed a joint Blunkett/Milburn statement. I felt it set a bad precedent, that ministers would have to go up on every potential terrorist situation. I called Milburn who was fairly relaxed, but agreed that if ministers were to do it, it should be to the House, and backed me. DB agreed provided there was no massive briefing around it.

We sorted the final version which went out at 3.15. Once it was out there, it was pretty much an all-day news sponge, which massively ate into the coverage which had been planned for TB's speech. Perhaps that was no bad thing in view of the fact following our overnight briefing of the speech, the US Embassy came on, alarmed at the way it was being presented as us trying to get them to broaden their agenda. I spoke to David Davies, and said I didn't rule the FA job out. He felt there was a way of doing it quietly if I went for it, which I doubted. We had a PMQs meeting on tomorrow being the first occasion for an earlier time. TB said if we had a decent Opposition, they really ought to be able to land some blows tomorrow. He said I must not discuss what he had said re GB yesterday with anybody. 'It can only happen when the waters are calm and it's least expected, and it must be a totally ruthless operation.' Like me, he had been shocked yesterday by Hilary saying, in front of civil servants and others, that GB was openly organising, and naming some of the people doing it for him.

Wednesday, January 8

Ricin enormous coverage. Up to the flat for PMQs meeting at 8. The new time slot of noon would change the rhythm of the day. We were expecting them to go on crime/burglary and the differences between Jack S and Geoff Hoon on Iraq, which was indeed what IDS did, though he was pretty crap. TB was still in pretty much of a rage about Derry and the burglary stuff, much more relaxed re GH/JS. I drafted him a note pre Cabinet tomorrow, saying that he had to reset the basic discipline and order, that there had been far too much thinking aloud, far too many politicians as commentators, and that we had to make clear again that the price of the privilege of serving in Cabinet was collective responsibility.

I had little input into PMQs, apart from one line, namely that what was one hundred per cent certain was that Saddam would be disarmed, as a way of getting round the slight problem Jack had given us with the percentage game. I made clear to the morning meeting that TB was pissed off both at the initial 40–60, also at Geoff's reaction and we had to get basic discipline back. We went over for PMQs and he successfully got up the public spending/cuts dividing line, then back to Number 10 and an amazing snowfall. TB, David Manning, Jonathan, Matthew Rycroft [private secretary, foreign affairs], Sally and I met to discuss Iraq. David was back from Oman and said he felt we had to give the inspectors more time now, but the US were impatient, felt the UN worked too slowly. TB said that if Blix found nothing, and the UN gave no specific sanction, it was going to be very hard to do. David said the Americans were very keen for a visit by TB at the end of the month. TB knew how difficult this was all going to be and felt we had to be out there fairly soon making the case, that it was only a matter of time before al-Qaeda get their hands on WMD unless we show how serious we are at dealing with the WMD issue.

TB was clear it was the right thing to do, and was on pretty good form, but also accepted there was not much support. Philip said to me later that there was next to no support for the war and the domestic agenda was in poor shape too. I had a meeting with Charles Clarke re some of his trickier issues. On student finance, he was confident it could be sold as an opportunity measure and we could get it done fairly quickly. He said he had been round to see the whole Cabinet one by one and that he had a lot of support, e.g. from Jack, Blunkett, Andrew Smith [Work and Pensions Secretary], Tessa, most of the others. The problem would be JP, because of the process, and GB because of the politics. But Charles was very confident, both about the arguments and the process. He was clearly a lot happier than when party chairman. He was also up for telling the NUT [National Union of Teachers] that no minister would go to their conference because they were not serious and did not properly represent teachers. Piers Morgan was apparently on *The World at One* describing Saddam as 'a benign dictator'.

Thursday, January 9

Very snowy, very icy, so ran in slowly. Iraq was running big with Blix to do 'minor' UN reporting today. The *Mirror* splashed on 'What is the point of Jack Straw?' The *Express* had a scaled-down version of the same thing, claiming to have been told TB had said Jack was extremely stupid re the 60–40 remarks and had authorised the Geoff Hoon attack. Even though TB was indeed pissed off, he did no such thing. Later GH apologised to TB, said he had just lost concentration and made a mistake. It was relevant to the Cabinet discussion. TB made the point that we were in much more difficult waters and that our opponents were constantly on the lookout for differences between us. He did a very tame version of the note I put to him suggesting he really lay it on the line and impose basic discipline. Instead, he said that we were a very tight and disciplined unit, but some resented that and we had maybe eased up a bit and got a bit lax. JP was a bit tougher, said there was simply no room for Cabinet ministers going out and giving their personal opinions and streams of consciousness. JP was very firm and very supportive but I could tell from the look on some of their faces, that they felt damage was being done to TB's authority by the fact it had taken John really to hit the message.

Then on Iraq, TB said that with Jack away in Indonesia, there was not much point in a major discussion and we wait till next week, yet he then allowed a discussion in which Clare accused Geoff and the MoD of briefing against Jack. She said she wanted a discussion of the military options because she did not believe that UK forces were needed. Yes they are, said Geoff. Well I don't think so, she said. Again,

TB just smiled rather weakly at her. I said to him afterwards that he had been really weak in there today, and his supporters left very pissed off. He just shrugged and looked irritated.

TB then had a very difficult conversation with GB re student finance. Charles was successfully winning round the Cabinet but GB was opposed and ready to move against by saying it was elitist because potentially it would punish the poorest first. He was making clear that TB could just plough on if he wanted, but he was adamantly against it. Charles was all bouncy and convinced he had cracked it, not knowing the depth of GB's determination to stop it. GB's view was that there was no real crisis in university funding, that it was just a way of them getting more money, and we didn't really need this big reform. Cabinet also had a very testy discussion on the Lords, Robin pushing at the 'democratic' end of things, JP, JR and DB very much against major reform that included an all-elected second chamber. Blunkett said we were sleepwalking towards constitutional gridlock which would stop governments doing the things they were elected to do and the public would give up on politics.

JR said we were not sleepwalking, but heading to disaster with our eyes wide open. Bruce said the reform and the make-up of the Lords was irrelevant without reform of the procedures, for example with no guillotine they could really screw us up. But again TB was not really directing the discussion so all we got was a collection of very different opinions. GB said next to nothing and left with Clare. Then to a meeting on health communications. We still lacked a clear top-line message. I was moving towards a 'personal NHS', also saying the statistics were hopeless for communications, which had to be rooted in the personal experience of patients. Milburn took me aside at the end, said people were getting really fed up of TB's tolerance of Clare in Cabinet. He said it was like having a bag lady in there just speaking out on everything.

TB saw Adams and McGuinness pm, then C came in. He told us that the Brits got on with Blix pretty well and we were a good buffer for the US, who were much less subtle. Blix knew that he was being 'cat and moused' but he was not on a mission. He was sure Saddam was lying but still felt he had to establish that for himself. C felt we had a better chance of finding the breaches than the US. TB, half in jest, said 'My future is in your hands.' The nightmare scenario, or one of them, was that there was a discovery that was sufficient for the US but not for us. C said the other risk was that we found the evidence of the breach before the US were ready to go to war. C felt that if the inspectors had another month with genuine access, the picture would be pretty clear. We were now pushing the line that they needed time and space to do the job.

I had a meeting with the Al Jazeera general manager and news editor who were over visiting the BBC. It was an interesting discussion. They did not appear overly hostile, but they said we had to face up to the fact that none of our arguments were really getting through to the Arab world at all. We were helped a little by the current row between TB and Israel over the Palestinian conference, but we were kidding ourselves if we thought our arguments were getting through at all. They said Gerard Russell was good and popular, but that they wanted and needed more access to ministers and military. They had been turned down for a facility on the [HMS] *Ark Royal*, which I sorted for them. They said we were not the US, and we should establish our own space. But nobody believed Saddam had WMD, or that he had any link with al-Qaeda.

Friday, January 10

The *Observer* sent me the magazine piece on me doing the marathon and Fiona went absolutely mental because of the ironing board being in the picture. God knows what that's all about. Crime figures – dreadful coverage, and there were the beginnings of the notion in the media that TB would get so fed up he would go. He was certainly pretty fed up and I went up to the flat just after 8. Cherie was there, much friendlier than before they went away, and neither of us mentioned those events. TB felt we had to make real changes. Even in front of the others now, he was talking about 'major reconstruction of the government', which was clearly code for GB. He also felt quite a few permanent secretaries should go. I said I felt he underestimated the negative impact upon him in looking weak as he had yesterday. He felt the problem was that the government was not sufficiently New Labour. We had defeated the hard left, but the instinct of most of them was to settle for that, not go much further, go for consensus politics with internal vested interests. That wasn't good enough.

We had a meeting – him, me, Jonathan, Peter H, Sally, Hilary C and Fiona – specifically to discuss him and his profile. Yet another discussion about how we reconnect him with the public. This couldn't be about gimmicks, initiatives so-called, and all the rest of it. It was about endeavour, constantly speaking the language of people's lives, but also being seen to be in charge and being seen to be on their side. It was yet another circular conversation of the kind we had been having for years. I said the question people were beginning to ask was whether he could change and do the on-your-side stuff in a way that broke through. He said that the big decision was whether to make the changes that would allow us to go for broke, but the truth was we could just end up with the 'broke' bit. He felt GB's game plan was to make him feel so miserable and paralysed that he would quit while he was ahead. But he was too strong to get rid of him right now.

Saturday, January 11

11.19 miles in. Ran round Islington, the Barbican, Embankment area and back up through town. There was a real sense of problems building up. Iraq obviously, with the party going offside, [anti-war] demo again, and the papers really hitting us on crime and public services. The *Telegraph* had a page 1 story headlined 'Campbell more spinned against than spinning', which spoke of a rift with TB and had a fair bit of accurate stuff, for example the row over the New Year's message, some of the background on Cherie/Foster. At first flush, it looked like Peter M's work, and there was a hint of that in their editorial looking forward to my leaving. Peter called later and said he thought it was probably Sally. My hunch was that it came from the Treasury. Peter M called and said I had to make it absolutely clear I was there for the long haul. TB called around 9 and said it was the usual lightning-conductor crap and nothing to worry about. We were going through a difficult period and it was far better we were seen talking about serious issues than the usual personality crap. We went over an outline script for Monday's press conference on the line of holding firm and sticking to our course. I was worried Clare would go off on one tomorrow so did a conference call with her and JR to go through the papers later. TB called again after returning from Germany [a private visit to Hanover]. He said the dinner with Schroeder had gone fine, but as the pressure grew on Iraq, the differences became more obvious.

Sunday, January 12

IDS was on *Frost* going for TB for 'wobbling' on Iraq. TB felt we just had to hold firm and take the difficult decisions needed. He said the Sunday papers were now beyond parody, not really worth bothering with, but that there would be a reckoning upwards before too long. We needed to decide whether to do a WMD dossier. He was in two minds about it, and so was I. John Scarlett told me on Friday he was keen, but the FCO less so because it gave rise to other difficult questions. TB was still going on about Derry's interview and said that of course, the liberal press would back him and therefore Derry would think even more he had done the right thing, when in fact he had given us a big problem with the public. He felt that on crime, Derry was not so much New Labour as Old Liberal. The *Independent* had a big story, including on page 1, on alleged concerns in the Civil Service about my diaries. The only person who had ever raised any such concern was GB, both with TB and Turnbull.

Monday, January 13

Clare Short's interview went pretty big as a combination of division/ warning to TB and the backdrop to the press conference was clearly Iraq. The tough question was whether there could be any military action without a second UNSCR. It was going to be difficult, lots of party in turmoil, diving polls stuff. The latest flurry about me was by and large confined to the *Guardian*, in which a minister was quoted as saying it was nonsense, and the *Mail* which did a full-page cocktail of bollocks, including yet another [Peter] Oborne piece saying that if I went it would presage the end of TB. There was a nice little leader defending me in the *Sun*. I texted [David] Yelland but then a bit later Rebekah [Wade] called to tell me she was the new editor and David was going to the US to do a business course.

At TB's Monday meeting, we were going round in the same circles. We just didn't have the necessary cohesion at the moment. PG did a very good note over the weekend identifying lack of trust, lack of a coherent narrative and lack of teamwork as our three big problems. I felt all the narratives in the world were not going to bring together the poor, weakened operation. Bruce [Grocott, Lords chief whip, Blair's former parliamentary private secretary] did me a note on the pros and cons of my leaving, said that the pros were all for me and the family, and all the cons were for others, especially TB. Tessa called, said she would do anything to support me, and to remember that if it hadn't been for me, we would not be in the strong position that we are. TB did fine at the press conference, no real news story, just pushing the line that we were backing the UN and we had to give the inspectors time. He also got up a good defence of tax rises.

He called later and said he had felt very strong at the press conference, felt that once we stood up to their arguments there was nothing much there. All that matters is making the right decisions. He felt that if we failed as a government, it would be because we were not doing enough fast enough, we were not being New Labour enough. I pointed out he still had to resolve GB. He said I can deal with that and if I have to I will. Dan Bartlett and I went over some of the projects they were engaged in.

They had similar but also different PR challenges, and the sense of the split between Powell and Rumsfeld was strong. They were also being criticised for not doing enough on North Korea because they were distracted on Iraq.

Six-mile run in, four-mile run home, sub eight-minute miles for the first time in ages. The press conference had done the trick in calming things down, and the Middle East conference was going far better than it might have done in terms of turnout and presence. GB was doing a tax credits launch and came out pretty hard for the line on Iraq. At John Reid's party meeting, we went over how to do the Tories on twenty per cent cuts, lines on the Lib Dems and a discussion of local elections slogan where we wanted the focus on crime and GB's people wanted schools and hospitals. JR was getting more and more confused about what we were meant to get out of these meetings. I had a meeting with Craig Reedie of the BOA [chairman, British Olympic Association], but my sense around the place was that we were moving away from supporting the [2012] bid. He gave me a big sell about the prospects of winning. I asked a fair few tough questions, and felt much more disposed to it afterwards than before, but I still felt it was going to be difficult to get Cabinet onside for it. Rebekah had gone to ground and the *Guardian* ran a line that she intended to be less close to us than Yelland. I did the conference call with the Americans, then fire, then diary meeting. Later to [broadcaster] David Frost's party. Lots of people I tapped for marathon sponsorship. A policeman was murdered in a terrorism operation in Manchester.[1] I made a few calls to get our response and handling agreed.

Got a cab in, ran home. Thirty-three minutes. The murder of the policeman in Manchester dominated the PMQs meeting at 8. It emerged that an asylum seeker who had had his case turned down was involved and so we assumed that would come out pretty quickly. The Tories were already on to the theme of border safety. As well as the obvious sympathy for the policeman and his family, TB was worried about the backlash, that this could be a tipping point re asylum and the public. We arranged for him to speak to the chief constable and also to write to the family. He had one of his regular

[1] Special Branch officer Stephen Oake had been stabbed in the heart by Kamel Bourgass, in a raid connected to the January 5 ricin raid. Bourgass received a life sentence for the murder of Oake and seventeen years for his involvement in the ricin plot.

sessions with the PLP, which went a lot better than it might have done, and which set us up for a much better than expected PMQs.

He filled me in on another bad meeting with GB yesterday re tuition fees. He felt GB's problem was that he saw everything through politics rather than life, so the child tax credit was a policy aimed at women, but actually showed a lack of understanding about how modern families work. I went back for a long meeting with David Wilkinson [Cabinet Office] and Bob Phillis [chief executive, Guardian Media Group], who was going to chair the GICS review. Bob felt, probably rightly, that I was not seeing Mike Granatt enough. David was very supportive, saying that I was expected by the PM and others to deliver strategy but didn't have all the levers. Mike had said I was on the bridge with TB when he was in the engine room. But I still felt it didn't really work.

At 5.15, TB, Jonathan, David, Sally and I went over to the MoD for a briefing on Iraq. CDS and all the other chiefs were there in uniform. We sat round three sides of the room. CDS said they expected Bush to make a decision for February 15 and they would go within twelve days or so to a massive air, sea and land operation. It was going to be called 'shock and awe', and the scale would reflect that. There would be hundreds of plane sorties from day one, aimed at wiping out his infrastructure and playing for a 'house of cards' effect. They went through where UK forces were most likely to be involved, taking out his defences close to the border. Substantial numbers of our ships and planes. A total of 42,000 UK forces possibly, 300,000-plus from the US. Then a slideshow briefing showed the scale of the attacks on the whole country, moving up to the capital. Oilfields were to be seized straight away, which, with the conspiracy theory about oil, would be difficult presentationally. [Admiral Sir] Alan West, ex-intelligence now naval commander [First Sea Lord], said there would be so much going on in the first day or so, that the international media would not know where to go.

TB pressed on whether Saddam would use chemical or biological weapons. They said they were buried so he might not be able to activate them quickly, but that was the reason [General Tommy] Franks had gone for the doctrine of overwhelming force. They believed Saddam was working on an assumption that it would be done by air strikes first, and then move in on land. It was interesting to see how much more fluent and confident Mike Boyce was in this setting. They knew the oilfield situation was difficult, and would require careful presentation. They said it was the right thing to do to prevent ecological disaster because Saddam might well go for blowing up his own oilfields as a way of causing chaos in the markets.

The planning was clearly well advanced, but it was still unclear whether the politics would allow any of it. But if this was going to happen as quickly as it seemed, TB said, then the work on aftermath questions had to happen now too. The intelligence people, including the defence guys, were pretty strongly of the view that Saddam would use WMD if he could. They warned of the inevitability both of civilian deaths and casualties of our own, but they felt in the initial attacks it was likely we would lose more through normal exercises than by being killed by Iraqis. They felt we would be able to strike very accurately but acknowledged the Attorney General might have difficulty in agreeing to some of the targets we would expect to hit. The scale of bombing meant that there were bound to be civilian deaths. TB also emphasised the need to get in place proper humanitarian support.

It was a pretty heavy-duty scene. It took place in the new MoD buildings, with everything very carefully laid out, typed name plates, tea and biscuits that nobody seemed to touch. On the way in, it had been like one of those scenes from darkly lit political thrillers where politicians and military and entourage are marching purposefully down a corridor, very little conversation, the only noise heels on floor, people walking too fast. It was pretty clear as we got into the cars and headed back to Number 10 that the Americans were going for this and TB had looked more nervous, particularly about the idea of UK military casualties and the possibility of large numbers of civilian casualties. It was pretty clear the Treasury were at it again. There seemed to be a pretty clear briefing against Charles' student finance proposals in *The Times* and against the Olympic bid in the *Guardian*.

Thursday, January 16

Jonathan's weekly meeting mainly on asylum and more 'why can't we just sort this out?' TB had met with front-line [Home Office] staff yesterday and regaled them with stories of people who were simply taking the piss in their attempts to come in, including the current fashion, which was to say they were from Iraq when they couldn't even speak the language. The main focus later would be the Iraq situation as Blix inspectors found shells and, though not yet public, notes of the nuclear programme. Stan Greenberg and Philip came in to do a presentation on polling. We were still seven points ahead, though the Tories did better on certain to vote. On the thermometer ratings, GB was slightly ahead of TB, while Bush was nestling between IDS and asylum seekers. When we briefed TB, his reaction was to say it could be a lot worse. We had been kicked about for months. The Cherie business had dominated pre-Christmas. On education we had been hit by the A-levels fiasco. Crime and asylum are gut issues that the people don't feel we get. And on Iraq, millions think we aren't listening. He said we have to win in Iraq and we have to be seen to be winning on crime and asylum.

Cabinet was fine. On Iraq, TB set out where we were. Trying to make the UN route work. Inspectors in there. Report back on January 27. He said the Russians were closer to the Americans than they say publicly, while the French do not particularly want to be left on the outside. But it was going to be tough. In the meantime, we build up the troops, and make sure that if it does come to conflict we are able to get it over quickly. Jack was pretty confident about the UN process, pointed out that a lot of people said we would never get a resolution in the first place but we did, on the strength of the case. Robin C said IDS had really sunk to a low point. He [RC] said we were in a tremendous position on the UN, 'thanks to you', he said to TB. He said the prospect of getting a second resolution was stronger if we do not rule out saying we may do it without one. One or two of them talked about the problem that Bush gave us with public opinion, but TB was clear we had to stay close publicly to maximise influence privately. There was a bit of criticism of communications strategy, with a feeling that because only two or three people were out there talking about it, the assumption was that the rest of the Cabinet were opposed.

At the end of the discussion JP did a very passionate wind-up. He said the discussion showed there was no real division 'so let's stop pretending there is'. He said the briefings and the 'talking out the side of the mouth' have to stop. He said the party doesn't like the idea of intervention but sometimes we have to make difficult judgements. If TB has the courage to put the case, we should get behind him and not give the press the opportunity to say there is division. Even Clare was reasonably measured. TB closed by setting out where he had asked for more work to be done, in three different areas – first, what offer we can make to the Iraqi people, e.g. re territorial integrity, lifting of sanctions, future prosperity; second, aftermath and the UN role in that; third, the unexpected and in particular the risk of WMD being used against our troops, or environmental catastrophe around oilfields.

John R left early to do the FPA briefing. TB was in a stronger place after a combination of the press conference, the PLP and PMQs. But the real discussion today came at the committee on the student finance review. Fourteen ministers there, with JP in the chair. Charles C put his case, and then a lot of the others expressed support. But then GB really laid into it, non-stop for twenty minutes, saying it was unfair, regressive, wasteful and not what the Labour Party was about. Charles gave as good as he got but was shocked when DB came in and backed GB. JP said it was clear they couldn't resolve it, it would have to be referred to TB who would have to decide. The whole thing had got very bloody. A lot of the things that GB said to TB privately were now coming out publicly for the first time, and the circle having been so wide, it was bound to leak soon. JP wanted to brief TB, said there were real differences and he would have to decide on the basic questions of fairness and the politics. TB was clear that GB was now really just on a mission to stall, paralyse, hold back. Charles then came in, really angry, said he had just told Ed Balls that he saw GB's intervention as a declaration of war. He told TB it was totally unacceptable behaviour and he should not allow it. GB was just trying to bulldoze his way to a solution that Charles strongly believed was wrong, and he felt TB had to stand up against him. TB headed off to [address Labour Party members in] Scotland after lunch.

I was working in the office when Charles called just after 4 to say that the details of the discussions had been leaked to the BBC. He was all a bit garbled and hyper but he wanted to go up and do a lobby briefing to put his perspective. I said he must be careful that this didn't just become a personality spat, but a serious issues-based analysis. I called JP who was in Milton Keynes. He agreed to Charles' briefing plan so long as it was treated as a genuine leak that he had to deal with, as opposed to the deliberate flaming of a row. When it came, it was actually not that bad for us. TB was reasonably calm about it. The storm passed fairly quickly before the news broke that Blix's people had found shells.[1] I spoke to Dan Bartlett and we agreed we would respond cautiously and let the media do the hoo-ha. Earlier, on the conference call, there was a pretty torrid row between Torie Clarke [assistant secretary of defense for public affairs] and Richard Boucher re next steps on the WMD debate, no doubt reflecting the argument going on higher up the food chain.

Friday, January 17

If it hadn't been for the UN inspectors' discovery of chemical shells, and TB meeting Blix today, the student finance row would have given us massive problems. Ian Austin claimed that the Treasury were really angry, that GB was furious that the discussions had been leaked, but nobody believed him. The fact that the *Guardian* was leading with a

---

[1] UN weapons inspectors had found eleven empty chemical warheads at the Ukhaidir depot, seventy-five miles south-west of Baghdad.

GB triumph, and that JP was wrongly stated as supporting him, left little doubt where it was all coming from. I had a long chat with JP who was outraged, and happy for us to let it be known he had not taken sides. He said GB had always operated like this and of course it was being put over as a pretty acute political problem between TB and GB. GB was setting himself up as the protector of the 'real' party interest. We chatted for an hour or so and he was clearly very onside at the moment, provided we kept in touch with him.

We did a conference call – TB, Jonathan, Sally, Godric and I – and 1. agreed we would say that we press ahead with publication next week, and 2. the arguments to put, namely that we had pretty much agreed everything, that universities could be able to charge more, that payment would not be upfront and the question was whether the individual paid back through future earnings or whether it was done through a collective pool. I did a visit to the CIC to get them better geared up on Iraq. OK but not brilliant. The FCO were not engaging as well as they had been. Later, Colin Powell said things would be clear in two weeks.

JP called me later, after I had gone to bed, said that he had spoken to GB after our conversation and things had to be resolved. The leaking of the discussions, and the nature of them even more so, had made it a very political issue and TB had to be supported. GB said to JP he intended to write something down overnight as a possible solution, and clearly wanted to calm it all down now. JP said he would talk to TB tomorrow. He was back in the referee role and clearly pretty fed up about it.

Saturday, January 18
Five miles on the treadmill, knee and ankle really bad. JP called again, said he had a pretty clear idea that GB had done the lion's share of the briefing. He said the problem we were getting into was that TB was worrying about legacy and GB only really cared about taking over and was frustrated the whole time. We had to get them to get their act together. Charles C put round an excellent note on the access issue, and the White Paper itself was in far better shape now. It also became public that the Blix inspectors had found nuclear papers which went pretty big.[1] We were in a much better place all round than a week ago, but it still wasn't great.

---

[1] 3,000 pages of documents detailing the process of producing enriched uranium had been removed from the Baghdad home of a leading scientist. The notes – on creating the substance using lasers – dated back to the 1980s.

Sunday, January 19

David Hill did us proud on *Frost*, plugging the *Observer* piece on the marathon and the [paper's] leader on Iraq. He was very nice about me, saying it was because I was good at my job that I was maligned. 'Agreed, agreed,' said Frost. Charles C was fine [on *Frost*] but he gave the figures people would have to pay back which was likely to cause a storm. There was a rash of dreadful asylum stories in the Sundays and DB decided to go on *The World this Weekend* to face them down. TB said he was looking forward to 'my reconstruction of the government'. He said he hadn't spoken to GB over the weekend and didn't intend to. He was simply not going to be halted any more, but it wasn't possible to do anything pre any action in Iraq. It was a terrible thing to say, he said, but he really did believe now that GB did not want him to succeed. Tessa came round later and said that when she finally got to see GB about the Olympic bid last week, she felt like she was being beaten up behind the bike sheds. He took her to bits, blaming her for getting the issue up in lights so that he would get the blame. She said he was so vile that even he recognised it and phoned her later to apologise.

Monday, January 20

Charles Clarke's interview on *Frost* had got up the issue of £21,000 and put TB in a total flap, made worse because during the day GB sent a long letter to members of DA [Cabinet Committee on Domestic Affairs] setting out objections, and a side letter to TB on the politics of it all and how we were 'getting it all wrong'. Andrew Adonis, Peter H and I went over to see Charles. You got the sense developing of something a bit personal between them, which we had to calm. Charles admitted that he had made a mistake on *Frost* by saying £21k. We needed to get over a message about opportunity and access and also spell out scenarios of how it would all work for different kids from different backgrounds. It also needed to be clearly in the box marked 'tough decisions', to which Charles added 'Like the euro, which he also wants to duck,' before laughing uproariously.

At TB's morning meeting he was seized about the whole issue, but also becoming increasingly worried about Iraq. The key question was what we did if and when the US went without the UN. There was a good response to the *Observer* piece [on AC's marathon run] and lots of cheques coming in now. TB felt that GB had effectively declared war and now intended to let him take the rope and put him out when nobody expected it, which is why he emphasised again that nobody said a word. He was in a total rage about asylum, felt the Home

Office just didn't get it. He was absolutely enraged by the fact that we kept pressing on this but it just didn't happen. We had a women's media reception, at which the women from the lobby were unbelievably aggressive towards TB, whereas the magazine editors were much more like human beings. Nice enough do, though. Then TB, CB, Fiona and I went off for dinner at DB's government flat at Eaton Place. David had been on at us for ages about wanting to return some of the dinners we had given him, and he was very proud of the house, the way he kept it, the way he managed on his own, though obviously he had help in for dinner. It was a bit of an odd evening though. Cherie, with me at least, was in a very odd, chilly mood and I reckoned relations with her were pretty well beyond repair. She was probably just responding to the fact that earlier we had tried to tone down her speech [to King's College Law School] for Thursday on children's rights. TB had said that if we thought there was a problem, and it needed changing, just change it, but she was not really up for listening. David was on OK form, though rather overdoing the host bit, while TB was being more serious than he might normally be at a social event, really wanting David's take on things. The conversation wasn't really flowing.

On student finance, I said nobody would believe that parents paid nothing if upfront fees went, because parents would feel responsible for the debts of their children. Cherie, perhaps not clocking the irony post Bristol flats, said she didn't believe that was the case. David seemed a bit ground down by the Home Office and by the crime and asylum agenda. He really never held back these days when complaining about the Civil Service, the lack of real grip and momentum, the difficulty in getting them to change their ways.

Tuesday, January 21

Five-mile run in, averaging 8.10 per mile. Up to see TB, really exercised about student finance now. He felt the exchange of [Cabinet committee] letters with GB had exposed the deep personal and political loathing coming from Gordon. GB was setting out a stack of objections in the policy, which he said was unfair and regressive and anti opportunity. He had spotted the way the *Mail* was going with it, £21,000 splash headline yesterday, and he was moving towards an argument that this was an attack on Middle England and therefore a political disaster. TB had a fair bit of time to prepare for his appearance at the [Commons select committee chairs] Liaison Committee. He kept coming back on the need to get together a proper political strategy on student finance. He wasn't clear we had it. I felt it lay in a mix of tough choices plus a dividing line on access. He feared the Middle England attack would really hurt, that there were just enough elements of the poll tax in this for it to be a disaster.[1]

He went off to the Liaison Committee, where he tried to get up the message that Saddam was weakening, also did lots on counter-terrorism. I had an OK meeting of the Iraq strategy group. There had been a discovery of lots of al-Qaeda documents seized in Afghanistan. One of the SIS guys felt there was more in there about a potential al-Qaeda link with WMD. We also had a discussion about what if anything we could do to build a better image for Bush and in particular break down the European hostility towards him. There was no doubt that though he was different to the caricature, as the main message-carrier he really hurt us. The conference call was a bit all over the place. I was trying to get a proper discussion going about oil, whether in fact we take on the argument about it all being about oil by saying that in part it is, because of its importance to economic stability, but it just wasn't the forum for a proper strategic discussion. We did however have a bit of proper discussion on Bush, where they needed to know the depth of the problem they had in Europe.

After TB came back, we had a long meeting on student finance, GB now trying to take out the proposal that they also be charged interest on the debt. TB was now demanding to see all the research from all the different systems round the world, also the comparisons between our richest and poorest universities. Then a meeting on the Olympics, where TB and I both made the point that we didn't seem to have the firm basis on which to make a decision. TB wanted clear advice but people were blowing hot and cold not according to hard fact and analysis. Tessa had definitely moved towards yes, others had moved away. The worry I sensed was that we would say no simply because it was easier than saying yes, and then regret it.

Then over to Derry's at the Lords to launch my appeal for marathon sponsorship. It was Derry's idea to hold it there, and it paid off with a terrific turnout, including some big cheques at the end of it. Dickie Bird [former cricket umpire] was an absolute hoot and ended up going back on the train with Mum, talking loudly all the way back about how much he liked TB, me, the government, etc. David

[1] The Community Charge, or poll tax, was a system of local government funding that moved away from the rateable value of property and placed a blanket levy on individuals. It was introduced by Margaret Thatcher's government in 1989 in Scotland and 1990 in England and Wales. It provoked significant anger, even leading to riots. Thatcher had chosen to front the policy herself. Her stridence on the issue contributed to her political demise.

Sainsbury [science minister and party benefactor], John Browne [businessman], David Frost, good turnout from News International and *Mirror* old and new. TB popped in and didn't look all that comfortable being photographed with me, and I sensed he was a bit bemused about how big the whole thing was going, he probably found it a bit odd when he wasn't the absolute centre of attention. Tessa, Peter M, Jackie Stewart [former racing driver], Trevor Beattie [advertising executive], Tony Ball [BSkyB chief executive] and his beautiful wife Gabriela. Did a little speech about John [Merritt], Lindsay and Hope.[1] Fiona and I found it a bit stressful but the kids were great, and we hoovered up not just cheques but some terrific auction items as well.

Wednesday, January 22

Cab in, but ran later, eight miles, after seeing Mel Cash, a physio who had been recommended, and who spends a lot of his time doing ballet dancers. Tuition fees and asylum were TB's big concerns pre PMQs. For once, he had watched last night's *Ten O'Clock News*, saw GWB saying he was sick and tired of the line, a clear message that he was losing patience with the UN, and they had pretty much decided it was going to happen and that was that. He felt there had definitely been a change in mood and it was pretty bad, and in addition the Franco-German forty years love-in today was more than symbolic, but also carried substance.[2] Stephen Wall had done an interesting note on it. TB read it, said what it means is that the French will get Schroeder into a basic anti-American camp, which is why Bush needs to do more to make it an international coalition.

Sally [Morgan] and I banged on at him again about the need to get them on a broader international route and even he, today, was saying how tough the situation was. He sensed that the inspectors would not necessarily come out with what was needed for absolute clarity, so we would have to face the prospect of going in without a UNSCR. Chirac was making it clearer than ever that he would be against war come what may, even with a smoking gun.

The anti-war mood was definitely growing and I raised it on the US conference call and pointed out the difficulty it was causing. It

[1] John Merritt, Campbell's closest friend, had died of leukaemia in 1992, as had his daughter, Ellie, six years later. Merritt's widow, Lindsay Nicholson, and Hope, their surviving daughter, attended the launch of Campbell's marathon run, which would raise funds for Leukaemia Research.

[2] At a press conference marking the fortieth anniversary of the Franco-German post-war friendship treaty, Jacques Chirac and Gerhard Schroeder announced their decision to co-operate against a US-led invasion of Iraq.

led to a rare proper discussion. I said they were going through all the gears for their domestic audience, and saying what Bush said yesterday, that gave us problems over here. Tucker [Eskew, White House media affairs], [Richard] Boucher and [Anna] Perez [now spokeswoman for Condoleezza Rice] all asked, genuinely as opposed to in irritation, what we felt they should do. I said it was back to the big picture about the UN standing up for itself, him being the guy that went the UN route, but are we serious or not? David also spoke to Condi to say the politics had got a lot harder and they had to be more sympathetic to international issues, pressures, concerns.

Dan Bartlett called and we spent half an hour or so kicking it around. We faced the same danger we had had re Kosovo and Afghanistan, namely moral equivalence, this time between US and Iraq. Dan realised they had a problem and wanted to do something. I was very frank, but he took it well enough. Condi told David that Bush wanted to spend some of the dinner discussing communications. Sally said to TB if we didn't take real care, this was the end of him. So far as the PLP was concerned, there had to be UN support, and they had to see real evidence. TB was pretty clear though that we couldn't peel off from the US without very good reason.

The other problem today was [Robert] Mugabe [President of Zimbabwe]. Unbeknown to me, on Christmas Eve Jack Straw had got TB to agree we would try to do a deal with France re EU sanctions on Mugabe.[1] He would come to the France–Africa summit in exchange for France agreeing rollover sanctions so that he didn't come to the EU Africa summit. I tried to get TB to look at it again, but he felt the other Europeans just didn't care enough about it. At the PMQs meeting, he was back raging about Civil Service performance, particularly re asylum. He was pretty poor. He then stayed in for Charles' statement on tuition fees, which he didn't feel had sufficient political message. He didn't feel we had set the expectations right. I worked on his speech for tomorrow and got Matthew Doyle [Labour Party press officer] out briefing the line that reform is the key. The message was becoming tired though. Godric came back from the afternoon lobby, having had a real hard time over Zimbabwe, because we had learned by then that TB and Jack having done a deal with the French on it, Clare [Short] and [Peter] Hain were both on record saying it was wrong.

[1] Though no agreement had been reached, France was pushing for EU travel sanctions against Mugabe to be eased to allow him to attend the Franco-African summit in Paris.

Thursday, January 23

Six-mile run with Hugh Jones. At Jonathan's meeting, we agreed now was the time to motor on the big argument on student finance. Charles C was up for it, but stupidly pulled out of *Dimbleby* [ITV]. I was really annoyed at the Mugabe decision, it was realpolitik at its worst and I was amazed that Jack had signed up to the deal. Robin was now lobbying hard against. Jack was in the US seeing Powell. We persuaded TB he would get absolutely fucked over and why on earth were we helping out the French like this? TB said his recollection was that Chirac was going to ask Mugabe, otherwise the others would not come, and then get TB to veto it. TB said he was OK with that, but Anna Wechsberg's [private secretary, foreign affairs] note on their chat didn't say that. TB had scribbled on it and his note was misinterpreted as going hard for the deal. He wanted Jack now to unravel it.

At the political strategy meeting, Philip said we needed more simple messages. TB asked Douglas, John Reid and me to put together a strategy paper focused on outcomes, and also wanted us to get a grip of a crime and asylum communications strategy. The recent [focus] groups had been poor, disconnected, not delivering, trust a problem, crime and asylum really bad, only the economy really accepted as doing OK. Cabinet was pretty low-key, Iraq, most people treading water before tomorrow's political Cabinet. Good stuff on the marathon front, *The Times* wanting a column on the build-up in exchange for cash for the fund, ten grand from Gavyn Davies [BBC chairman]. TB lunch with Bertie Ahern, cooked by Jamie Oliver [TV chef]. I was just trying to plough through paperwork as they talked over where we were with the IRA. They were still thinking it was possible for a big-bang solution to end the IRA.

I left early for Rory's parents' evening. He was doing well but apparently talks about Manchester United too much. Ken Clarke on *Question Time* came out against our [Iraq] policy and said we were the fifty-first state of America. I called TB to make sure he knew. He said there was no doubt we were going to go through a bad phase, be more unpopular, but we were doing the right thing and would come through it. At our best when at our boldest, etc.

Friday, January 24

Ran in, thirty minutes. Brief meeting with Douglas on the draft communications plan we had worked up on asylum. The *Today* programme had an Iraq story about chemical weapons which went OK, and we didn't overdo it. Probably came from the CIA. One of those days when there was too much stress and pressure, too many things to deal with. Cabinet was pretty poor in terms of the discussions. TB flat, GB a bit tired, Milburn and Reid probably the best contributions. JP strong re discipline but also saying we needed more Cabinet committee discussion on policy. Clare offside, the rest pretty average. Hysterical moment at the start. Someone in the previous meeting had broken the back of a chair. JP carried it round to where GB sat and said 'Let's see if he notices, and let's see if he laughs.' He didn't want me to change it back, said leave it, and let's see what happens. When GB came in, JP was watching to see how he reacted. He sat down, the broken piece fell away and again he showed himself pretty much incapable of laughter.

TB said we were strong on the surface but get beneath it and on the issues – Iraq, crime, asylum, public service delivery – we faced a lot of problems. He felt now was the time to be facing up to the tough decisions, not ducking them. The background, Iraq and tax rises coming in, would make it difficult, and we were in for a testing time. GB said they were the biggest tax rises ever under Labour, £12 billion, and we faced a number of important economic challenges. He warned fifteen per cent of the extra money would go on public sector pay. We just had to defend the tax rises for health. He felt taxes were now set at the right level, and we could campaign against the Tories on cuts. He said the main theme running up to the Budget is modern prosperity for all. He went into no detail, said it would go through an economic subcommittee. He felt we needed to decide department by department the key achievements of the government. And on the euro, he emphasised the comprehensive nature of the tests.

Jack pointed out that we were coming up to six years in power and we were still more popular than past Labour governments. They failed because of division and lost momentum. JP said it should be possible to discuss and debate policy differences without Cabinet committees becoming a battlefield. Honest debate is good, division and briefing is bad. Milburn felt we were losing trust and momentum. He felt we were being protected by the uselessness of the Tories and politics would be transformed if they got a half-decent new leader. He felt that would help because it would challenge the massive sense of complacency in the PLP. He said we needed a course to stick to but we need the political sense of purpose. Charles on tuition fees, Alan on foundation hospitals, Andrew Smith on welfare reform, we had to tie it together around our values. 'We have thousands of administrators, but we are the politicians and we have to lead, get back to locating policy and values.' He felt the Tories were trying to place us as big state, and the values of public service were the answer to that. He said that Blunkett had the most difficult job in government and that crime and asylum were not just his issues, they were health issues, education issues, housing issues, and we need to restructure government systems to recognise that. Margaret [Beckett] said virtually everyone who came to her surgery last time was an asylum seeker. Peter Hain diddled a bit, said he wasn't advocating jettisoning New Labour, but said we had to accept we weren't new any more, do a better job at talking to party and public.

Helen [Liddell, Scottish Secretary] said she felt there was a corrosive sense of division and self-indulgence. Cue Clare. She said the record of the government was fine, but the style and presentation damaged us and the PLP was troubled. JR said the basic narrative – strong economy, fairness, public services, rights and responsibilities, Britain strong in the world – is still a strong one for us, and does relate to our values. The PLP was a problem because too many of them do not get the narrative and yet they are an important messenger. TB said that we could win on jobs, health and education. We couldn't win on crime and asylum, but we can lose on them and we have to deal with them or pay a big price. But it was a basic tough-decision message, if not put over terribly energetically. A pretty desultory discussion re the Olympic bid with Tessa in favour but far from clear where the rest of the Cabinet were, and a real lack of clarity about whether we thought we could win.

On Iraq, TB was due to speak to Bush and sent through a note in advance. He was clear that so far as international political support was concerned, we did not have it without Blix finding a smoking gun and we needed more time. His proposal was to give them another month during which Blix would do two more reports. He was sure that in time we could turn opinion. Bush was pretty clear there would have to be a war, because he did not believe Saddam would ever comply, or that the inspectors would ever be allowed to do the job. As TB said, this was Bush in a different mode. They have very different problems to us. We are getting criticised for being too gung-ho. They are criticised for not being gung-ho enough. Condi explained Bush was going down in the polls because he was keeping the troops out there too long. TB and I felt it was more likely he was getting hit because he was not winning support for going without the UN. TB, who was wearing shorts and tennis shoes and about to go to the gym, was a bit taken aback. Also the Saudis were saying that the US didn't need a second resolution, and were saying something different to us.

TB wasn't terribly amused by Jonathan's characterisation of his current position, as set out in his note, as 'wobble and delay instead of shock and awe'. TB was confident we could get Bush to the position where he stayed long enough for a second UNSCR. There was also a real danger the Attorney General would resign if he thought the plan was disproportionate force. He was clear with the Cabinet it was important to stay with the Americans, and emphasise that closeness as a way of influencing the debate there, and he wanted to do a big pre-Camp David diplomacy round. He set out what he saw as the political and other realities. He felt Bush deserved praise for showing strength in forcing Saddam to the position of getting the inspectors in, but said we didn't have enough international support and we needed time to build it. He was also clear with Bush that not only did he not have support in the country but as things stood he couldn't really call on a majority in his own Cabinet. He set out the case for delaying military action to give the inspectors more time, during which it would be clear they were being obstructed. Blix would report two or three times up to March, which would almost certainly show they were not being given full co-operation, and meanwhile we would carry on the military build-up and meanwhile build diplomatic and public support and get Arab leaders to push hard for Saddam's removal. He still believed it would be possible to get him out without war, but the option had to be there, and the threat had to be real.

It was a very well-made, carefully constructed argument that made sense and it was clear Bush had read it. When I asked TB if he thought Bush had basically decided there was going to be a war, TB said if that call was anything to go by, pretty much. He remained hopeful he could keep things on a multilateral track but it was not going to be easy. He was facing a very tough call indeed, about as tough as they get.

Saturday, January 25

Sixteen-mile run with Hugh, steady then slow. [Bill] Clinton was in town and explicitly told TB something I felt already, namely that Bush was not winning support for his strategy because people in the States felt it was a political strategy dreamt up by Karl Rove [senior adviser to Bush], not a principled foreign policy. We put together TB's briefing for *Frost* and in particular on asylum where he wanted to signal change to our obligations under the UNHCR [UN refugee agency] and ECHR [European Convention on Human Rights]. He felt, particularly on the back of the BNP win in Calderdale, that we had to get a grip of this and be seen to get a grip.[1] He was worried that

[1] The far-right British National Party had won a council by-election in Calderdale, West Yorkshire, pushing Labour into third place.

DB had too much on his plate and was unable really to crack it. He was in no doubt that we had to toughen our approach and he intended to send out a very strong signal. On Iraq, he was clear about the message, that we had to set out a pre-Blix positioning, to show that the onus was on Saddam.

On the Olympics, TB was warming to the idea. We had received a whole stack of handwritten letters from some of the athletes, and it definitely had an effect on him. He now felt it was the right thing to do but we would see where the Cabinet flowed on it. Then to Brentford vs Burnley with Neil [Kinnock], Calum and Charlie [Enstone-Watts, Calum's friend]. We didn't deserve to win but took all three chances. Good day. Back for [Fiona's mother] Audrey's birthday party, mainly talking about Iraq with Glenys [Kinnock] and Lindsay [Nicholson]. Lindsay had written me a really nice letter after the event on Tuesday, saying she couldn't have got through everything without me and Fiona, that John always worried about me but if he had seen me on Tuesday he would have stopped worrying, that the persona there on Tuesday night was my political and personal beings coming together as a whole, saying this is what I am, and if the breakdown was the low point, now I have planted a flag on the summit of recovery. Kind of how I felt, and a really nice letter.

Sunday, January 26

Up before 7 and in to see TB to go over all the running stories pre *Frost*, and agree messages on Iraq, Zimbabwe, asylum, GB/TB. He was, despite the real difficulties we faced, much more confident. Strong on tuition fees, very good on Iraq and asylum, and generally empathetic with pumping out message. His body language on GB was not great, but he didn't mind that. He didn't much like the way the press were presenting the TB/GB situation as six of one and half a dozen of the other. As Neil had put it, it was more like three of TB and nine of GB's lot. I went back with him, and did a conference call with Tom and the press team and agreed we would push out more intelligence on concealment and push in certain quarters the idea of radical action on asylum including looking at the ECHR.

Most people I spoke to seemed to think TB did fine, some that he was back to his best, which was probably overstating it. Neil and Steve Kinnock were at home when I got back, dropping off Grace who had been staying with them, and Neil said something interesting, that TB always seemed more comfortable when he was defending something thought to be unpopular. News-wise, the interview ran fine but our problem was that GWB seemed hell-bent on war and we looked like we were doing things from a US not UK perspective. TB was talking about going to Spain and Italy to show that Europe was not just France and Germany. During the afternoon I spent hours signing Leukaemia Research letters to appeal for funds.

Monday, January 27

Clocked up close on forty-five miles last week, did ten today. *Frost* came out as a mix of Iraq in most of the heavies, with the briefing on intelligence going well, ECHR in the right-wing papers but lots of doubt as to whether we would do it. TB cancelled his morning meetings and called in experts and lawyers from the Home Office and the Attorney General's office and spent literally five hours non-stop being taken through the system from start to finish. At the end of it, it looked even worse than when we started. As Jonathan said, it was like the NI peace process in that every time you thought you had it sewn up, you could pick a thread and pull it for miles. The only interruption he allowed during the five hours was an 'encouraging' Putin call in which it was clear Vlad was really losing patience with Saddam. Despite yesterday people were still applying the yardstick that the inspectors would have to find WMD rather than simply that Saddam had to co-operate.

On Zimbabwe, Liz Lloyd [policy adviser] was blaming me for getting us into a different position, she hadn't felt the original deal was defensible. I was up to £76,000 on the marathon front, and today I finalised my deal with *The Times*, also cheques in from Sarah Brown and Sinead Cusack [actress]. The *Sun* was getting a lot worse on asylum. There was a piece by [Trevor] Kavanagh which DB condemned as racist. Rebekah [Wade] came on about that. She had just had her weekend with Murdoch getting her orders. I said she was being totally irresponsible by inflaming asylum as an issue and pretending there were simple solutions when there were not. It was pretty clear she was going to be difficult, probably more difficult than she actually wanted to be. Blix came out at 3-ish and it was OK. It made clear that Saddam was not really co-operating.

Probably the most noteworthy meeting of the day was when Ed Balls came to see me at 3.30. No small talk. I asked him what he intended to do to help get TB/GB on a better footing, because things are really bad and a lot of it is down to their modus operandi. I told TB I was seeing him and he agreed I should say he had never imagined fighting three elections, that he had always imagined he would hand over to GB during this term but that GB would not have that conversation. He felt that GB did not want to work with him, particularly on public service reform and the euro, and the relationship had become – my word – dysfunctional. Ed agreed it was bad and dangerous. As so often before, their view was that Peter M was responsible for a lot of the bad stuff that appeared in the media. I dismissed that. He talked about the coverage today as if we had planned it deliberately. He insisted there were people around TB who saw GB only as a problem.

I said it was only happening because the relationship between the two of them had become more dysfunctional. If they worked together, and JP was on board with them, we could do pretty much anything, but it simply wasn't happening. The meetings were dreadful. The so-called strategy discussions weren't strategic. He said GB felt that TB was tolerating and even promoting factionalism, as with foundation hospitals – for which again he blamed Peter M as well as Milburn – and now top-up fees. GB profoundly disagreed with the policy. There had been no strategy for its preparation. We didn't need it. It was right wing and would give us a problem right up to the election. GB just couldn't understand why we were doing it.

I said TB felt that GB believed he could do the top job better, that he now neither liked nor respected TB, and that made it hard to feel they could work together. It would be a lot harder to help him get the job if he thought he was being pushed out. Ed said that GB of course wanted to be PM but it was nonsense to say he had an operation to achieve that or that he was trying to undermine TB or his legacy. He said I only heard TB's side of the story. I said maybe if GB spoke a bit more, that wouldn't be so. He intimated, and later said outright, that GB was offended before the last election, and afterwards, because TB was making clear that his departure was conditional on GB saying yes to the euro and us going in. It sounded to me like a line they were developing in the event of GB being forced out.

I said between us we ought to be able to do something to improve things because what was happening now was mutually destructive. He said that he had offered regular meetings with me but he sometimes felt I didn't think he was senior enough. I said no, we just do different jobs. I would like to have better relations and of late I've had no relationship with GB at all, and that is his choice. I said I felt he was playing a dangerous game placing himself to the left of TB, to which he retorted that it was TB who was placing himself to the right, with some very Tory policies. I said he always wanted to be cutting edge, but before they had been able to do it together and that is what we had to get back to. I said they had to cure themselves of their obsession with Peter. He said I was blinding myself to the obvious, that Peter was wreaking revenge on all of us.

He denied they had an operation and said there was no way the Labour Party would ever allow someone who was disloyal to be made leader, so it would be crazy for GB to do that. He had genuine policy and strategy differences. He couldn't believe that TB had not replied properly to his note on tuition fees. We agreed we had to get back on a proper TB/GB footing, and he and I would mull over how. We had had a proper frank discussion for the first time in a while, and both had shared analysis if not entirely shared views about how to address it. Then to see TB who was still talking about asylum, even more worried after a meeting with some of our MPs who had told him it was raging. His big worry was that it was going to turn the country against us.

Tuesday, January 28

Blix had changed the dynamic a little but it was still very difficult. TB was pretty well geared up for the US trip but realised we were in a very tight spot. We got up the idea of 'material breach' [of obligations under UNSC resolutions] which Jack did today, and later at the press conference. We really had to motor on Blix, get out lots of material about what it meant, the potential capability of the materials he was talking about. The morning meeting was a lot chirpier than recently, though asylum continued to be really grim, particularly in the *Sun*, where Kavanagh was now clearly driving the policy of the paper, hard, in a pretty inflammatory way.

I had a long chat with Dan Bartlett re Bush's State of the Union address. David Manning had a couple of difficult calls with Condi because they were getting really impatient now. TB felt that there would be more Blix reports revealing greater non-cooperation, and then there would be much more solid international opinion. But they [the US] were clearly growing tired of waiting, already felt they had bowed to us on this and now they were going to be hard to persuade. TB and I agreed that probably what made us most angry was that they were doing the right thing but in the wrong way. Another good Iraq strategy meeting. At least we were using these meetings to develop proper strategic message, on Islam, outreach, oil. The SIS guys were very good on this, John Scarlett a bit more cautious. But everyone seemed to think we were heading for war, and it was only a question of how and when. We had got hold of all the Iraqi 'lines to take' and when I said they weren't great, one of the SIS guys said that Iraq lacked meetings like this.

I saw Philip, told him about my meeting with Balls. He said I had to get a grip or TB was going under. He had noticed I was more detached and assumed that the marathon was part of an exit strategy, raise my profile then get out. I said maybe it was a strategy to keep me in, give myself other challenges that weren't just the ones that did my head in here. He said I had to imagine what it would have been like five years ago if we were in this state – you would be motoring, working out plans, getting people going, firing them up, really going for it. We were tired and worn down. He felt we used the TB/GB thing as an excuse not to motor. There was something in what he was saying.

Balls sent me an email saying that Gordon had been 'encouraged' by our meeting and should we do the same next week. Yes. I put to TB what Ed had said about the euro being a condition of succession. TB said 'That's a lie. He always says that. He says to me, so are you saying you won't go unless I do the euro and I say no, I'm not, I'm saying that I'm entitled to be able to have an honest conversation with you about it.' I asked if he thought it was worth it me trying to develop relations with Ed to put something political back together again. He said yes, but it must be on the basis that whilst we must discuss everything, ultimately he must be allowed to decide. Also they have to get over their paranoia that we are somehow responsible for anything bad that appears about him in the press. He felt Ed's claim that they didn't have an operation was ridiculous. He felt GB was worried, now realised that TB might just dare to move him. 'I know what I have to do. If I don't do it, I won't get the job done in the way I have to do it. This is the key to reconstruction and renewal.'

TB spoke to Chirac later and Chirac was doing his usual high-falutin' stuff, lots of blather. At one point, TB held up the phone with his hand over the mouthpiece, turned to me and said 'I can't be bothered with this any more. Bullshit.' He talked to John Howard [Australian Prime Minister], who was really worried we wouldn't get a second resolution. Then to [Costas] Simitis [Greek Prime Minister], who was hopeless and totally with the French. [Peter] Foster deported.

Wednesday, January 29

Having tried to develop a better relationship with Ed, the first test came today with the *Telegraph* front page, saying GB was constantly asking TB to step aside. GB/Ed wanted us to issue a total denial. I said that was difficult because TB was clear to me that it had happened often enough. Ed said not. I also said TB had disputed their version of events re the discussion on the euro, that he never linked the idea of the job to this or any other policy. Ed was sceptical. We agreed to be totally dismissive of the *Telegraph* story. PMQs meeting was largely about asylum. TB felt he had been right to deliver the signal he did on *Frost* and wanted to signal more now. For obvious reasons, Iraq was worrying TB more and more. He wasn't sure Bush got just how difficult it was going to be without the second UNSCR, for the Americans as well as us. Everyone TB was speaking to, including the tough guys like [John] Howard, was saying they needed a second resolution or they wouldn't get support. TB felt that was the reality for him too, that he couldn't deliver the party without it. David was in the US today and saw Condi for three hours to go over the whole scene, tried to make her see that rushing our fences was not sensible, stating in terms that TB would not be able to deliver Cabinet or Parliament as things stood. We did however have a rare, for these times, PR hit in the form of an article signed by, eventually, eight European leaders about standing alongside the US in standing with us for Resolution 1441 [on the return of inspectors to Iraq].

I had a long chat with Dan Bartlett re the European signed article and also going over what we hoped to get out of Camp David. I was trying the whole time to get over to them just how bad the politics were. TB really exercised at the moment, said he sometimes wondered if they really got it at all, spelled out some of the risks of going without a resolution. 'What on earth do we say or do if something goes wrong, which it's bound to, e.g. there's nothing to stop Saddam killing kids and saying it was us.' He was gearing up to be very frank with Bush. He had an OK meeting with [Silvio] Berlusconi [Italian Prime Minister], full of the usual flouncing.

Thursday, January 30

Matthew Rycroft, Danny Pruce and Steve Morris [Number 10 officials] had done a terrific job on the *Wall Street Journal* article which was leading the news, and lots of the other papers followed up. But the build-up to Camp David was going to be tricky. The sense was that the US were totally decided and we just had to go along with it. I did the morning meeting, and chatted with the SIS guys re the report on Iraq's infrastructure of concealment. Lots of meetings with TB, first on asylum. He was worried by DB at yesterday's meeting, felt he had been floundering a bit, was just raging at people, not clear what the plan was. CDS, GH, JS and JP came in for a meeting re Iraq. Jack said several times TB had to make clear we couldn't do it without a UNSCR. He also felt that the Attorney General would not let us hit most of the 'shock and awe' targets because he would feel disproportionate force was being applied. The politics of all this were dreadful.

CDS warned that he was worried the Americans felt they would be seen as liberators. It just wasn't so. They would be resented. We went through the strategy for the next phase. [Colin] Powell's speech to the UN, then the next Blix report, TB clear that he wanted to try to get GWB to a second UNSCR, clearly getting the message that we couldn't do it without one. He felt we needed two or three Blix reports, and more time for Arab leaders to push Saddam out. Even Geoff, much more than before, seemed worried, telling us that Rumsfeld was saying inside the administration that the problem with the UN route was that it was open-ended, that other countries just used the process to ensure nothing ever happened. JP and I exchanged very worried looks.

The Iraq discussion in Cabinet was a bit scratchy. Jack said the Blix report was pretty devastating for the regime, and it covered missiles that were banned, weaponised VX [toxic nerve agent]. Clare said we were losing the public because people thought the Americans were hell-bent on war. TB was clear that his role was to pull the Americans into the right position re the UNSCR. GH said 1441 changed the terms of the debate. Clare and JR snapping at each other, Clare having a go and John saying why was it she could say what she liked but if anyone said anything she disagreed with, all she could do was heckle. Robin chipped in to support Clare. Robin was very spiky, in part perhaps because he was sulking over TB and the Lords yesterday.[1] Then JP on fire, making clear he didn't favour anti-strike legislation. GB said the unions had been totally behind the curve. He said the trade union movement does not understand what is happening to it out in the country. 'There's a shock,' said TB, to laughter.

Then a discussion on the Olympics. Jack reported on the committee meetings so far, the £2.6 billion estimated costs, the rise in London council tax, some of the pros and cons. JP said we were more experienced than we were at the time of the Dome but what was absolutely essential was that if we went for it, we all went for it, that there could be no division on this. He was broadly positive. When he mentioned the Dome, Clare chipped in 'Most of us were against it,' and he gave her one of his snorts. TB said he was struck by how pro the London MPs were. Nobody was saying go for it irrespective, but we had to pin the details down. GB said, very finance director-ish, that it would be desirable to go ahead if the finances are sustainable. DB was

[1] To Cook's chagrin, Blair had said the true options on Lords reform were either a wholly elected or wholly appointed House of Lords. He told Labour MPs 'I personally think a hybrid between the two is wrong and will not work.'

sceptical, Paul Murphy [Northern Ireland Secretary] pro. TB had to leave halfway through to take a call from Bush, from which he returned looking very worried. Overall the Olympic discussion was more negative than I thought it would be. Tessa pro, Charles pro, GH pro, Alan M basically pro. Lots of yes-buts, but the buts were very heavy, particularly on finance, with Andrew Smith and [Alistair] Darling both very clear no's. John R very opposed. JP less sceptical than before.

It was snowing as we set off for Madrid [for talks with Spanish Prime Minister José María Aznar, en route to Washington]. On the plane, TB worked on a new note on strategy for Bush. He was clear in his own mind about policy and strategy, but worried Bush would not go for it. David [Manning], back from the US overnight, reported they were really impatient with the UN. TB saw his challenge as persuading Bush that it was in America's interests to stay with the UN. He felt it would be total madness not to, and he was right, but it was not going to be easy. He was aiming to persuade Bush to wait till the middle or end of March and support a second resolution before action. He went through it all in his note, the military, the diplomatic, the propaganda questions, plus early planning on aftermath. Very simple lines and questions that we had to get answers to.

He was worried after the phone call today because Bush sounded much more frustrated re the UN, definitely listening more to those saying he had to go for it. He wanted to be able to take him to one side and go through the whole thing. They may not like it, but Blix was the key, and they had to see that. They couldn't just bully here. Blix had to get the evidence of non-cooperation and we had to get the argument round to non-cooperation being a breach, but we needed two or three Blix reports to get that. He also emphasised that the 'other agenda' was important, particularly MEPP. He had pretty much given up on Schroeder as being opportunistic, felt that Chirac was going to use whatever happened to do us in, so was keen to build up the other Europeans, hence off to see Aznar.

Landed, helicopter to Moncloa [palace], meeting then press conference, then back on to the plane for the flight to the States. TB was now focusing his mind on crunching down the arguments. He said this is the toughest spot yet. I have to persuade him to stay on the UN route. He wrote another note, said that Blix could put down questions, report on February 14, then again on February 28. If co-operation gets harder and harder to achieve, by March 5 we declare Iraq in breach and maybe go for another UNSCR. We give the Saudis ten days to mobilise Arab opinion to get rid of Saddam. March 15, military action. He then laid out the potential problems on the way

– e.g. Saddam uses WMD, attacks Israel, destroys oil wells, or there is major civil unrest. He went through the aftermath questions, organisation of humanitarian aid, role of the UN. On propaganda, Powell at the UN, the history of Iraqi non-cooperation. The WMD threat more generally, the link to terrorism, the growing worries in the intelligence. They have to understand that Blix is key – I lost count of the number of times he said it during the flight. We were also feeling the beginnings of the global split, Chirac trying to get a little group going of France, Germany, Russia and China, saying the priorities were Afghanistan, MEPP, AIDS, poverty.

TB then set out the forward diplomatic strategy, then asked me to fill in on communications. He also asked me to draft what we would view as ideal GWB clips out of the meeting. I felt we had to get him as close as possible to a second UNSCR, and tone down the rush-to-war talk. TB was in OK mood, but really worried. He just didn't know how Bush would be. He said he wanted as much time on his own as we could get, to persuade him he was more vulnerable than he thought. There was a risk of hubris. He needed world support more than he thought, especially if something went wrong. Shock and awe, then Iraqi kids dying, Saddam would stop at nothing and would happily inflict civilian casualties and we would be on the back foot straight away.

We went round the Cabinet one by one to assess who would support him without a second resolution. We could probably just about get to a majority but it would be difficult. It was pretty much 'future on the line' time. On Clare, TB said he knew the Cabinet hated the way he tolerates her but he didn't want her outside, as that would be even worse. I said appeasement never worked. He said sometimes it worked better than the alternative. David Manning was telling him we had to fight hard for more time, that we should persuade them it was in their own interests.

Friday, January 31

Poll in the *Mirror* said two per cent felt a war on Iraq would make the world a safer place. I made sure Dan [Bartlett] knew and made sure he told Bush just so he knew we were up against it. TB had also slept badly and was up and about, going over the same questions again and again, kept saying we needed a clear intellectual construct which was that 1441 focus should be on the co-operation issues, if the Iraqis didn't co-operate and Blix makes that clear repeatedly, we should say so and then we go for a second resolution and action could follow. We had allowed the goalposts to be moved to the smoking-gun issue, and instead it had to be about the inspectors not getting co-operation. We typed up all the relevant past resolutions, so he could read from them, particularly 1441. I had a long chat with Dan, made clear the issue for us was the second resolution, that that was where the press would go for the gaps and therefore we should try to close them. It was difficult because of course in the US the UN was not popular. Also Peter Reid [embassy official] was worried that the UK stories of TB trying to press GWB would backfire. 'They hate being pressured.'

We had a long chat in TB's bedroom with him, DM, Jonathan, Sally and I. The French officials were apparently really worried about France being left behind and some evidence that the Germans were looking to get into a different position. David had been shuttling between us and the Americans and they certainly had the message that we had to keep pushing for a second resolution. They felt 1441 was all they needed. Goldsmith was making clear that he didn't agree. Over break-fast, TB kept asking what we wanted out of today and I kept saying 'Bush moves towards second resolution.' We joked about this being his last visit to the States as prime minister. [Sir Christopher] Meyer [UK ambassador to Washington] said TB could make a fortune doing lectures.

Blix's interview was a bit iffy but he did have the line that there had been no change in Iraq's attitude. TB went off to the gym. I read a JIC note that made clear they held out little hope of Saddam just giving up, whilst there was every prospect of him doing something crazy like setting off the oilfields. The weather was apparently terrible at Camp David and meant we couldn't go there by helicopter so we were grounded in Washington and at 1 we left for the White House. While TB was seeing Bush, Tom Kelly and I saw Dan and I gave him a very frank assessment of the politics for us, said that our balls were in a vice. He said they believed that both politically and legally they could go without a second resolution. Again, we went over the issue of anti-Americanism. 'My guy's not doing you a lot of favours is he?' No, I said, it used to be Rumsfeld, now it's the president but I can see why you can't keep HIM off.

We went up to wait for TB and GWB. The question to resolve pre the press conference was what to say about a second resolution. GWB and Condi were both up for the idea of him saying he was 'open' to a second resolution, but Ari Fleischer [press secretary] pulled him back, said it would be seen as a shift in US policy, and then tried to push him back the other way, said that I was worried after what TB said in his interviews earlier, it would be a split story. It was a very odd scene. Me standing next to Bush, Condi and Ari next to TB, Ari and I trying to push each other's leaders in a different direction. Bush said he could say a second resolution would be 'welcome but not necessary'. TB and Bush having had a lot of the discussion without us there, it made it harder to push back without them stating the nature of the discussion they had just had, and in any event Bush was impatient to get on with it. As a result, we didn't really have the lines properly prepared. 'Let's just do it,' said Bush.

They both dispensed with opening remarks, which I think was a mistake because they gave no real context. The overall impression was poor. TB didn't really answer the question about a second resolution. And though Bush said it would be 'welcome' he looked uncomfortable and the body language was poor. Whatever people said about him, he is actually a very direct personality, which meant that he wasn't good at hiding what he thought or felt. Even though the words were kind of OK, the overall impression was not. As they wrapped up, Sally and I caught each other's eye. She grimaced. Tom managed to spin our lot [travelling UK media] to a more positive position by saying Bush was making clear he was open to a second resolution. TB said afterwards that in fact it had been the best meeting they had had in terms of substance, that they got on well, that Bush had read and digested his notes and was more on the same page than we thought, said he intended to work hard to get a second resolution and work to get a majority for it. TB repeated that if we didn't have the cover of the UN, when the Iraqis were bringing dead babies out of bombed buildings, having killed their own people, we would be in real trouble, so we had to go for it. But the politics of the UN on this were the opposite for him. David's note on the meeting made pretty clear they had made their minds up and that the campaign was going to start March 14, later than originally planned. For Bush, the diplomacy had to be based round the military campaign, not the other way round. We had very short timelines now.

The press conference over, we went to the family dining room for dinner – Bush, [his wife] Laura, Condi, George Tenet [CIA director], [Dan] Fried [National Security Council], [William] Farish [US ambassador to London], Dan [Bartlett] – TB, C, AC, Jonathan, [Christopher] Meyer, David M, Sally M. We talked a bit about the Democrats. He reckoned [Senator John] Kerry was the front-runner [to be Democratic presidential candidate in 2004], the guy who was married to the Heinz heiress [second wife Teresa] who would be able to put up millions from front organisations. He wasn't impressed by [Senator John] Edwards [another Democratic contender]. We had a good laugh on the Olympics when I persuaded him to say that London would be a great choice. Jonathan ruined the whole thing by pointing out that New York was going for it. Bush reckoned Hillary [Clinton] could go for it [the presidency] in 2008. Laura was pretty quiet all evening. Bush was playing up his daft image again, saying his favourite leaders were Who and No because he could pronounce their names properly.

TB was due to do a couple of interviews at Andrews Airbase so Tom and I travelled back with him. He said he was confident of getting a second resolution. We had to cancel an interview with [George] Stephanopoulos [TV journalist, former Clinton adviser] because of the fog. George was in a terrible state so I agreed he could come over to do it in London or Chequers on Sunday morning, though that eventually got cancelled because of the space shuttle crash.[1] I had told Dan that people in Europe really questioned their motives, and TB came away feeling their motives might be questionable, but he was adamant that it was the right thing to do to get rid of Saddam and send out a message that we were determined to deal with WMD. But he knew how tough it was going to be. Expressing confidence on a second resolution was the best way of dealing with that.

On the plane, as we flew home, I was taken aback by the extent to which the press thought the body language between them had been bad. We briefed hard that this was the US playing hardball, the message directed as much at the French and the Russians as anyone else. What was really annoying was that both Bush and Condi seemed fine about saying they were open to the idea of a second resolution, but that Ari [Fleischer] had pushed him back, and by the time he was out there, his body language was terrible. TB felt things had gone about as well as they could have done, but still felt they were doing the right thing in the wrong way, and just wished they could improve the way they put their case to the world.

Saturday, February 1
Got home, felt ill, went to bed. Space shuttle crash pretty much overwhelmed the media agenda. Out for dinner at Tessa's. David Mills [her husband] massively against the war. There was definitely a feeling there that we weren't doing the right thing, or if we were, we weren't doing it for the right reasons.

[1] The space shuttle *Columbia* disintegrated over Texas during re-entry to the earth's atmosphere. All seven crew members were killed. President Bush addressed the United States, saying 'This day has brought . . . great sadness to our country . . . the cause in which they died [space programme] will continue.'

Sunday, February 2

Did fourteen miles in just over two hours, took the total for the week to forty-seven. Press very low-key on Iraq because of the space shuttle. Spoke to TB who wanted to make clear he had no problem with Robin and others criticising his position on reform of the Lords, the Sundays having a few stories about Robin shaping up to quit. He wanted to go out early to Le Touquet for the Chirac dinner, but Chirac didn't want to move it. Tuesday was going to be tough. Spoke to Catherine Colonna to discuss how we avoided *la bagarre* [trouble].

Monday, February 3

Space shuttle still huge. TB's statement on Iraq was running fine, alongside the Pentagon briefing on the scale of the military attack planned. GB was making a speech [to the Social Market Foundation] emphasising we were OK on the economic front, though there were a few pieces around on his reputation falling, which was a bit of a current theme. Andy Marr [BBC] called, claimed that he was being wound up by the Treasury to present GB's speech as a split with TB, with a big attack on markets and a different tone on Europe. I called Ed Balls and we agreed a line to push, that it was pro market, pro reform, pro PFI. TB read it, all forty pages of it, and felt it was fine but it just didn't take on the arguments in the way that he needed to.

We had another firefight re Zimbabwe. TB was calling Chirac at 11 who mentioned that *Le Monde* had got hold of a telegram that revealed that Straw and [Dominique] de Villepin [French foreign minister] had agreed to Mugabe going to Paris and that TB was aware. Our immediate suspicion was that the French had done it deliberately. Catherine Colonna called me after the call and said please believe me, this was not an official leak and they were very embarrassed about it. It clearly put TB in a bad light and she said they would probably say nothing about it. Our line was basically that there had been discussions at various levels but we had been unable to agree, which was why there was continuing discussion in Brussels and our bottom line was sanctions rollover. The money was beginning to come in for my marathon appeal – £5,000 from [David] Sainsbury, £2,500 from the GMB [union], £500 from Jackie Stewart.

TB felt on Iraq we had finally got the focus where it needed to be, on the issue of co-operation with Blix. He did calls with Putin and Simitis, which were better. The joint article had had the desired effect of the French and the Russians taking us a bit more seriously. [French ambassador Gérard] Errera's brief for the summit was that TB was weakened but still the only show in town because the Labour Party needed him more than he needed them and his prediction was that TB would be PM for some time. We went over to the House for the post-US visit statement and spent longer than usual going through the difficult questions, many of which just didn't come up. In any event he did well, a lot of passion and personal commitment, making clear he was doing this because he felt it was right.[1] I got back for an honours meeting, usual bollocks where anything too radical was blocked and the usual Establishment lot put forward. I sometimes wished TB took more of an interest in changing all this, but at the same time could see why he didn't want to spend time on it. His hopes for the Chirac meeting tomorrow seemed a bit unrealistic. He wanted a really positive outcome, but it was hard to see where it would come from.

Tuesday, February 4

The Anglo-French summit at Le Touquet was being built up on the assumption of a big bust-up. Catherine Colonna and I were talking the whole time, and were on the same track in trying to get things in a better place. We were both using the line that more unites us than divides us. We left at 8.40 for Northolt, flew out on a tiny plane that Chirac wouldn't be seen dead in. Stephen Wall had done a good draft for the press conference which I topped and tailed. TB was convinced that the pro-US EU leaders' joint letter had been the right thing to do and would find Chirac in a better position vis-à-vis us, because if there was one thing he understood, it was strength. It was very cold on arrival. We were driven to the town hall, a huge scrum of media and public around TB and JC. Then in for the main bilateral, [Jean-Pierre] Raffarin [Prime Minister of France] also there, in the room normally used for marriages. It was when you saw French president and prime minister together that you were most aware of where the real power lay. Chirac, who could be overbearing at the best of times, was even more so in the presence of his prime minister, and although TB was his political opposite number, I think psychologically he tried to make TB think in terms of being Raffarin's opposite number.

They went through some of the difficult non-Iraq issues first, defence, CAP [Common Agricultural Policy], climate change, Africa.

[1] Blair told MPs 'Eight weeks have now passed since Saddam was given his final chance. Six hundred weeks have passed since he was given his first chance. The evidence of co-operation withheld is unmistakable. He has still not answered the questions concerning thousands of missing munitions and tonnes of chemical and biological agents unaccounted for.'

On EU institutions, Chirac claimed close agreement, at one point even claiming that on the reform of the institutions his position was '*plus Britannique*' than German. He said we had to convince the smaller countries that they do not lose by having a full-time president of the Council and we had to strengthen the Commission and Council at the same time. TB said he had had lunch with Giscard [d'Estaing, former French President] last week and that he had done a good job. Chirac – '*Je t'ai dit que c'était le meilleur.*' [I told you he was the best.] TB – '*Tu avais raison.*' [You were right.] Chirac – '*Comme d'habitude.*' [As usual.] Things got trickier on CAP, Chirac absolutely clear that he wasn't going for the kind of major change we wanted. He said the British view and the French view of farmers was very different, that France was the second biggest agricultural exporter in the world, that in England agriculture was not popular, that in France it was. Chirac was at his patronising best or worst, depending how you look at it, and TB had a big smile as he spoke. 'I think you are a very fair man, Tony, and it would be good to see if we can get you in a better position on this.' '*Si non, on arrive à un moment où on s'engueule. Tu comprends s'engueuler?*' [If not, we reach a point where we are rowing. Do you understand 'rowing'?] TB – '*Je comprends très bien. Surtout maintenant.*' [I understand very well. Especially now.] The joint letter had definitely got to him, and he emphasised that prior to the spring summit there should be a joint letter from UK, France and Germany, even though '*je me méfie des lettres*' [I mistrust letters]'.

On Zimbabwe, he [Chirac] apologised for the leak, said there would be a leak inquiry 'which will not find out anything'. Again, he gave the impression that we were opposing for the sake of it. On the Middle East, Chirac was sceptical that the Americans would do anything, said power was not in Washington but in the Jewish population in New York. When TB said he believed Bush would do something, Chirac looked upwards rather dramatically. '*Que Dieu t'entend.*' [May God hear you.] They weren't much closer on Afghanistan. Chirac pessimist, TB trying to see the bright side.

Then Iraq, where Chirac said 'I'm not going to convince you, you won't convince me, so we can explain that one easily.' He said tomorrow we get the 'famous American revelations, namely *rien du tout* [nothing at all]'. 'Is that because they are American?' asked TB. No, but if there were real revelations, we would know them too. He said they would listen with respect to [Colin] Powell, then Blix and [Mohamed] ElBaradei [director general of the International Atomic Energy Agency]. He said there was no point pretending we were in the same position, other than agreeing that we wanted to disarm Iraq.

They thought 1441 and more time for the inspectors. If Powell has important things to say, he should let the inspectors examine it. On a second resolution, if there was a war, we would need one but we do not need one at the moment because we are going through 1441. He came back to the letter, and TB said there was little point commenting on it. 'But it created a lot of noise. We should show some humour on that, otherwise we will appear imbecilic or hypocritical.' Catherine chipped in and said sometimes your humour does not travel with the press, Mr President. He asked what she advised. '*Dire rien.*' [Say nothing.]

He said war had to be absolutely the last resort because the consequences – political, human and economic – were terrible. It was a tense, pretty spiky meeting and at the plenary as well, though people were pretty much going through the motions of saying what they discussed at the various bilaterals, the atmospherics were poor and flat. Only the chiefs of defence seemed to have got on. When the French CDS [General Henri Bentégeat] said that Boyce was shortly leaving his job, it set Chirac off into a huge, obviously pre-planned, and for us rather embarrassing, tribute to Boyce. Chirac was even more full of Gallic gesture than usual. His face seemed to get more lined with every meeting. TB was tougher than usual, felt the letter had had a genuine and desired impact, that he now knew if France and Germany tried it again, we had the wherewithal to build alliances elsewhere. TB and Chirac had lunch together.

I was with Catherine, who had been with him about the same time I had been with TB. We agreed to get them away from the others before the press conference to try to get the focus on the need for Saddam to disarm, and the importance of the UN, also to try to minimise the differences on the tough questions, e.g. second resolution. Both did pretty well, good body language, no attempt to deny differences, but Chirac brilliantly fobbed off the really difficult questions, e.g. on material breach, US–UK. TB was keen to get back to vote on the Lords, so we got some of the ministers out doing end-of-summit interviews. Chris Meyer sent over a bootlegged version of Powell's presentation. Tony Benn [former Labour Cabinet minister] had done an interview for Channel 4 with Saddam [in Baghdad], which was nauseatingly toadying.[1]

TB was pleased with the way the day had gone, felt that particularly over lunch Chirac had been warm and making an effort. TB called

[1] Benn described the interview as 'Very historic for all of us' and asked Saddam to 'Help me see what the paths to peace may be.'

again later, said he felt he could now see a way of getting to the same place with Chirac. I said surely the best thing for Bush was to get Saddam out without a war. TB said that was his whole strategy, get the Blix report, then a second resolution, then get the Arabs to press him to go.

Wednesday, February 5

The Powell presentation to the UN was going to be the focus of the day but [Andrew] Gilligan [BBC] had a so-called secret DIS [Defence Intelligence Staff] paper suggesting there was no real link between Iraq and al-Qaeda.[1] Up to see TB for PMQs preparation and we were assuming they would do the Lords after last night's debacle.[2] And maybe Iraq pre Powell. We had a meeting of the Iraq communications group to go over how we dealt with Powell. I saw Ed Balls who returned to the theme of the so-called leadership/euro deal, allegedly done by intermediaries, by which I presume he meant Anji [Hunter] and Sue Nye and from which, he said, he and I were to be excluded. I said for God's sake, let's get real. He said GB was still obsessing re why TB did not reply to his note. The reality was there were real policy differences between them.

I said we needed proper structures for discussing strategy and we had to be honest with each other about the problems. I felt he, Philip, Douglas and I should meet regularly. He wanted to add Spencer Livermore. I said the most important thing was that we agreed things and then stuck to them, instead of constantly moving the arguments to slightly different places. I'd had a session with Arnab Banerji [recently appointed economic adviser to Blair], who I think was finding it difficult to work out exactly what his role was meant to be, but he said the Treasury was full of angst and vibes that TB would try to move Gordon. I sensed from Ed that GB was a bit more nervous. He kept saying we stand or fall together. His line about TB doing a deal, that he would go if GB helped him do the euro, was probably the line that they were developing for public use if TB did try to get rid of him. It was a good meeting though, and we always worked better if we worked together. Then a meeting with Peter M, Philip and Peter H where we agreed that things had got a bit cavalier and slipshod, that we weren't properly knitting together policy, politics and

---

[1] The three-week-old 'top secret' document stated that the 'aims [of al-Qaeda] are in ideological conflict with present-day Iraq'.

[2] Both Houses of Parliament had voted on the future make-up of the House of Lords. Eight reform options were defeated in the Commons, while the Lords voted for the status quo.

communications. On the GB front, Peter M was against my closer co-operation strategy, said that all they did was use these meetings to hoover up intelligence and use it against us.

Thursday, February 6

The Powell presentation to the UN re WMD had gone well and there was a sense of things moving back to us. The first meeting of the day was with JS and GH who had a bit of a spat about the DIS leak. Then CDS, C, Eliza [Manningham-Buller], John [Scarlett] and the main MoD targeter. They took us through a presentation of 'shock and awe' making clear that the aim was an overwhelming immediate effect. Jack and I both felt the words 'shock and awe' were ghastly and I spoke to Dan about it later. Boyce said it was the first time we had done an effects-based campaign. The aim was to isolate Baghdad. Hit bridges, deny WMD capability as the risk would be at its highest early on. Some of our guys to go forty-eight hours before the air campaign starts. They envisaged sixteen days between the start of the air campaign and a ground campaign, but want to get that down to as low as five days if we can get the regime to collapse early. Scarlett warned that there would be civilian casualties and that Saddam would use them to create political problems here.

TB asked about the assessment on collateral damage. Geoff said some was inevitable but the missiles were far more effective, even since Afghanistan. It had to be clear we were targeting Saddam and the regime, and also focusing on the aftermath and the humanitarian. When Geoff said that Rumsfeld was going to be running the humanitarian side, he was met with laughter mixed with shock all round the table. Shock and awe humanitarian. C reported that Blix was making clear there could be no aggressive inspections in mosques and cemeteries. He also said no serious interviews had really taken place at all because there had been so much intimidation. Eliza gave a very gloomy picture of the terrorist scene here, said that even though al-Qaeda were not directly linked to Iraq, they would use an attack on Iraq to step up activity here. TB was looking really worried at that point. There was also a lot of intelligence around on a planned hit on Heathrow. TB said he had no doubt that trying to remove Saddam quickly in the event of action was the best way, but he wanted to know what he was in for. C and John said there were suggestions that the Republican Guard were to be kept out of Baghdad because Saddam didn't trust them fully. Then to Cabinet, after a brief wash-up session with a worried-looking TB.

Cabinet was fine though as Tom Kelly said to me, Clare Short was like the granny who sat in the corner talking through the important bits when the family was trying to watch TV. TB reported on Camp David and the Chirac talks, put a pretty optimistic face on both. Jack went through what was happening at the UN. Robin was quizzing on the parliamentary process, Clare on India/Pakistan and rebuilding Iraq. JR said he was troubled about the lack of domestic consensus, that there was a sense of people losing their moral compass about the nature of the Iraqi regime. Tessa said she didn't know anyone under twenty-five who supported action and we had to do better at countering the scepticism.

Then Blix and ElBaradei came in. TB asked Blix how he was with the weight of the world on his shoulders. 'A lot is on yours,' said Blix. He felt Powell had done well but he was avoiding comment. He was pretty cagey all the way through, made clear his job was to be sceptical. TB said the issue was whether they were co-operating or not. At the moment there appears to be some, but there must be full co-operation. Blix said they had discussed the idea of enhanced co-operation. They were trying to resolve the issues of anthrax and VX. On the remnants of old programmes, they should be able to tell us. TB said that the reason we believe they are not co-operating is that we have no more documents, and they are resisting proper interviews. Blix described it as a moment of truth, but also said he did not want to be put in a particular arena. He felt the 14th of February was a little early to report to the UN [Security Council] and that they had a meeting of the College of Commissioners [of UNMOVIC] on the 12th.

TB said he felt Iraq would come up with some surprise to split the international community, that intelligence showed he would regard giving up WMD as a total humiliation, that it was essential to his internal grip. Blix said the South Africans were sending a delegation to tell them how to give up WMD. Blix said Iraq had definitely been hampered by inspection. He said they had been to some of the places named in the dossier, and it could be they had been sanitised, but they found nothing. The indication was that come February 14 he would be saying they had not found WMD but there was no real co-operation. He didn't want to name scientists for interview for fear that they would be killed. He was a lot less bullish than last time and clearly fed up with the feeling he was being bullied by America. He didn't want to pose any new questions because they would take so long to answer.

Then TB saw ElBaradei. He was quite open and chatty, less nervy than Blix. He said the Iraqis claimed they had never tried to get uranium but it wasn't true. He didn't think many tears would be shed in the Arab world if Saddam went. He was worried that Iraq would claim they were being attacked not because of weapons but because they were a Muslim country. He felt it better if TB and Bush could say it was part of a vision of a zone free of nuclear weapons. Also, it was important the aftermath was a UN administration, multilateral, not the US. He said their strategy was to force him into co-operation, though he doubted it was possible. But he came back again and again to the theme that American public diplomacy wasn't working.

TB said we had to sort out Saddam in as peaceful a way as possible, but above all sort out MEPP. He said Saddam's duty was one hundred per cent co-operation, not hide and seek. ElBaradei said we needed intrusive inspection but it can't be done without active co-operation. TB said if there was a breach, there would be a second resolution and then we could build pressure on him to go. I caught the news later, ElBaradei making clear that the Arab world wanted Saddam out and they would help him on his way if they could. Blix was less impressive, came over as very ponderous and bureaucratic.

TB and I left for Northolt to fly to Newcastle where he was doing a two-part [BBC] *Newsnight* special, first on Iraq with an audience of critics and then on public services. It was a good setting, with a view out over Gateshead and Newcastle. He was very strong on Iraq, not so good on public services. Meanwhile Channel 4 ran a story that the CIC paper on the infrastructure of concealment, which I'd commissioned, had included passages plagiarised from a Californian document, and claiming we had made it look like intelligence.[1] It gave them another spin story, which was a real pain.

Friday, February 7

The CIC dossier was causing a lot of embarrassment. Seemingly whole chunks were lifted off the Internet. I wrote a note to the CIC to emphasise the importance of quality control and to make clear that this shouldn't have happened. It was a bad own goal, especially as we didn't need it given the very good intelligence and other materials

[1] *Channel 4 News* had broken the story of what was dubbed the 'Dodgy Dossier', a briefing paper compiled for the Sunday papers by CIC civil servants. Cambridge academic Dr Glen Rangwala recognised plagiarised passages from writings available on the Internet, particularly 'Iraq's Security & Intelligence Network: A Guide & Analysis', an article written by political scientist Dr Ibrahim al-Marashi, and published in the *Middle East Review of International Affairs* in September 2002.

we had. Definitely no more dossiers for a while. I called John Scarlett who was very nice about it, but also rightly emphasised how careful we had to be. Then another major PR problem emerged, namely Derry's pay rise as part of the pay review bodies. Derry's pay was linked to the Lord Chief Justice who was linked to the performance-related pay of permanent secretaries and it meant he would get a £22,000 rise. The feedback from *Newsnight* was good, though the dossier was a real setback. It also came to be stated as a fact that it had been put together by Alison [Blackshaw, AC's PA] and John Pratt [press office assistant]. Ridiculous, but a sign of how difficult it was going to be to get our message across. *Newsnight* had pulled in 4.2 million viewers, way up on usual, almost matching BBC1.

Then to the LSE [London School of Economics] where I was speaking to Philip's students. There were a few Trots around but nothing like the trouble they had feared. During my speech about twenty came to the stage and held up banners urging NO to conflict, but I was perfectly polite to them and they just stayed there, largely ignored. I felt the Q&A session went fine. At the end Philip called one of the protesters to ask a question and I really laid it on the line about Resolution 1441, the authority of the UN. I asked him if he believed the UN was the best place to resolve it. He said the UN was a front for American imperialism, at which the audience groaned, and he was dead. I went through the whole Iraq story as reasonably and dispassionately as I could, and was surprised to get very warm applause for it, as also for a passionate defence of politics and the centrality of communications to any programme of progressive change.

Saturday, February 8

Times magazine did a good piece on the marathon with a good appeal at the end. TB called early on in a rage, adamant he had not signed off Derry's pay rise. We didn't quite know how it had happened, but when I called Derry it was pretty clear to me he had no intention of giving it up because of what he saw as a hoo-ha in the tabloid press. Derry was very clever but sometimes lacked very obvious politics. JR called to say he was confident we could fight our way through Iraq but how do you defend this when you are telling soldiers, teachers and firemen to settle for less? JP called, asking if it was worth us trying to get him to change his mind. I said I didn't think so but we could try. JP spoke to him, said he wasn't just the head of the judiciary, but a member of the Cabinet that was agreeing the pay of other public sector workers, that he had to get political because this was damaging government and party. JP said Derry put the phone down on him. JP was also asking GB to call him but he never did and then I had Ian Austin on asking if I could get it sorted because GB was on *Frost*.

Jeremy [Heywood] was on the case and worked a way out, namely to review the salary link in the light of performance-related pay and also review whether in fact the Lord Chancellor's salary did have to be higher than the Lord Chief Justice's. Derry still didn't want to budge, saying to me 'I'm buggered if I'm going to do something because of the tabloid press.' But as TB said, we all hate the press, but it doesn't mean they are always wrong and they are right about this. It is indefensible in the context of our overall policy on pay. JP made clear that both he and GB would find it impossible to defend in their various interviews tomorrow. But it took two more very difficult conversations.

I then spoke to JP, JR and Ian Austin to tell them about an hour before the statement went out. It missed the first editions, apart from the *News of the World*, presumably tipped off by Austin, who headlined it as 'Brown blocks Derry rise'. I raised it on the conference call later, said to JP we didn't want this to be anything other than Derry's decision, that nobody should spin it to damage him. JP called GB and said it must be his camp who had tipped off the *News of the World*. GB of course denied it and even claimed he had told us to deny the story.

Sunday, February 9

The CIC dossier was still rumbling on. Alison even made Rory Bremner [TV satire show]. Following JP's call last night, GB denied he had pressured Derry, telling [David] Frost that it was all Derry's idea. But of course the story that ran was GB denying putting on the pressure, which increased the sense that he probably had. It was not a great interview for either of them. GB a bit predictable. TB called to complain that he had so much work to do over the weekend. He cancelled his morning meeting tomorrow, and said he wanted to talk about how we get more politics back into the office. Blix was in Baghdad and ElBaradei came out with more positive comments re co-operation. The other big story was the Franco-German 'peace plan' and there was a lot of build-up to the march next week.

Monday, February 10

TB called me up with David Manning and Jonathan as soon as he arrived. He looked very pissed off, for once grumbling that Jonathan and I were both in sweaty sports gear. He was harassed and fed up. The Franco-German plan, which presumably Chirac knew all about when we met at Le Touquet, had wrong-footed us. It looked reasonable and the Russians seemed keen to support it. David M said the French denied saying there should be a UN force, the Germans had denied it, but still it ran. We also had a problem in NATO with France, Germany and Belgium blocking Patriot missile defences for Turkey. TB thought it unbelievable that these countries were putting the transatlantic relationship at risk. It had definitely been a few steps forward and a few steps back, Colin Powell and TB on *Newsnight* taking us forward, a combination of the dossier and international division taking us back. TB said we needed a proposal. I said the problem was people felt we were driven by a timetable dictated by a desire for war rather than by a desire to disarm Iraq.

TB was looking more worried and harassed than I had seen him for a while. I looked at his diary and really felt for him for once. Today alone he had meetings on Iraq, on asylum, where Blunkett was giving him grief, feeling he was weakened by TB driving the policy, a big meeting on terrorism, a difficult meeting with the military on Northern Ireland pre Wednesday's plan, Ruud Lubbers [UN high commissioner for refugees] for a meeting re refugees, the trade unions re two-tier workforce, and a lot more besides. I went to his meeting on the Olympic bid. He was still keen but we agreed that a combination of Cabinet opposition, the usage of political capital, uncertainty about costs, GB likely to be against made it very difficult. But he remained keen.

At a party meeting with Hilary A, JR etc. Hilary said it was really grim in the PLP on Iraq. TB did his 'Oh well' look but beneath it I could tell he was concerned. Then to a meeting in the Cabinet Room with a huge group of ministers, spooks and police. TB, JP, GB, DB, AD, Lewis Moonie [parliamentary undersecretary for defence], C, Eliza, Scarlett, GCHQ, [David] Veness [assistant commissioner for specialist operations] from the Met. There was a mildly embarrassing moment at the start when JP walked in and said to me 'Did you see Gordon's first answer on *Frost*? What a laugh.' I then nodded to the other side of the table where GB was sitting, staring down at his notes, pretending not to hear, JP not having seen him. There had already been a Cobra meeting on the threat of a surface-to-air missile attack on Heathrow on Wednesday at the end of Eid.[1] The choice was

---

[1] Eid-ul-Adha, 'Festival of the Sacrifice', the Muslim festival commemorating the prophet Abraham's willingness to sacrifice his son for God.

a difficult one. Carry on with the programme of arrests that was underway; do that, plus step up security at Heathrow, visibly and overtly with a public announcement, or three, close the airport. As far as TB was concerned, the last of these was unacceptable, though we had to be clear about all the things we had said about how we would respond to specific threats in intelligence.

DB was very grumpy, clearly had very little confidence in the ability of the police and security forces to handle the public communications on it, constantly warning how their briefings went wrong. His basic pitch was to say as little as possible. AD talked about the need to make sure our political flank wasn't exposed. He was also worried that once we announced it, we didn't have the airlines and insurers all going crazy. Eliza was very clear that the threat was serious and the decision that had to be made now was whether TB/MoD authorised the operation for the airport tomorrow. We then agreed that Veness rather than ministers should announce it. Afterwards, Veness and I went to my office to agree words and lines to take and then planned the Q&A. Then a mountain of comments came through, including AD not wanting to say in the Q&A that Heathrow was safe, DB, ludicrously, not wanting to mention Heathrow at all.

On Iraq, Putin and Chirac put out a joint position. TB's 'bridge between Europe and America' was looking pretty shaky and the media was working itself up into going crazy about TB being isolated. People were even beginning to say that his premiership was now on the line. In the conference call with the Americans, I briefed them on the dossier problems and tried to get a proper discussion of all the different divisions, but all we got was the usual crap about who was doing what today.

The fallout from the CIC dossier was continuing. C and John Scarlett both said they were getting a bit of grief from some of their clients who were less signed up to the openness strategy than they were. Michael Jay [FCO permanent secretary] came to see me to say he felt we had to tighten up, get the CIC people more closely bound in to the FCO on policy, go easier on 'product-led material'. TB could barely be in a more exposed place now. PLP tricky. Massive march being planned. France and Germany right out there now, open in their hostility, Russia difficult. We were in danger of looking like we were the bad guys prepared to disobey international law. It was one of those days when I really felt for TB. Any one of the issues he was dealing with – Ireland, security, terrorism, asylum, some of the diplomatic stuff – was enough to lose you sleep, and he had a stack of them. He looked absolutely shagged out and was clearly feeling a bit isolated.

Tuesday, February 11

The Heathrow situation low-key at first but became huge once they had pictures of troops and tanks at the airport. The briefing on it was OK but got a bit too detailed. Godric was stitched up at the four o'clock, his words on the specific threat twisted. I had another Iraq communications group meeting, and a bit of an inquest into the CIC dossier. John Scarlett and Nigel Inkster [SIS] said there was some dismay among colleagues but John was clear they still understood the need for the [intelligence] agencies to help in public communications. But it was a blow, not least because it was being pinned at my door and would be used to change the general modus operandi. At least TB was being robust about it. He was about to speak to Bush. He had looked at the Mirage report in *Der Spiegel*[1] and decided that maybe we took the wrong line, that maybe we should say it was interesting because it accepted that conventional inspections would not work and was effectively arguing for taking the country over without saying so.

We grasped our way to a plan that was basically wait for Blix, then surface the elements of a second resolution that included the ultimatum, then Saddam to go, and if he didn't we were going to go for it. He spoke to Bush at 12, who was very solicitous re TB's political position, said he was determined to help get a second UNSCR. He was livid with the French and Germans, less so with the Russians. But he was just as worried as TB was. TB could not quite believe that the French and Germans were so flagrantly damaging their relationship with the US. He said the problem was everyone accepted Saddam was bad, evil, and a threat, but they didn't necessarily believe that gave you a reason to go to war. We had to be the people putting forward one last push for peace. TB also wanted to get European leaders to our cause in advance of Monday's council meeting. But we were looking shaky. I had a good meeting with Jack who was on form at the moment. Ditto Jeremy Greenstock [UK ambassador to the UN], who filled us in on where everyone was re a second resolution. He said the sense of America vs France and Germany was really big. David Omand, with whom I had a perfectly civilised discussion on

---

[1] *Der Spiegel* reported a Franco-German plan, 'Project Mirage', to prevent war by sending UN regulars into Iraq to strengthen weapons searches, declare the whole country a no-fly zone and increase trade sanctions. Iraq would have become, de facto, a UN protectorate, forced to disarm.

the CIC document, sent round a letter re new rules on the handling of intelligence which was fine, if an obvious attempt to retrench.

Wednesday, February 12

At the PMQs meeting, we reckoned it would be a mix of dossier and asylum. Iraq was grim at the moment, we just weren't making headway. TB said again that the problem was people couldn't see the case for war based on a threat to us. We went over to the House and then heard that JR had said we were facing a threat on the scale of 9/11. In fact he hadn't said that, but it was how it was taken, and we had to wrestle with it all day. Then both Blunkett and [Sir John] Stevens [Metropolitan Police commissioner] said we had considered shutting Heathrow, which added to a feeling of raggedness. The build-up to the march was growing and clearly it was going to be huge. TB was still saying he could win people round. With TB gone, I tried to clear the mountain of paperwork that had built up. I didn't feel like I was motoring at the moment. I had done my first marathon column for *The Times*, which they liked.

Thursday, February 13

I ran in with Lauren Taylor [ITN] and a camera crew on a cycle rickshaw. 6.3 miles. Later did another 9.2, running back from seeing the podiatrist at Roehampton, who said I had totally flat feet and needed orthotics. The terrorism stuff was being covered ludicrously, cranking up the idea of 'mixed messages' and also still pumping the idea that we had basically sent tanks to Heathrow to scare people re Iraq. I got in for the end of TB's breakfast with John Howard. UNMOVIC had found a missile in Iraq that breached the allowed range. Howard was impressive if dull. They did a very good joint doorstep on Iraq and terrorism, though the media were getting a bit frenzied again.

I took Howard to say hello to [Rupert] Murdoch, Les Hinton [News International chairman] and James Murdoch who were in for a meeting with TB. After he left, we kicked a few things round on the international scene before TB looked very sharply at Les, and said 'What about all this other stuff then?' and we got into a pretty spiky exchange in which TB said it's not much good supporting us on the international agenda if the domestic coverage is so hostile. We argued our corner on health and education and I felt TB did it too much from the perspective that this was an agenda they should back, e.g. a liberal market in public services rather than these were the issues we really believed in and they should support us because it was right for their readers. TB went off for a meeting with Clare, trying to get her back in line, though there was no doubt where it was going to end.

Then a meeting with Jack, GH, Clare, CDS on the humanitarian aftermath planning. Jack was giving me a very hard time re the dossier which had indeed done us some harm. I was prepared to take responsibility for it, but truth be told it was as much a failure of internal quality control. But his point was that they saw themselves as answerable to me, and therefore tended to work outside FCO systems. Cabinet was pretty heavy, DB on terror, TB and JS taking them through where we were on Iraq pre Blix. Then RC reporting on a meeting of the PES [Party of European Socialists] . He really played up the extent of the opposition and I sensed he was putting down a marker that he might actually bugger off. He was clearly very offside and had become more so. Clare was chuntering away the whole time. Then Northern Ireland, which was also tricky. Then TB called in AD and DB to say we had to learn lessons from the handling of the Heathrow threat. Gently, but they got the message.

Life seemed to be a never-ending round of meetings on really difficult issues. Next Jack on tactics re a second UNSCR, and whether to table it before the European Council. I was impressed by Jack at the moment. He was really on form, on top of the detail, but not in that obsessive way that he sometimes gets. TB, like me, had sensed that Robin had moved to a different position, a different tone, and was gearing up to go. TB went off for a visit in Yorkshire, then called about whether to do media on the security situation after IDS went on the rampage. Then a Venezuelan was caught with a hand grenade at Gatwick. TB called again from Yorkshire while I was at the podiatrist. He felt we had to get up the humanitarian theme and at least give the marchers something to think about, and something to put them on the defensive. They may not like to think of it in these terms, but they might like to reflect on the penury, the poverty and the cruelty, and that as far as Saddam was concerned, these big explosions of public protest were seen as helping to keep him in power.

Friday, February 14

At the morning meeting we agreed we needed to get up more of the humanitarian side of things ahead of the march. Catherine Rimmer [Number 10 Research and Information Unit] had a good line, that even if there were one million people on the march, it was still less than the number of people whose deaths he had caused. But it was going to get very tough. Left for City airport [for Edinburgh and the Labour Party spring conference in Glasgow], the plane slightly delayed. Matthew Freud [communications executive, husband of Rupert Murdoch's daughter Elisabeth] called to say that Murdoch had left yesterday hugely impressed and telling everyone TB was the man, not GB. I did the conference call on landing in Edinburgh, then up to see TB who was working on the speech.

I watched Blix [deliver his report to the UN Security Council] on the TV in my hotel room. He leant this way one minute, the next way the next, but it was obvious he was not going to come down as clearly as he had before. There was not much co-operation, yet he was not saying so. You definitely got the impression that he was deliberately siding with France, attacking us and the US. At one point he picked apart some of Powell's presentation. And even though he said there were clear issues of breach, for example proscribed weapons, he was signalling that inspections could work. I went through the main points with TB who said he wanted to read a full version, did so, said it was a total disgrace, that he should just have told the truth and the truth was Saddam was not co-operating. We were in a very tough place now. TB felt the Americans had fucked it up by failing to manage relationships properly. But the French would now be cock-a-hoop. TB showed no signs of changing tack though, said we were doing the right thing. But whether we liked it or not, we were moving towards a regime-change argument.

TB felt we had to make more of the moral case but we agreed he could not really set out the forward plan he had devised on the back of this, because it would look like weakness. We were getting very close to the argument, which itself was politically dangerous, that the marchers were pro Saddam, that they plus international community divisions would keep him in power. He, Sally and I had dinner in a private room downstairs at the Caledonian. It was our favourite Scottish hotel, but there was something odd and rather dingy about the room and it was all a bit sad and depressing. Then when we started to work on the [spring conference] speech, he couldn't find his glasses and was scrabbling around on the floor. We worked pretty late. There was a lot of American reaction to Blix, with Powell very emotional, Bush on much the same line. We were told there would be big protests tomorrow. TB was clear we just had to hold our line and defend ourselves from a moral point of view. But we were already into the black humour, speculating about what he would do in a few weeks when he was out of a job.

Saturday, February 15

The first thing TB said was that he had slept badly. So had I. He knew that he was in a tight spot. 'Even I am a bit worried about this one,' he said. The problem was that for the moment it looked every part of the strategy was in tatters – re the EU, re the UN, re the US, re the party, re the country which was about to march against us. We rewrote the speech to get even more focus on the humanitarian side of things. We had had letters from Iraqis urging him to carry on, which we decided to use in a strong passage pushing the moral case for action. One of the people who had written was a Glasgow doctor who we got to come over and see him. We had to involve Iraqi exiles much more. The moral case for peace was being put on the march and that gave us the right backdrop to make the moral case for action. I put in the final bits in the speech about the inhumanity of keeping Saddam in power doing the dreadful things he does. We struggled to get the broadcasters to take the Iraqi exiles and I wrote a letter of complaint to the BBC and Sky that important voices were being ignored unless they opposed the government.

We drove through to Glasgow, went over where we thought weaknesses in the Cabinet were, who we had to win round. The speech was pretty strong and we joked about it being his last as leader. There was massive security around the conference centre. The speech was heard in near silence. He wasn't playing it for applause but to put over a rounded argument. It was well received, not least because it was so serious.[1] Meanwhile TV was wall-to-wall, uncritical coverage of the march and the usual over the top claims about its size.[2] What was clear was that it was very big, and I got more and more angry about the claims being made for it, e.g. the *Mirror* front page with a dying Iraqi child and the headline 'March for him' as if he was starving because of us.

The speech went down well with the media and we got as many front-page leads as the march, which was a surprise. TB was confident and felt we had the right argument and we now needed a big strategy to put the case properly. I got home, then later down to the canal and did an eighteen-mile run at just over 7 mph. On the route back, I bumped into no end of people coming back from the march, placards under arms, faces full of self-righteousness, occasional loathing when they spotted me.

[1] Blair told Labour delegates 'It is still possible for Saddam Hussein to prevent military action by co-operating, and fulfilling his obligations as set out by the United Nations.' Blair dismissed Saddam's invitation to South African officials to visit Iraq to advise on disarmament. 'The concessions are phoney, the weapons are real.'
[2] Police estimated that at least 750,000 people had taken part in the London march. Organisers put the figure at nearer two million.

Sunday, February 16

Carole [Caplin] had done an interview in the *Mail on Sunday* but TB was in so-what mode, said it would only blow up if we responded, that he was absolutely sure she would not set out to harm us. I said the problem was that people would question his judgement over it. Fiona had pretty much lost respect for both of them, and a lot of it because of Carole. He said she wasn't a bad person and he didn't accept she was trying to damage him. On Iraq, he felt more confident than he had for some time, because he felt confident in the argument he made yesterday, that it gave us a chance to get back on higher moral ground. The press on the march was not nearly as bad as it might have been. But that was an awful lot of people who took the trouble to go out, which meant that there was a hell of a lot more who thought about it. We really had to push the humanitarian arguments harder.

Monday, February 17

The media on Iraq was still an uphill battle, but the commentary was a lot better and I think the serious people were thinking the coverage of the march had just been too one-sided. TB was really nagging me about getting out more on the humanitarian side, getting better material out of DFID and the CIC. At TB's weekly Monday meeting, we went through the usual and continuing irritants – red tape, complexities of the asylum system, lack of drive in departments on public service reform. On Iraq he was keen for a major upgrade of our communications and believed we could win the argument as set out at the weekend. David M reported Condi as saying that we could go for a second resolution, that she had been told by Blix he felt it was unfortunate his report had gone too far the other way. I did TB a long note on the need to get the US to talk in our language. A lot of the antagonism they caused was by the manner of what they said as much as content, Blix was a case in point. I got the very strong impression that he thought we were OK and they were anything but, yet we were pretty much saying the same things.

We left for Brussels [EU summit] at 3 and agreed that TB would do a doorstep setting out the basic line that now was not the time to weaken. It was one of those summits that nobody really wanted but we were there and we had to get a recommitment to 1441. We did so, and then Chirac was doing the usual posturing, saying there could be no second UNSCR. It was interesting how keen some of the other countries were to make clear they were basically on our side – Spain, Italy, the Dutch, the Danes and the Irish. Jack was taking notes of the discussions which he was getting sent out to me and enabling us to brief as we went. Later more and more people were out on our side. Chirac was slightly losing it, later issued a pretty clear threat to the enlargement countries trying to come in, said they should be careful, they were too pro US and may not be able to come in. Things were going our way much more than we had expected and it was quite a productive day, Jack getting the notes out to me, me turning them into briefings for Godric and Danny [Pruce], who were just working the press centre the whole time. It definitely gave us the feeling that with momentum, we could turn the argument.

Tuesday, February 18

Chirac was widely felt to have made a big mistake attacking the ten candidate countries who felt they were being bullied.[1] Of course he was getting a great press at home and reviving a sense of Gaullism. Needless to say our press were keen to build him up at TB's expense. Our plan was to consolidate the actual success of yesterday, restate the basic case and get going re Iraqi exiles. I had a meeting with the Iraq communications group. There was a clear understanding that we were widening to take in the bigger dimension of the moral and humanitarian side, and we had to be clear about whether this was shifting to a regime-change position. We had to be clear that it didn't, that the basic rationale hadn't changed, but equally we were entitled to make the case that the world would be better without him in power.

I was worried about the CIC which was not working as well as it had been. Gerard Russell's Islamic media unit was doing fine but the CIC as a whole was not producing as it should. We were beginning to get good email responses from Iraqi exiles. At the press conference, TB was relaxed and confident, even though the story was building that his own future was on the line. He seemed relatively unconcerned. Then another meeting on Iraq. The US was still giving out the message that it was going to happen and the rest was just giving us cover, e.g. saying that a second resolution wasn't absolutely necessary but they would try to get it. Maybe they were just getting irritated with us for having taken them down the UN route in the first place.

Wednesday, February 19

TB called on the way to Chequers after what he described as a truly dreadful meeting with GB. He said it wasn't even worth talking about.

---

[1] The ten East European and Mediterranean countries due to join the European Union in 2004 had signed a letter of support for the US stance on Iraq.

He was at a genuine loss to understand why Chirac was prepared to go so far out in damaging his relations with America. It could be Chirac had just decided to go for it as a way of building national identity, but it was a high-risk strategy and he thought it would backfire badly. John Reid was doing a tour of local parties and said he genuinely felt we could persuade people. I spoke to Piers [Morgan] to try to get him to take a piece from John as I knew they were meeting tonight. Of course he wanted TB, but agreed to take JR as a first step. This followed our meeting with Victor Blank [*Trinity Mirror* chairman] yesterday who had suggested JR as a possible link to Piers. TB was pretty frank with Victor, told him he found it very difficult to have a serious conversation with Piers, as the only thing he was really interested in was himself.

TB sent a note through to Bush setting out the basic strategy – that we put down a UNSCR, not push to a vote, instead use it like an ultimatum, give him two weeks or so to take us to the French date of March 14. He spoke to Bush later, said we couldn't dispute that public opinion was against us but he strongly felt the French and Germans were in the right place for public opinion but in the wrong place for the world. Dan [Bartlett] was clearly feeding in our conversations because Bush referred to the fact that I had said he was giving us real problems because they just didn't speak our language. TB felt it was a good call, which ended with Bush raging at the churchmen, this on the day that our church leaders were having a go at us too.

Thursday, February 20

TB was getting more and more worried on Iraq, and with good reason. He called from Chequers saying we really had to think through the strategy on the theme of 'the last push for peace'. He wanted a strong media plan to underpin it. Dan Bartlett was in agreement we had to tone down the war rhetoric and tone up the push for peace. I said we couldn't emphasise enough how we needed the sense that we were trying to avoid war, not rush towards it. TB called later, asked for a call on the Brent [secure phone], later joined by Jack, to discuss rumours that Blix had been saying he intended to report that Iraq was complying when our evidence pointed in the opposite direction. TB later spoke to him. He felt we needed to get the US, UK and Spain putting out a second resolution. I felt we also needed someone unexpected on it, like Mexico or Chile.

Jack wanted to do a parliamentary debate next week and we went over when to announce it and what kind of motion. We now had to get the second resolution, and put down the ultimatum, that amounted to Saddam being forced to answer the questions he had not yet answered or even been properly asked about the leftovers, interviews with scientists etc. We had to get the tone straight prior to the Bush/ Aznar meeting on Saturday. Andrew Adonis had sparked another flurry with the Treasury. Ed Balls was complaining about a story in the *FT* based on TB's progressive governance article about co-payment.[1] Andrew was adamant it referred to what we were doing on tuition fees, but the Treasury were cranking it up as a threat re the NHS. I explained all that to Ed but he was equally adamant it was a hostile act.

David M's conversations with Condi were getting more and more scratchy. Condi was keen to be pushing towards conflict whilst we were emphasising the peaceful route still. Dan and I spent quite a while working on an agreed script.

Friday, February 21

TB called en route to Rome. He really felt everything now had to be set in the context of pushing for peace, that we wanted to resolve it peacefully. He said he really wanted me to work on Dan Bartlett, and get properly agreed message scripts, which I had been doing much of last night and this morning. By the end of it, we had a very strong four-page Sunday briefings script, which if everyone stuck to it, would get us in a far better position. He called me later and I gave him an example of where words that seemed commonplace to them gave us major public opinion problems here. Rumsfeld leading the news here simply by saying 'We're ready', that totally cut across our message that we were trying to avoid war not rush into it. I had the idea of the ultimatum in the briefing note. TB was happy with it and so was Jack until he spoke to Powell who said that the real ultimatum would be made just before action when we tell Saddam to get out of town. I was fine with cutting it, though it weakened it.

Late pm I got a message that the Americans wanted a conference call – Condi, Dan, Steve Hadley [Deputy National Security Advisor] on their side, with David M, Jonathan and me. They clearly had worries. I set out why we wanted to frame it this way, set out the process including a side statement directly challenging Saddam. But Condi feared that setting it out as a final chance – again – or a challenge to Saddam, suggested there was something here beyond 1441. She said 1441 was all that we needed. We tried to use the call

---

[1] Payment made by an individual, usually at the time a service is received, to offset some of the cost.

to get over the need for a different sort of language on this, but they really didn't get it.

During the day I had had three long calls with Dan, a difficult but productive conference call with Condi, a totally useless thirty-minute conference call, yet despite all that we were not really in the same place. I could sense Condi felt we were weakening. She really didn't like the final, final opportunity line, couldn't see that it was simply a way of trying to show we preferred peace to war. TB had done a very strong message at his press conference with Berlusconi, strong on the moral case again. He called to say he felt much better placed on the arguments but it was all still very tricky. John Williams [FCO] had already suggested prior to the Condi call that we say the gap between tabling a resolution and a vote was the closing of the final opportunity for 1441. It was a bit convoluted but we went for that, though Condi kept coming back with noises and a voice that seemed to get shriller as the call went on, that she was concerned we weren't firm enough. I said she had to understand that we were hit hard here because people felt we were rushing to a timetable set by others. The ITV programme on me and the marathon was fine and seemed to get an OK response.

Saturday, February 22
TB was seeing the Pope [John Paul II]. He called but then said as he was on a mobile, to say nothing. Bit of a pointless call really. Tom briefed strongly on 'the last push for peace' while I listened in to a TB/Bush/Aznar/Berlusconi call, livened up a bit by Bush saying he planned to get out his biggest guns and cowboy hat to help Aznar's rating in Spain.

Sunday, February 23
TB was full of it re the Pope, had clearly found it very special. He was for once asking about the marathon. 'Are you really going to run twenty-six miles?' That's what a marathon is. He wanted us to keep pushing on the push for peace, but said we kept being undone by the Yanks and their mode of communication. I called Alan Milburn to suggest he try to cool the public spat going on between him and GB. I watched Rory Bremner which had me and Condi swapping places and was moderately amusing.

Monday, February 24
Iraq was totally dominating, but at TB's morning meeting it was the usual whinge about asylum, crime, health and all the dreadful figures

that were coming out. He was really fed up with it all, in a rage at departments who he felt took their feet off the accelerators once we were all occupied with something else. On Iraq, I said I felt we needed to add some substance to the 'last push for peace', which at the moment just sounded vacuous, something to say to get us through a bit more time. We needed something concrete, like signs of Arab pressure on Saddam, or a new diplomatic effort that meant something. He said the last push WAS the pressure being applied, or the pressure was the last push. But I still felt it looked like we were trying to meet a US timetable, not genuinely trying to avoid war. But all the US politicians did was communicate an impatience to get to war. Hilary A was a little bit more confident about the Commons [vote], but said it was all going to be tough. She, Jack and I negotiated the final motion, which was fine, not explicit re military action or UNSCR.

I think TB was beginning to think I was a bit distracted by the marathon, and maybe I was, though I felt the training was on balance a bonus for the job. It was the focus on the event itself, the build-up and the fund-raising, that was maybe taking my attention away. I discussed Carole [Caplin] with him again. The *Mail* were doing a string of stories at the moment that seemed to be coming from her or someone close to her. He was still maintaining she was a victim in all this and that she would do nothing to harm them, and was upset by the way these stories were coming out. Even after the TV documentary, he was saying she was victim in all this.

I had a meeting with some of the SIS people, including a former member of the Iraqi government who had some good insights into the way we were putting our case, the messages that were likely to get through, and those which didn't. He was clear a lot of the US messages were undermining what we were trying to do. We also needed to emphasise we didn't want to be there for long, and that the commitment to the MEPP was absolute. No matter how closely you read all the briefing and the intelligence, it was always a help to get this kind of verbal face-to-face analysis. He was interesting on the way the regime worked, and felt we should be getting messages into Iraq re that – how they worked against the interests of business, against families – e.g. by using them to spy on each other – and against women. He claimed Uday [elder son of Saddam] raped a different woman every day.

I went to [David] Yelland's farewell [as *Sun* editor]. TB popped in briefly. [William] Hague [former Conservative leader] very nice re my marathon efforts and sponsored me, along with a few others there.

The SCR [draft UN Security Council resolution] went down. Jack and [Sir Jeremy] Greenstock were both out on it but what the French would do was not clear. We put it down with the Americans and the Spaniards, while the French put down a memorandum with the Germans and the Russians. TB was keen to rubbish it but not go OTT. But the main perception of the whole thing was a riven international community and the perception for TB was pretty grim.

Tuesday, February 25

Saddam interview with Dan Rather [American TV news anchor] was going big, both saying he was NOT going to destroy al-Samoud [missiles, with a range in breach of UNSCR 1441] – though we knew he would – and also challenging GWB to a TV debate, which was hilarious, but also a good way of getting up a clear and straight line. I went up to see TB who was fairly relaxed re the French, just wanted us to keep making the case, setting out the whole background. At the Iraq communications group, both John S and I were stressing that the regime-change argument was more productive than the technicalities of 1441. Over to the House for the statement [on Iraq].[1] He was on form, and had a lot of Tories strongly supporting.

Later, TB had a meeting with GB and Balls on the euro. Yet again, he said at the end it was the worst yet, that 'I just can't be bothered with it any more.' He said GB talked to him like he was a five-year-old. If it was serious, he would be worried, but it's a total joke. If he had any sense, he would just be totally, absolutely, totally supportive on the war. GB had sent a copy of TB's progressive governance [FT] article to JP, with bits underlined, and was saying a lot of it could be said by a Tory. JP was onside at the moment. TB said 'I'm afraid I have reached the position where I trust nothing he says because everything is worked out through the prism of his own position.' There was real contempt in his voice.

TB called during the Juventus vs Man U game. He said it was going to be really tough from now on in. The truth was we may well have to go without a second UNSCR, or even without a majority on the UNSC. The Bush poodle problem would get bigger. We were giving the Lib Dems a big opening, but he was adamant it was the right thing to do, and worth the political consequences. I said what

[1] Blair told MPs 'The intelligence is clear: [Saddam Hussein] continues to believe that his weapons of mass destruction programme is essential both for internal repression and for external aggression. It is essential to his regional power. Prior to the inspectors coming back in, he was engaged in a systematic exercise in concealment of those weapons.'

if a hundred of our own MPs are voting against the government and he said fine, they're mainly the dispossessed and disaffected. He knew it was more serious than that but was pushing the argument now that those against us had to face up to the fact that the consequence of their actions was Saddam staying in power. Hilary Armstrong called and said things did not look good. He must be worried about the growing talk of his job being on the line over this. He was getting a good response for doing well in the House, but an awful lot of our side were already publicly committed to rebellion. The question they were asking was is Iraq a threat to us, and now? TB was dismissive of Blix. He said his job was to set out the facts, but he now saw his mission as to stop war.

Wednesday, February 26

Jack went a bit loopy re a JR interview in which he seemed to suggest today's [Commons] debate would be the last vote before action – it wasn't. With the debate straight after PMQs, that was almost all we discussed at the PMQs meeting. I did though have a meeting with Alan M and Darren Murphy [Milburn's special adviser] to try to get them in a less confrontational position re GB, which was doing nobody any good, and to try to get the dividing lines back to being about us and the Tories, not internal. On Iraq, Alan was very much of the view that we should get on with it.

TB was good at PMQs, and [Charles] Kennedy [Liberal Democrat leader] was so opportunistic it would begin to damage him soon. JP meeting, where he was very supportive, and urging TB to do more of the direct communication, both with MPs but also on the media. There was a sense among most people that if the uncommitted and unsure could hear the arguments direct, unmediated by a cynical media, we would win over more people.

Then all eyes on the vote. Through the day, we got the indications the majority would be bigger than we thought initially. Dan Bartlett sent through lines from Bush's MEPP speech for us to start briefing from midnight to try to build it big from the morning. It was imperative our people felt there was something substantial involved in this. Then back for Burnley–Fulham [FA Cup replay at Turf Moor, Burnley]. We were on great form, 3–0, and I had avoided the nightmare of not being able to go. The Iraq debate itself was good, though the dangers were very clear and there was a growing sense of menace in the voices of the disaffected, particularly former ministers. Frank Dobson [former Health Secretary] was now pretty determinedly anti, and as Alan M said, we had handled him disastrously. There was also Chris Smith,

Peter Kilfoyle, Kate Hoey, Glenda Jackson [all former ministers], the list went on. At least we ended up with a majority of the PLP, though David Miliband said to me he reckoned there were about ten backbenchers who were actually totally supportive of TB's position on this. Jack did a good job in the debate and probably helped keep a few on side. Ann Clwyd [Labour MP and Iraq expert] was absolutely terrific and we needed to hear more of her. She brought a real passion to the debate and everyone knew it went back a long way. But the result was pretty tough.[1]

Thursday, February 27

TB was exercised re the French. 'They are really going for it now. This is war by other means.' TB remained reasonably chirpy, said he felt comfortable with the arguments and we just had to keep making them. Philip told me that the groups were far less cynical than the media. They were looking to hear TB more, and when they did, they just about gave him the benefit of the doubt. There was an instinctive understanding that no prime minister would do anything as difficult and unpopular as this for the hell of it. The public wanted a deeper sense of engagement. They were actually ready and willing to listen to deeper arguments on it. There was a hunger for debate on the substance, not just the media headline stuff. TB felt we had to be pushing on two main arguments – the moral case, and the reason why the threat was real and current, not because he could whack missiles off at London but because he could tie up with terrorists and others with a vested interest in damaging us and our interests. But we should understate rather than overstate, a point I made on the conference call. The Americans' saying there was a direct link was counterproductive. Far better to be saying this was a possibility and one we were determined to ensure never came about.

TB, JP, Jack S meeting at which we went over the distinct possibility of no second resolution because the majority was not there for it. TB knew that meant real problems, but remained determined on this, and convinced it was the right course. He said later that he felt only now was Bush really aware of the full extent of the stakes here. This had the potential to transform for good America's relations with Europe and the rest of the world, and in a worst-case scenario was a disaster for everyone. He wanted to get the thing done quickly, but he also wanted them to understand better the broader agenda. He

[1] The amendment arguing that the case for military action against Iraq remained unproven was defeated 393 to 199.

felt Bush had moved a good deal on that but was less convinced it permeated throughout the administration.

At Cabinet, things were pretty much rock solid. TB looked very tired and I could sense a few of them only fully realising, when they saw him close up like this going through the arguments, the enormity of the decisions, and the enormity of the responsibility involved. Robin was the trickiest, and was delighting in giving the sense of how isolated we were from normal traditional partners. Clare was doing her usual interruptions and mutterings but a bit less provocatively and for her was relatively onside. She wanted to do a big number on aftermath preparations but TB was there ahead of her. He was very calm, matter-of-fact, just went through where we were on all the main aspects of this. Margaret Beckett, who had been excellent on the radio this morning, made a very strong intervention. She was a useful barometer and she was very supportive. Nobody was really looking to make TB's position more difficult out of today, with the possible exception of Robin, who was moving towards exit.

Later I headed with Sally for the airport to meet TB, who had been at the archbishop's enthronement at Canterbury.[1] There was a cock-up over the planes but we finally met at the Hounslow Suite after a long bus journey and went over themes for the speech in Madrid tomorrow. He had a cold and was surprisingly OK considering the delay. He did an OK interview with Jackie Ashley [*Guardian*] on the flight, and was strongly putting the moral case, but whether it was his cold or her rather irritating manner, he didn't really get into his stride. It was OK but no better and would be unlikely to change Guardianista opinion. I'm not sure anything will at this stage. When I told him that Fiona felt he was on some kind of kamikaze mission on this, he said sometimes when you were in the top job, you just had to do what you thought was right, even if you knew so many people thought you were wrong. We finally got to Madrid, then by helicopter to Moncloa [palace]. He said he knew the risks but he was clear we were doing the right thing.

Friday, February 28

The Ritz Hotel [Madrid] was a bit faded and jaded, and for various reasons I didn't sleep as well as I had hoped to. I went out for a run early on, and gave up after three miles, just couldn't get going. I had worked late on TB's speech for Wales, in particular trying to explain in ways that would connect why he cared so deeply about this, why

---

[1] Dr Rowan Williams had been anointed as the 104th Archbishop of Canterbury.

February '03: Cabinet fairly rock solid

he was willing to face potentially disastrous personal and political consequences for this one issue. I was struck more and more by how many people, mainly but not limited to critics, said they couldn't understand why it seemed to matter so much, and that was what we needed to explain. All the rational arguments were out there and yet for a lot of people this had become emotional as much as rational. It had to be in the area of the nature of the threat, but also the lessons of history when it came to failing to stand up to danger.

Blix was now causing us significant problems. He was talking now about Saddam's line on [potential decommissioning of] al-Samoud missiles being a significant piece of disarmament. TB was raging again, said the man was supposed to be a civil servant, but had decided to behave like a politician. He is just desperate not to be seen as the person who allowed a war to start, but his job is to present the facts. He felt Blix was being bullied successfully by the French who, he was now convinced, wanted as their main foreign policy objective to build Europe as a power rival to the US, and determined to shaft TB as the, or a, main player in Europe. He was also worried that Kofi [Annan, UN Secretary General] was getting closer to the Franco-German position from where we thought him to be. At last night's dinner with Aznar, he told TB that Chirac had said directly to him that there were two possible visions for Europe – in one, close to the US; in the other, as a rival. Chirac knew which he wanted. Aznar knew which he wanted too, he said, and it wasn't that.

In Spain there was four per cent support for action without a second UNSCR, twenty-three per cent with it. TB said to Aznar that four per cent was roughly the number you could get in a poll for people who believed Elvis was alive, so he had a struggle! Aznar seemed as determined as TB though. TB's cold had got worse and he had stayed late in bed. The Jackie Ashley interview disaster went on. After all the travel nightmares of yesterday now it transpired the tape hadn't worked, so TB had pretty much wasted his voice. Godric, Sally and I tried to help her out from notes and memory, but it was another pain we could do without. His cold cannot have been helped by all the nonsense of yesterday, broken planes and buses to get scheduled flights and the rest of it. As Jack Straw said, 'He is effectively vice president of the free world, and has to travel around like a cost-cutting tourist.' I had a similar feeling at the Moncloa, which was a beautifully designed and expensively built complex for the PM and his staff and the kind of thing that would provoke an absolute outcry if we went for something like it. Downing Street had a lot of advantages, but set against this, it had a lot of disadvantages too. The Aznar breakfast was the usual going through the motions on a communiqué which would get very little attention at all, and then focusing on the questions likely to come up, which were all pretty obvious. It helped that generally on Iraq they were in the same place, and able to offer a bit of mutual support. Aznar was determined to reshape Spain's relations with the US. The press conference was good, and between them they got up the right message.

We set off for the airport, TB now turning his mind to the [Welsh Labour Party conference] speech, in between continuing to vent his spleen at GB. He was convinced that GB and Co. were running the line to the media that the reason TB couldn't persuade people was because of the general TB-trust issue. 'It is actually wicked.' There was another story in *The Times* today about TB planning to overrule GB re foundation hospitals which sparked another little wave of Treasury briefing against Milburn for having stirred it up. Back on to the small plane taking us to Wales where TB wrote out in long hand the Iraq section of the speech for Swansea. Very strong. The nature of the threat plus the lessons of [Neville] Chamberlain as 'a good man who made the wrong decision' [appeasing Nazi Germany]. I reordered it and we signed it off on the thirty-minute drive to the conference centre. Fairly big demos. His voice was really bad now but he just about held it together for the speech, which went OK, both in the hall and media-wise. On the plane back we were talking through general positioning. Blix was not making things easy in one direction; the Yanks were making it difficult in the other. This is tough, he said, very tough, about as tough as it gets. He asked what I thought the chances were of it killing him off. Twenty per cent, I said. 'I'd say nearer thirty the way things are right now.'

Saturday, March 1

I did a twenty-mile run, my longest yet, stopping only once when TB called for a chat re Blix. A combination of Blix and the recent moves by the Iraqis had got us on the back foot again. He felt it was all now about the politics of the UNSC, and would come down to a hard-headed argument for votes. It was all going to ebb and flow but we just had to keep going. He was clear that the consequences of not being with the US now were incalculable. I said I felt there had been various points where we could have done something different vis-à-vis the US. He said no, the only way to have had influence with them was to be clear from the start we would be with them when things got really tough. He was clear our interests were aligned.

Sunday, March 2

Yesterday's news of the arrest of al-Qaeda's Number 3 kept the media off our backs for most of the day, but in general I felt things moving away from us again.[1] Saddam was definitely outwitting us on al-Samoud missiles and getting us in the wrong place. We didn't have the armoury to hit back hard. It was partly my fault because I hadn't been motoring as I had in previous full-on communications situations. We were doing OK on the sustained arguments material, but on the quick tactical stuff I didn't feel on form, and I think that hit TB's confidence on some of this too. I had to decide re the FA [chief executive job] because they were starting interviews tomorrow, but I had pretty much reached the conclusion it wasn't possible. PG said it would be seen as a disaster for TB, just when he didn't need anything to add to his problems. The latest polling was not as bad as it might have been considering.

Monday, March 3

TB called me up at 7.45 as he was due to leave for Belfast at 8.15. He was even more worried than he had been on Friday. He felt things just were not where they needed to be. David M and John Scarlett came back from their weekend trip to Mexico and Chile and felt both countries were very firmly on the fence and could see no reason to come off it. TB said it was still possible we could get a majority on the UNSC but if it was in circumstances where people felt we bullied and arm-twisted, the French would be less worried about putting down a veto. The Americans were frankly alienating people by their tactics. David M said the message these smaller countries got was the basic assumption from the Americans that they would come over in the end.

I said to TB that our problem on the communications front was largely caused by US friendly fire. Just when we started to get a message through, they would come up with something different which would pose a real problem for us. They looked the whole time like they were desperate for war. We at least didn't look like we were desperate for war, but we did look like we were desperate to be with them, so to a lot of people it amounted to the same thing. TB said he would have to tell Bush that it was not possible to get the votes at the moment. It was totally what they didn't want to hear but they had to hear it from someone. He was very down on the Americans

[1] Khalid Sheikh Mohammed had been captured by the Pakistani secret service in Rawalpindi.

at the moment. I was feeling much as I had done for some time, compounded by another totally useless conference call which was becoming little more than a telephonic multinational diary meeting. Also I sensed they were becoming irritated with us. I told David I wanted to be frank with them that Bush, not just Rumsfeld, was the main communication problem. With TB away [in Northern Ireland] for the next day or two, I did a series of meetings on the structures we had, and also trying to analyse which of our key messages were actually getting through, both here and in the regions.

I had a meeting with Ed Balls, still going on about Peter M urging Milburn to be a rival to GB, still claiming that we were encouraging columnists to write that GB could be for the chop. He claimed GB wanted to do more on Iraq, and I said the more he did the better. But I always felt he would only do it on his terms. I also suggested he and Milburn do something public together in the run-up to the tax rise. TB called in once or twice re Iraq. Blix had effectively become a commentator as well as a player. Saddam's games were playing well for him and whether they tried or not, the Americans just weren't helping us in public opinion terms. Sally felt the party was with us up to the point of the destruction of missiles, which tipped the balance towards giving the inspectors more time. TB was moving to the Canadian position of a bit more time to get the questions finally answered.

I was beginning to fear that if we went to war without a second resolution, TB would fail to get it through the Commons, and he would be dead in the water. 'I've just got to tell Bush clearly that if he does this wrong, he'll have governments toppling all over the place and cause absolute chaos.' There was a poll in Spain showing ninety-five per cent opposition. Opposition in Turkey was enormous.

Tuesday, March 4

TB still in Northern Ireland. The Iraq meeting was fine though I felt we needed to do more to get up the bigger argument about democracies versus dictatorships. We were in a very odd period where there was a strong sense of momentum towards war come what may, but with the dynamics feeling as though they were totally against us. He was doing OK in Belfast, though [David] Trimble [First Minister of Northern Ireland] walked out at 7 and Sinn Fein kept chiselling away. They kept at it till gone midnight and TB didn't get back till 3am. I had some good cheques coming in – [Michael] Heseltine [former Conservative Deputy Prime Minister], [Jeremy] Paxman [BBC]. Ed Balls called, clearly having spoken to GB, and said he thought if he did something with Milburn, the story would be division not unity. Depends how you do it.

Wednesday, March 5

TB had just a few hours' sleep before his meeting with [Igor] Ivanov [Russian foreign minister]. David M had raised with Condi the idea of TB going to Chile and Mexico and trying to get them to co-present on the day of Blix the idea of a final ultimatum and taking the clusters document [a paper setting out where Iraq had not complied with its disarmament obligations] from Blix to get out what needed to be done. She was not dismissive, though they may be sensing that we felt they lacked the subtlety required. TB felt strongly these countries needed to be given a reason for coming on board more than fear of US bullying. The idea would be to say after Blix reported that it was clear Saddam was not co-operating and now we would set a date by which the UNSC would decide it was clear he had not taken the final opportunity to disarm. Ivanov was clear that Putin would like to be more involved. David felt there was a case for going to Chile as early as tomorrow.

TB was pretty good in the House today, considering how little sleep he had had and how difficult the issues were. France, Germany and Russia issued a joint statement, de Villepin driving it mainly. Earlier Jack came over for a meeting with TB and told him 'If you go next Wednesday with Bush, and without a second resolution, the only regime change that will be taking place is in this room.' Written down, it sounds more menacing than it was. He was trying to be helpful. TB's call to Bush was OK, though as I stayed in TB's room, I only heard his side, saying we had a real problem with world opinion, that these countries needed a reason to come round, that he wanted to go to Chile and set out the outlines of an amended resolution with a deadline so it was clear there would be war if Saddam hadn't responded. Blix was out again today, as much commentator as civil servant. TB felt the UNSC had to take control of this now, not Blix.

When the call ended, Jonathan walked in and said that was a 'fuck me' call, in that they actually seemed far apart. TB said it was not as bad as that. He told Bush we would be with them come what may but these other countries needed help to come over. He also said Bush needed to work more on Putin, not just write him off. TB then did the [Chilean President Ricardo] Lagos call and put the same idea. Lagos didn't totally go against it but was not exactly wild and we certainly had to put on hold the idea of going tomorrow. By the end of the day, not only did he think he should go to Chile, but also

Moscow and another visit to Bush. So the wanderlust was on. 'We are in this, and nobody must think we would ever wobble.' But the Americans were not helping. They claimed they had already slowed down as a result of TB, that Bush had wanted to go as early as yesterday but TB had made sure he didn't. It was a pretty grim scene, and no matter how grim, TB was still saying constantly it was the right thing to do.

Thursday, March 6

I ran in, slightly different route, almost five miles, then up to see TB in the flat with David and Jonathan. He was looking a bit more worried. He said the frustrating thing is that he felt that if we were in charge of it all, we would have sorted it by now. David said the Americans were much more confident they had the votes for a second resolution. TB was keen the Americans reach out far more, especially to Putin. He was also keen that we 'rise above Blix' and a meeting with Lagos might be the way to do that. Jack came over and we discussed pre-Blix positioning. We needed to get out the idea that we wanted the clusters document out there, also the sense that Blix was just inhaling the politics in all this. We agreed we needed to publish a version of the clusters document which would help turn round the argument. I was impressed with Jack at the moment. He could sometimes be very nerdish, and wood-for-trees, but his grasp of the detail was a help, and his political feel was currently good. We discussed with JP the idea of going to Africa to see the three leaders there.[1] He was off to New York on Concorde at 9 with the message from TB that we needed to turn the Blix clusters document to our advantage.

Cabinet was scratchy, Robin and Clare both a bit bolder in setting out their concerns, Clare saying that the idea of horse trading and bullying was bad for the authority of the UN. TB hit back quite hard, said it was not just the US who were bullying and intimidating. What about the French telling the Bulgarians they would not be able to get into the EU if they sided with America? Robin was diddling rather more subtly whereas Clare was just doing anti-Americanism. John R hit back hard as well as TB. I walked through with TB to his office at the end. He said 'God, you wouldn't go into the jungle with them would you?' The mood had generally been OK, though there was clearly a lot of concern about our position.

[1] Angola, Cameroon and Guinea supported continued inspections, but were thought to be against taking a stand on disarmament by military action.

We set off for a studio in Wembley, where he was doing an MTV special. He was fairly relaxed and it helped put out a tough message, the idea that it was going to a vote and people had to decide.[1] The audience was pretty good, not the usual rent-a-crowd. He spoke to the Cameroon president [Paul Biya] in the car on the way back and offered him a visit to the UK. Then the call to Lagos, and the idea of the visit was clearly not on as things stood. There was a rumour doing the rounds that Bush was about to address the Americans to say they had captured Bin Laden. I called Dan. It wasn't true. He intended to say they were confident of a second resolution and he intended to be positive re MEPP. We agreed there may be a case for going for Blix tomorrow.

With the Chile trip off, TB was keen to go and see Bush soon. I said we had to be clear about a purpose, because there would be such focus on the visit. He said it was to get them to do the right thing. I said but they were already very clear about their purpose, which was to go for it. I said 'Are you not sure that your frustration at the way others are dealing with it is just producing a kind of wanderlust?' He said no matter how many times you spoke on the phone, there was no substitute for face-to-face meetings. He said don't worry, we'll get through this fine. I asked him, if at the end of this he was history before his time, was this issue really worth sacrificing everything? He said it is always worth doing what you think is the right thing to do. Iraq is a real problem, Saddam is a real problem, for us as much as anyone, and it's been ignored too long.

Friday, March 7

Up to the flat to see TB with David, Jonathan and Sally. Condi had told David overnight that Putin had been clear with Bush that they would veto the second resolution. Also we still didn't have a clue whether Chile and Mexico would come over. The mood was gloomier than ever. TB was keen to get up the clusters document and also move towards the sense of an ultimatum. He and David were both now expressing their irritation at the US. David was even of the view that we should be pushing the US to a version of the Franco-German idea of inspections with force, a blue beret [UN] force involved in disarmament. TB spent hours on the phone, including an hour with Putin, a long call with Jack and later with Bush. He wanted to give

[1] Blair told the MTV audience 'If we don't act now, then we will go back to what has happened before and then of course the whole thing begins again and he [Saddam] carries on developing these weapons . . . dangerous weapons, particularly if they fall into the hands of terrorists.'

him a clear message about the political realities, namely that we could not do this without a Commons vote and it was not going to be easy without a second resolution, or with a resolution that was vetoed. The Russian veto was a new element. Everyone expected the French to be ultra difficult but thought the Russians might be more prone to be neutral, but Putin's position had clearly hardened. During their call, Putin was very clear that he felt taken for granted by the Americans, and he felt he got a lot of talk from them but very little delivery. Jack was doing his UNSC speech and did it well and with passion. Bush was agreeing to a slightly later deadline, March 17.

TB, Jonathan, Sally, Pat [McFadden] and I had a meeting to go through some of the what-ifs, including him going if we lost a vote. TB said he felt that there had to be a vote on a second resolution and if it was about the use of troops and he lost a vote on that, he would have to go. The Tories were making clear they would support us on a war motion but not on a confidence motion. Andrew Turnbull was quietly looking into how a JP caretaker premiership would operate. Even though we were talking about his own demise, TB still felt we were doing the right thing. He said even though we were all rightly irritated by the Americans, it was the French we should be really angry with. Bush told TB he would certainly go for a vote. He was still making clear he didn't feel he needed a UNSCR but he wanted to go for it.

Jonathan described the whole thing now as an enormous game of diplomatic chicken. TB said we could not flinch now, that if any weakness was signalled, we've had it. He was making clear to Bush, not in personal or moaning terms but as a reality, that his job was on the line, that if we didn't get the Commons vote, there could be no using UK troops, which the Americans needed. Black humour was setting in. TB said his future was now in the hands of the dying president of Guinea [Lansana Conté] and the diplomatic judgement of Jeff Ennis [Labour MP]. We were sending JP to a president's deathbed to keep the British government alive.

Bush was at least conscious of the difficulties they gave us. He said to TB don't worry, I'll be more subtle than you fear. 'I'm not going to say to Lagos – hey you mutha, I'm gonna crush you like a Chilean grape.' TB said afterwards that the reason he liked him was that he was actually so straight, and understood his own weaknesses as well as strengths. He happened to be right on the issue even if they didn't always handle it well. I said all that being said, TB did need to think about his own position, not get pinned into just doing what Bush wanted. TB was clear with him that we needed a bit more time. I reckoned the chances of him being out within a week or two were about 20–1 now. Parliamentary arithmetic was complicated, and not yet entirely clear.

Jack called from New York and pissed me off when he referred post CIC dossier to the 'discredited Downing Street machine' and said he didn't want to put out our short clusters document. We did it anyway, with Tom going over to the gallery after Blix. We were all outraged at the Blix report. TB said it was political and dishonest. Dan Bartlett said we don't care what he thinks, his job is to tell us what he knows. Scarlett said he was wrong in saying the Iraqis were trying to co-operate more. TB was very philosophical about it all. As I sat listening to him on the phone, I lost count of how many times he said: 1. we are right on the issue; 2. we have to see it through; 3. I'm philosophical about what it means for me and whether I survive or not. TB was keen to push the idea that the only reason the concessions were coming was because of the pressure we were applying. But there were real divisions and dangers and the UN was on very dangerous terrain. There was a very clear picture, clearer than ever, of the US in one place, us in another, the French in another, the Russians in another, and the UN as an organisation really worried about where it was heading.

Saturday, March 8

Blix didn't come out as badly as it might have done. In a sense he was almost irrelevant now. I spoke to TB to agree the lines to push for the Sundays – namely there are two routes by which he can avoid conflict: 1. he disarms, or 2. he goes. TB was working the phones pretty much flat out, especially Lagos but also the Chinese and keeping in touch with Bush. We were pushing hard for the second resolution. We were discussing whether JP should go to Africa to work the African countries on TB's behalf. I tried to get Jack out for the *Frost* programme but he said he was desperate for a day off. I spoke to JP who agreed to come down from Hull to do it. JP was totally onside at the moment. TB felt the PLP was at best shaky. He remained sure we were doing the right thing and it helped internally that JP was as solid as he was.

Later I did a conference call with JP, [Patricia] Hewitt and [Peter] Hain who were also on the [Sunday] programmes and went over some of the problem questions e.g. on second resolution and also the issue of a Commons vote. By the time the papers came in, the main story was a mini wave of threatened resignations by PPSs [parliamentary private secretaries]. JP was totally scornful, said they were cowardly and pathetic. When it was pointed out that Anne Campbell was one of them, JP said 'Who is she PPS to?' 'Me,' said Patricia. 'Who is me?' said JP. 'It's Patricia here, John.' I managed to get in a long run earlier, twenty-one miles or so, and was feeling in good shape pre marathon. But Rory was racing at Brighton and had a massive allergy attack which had Fiona really worried for a while. Again, I felt bad that work had kept me from going down there with him, but he seemed a lot better when they got home. The key now was winning the necessary votes at the UN but in some ways the situation was in limbo. TB was clear we just had to keep our nerve and keep striving to get their votes.

Sunday, March 9

Up to watch JP on *Frost*. He was fine on the basic lines we had agreed though the resignations were the main news out of it. Andy Reed [PPS to Margaret Beckett] duly resigned as I was driving with Calum, Philip [Gould] and Georgia [his daughter] to Watford. I was troubled all the way by the possible clash between the marathon and the [FA] Cup semi-final if we got through and were playing on the Sunday. But the problem never arose as we played poorly and went down 2–0. I had agreed to do a piece for the *Mirror* which I dictated rather half-heartedly on the drive back.

TB spoke to Jiang Zemin [Chinese Premier], and the Chinese put out the line that they were calling for more time for inspections. Then at around 5.30, just as I was settling down to do some work upstairs, Clare Short called me. She hardly ever called me, so I was surprised when Switch came on with her. She was friendly enough as we did a bit of small talk, but then got to the point. She had done an interview with Andrew Rawnsley for the *Westminster Hour* and had said she would resign if we went to war without a second resolution; that we were allowing our own policy to be dictated by the US; and that we were not doing enough in the Middle East. She said it all very matter-of-factly, as though she was telling me a few football results. I was conscious of myself shaking my head as she spoke, and then making a mental note to myself not to let my loathing of her pour out, but I said I was at a total loss to understand how she thought this kind of public conversation helped the government make and implement sensible policy. I also reminded her that nobody, as she herself had said, had done more than TB to get this down the UN route.

She said nothing at first. Then I said I also thought it absolutely extraordinary that she should be saying this to me, rather than to TB. 'I thought I would call you because I knew you would be angry and

I thought I'd rather get the anger direct than through the media.' The whine in the voice was whinier than ever. As if TB was going to be doing fucking cartwheels. I said I found the whole thing extraordinary. I thought the deal was that if you were a Cabinet minister, you spoke up in Cabinet if you had concerns, that was the place to do it, and then a policy or a line was agreed and everyone stuck to it. I said I had never heard her say in Cabinet she would resign. She said – rich this, considering how often she spoke – that she tended not to speak in Cabinet in case she was briefed against. I said there was no point her talking to me; she would have to speak to TB. I would call him to see if he wanted to speak to her. She said she was going out shopping with her mum but she would take her mobile with her. How considerate.

TB was at church so I sent through a note to be given to him when the service ended. I called JP, who was due to meet TB at 7. He said the whole thing was typical of her – she was a coward, couldn't cope with pressure, and so ended up doing it like this, hanging her conscience out to dry. Jack called after learning Mike O'Brien was going to be played the tape of her interview on the programme. He said this was the result of years of her being allowed to do what she wanted. It was a disgrace. I spoke to Mike and we agreed he would simply stress the line we were working for a second resolution and not get drawn into a detailed conversation re Clare. TB finally called after he got back to Chequers from church. He was as appalled as I expected him to be. 'It is disgusting, totally disgusting.' It was the same word virtually every minister who called to complain used. TB said he was appalled for a whole stack of different reasons: 1. at what she had said and done; 2. that she had done it on the radio rather than talking to him; 3. that she had called me rather than him, and 4. most importantly, that it totally undercut his strategy to build UN support. He felt it showed there was a willingness among some – her included – to push him out over this. I was less sure it was a thought-through thing at all.

I said I cannot see how you can keep her without looking weak. He said in process terms, there was no doubt about that. The BBC had told Mike O'Brien that she called them up and volunteered to go on. He spoke to her later, and said simply he would reflect. We agreed to a public line that simply made clear she had never spoken in these terms within Cabinet or to the PM. There was no point rushing on this. JP spoke to her a couple of times. He said what she was saying was that she didn't have confidence in the PM's strategy, or his ability to pursue it. She claimed it had not come out as she intended, which was bollocks. I now had the transcript and went through it with JP. He said he didn't see how he could keep her in those circumstances. She was clearly limbering up to go. He thought it was not impossible GB knew what she was planning and that she might be thinking in terms of a stalking-horse challenge at conference. I went with Fiona and the kids to Pizza Express, but the phone just never stopped, usually another minister to go on about how beyond the pale she was and had to go.

TB called again, said Saddam would be laughing his head off when he heard about it. Later a secure conference call with Jonathan, David M with Condi, Dan and Andy Card [White House chief of staff] to go through the various scenarios: majority with no vetoes – fine; majority plus veto(es) – manageable but difficult; no vote; no majority. We said if we got a second resolution we would put it to a parliamentary vote quickly. We could live with a French veto, because people expected it, but we couldn't live without a majority. If that happened, we would probably have to put it to a vote, and if we lost it, there was a danger we would lose the prime minister. The Yanks said that if we got a majority with vetoes, Bush wanted to go straight in, within days, even short of the March 17 deadline, would say the UNSC had failed to act, and get going, on the basis of 1441. We made the point that we needed the second resolution. Without it, we had real problems in Parliament. They said continually they wanted to help us but of course what they really wanted was the use of our forces.

Jonathan and I continually emphasised we needed the second resolution. We had seven definite votes still, but Condi was less confident re Chile and Mexico. She said [Vicente] Fox [President of Mexico] was in a state of torture because it was such a big thing to stand up against the US. They basically wanted by Tuesday/ Wednesday to say we had exhausted every effort and now the diplomatic window had closed. We said if we got the majority for a second resolution, even with vetoes we would have to go through it, including with the timetable. Andy Card said he feared the president's response would be 'Here we go, another final opportunity, a final final opportunity and this time we really mean it.' I said TB's job was on the line and we did not want to lose him. 'No, nor do we,' said Condi. I think our concern was probably deeper. I called Jack Cunningham [former Cabinet minister] who was doing the media in the morning. He was scathing re Short, Chris Smith, Kilfoyle, Dobson. There were two groups ranged against TB, he said – those who never wanted him, and those who felt he didn't share their own high view of themselves. But the mood out there was not good, and this was a 'dangerous moment' for TB. I listened to Clare's interview and the disgusting self-indulgent whine made the words even worse to the ear than they were in print on the transcript. It was clear she was asking to go, but wanting the moral high ground when it happened.

Another rash of ministerial calls after it went out – JP, JR, JS, DB – all saying she was an outrage and there had to be decisive leadership about this. JP said to her afterwards that he had been sitting in the room with TB as he called some of these leaders and she totally undercut his strategy. Phil Webster [*Times*] told me every single broadsheet had been planning to lead on TB trying to go the UN route, and then Clare does this. I listened in later to the TB/Bush call. TB started by saying he was 'fighting on all fronts'. 'Attaboy,' came the reply, a bit too patronisingly for my tastes. TB said one of his ministers was threatening to resign, also that Chirac told Lagos that the Africans were 'in the bag'. I hope that's bullshit, said Bush. TB had spoken to the four leaders who made up the 8 plus 1. [Pervez] Musharraf [President of Pakistan] was with us but it was difficult for him. Cameroon said absolutely. Guinea's foreign minister coming tomorrow. [José Eduardo] Dos Santos [President of Angola] solid.

TB was doing most of the talking, said he felt Lagos was trying to move. We had been working on the idea of laying out a series of tests re what we meant by full co-operation. He felt Bush needed to work some more on Fox. He felt if we could get them to accept the idea of the tests, other countries would also come with us. But Bush said he was already putting enormous pressure on Mexico. He said he had also been twisting Lagos' arm, 'but gently because I respect you'. GWB said he could be in no doubt that if there was a vote, they would have to use it. TB said the Chileans felt any tests should be agreed through Blix. Bush not happy. Bush said Saddam was very adept at exploiting weakness and Blix was weak. These countries need to see we want to do this peacefully. He wants the vote to go through but not on an unreasonable basis.

TB said the public opinion problem stemmed from people feeling the US wanted a war. We have to put up the genuine tests of disarmament, show the determination to try to do this peacefully. Bush said he had never come across a situation where the dividing line between success and failure was so narrow. He said we want it done peacefully, or any other way. His tone was very different to TB's. Bush was talking the diplomatic talk whilst clearly irritated by the whole thing. His worry was that we were negotiating with ourselves, that we get a resolution with a timeframe, everything they want, and we get nothing for it. He said he couldn't believe Chirac said he had the Africans in the bag. 'I can,' said TB. 'I have a lot of experience of them.' He [Bush] was clearly aware of how tough things were getting for TB. He said if the swing countries didn't vote with us 'my last choice is for your government to go down. That is the absolute last thing I want to have happen. I would rather go it alone than have your government fall.' 'I appreciate that,' said TB. 'I really mean that,' said Bush. TB said it was also important he understood that he really believed in what they were trying to do. Bush – 'I know that but I am not going to see your government fall on this.'

TB said 'I've got our troops there too. If I can't get it through Parliament, we fall, and that is not exactly the regime change I want. We have to work out what Mexico and Chile need.' They agreed to speak again to Lagos and Fox. TB said we were in high-risk, high-reward territory. Bush said he was being eroded domestically by inactivity. He also said he felt the hardest part would be after Saddam. Then Bush did a number on the changes in the Arab world that could follow. TB said the biggest concern in not going with the UN was the lack of support if things went wrong. [US General] Tommy Franks had said ninety per cent of precision bombs are precise. That leaves ten per cent. But Bush was left in no doubt TB would be with him when the time came. Bush said 'I'm not going to let you down. Hang in there buddy. You are doing great.' What had been interesting was that Bush listened far more intently to TB. TB did not make too much of his own problems, and was stressing he thought we were doing the right thing.

Monday, March 10

Needless to say Clare was leading the news, amid lots of assumptions we would sack her. The papers, as expected, were fairly grim. I went up to the flat where David was briefing TB on Jeremy Greenstock's meeting with Blix. Blix was just about up for the clusters plan. TB wanted Jeremy to work on Blix and [Dimitri] Perricos [Blix's deputy] to get them signed up to it. It was the only show in town and the only one likely to lead to a majority of the UNSC. He was still working on Lagos and worried about him. Re Clare he said he viewed it as an act of personal betrayal to do what she did, without warning, when he was in the midst of negotiating on this. TB's real anger with the French had been the sending of mixed messages to Saddam, and that is what Clare was doing too. He was minded to sack her but on the other hand felt there was no point in doing anything other than

Tony Blair (*seated*) before the Commons debate on going to war with Iraq; with him are (*left to right*) Jonathan Powell, David Manning, Peter Hyman and Alastair Campbell.

Campbell watches Blair's speech live on television from the Prime Minister's office.

US–UK talks at Hillsborough Castle; clockwise from bottom left: Colin Powell, Alastair Campbell, George Bush, Tony Blair, Condi Rice, Ari Fleischer and Jack Straw.

Though the run-up to war preoccupied everyone, Campbell found time to train for the 2003 London Marathon (*above, left*, at the finishing line with Fiona), raising half a million pounds for Leukaemia Research in memory of his best friend John Merritt (*above, right*), and prompting the charity to remind him of his day job (*right*).

RIGHT CATHY,
WE'VE GOT THE CHEQUES
FROM BUSH AND BLAIR, HAVE
YOU FOUND SADDAM'S @**!@
ADDRESS FOR ME YET?

PVGH

Thank-you so much for your outstanding contribution to the work of the Leukaemia Research Fund in the Flora London Marathon 2003.

LEUKAEMIA
RESEARCH

(*Facing page*) The march against the war, February 2003; and two ministers who eventually resigned in protest: Clare Short and Robin Cook.

Saddam is toppled; Blair thanks the troops.

2, 11·07·03 *To Alastair — with appreciation* • *My Mother Donald*

Bill Clinton (*above, far right*) works on a speech with (left to right) Peter Mandelson, Philip Gould and Alastair Campbell; and (*right*) a cartoonist links Clinton's past problems to Campbell's current ones.

(*Above*, *left*) John Scarlett, the spy forced out into the open by the row over (*above*, *right*) weapons inspector David Kelly.

(*Left*) Alastair Campbell, with Jonathan Powell behind him, leaves Number 10 to give evidence (*below*, *right*) to the Foreign Affairs select committee.

Lord Hutton (*left*) headed the inquiry into David Kelly's death. BBC reporter Andrew Gilligan (*above*) and Campbell (*below*) arrive to give evidence. The artist's impression (inset) shows Campbell being quizzed by the inquiry's counsel, James Dingemans QC.

Campbell arrives home on the day of his resignation, 29 August 2003, an event enjoyed by *Private Eye* (*right*).

being totally hard-headed and ruthless about the issue, in which she was something of a sideshow.

I got Jack Cunningham, Bev Hughes [Home Office minister] and Alan Milburn up all making the point that it was odd to do this on the radio rather than speak to the PM about the threat to resign. JP spoke to her twice last night and again this morning and sensed she had concluded we were definitely going to war and she was going to position herself to resign with maximum damage. He even wondered whether she wasn't setting herself up as a possible challenger to GB. I took JP up to the flat. He said it was on balance not sensible to help turn her into a martyr, which is what she wanted, but instead leave her hanging in the wind for a while. He went off to speak to her again and later TB spoke to her, told her she had committed an act of gross betrayal, that he was at a total loss to understand how she could do that. Her defence was that she felt in recent weeks his approach with her was to listen politely but take no notice. He said to her who do you think got us down the UN route, who is the one still pushing on that, who is the one trying to use this to get the MEPP going again? She was totally beyond the pale. He had decided however that he was not going to sack her. JP and I were usually at the front of the 'get rid of her' queue but agreed that on this it would be a mistake. JP said it was all about her position, nothing else. She did say sorry at the end of her conversation, but in that whiney, drippy way that was designed to convey she was sorry that he couldn't see things as clearly as she did.

Jack C was excellent on the media. TB and I prepared for the ITV programme which was pretty dire because the usual so-called representative audience was packed with the usual activists. TB meeting with Hilary A, John R, David Triesman. Hilary said that if we didn't get a second resolution, or if there was a French veto, we were in trouble. So the PLP was willing to subcontract foreign policy to Chirac? We headed over to the FCO for the ITV special. I knew the moment we arrived the audience would be a problem. You could smell the mood. They were not so-called ordinary people but a group put together to give TB as hard a time as possible. Trevor McDonald didn't chair it very well and the whole thing became not just difficult on the substance, but also pretty undignified. When all is said and done he is the prime minister and one or two of them were talking to him like he was a piece of shit on the pavement. He kept calm and dealt with it fine, deciding in the end just to absorb it all but as he came out he gave me a look that could kill. It was a pretty shoddy operation and Peter Stothard [former *Times* editor], who was following us around for the *Times* magazine with [photographer] Nick Danziger, reckoned that not only was the audience slanted, but they had wound them up beforehand.

Then a meeting to discuss whether we could get going on a revised amendment with the challenges to Saddam. [Igor] Ivanov had said the Russians would veto and Chirac did the same. Pakistan indicated abstention. TB told Lagos that if Chile and others moved, the French would pull back but that looked doubtful. Chirac was clearly up for the kill on this, really felt he could damage TB and alarm some of his traditional allies. Chirac was now out with the veto message. TB was on and off the phone to Lagos who said he was eighty per cent there but worried about France and Russia. TB spoke to Greenstock, then at 9.50 did a long call with Bush. GWB kicked off 'Did you save your Cabinet woman?' TB said she was still in for the moment, that she met every description of self-indulgence 'but we have to carry on'. TB did most of the talking, set out where he thought all the different players were. GWB reckoned seven votes solid 'locked up' but Pakistan and the Latins were difficult. He felt Chirac was trying to get us to the stage where we would not put to a vote because we would be so worried about losing.

TB said he felt Lagos wanted to come, but he needed to be able to say he had achieved something, even winning a few days more. But I could sense in his voice and the manner of the discussion that Bush was less emollient than yesterday. He felt Fox would do whatever Chile did. TB said Lagos wanted to come with us but he was very nervous. TB had spoken to him several times. He was biting but wanted to know what the inspectors would say. Lagos was asking do we have to accept military action if he fails these tests? Bush asked re timeframe. TB said they would want to kick us back a few days as a way of showing they got something out of this.

The French and Russian strategy was to play it so hard that we end up thinking we cannot even dream of getting to nine or ten votes. But TB said if we can shift Chile and Mexico, we change the weather. If we can make these tests the basis of an ultimatum, and then the French and Russians have to veto, with Chile and Mexico behind us, and the numbers right on the UN, I think I have a fighting chance of getting it through the Commons. Bush was worried about rolling in more time. TB held his ground, said the Latins had to be able to say they got something out of all this talking to us. They need to be able to point to something that they won last minute that explains why they finally supported us. Bush said the first resolution was also tough – total and complete disarmament. 'We can't weaken.' 1441, he said, we should just put it down again.

TB felt the second resolution was important and this was the best way to get it. He felt that we needed UN backing, or at least a majority, on the assumption France and Russia would veto. Bush said 'Let me be frank. The second resolution is for the benefit of Great Britain. We want it so we can go ahead together.' His worry was that we would get rolled over on timings and also the inspectors would get used by Saddam again. There was something crazy and random about what was going on. It was a pure accident of timing that suddenly made Chile and Mexico the focus of so much diplomacy, TB working on Lagos, Bush on Fox. TB said when this is over, we need to take a long hard look at the reality of how the UN works. These countries suddenly had a lot of power but seemed unsure how to use it. TB felt the Russians, French and Germans now had a bit of a swagger, felt they were showing that the Americans can be taught a lesson. TB felt if we swung over Chile, Mexico would come, then we could go to Putin and say let's be reasonable.

Bush said he'd had a bad conversation with the Turks. [Recep Tayyip] Erdogan [new President of Turkey] had basically given him a lecture on world events when Bush called for [military] overflight rights. He said he would have to go to Parliament. Bush said 'It was not friend-to-friend, far from it. Maybe the interpreter didn't get the nuances, I don't know, but it was a bad call, no camaraderie.' He said again we must not retreat from 1441 and we cannot keep giving them more time.

I was by and large signed up for the policy but it did make me feel a bit sick the extent to which our problems were US-created, and our politics now so dominated by their approach. TB had not really wavered at all but as the time got nearer the politics got tougher. Bush said 'It's time to do this. We have sent tough signals and he knows that. So no more deals.' He had told Rumsfeld to move the ships. We had Schroeder coming over and Bush told TB the Germans needed to know the real lie of the land. He said he took Schroeder's election antics personally.

Bush said again he had no problem with TB presenting him as the US hard cop against his persuading soft cop. He then said 'It makes me sick the way these people are trying to divide us so that we help save Saddam's skin.' Bush said 'If you ran for president over here, you'd whip my ass.' Laughter. TB said he was sure we were doing the right thing and we had to see it through but it was going to be really tough. Bush signed off with 'Hang in there friend.'

Tuesday, March 11

Growing sense of crisis, what with the Chirac veto, talk of a challenge to TB and the dynamic moving away from us the whole time. The press was about as OK as it could be re Clare, but generally things were getting more not less difficult. TB was seeing the Portuguese PM [José Manuel Barroso]. I missed the start because I was doing the morning meeting, but went in for the end, and said there was the case for going at the French with the concept of an 'unreasonable veto'. TB laughed and said to Barroso 'He is the Roy Keane of the operation.' When he said that Barroso would be more diplomatic, I said I know, because he is the Eusébio [great Portuguese footballer]. The doorstep was fine, TB saying Chirac risked letting Saddam off the hook by saying they would veto *'quelles que soient les circonstances'* [whatever the circumstances]. After Barroso left we had a meeting with JP, JR and Hilary A to try to get more politics into all this. The party was going to be important and we were neglecting things.

TB asked if we should not be a bit nicer to Clare and was met with a row of uniformly horrified looks. JP looked at him as though he was mad. TB briefed them on the diplomacy and we agreed I should do a briefing note to go to the whole of the PLP. JP and I also agreed, having persuaded TB to do more difficult TV, that there was a danger it was going too far, that Operation Access had become Operation Masochism and there was something a bit undignified about him getting beaten up too much. [Peter] Goldsmith had done a long legal opinion and said he did not want TB to present it too positively. He wanted to make it clear he felt there was a reasonable case for war under 1441. There was also a case to be made the other way and a lot would depend on what actually happened. TB also made clear that he did not particularly want Goldsmith to launch a detailed discussion at Cabinet, though it would have to happen at some time, and ministers would want to cross-examine. With the mood as it was, and with Robin and Clare operating as they were, he knew that if there was any nuance at all, they would be straight out saying the advice was that it was not legal, the AG was casting doubt on the legal basis for war. Peter Goldsmith was clear that though a lot depended on what happened, he was casting doubt in some circumstances and if Cabinet had to approve the policy of going to war, he had to be able to put the reality to them. Sally said it was for TB to speak to Cabinet, and act on the AG's advice. He would simply say the advice said there was a reasonable case. The detailed discussion would follow.[1]

[1] Lord Goldsmith was later to tell the 2010 Iraq Inquiry that he had strengthened his legal view of the Iraq War after a visit to the US, for discussions with lawyers there. He described suggestions that he did so because of political pressure as 'complete nonsense'. The former Attorney General said he had believed it was 'safer' to get a new UN resolution but gave the 'green light' after deciding force was justified by UN accords dating back to 1991.

March '03: TB – 'Should we be nicer to Clare?'

Alan Milburn called me later to say RC told him he would resign if we didn't get a second resolution. Of the two, RC was easily the more serious and the more thought through. Peter G told TB he had been thinking of nothing else for three weeks, that he wished he could be much clearer in his advice, but in reality it was nuanced. I had a polling meeting with Stan Greenberg. The Lib Dems were on the up a bit. Tuition fees was a growing problem. The figures on right/wrong direction were not great. Asylum was still number one problem area, then crime, and the two were becoming linked in some people's minds. We were losing young people, London swing voters, plus middle class. The Tories had the beginnings of a message that was getting through. Of those who voted for us last time, only sixty-three per cent were still solid. Stan was very sceptical about what we were doing with the Americans. He felt we were being used as part of a US strategy.

TB did a call with Lagos, who was still moving about, then to a meeting with JS, GH, CDS and the AG re the military plan. GH said he would be happier with a clearer green light from the AG. Andrew Turnbull really irritated TB when he said he would need something to put round the Civil Service that what they were engaged in was legal. TB was clear we would do nothing that wasn't legal, and gave him a very heavy look. Peter [Goldsmith] did a version of the arguments he had put to TB, on the one hand, on the other, reasonable case. GH raised the US request for use of Diego Garcia and [RAF] Fairford, saying we should not say it was automatic but had to go round the system. TB said he did not want to send a signal that we would not do it. GH and JS were trying to press on him that the Americans were thinking about doing this very soon, i.e. even at the weekend, and that some of our forces would have to be in before.

CDS said his formal military advice would be that it was not sensible to go on the 17th because of the full moon. We would have to get in before any bombs with night vision and buggies. Our forces were to be involved in the operation to secure the oilfields and prevent the Iraqis setting off an environmental catastrophe to hit the oil markets. We desperately needed some change in the diplomatic weather. The best thing may in the end be to go in without a vote because of the timings, and that once troops are in there the mood changes. But short of that, which was risky enough, it was hard to see how the dynamic changed. There was another small step back with the news Guinea would not be coming with us because they were now in the chair. The system is crazy, like pot luck as to who is in a voting seat at any one time, though I guess it is just about the only way they can make all countries feel more or less involved.

Then came another Rumsfeld disaster. He did a press conference at which he said he and Geoff Hoon had just spoken and went on to indicate that we would not necessarily be in the first wave of attacks because of our parliamentary difficulties. It was not entirely clear whether it was deliberate – i.e. a warning shot that they could and would do it without us – or a fuck-up. We all assumed the latter. He just didn't get other people's politics at all. David M said it made it virtually impossible to have a shared strategy with them. Hopeless. Yet another communications friendly fire. TB went bonkers about it, then called Geoff, who admitted he had put the thought in Rumsfeld's head because he was trying to be very explicit about our difficulties as a way of reining him in. Rumsfeld must have thought he was being helpful, God knows. GH got on to the Defense Department and got them to put out a retraction, making clear we were with them. But it was all very ragged, and indicative once more of the difficulties.

TB had an audience with the Queen at the Palace which usually cheered him up a bit, but he came back still in a real fury re Rumsfeld. He spoke to Geoff, then Lagos, before going to JP's flat where he was having dinner with him and GB. As if he didn't have enough on his plate he was also in the midst of another 'let's sort GB and the future' phase. He said afterwards it was all very odd because they didn't really get to the point. He said he felt something close to contempt for GB at the moment, the way he was manoeuvring even on this. Hilary A had told him earlier that there were people in the PLP not sure which way to go because they were unclear where GB was, and whether it would affect their future chances if he took over. It was a bad scene, really bad, and one which TB felt reflected badly on GB's leadership credentials.

Sally and I were both working late and waiting for his 11pm Bush call. We saw him in the flat when he came back. He said he couldn't believe how the US kept fucking things up, the Rumsfeld thing just the latest. TB was pretty mellow, probably a bad sign. He had suddenly had a load of energy drained from him. He also took a call from Murdoch who was pressing on timings, saying how News International would support us, etc. Both TB and I felt it was prompted by Washington, and another example of their over-crude diplomacy. Murdoch was pushing all the Republican buttons, how the longer we waited the harder it got.

TB/Bush call, 11pm. Bush referred to Rumsfeld's latest gaffe. 'I want to apologise for that – one of those attempts to be helpful that

490 First he is in the

March '03: A 'Rumsfeld disaster'

wasn't very helpful.' These things happen, said TB, but with enough irritation in his voice for the message to be clear. GWB described his latest calls with Fox and Lagos as 'difficult'. He had said they had to give us their votes, that we had to get this over with. There were two options – the soft resolution, or no resolution, but there needs to be an up-and-down vote. He was determined we could not let the date slip. He told them they could have a week. He said the Africans were under huge pressure but solid. Pakistan looking for a way back. 'I just don't understand these guys.' He said Lagos and Fox were clearly happier with no vote. TB said we needed to hold their feet to the fire. Bush 'I'm waiting your instructions. If it falls apart I'm going to make a speech to the American people saying I tried, and now Saddam has forty-eight hours to leave the country.' TB said he still felt Chile would come round and not walk away.

Bush felt seven days was too big a stretch to give them. He said Congress was getting restless and all the polls were showing criticism of the UN for inaction. 'We just got to go.' TB said we had to do something to change the diplomatic weather and get on the front foot but if we can't get anything, we're in real trouble and there is no point pushing the UN beyond what it will take. Bush said 'We know he's not going to disarm. We already had benchmarks. I said to Ricardo [Lagos] that it is time to stand up and be counted. I want your vote. He said no. I said I'll tell Tony and he said no, I'll tell him.' He sounded pretty much at the end of it. TB said he would speak to him again and that a week's delay was the top end for us. As Condi had said, the danger is losing altitude but if we were on the front foot we would gain it again. But Bush said these guys were just playing for time. He felt maybe we stand on Thursday and say there could be no new UNSCR, that it had failed in its mission so Saddam has forty-eight hours to leave. He did not feel the need to buy more time. He was more impatient than ever. TB said he felt a bit more give on the last Putin call but Bush wasn't really listening to this stuff now. TB felt the problem was that the Chiles and Mexicos were not used to making decisions as big as these. But he felt Mexico was making a big mistake siding with the French against the US. Fox was less like a leader than an official. All we got was 'I'll get back to you.'

Wednesday, March 12

Jack S said that Rumsfeld's idiotic comments gave us a way out, namely that we could not be involved at the start but could do humanitarian afterwards. TB was not keen but Jack was very blunt. He said we were dealing, however right we thought it was, with a

US 'war of choice' and we had to understand, as Powell told him the whole time, that some of these people around Bush could not care two fucks about us whatever, and that went for TB as much as the rest of us. Jonathan and I agreed that last night had effectively been a pincer movement. Rumsfeld fucking up had forced us to come out strong. TB felt the Murdoch call was odd, not very clever. Jack had clearly been wound up big time while he was over there. He said we were victims of hopeless bullying and arrogant diplomacy. David M also felt yesterday had been a rather crude attempt to shaft us. He came to see me later and said we really have to work hard to keep TB in position. He was so earnest about it but adamant that both America and France were so capable of doing the wrong things for the wrong reasons that TB was absolutely key to keeping the international community together. David felt he was in a different league to the rest and could not be sacrificed in all this.

David felt we should say to the Americans they could only use our troops after the first effort and also on humanitarian duties. TB did not want to go down that route, no matter how much he agreed the Americans were not being helpful. Jack was absolutely vituperative about Rumsfeld and said we were being driven by their political strategy. TB said maybe, but it was still the right thing to do. After Jack left, we went down for a meeting with JP, HA and JR. TB admitted things were not going in the right direction at all. We agreed we were going to put out six tests[1] for Saddam today and also emphasise we were in this because it was right, not because the US wanted it. That was a point I made on the conference call where I didn't hide how pissed off we were with Rumsfeld, and said we couldn't have a situation where they were commenting on our politics.

TB had a couple of meetings with GB who was being brought in more closely on Iraq now, thanks to JP's meeting with him. We agreed that we really had to put it to a vote in the Commons even if we didn't get a second resolution because that was what we had promised and TB would just have to go and fight for his life on it. JP and Hilary both felt the note I did for the PLP was helpful and suggested I do

[1] The tests demanded: a statement from Saddam admitting the concealment of WMD and undertaking not to retain or produce WMD in the future; that at least thirty scientists and their families should be delivered for interview outside Iraq; the surrender of anthrax, or evidence of its destruction to be provided; all al-Samoud missiles to be destroyed; all unmanned vehicles to be accounted for, including details of any aerial devices for spraying chemical and biological weapons; all mobile chemical and biological production facilities to be surrendered.

another to update facts and arguments. I also put round a note to Cabinet on arrangements and structures for communications in the event of war. At PMQs, TB was on form and IDS was awful because he tried to exploit the Clare Short situation. There was a suggestion that the French may try to put down a resolution based on our tests. TB agreed my note on the tests. Jack at the PLP set us up well and we were now clearly saying 1441 gave us the legal cover we needed.

Chirac had effectively said he would veto anything, so even though we were continuing to work for it, it was hard to imagine getting one. The French were clearly worried. Just before PMQs, Matthew Rycroft took a call from [Gérard] Errera to say the Elysée wanted to make clear that 'whatever the circumstances' was being taken out of context. They were clearly backtracking. Then to the secure room to listen to the Bush call. Bush said his people had watched TB at PMQs and said he was brilliant. TB said he had spoken to Lagos and the Chileans were buggering about. Bush said Fox had told him he would get back to him within an hour, and then went off to hospital for a back operation. TB laid it on the line that we had to have a vote in the Commons. He said we couldn't pull the plug on UN negotiating because the bigger the gap between the end of the negotiation and a Commons motion, the worse it was for us. We had to keep trying. Bush said when do you anticipate a vote? TB said we had pencilled in next Tuesday. Bush: 'Erm.' Long pause. TB: 'You want to go on the Monday?' Correct. TB: 'My military have given me formal advice re the full moon.' It's not a problem, said Bush. 'What – are they taking away the moon?' TB said he would have to check it out. There was clear tension between Bush wanting sooner and TB wanting later.

Bush was clear that the French position meant no UNSCR. But we were still trying to be reasonable. He felt that on withdrawal of the resolution he would give a speech saying the diplomatic phase is over, issue a 48-hour ultimatum to Saddam, say late Friday, which takes us to Sunday. TB went over the politics here, how we were pulling out every stop. TB said there was a danger the Tories would see this as their chance to get rid of him, support us on a war motion, but not a confidence motion. Bush said they would make it clear to the Tories that if they moved to get rid of TB 'we will get rid of them'. He said he wouldn't speak to 'Iain Duncan Baker' himself – TB didn't correct him – 'but he'll know my message'.

The French had definitely allowed themselves to be presented as the unreasonable ones, which was probably swinging opinion our way a bit, but it was still very difficult. TB said it was important we still showed we were trying to be reasonable. But he said if Bush could delay his broadcast till after our Commons vote, it would help. Sunday, say you've tried, the French are being impossible, we are working the phones. Monday, we take it to Parliament and say we must bring this to a conclusion. Vote Tuesday. Forty-eight hours you go to their people and say war. The best argument we had is that we don't want our foreign policy decided by the French, though TB was clear again that Rumsfeld's comments had given us a problem.

He then started to press on the Middle East and said that if Bush would commit to publishing the road map, that would be a big breakthrough. We needed a fresh UNSCR on the humanitarian situation post conflict. Nobody doubts us on the tough side of things, but it's Middle East, humanitarian, democracy in Iraq, that people here want to hear about. TB spelled out the symbolism in the road map. Bush didn't quite get it but was willing to do it. He said if you took a poll here they'd think the road map was a local atlas. He said he had never shaken hands with [Palestinian leader Yasser] Arafat and he was never going to kiss him either. But TB really pressed on him and he got it by the end. Bush said we had to watch out for the French, that they would be worried they had got themselves in a ridiculous position.

I then had a long call with Dan Bartlett, who said there was some talk of a Bush/TB/Aznar meeting on neutral territory at the weekend to show continuing commitment to diplomacy. TB was now worried that the French would put down their own resolution aimed at getting support for delay and forcing the Americans to veto it. We were now in a position of not having a second resolution put to a vote at the UN, but then having a vote in the Commons for military [action] without a second resolution on the grounds everyone knows the French would veto it. I was very frank with Dan, said that the chief American voices had been doing us real damage. Hilary Armstrong came in for a chat. She was very stoic about it all and said it was going to be difficult.

Thursday, March 13
Greenstock put down the six tests at the UN at 2am. Before anyone had even had time properly to discuss them, de Villepin rejected them, allowing us to go to an aggressive position re French intransigence and their 'whatever the circumstances'. We needed to keep going on the tests through the day. We also wanted it that Blix wanted the TV address rather than us. I had a brief chat with IDS before he saw TB for a Privy Council talk re where we were. I just could not imagine him in there as PM. Jack and JP had both spoken to Robin and were clear he was going to quit if we didn't get a second resolution. It was

a matter of when, not if, now. TB was due to see Robin and Clare before Cabinet and JP emphasised how important it was to make clear today was not the final Cabinet before any action, that there would be another one if the UN process collapsed. The political argument we needed now was that the French had made it more not less likely that there would be conflict. This was the way some of our MPs could come back. The other thing all of us were pushing on our US counterparts was the importance of publication of the road map. Dan and I had taken to calling it 'the Detroit A to Z' as a way of me trying to get them to understand why it mattered so much to us. Jack agreed to go out and do clips on the French.

Cabinet was delayed while TB saw Robin and Clare. When he came in he said 'Good morning,' and they all – or almost all – did a schoolkids-type 'Good morning' back which at least lowered the temperature a bit. TB talked through Iraq. Gareth Williams [Leader of the House of Lords] said there would be a debate on the legality. Clare said the AG should come to that. TB said of course he would. He said that the French had exposed fully how intransigent they were. Chirac's 'whatever the circumstances' was a mistake, and the wrong approach, and people were angry about it. They had also now rejected the basis of the tests we were proposing without any discussion or consideration. He felt Chirac's desire for a 'bipolar world' was leading him to turn away from discussion of any kind on this. He promised another discussion before a vote. Jack reported on UN activity. Clare chipped in 'Why can't the US give more time?' GB came in very strongly later on, on the French in particular.

RC said we should not 'burn our bridges' with the French, made clear that though there may be a legal base for action, there was no political case without a second resolution and we must keep working for it. He spoke very deliberately, as though he had rehearsed and of course everyone was listening for tone as well as content. It was a very clear marker that he would quit if there was action without a second resolution. He felt that without it we did not have the moral, diplomatic or humanitarian cover. Clare was even heavier, said we needed the road map published, lambasted the 'megaphone diplomacy' but as ever gave the impression it was just us and the Americans who engaged in it. She said the world community was split because the Americans were rushing. We should not be attacking the French but coming up with a different kind of process. 'If we can get the road map, we can get the world reunited behind it.' She was calmer by the end and my sense was RC would definitely quit, but she might stay.

I did a secure call with Dan. They were still keen on another meeting. Bush was prepared to come to London. I said I was not sure that was the right thing to do. The best thing you guys can do for us is publish the road map. I mentioned the idea of the Bush visit to TB. He was tempted but finally agreed GWB on UK soil in the run-up to the vote was not what we needed. The satirists would have a field day, 'I've come over here so that Tony and I could hold joint prayer sessions with your troubled backbenchers, so they can see the light. I like Tony so much because he is so much not a socialist,' etc. Definitely not what we needed right now.

TB was sure the French had something else tricky lined up. I did a note for TB post the chat with Dan, emphasising the need to keep driving a hard bargain from the position we were in. We agreed a plan – road map Friday, maybe visit Saturday. Talks expected to collapse Monday. Tuesday vote. Action begins immediately after the vote, then war declared, though no bombing yet. Then bombing and the POTUS [President of the United States] call. I went over to SIS to go over a few things, and what they could do to help once we got going. They were focused on the need to make sure the MoD documented properly all the atrocities, WMD, torture incidents etc. They were a pretty impressive bunch. We went over a lot of the obvious stuff, but once the discussion got going, I felt they got far better than other parts of the government machine the importance of dominating the media battle and also the need to stay robust whatever else was going on.

He was due to speak to Bush. Bush said that they could do the road map, give it to the Israelis and Palestinians once Abu Mazen [about to take over as Palestinian Prime Minister] accepts the position. TB said that could make a big difference, anything up to fifty votes. 'It'll cost me 50,000,' said Bush. TB said he had just seen a group of 'wobbly MPs' who were all clear the road map would help. There was a totemic significance to this. TB said it might also help him hang on to a couple of Cabinet ministers. GWB suggested he might be better off without them. He clearly could not fathom why the road map mattered so much. He had been reluctant because of Arafat. He then said 'Tell Alastair, like I'm telling my boys, that I don't want to read a word about this until I've said it. It is in our interests that I come out and say this, and it's clear I mean it.' TB said the French thought they had lost the initiative and were getting worried. He felt we had to keep in very close touch with Mexico and Chile over the weekend. He was worried the French would come up with a counter-proposal and win them over. Bush referred to the discussions Dan and I had been having. 'I guess me coming to London might create a stir.'

They kept going back to the parliamentary arithmetic. TB said it was knife-edge, that we were maybe twenty-five short of comfort. He said I know you think I've gone mad about the road map but it really will help. Bush said that Rumsfeld had asked him to apologise to TB. He said after the diplomatic process collapsed he would do his ultimatum speech. Nothing military will happen before our vote. After our vote, if we win, the order goes to Rumsfeld to get their troops to move. Ops begin. He said he would not be doing a declaration of war. Wednesday 8pm in the region, 1pm US, 6pm UK 'They go. Ten hours of operations before anyone finds out what is going on.' He intended to wait as long as possible before saying the troops were in action.

Dan called later to say they were postponing the meeting to Sunday because Spain had big demos on Saturday and Aznar felt he should stay for that. Aznar didn't like the idea of Bermuda so we settled on the Azores.[1] I had a meeting with GB and his people to go over all the difficult lines and to engage him in more media. We had to pin this on the French now. Then another chat with Dan to work out how we fill the void in the coming days. I asked him to make sure Bush did not wear any of his bomber jacket-type stuff. Things were pretty rocky with Fiona, who was really pressing for departure now, and I was feeling pretty stressed. I called Neil [Kinnock] in Rome and asked for him to have a word with her, and just spell out the kind of pressure I was under, and why I needed her to hang in just a while longer.

Friday, March 14

A real sense the diplomatic scene was going nowhere but we kept going with the line we were working flat out for a second resolution. To a meeting with TB, JP and GB. Gordon was far more engaged, pressing for constant meetings, election-type hours, working with me on the arguments and lines, agreeing to do more media. I was keen we somehow avoid the Azores meeting being seen as a council of war but it would be hard. A message came through that Chirac wanted to speak to TB. It was a lot friendlier than it might have been and he said we should strive for good relations. He was straight on to the point TB expected, namely he could see a way of co-operating on the tests but it must be the inspectors who decide if Saddam is co-operating.

[1] A special summit would be held at the Lajes airbase on Portugal's Azores islands, attended by Bush, Blair, Aznar of Spain and Barroso of Portugal.

He said he could not support an ultimatum or anything taken as support for military action.

TB said the problem with that was that it meant he could have as many last chances and as much time as he wanted. There had to be automaticity [trigger for attack]. Chirac said there could not be automaticity. They agreed Jack and de Villepin should talk but TB issued instructions to Jack to concede nothing. There was intelligence suggesting the French were seeking to get the undecided six to go for tests plus more time. TB suspected Chirac would move to a position of automaticity but inspectors are the sole judges of compliance.

Robin called to discuss 'rules of engagement' in the event of his resignation. I got Sally to join us when he came over. We were pressing him to stay, saying we couldn't have the French running our foreign policy, telling him Bush was about to do the road map. He said it would make a bit of difference but not much. He said this went deeper. He felt we were too close to a unilateralist right-wing US government that didn't care two hoots about the UN and didn't care two hoots about Tony, other than for his skills as a better politician and communicator than they are. He felt it was dishonest for him to pretend he supported them any more. He couldn't. He said he did not want to be awkward and was clear he wanted TB to stay. 'I do not want to be part of a process that sees Gordon become prime minister on the back of this.'

I said I thought if his mind was made up we should tie it all up before Monday's Cabinet. He said fine, that he was sad but felt a great peace of mind having made the decision. He wasn't questioning the integrity of those with a different view but he was doing what he felt was the right thing. He said he valued the good relationship we had and 'Could we agree a pact of no rubbishing on either side?' Absolutely. 'Can you ensure John Reid is part of that? The man can start a fight in a paper bag.' He intended to do a personal statement and speak in the debate. We agreed to consult re draft letters over the weekend. I said I would ensure TB was warm about him and he should be warm about TB.

I then went to another meeting with TB and GB. TB said it was extraordinary how much more dangerous the world seemed, when in fact more people were enjoying peace and prosperity than ever before. He had to leave for a few minutes and GB and I watched Bush doing his road-map statement. He did it pretty well and put the tone in as we had been suggesting. GB asked me what I really thought of Bush. Complicated, I said. Bits of him I like, bits I don't.

But he has got a long way by being underestimated. I was conscious of putting a bit of a line, even with GB, because you never quite knew how he stored these things away and used them. We spoke fairly openly but there was none of the old flow and warmth and laughter. Sad really. I worked on TB's draft words for the MEPP press conference. The Palestinians were being negative post Bush. TB said if they carry on like this they will lose the opportunity they've been given. It had a feel of Northern Ireland about it.

Then to the secure room to listen to another TB/Bush call. He kicked off with a 'Tell Alastair we're grateful he didn't leak anything. Tell him we're watching his every move, heh, heh.' He and Cheney had spoken to eight Arab leaders. TB reported on his call with Abu Mazen. Bush said 'If he plays his cards right he will be here in the Oval [Office].' Then on to the vote. It was already in the US press that it was on Tuesday. Bush said he was predicting a 'landslide, baby!' TB said it was too close to call. Bush was pissed off with Clinton, felt he was being difficult. The Azores was on. TB said we had to be seen striving all the way even if we felt the French had made it impossible. Bush said it was a 'moment of truth' meeting after all the previous last chances. TB said we must not let it be built up as a council of war. The more we talk about the UN and the aftermath the better. Bush said Dan and I were working on the outcomes for the media and we were getting Cheney to set the context on the Sunday shows.

TB briefed on the Chirac call, said the divide was between those prepared to consider military action and those who were not, who would give him as much time as he wanted. Bush said he did not trust the French but we had to do a slow waltz with them in the next few days. He felt they thought America was more guilty than Saddam. TB said the French appearing to be so unreasonable had been a big mistake by Chirac. I did another call with Dan re the arrangements for the Azores then a stack of calls, a last meeting with TB and headed home. TB saw Clare again and was confident he could keep her in. He was resigned to losing Robin.

Saturday, March 15

In for 8.30 meeting. Up to see TB in the flat. He was in the bath and Jack was pissed off not to be able to speak to him when he called in from Blackburn. TB was in very odd-looking shorts as he finally came down, said right, sorry I'm late, sat down and got going. He said it was clear now what the French would try – yes to the tests, even to the possibility of military action, but they would push for a later date.

We had a pre-meeting with JP, GB and DA downstairs before all the officials came in. GB was beginning to motor a bit, firing with good media and political lines. He also felt we needed to explain more clearly why we had been so keen to get the second resolution when now we were saying we didn't need one. The answer lay in the pressure we had been putting on the Iraqis, through the building of international support. He also felt we should be pressing publicly over some of the questions he still felt Blix had not fully answered.

Goldsmith was happy for us to brief that in the coming days he would make clear there was a legal base for action. We now had to build up the Azores as a genuine diplomatic effort, which was not going to be easy. It was running as a 'war not peace' situation. John Scarlett joined us, reported signs of the Iraqis really hunkering down, said there were reports of summary executions. Godric and I were briefing ministers and then the media re the coming AG advice. A few decisions having been taken, the travel of direction clear, we felt in a stronger position. Robin sent over his draft letter which was pretty negative. I worked on TB's, set it in a place that would make Robin want changes in both. TB went off to call Lagos. I got home in time to listen to a very long TB/Bush call. 'Hey Tony, how are you?' 'I'm very well.' 'That is what I want to hear every time.' He accepted we had done the right thing pushing him on the road map. 'Good advice and it has helped a lot.' The *New York Times* had it as 'Blair insistent, Bush responds' but it was a good move.

Bush was pretty vile about Fox, Chirac and Schroeder and to a lesser extent Lagos. He wanted to go for a 'coalition of the willing' meeting next week, but exclude France and Germany. He was venomous re Fox, said he could not believe they were not supporting us. He had guys like the Danes saying they were trying to help but had constitutional difficulties. Or Musharraf with all his problems saying let's get it over with. TB said it was time for the UN to show it could do its job, Bush that anything that weakened 1441 was not on. His plan now was: 1. get through Monday; 2. get through our vote, then 3. coalition of the willing. He and TB then came up with the idea of doing the press conference before rather than after the meeting in the Azores. I was opposed, felt it would fuel the idea that this was all a bit of a charade. There was the odd flash of Bush humour in there. He said he would call some of our backbenchers and tell them he was converted to Kyoto, planning to go vegetarian, would legislate so that all fertiliser could only come from cows and horses and campaign for an agrarian society.

His main line was that anything that takes us back from 1441 was not enough. This was the final stage of the diplomacy. TB said the UN had to be seen to do its job. Bush felt the TB line re the divisions being between those prepared to use force and those who were not would come best from TB not him. 'People kind of know where I am on force.' He said we have come to a conclusion at the UN. If we issue an ultimatum and the prospect of force, and France says no, it becomes impossible. TB said he still thought Chirac might say yes, but with a delay. Bush said if he went for yes with twenty-one days, he would reject it. They are the ones being unreasonable, not us. TB said he would definitely lose one minister, RC. 'What does he do?' Was Foreign Secretary, now Leader of the House. Bush said the ranks of the disaffected swell after a time.

Then going over the various timing issues again. TB said he was not sure where Kofi was. Bush said he had totally different problems to us re the UN, that the pressure in the States was to bury it. Then 'I told Fox he has seriously messed up. He has really let me down on this.' He then went off on one about the just demands of the free world. Was the UN really serving the world as it should? It had been pathetic in Rwanda. Then a discussion about anti-Semitism in Germany. TB said as things stood he was probably the only EU leader whose natural instincts were to go out and defend Israel. TB said the view here was of an all-powerful Jewish lobby in the States which could prevent a president moving on MEPP. Bush reckoned he had ten to fifteen per cent of the Jewish vote so it was all a bit of a myth. He had a lot less to lose than a Democratic president would.

Briefly they discussed proliferation of nuclear weapons. We do not need Saudi Arabia popping up with nuclear weapons, said Bush. The IAEA is pathetic. It's got Cuba on its board. He said he was convinced we would help world peace and at the end said 'It has been a great conversation. Let's get a bit of exercise and rest up for the Azores summit. It will be historic. And I'll be nuanced, I promise.' TB: 'We don't want anything unnatural now.' I went out for a longish run before getting back for Neil and Glenys coming for dinner. Neil was pretty much with me on Iraq, Glenys against, but we managed to avoid a big flare-up. Neil told me he had written to Robin saying don't resign, that he ought to stay in there and be part of the dealing with the aftermath.

Sunday, March 16

In for a long meeting in David Manning's office after TB came back from church. First just David, Sally, Matthew [Rycroft] and I, then GB, JR and HA joined us. We were trying to boil down the central arguments and dividing lines now. I suggested we say we intend to go back to the French and test their position – do they support any element of what we are saying? Are they really saying there are no circumstances in which they would support anything seen as a threat of military action? If they are, we go. If not, we have to look again. David M said there was no indication the French intended to shift. GB did *Frost*, and came back saying the really tough questions were in the field of legality. GB also said if we are saying this is the final shot at diplomacy, what are we actually saying we are going to do after today? Bush didn't want a process story but I suggested one, namely a last round of contacts at the UN post the Azores meeting. I spoke to RC. He said he had thought about the changes I had suggested to his letter. He was happy to say TB had helped keep this on the international, multilateral track. He was happy to make clear he felt TB should remain as leader.

It was now time to leave. There was the usual last-minute stuff to do before we got into the cars and set off for the airport. Pretty big media turnout in the street but we pretty much ignored them. I travelled with TB in the car to the airport and first he spoke to Margaret B, then a call with [Jan Peter] Balkenende [Dutch Prime Minister]. Then we just chatted a bit. This was as tough as any decision we would have to make, he said. He felt it very deeply. It was a tough, tough call. He was still angry at the way the US had handled it. 'If we had been totally in charge of this, I am absolutely sure we could have won the French round,' he said. I felt the US and France both, for different reasons, did not want to meet on this. We got on to the plane and for most of the flight were working on other papers and TB's message for the press event after the summit. It felt a bit insubstantial, especially given where it all now seemed to be heading. It was an opportunity though to set out the whole story, how we got to here, the French intransigence and so on.

It was a four-hour flight and the media were pretty much in 'council of war' mode. It was hard to sell this as a genuine diplomatic effort. Clinton sent through a draft of an article for the *Guardian*. He was trying to say he supported TB but the unspoken message was that he didn't support the war. TB asked me to work on a different version. I was also working on the Iraq vision document and the RC letters, and shifting paper. Alison [Blackshaw] said she was always amazed how much work we seemed to get through on planes, and this one was particularly prolific. Re RC I put in a reference to his support for Operation Desert Fox [1998 bombing of Iraq], and Kosovo, and also hinted he could go on to another big role, having successfully got the

Sunday Times to do a story saying he might go to Europe as a commissioner. We were also still negotiating the texts for the summit. DM felt there were too many references to terrorism and the language – e.g. peace-loving people – was too American. Also on the road map, they were saying it was a prospect. We needed it clearly there as a fact, something that was happening. They were pretty low-key re UN aftermath involvement and David was getting very fed up with them. I said why can't we just say we will work for new UNSCRs on appropriate post-conflict government? We arrived in the Azores for what was going to be a fairly odd meeting. At the airbase we had a meeting with Barroso, then joined by Aznar. TB spoke by phone to Kofi who was pretty much in agreement that the French had fucked up. He agreed to see him in New York later in the week. Then we heard Chirac was intending to set out a new proposal, but it turned out simply to be calling for more time, thirty days. It was clear now, said TB, that the French did not intend to move.

We hung around for Bush to arrive and once he did we all moved to the US part of the base. TB travelled with Bush in the presidential limo and the ludicrously large motorcade. We sat around a fairly small square table. The mood shifted regularly from serious, e.g. going through texts, running over difficult arguments, to light-hearted. Bush at one point just looked over at me and said 'You're just like a faucet. Can't stop leaking.' I said we called it tap. Barroso did a long and ponderous opening and said we had to make the last effort for peace. Everyone kept going on about it being 'the last effort for a political solution'. But there was a more than slight feeling of going through motions. The meeting itself was in an odd room, way too big for the numbers, with a kind of weird grey crazy paving-type set-up on the walls, thick white tablecloths.

Bush talked about it being a last effort. But he said it was important the world saw we were making every effort to enforce 1441. He said everyone had to be able to say we did everything we could to avoid war. But this was the final moment, the moment of truth, which was the line most of the media ran with. He stressed he wanted the UN to play an important role in the post-Saddam era. He was clear we had to emphasise Iraq's territorial integrity. He was emphasising he would really move on MEPP. He said again TB had been right to push him on the road map, and said he intended to spend a lot of time on this. He said re Chirac 'I don't want to provoke him into unreasonableness.' He was however keen to say he wanted the UN properly involved in the post-Saddam era. He would not deal with Arafat though. Condi and Karen [Hughes, AC's opposite number] later showed me the current draft of GWB's ultimatum speech which I felt was a bit too warlike. Too much war, not enough ultimatum.

TB said we had reached the point of decision for people. We had been here before, but there really had to be a decision. How many times could there be a last chance, serious consequences for material breach? He reported that Kofi had said the French and Russians would not rule out force but would not agree to an ultimatum, which was an odd position. He really hit the UN buttons post Saddam, and was trying to force Bush to go further on that. 'It has to be a UN-authorised government.' He was also hammering home the advantage on MEPP, but I wasn't convinced it would happen. We needed some kind of process story. I suggested to TB they all instruct their ambassadors at the UN to have one last go, see if the position of the others has changed. TB was constantly emphasising final appeal, final opportunity for the UN. Bush was scathing re the Turks, said Erdogan 'just doesn't get it. The Turkish military are setting him up.' He was pretty keen to get on with things now, wanted to pull down the SCR now. He then said he would address the American people tomorrow – say diplomacy had failed, issue the ultimatum. He said to TB we should say we were issuing one last set of instructions to UN ambassadors to have a go at securing agreement. Aznar said he was concerned the French, Russians and Chinese would come up with a proposal. Bush said he would be happy to veto if they did. He was even talking about not going to the G8 summit.

Aznar was really pushing the importance of the transatlantic alliance, but he was in even more political hot water on this than we were. I introduced Bush to Godric, said he was our Ari Fleischer. 'You gotta be bald or something to do these spokesmen jobs? Or is it the job makes you bald?' TB had vanished to the loo. I said we've lost the PM. 'I hope not,' said Bush ''cos he's the reason we're all here on this island on a Sunday.' He asked about the vote, said he was confident we would win. I said Robin C might shift a few. As we left I said to Bush, if I do a sub-four-hour marathon will you sponsor me? He said 'If you win the vote in Parliament, I'll kiss your ass.' I said I'd prefer the sponsorship. Over to the press conference and now he went into 'bastards' mode in a kind of imitation of me. Dan said he was amused by the fact I dealt with the press in the way I did. He saw them as bastards too, but in the US nobody dare say it.

The press conference was very well set up and at least the Yanks knew how to do these kind of things. They did their statements, then one question from each country, and all on-message though Bush went off on one a bit re Chirac. He did his 'moment of truth' well, but there was something very odd about his manner today. Bush had just about had enough of the serious talk and we had another half-serious, half-jokey conversation re marathon training. The last hour or so dragged a bit and we were basically just chatting, filling the time while the hacks all filed before getting back on the plane and heading home. In the car to the plane TB seemed to think it had gone OK, though we were all pretty clear the US had decided and nothing that came out of the French or anyone today would have changed their approach. I told him re the kiss-ass threat. He laughed, but then said it is not that often that a major US policy depends on a UK parliamentary vote. Sally reported from Hilary A there had been some movement our way.

We saw the press on the plane, and we were making clear the French had to come back and say whether there were any circumstances at all in which they might support military action. I lost it with the staff when I learned the texts and documents had not been issued at the right time. TB was seeing David Margolick [*Vanity Fair*].[1] TB was still saying it was the right thing to do. I had lost count of how many times I had heard those same words. We started work on his speech for Tuesday, which was going to have to be one hundred per cent.

Monday, March 17

The summit came out not too bad, Bush's 'moment of truth' the best top line, the overall sense that the diplomatic process was going nowhere and now we had to gear up on the military side. There was the not insignificant matter of our vote, mapping out in my head a note to send to Dan with an overnight press summary, schedule for the day and stressing how important it was that Bush's 1am speech did not create problems for us. I said GWB was unlikely to pull any of our people back, but he could push them the other way. I leavened it a bit by telling him the *Guardian* had said Bush was better than Blair yesterday. He called later, said they had built up the ultimatum as I suggested and also injected a lot of conditional material so that it was not simply seen as a declaration of war.

Then to a meeting of TB, JP, GB, JS, JR, HA plus the usual lot to go through the day. Jack was irritating TB a bit by going on about process the whole time and irritating JP who was trying to get a

[1] This was the interview from which would emerge one of Campbell's most oft-quoted statements. When, at the end of a long interview, Margolick asked Blair about his religious faith, an impatient Campbell interjected, 'We don't do God.'

straight answer to the question of whether RC should do a statement tomorrow or today. Jack and I both felt today was better, on a day of massive events, then GWB in the morning, rather than before TB's speech. We agreed Greenstock would put down the SCR at 10.15 New York time, that we would say at the 11 there would be a Cabinet at 4, Jack's statement later and also that the Attorney General would publish his view that there was a solid legal base for action. Jack would go through the motions of talking to his opposite numbers but basically the game was up. De Villepin had rejected it again. GB said we needed to get up the Blix unanswered questions as well. TB was fairly quiet, worrying about his speech and about rebels. We agreed Margaret B should do media so I spoke to her to brief her, then sent over the AG's opinion and our various texts from yesterday.

I was working on a draft exchange of letters with Clare in case she went. JP went off to see her and reported back that she was probably going. It was all playing totally to her attention-seeking. Jonathan emailed me about the draft exchange of letters, saying 'Probably better not to have them drafted by someone who so clearly despises her.' Probably true. Robin called re my draft. I had mentioned the various military situations we had been involved in – Operation Desert Fox, Kosovo, Sierra Leone. He was very funny about it, said 'I can see why in these circumstances you want to present me as a heroic war leader, but I wonder if you couldn't put in one or two of my humanitarian triumphs as well.' He was keen that we make mention of Lockerbie and the International Criminal Court, and also wanted to make clear that he wanted TB to stay on as leader. It was so different dealing with him rather than Clare. He felt she was in a totally ridiculous position. TB was working to keep her in, even suggesting we get Kofi to call her. RC came to see TB and they agreed there was no point in him staying for Cabinet. So Robin and I went round to my office to agree the process. We agreed we wouldn't put the letters out until 4.15, once Cabinet was in.

We joked about the fact that it was the first resignation letter I had not written. 'I'll race you to see whose memoirs that appears in first,' he said. He was very friendly, seemed liberated, also clear that he had a strong if very different political future ahead of him. He was also very nice to me personally, said we had been through some very difficult times together and he always valued my advice and support. He said there was something oddly fitting about the fact that we had worked so closely at the end of his marriage and were working so closely again at the end of his ministerial career. He wanted to leave by the side door so I walked down with him, we shook hands, he said 'I really hope it doesn't all end horribly for you all,' and headed off to Birdcage Walk.

TB started Cabinet, introduced Goldsmith, then Clare came in and asked Sally where Robin was. 'He's gone,' said Sal. 'Oh my God.' TB's only reference to Robin was to say that he had resigned. He said French intransigence had made it impossible to get a resolution. We were at an end of the diplomatic process. We intended to issue an ultimatum and seek an endorsement for action if it was necessary. He said we had tried everything to avoid this course. The other big issue was MEPP, and the US had undertaken to publish the road map. He also emphasised the planning that was going on on the humanitarian front. He said Jack and the FCO team had done a brilliant job but an impasse is an impasse and the French block is not conditional but absolute. Jack said nobody could have done more than TB did to keep things within the UN.

I was in and out agreeing final changes to the article Bill Clinton was doing for us for the *Guardian*. I got back in as Peter Goldsmith went through the answer on legal authority to use force. Clare asked if he had had any doubts. He said lawyers all over the world have doubts but he was confident in the position. One by one, a succession of colleagues expressed support, then Clare said she owed them 'a short statement', that she intended to reflect overnight. She said publication of the road map was significant but we shouldn't kid ourselves that it means it is going to happen. She said she admired the effort and energy that had gone into getting a second resolution but there had been errors of presentation. 'I'm going to have my little agonising overnight. I owe it to you.' JP, John Reid and one or two others looked physically sick.

JR spoke next, said never underestimate the instincts for unity and understand that we will be judged by the Iraq that replaces Saddam's Iraq, and by the Middle East. Derry said he felt we would have got a second resolution if the French hadn't been determined to scupper it, and said we had made so much effort to get a second resolution that it had led to people thinking we actually needed one. Paul Murphy was just back from America and said what an amazing feeling there was towards us there. 'It's not quite the same here,' said TB. JP pointed out we were on the eighteenth SCR dealing with Saddam and it was about time we moved to uphold the UN's integrity. He said the only reason the Americans went down the UN route at all was because of TB and now he is getting them down the road of the Middle East peace process and deserves all the support we can give.

We had agreed JP would speak in the street post Cabinet. I had drafted a script and he went through it with me and Jack. He went and did well. TB felt Cabinet had gone well. JP had been terrific. Only Clare was ridiculous. Fittingly, when she spoke, huge gusts of wind had blown through the open window. TB had another call with Bush, fairly inconsequential, mainly about the vote. TB said at the moment we had 190 backbenchers against us and we wanted to bring it down to 150. Bush seemed genuinely surprised when TB said his comments on the Middle East had helped. They both felt the French had mishandled things. He was in very folksy mode, said that TB had 'heart in your voice and a spring in your step, so that's fine by me'. He asked TB if he had to be in there in Parliament for ten hours of debate. TB said you get the odd comfort break. GWB laughed. TB said it was tough and would be tight and that French intransigence, plus the Middle East moves, had helped, but also we had to keep the UN in play. He said a lot of our backbenchers were mildly obsessive about the UN and the post-war issues. Robin did his resignation statement, did it very well, a really powerful Commons moment and got a fairly widespread standing ovation. Margaret [Beckett], who was about to do *The World Tonight* [BBC Radio 4], was unimpressed. She called me, felt it was typical Robin, said he would support TB and then call directly on people to vote against action, which, if carried, would defeat the PM and the government. She wanted to go for him but I said it was better simply to say that TB would also be going to the House and would make a case that was logical and powerful and strong. I was surprised at how angry she was with Robin. She said she hoped she could hold her tongue. TB was working on his speech for a good part of the day and it was in good shape. Neil [Kinnock] called and said Robin was one of a very small number of people who could bring catastrophe to the government and even though it was difficult, we should try to keep a bridge out to him. It was pretty clear by now that Clare would be on her way too, if with a lot less impact.

Tuesday, March 18

Debate day dominant. GWB's statement overnight had come out fine. They had taken in all our changes, the ultimatum was calm and strong, the tone towards Iraqi people compassionate, the commitment to the Middle East peace process was in there strong, and all the bellicose stuff either taken out or conditional. So to be fair, they had delivered big time for us. The Robin resignation speech, and the standing ovation in parts of the House, was still getting a lot of play but I sensed that was the high point of the rebellion. I ran in, then up to see TB in the flat. He was on the phone to Blunkett who was warning him that John Denham [Home Office minister] would resign. Also Philip Hunt [Lord Hunt, junior health minister] went on the radio to resign. That seemed to be about it at the moment. TB was in a pretty calm mood. He felt we were winning some people over on the arguments, but we had a problem in that there were a lot of our MPs who had promised their local parties that they wouldn't support without a second resolution. This was the unintended effect of the point Derry made yesterday, that we fought so hard to get one that people assumed we needed one before action.

TB had been up early and had rewritten the speech so it was much more his voice. The only ongoing discussion was about whether to keep in the passage about the 1930s [appeasement], or whether really direct comparisons might backfire. It was not yet clear what Clare intended to do. Then we heard a rumour that she was planning to make a statement, which we assumed was a resignation but then learned was to be an announcement she was staying. We had a meeting to organise a pretty much all-day blitz of the airwaves including getting GB live on some of the bulletins. We had Margaret out and about all day doing well. Whether in the House or out, we were at least making the arguments but Hilary said it was still too difficult to judge the outcome. I worked on the Queen's message to the troops, and spoke to Dan [Bartlett] a couple of times to go over the exact timings of military action. There were going to be a lot of special forces operations around the oilfields, then wait till Friday for a proper announcement. Clare was making a complete fool of herself. TB had done very well keeping her there, but she was now viewed as humiliated. She was pretty much finished. [William] Hague was on to it, had an absolutely brilliant line in the debate, how TB had 'taken his revenge and kept her'.

TB's speech in the House was one of his best.[1] Very serious, full of real argument, confronting the points of difficulty and we felt it moving our way. He did a brilliant put-down to the Lib Dems ['unified, as ever, in opportunism and error'] which helped the mood behind him. I did another secure call with Dan. It looked like Wednesday late, special forces. Thursday, preparations underway. Friday, 'A' day, first Bush, then TB, recall Parliament. By the time I got back in, Sally said there were definitely some people turning

[1] Blair told MPs 'This is the time for this House, not just this government or indeed this prime minister, but for this House to give a lead, to show that we will stand up for what we know to be right, to show that we will confront the tyrannies and dictatorships and terrorists who put our way of life at risk, to show at the moment of decision that we have the courage to do the right thing.'

back to us. I got GB out on the media again. He called me into his office for the first time in ages to discuss the line to take on Clare. Stay nice to and about her and not put the boot in. TB's speech had gone fine and the reaction was good. It was one of those days when people out in the country were actually following what was going on. IDS and Charles Kennedy had both been poor. There had been some excellent back-bench speeches but the interventions didn't really zing, TB had definitely come out on top.

There were a lot of protesters outside, so I faced a bit of abuse going in, then up to JP's office to agree the line that we push from the moment the vote was over, that we won the vote, because we won the argument, and now the country should unite. JP asked me to stay back and asked if I had a problem with him. I said no, why? He said he felt I was angry because he screwed up this morning in going for Robin and Hunt and I had kept him off through the day. I said not at all, but it was one of those days when GB seemed up for it and I wanted him out and about as much as possible. We had also used Peter Hain a lot as well. We ended up having a very friendly chat, then going down to wait for the vote, which for the government motion was 412 for and 149 against, and for the rebel motion 396 voting against and 217 for. 139 Labour MPs rebelled. I called Dan B with the result as it came through.

I was in the front office of TB's Commons office, MPs coming and going, the staff all pretty relieved. TB came back and called everyone in to say thanks. He said we had pulled out the stops and we had to. His own performance today had been superb. All of us, I think, had had pretty severe moments of doubt but he hadn't really, or if he had he had hidden them even from us. Now there was no going back at all. He had to give authority for our forces to go in and by tomorrow night it would be underway. Everyone was assuming the Americans would start a massive bombing whereas in fact the first action would be some of our forces acting to prevent an ecological disaster. I got to bed by 1am.

Wednesday, March 19

TB got the best press he had had for ages, because of the quality of the speech and the fact that he had seen it through. As Bush said on their call later, other leaders would look at what he did, and the power with which he did it, and really learn lessons from it. 'Landslide,' he said, referring to the road-map publication as 'genius'. He referred back to what he called 'the *cojones* conference' at Camp David. 'You showed *cojones*, you never blinked. A leader who leads will win, and you are a real leader.' He said the object is regime change and once Saddam is in hiding, that is the beginning of the change. TB felt the next stage after winning the war would be to work out the geopolitical fallout and repair some of the divisions. Bush said Condi had this line that we should 'punish the French, ignore the Germans and forgive the Russians', which was pretty glib. TB didn't comment at the time but later said he didn't agree. We should try to build bridges with all of them. We finally got Bush to agree that there was no point TB going to the US at the moment, that we should wait until the fighting starts. 'You're one of the few leaders they let me see,' said Bush.

De Villepin called JS to say that Chirac was 'pained and shocked' at the way we had misrepresented what he had said, that this was not what was expected of an ally and it showed TB lacked courage. Chirac was clearly going up the wall and we were getting a lot of signs that he had basically been hoping TB would fall on the issue. Bush said that the Iraqis would now be 'shredding documents like crazy'. When he heard about the prisoners who had had their tongues cut out, it 'made me vomit'. He said the road map would be published today when Abu Mazen was confirmed. He would call and congratulate him.

I went to see David Manning then chatted to C and John Scarlett. Desertions were beginning in Iraq. The Republican Guard was moving to Baghdad. Nobody seemed to have a clue where Saddam was hiding. It was possible to feel the planned operation moving through the gears. First we had the ad hoc ministerial meeting where John S went through the intelligence, and CDS was clearly reluctant to go over the military plans in detail. I also found myself holding back with Clare there. TB saw her afterwards to tell her not to worry about the savaging she was getting in the papers at the moment. I felt her credibility was now totally shot but he still wanted to keep her on board and she was off to New York.

Fiona came to see me, said she couldn't stay in the job any longer and started crying. She said it wasn't the war per se, but it had been the last straw. She felt it was a waste of time her being here, that she wasn't happy doing what she did. I said she should go if she wanted to, and if she didn't support what we were doing, to try not to do it in a way that makes us an issue. She said but you are a big issue, which meant that there was never a right time to go, but she really didn't want to stay. She went to see Sally, got very upset. Sally said she felt it was as much about Cherie/Carole as being about me. It was about not being valued. I didn't quite know how to deal with it. It's true there was never a right time, but this was about as unright as it could be, in terms of us being made an issue. It didn't exactly help that the message from the security people was that patrols around the house would be stepped up while the conflict was going on.

I wrote letters of complaint to the BBC, first from me to [Richard] Sambrook [director of news] on various issues re [John] Humphrys, [Andrew] Gilligan and Rageh Omaar [BBC journalists] on the nature of their coverage. Then drafted a letter from TB to Gavyn Davies [BBC chairman] and Greg Dyke [BBC director general], attaching articles from David Aaronovitch [journalist] and [John] Simpson [BBC]. PMQs was low-key after all the drama of yesterday but TB did fine, pushed the general vision stuff, also explicit about regime change for the first time. TB called me in later to discuss France, what to do at the summit with Chirac. He was clear we shouldn't go running after them, that they should come to us. But there was no chance of that at all.

I told TB about Fiona. He reacted, as I knew he would, by saying he couldn't understand why people got so emotional about this. I said well, it's going to happen so I have to work out how to handle it. I said it's true she wasn't happy with the war, but there were other issues too, chief among them that she now had a bad relationship with CB, despite having successfully helped build a very positive image for her. She felt we had next to no life outside work, and that I gave too much for too little in return. He went into 'this is ridiculous' mode. I said Tony, you are talking about Fiona and I won't have it. He said for God's sake, I was always saying things about his wife, but this stuff was very difficult, when big political issues were swirling around and they got mixed up with relationships. But if she went and said it was about Iraq, that would look very odd for me because people would think that was my position too.

I said it's probably a consequence of a build-up of neglect, some of it mine, some of it Cherie's. He said it was a bit much to have all the things he had to deal with and be expected to keep everyone happy all the time. I had the weekly meeting with Peter M, PG, PH. Peter M was interesting on GB. He felt GB had come back to us a bit because he was worried about Clare, in that if she went it was his last out-and-out support in Cabinet. Whatever the reasons, he was a bit more back on board. TB called me out for another chat on his way up to the flat and we went into the Number 11 study. He said he felt Fiona was probably fed up with being in my shadow and needed a role independent of me. He asked me what I wanted to do. I said if he was going before the election, I may as well go sooner rather than later because I couldn't imagine working in the same way for a different leader or prime minister. He said in the big moments, like now, I gave real added value, and I shouldn't underestimate how important that was to him. So all he asked was that if I did go, I helped find someone who could replace me.

I asked what his plans were. 'I really don't know. I've never really wanted to fight a third election, but I don't know, I might.' I asked if he had done a deal with GB. Not at all, he said, but he didn't rule it out. He said it was interesting that GB had been more co-operative recently and said JP had been the key to that. JP had basically told him that if TB didn't want him to get the job, and JP was agin it, it would not happen. In the end, he said, I think it's wrong for me to think I can pick the next leader, or control what he does. But I do worry about him. I worry about the party and do want it to be well led. Things were definitely in flux again, and it was odd how often it was the really big moments that brought out these situations.

It was a friendly enough chat and although inevitably he was thinking about his own interests too, he did seem to be applying his mind to a decent way out for Fiona. As for me, I said I wasn't that excited about the euro, which might be the next big thing, and I wasn't sure I could face doing another election in exactly the same job. Maybe I could leave and come back for that. I told Godric about the Fiona situation. He felt it was potentially bigger than Cook going, because it played into so many different parts of the soap opera, which in the end is what the press love most.

Thursday, March 20

After going to bed late last night, then another row with Fiona over my leaving, and her demanding a departure date NOW, I was woken at 3am by Godric. Did I know action had begun? Then media calls started. GWB had gone on TV to say that preparatory action had begun, taking the MoD totally by surprise, and most of us in Number 10. It transpired that Condi had indeed told David [Manning], who had passed it on to TB, but neither thought to pass it on. It meant we were not ready in the way we should have been. We put together a line that said TB was told just after midnight, and when there were operations with substantial UK involvement, we would say so. GWB later apologised to TB who said all he really cared about was that we now got on with it and won. It turned out the US had some late, sudden intelligence re Saddam's whereabouts and took the decision to go straight away. They reckoned later he may have been injured, and certainly there was real angst and turmoil being reported from his inner circle. I was up most of the night, got a couple of hours' sleep and then in for a 7.30 meeting.

TB had a meeting of his inner team (Jonathan, DM, SM, AC) with C, CDS, John Scarlett to get a military and intelligence briefing before being joined by JP, JR, GB, DB etc. John said there were reports of growing internal strife, e.g. pilots being ordered to carry out suicide missions; one-fifth of the Republican Guard deserting. We discussed whether TB should do a broadcast. With our Marines due for action taking a peninsula towards Basra tonight, it was madness to think we could wait another day before TB did a broadcast, so we went ahead with setting it up. Peter H had done a draft but TB was keen to do his own, into which I wrote a couple of clips, but it was basically very much his own voice.

We got hold of the Speaker and GH offered a statement. We were clear we would not be giving a running commentary but statements in the House were going to be an important part of the overall communications. Cabinet was fairly sombre and subdued, and so much better without Clare's constant muttering and interruptions. Sally and I were chatting about what I should do re Fiona. TB, JS and GH all did a fairly basic reporting job on what was happening. Lots of praise for Hilary A on the whips' operation. There was a pretty united mood and a lot of understanding for the enormity of the decision, and the pressure on TB now. He still hadn't decided on RC's replacement. I was feeling the stress today, just a bit wired, and burdened. When these big moments were on, everyone seemed to want to call, or pop in, and it all just added to the sense of pressure.

We recorded the broadcast at 3pm. TB did fine, though he was blinking a lot. We did it in two takes, and I was watching the camera crew to get a sense of their response. They were definitely following the argument, and I sensed the effect was positive. Then straight to the Bush call. GWB reported on the strike, said they very nearly struck lucky. They were still hopeful. They had another discussion re France and Russia, and Bush signalled he really wanted to go over all that in detail at Camp David. He felt it would be a vital discussion for the future of the world, because these relations were central to the direction the world took. He wanted to get back on decent terms with Putin in particular. Then, apropos of nothing, he said 'And tell Alastair I am NOT going to kiss his ass, even though you won the vote.' TB laughed, and said 'I think he'll be relieved. He was not exactly looking forward to it.'

On the flight to Brussels [EU summit], Jack S and I were chatting re the French. His basic view of Chirac was really negative. At the meeting, Chirac seemed to be avoiding TB, and wanting it to be noticed that he was avoiding him. Later, with Chirac sitting at his desk in the meeting room making a call on a mobile, TB went over and shook him by the hand. But it didn't exactly warm things. When we left the building at the end of the session, we had to walk by Chirac and his entourage to get to the cars, and on seeing TB, he just turned away. De Villepin did likewise. The atmosphere generally was dire. The meeting room was being kept pretty tight so I was relying on Jack's notes to follow what was going on. Jack came out to tell us that Chirac was trying to remove any reference to Iraq being responsible for the crisis, and [Costas] Simitis [current EU President] was letting him. TB did not say much, and on the occasions I popped in, they seemed to be splitting into groups rather than getting things sorted round the table. It was not a nice atmosphere at all. But in terms of outcome, it was OK for us, and the French did not have as much support as they had hoped for. I had a chat with Schroeder's team who thought TB's speech had been 'brilliant'.

Friday, March 21

Nick Matthews [senior duty clerk] called me early to say that eight UK Marines and four US servicemen had been killed in a helicopter crash inside Kuwait. Worst possible start to the day. I went out for a run, then back to see TB in his bedroom. He was getting dressed, and reflecting on the news we'd just had. We agreed he should not say anything about it till the press conference. He said that people will be saddened but they understand that these things are going to happen. I sensed he was hiding how he actually felt. He said what mattered now was that we saw through the military campaign. At the summit centre, Schroeder was the first to come over and offer condolences, followed by others. Chirac wrote TB a little note, which was nice of him, and his words were totally devoid of any side or politics. It was interesting how many of the smaller countries were just not prepared to take the Franco-German line on things, and Chirac was definitely weakened around the place.

TB and I discussed euro/GB. GB had definitely been more co-operative recently, and that was largely down to JP. But GB was now keen to include the euro assessment in the Budget, and TB felt he was going to be in a 'yes but' position, that there were a number of changes that had to be made, e.g. to the housing market, before we could consider it. We were in the middle of this conversation, just outside the main meeting room, when Chirac came out to have a pee. He walked past us, went to the Gents, and when he came out he and TB both smiled warmly at each other. Chirac went back into the meeting room, but then came straight back out and walked over to us. *'Tony, est-ce qu'on peut avoir un mot?'* [Could I have a word?] I stepped back a little, Chirac put his hand on TB's back and steered him a little way down the corridor, where there were fewer people. But most were looking on, whilst trying to look like they weren't. They chatted for ten minutes or so, and the body language of both was tense.

Chirac said it was time to calm the atmosphere, lower the temperature, that there was nothing to be gained from the kind of mutual aggression we had been showing. He said he could not understand why we had been so aggressive towards him and it was time to call off the press attacks. TB said he could not understand why they had been so aggressive diplomatically. They agreed it was time to make up. But Schroeder's people were clear with me that Chirac had been hoping to destroy TB on the back of this, and failed. TB had been down at one point but bounced back quickly and won a surprisingly high number of plaudits from fellow leaders here. On the way out to the airport, he said 'God, it is awful, this war business.' 'Yes, that's why it is usually best to avoid it.'

Then to the Bush call. He said he was sorry about the deaths, then added 'It's called sacrificing for peace and freedom.' He said he thought they had secured the southern oilfield. Rumsfeld reckoned eighty-five per cent of Iraqi oil was secure, so the danger of a self-inflicted environmental attack, or a huge impact on the markets, was limited. We occupy thirty-five per cent of the country. The Scud baskets are under our control. The ground campaign started early. 45,000 troops, US, UK and Australian forces marking the way. Basra should be surrounded today. The Iraqi Army in the north has surrendered. Inside Baghdad there is chaos. There are defections. Saddam's circle is fracturing. It all sounded a bit too good to be true.

There were worries re Sunni/Shia divisions, worries re minefields, worries re oil platforms, though he said the Brits had done a brilliant job securing the offshore platforms. Bush sounded very bullish, said that where there had been combat, the force had been overwhelming. TB said it was important that we underclaimed and overdelivered. Bush said 'Yes, we only have forty per cent of the country.' It had gone up five per cent in two minutes. TB felt most Iraqis would not be waiting for Saddam to topple, that they did not need to flee. Bush said the Brits had been great. He said Clare Short had been given a briefing and was apparently surprised that the Americans only had one horn coming out of their heads. TB filled him in on the summit, and said how strong the accession countries were generally. TB felt the French were trying to come back to us a little bit. At the War Cabinet, C said there were some suggestions – alluded to by Bush earlier – that Saddam had been hit. He may be injured, and there were definitely signs of the inner circle turning on each other.

Saturday, March 22

In for the War Cabinet. Another helicopter crash, and also Terry Lloyd of ITN [correspondent in Iraq] was missing. News-wise, things had moved to the region and the overall sense was of things going pretty well. TB set off for Chequers, saying he felt we were in much stronger shape than we might have been. I went home, set off for a run but had a bad asthma attack and walked back after a mile or so. Whether it was the air, stress or both, I don't know.

Sunday, March 23

I got up early, flicked through the papers, but as often when there was a real and moving international story, the impact of the papers was lessened as events drove the agenda. TB called and he wanted to change the planned broadcast to the forces into an interview, so Emily Hands [press officer] and I worked on that. There was a spate of stories of troops being captured, tortured, etc. In the end, we established there were ten US soldiers captured [in an ambush at Nasiriyah] and later they were paraded. The big battle seemed to be taking place around Umm Qasr [port in southern Iraq], and there were pockets of resistance elsewhere. ITN, not surprisingly, were going crazy re Terry Lloyd. Stewart Purvis [editor-in-chief] called to say that the MoD were being hopeless but it seemed that Terry had gone too far behind enemy lines [near Basra] and was shot by US special forces dealing with Iraqi troops at the time. Purvis called again later and said they now had pictures of the body and would be putting out a statement shortly. I said I would organise a TB tribute. I knew Terry reasonably well and liked him.

In then for a War Cabinet meeting. CDS on the military update and the latest on casualties. GH explaining what they had tried to do re Terry Lloyd. C still not clear on Saddam's whereabouts or well-being. CDS said things were pretty much on track but there had been a number of accidents and the going was hard. As we wound up, the Iraqis were parading the [captured] American servicemen on TV. Dan called to say Bush was intending to go on TV and say this was a flagrant breach of the Geneva Convention. We agreed TB would echo that in his forces interview with BFBS [British Forces Broadcasting Service]. He said to me as we came away from the interview 'How do you really think it's going?' I said from everything we could gather, fine, but it is going to be really tough. There were too many signals that the US did not really want the UN to lead on the humanitarian effort. TB said his next meeting with Bush was going to be vital in terms of all the big strategic questions, and how we planned for the future. He was clearly worried.

At the end of the War Cabinet he had taken Boyce aside for ten minutes or so, just to try to get a real fix on his analysis and how he thought the Americans were doing. Boyce did not hide the difficulties ahead. There had been a bit of street fighting going on. Then we heard that a Red Crescent [medical aid] hospital may have been hit by an RAF bomb, with possibly as many as seventy dead and fifty injured. In briefing, I was simply saying things were on track despite the accidents but there was inevitably a lot of focus on the accidents and less on the 'on track'. The truth was the strategy was on course, but they were meeting greater resistance than anticipated.

Monday, March 24

Four days in and our ridiculous media were all on 'setbacks'. As I said to TB, if we had had 24-hour news during World War Two, we would all be German by now. The main news overnight was two UK soldiers missing, big stuff on PoWs paraded, so all quite tricky. I got the cab in, and up to see TB and Jonathan. He was generally worried. Jonathan and I were both pointing out that this was the fog of war, and it would take time for a rhythm to be established and we had to hold our nerve. The media were pushing hard at the limits of what they should know and then deliver instant comment on everything. At the pre-meeting CDS said things were still going pretty much according to plan though there were Fedayeen [Saddam paramilitary] fighters in Basra causing a fair bit of trouble. C said there were some reports, as yet unclear, of an enormous civilian disaster in Basra, with dozens possibly killed. In general, the bombing campaign was more low-key than people had expected, and very targeted, but the fighting was going to be tough, especially when our forces reached the Medina troops on the road to Baghdad.

Then through to the broader meeting, where John Scarlett ran through things and there was a run round the block on the issues already discussed in TB's office. These meetings were not great. John and CDS obviously felt they were being asked to repeat themselves; those not at the earlier meeting assumed there was something else going on they didn't know about. David Blunkett was in a pretty bad mood and went off on one, saying he needed to know whether Basra was going to become like a medieval siege. TB just said 'No.' David was so down on his own civil servants most of the time that he had slightly got himself into a habit of messenger-shooting, and these guys didn't particularly like it. John R asked whether we shouldn't be moving to messages and tone that suggests longer not shorter term. He felt we had been caught a bit behind the curve and needed to get ahead again. I picked him up on it at the party meeting later, said 'Aah, the man losing his nerve.' 'No,' he said, 'just keen to ask questions because we have to make sure we can sell this policy to party and public.'

I said we had to communicate that there was a plan, it was unfolding, there would be mishaps and accidents but the basic plan would be seen through, and this was not a time to communicate nervousness to generals, which I fear is what they took away from the meeting this morning. He and David B both denied panic but it seemed close to it to me. Later another meeting with C and CDS who assured TB things were generally on track, but there was going to be heavy resistance and a lot of fighting. He and C both said that the 24-hour news was making it much harder in the field. We discussed with CDS and GH the idea of the main Baghdad switchboard being bombed, as it was central to the working of the regime. We also discussed a new missile that could wipe out the power to broadcast on Iraqi state TV, but GH was worried about it.

Then working on TB's statement to the House. He was very focused, but also worried and wanted to walk round the garden to go over it. He was starting to think ahead to the meeting with Bush. He felt Russia had behaved really badly, and though there was an explanation he felt it showed they could not really be trusted to be strategic partners. It was sad, he said, but there we are. We were also picking up all kinds of signals that Cheney and Rumsfeld in particular were not that keen on us being too involved in the UN/aftermath issues. TB felt there was some sense to the really hard US approach. Why should the French and the Russians come in at the end and clean up? Condi was giving the French a very hard time. We were in for a very foggy few days and we were going to need a lot of nerve around the place. I had a long chat with Dan B re the visit and how we intended to handle the public side of things.

Tuesday, March 25

I still felt we did not have a big picture out there, and the problem with the embedded media was that they were just putting over little snapshots from where they were, all competing to get on, but with no sense of an overall strategy. I also felt the military were going a bit native with the media, giving them too much access, letting them get in too close. GB asked to see me, and we met next door. He said the War Cabinet meetings were hopeless. You had Clare just blathering away, DB and JR behaving like armchair generals and giving out weakness vibes to the real generals. He felt we needed to structure things much more like a campaign. We needed to be clear what it was we were pushing every day, e.g. today would be push on Baghdad with a line out on humanitarian and reconstruction. The problem was there were currently too many places and people capable of setting an agenda from somewhere. I asked if he thought the party was OK on this. He said the party is fine on Iraq. 'It's other things they are worried about.' He said there were real worries about the direction of domestic policy and I needed to rein him in a bit.

I got back to the pre-meeting at Number 10. There were more friendly fire incidents today, including UK on UK. The Saddam broadcast on Iraqi TV had the effect of pushing the message he was still in power, which might set us back on the internal opposition to him, which had been growing in confidence a bit.[1] TB and I agreed that we had to reimpose a big-picture message, and he would have to be the one to do it. I had done a script overnight that set out the overall mission and purpose, update on the military front, humanitarian. The War Cabinet was possibly the worst yet. John S and CDS went through the motions of telling us what they had already told a smaller group of us in the pre-meeting and then we meandered around for a bit, with Clare, JR and DB asking a few questions. I scribbled a note to John S 'How many of these would you take into the jungle with you?'

They reported that the Fedayeen were being organised by Chemical Ali.[2] CDS reported continuing difficulties with the Turks re requests for access. He also warned operations may have to be scaled down because of the weather. David B had a go at one of the UK military spokesmen who had been on. 'I would get him off the airwaves if you can.' GB said to me afterwards that TB needed to take DB and JR aside, tell them these were supposed to be meetings on military strategy and we should have a separate meeting on political strategy. John's and David's questions did tend to be about the politics of where

[1] Saddam had urged Iraqis to attack the US and British enemy: 'O Iraqis, fight with the strength of the spirit of jihad . . . strike them, and strike evil so that evil will be defeated.'

[2] Ali Hassan al-Majid, military commander and chief of the Iraqi Intelligence Service, who had deployed chemical weapons in attacks on the Kurds. Later convicted of war crimes and hanged.

we were, but the overall impression for the military and intelligence guys was not good. TB went off to the NEC, then back to prepare for the press conference. They were all going to be on the 'Why is it all getting bogged down?' theme, which was easy to deal with. The tough questions related to differences with the US on the UN role, where we were not in the same place. We had stated clearly there would be a UN role in the aftermath, but the US signals were not as clear. We just had to go back to the Azores words on this. It would be so much easier if Powell, not Cheney and Rumsfeld, was driving the policy in the States. The press conference seemed to last an age. I watched downstairs. They were running a split screen with TB on one side, and bombs being loaded at [RAF] Fairford on the other. One of the girls in the office said the whole thing was being presented like another form of reality TV show, round-the-clock coverage of anything and everything and the prism was 'setback' and 'bogged down'.

On the conference call, I was pressing for more strategic communication and less focus on one part of the picture. There was next to no context out there for the briefings and pictures. They were like random scenes. The briefings in Qatar, and at the Pentagon, kept taking us to our weak points, e.g. PoWs and casualties. TB did the big picture OK today but there was precious little sign of it anywhere else. Also we had real problems on the diplomatic front, particularly re the UN. We had a good meeting of the Iraq communications group, and we agreed to get a message to all those with access to media in the field about the need to stay plugged in to bigger message and overall strategy. We also agreed to press internally for strikes against Saddam's TV output, which was integral to his command and control, part of his infrastructure of fear, and a legitimate target.

We had a lot of problems – sense of setback, bogged down; UN role; humanitarian crisis growing; Basra very tricky. It was a good meeting though and I felt if this group was in charge of the whole communications operation, we would be in a better position. We had to step up even further the contacts with the US. I commissioned a message note justifying attacks on their TV station. Then to the Bush call, and lots of comforting noises to each other, TB saying things were going as well as they could be expected to, Bush saying our troops were so much better than theirs and it was going well. TB said there was a chance the whole thing would collapse quickly like a pack of cards, but we shouldn't bank on it. There would be a lot of fighting, but eventually people would notice change happening, different people in control and if we handled the relations with the

Iraqi people well, change could come quickly. Bush said that if the word went round that Saddam was incapacitated, and also when we 'kick the crap out of the Republican Guard', that will have a profound effect around the country. He was in pretty bellicose form. They discussed Putin, and Bush said he was going to be looking for advice on how to deal with him from now on in. TB said [Hosni] Mubarak [Egyptian President] was nervous and what these guys wanted more than anything now was for the job to be done quickly.

We then left for the MoD for a presentation by CDS, [General Sir] Mike Jackson [Chief of the General Staff], [Admiral Sir Alan] West, [Air Chief Marshal Sir Peter] Squire and [General Sir John] Reith from PJHQ [Permanent Joint Headquarters]. Reith was very impressive but it was absolutely clear this was going to be a lot tougher. Reith felt the US had been excessively optimistic about the collapse of the regime. The hard core and the Fedayeen were absolutely up for the fight. They had nothing to lose, and would not just give up. TB asked about Baghdad. They said it would be split into forty sectors, and our forces would try to take them one by one, before sending in regulars. It would take several weeks, and there were a lot of dangers attached. Jackson said it was the only possible plan. Reith was excellent on the overview, but said that at Basra for example, it was not yet clear the best way to proceed.

The most important thing for TB was to communicate to the Iraqis that we would see this through, that they would benefit from the fall of Saddam. But we should not expect them to welcome with open arms, because they will find it hard to believe the Saddam era is ending. We were doing OK with public opinion in our own country, but we were nowhere in Iraq. Reith said we had to separate regime from people, and that meant taking out his media. The march on Baghdad was going OK, but they expected a lot more fighting. Our forces were busy in the Western Desert dealing with his Scud facilities to prevent them trying to draw Israel in. West went through the navy role and said [trained] dolphins were being used in minesweeping. Back at Number 10, TB was clear it was going to take longer than anticipated. Shock and awe had not really happened. So we had taken the political hit of a stupid piece of terminology, and then not actually had the military benefits. He felt reassured by the expertise of our military.

Wednesday, March 26

More delay in Basra. War Cabinet was awful. C told me later he found the whole thing ridiculous, and it was. It was necessary to involve

March '03: US too optimistic about collapse of regime

the key ministers and keep them up to speed with everything, but the nature of the discussion did not inspire confidence. Clare blathered away, DB was a bit better today, whilst JR did come over a bit as an armchair general. The truth was we were not totally clear about the picture out there. TB had a bilateral with JP, who said Clare's behaviour at these meetings was intolerable and he should not put up with her for too long. TB never quite agreed with us on that and he had another meeting with her later, going out of his way to keep her involved and on board, as much as she ever would be. His concern at the moment was that there might be more support for Saddam than we thought, and that explained the level of resistance. Then later, when a bomb hit a Baghdad market, and the Iraqis started to pump out pictures of it, we were looking a bit shaky.

I was doing an email exchange with Dan on the visit, and it was clear Bush was pissed off at the *FT* story suggesting TB would press him for a bigger UN role. They were sensitive to the idea that TB was shaping their strategy, which was understandable. TB asked me to send a message back that this was our media seeking to open divisions. We knew of a Rumsfeld memo to Bush saying that TB would demand a bigger role for the UN, but that they should resist. Jack said Powell was on our side in this, and was trying to put a halt to the neoconservative stuff. TB's worry was the military campaign. He felt the Americans lacked the absolute single-mindedness needed to get the job done quickly. He said it was beginning to remind him of Kosovo. As we headed to the airport, the market attack was really taking off as a media and political issue, though there were suggestions the Iraqis may have been involved themselves.

TB was working on a long note for Bush on the plane, and I left him to it and had a long chat with Jack, going through all the difficult areas. He was worried just how far out on a limb TB was pushing himself, but was still totally on board for where we were. The main message in TB's note, when you boiled it down, was that there was a lot of support for the aims of the campaign, and we totally believed the policy was right, but there was real concern at the way the US put over their views and intentions, and that rested in people's fears about their perceived unilateralism. He was urging him to do more to rebuild with Germany, then Russia, then France, and saying he should seize the moment for a new global agenda, one to unite the world rather than divide it. A distorted view of the US was clouding everything – look at how much cynicism there was at their efforts in the Middle East. We had to break that down. Why had Mexico and Chile gone the other way? Why did so much of Europe?

In the end he wrote a twelve-page note that was both subtle and blunt at the same time. It was a good piece of work and if Bush took it on board would have a good effect. But he still had his own internal battles to deal with. I didn't really feel Bush had the will to deliver on this new international agenda TB was talking about, but we would see.

We landed in pretty miserable weather conditions, then flew down to Camp David, Bush seemed more nervous than usual, and it came out in that over-cockiness that sometimes spills out. 'We're gonna win. I'm sure of it. Basra will fall. The people will rise up, and choose freedom.' Overall, he was confident we were going to win. He made a jokey little reference to the *FT* story, when TB said we had not been pushing that line. 'Don't worry, I blame Alastair.'

Thursday, March 27

GWB had clearly read TB's note and was going through it virtually line by line. He was fairly strong on MEPP. He said he knew there would have to be a reckoning in their relationships with others. He seemed a lot more on top of the detail and in the discussion on the complexities of the Arab world seemed less one-dimensional than before. TB's note was saying that in essence the US had a choice about what it wanted to do with its power. They had to face up to that choice. The power was a given but how it was used was a series of choices. Jonathan and I were staying in Redwood – the cabins were all named after trees. We went over to see TB who was worrying about the whole UN scene. I felt we had it parked fairly well and there was no real need to take it forward at the moment. We walked down to Laurel where the meeting was to be. At first there was just me, TB, Jonathan and DM. TB felt on the war that we had reached the point we did in Kosovo where it felt like we were holding back slightly and not really going for it. In Kosovo the point came a bit later but it did feel similar.

On the UN Bush had said last night he was happy for a UN role but he was pretty scathing, said their handling of some issues was woeful, that some of them couldn't run a garbage service. It was a recurring theme. He just wasn't up for it really. It was interesting how Bush liked to take in different views and experiences round the table. He wasn't status-conscious in these meetings. He was also prone to go off on conversational tangents, asked me a few times re my running, and telling me he had been doing seven-minute mile pace round the Camp David track, which was faster than I could. They had another confined session then came out to discuss

March '03: Bush more nervous than usual at Camp David

how we dealt with the press. Condi said we should go over the aftermath issues.

Bush said he understood there had to be some kind of role for the UN but he didn't trust their competence. He said on Kosovo the UN had been all over the place. Jack said 'With respect Mr President, Kosovo is not the only model. There is Bosnia, where the UN was light touch. There have been others which they have done well.' They agreed Sérgio de Mello [UN high commissioner for human rights] would be a good guy to do the UN job [Secretary General's special representative in Iraq] but Kofi may want him to stay on human rights. Pre the press conference TB was worried re the body language. I said the most important thing was the issue of resolve, and a message to the Iraqi people about seeing it through and being with them for the long term.

As TB walked back to Dogwood cabin afterwards he said to Jonathan and me 'He's not wrong about the UN you know.' I said he may have a point but it doesn't mean he is a hundred per cent right. We were driven by buggy up to the hangar where the press conference was being held. Dan had told him that I referred to them as 'the bastards' and Bush was saying 'bastards, bastards' loudly. I had done a script for TB and created a bit of a problem maybe by referring to the dead soldiers being 'executed'.

TB and Bush went off for a walk and then came back for lunch. Fairly relaxed and informal. GWB was geeing me up re the marathon, said I would love it, that it was one of the best things he ever did. TB and Bush then went out on the terrace for a genuine one on one. TB said afterwards they had discussed US politics and the pressures from the hard right. Bush had changed into a tracksuit. He did casual gear a lot better than TB but I guess the White House logo on everything helped a fair bit. He looked very fit for his age though the media had felt he looked tired at the press conference. I had an interesting chat with Dan about how Bush worked. He was a real early to bed, early to rise man. He was obsessed about punctuality and would really go for people who arrived late for meetings. He liked to read a brief, then discuss, then decide. He was open to ideas. He was very religious. He was loyal to friends but once you fell out with him, that was that. We were just whiling away the time while Bush and TB chatted. After half an hour or so they came in and we walked up to the helipad. TB was pleased and excited that Bush seemed to have moved on the road map. He was saying not only that he would publish it but take the lead in implementing it. We had a nice enough journey to New York with a fantastic view out of the helicopter. To the UN to meet Kofi. The main focus was post-conflict and Oil for Food.[1] Kofi was really pleased TB had gone to see him rather than the other way round. It was clear the politics were getting harder and harder. Bush was heavy enough but Cheney and Rumsfeld were even heavier. Back to the plane by chopper.

Friday, March 28

There was definitely a changed mood, lots of it media-driven. The morning meetings were developing a rhythm. First a pre-meeting with TB, GH, JS, C, CDS, John S and the key Number 10 people and then through to the broader meeting. CDS was confident things were going OK though it would be a while before there would be a commonly understood acceptance of military success. The weather was not helping and there had been more resistance than predicted. Not all bad news but there had been another friendly-fire incident. TB felt the Bush visit had been good and yet again today we saw how the propaganda could quickly go wrong. There was another attack on a Baghdad market. No evidence it was ours but the Arab media were straight out saying it was. At the morning meeting, we had a long discussion about how to improve outreach to the Arab media and also how to deal with the embedded media. As I said to TB, the problem was that the military had gone native on the media, rather than the other way round. They were all getting too much access and putting over little snapshots, so that there was very little communication of a big picture.

War Cabinet was pretty grim, with Clare blathering on about the UN. It was quite clear she was going to quit. She kept saying the issue was not fudge-able because it was a question of legality. TB said nobody was saying we were going to do something illegal. But she said there was a US draft that did suggest that. She said it was a matter of principle for her, and it should be for all of us. TB and Jack both had a go, not really clear what she was on about. C and John S said to me afterwards it was extraordinary that she behaved in the way she did. James Harrower [Number 10 security] and Mohny [Bahra, protection officer] called about how to handle demonstrations at home. James said the police were also discussing the possible need

[1] The UN Oil for Food programme had been set up in 1995 to enable Iraq, despite economic sanctions aimed at demilitarisation, to sell oil on the international market in exchange for food, medicine and humanitarian supplies. The programme was suspended by Kofi Annan prior to the invasion, and eventually terminated in November 2003.

for security on the marathon route. TB was planning to speak to Chirac and Schroeder tomorrow. He said we needed to start putting together the main European relationships again. [Royal Fleet Auxiliary ship] *Sir Galahad* finally docked at Umm Qasr [delivering humanitarian aid, after being delayed by mine clearance].

Saturday, March 29

In for the 9am meeting. The head of the Iraqi air defences had been sacked because of malfunctioning air defences, which may have caused two explosions in Baghdad. 24-hour news was a bit of a nightmare at the moment, as they covered it like any other story, with a mix of hysteria and comment the whole time, and the settled view was that it wasn't really happening. They seemed to think wars should only last a few days and then they should get on to the next thing. There were suggestions the public were getting sick of all the comment though, and making up their own minds. But a combination of dead soldiers, friendly fire, lack of progress towards Baghdad, Rumsfeld mouthing off re Syria [warning Syria not to aid Iraq] was not great. Dan told me they were delighted that Richard Perle [Rumsfeld-appointed Pentagon adviser and neoconservative lobbyist] was having to resign as chairman of a defence group [Defense Policy Board Advisory Committee, Department of Defense], though he was staying on the board.

At the War Cabinet Jack said we would be in a better place if Bush was not surrounded by 'loonies'. ORHA [Office of Reconstruction and Humanitarian Assistance, established by the US to become a caretaker government in Iraq] was in a state of chaos because of internal US difficulties. They appeared unable to agree on anything. TB asked me afterwards if I thought the propaganda effort was working. I said not. He agreed. The problem was the US were pretty much doing their own thing, and they lacked coherence at the centre. The embedded media were treating the whole thing like scenes from a war movie, and there was no place for the big picture. The media here were pretty much set on presenting things in the worst light. So the mix was not good. We had to raise our own game, but also get the US and the military to raise theirs, and co-ordinate better. The pressure for instant comment and analysis was a real added problem in modern conflict situations.

Sunday, March 30

The papers were not good. The overall impression was that things were not really going our way. TB and I had both come to the view over the weekend that we needed to beef up the whole communications effort. If we were moving from 'shock and awe' to a message of steady progress, it required a different communications plan and approach. I went to Greenwich to run the first half of the marathon course with Hugh Jones [runner]. Did 14.08 miles in two hours flat. I quite liked the course and could see no real problems in it.

TB called a couple of times later, as he was preparing another note, including on the media, and we tossed around a few ideas. The Americans were still causing us problems on the media and political front, e.g. Rumsfeld suddenly turning on Syria had apparently also been a shock to the White House. Things not great with Fiona, and were unlikely to improve until I was out of it. Even with all this going on, there was a large part of me wanted out. I had pretty much lost it with the media, had very little time or respect for any of them, which was not a great position to be in, and maybe it was time for someone else.

Monday, March 31

In for the usual morning meetings, with both CDS and C more hopeful. John Scarlett also reported that the general picture was a lot better. TB later saw CDS and a general from the campaign and said he got more talking direct to the general than he had from weeks of meetings. The truth was that the military and intelligence campaigns had not been wholly successful. The morning meetings were not very productive, and the mood at the War Cabinet was the usual mix of sullen and concerned. Then to TB's meeting with JR, HA, DA, Peter H, Jonathan, Pat McF, Sally, David Hanson [Blair's PPS]. TB went through what he wanted on the political and media fronts. It was basically a war room à la Millbank, with all the main tasks being overseen from there, and everyone knowing what was going on in all the different parts of the operation.

I then spent most of the day in a series of meetings working out how to put it into practice. I called in the key people from CIC, FCO and MoD, and explained we needed much more centralised co-ordination. We were heading for another version of the Kosovo model, though as I pointed out to TB, getting real co-ordination with the Americans wasn't easy because their own internal co-ordination was not there. Another TB/Bush call, which was basically just going through TB's note. A lot of the discussion was about presentation and Bush said he would speak to Dan 'who is kind of responsible for this'. He did so, because Dan called later and said TB had really got GWB 'spun up', because he was asking what we were going to do to grip it. I said we had to have a real exchange of people and we also needed them to get their act together internally. He said the reality was they had no real grip of Rumsfeld. The main story of the weekend was division between Rumsfeld and the military over the way the campaign was being waged.

TB called later and asked if I thought it had been OK to raise the comms and media issues like he did. I said it was, but don't under-estimate how hard it will be to grip. We have our own internal prob-lems but they are nothing compared with the Americans'. He had to be more direct with Bush because at least he tended to get things done when he cared enough about it. I sensed on the call today that Bush was maybe sharing TB's feeling that the military campaign was not quite right. They were both desperate for better communications. The BBC was a bit better today but we had to do more to slow the rhythm. Shock and awe had to become steady progress.

Tuesday, April 1

I did a note overnight on the communications effort for TB. Last night had been better but we were still having real problems with the BBC, particularly the reports out of Baghdad and the embedded reporters. TB was involved in a series of meetings with GB re EMU. GB had suddenly announced last week that he wanted to do the euro assessment in the Budget, and say that four out of the five [economic] tests were met, and set out how we intended to meet the fifth, plus there was the suggestion, from us, that we could do the [euro] referendum bill. Andrew Adonis and Peter Hyman in particular were against it, felt it would be seen as sneaky. I felt it was big and bold and TB should use GB's desire to do it now to extract maximum leverage for a pro position. But then after one of the sessions, TB said 'God knows what he's up to. I just can't work it out.'

The military campaign was going better. There was a classic Clare moment at the War Cabinet when she asked CDS if we shouldn't be talking to the local military down there. 'We're killing them, not talking to them,' he said. She was more and more ridiculous at these meetings. At the pre-meeting TB raised the *Guardian* splash that the US was going to run Iraq from Kuwait. We worked up a line 'Iraq for and by the Iraqi people'. But most of my day was taken trying to set up TB's war room. I got him to raise it at the War Cabinet so ministers and top brass knew we would be changing things on the comms front. GH said he would like to have it at the MoD.

I chaired a ninety-minute meeting to work through all the things we would need for it and started to bring in the people we would need to drive it. Anne Shevas [chief press officer] found premises at the FCO and rebuttal in MoD. Things were feeling better at the moment, and it was also the case that sometimes if we got the communications right, and the PR situation settled, things then improved in reality because people could focus better. We had intelligence, which I wanted to use, that Saddam was planning to attack holy sites as a way of generating real anger against us, not exactly difficult in the Arab world at the moment. CDS said we had to wait for the US to agree never to attack holy sites, even if they were being used to store weapons.

We had an internal meeting on some of the domestic policy issues, foundation hospitals, asylum, health and NICs. There was a lot to be sorting on the domestic front but most of our time and energies were going on Iraq. At the lobby we were starting to use the basic narrative set out in TB's note – 1, strategic grip, 2, steady advance then 3, end of regime. It was the best way to slow the media rhythm. I was working on humanitarian stories for tomorrow. Clare did [Jonathan] *Dimbleby* on ITV and was talking about the illegality of the US approach. We were making good progress finding out what happened at the first Baghdad bombing, enough for Jack to say it was 'increasingly probable' it was caused by Iraqi missiles. The sense of strategy was finally beginning to get communicated through the media. I lodged another complaint with the BBC re their output from Baghdad from [Andrew] Gilligan and Rageh Omaar.

Wednesday, April 2

Definitely a sense that the military campaign was going better, plus we had a strong humanitarian message running alongside. The major news overnight was the battle getting closer to Baghdad, and also the rescue of a female US PoW [Private Jessica Lynch] by the Marines. Jack sort of got up the holy sites issue on the *Today* programme. I got a cab in and on the way up the street Alisdair Macdonald [*Mirror* photographer] showed me a picture he'd taken of Geoff Hoon yesterday as he left Number 10, with a 'Top Secret' paper facing the camera, and with the text legible. I thanked him and later spoke to Geoff about it. We had a fairly brief PMQs preparation meeting. TB now had maps of Iraq in his room. At the pre-meeting the picture given was a lot better, particularly in Basra. CDS made a revealing comment when he said in Basra we were using lessons from Northern Ireland. Troops were getting to know people, finding out who the ringleaders were, then seeking them out. 'Did you do that in Northern Ireland?' I asked. Laughter.

The War Cabinet proper was the usual blather. At the political meeting we agreed: 1. big push on holy sites; 2. pull back the military narrative so that it did not appear like we were about to win any day now, and 3. more out there re Iraq vs Iraqi people. I was working on a TB speech re a future vision for Iraq. Jack S called to say he was intending to go to ORHA. He said not to mention to Clare because she would want to come and it would change the whole tone and nature of the visit. Then to a meeting with John Reid and Douglas [Alexander] to see how they would fit in the war room. We agreed Douglas would be semi-permanent, JR in and out, though later TB told me he was thinking of moving JR to Leader of the House and Ian McCartney [pensions minister] to party chairman.

Over for PMQs which was fine though it was interesting that there were no questions on the conduct of the war – it was all about the post-conflict questions. I got back and started to insert people into different parts of the war room. The conference call was a mix of wandering conversations and pipe dreams about how well we were doing. I just didn't see it. I had a separate chat with Dan re the Northern Ireland visit. We were thinking about a joint interview, and also getting over their guy from Homeland Security. TB saw GB again re EMU and was clearly now thinking he was being stitched up to do something he didn't particularly want to do. I saw Peter M, PG and PH and discussed the BBC coverage. I got a nice letter from Neil [Kinnock] saying his favourite game at the moment was imagining how the BBC of today would have covered World War Two. 'Hitler would have lived to 1978.' PG felt the public were making up their own minds and that TB was in OK shape. The public liked TB being so big in the States and he felt we should build that side of the profile even more. My big worry was the Arab media. We were kidding ourselves if we thought we were making real inroads.

Thursday, April 3

TB had issued instructions to ministers in the War Cabinet that they couldn't go on holiday at Easter. When I mentioned it to Fiona, and said we needed to work out how to handle it if the press came after me when we were away, she snapped back 'I suppose that's a polite way of saying you can't have a holiday.' I couldn't understand why she felt we both had to leave. We still had a lot going for us. But she didn't really believe we could get our lives back until we were both out of their [the Blairs] shadow, and maybe there was something in that. I got Sally to speak to her, and Peter M. Both felt that her anger with me for being a driven, obsessive, selfish bastard had boiled over but because she basically wanted us to stay together she preferred to express it as hatred for TB and CB who in turn gave her lots of ammunition. But it was really grim at the moment.

On the war front, things were going better. The movement towards Baghdad was quickening, more people were deserting, and more was coming out re the nature of the regime. TB was late for the pre-meeting because he had another euro meeting with GB. He was now firmly of the view that GB was trying to bounce him while his eye was off the ball because of Iraq. GB was now trying to make out that he had always intended to do the assessment now, and that TB had agreed to it a while back, which he hadn't. Also that it was somehow TB's fault Iraq was 'taking so long'! And he was back on to a Peter M kick, saying that Peter was responsible for foundation hospitals and the division they were causing. So it went on.

There was an established meeting rhythm now – TB with me, Jonathan, DM, sometimes Sal, then pre-meeting with CDS, C, John S, then the War Cabinet, then a mop-up, and today full Cabinet as well. The mood was OK. TB went through the whole picture and was emphasising steady progress. I helped GH with his Commons statement and then went over to the war room. Dickie Stagg [director of public services and information, FCO] had done a great job and it was pretty much all there now, now needed the fine-tuning and the drive. It would definitely make a difference and we had some good people in there already. I worked on TB's 'message to the Iraqi people' and we brainstormed on the different ways to get it across. TB was out on a troops visit so I tried to clear my in tray.

TB had asked GH and others to work on a counter-plan on the future of Iraq to offer to Bush that was not Rumsfeld's eccentric ideas. TB said there was no point just going on about Rumsfeld the whole time. We needed a counter-plan. David M, Jonathan and I did a secure videolink with Condi, Dan and Karen. They agreed that on Tuesday we should publish a joint statement similar to the Azores. We also discussed [Bush visiting] Northern Ireland. I asked what the US media would make of GWB pitching up there. They said their approach was to say it was to show those involved in the MEPP that peace processes can work. Good idea. It was a good discussion, pretty frank about each other's difficulties, so at one point we joked about swapping Rumsfeld for Clare. But I sensed we were at least gripping some of the post-war issues and had a sense of a stronger strategy going forward. Then a rash of calls on the euro, as GB's lot seemed to be putting it about that there would be something on it in the Budget, which confirmed the suspicions this was an attempted bounce. TB got back at 6 [from Aldershot and RAF Lyneham] and we went through the outstanding issues. HC [Hilary Coffman, special adviser] said he had been terrific with the troops.

Friday, April 4

More EMU meetings and TB was reverting to his original view that it would be seen as sneaky to do it in the Budget while a war was going on. Jeremy [Heywood] had been up until 1.30 negotiating with Ed Balls and trying to make the language more positive. After all the morning meetings TB called an office meeting and he looked pretty fed up. While GB's rationale to TB was glass more than half full, it was the empty bits that would get the attention. TB saw him again later and said it was the worst meeting yet (again). GB said the assessment was done and he was not having it rewritten 'for political reasons'. He was back to speaking in code again. He said 'I know what your plan is' – i.e. you are going to sack me. TB tried to get him to say that was what he meant, but he didn't. TB said he was not prepared to be bounced into something that he felt was wrong. His instincts were telling him this was the wrong way, and the wrong time. He had discussed it with JP who had said he should follow his instincts, and also that there had to be more time for the Cabinet to be brought properly into the discussion.

GB said he was not prepared to let them rewrite the assessment and if that was what we intended, he would have to go. 'There's the door,' said TB. GB claimed he had been trying to have these discussions for ages, which was total balls. The Treasury had already prepared for printing, and now sent to the printers, 3,000 pages of background material. TB said he had been trying to discuss this for months and GB had resisted, all the time preparing for this decision and announcement, and we had to wait for something written by someone called Dave Ramsden![1] Sally said it would be hard to win a referendum campaign without GB. But what he was doing was ensuring there wasn't one for the foreseeable future.

TB and I went out on the terrace later. 'One thing is for sure,' he said. 'At the moment he is crackerjack. My big worry is that he will bring the whole show down.' I saw Ed Balls later and although we were able to talk in a civilised way about it, there was no getting away from how grisly things were between them at the moment. I

[1] Treasury official then leading work on the assessment of the five economic tests.

had told TB I was seeing him and he asked me to get over the message that he didn't want to sack him, they had to work together but he did not fear him any more. I discussed my own situation with TB. He said if things were bad and I was feeling demotivated, I had to decide what I really wanted to do, but he felt I would regret it if I left. The truth was I didn't really know if I wanted to leave or not. He had a lot on his plate at the moment. Iraq, then the euro suddenly thrown in and I felt bad adding to the problems, but I really need to resolve in my own mind what I intend to do.

The Iraq situation was better. The airport at Baghdad was eighty per cent under control. The Republican Guard was on the run. The broadcasters there were finally beginning to accept that we were doing well. There were signs now of regime collapse. Our main media focus today was the [BBC] World Service Arabic Service and Abu Dhabi TV. The Islamic media team were doing well. We also had some good Iraqi exiles in who were able to talk about the regime far more convincingly than we could. We signed off the TB letter to the Iraqis which we were going to be getting out through the military. The main message for the interviews was that it was a war on Saddam not Iraq. We were also pushing the line that Iraqis wanted to see money spent on schools not palaces. Pictures came in of Saddam out on the streets but it was not entirely clear that it was him rather than a lookalike.

TB did a video conference with Bush. Dick Cheney, Condi and Andy Card were also in the shot. Cheney said next to nothing, just sat there looking menacing. I couldn't work out whether he always looked like that or it was an effect he sought to create. They went over the Middle East again, Russia, military update, but TB said afterwards he preferred the one-on-one phone calls to the video conference. There was something about it that made him feel constrained, unable to speak freely. There was also something a bit surreal about the fact that while we could see them on the main screen, there was an ordinary TV screen to one side, Peter O'Toole starring in some old-style Zulu war film [*Zulu Dawn*, 1979].

I saw TB again before he went up to the flat. He was concerned GB was setting himself up to walk by claiming TB had sought to rewrite the euro assessment politically. TB's view anyway was that it was a political process based on economic judgements. The assessment per se could not decide. That had, ultimately, to be a political judgement. Dan B called as I was leaving to say AP [Associated Press] were on to the Belfast visit. I knocked up a quick briefing note with Ben Wilson [press officer] to use it to get out basic message on Iraq, MEPP and NI.

Saturday, April 5

The military picture was changing fast. As I arrived at the office for the 9am meeting, Sky was showing US tanks going through Baghdad. Things were also going a lot better in Basra and the mood was much improved all round. The regime was refusing humanitarian help. However, the post-conflict issues were looking really ragged. Though we were trying to minimise the differences, the truth was there were differences between us and the US, and differences between the White House, Powell and Rumsfeld. TB said to me he couldn't understand how I could think about leaving when we were in a position to sort the big geopolitical questions for the next generation, and surely it was right to see the whole thing through.

At the War Cabinet, issues to do with the future of Iraq were becoming more difficult. Clare's tone was becoming more menacing. Scarlett said there was a possibility Chemical Ali was dead. I went up to Mum and Dad's with Grace and did the conference call from Robert's [Templeton, sick relative] bedside. I raised the issue of a planned ORHA briefing for Monday which I said would be a bad thing at the time TB was seeing Bush. Dan and Tucker [Eskew, White House media affairs] both agreed and we would try to move it. The military situation was getting better all the time but as the prospect of winning came closer, the aftermath issues became more pressing.

Sunday, April 6

David M and Matthew Rycroft were pulling together the post-conflict arguments for TB. It was difficult. David called when I was on the train home and said we were meeting a fair bit of American resistance. I got home and Fiona and I had another heart-to-heart. She thought the kids were fed up with it and she was determined that we should leave together. I don't suppose I handled it very well, just raged about how I hated being pressurised like this when I had so much on my plate at the moment. The reality was I was unsure what I wanted to do. I was very torn.

Monday, April 7

Fiona picked a fight this morning as soon as I went downstairs with some jibe about 'the thought police'. I said it was time she got a grip of herself. She ended up calling me a bastard and throwing a cup at me, which smashed on the floor at my feet. She was more angry than I had ever known her and taking it all out on me. Part of me understood. Part of me resented it. But I had a terrible sense of foreboding about it. I left for the office feeling like shit. At the intel meeting, the news was overwhelmingly good. Basra was going according to plan. Around Baghdad the US troops were really going for it now. All our problems really related to the future of Iraq. [Ahmed] Chalabi [expatriate Iraqi dissident], a friend of Rumsfeld and [Paul] Wolfowitz [Deputy Defense Secretary], was putting himself around the whole time as a key player, possible future leader, when the reality was he would be unacceptable.[1] The nature of a UN role was becoming the key difficulty. The Americans didn't want the French in particular to be involved, and because of the reality of the P5 [permanent UNSC members – US, UK, France, Russia and China], that meant the UN. Their general take was that they had given the UN the opportunity to deal with this, the UN had fucked it up, and didn't deserve to be straight back in the game. But TB was firmly of the view they should be rebuilding relationships, not keeping them broken. He said at one meeting of the inner group 'I did Iraq because I thought it was right and I am prepared to take whatever comes my way to do what I think is right. But I'm not prepared to stand up for something I think is wrong.' He was back to the notion that they were doing the right thing in the wrong way. We wanted an interim authority that was mainly Iraqi, then a truly representative government. TB felt his job was still to keep the US focused on the UN route but the pressures in the States were all the other way, to present the UN as a bad thing that shouldn't be allowed near the place. Dan called to say Bush had agreed to our idea of a joint Iraqi TV broadcast with TB so I worked on a script. Then domestic problems took another bad turn, Fiona sending Jonathan an email saying she intended to resign. TB said he would see her on Wednesday when we got back.

On the flight to Belfast TB worked on a note for Bush setting out why it was so important to get the UN properly involved – to show our commitment to rebuilding after the divisions in the international community, for the Arab world, for Europe. It was a two-page note, very clear and rational. We landed, got a helicopter to Hillsborough. As I was making a few calls in my room, TB called me through to

[1] Chalabi and his organisation the Iraqi National Congress provided the US government with intelligence material about weapons of mass destruction and links to al-Qaeda, the majority of which was used in good faith in making the case for military intervention. It later turned out to have been fabricated by an Iraqi defector codenamed 'Curveball'. Chalabi would be appointed president of the interim governing council of Iraq in September 2003. He would later dismiss the fabricated intelligence, saying 'We are heroes in error. As far as we're concerned, we've been entirely successful. That tyrant Saddam is gone and the Americans are in Baghdad.'

his room. He asked how my situation was at home. I said that unless I had an exit date, I had no 'marriage'. He said he was really saddened and disappointed, but he understood. He would not put me under pressure to stay. He felt it was a bad move for me, that I would forever regret not seeing the whole thing through to the end. 'But you need to know you have done more for me than anyone, more than I could have asked for, I could not have done it without you, and I will not feel let down, so let me relieve you of any pressure you may feel on that front.' But I did feel it, because I knew he valued the close team around him and I knew I made a difference. I felt it very strongly here at Hillsborough because there had been so many good and bad moments here, but I knew I had helped with both.

We stood at the window and I reminded him of the time we came here in Opposition and he looked out over the grounds at Hillsborough and said the Tories were not going to give it all up without a real fight. We had won that fight and I knew a lot of that was down to me and the work I'd done for him, and it was not easy to walk away from it. He asked me when I wanted to go. I said summer at the latest, maybe conference, maybe before. He just nodded. We went round in circles for a while and then he said I would have to help him find a successor. I felt David Hill [former Labour Party chief spokesman] was possibly the only option. We went downstairs to wait for Bush and Co. to arrive. They flew in, then drove up, GWB, Powell, Condi and Andy Card in Bush's car. TB and Bush having a fair bit of time together. At one point they came back from a walk and Bush was talking about his favourite presidents – Washington, Lincoln, Roosevelt, Reagan. He said Reagan made the country feel good again and he saved the Republican Party.

I tried to go out for a run but was stopped at every second tree by bloody American security men jumping out from trees. Gave up after a couple of miles. Bush seemed to be going in the right direction on MEPP, said he intended to put real pressure on Sharon. He was still not in bridge-building mode elsewhere, said that he didn't want TB to accept Putin's invite to meet VP, Chirac and Schroeder at St Petersburg. Meanwhile Clare had sent through a note listing all sorts of points she wanted TB to raise with Bush. Jack was of the view that it didn't matter too much if she went. TB felt it was a good discussion but he was concerned that Bush was in such a different position re the UN and trying to rebuild relations. Jack felt they really were pressing for a right-wing government there, though Bush seemed to be pretty clear [Ahmed] Chalabi was a non-starter.

Tuesday, April 8

TB said 'this neocon stuff' was crazy. I had asked Dan last night what 'neocon' meant and he said it was the belief that government had a moral purpose. I said does that mean moral purpose can only be right wing? TB felt today's meeting with Bush was going to be tough. It was clear Condi was pushing a fairly hard line re the UN. We had a fight on our hands to keep in a 'vital role' [in the press conference script]. She wanted 'important' which sounded too grudging. 'It's meant to be,' she said. My other worry was that it might be briefed they had downgraded it. TB was determined we had to get something out of this and in the end, largely thanks to Bush, we did. Bush was excellent on Northern Ireland, and on MEPP, linked the two well by saying he would spend as much time and energy on MEPP as TB did on NI, then excellent too on the UN role. He was good on the war message too. The general feeling afterwards was that it was the best media performance he'd done.

It was interesting to watch him in the main meeting today, where he was letting TB do a lot of the talking, then taking in Powell's and Condi's views in particular, then more or less saying what we expected him to in the first place. He seemed restless too, a bit fidgety. He and TB were in the big armchairs by the fireplace, the rest dotted around the room, Jack and Powell on the sofa together. Powell was talking at one point when Bush got up, got himself a coffee, asked me if I wanted one and came over to talk to me about the marathon. When is it? What time will I do? How much money will I raise? Dan pointed out that I had a piece in *The Times* on it and Bush picked it up and read it, getting to the end plug for Leukaemia Research. 'You doing it for leukaemia? Did you know my sister died from leukaemia? Would you like me to give you a cheque?' I certainly would, I said.

He went to the door giving on to the lounge, opened it and shouted out 'Blake [Gottesman, aide], get my chequebook.' Later the cops said he created an absolute stir because nobody had a clue that he had a chequebook with him, let alone where it was, though they did find it eventually, and he wrote out a cheque there and then. He said his sister was called Robin and died aged seven when he was four. 'I will do this because you are my friend,' he said, 'but I am also doing it for her.' I asked if the charity could publicise it. Sure, he said. TB came over and asked what I was up to. I said the president had just given me a cheque so where's yours?

Bush seemed seem to buy into TB's line that he had to develop a bigger international message that was not just terrorism but MEPP, world poverty, environment, etc. He was pretty vile re Chirac, said he felt betrayed, that Chirac had gone against him not on the merits but as part of a general anti-US strategy and he would never forgive that. 'The only thing that would swing me round to France is regime change.' Bush said he would maybe rebuild with Schroeder first but he wanted TB to make sure he knew he felt personally affronted and he would only think about putting things back together with them on the clear understanding German foreign policy was not run by the French.

TB seemed to have worked a fair bit of influence on him because the general reaction from the press conference was that Bush went well beyond what was expected. He also tore a bit of a strip off Condi at the pre-meeting when she was still picking away at him, and he suddenly said 'There is too much tension in here.' He asked everyone to leave apart from me, Blake and Magi Cleaver [Number 10 press officer]. TB and Bush also had a fairly long stroll, just the two of them while Jack continued to work on Condi, Powell and Dan Fried [National Security Council], saying that the warmer the words re the UN, the greater the influence within it. Jack and I both fought very hard to keep 'vital' in the text, and eventually they agreed to it. Later Dan said, only half in jest I think, 'Can we win any of these arguments at all?' He obviously had the counter-worry, that if Bush was too warm re the UN, he would get hit at home. TB said to Bush 'that was a very rash promise' – to spend as much time on MEPP as he had on NI.

Bush knew he had done pretty well. I was trying to get them up to do the Iraqi TV pieces to camera straight away while they were still in the mood. Bush's crowd were gathering round him clearly telling him he had gone too far in our direction. Both Condi and Dan looked slightly panicked, though he was holding firm and seemed not to be bothered. During the press conference Powell had slipped a note to Condi saying they would have to send a 'Rummygram', to warn Rumsfeld of what he was saying. Jack was trying to joke with Condi about it but she was clearly not happy. She said he had risked bad US reaction re the UN and they would have to make some calls to see how bad it was. Bush overheard and snapped back at her 'I don't want any pulling back on this.' We were due to do the broadcast recording on the same floor as the bedrooms. I went up with them, and went in to TB's room while he tidied himself up. Bush came in after a while. 'Hey, they didn't make your bed yet.' He said he was getting a bit of grief from his people but he was fine with what he said. TB said it was the right thing to do. We sorted the filming logistics, then down to meet Bertie [Ahern] who was arriving for lunch, and then the other parties. The press conference was running pretty much word perfect for us.

We gathered the parties, including [David] Trimble, [Gerry] Adams, [Martin] McGuinness, [David] Ervine [leader, Progressive Unionist Party] etc., in a rough circle inside the main dining room. Bush did the rounds and was pretty good at it, and did a little general number, saying he was there in the hope he could put some wind in their sails, and that when NI finally moved to lasting peace, it would be seen as a symbol of hope around the world. I was chatting to Powell about the French. He said even he found them impossible to deal with, that he found de Villepin arrogant and condescending. The meeting went fine, and they all seemed to think it had been worth him coming. TB and Bush then walked down the hill to the helicopters. I was following on behind with Condi. We joked about the next venue, maybe Cyprus. I said I thought it had gone pretty well, but said she seemed a lot more wound up than before. They flew off and TB went back in for meetings with Bertie and the parties.

TB was full of himself on the flight home, really felt it had been good and positive, pretty much on all fronts. GWB was definitely moving a bit on the international agenda, and buying into the need for a new approach, but the tensions internally had been very clear. TB felt Schroeder had a chance of getting back in with Bush, but not Chirac. TB was even more firmly of the view now that Chirac's world view built around rival poles of power was crazy. Chirac had put himself out on a limb and would see France's power diminish. The question unresolved from today was when to declare victory.

Wednesday, April 9

Today was the day when things really started to turn. While we were having a meeting on the humanitarian issues, which I wanted to badge as a return to normal life, the US forces were now motoring big time, and the Iraqis were spilling out on to the streets in greater numbers and with more confidence. The BBC reporters and David Chater [Sky] were beginning to change their tune. The main focus for the media was the toppling of a statue of Saddam, all the more dramatic for the time it took, but the effect ruined in many ways by an American soldier getting up there to put a US flag round his face. They just don't get it sometimes. I could appreciate the emotion that led him to do something like that, and these guys are soldiers not diplomats, but even so, surely someone nearby would have reckoned on how what plays well in the States goes down like a lead balloon elsewhere. The PMQs pre-meeting was strangely flat and desultory and they could tell TB's mind was elsewhere now, moving on to the next set of problems.

War Cabinet. Signs of regime collapse were all around now. It was still not clear where Saddam was but they believed both he and Chemical Ali were alive. Clare was rabbiting on more than ever. I slipped TB a note about the time Saddam shot his health minister at a meeting because he was annoying him and did he want me to get a gun? Yes, he scribbled. We came out of the meeting straight into another GB-inspired mini crisis. Jeremy had discovered late yesterday that GB planned to include in the Budget a review by [Sir] Derek Wanless [banker] on health inequalities, obviously with a view to making big changes in the future. He hadn't discussed it with TB or with Alan Milburn, who hit the roof when told about it, and demanded it be removed from the Budget. Of course GB being GB, it was too late to unpick fully, the background documents having been printed we assumed, and Wanless having been lined up. We did though get it pulled from the statement and got the Treasury to agree Milburn would be in charge of the review.

TB and I were in many ways so used to it that with everything else that was going on, we didn't let ourselves get too wound up, and we were trying to make light of it when Alan came in to see TB pre Cabinet. He was totally on the rampage. He said it was just unacceptable to have a Chancellor behave like this, to announce major change in someone else's department without even discussing it. He could see TB was not going to get too wound up and so added 'And it weakens you in the eyes of others that you let him get away with it.' He said the NHS was more monitored and reviewed than any other part of government and if this was to be another great review, he would put out a statement denouncing it. 'I am just not having it.' We tried to get him down from the ceiling but he said he intended to raise it in Cabinet.

I had to leave to chair my Iraq morning meeting which went on a bit so I missed the start of Cabinet. GB was in full flow when I got back, going through the Budget. He got an OK if not overwhelming response. TB said we were doing better than most countries, but there had to be a continuing emphasis on the changes we needed to make for the future. DB made a joke about being upset at the rise on wine. GB said sparkling wine was frozen. 'I don't like that. I like red,' said David. Charles asked about 'the speculation that we would be doing the euro tests today and what is the answer on that?' 'The answer is no,' said TB. Then Alan got in there, made a few political points, e.g.

that as the Tories tried to stake out a low tax position, we had to win on value for money and he would circulate a paper to colleagues about where the money was going in the health service. He then said he wanted to raise a process point, that there was to be a second Wanless report announced in the Budget. He said that at ten to nine he got a call from Paul Boateng [chief secretary to the Treasury] to say there was to be this review, and it was totally unacceptable and it was unnecessary for the Treasury to operate in this way. Of course having been there as chief secretary, he knew that for something like this to be included in the overall package it will have been known about for some time, and he stated several times it just wasn't necessary to behave like this.

Ian McCartney [newly appointed party chairman], who was at his first Cabinet after the mini reshuffle involving him and John R, came in with his first intervention, which was pretty telling. He said it was important that colleagues (i.e. GB) did not make things even more difficult than they already were for other ministers. He felt there were sufficient reviews of the NHS going on already. He was not clear what the purpose of this one was, or its agenda. And though at times he was coded, he laid down a marker that he thought GB was exploiting the foundation hospitals issue to be divisive in the party. GB totally ignored the point when he was summing up. As the meeting finished and we went through to TB's room, TB sat down in the chair by the fireplace, shaking his head. 'I just don't know what you do with him. On the one hand, there is nobody else there who has the breadth and the reach that allows you to put together a Budget like that. On the other, why is he incapable of working with other people unless they are wholly owned disciples?'

PMQs went fine. The Budget a bit of a monodrone. Peter M came over for a chat re my situation. The TV was on in the background, Saddam's statue coming down. He felt Fiona in some ways resented the way I was seen as such a big figure, when she was every bit as political, and she felt let down personally by TB and CB. We perhaps had more realistic expectations because when all was said and done he was a politician and a human being with weaknesses as well as strengths. Fiona was very unforgiving of others' weaknesses, he said. Also she had got herself into a mindset that could only see the downside. He said I was a figure in political history and that only came about because TB gave us that opportunity.

TB was seeing Fiona and seemingly told her he was sad things had reached this point, that she had done a good job, and he knew these were very high-pressure positions. She felt he was fine about us leaving but not yet. She told him she thought the political side of our operation was weak, that too much fell on me. She said it was fine on one level, but the reality was she didn't much like him or respect him any more, and she was convinced we had to get out. I felt that considering everything else he had to deal with at the moment, it was a bit much to expect him to be on top of all the internal personnel issues too, even those involving us.

He had a stack of calls post PMQs, including Chirac and Kofi and he was clearly going to be a feature if not the key player in the aftermath. David Blunkett came round for dinner and Fiona was now pretty open about how she felt about things. He said to me when she was out of the room 'You must not let her push you out. TB has to have you there, and so do the rest of us.' He was making clear he thought TB had to grip GB. He realised he couldn't sack him but he could swap him with Jack. GB might see it as a downward step but you cannot be Chancellor forever and Foreign Secretary is the other big job he could do.

Thursday, April 10

Jonathan had stayed out in Northern Ireland trying to get the final pieces in place for a deal but it didn't work out, so we aborted the plan for TB to fly out. Jonathan called early to say that they couldn't do it. TB worked on it for a while, tried out various forms of words, but in the end the IRA were not going to deliver. GB got a fairly good press out of the Budget but on Iraq, the media were moving effortlessly from 'victory' to lawlessness and humanitarian disaster. Their determination to ensure TB got no credit at all for Saddam's fall was pretty intense. Jack was chairing meetings on the aftermath issues and said to me later that having Clare there was like having a fifth column, that he felt the whole time she was trying to sabotage.

The mood in the War Cabinet and Cabinet itself was better but still not great considering the progress made. We still had major problems ahead – e.g. where were the WMD? What do we do to repair the divisions in the international community, particularly between the US and the EU? TB had another difficult call with Chirac.

De Villepin told Jack that as far as France was concerned, the US and the UK were 'the demandeurs' so they clearly felt it was up to us to make the running in trying to repair things. Schroeder was trying to get back onside. There were signs of Putin doing the same, but they all would delight at the fact that 'victory' was messy and not universally seen as such, and that now we had to involve them more. GH said there were plenty of other countries wanting to help but they needed UN cover for their internal politics. It was blindingly obvious and yet we were still struggling with the US on this.

John Scarlett's military and intelligence update was overwhelmingly positive. By contrast Clare was exacerbating problems as much as she could, winding up the International Red Cross, or being wound up, and the DFID website was pretty much unadulterated bad news, dreadful about everything. After Cabinet I left with Charles Lindsay [one of TB's protection officers] for the Tower Hotel. Charles was doing the marathon and at the security review it had been suggested he run with me, whilst the cops on the route would also get an alert when I was in their area. Deep down I did not imagine anything would happen, but you couldn't be sure in the current mood. I did a photocall at Tower Bridge, then a press conference and interviews. The organisers were a good crowd and seeing the HQ brought home how close it was now.

Then an Iraq update meeting. CDS was very clear that a near-philosophical difference between us and the US was responsible for some of the disorder problems we had. We believed in peacekeeping. They believed in war fighting. We were good at both. They were only really focused on one, so didn't adapt quickly enough to changed circumstances. *The Times* had done a story re Bush's sponsorship cheque, and having seen it, TB said 'I suppose I'd better sponsor you too then.' He was totally at a loss re GB at the moment. JP had told him it had to be sorted one way or the other, that it could not go on like this much longer. TB agreed in theory but was unsure in practice what that meant he should do. He felt the euro business had become a bit of a nightmare now, and could easily have been avoided if there was genuine trust between them.

Friday, April 11

A few OK pictures from the marathon photocall. The main news overnight was lots of looting going on in Iraq, the BBC hyping for all it was worth. Gilligan was saying there was more fear there now than there had been before. The main focus both of the pre-meeting and the War Cabinet itself was the disorder, and there were still problems re ORHA. [General Sir] Mike Jackson was saying that if only the US would operate in Baghdad as we were in the south, we would all be better off. But they didn't, so things were becoming very messy. In reality, the operation had been an enormous military success, but it didn't seem like that. We were having to dance around perfectly legitimate questions re when ORHA was going to be up and running and what we were supposed to be doing there. I could hardly believe the marathon was just a couple of days away, that I had all this other stuff to keep me awake, but the one recurring dream I had been having was that I lost my race number on the way to the starting line. TB went off to Sandhurst [Royal Military Academy] where he was speaking at the passing-out parade. Geoff Hoon called re Terry Lloyd. It was pretty clear US forces had killed him. Amid all this, we then had the people from *The Simpsons* in to record TB. The writer [Al Jean] was a really serious type who clearly worried himself a lot about his work. He and I had been batting scripts back and forth and it was fine really, though as TB said, there would be plenty of people willing to slag him off for doing it. But hell, he said, there aren't many perks to the job worth having, so how can you say no to a bit part on *The Simpsons*?[1]

Saturday, April 12

I was determined to be in the best possible shape for the marathon tomorrow so rested up a lot of the day, didn't go in for the morning meetings, watched Man Utd vs Newcastle on the TV and took Grace to see *Maid in Manhattan*,[2] which had a seriously silly plot, though the relationship between the politician and his spin doctor was moderately amusing. TB left me pretty much alone, though he did call to ask why I hadn't been to the meetings. I said I really wanted to get my head in gear for tomorrow, and in any event Jonathan had filled me in. Baghdad was still looking grim, though things were getting better in Basra. I was getting loads of Good Luck messages and I was getting really psyched for it. I ate a ton of pasta, then went to bed, after laying out all my gear for the morning. I was really pleased to have got this far, and pretty confident. I think part of me was glad to be doing something to keep John's [Merritt] memory alive, but part of me was glad too to be doing something that was in a way independent of the job, even though I had managed to raise as much as I had because of that, though the biggest donation was £50k from the Bridges [neighbours].

Sunday, April 13

I had my recurring dream about losing my race number, only this time there was a different twist. It rained at Greenwich, the ink on the number ran and it became illegible and I was stopped from

[1] Blair became the only head of government to guest star in the animated comedy series, welcoming the Simpson family to London in the episode 'The Regina Monologues'.

[2] Romantic comedy film starring Jennifer Lopez.

running. Relieved to wake up, I turned on the radio and they were talking about me doing it, which I took as an omen I would do OK. It was a nice day, fresh but looked like it was going to be sunny, and the mood up at the start was terrific. There were two starting points and Charles [Lindsay] and I were starting from the one with the smaller numbers, which was a bonus. We were taken to the VIP tent to wait and I chatted to the Slovak PM [Mikulas Dzurinda] who asked me if I would do a race out there. I was peeing every few minutes, a mix of nerves and all the fluids of the last couple of days.

The start felt great, and I reckoned I was in OK shape for sub four hours, which is what I really wanted. I did the first mile well below eight minutes without even really trying, which was probably the adrenaline getting me to start too fast, the second mile bang on eight, and then into a fairly steady rhythm for a while. After three miles Charles said I ought to run on ahead on my own. The hardest points were nine miles, fifteen and twenty-one, but the bands and the crowds were great. 'Rockin' All Over the World' [hit record by Status Quo] got me through one tricky part. A Jennifer Lopez song playing made me think of Grace at another and got me through. The crowd were fantastic all the way. I didn't get a single adverse comment, which surprised me considering how much war divisiveness there had been, and loads of encouragement. Philip and Georgia [Gould] popped up a couple of times on the route. Andrew Turnbull, Alun Evans [Cabinet Office], others from the office though I missed Alison [Blackshaw] and her crowd at Canary Wharf. I had been warned Canary Wharf would be quiet but it was about as noisy as anywhere on the route and I got a great lift there. There were no quiet and lonely miles at all. Also, on a couple of occasions when I was struggling one of the other runners would come alongside and help push me on, including a woman from Dulwich who suggested I 'lock on to her' and follow step by step which, as she had a near-perfect bum, took me through another tricky mile before I recovered my strength and eventually left her.

The last few miles from the Tower were hard and exhilarating in equal measure. I hit twenty-two miles with fifty minutes left to break four hours so I knew I was going to do it and could relax a bit. The crowds by now were just a wall of sound and encouragement. I was worried I was going to cry on crossing the line, so forced myself to do it as I ran towards Big Ben, lost myself in a crowd of runners, and just let the emotion come out, imagined friends on one shoulder, enemies on the other, friends pushing me on, enemies failing to hold me back; thought about John, thought about how long left my dad

April '03: AC's tears as he completes marathon . . .

had, thought about the kids, really piled it on and cried for a bit as I ran, and then felt fine on the last mile.

I had trained hard in really difficult circumstances work-wise and I felt a real sense of achievement. I wondered around twenty miles if I could beat Bush's time, but as I tried to pick up the pace, the pain in the hamstrings really intensified and I just went back to my steady plod, and settled for sub four. I didn't realise the cameras were on me for the last couple of minutes, by which time I was swearing at myself the whole time, push yourself, faster, fuck it, keep going, push, etc. The last few hundred metres were a mix of agony and joy. The pain was pretty intense but by now virtually every second someone was shouting out encouragement, from 'Do it for New Labour' to 'I forgive you everything Tony Blair has done' to endless 'Go on, you can do it, not far to go.'

I was siphoned off at the turn into the Mall and could now hear the commentary. I spotted Fiona and the kids right at the end in the stand and ran towards them. They were screaming at me to head straight to the finish but I was seven minutes inside my target and just so pleased to see them. My legs buckled a bit as I stopped and my voice was unbelievably weak, but it felt fantastic to have done it. I posed for a few pictures for the snappers, did an interview with Sue Barker [former tennis player turned sports commentator], dictated my column to *The Times*, and also did a briefing at the ICA [Institute of Contemporary Arts], by which time my legs had pretty much seized up. We got home, by which time I had a massive dehydration headache, and was drinking gallons of water. We went out for dinner with the Goulds. Philip had reminded me of the Woody Allen character[1] today, popping up in incongruous places along the route. But I felt really happy at having done it. Grace said she had felt so proud of me, and did I know what a fantastic thing I did for John? I was really touched, especially as she had never known him.

Monday, April 14

Good enough coverage of the marathon, including some nice pictures with Fiona. TB was seeing the Slovak PM, and said he hoped that now I would get back to getting HIM good media coverage, rather than me. He said it with a smile though and the response in the office was really warm. Loads more cheques were coming in today on the back of the recent interviews. The war meeting was fairly low-key.

[1] Zelig, the mysterious title character in Allen's 1983 mockumentary, who sidles into camera shot for most of the major events of the twentieth century.

TB was getting more and more exasperated with Clare. When CDS and Mike Jackson said that the humanitarian scene was not as bad as the [International Committee of the] Red Cross were saying, Clare snorted and said 'I believe the ICRC.' TB said she was a total burden. He also felt that now, if he got rid of her, there would not be too much of a fuss. There was still no sign of WMD, no sign of Saddam, and a considerable humanitarian challenge. A little boy named Ali was getting a huge amount of media attention, and becoming something of a symbol.[1] We were going to have to resolve his case pretty quickly.

I missed the Bush call but TB said GWB had said to congratulate me on the marathon and to say that my 'bleeding nipples' were all over the US media. TB told him that I had also been covering my balls with large amounts of Vaseline. Bush said 'I think I have heard enough about his body now.' The conference call was not great. Syria was a problem[2] because it was clear we and the US were in a different place on substance and on how to handle it. Then a TB/Milburn meeting on foundation hospitals. TB felt the whole thing was looking very ragged, that we had made clear the direction of travel we wanted, but the Health/Treasury conflict was forcing us to a bit of a muddled compromise.

Tuesday, April 15

Nice email from Keith Blackmore [*Times* sports editor] who said he thought my pieces for them had been the best marathon column he had ever read, and if ever I wanted a career in sports journalism, I knew where to go. My legs were still stiff and sore and I had to walk downstairs pretty much sideways. I got a cab in and the driver was really friendly, and full of congratulations. He was also totally onside re Iraq. The War Cabinet was OK, though Clare was still causing us as many problems as she could. It was perfectly obvious she was going to end up going. TB wanted me to go on the trip to Germany, but agreed I could come back after that. He wanted to discuss the media and political plans for the next phase, and we often managed to get some decent work done on these plane

[1] Ali Ismaeel Abbas, a twelve-year-old Baghdad boy, had lost both arms when an American rocket fell near the family home, killing most of his family. His case became a symbol for media and other commentators of the suffering of ordinary Iraqis during the invasion. He would later be flown to Britain for treatment.
[2] Syria's President, Bashar al-Assad, had urged non-Iraqi volunteers to take up arms in support of the Saddam Hussein regime.

journeys. By the end of the day I had put together an OK plan for the next few weeks.

As we drove to Northolt he must have said three, maybe four times, that he was just at a loss to know what to do about GB. He felt that he was now of a mindset that he needed to wage war on pretty much every front. To create the circumstances to depose him, he felt he had to create and win power struggles. I felt if that was the case, it was totally the wrong approach. If I were him, I would love TB to death, support him so closely that TB felt a certain pleasure in handing over power. As things stood, he was making it harder and harder for him to do it. He seemed to want not only to get rid of him, but also destroy any sense that TB had a legacy worth the name.

At the War Cabinet, Clare had said she had been talking to the French and German development ministers and 'they just need lots and lots of talking to', to which TB replied 'Well I'm all in favour of therapy but I'm not sure it constitutes a policy.' I asked if he finally accepted my long-held view that she was bad news. He did. He said what she did re 'reckless' was an act of treachery.[1] He believed GB was now calculating the potential implications of her resignation, that he wanted her to resign over 1441. TB said he was still of the view he didn't really want to serve a third term but he couldn't see how he could hand over to GB.

I was urging the MoD to do something about the young boy who had lost his arms, Ali, who was getting enormous media attention. We flew up to Scotland with Helen Liddell [Scottish Secretary] and Catherine MacLeod [*Herald*] who was interviewing TB. We landed, drove to the Burrell Collection [Glasgow art museum], where the speech [for the Scottish Parliament elections] went fine, then off to RAF Leuchars [Fife] to see the families of pilots out in the region. The people there seemed genuinely appreciative of the support TB gave them. Of all the various services we came in contact with, I would say the military were consistently the best to deal with. Then to see the team on permanent standby for a terrorist incident or a hijacking. A great bunch of blokes, who admitted that a lot of the time they were bored stiff, but they knew they could be called on any second, and had to keep mentally alert the whole time.

Back on the plane and off to Germany. TB was reading the

[1] In a BBC radio interview, Short had been asked if she thought Blair had acted recklessly. She replied 'I'm afraid that I think the whole atmosphere of the current situation is deeply reckless; reckless for the world, reckless for the undermining of the UN in this disorderly world, which is wider than Iraq . . . reckless with our government, reckless with his own future, position and place in history.'

intelligence and briefings pre the meeting [EU summit] in Athens. Chirac was up for causing as much trouble as possible on Iraq and ESDP. Schroeder was seeking to be more constructive, and even to become the bridge to France/Russia. But Chirac basically wanted us to be left out as much as possible. TB felt it was as though Chirac had 'found religion', that he had become fixated on a multipolar vision of the world, and it was a recipe for disaster. 'It is madness. It is like a rerun of the Cold War, and yet there is no real balance. If you say US or France, what is he talking about, what is the choice?'

Chirac was intending to try to stuff the Americans over ESDP by backing a ridiculous Belgian idea of a four-way defence summit with France, Germany, Belgium and Luxembourg. The French were assuming that we would not want to upset them, and so were intending to try to push the whole defence debate in a different direction. It was the wrong assumption, and the wrong time to make the move. Luxembourg for God's sake. TB had a good meeting with Schroeder in Hanover. He said he did not subscribe to the Chirac multipolar view and also that he was looking for better relations with the US. Then a three-hour flight to Athens, during which I worked on a note to get TB back focused on some of the domestic issues that had gone off the boil during the height of the Iraq business.

Wednesday, April 16

Overnight in Athens and I woke up to open the curtains of the hotel room and behold the most beautiful blue sea imaginable. It was hot without being unbearable, and I sat out on the terrace and finished the note I had been working on on the flight down. Then the media monitoring note came through and Short had given us another problem, this time saying time will tell if TB made the right decision and whether we should have given Blix more time. TB was pretty close to the end of his tether with her.

TB had a breakfast meeting with [Romano] Prodi [President of the European Commission] who was mumbling and rambling more than ever. At the end of the meeting, even his own spokesman said to me 'What on earth was he talking about?' TB spent a lot of the meeting just nodding and I don't think he could hear much of what Prodi was saying either. Very odd. Then to a meeting with Kofi, who made a beeline for me on arrival, said 'Ah the marathon man, and such a good time.' I think TB was getting a bit pissed off with the attention it had been getting. To be frank, I was beginning to feel a bit of a void without the training routine and the day to aim for, and would need something else. I had been kind of hoping work would fill it again, but things at home made that difficult. We were due to go off for a week in Majorca and tonight I had promised to take Rory to Arsenal vs Man United and was fretting about getting back in time, particularly when the plane back was delayed. I left the summit early with Kate [Garvey, events and visits team], got to the airport and just made it back. I told Kate I was feeling myself heading towards the exit door.

Thursday, April 17 – Thursday, April 24
We had a nice enough week in Majorca, but Fiona and I had said too much to each other that was hurtful in recent weeks and we weren't really getting on that well. At one point she said in terms that she sometimes felt that I had left her for TB, that that was where all my emotion and energy went, and that any left over went on the kids but not her. It was a pretty harsh thing to say, but I knew what she meant. I could only do the job full on or not at all, and full on meant staying on top of things round the clock. Whenever I didn't, I felt things slipped backwards. Her view was that I had been to some extent brutalised by politics, that I had put up so many barriers around me as a way of making myself immune to the attacks that came my way, but it had carried over into our home life too.

The kids were brilliant though, and seemed to have a great time. I had a couple of heart-to-hearts with Philip, but his main concern really was that I stay involved. TB called a few times. He had had another session with GB at Chequers which had been better, but then it was all briefed into the *FT* as a discussion of the euro tests, saying how TB had agreed it would be very difficult to do this parliament. It was intolerable if they could not have private discussions on issues like the euro without it all being spilled into the media.

Friday, April 25
We got back last night and to Fiona's annoyance I went in today for a whole stack of meetings, first on health policy, one on foundation hospitals then PCTs [NHS primary care trusts], then Charles C in for a session on the choice agenda for schools, where he and TB pretended to be in the same place but weren't in reality, then on the euro. TB was determined to ensure a more positive tone to the assessment. He had read all the texts now and felt it was OK and reasonably positive. Arnab [Banerji, economic adviser] was of the view that it would and could be presented as a case for entry. TB also went through how it could be presented positively. But GB would present it in a negative light. TB said we needed to get the focus on fact – he would be saying

four out of five tests were met, measures would be taken to meet the fifth, there will be a changeover plan and a referendum bill. Provided there was warm body language alongside that, it could be a big step forward. But it was not clear to any of us that he and GB were on the same pitch. He did the *FT* interview and though we didn't really want the euro to be the story, he was pretty forward on it.

Iraq was looking a bit messy though Tariq Aziz [Iraqi Deputy Prime Minister] was in the hands of the US. I went to another meeting on Iraq but wasn't really focused, and I suddenly realised how much of my thinking was about leaving. When Phil Stephens [*FT*] pointed out to me earlier that TB had been leader for almost nine years, it came as something of a shock, stated in those terms. I liked a lot of the people in the office, and was pleased with the team I had built, but was that enough to keep me? I don't think so. Was the closeness to TB and all that meant enough? Not any more.

Then to a reshuffle meeting, TB, Pat McF, Sally, Peter H and I. TB was clear Clare would go, so would Scotland and Wales as separate jobs. He was also intending to reshape the Lord Chancellor's Department and say farewell to Derry [Irvine], which would be quite a big thing to do. He was clearly feeling in bold mood. But he still felt the difficulty on public services was the paralysing effect of GB when he didn't want to go with TB's agenda. Home, and another humdinger of a row. Fiona said either she leaves and I stay, which she thought was a recipe for disaster, or we both go and I always blame her for forcing me out, which did not exactly make her feel good about the future either. A story came in later which would reinforce her view of how CB had changed for the worse, namely that she had been invited to a store [Globe] in Melbourne [Australia] and walked out weighed down by stuff. 'I wish she didn't have this thing about a bargain,' TB said when I told him.

Saturday, April 26

Grimsville at home. I was feeling really down. I couldn't let things get so bad we split up. I went out for a run, and came across a scene in Golders Green that underlined how much I didn't want it to happen. A young boy was screaming as his mother tried to hand him over to his dad, because it was 'his weekend'. We had another flare-up on the way to the Landmark Hotel, where we were due to meet Alex [Ferguson]. We managed to have a nice time despite it all. We met Carlos Queiroz [assistant manager, Manchester United] who seemed a decent sort, Tony Coton [goalkeeping coach] and some of the players. Alex was clearly losing it with [David] Beckham. 'He's upstairs preening himself.' He said when he dropped him Real Madrid knew about it within minutes. He felt Beckham was addicted to the press profile, couldn't exist without it. He said even Gary Neville [teammate] was losing it with him a bit.

It was a nice enough hotel but he ended up complaining about the wine. 'Govan boy complains about the wine,' he said. 'That's New Labour.' Fiona said she held him responsible for me still being there, because he had been so adamant at the time of the election that I should stay. He said 'No, what I said was do what you're good at and if you're still good at it, carry on, but always be in control.' He reckoned if I knew what else I would rather do, and I would be happy away from it, I should go. Fiona was a lot calmer talking about these things when it wasn't just the two of us and now she was saying she'd be happy for me to stay till the next election provided she was absolutely clear that that was it. Alex was talking through who might be his successor. Maybe [Roy] Keane [Manchester United captain] – 'the most intelligent player I ever worked with'. On GB, he felt he was clever but lacked Tony's presence.

Sunday, April 27

TB called first thing, after two long conversations with GB, and said they'd been awful. On foundation hospitals TB said to him 'Am I supposed to believe that Frank Dobson and Bill Morris [TGWU general secretary] just stumbled across these arguments against foundation hospitals?' For example Dobson had written to MPs on foundation hospitals and referred to the J-Curve theory [of how nations rise and fall]. On the euro TB thought that GB was buying into the idea of a rewritten assessment of the euro but when Jeremy went through it with Ed Balls, it went nowhere. It had taken TB almost forty-eight hours to get hold of him. When he did at least they were talking but he said GB was just creating non-arguments. It was draining and on the fundamentals they couldn't agree.

TB felt GB clearly believed that TB was going to move or sack him and this was all about protecting himself. He'd said to him 'I know what you're up to. I know your plans.' TB said to him 'I don't have a plan. I would like to work with you.' He said it then went into a 'no you're not, yes I am' routine. He said to me later that he was really unsure about fighting another election but he said there were a lot of people in the party saying to him 'You cannot hand over to this guy. You've made your mark but we have to live with him after you've gone.' TB had read the euro assessments himself and actually felt they were broadly positive, but Balls had put enough in there to present as anti. TB said the second of the conversations was 'mono-syllabic'. He said he really didn't know what to do. He said he had never wanted to fight a third election, but it was difficult to hand over to someone who was behaving in such a crazy way.

We also had the problem of Melbourne and CB's shopping spree. A clothing company had asked her to look at some goods and she ended up with sixty-eight items and we had another freebie story to deal with. TB suggested to her that she get someone else to help her with the PR and she called David Hill. He, Hilary C and I were all of the view that it was best to do nothing, say nothing, and just wait till it went away. She had told TB that she hadn't asked for any of this stuff and it just turned up at the hotel. We were heading for a rocky patch all round, and this didn't help.

Monday, April 28

Iraq meeting. We were being warned of the possibility that Saddam had got rid of WMD and certainly most of the documentation, before the conflict. How big a problem was it if it turned out to be the case that we found none? Very difficult. It seemed the best we could do was defectors saying that it had all been destroyed. WMD were not being found and that was a problem. At the War Cabinet, Jack S and Clare had their standard row about the ORHA [post-conflict] operation. Clare said Jack wanted to throw people at the organisation 'regardless of effect' and Jack said she was talking nonsense. Clare was looking and sounding more and more ridiculous. TB did OK at the press conference and though the BBC decided early on that WMD was the story, later they moved to the domestic agenda stuff. Peter M called me, said re EMU he felt GB was doing the wrong thing for the wrong reasons. He felt we were being cowardly.

Tuesday, April 29

Iraq, and where were the WMD, was back as a problem. Yesterday John Scarlett called and asked me how big a problem would it be if we didn't find any and had to rely on ex-scientists telling what had been there and what they knew. Big problem. I got a cab in to meet up with TB then into the car and off [to Russia]. He said he felt good at the moment but the GB situation was like a permanent dark shadow. 'I just don't know what to do about it.' He said the problem was he just didn't believe what he said to him any more. 'I cannot fathom why he has to be so destructive.' We had a tiny but revealing example. John McFall [Labour MP, chair of the Treasury Select Committee] told us – simply as a matter of fact, no agenda and no reason why it shouldn't have happened – that he had discussed the TSC report with GB. GB told TB he hadn't. Why? TB said surely Gordon must realise he is making it harder not easier to hand over to him. What is unfathomable is that it is such a not clever strategy.

The visit had been Putin's request and it was an OK thing to do but there were some very difficult issues, particularly divisions over the UN role. Iraq generally would be difficult. TB saw the press on the plane and I was warning them not to expect major league front-page stuff. But unbeknown to us Putin was gearing up for a direct big whack on WMD and plenty else besides. TB's basic case at the moment was that the world had to come together. That the US was the only superpower and it was better that we tried to work together rather than try to be setting ourselves up as rivals. But France, Russia, maybe China and India wanted to check that power as a matter of policy.

On arrival TB, David M and Tony Bishop [interpreter] were taken up to the Putin dacha while the rest of us were taken to another building. We were hanging around with some of the Russian officials and it was a pretty tough atmosphere. When we did the pre-meeting with TB and Putin I was very clear that our press would be looking for the differences on Iraq and WMD. I asked Putin what he was likely to say. He said he would simply say we should carry on looking. But he definitely had the steely look in his eye and TB was looking a bit on edge. When it came to the event he let rip in the opening statement, made clear he doubted WMD were there and painted a comic picture of Saddam in a bunker somewhere sitting on his arsenal. TB was doing his best to look unfazed. The press were suddenly all terribly excited. Trevor Kavanagh [*Sun*] and Charles Reiss [*Evening Standard*] had big smiles over their faces as they took notes of what Vlad was saying. They sensed a diplo-disaster which of course it was, especially as Putin had invited TB and we thought we'd agreed lines.

David Manning was taken aback and angry, said he felt it had been deceitful of Putin to agree what he intended to say then go off on one like that, clearly pre-planned. He said the one-on-one session had been very tough and that Putin was in no mood to listen to pro-US messages. I noticed too when they came down that he just looked angrier than before, was less chatty and relaxed. He was also putting on a bit of weight and acting in a much grander fashion. He had his own stables now and had showed off the horses to TB who felt he was showing signs of becoming the traditional Russian leader in terms of interest in lifestyle, luxury and so on. The press conference was pretty stunning. The mood when we regrouped was very chilly. TB took me to one side, said how do we deal with that? I said not much we can do to stop them going into overdrive.

TB said 'I almost felt like interrupting him and saying "Hey – you invited me out here. I didn't expect to get stuffed by you like that."' Then TB, Vlad, the interpreters and I were taken into a little side room. TB said to me, very deliberately and inviting absolute honesty, 'What did you make of that?' I said it was very explosive, our media would be very excited. Putin looked a mix of surly and worried. He could sense TB was angry but he was also totally unapologetic. He said the US had created this situation. In ignoring the UN they had created danger. They were saying there may be rules, but not for us. Time and again he made comparisons with the situation he faced in Georgia, used as a base for terrorists against Russia. 'What would you say if we took out Georgia or sent in the B-52 bombers to wipe out the terror camps?' And what are they planning next – is it Syria, Iran, Korea? 'I bet they haven't told you,' he added with a rather unpleasant curl of the lip. 'Also there is no consistency. Saudi and Pakistan are problems but for different reasons the Americans prop them up'. He said other parts of the world felt pressure to go for Israel. He said he didn't support that 'but these are dangerous games'. He said the Americans' enemy was anyone who didn't support them at the time. Anywhere from Algeria to Pakistan. Then what about the new powers like India and China, do their views matter, or is it only America?

TB had given as good as he got at the press conference and did so again at the dinner once he realised that the diplomatic approach was not exactly working. He said there was no grand US plan for global domination. There was a series of choices. On MEPP they were deciding whether to engage or not. On Korea they were deciding whether to engage diplomatically. On a lot of other issues they were deciding whether to approach them on a unilateral or multilateral basis. 'We have to help them choose the multilateral route. But you have to understand that September 11 changed their psychology and it changed Bush's psychology personally. Before, anti-Americanism was just an irritant that they put up with. Now it became a threat.' Putin said that meant anyone who disagreed with them on these choices was a threat. 'That is ridiculous. I am a Russian. I cannot agree with the Americans on everything. My public won't let me for a start. I would not survive two years if I did that. We often have different interests.' TB said but you have to build a strategic partnership with them. He said he was tired of trying. 'They don't listen. They only hear what they want to hear. Some of them are crazy.'

Putin said the South Koreans had told them the Americans had said they were prepared to use nuclear weapons on the North. Crazy. He said they would end up killing people in the South too, 'and that is on our border'. Vlad was in full flow. He said they had asked to run reconnaissance flights along the Russian border during the Iraq crisis 'as a counter-terrorism measure – what nonsense. It was to intimidate us. We told them it was an unfriendly act. They did it.' TB asked him if Bush knew and Vlad said his people knew, but the question was why did they do it? Because they think they can do what they want. Others have to operate by the rules but not them. China might feel it should be able to sort out Taiwan. But it feels constrained by the UN, by international opinion. India and Pakistan might like to set off nuclear weapons at each other but they feel constrained. Time and again he referred to Georgia and Chechnya and said 'Why can't I go in alone – because of international pressure. Yet there are people threatening our people, killing people on our streets.' TB said Iraq was different because there were nineteen outstanding UNSCRs on Iraq. The UN had made its demands and for once they should be upheld. Putin said the US was thousands of miles from Iraq. So was the UK. Saddam was a monster but he was not a direct threat.

TB went back to his argument about September 11. Putin went back to his line that if we were saying anyone who disagreed was a threat that was ridiculous and dangerous. TB was pretty taken aback by the vehemence. Normally there would be a bit of levity, a bit of banter, or if things were heavy I might throw in something lighter. But this was not that kind of meeting. I could see David [Manning] feeling more and more intense about the whole thing. We agreed afterwards that it had been a real privilege to have been in on a discussion like that, where the raw politics and feeling of a country like Russia came pouring out. There were even short periods of silence as we ate – caviar, a nice enough fish plate then some horrible cold meats including one that looked like dogshit and tasted pretty dreadful too. Then a nice mix of ice creams. Lots of vodka being poured into different glasses but little of it was drunk.

There was no give at all. Putin's face was tight and his eyes really piercing. His cheek muscles clenched whenever TB defended the US or the policy on Iraq. He said partnership was a two-way thing and the Americans care only about themselves. There had to be a role for both partners, not just one partner doing whatever they wanted. That was the central message, again and again and again. TB kept asking him – so what do you do, how do you resolve it? – and then would come another wave.

I kept thinking of Fiona when she was really angry with me, telling me it was all one way, all on my terms. I took her for granted and she'd had enough of it. This was someone who felt he deserved to be treated as an equal, and he wasn't being treated as an equal and he was angry, and TB was the person who was going to cop the anger. At one point Putin said the whole post-September 11 response was designed to show off American greatness. They don't care what anyone else thinks. TB was about to respond but he didn't let him 'Don't answer – there is no answer. That is the truth Tony, and you have to know it. There are bad people in the administration and you know it.'

David said as we left 'Fascinating, absolutely fascinating.' I said that was the death of diplomacy. It certainly was, he said. There was no effort at all. TB was a bit subdued as we went to the plane. He said he thought ultimately Putin would do a deal on the UN but he felt Iraq was clearly going to have to be sorted as a coalition of the willing. He felt we should put together a plan that tried to meet the points the Russians were making, but if they were basically just going to bugger about we should say OK, we will have to do it on our own. TB had been taken at one point to see Putin's private quarters and what he saw worried him. He said it was like something out of the Roman Empire, that it had been transformed. An Olympic-sized pool for his own use only. Stallions. Horses with butlers! I had felt too that Putin was far grander than before, much more up himself, a bit peevish.

I drove to the airport with TB and though we assumed the car was bugged, we had a pretty frank discussion. He was less shocked than David and I had been and said they had an argument different to ours and it was far better we have it out like that. But in the end they are wrong. You cannot just walk away from the US. It is a mistake. The reason they will go it alone on some things is because they can. He was blaming Chirac a bit for getting Putin more wound up. Chirac was even saying the US was a bigger threat than al-Qaeda. He was really keen to see TB fall flat on his face over this one. What was very clear was that it was going to be difficult to put things back together again. These were pretty deep fissures we had been witnessing. By the time we were flying home, TB was saying 'what a day. He invites me out there. I go. He insults me publicly and privately. Then I come home. Bloody brilliant.'

He thought a lot of it was driven by Russia no longer being seen as a superpower and the anger that aroused. They were angry and humiliated and they needed to let out the anger. I said though that

Putin had a point – the truth is the Americans do tend to treat people like shit unless they agree with them and that their vision of democracy was stars-and-stripes-coloured. Everything was seen through their own prism. TB said that the answer was not to rival them, because they were now the only superpower, but to build a partnership, support them but in exchange for support be listened to and gain influence. Tony Bishop felt Putin had missed an opportunity to build bridges and he seemed genuinely disappointed that Putin behaved as he did. The press were as shocked as we were and had loved it.

TB said what it showed was real deep anger but the question was how was it to be channelled? How do we use it to get the world on a better footing? He could see some merit in Putin's argument but he seemed to be saying the Americans were not entitled to use their power for their own ends. I said he wasn't saying that, he was saying others had the right to be treated with respect. That their status as the only superpower – something Vlad never actually acknowledged, I noticed – gave them an added responsibility to think of others. I had sat in on so many TB meetings but this had been one of the most memorable. David M and [Sergei] Prikhodko [Putin's foreign affairs adviser] both agreed afterwards they might as well not have been there because the normal diplomatic niceties were out of the window.

Wednesday, April 30

Grace's birthday, stayed home to do her presents etc., then took her to school. It reminded me how rarely I had done so, whereas with the boys it had been pretty much an everyday occurrence, particularly Rory. The [Middle East peace process] road map was finally being published today but all a bit overshadowed by a suicide bombing [in Israel].[1] Then it transpired it was carried out by two men with UK passports, which gave it an added difficult dimension here. TB apparently told the PMQs pre-meeting that he felt yesterday was not as bad as it came across on the media, but though the Russian media was not quite so bad, it was certainly not a diplomatic success story.

I went straight to the Commons where TB was doing the PLP. He said it was better than expected, also that it was more obvious than ever that the anti-foundation hospitals argument was being run out of the Treasury. Hilary A told me that John Healey [economic secretary

[1] Three people were killed and sixty injured in the blast at a bar in Tel Aviv. Asif Muhammad Hanif, the suicide bomber, and Omar Khan Sharif, his accomplice, were both British citizens. Hamas and the al-Aqsa Martyrs' Brigades of the Tanzim Fatah declared joint responsibility.

to the Treasury] had apparently told Jon Trickett [Labour MP] to vote against it. GB was using Healey, Ann Keen, Kevan Jones, Doug Henderson [Labour MPs close to Brown] and others to get up the argument that this was two-tier, divisive. I saw Peter M later and we agreed the time was coming when this had to be exposed for the operation it was, that it all depended on those who knew what was going on remaining silent, including the hacks who got fed this stuff the whole time.

PMQs was a score draw on public services. TB was strong on foundation hospitals but GB was lukewarm at the Treasury Select Committee which was going to spark another TB/GB rift round. Back for an Iraq communications meeting. We agreed to keep them going. I was worried though that ORHA lacked strategic message and capability. Emily [Hands, press officer] was back, and now Ben Wilson was out there and both were saying how hard it was to grip it. But I still felt there were very basic things we could be doing to communicate very basic messages, whatever the security nightmares. Rumsfeld made a visit to Baghdad and [US General Jay] Garner [director of ORHA] did a big chest-thumping number all about being proud to be American. All yuksville stuff for audiences outside the States. Margaret Tutwiler [US State Department] was in charge of the media side of things there and I fixed a call with her for tomorrow.

TB was heavily focused on Northern Ireland, where we were in a bad place again, heading towards cancellation of the elections, which we would do tomorrow. TB said he was determined to treat Sinn Fein politicians like any other. His big worry was that SF would not deliver on the final steps. The other big story was the *Times* exclusive on Special Branch transcripts of calls between McGuinness, Jonathan and Mo [Mowlam, former Northern Ireland Secretary], clearly genuine.

Peter M had been attacked in the *Sun* and wanted to do an article. He sent over a draft which said that both TB and GB had said we MUST join the euro and that it was a matter of when, not if. It took me twenty minutes to persuade him this was not the time, that the second line was an important strategic plank of the assessment, and he should wait. He finally, if reluctantly agreed. He was clearly fed up though. Another discussion about the Olympic bid. TB moved from very pro to neutral and back again. He feared a big hit on the whole Pride in Britain theme if we didn't go for it. On the way out I bumped into Sarah Brown with a group of wives of Norwich City footballers. She introduced them to me as wives of Norwich United players.

Thursday, May 1

Back running regularly, twice today, feeling a lot better after first reasonable chat with Fiona for ages. She had seen Jonathan yesterday to say she was leaving definitely in September, whatever I did. At my morning meeting, Ian Austin [Brown's spokesman] reacted very defensively when I asked why GB didn't simply say that he supports the policy on foundation hospitals. Ian protested that he did, and said people were briefing against GB. Both the *Sun* and *The Times* had leaders today attacking him for not being reformist enough, leaning to Old Labour, which was clearly Murdoch's line.

We had a brief political meeting, with TB and the core political people, back to the argument why public service delivery isn't happening at the rate we want, why no overall narrative, where is the sense that education is still the number one priority, where are the values driving what we are doing? We were also still miles apart on the euro. The Treasury sent over a draft structure for the statement, which was hopeless.

Cabinet was pretty dire, a fairly desultory run around the block on European elections, Northern Ireland, fairly lacklustre discussion about Iraq where Clare made even by her standards a ridiculous intervention, that seemed interminable, about a museum in Baghdad.[1] JP was barely containable. TB then had a meeting with Milburn who was in a total rage re GB. 'It's fucking not on. He's actually encouraging people to vote down a government bill [Health and Social Care Bill, containing plans to introduce foundation hospitals] that's been agreed. He's just sent over a long document with new queries and problems which in fact have already been answered. You wouldn't tolerate it from anyone else but you have to realise this is an attack on you, Tony, and you can't just stand there and take it, you have to do something.' All TB could do was say he had spoken to GB who had assured him he would get in there and support the policy. Alan's face betrayed the reality, that it was wishful thinking. Hilary A said it was becoming a settled view that GB was using this to damage Alan but it was also damaging TB.

Alan came round to see me afterwards and said if this kind of thing happened again, he would walk. I had the phone call with Margaret Tutwiler in Baghdad. She had a very broad, slightly weird accent and was prickly and defensive. I got the impression she didn't

---

[1] Short suggested that, by failing to prevent looting at the National Museum, US troops had violated the 1907 Hague and 1949 Geneva conventions, which required occupiers of countries to maintain civil order.

really understand why she had to speak to me. I tried a bit of charm and flattery, but all I really got back was a litany of difficulties, how the lack of communications and security made it all very difficult. The impression I got was of a pretty chaotic approach. I said I just wanted to help as much as I could because I feared there was a lack of positive strategic communication and the media would fill the vacuum. She said she thought the best thing would be if we could persuade the press to leave because everything was so chaotic! It was a pretty hopeless discussion.

We had Rumsfeld due in tomorrow. I agreed with his office that there should be no media. TB with Rumsfeld was the last thing we needed right now. We went out for dinner with the Kinnocks. On Iraq, it was very much Neil and I on one side, Glenys and Fiona on the other. Neil had a great line, said he thought we had the best possible outcome, that Saddam was both dead and alive. The only point he slightly lost it was when Glenys said we were following the Bush doctrine. He was pretty down on GB at the moment, said he had told him that the only thing that could stop him becoming leader was himself.

Friday, May 2

The local elections were better for the Tories than expected. BNP strong in Burnley [from three council seats to eight]. We did badly without it being a disaster.[1] TB felt that for midterm, second term, it was OK. I ran in and at the morning meeting had to contend with Ian Austin's anger at the coverage on foundation hospitals. Both the *Sun* and *The Times* ran stories that GB allies, with John Healey named, were orchestrating the opposition. The Treasury put out a denial and Healey called me later to say it wasn't true. 'You know me well enough to know I wouldn't do that.' He said he had been accused of stirring both Dobbo [Frank Dobson] and Doug Henderson but was adamant he had not spoken to them about it. TB, though he had asked us not to stir it, didn't exactly complain about the coverage. It was interesting to note again that it was only when their antics risked being exposed that they occasionally started to pull back.

TB was seeing Rumsfeld at Chequers. But I emphasised to TB he needed to make clear to Rumsfeld how urgent it was that they got their act together at every level. I had been alarmed by the Tutwiler

[1] Labour lost 833 council seats, the Conservatives gained 566, taking control of Birmingham and Coventry, and the Liberal Democrats gained 193. The far-right British National Party gained eleven nationally, giving them a total of thirteen.

call. She was very defensive. Dan [Bartlett] called me later, fresh from the spectacular impact of Bush landing on an aircraft carrier in a flight suit to deliver a victory speech, and said she [Tutwiler] had never really wanted to go there.

On foundation hospitals, I met with my team to plan the next few days, with Darren Murphy [Milburn's special adviser] sure we would win the vote, Simon Stevens [health policy adviser] less confident. We hadn't really got up the argument well about how this was helping to deliver Labour goals. TB had a pretty daunting workload at the moment, Iraq, UN, euro, NI, asylum, public services, European Convention, all of them really eating into his diary, with the GB business constantly in the background. Looking back at the week, I didn't feel we had achieved much.

Saturday, May 3

The *Times* magazine ran Peter Stothard's piece [on TB at fifty] which was pretty fair. The other thing running was follow-up to the line in *Vanity Fair* of me saying 'We don't do God' when I tried to shunt David Margolick to the back of the plane [see March 16]. Allied to Peter Stothard's line that TB had wanted to say 'God bless you' at the end of his Iraq broadcast, there was a bit of a running theme in the media about me trying to stop him talking about God. TB seemed reasonably relaxed.

His current refrain was that the only radical policies were coming from the centre. Even the departments we felt were pretty good, like Health under Alan and Education under Charles, didn't really drive forward change. The machine at the centre was trying to push forward all the time, and the bureaucracies in departments trying to push back. It was really frustrating him. He was disappointed that Charles and David Miliband had allowed the schools funding situation to deteriorate. Whilst he had been so focused on Iraq, others had taken their foot off the accelerator.

I spent part of the day drafting a note on all the strategic challenges we face, viewed through what goals we would like to meet by the summer, just twelve weeks from now. Iraq, MEPP, Afghanistan, Africa, on the geopolitical front, the polar world division with the French, euro, IGC [EU Intergovernmental Conference], all the big domestic issues, also trust, TB. I did it partly to force myself to think it all through but also to draw attention to what I thought was a gap between the scale of the challenges and the lack of capacity in departments and at the centre to meet them. I was trying to get TB to shake up the system, not just rest on his being so sure that it was all about policy. I sent the note through and he called a couple of hours later. He said he had been thinking the same thing. Six years in, almost to the day, we were facing more or less the same problems. It was all about delivery of the machine.

He felt re the politicians, that we had some OK ministers but too many of them were basically European social democrats, who tended to look for partnership and compromise rather than face up to really difficult decisions. He didn't like fighting on too many fronts. He felt re the argument on foundation hospitals that it actually wasn't that radical. He felt that the controversy of the schools agenda was also not matched by the radicalism, that we were being held back by forces of conservatism. I said again I felt we should have stuck with that argument. I put a worst-case analysis – at best what could be called the variable quality of ministers, GB paralysing reform, senior civil servants often resistant to change.

We also faced a big loss when Jeremy [Heywood] went [to join Morgan Stanley investment banking division]. TB had deliberately sought out David Manning and Stephen Wall and that had made a difference. He had to do the same with Jeremy's replacement. If the Civil Service wasn't so status-conscious, it would be possible to get one of the best permanent secretaries, Gus O'Donnell or Michael Jay even, but neither would be keen because it would be seen as a demotion. But at least he was focusing on these personnel issues.

Sunday, May 4

Calum and I went to Wimbledon vs Burnley, last game in the season, Wimbledon's last game at Selhurst Park and a bit of a sad affair all round [Wimbeldon 2, Burnley 1]. Leeds beat Arsenal, leaving Man United the champions. Alex F and Rory both mildly delirious. I watched a bit of [political journalist] John Sergeant's BBC programme to coincide with TB's birthday. It was very funny in parts, though Mo [Mowlam] and [Peter] Kilfoyle were exceptionally bitter. Overall TB came over fine.

Monday, May 5

TB called first thing, wanted to talk again about the strategic challenge note I had done. He said it was the right analysis. He wasn't sure how widely we could discuss it because it was about policy and personnel. He was aware that things weren't working as well as they should be. He reckoned we had a year really to get it moving, really to be in a position at the next election where it was accepted that public services are much better. We agreed we were nowhere near that. Education had gone backwards. Health is better but it's patchy. Ditto crime. Transport is a disaster. He then said he was thinking about making this a five-year term, really get these issues sorted, 'particularly if I decide I don't want to fight a third election'. He still hadn't decided but said he couldn't understand why there was now this assumption that a term was four years when the option of five was there. He was also thinking about a reshuffle just before Whitsun followed by a major drive on reform. He knew we would lose some of our coalition over the euro but was confident we could win over others on reform.

He was also still making up his mind about GB. He acknowledged he had ceded too much to him. He said it sometimes felt like we were driving with the handbrake on, because he thwarts reform, not necessarily because he is against it, but because he wants to make life difficult. It was obvious that TB wanted to go a lot further on public services, open them up to real innovation and competition. He was working on a note of what he wanted to see in the statement on the euro assessment. As far as he was concerned, this was a big test of whether GB was serious about working with him. 'If he's not, then I'm prepared to do the deed. I'm not prepared to be held back from making a change I believe it may be in Britain's interests to make.'

The note had at least provoked, or at least brought to the open, some pretty big thoughts. What we actually did about driving change in these big departments was less clear. He felt the Foreign Office was pretty good, Treasury good but limited and sometimes malign, but that overall we didn't have good domestic departments. What he was signalling was that 1. he intended big policy changes, 2. a big reshuffle, 3. longer term, he seemed to be keeping open the option of someone else leading us into the next election. He said he had not ruled out standing again but 'I kind of think eight years is enough for this kind of job.'

Tuesday, May 6

We were building up to the foundation hospital vote tomorrow and used TB's speech to the Newspaper Society to get up some of the arguments on that.[1] [David] Bradshaw wrote in quite a funny section

[1] Blair warned the audience of newspaper executives that Labour rebels voting against NHS reform and foundation hospitals would be 'a collective mistake of historic proportions', and that reforms would give more freedom to bring 'new providers into elective surgery to reduce waiting times for NHS patients, whether those providers are from the NHS, the private sector or abroad. For the first time giving patients real choice to go elsewhere for treatment, paid for by the NHS, if they are waiting too long.'

on TB being fifty. TB started his day with a ninety-minute session, one-on-one, with GB on the euro. He said afterwards that it was a 'real crackerjack job'. He had asked him for a completed copy of the draft statement on the EMU assessment. GB said not until they had sorted out their differences. So here we were, a few weeks before what might be the momentous decision of the parliament, possibly of TB's premiership, and his Chancellor wouldn't tell him what he intended to say. 'It's like dealing with a child,' he said. 'I said to him that I wanted him to work with me. He says I am working with you. Then, no you're not, yes I am. Then he's back into "I know what you're up to" and he does all this stuff about me wanting to get rid of him.'

TB said he had told him that it felt at times like driving a car with the handbrake on. 'That's a very significant statement,' said GB. No it's not, it's obvious, said TB. He said he just couldn't see a way out of it at the moment, also that he believed GB was actually intent on destroying the health bill. Alan was making clear he would resign if we lost the vote tomorrow. We signed off the speech, then into the car where Putin called him to say happy birthday, which suggested he was trying to calm things down a bit after recent events.

Wednesday, May 7

Ran in and the morning meeting was pretty much all taken up with foundation hospitals. The whips were still worried that if the Tories really went for it, we could lose. The rebellion could be bigger than we thought. TB had breakfast with John Howard [Australian Prime Minister], mainly Iraq and Zimbabwe, then to a meeting with Charles C on schools funding. Charles was clear it could be sorted but he may need more money. We went over for PMQs and though TB did well, and IDS was crap, the signs were still of a very big revolt. I got back for an Iraq communications meeting and we were really focused now on how to try to get a UK operation properly inserted into Baghdad. I called [Major General] Tim Cross [senior British officer, Coalition Provisional Authority] who said that he couldn't properly express to me just how useless the Americans were. They had no idea. He said there were people working hard but who couldn't deliver. He felt we should try to get a CIC-type operation inserted in there. I had been led to believe he was very protective of the US there, but in reality he could barely conceal his contempt. 'I'm afraid they are very capable of snatching defeat from the jaws of victory because they are just useless at the things they now need to be doing.' On the communications side, he said somehow we had to make it work. We agreed to try to get more of our people there. It would help when we got John Sawers [UK ambassador to Egypt, Blair's former foreign policy adviser] there as the UK envoy.

Then it was a case of hanging around for the vote. TB said 'This is classic. The Labour Party and a group of bone-headed MPs making historic errors that will help put us out of power and leave others to do the reforms that we should have done.' He said it was a different issue but a rerun of *In Place of Strife*.[1] If we lost, he wanted us to come back with a bill that was more reformist, not less. He felt it was crazy for Alan [Milburn] to talk about resigning and that he was far too prone to the cavalier and dramatic. But I spoke to Alan who said he had thought long and hard about it and he would definitely resign. 'There have to be rules. This is my bill and if it's rejected I will have to go.' When it came to the vote, it was 304 for the bill to 230 against. The wrecking amendment was defeated 297 to 117, with sixty-five Labour rebels.

Thursday, May 8

The foundation hospitals vote was fading away but it emerged during the day that Clare hadn't voted. She claimed it was because she thought the vote was at 10pm. Nor did she come to Cabinet, claiming that she had to read intelligence briefs before a meeting with the leader of Rwanda [President Paul Kagame]. TB had another euro meeting with GB, who seemed a bit troubled. Last night's vote was not great for him. TB told him that the reshuffle would be after the euro statement, which he hoped would bind him in a bit. TB seemed a bit more confident on the substance.

Cabinet was awful, even without Clare. Iraq, Northern Ireland, then a truly awful discussion of the local elections. Ian McCartney was not too bad, very factual about the results, where we had done well, where we had done less well, some quite good analysis, but then a whole load of interventions displaying considerable knicker-wetting. Alistair D was clearly in a bit of a flap about the Libs letting the Tories in, Blunkett on the BNP and the need to reinforce what we were trying to do on the crime agenda, and above all the need to tackle asylum. Patricia [Hewitt] saw it all through the prism of the electoral behaviour of women. JP left before the discussion had finished, muttering that he couldn't stand any more of this.

---

[1] In 1969 Harold Wilson's Labour government issued a White Paper, *In Place of Strife*, that proposed the reform of industrial relations. Divisions in Cabinet and the Parliamentary Labour Party over the proposals led to them being dropped.

TB agreed afterwards that it was a pretty awful discussion but equally he should have given more of a lead. I went off to speak at lunch for all the EU ambassadors. I was on good form at the Q&A, where the questions were mainly on the euro, fallout from the local elections, TB's future intentions, EU–US, and defence. It was definitely worth doing. The German [Thomas Matussek] and the Greek [Alexandros Sandis] asked afterwards why I didn't do TV briefings because they felt that apart from TB, nobody really explained foreign policy so clearly. Only the French sent a deputy rather than the actual ambassador.

Back to Number 10 for TB doing another series of public services meetings, first health, then education, really trying to press his own people and the departments to think more radically. I was also worried that what Jonathan, Jeremy and Andrew [Adonis] were badging as ever more radical, felt to me like radical right wing. We had a brief political strategy meeting, at the end of which Philip said to me he thought TB had been a bit too unyielding – he was right, everyone else was wrong, he was now going for broke. I think it was just an expression of his frustration at lack of delivery. Fiona was having a dreadful time with Cherie, first of all, Cherie seemed to hold her responsible for TB not having a birthday party, whereas in fact all of us had been clear it was the wrong thing to be doing, no matter how privately intended, while Iraq was still as intense as it was. Now, another problem. We had *Marie Claire* [women's lifestyle magazine] in for an interview and picture session and Fiona had told Cherie not to let them in the flat without her being there. Not only did Cherie have them up in the flat but allowed them to photograph her in the bedroom with Carole [Caplin] putting on her lipstick. Fiona was convinced she would be better out of it sooner rather than later. The way I was feeling, I was keen to get out pretty soon too.

Friday, May 9

TB was up in Sedgefield and called a couple of times. I was more conscious, after Philip's observation, of how regularly he said 'I know I'm right about this.' In truth, often he was, and I was as down on departments as he was, but equally I was beginning to get less and less motivated. We were already beginning to talk about elections and it just didn't hold out the excitement it once did. Also Rory had an interesting take. He said he reckoned I wasn't as good as I used to be, that if I left soon, I would be a legend, the first person really to take communications to a level that made an actual difference to politics, whereas if I stayed, it was downhill all the way. 'You're not enjoying it as much as you did, you're not doing it as well as you did, and never forget that the reason [former Manchester United footballer] Eric Cantona's a legend is because he left at the right time.' I had a long call with Dan Bartlett, who was as seized as I was with the need for change in ORHA's modus operandi. I offered to put a team of UK people at his disposal. Paul Bremer was replacing [General Jay] Garner [as director of ORHA], [John] Sawers was going soon so it was possible we would improve things but we really needed to up our game. Calum finished his SATs [Standard Assessment Tests] and was particularly happy with a question about Henry V being a lower-league football manager, and how would he prepare to play Arsenal in the Cup Final.

Saturday, May 10

I spent most of the day taking the boys to various sport events, then later the Goulds came round for dinner. Philip, who could normally be relied on for a bit of optimism, said that for the first time he could see TB losing the election, that he seemed a bit out of steam, not getting things like he used to.

Sunday, May 11

The *Mail on Sunday* had stuff on Cherie and Bermuda.[1] It seemed to us that whether knowingly or not, Carole was shipping stuff to the Mail group.

Monday, May 12

TB was seeing GB the whole time, trying to get him to be more positive about the euro assessment or at least be positive about the idea of a referendum this parliament remaining a possibility. TB called me to the flat first thing to say he was really worried about Cherie. There was someone very close in putting stuff into the press, this weekend again with the freebie story in the *Mail on Sunday*. He noticed for the first time that the kids were getting worried about it. He wanted to know if I thought Fiona was still able to help her. I said Fiona felt she had been let down, that Cherie had changed and that Carole was a bigger problem than either of them were prepared to concede. I said Fiona was definitely leaving. He asked what she would do. I said that depended in part on me. He asked what I wanted to do. I said I would like to go fairly soon. I wasn't enjoying the job anything like

---

[1] Cherie had agreed to give a speech to the Bermuda Bar Association and intended taking her mother and children.

as much as I did and I wasn't doing it as well as I could. He said he thought I had done it well during Iraq, and he was sure I was doing it better than anyone else could. I said the public service reform agenda was not really my thing, and in any event I wondered whether some of our media problems might be helped if I went. He said he realised why I felt the way I did, because there weren't that many really high-pressure jobs, but he had one of them, and I had another. He really wanted me to think it through very carefully. He was not sure yet whether he would fight another election. A lot depended on GB.

Later, when he saw Fiona again, he said he was unlikely to stay but he couldn't be sure. She spent an hour with him and though he started off very defensive about Cherie, he admitted that in part because of the pressure of the job, he had neglected her, but he also knew that things had to change. TB and I had been talking about it just before 10 and Jonathan and Andrew Turnbull came in.

Suma Chakrabarti [permanent secretary] had called from DFID to say that Clare was about to resign. From then on we were set for a day in which she would do as much damage as possible. She got a line out to PA as soon as she resigned, then interviews, later a statement. Every part of it was very bitter and designed for maximum damage. TB though felt it was the best outcome. He was intending to sack her, she probably knew it, so she walked, but with little credibility. Her letter of resignation was pretty bitter. I worked on TB's reply, conscious of the fact I had waited eight years for this, but now it came to it I felt very little satisfaction from it. She wasn't worth it. I watched her Commons statement and she got more and more bitter as she went on, spreading the attack on Iraq to the whole style of government. She was heard in near silence with the occasional gasp as the boot went in.

TB said afterwards that he had bent over backwards to be nice to her and about her, and if there was a criticism to be made of him, it was why he let her stay so long. 'I doubt that any Cabinet minister has ever been indulged so much by a prime minister.' There was no point pretending it wasn't a bad day but she was such damaged goods that it wasn't that bad. Adam Boulton [Sky] said few people could swallow it all without gagging. She was pretty powerful as a speaker but nauseated a lot of people. Valerie Amos[1] took her job. The main thing the politicos were on to was any input GB had. She said on TV that she had discussed her position with GB which begged

[1] Baroness Amos, FCO minister, became the first black woman in the Cabinet.

the perfectly fair question, why he hadn't mentioned that to TB. We were going through a pretty vulnerable phase. GB, euro, reform, rebellion, Iraq.

Tuesday, May 13

Al-Qaeda bombings in Riyadh [Saudi Arabia, thirty-five killed] which were pretty massive. I spoke to John Sawers through the day about ORHA. He was due to have dinner with Paul Bremer and I suggested that he proposed to Bremer that we send a UK team to support their media operation. The papers were needless to say full of Short but the commentariat wasn't greatly in favour of her. I felt CS herself was not so damaging but the GB resonance was and there was a bit of focus on why he hadn't alerted TB to what was going on. We were trying to persuade TB that he did have to do more to get back in with those parts of the party drifting off, but he was more and more determined that reform was really all that mattered. The BBC called me out of the blue to ask if I would do a documentary on Paula Radcliffe [world record-holding marathon runner]. I obviously couldn't do it now, but it underlined again that I wouldn't be short of offers of work if I left.

Sawers called me after his meeting with Bremer who had asked if I could go out there and help set up the new system I was proposing. Lunch with Piers Morgan. We met at the Savoy Grill. He was in appeasing mood, said he had ballsed up the war, had lost 60,000 readers through that, 120,000 to the price war and he accepted he had fucked up. He knew he wasn't in a strong position with us but said he wanted to come back in a bit, needed to get rid of [John] Pilger [journalist and polemicist], cut down on [Paul] Routledge [columnist], stop whacking CB, get back to being more positive on the domestic agenda. He denied there was a pro-GB agenda at the *Mirror*. He viewed TB as a formidable politician who won things through argument. He was sure that if ever it did go to a TB/GB war, TB would win and the *Mirror* would be on our side. Back for a meeting on the Olympics. I sensed we were moving in the yes direction. I had a chat with Sally who said TB didn't believe that I would go, so if it was serious, I maybe ought to have the conversation again.

Wednesday, May 14

Alison [Blackshaw] spent much of the day trying to sort flights to Iraq while I was talking to John Sawers, then a series of meetings and conference calls on what we needed to do if I got out there. I was starting to ask some of our people, like Simon Wren [MoD] and

Darren [Murphy], if they would go to Baghdad. I got the sense that with Bremer there to replace Garner there was the chance to move in properly, though everyone agreed it would not be a good story if I actually went out and ran it.

TB was still thrashing out the euro with GB. He wasn't at all happy with the process and nor were we, but it was about all we had. Charles C had a bit of a rough time at the PLP because MPs felt the Tories were on to something re tuition fees. Fiona had a face like thunder when I told her I might have to go to Iraq. Then a problem with the Olympics. Yesterday we were clear that we had sorted out the answers to all the financial questions we needed to be clear about for now, but today GB told Tessa that it was definitively not sorted. Both Andy Marr and Martha Kearney [BBC] were chasing me on the euro. Then Simon Buckby [pro-euro campaigner] called me at 9.30 to say the BBC were getting him on to respond to a report by Marr that the assessment had happened, it was negative and it was definitely not happening this parliament. This was clearly the next stage of the bounce. I called TB who said I should call Marr and say he could end up with egg on his face if he was definitive about this parliament.

Andy said he had been briefed by someone with 'iron authority', which I assume was his way of saying it was GB. GB denied briefing Marr. I put in a call for Ed Balls who came back just as the bulletin began. He was on a train. He said unless GB was a kamikaze pilot there was no way they would do this the day before a Cabinet meeting that was already going to be difficult. He was adamant that neither he nor GB had spoken to Marr. I said Andy could not have done a story so definitively unless it was one of us four, or Jeremy or Jonathan. I knew it wasn't me or TB and I didn't for one second think it would be Jeremy or Jonathan, both of whom were in a state of outrage.

The upshot was that I was taking calls till well past midnight. The best line we could deploy was that a very small number of people knew what would be presented to Cabinet tomorrow, Marr was not one of them and whatever he said the final position was not decided. TB felt GB was worried at the moment. He knew that Clare had damaged TB, but felt she damaged GB too. 'If this thing ever was pushed to a contest, the fact is I would win. People would not want him if he was trying to force me out. He also knows now that if I wanted to, I could get rid of him and I've decided unless he starts being more co-operative and more supportive, I will do that.' He sounded pretty steely. When I finally got to bed, the phone went again and it was TB again, saying he was sorry I had been kept up late.

The euro stuff was not taking off in the press, but it was still leading the BBC and we had to get ourselves in a better position. TB came down from the flat and after the usual bound down the corridor, we got into his office, sat down, in the armchairs, and he looked really fed up. I asked him what was wrong. He said he and GB were in a different league to the rest of the Cabinet as politicians, and GB was the only one who got anywhere near him in terms of ability, which was why he still felt he had to be next. But he couldn't see a way out at the moment. He felt if they fell out terminally, and he felt he had to get rid of him, that was the nuclear option. 'I would probably be left standing but there would be plenty of big holes in the floor around me and the party would be damaged for quite a while.' He sat down at one point with a pad and made a joke of it, saying let's do the pros and cons.

Cabinet was going to be tricky. Jeremy had worked out a stage-by-stage process. They had to have a sense of involvement in the process. So we would give them the eighteen documents, and follow it with a series of trilaterals with TB and GB, followed by another Cabinet and finally TB's statement to Parliament. JP and GB came over and we signed them up to the process. TB believed that GB now thought that if he didn't do what he wanted on the euro, he was prepared to move him. He said he would still be a pain in the arse at the FCO but he couldn't do as much damage there. They had another one-on-one after which TB claimed GB was on the same pitch, but we doubted it.

Into Cabinet. First FBU/troops, then Iraq/MEPP, then TB set out the process on the euro and you could sense the relief round the table. He said that everyone within the Cabinet would be engaged in this discussion and whatever the press briefings coming out, he said the final decision had not been made. A number said explicitly how pleased they were at the process. It meant TB was wrestling back some of the control in this, though GB couldn't resist saying there would also be meetings of the economic affairs subcommittee. TB said there would be another full Cabinet on June 5 or 6 and his statement would probably be on June 9. He urged them to ignore anything they heard in the media until this process was through. TB chaired the discussion well.

Then on to the Olympics decision. TB set out the basic case, Tessa the process and also the need to learn lessons from the [Millennium] Dome and Wembley [Stadium]. JP said everyone had to support it if a yes decision was taken, that there could be no mixed messages.

Both Blunkett and Straw, then McCartney, said what a huge benefit it had been to Manchester to host a successful Commonwealth Games. GB then said, in a pretty barbed way, that it was important the business community get the message that things will be asked of them. We had agreed that JP would do the media at lunchtime on the euro. JP went through to see GB at Number 11 and shortly afterwards Joan Hammell [Prescott's special adviser] came out and asked me to join them. We went over what JP would say, then GB said to me 'Where do you think the BBC story came from?' Before I could answer, he said it was not him or Ed – 'I absolutely guarantee you.'

I did a note to John Sawers on what we could offer Bremer, and on what approach I should take. I had another long chat with [Margaret] Tutwiler who seemingly had delayed her departure by a week in case I went out there. I was really trying to help but practically anything I suggested she would say that they already had it, even if I knew they didn't. I got the very strong impression she saw me simply as an irritant. Charles Heatley [FCO spokesman in Baghdad] told me that whatever John Sawers said out there, there tended to be an immediate US push back. He also said there was a lot of chatter there about me trying to take over the communications side of things. He felt there was no way I would get them to accept everything we wanted.

Tutwiler gave me a long list of all the things she said were being done, but in the end what mattered was output and in so far as opinions were hardening, they were hardening against us. She was due to be the next undersecretary for [public diplomacy and] public affairs [US State Department] and was going through the approval process, so clearly didn't want to be seen as part of any failure. Her attitude was 'we're not doing perfect but we're doing OK considering'. John fixed a call with him, me, Bremer and Tutwiler. I did a five-minute pitch, then said I would write him a note overnight on what I felt they needed and what we could offer. I was beginning to think it might be a bad idea actually to go out there, partly because of home, partly because it would be seized on as a big bad story, but most importantly because it did not feel like what the military call a permissive environment.

TB and I had a cup of tea out on the terrace. There was a rumour around that the *Mail* had some big Carole story they were saving up to do damage either during a euro campaign or the next election. TB said he continued to believe she was basically straight and didn't want to harm them. Sally sensed he was more worried about it than he was letting on to us. GB was now causing grief on the Olympics.

He said to TB 'Do it anyway, you've already made up your mind.' I saw Les Hinton [News International chairman] and without being absolutely explicit, told him I was thinking about leaving. He started to go over the sorts of things they might ask me to do, columns in the *Sun* and *The Times*, books, speeches, etc. He was the first person outside the immediate circle that I had raised it with, albeit obliquely. The only thing really holding me back was a basic loyalty to TB, my fear that he would be weakened, and GB emboldened if I went.

Friday, May 16

On the one hand, the papers came out fine for TB with a sense that he was back in control of the process and that the Cabinet was being used to shift to a more pro-euro position. On the other, there was still the sense, e.g. *The Times* and the *Guardian*, that GB was clearly set against a referendum in this parliament. TB called an EMU meeting for 11, just before he left for Chequers. He said we had to correct the impression, by the weekend, that GB was against a referendum in this parliament. I said that was easy enough for me to say to people but I couldn't deliver what GB said. I suggested that I try to negotiate an agreed statement with Ed. I discussed it with him and with Jeremy and then drafted something. There was a risk of course that it would be seen as protesting too much. I felt we should get TB to echo their usual line – not dogmatic and emphasise the tests – whilst GB should echo ours, namely that he would fight for a yes vote if the tests were met and it was not the case that in principle he was against a referendum in this parliament.

It took an hour or so. When I read it to TB, he was fine. GB came back with a couple of changes that were relatively insignificant, there basically just to clutter it up, but we kept the basic thrust, i.e. unity and a position more subtle than was being ascribed to both. Phil Webster [*Times*], who was usually my first yardstick port of call on tricky issues like this, thought it did the job well. [Trevor] Kavanagh's response was that it showed GB had seen off TB, a bit odd given that I had written it, and in the end it was probably not one of my greatest triumphs, but further evidence of the dysfunctional nature of their relationship.

I got a message to call TB. He asked 'Are you on a landline?' I said yes. 'I think there may be a case for moving him come what may. It's just not tenable like this. He is impossible to deal with at the moment.' The press as a whole were not totally convinced by the statement but at least they knew we were trying to keep the act together. I was also dealing with getting more of our people into Baghdad by Monday.

Conference call with JP before the *Today* programme. The euro was tricky but he was fine. TB felt the statement we had done went well. I felt that it had given the press the chance to take the piss in saying we were protesting too much. We did however get up the message for the party and the rest of the government that we were trying our best to be united on this. I had been a little bit troubled by something Matthew Freud [PR] had told me last night, namely that there was talk around I was thinking of leaving and that I would be absolutely mad and I had the best job in the world for anyone interested in politics and the media, and nothing I ever did afterwards would replace it. Fiona was pressing for a kind of 'road map' re my leaving, but it felt like we were going round in circles a bit. I wanted out, but I felt bad and guilty about it. Philip was strongly of the view that GB would feel it would be easier to go for TB if I wasn't there. But then again, after nine years, surely it was time to get a life back, and get things with Fiona back on track long before the kids move away.

We also had another Leo [Blair] episode to deal with. Some of the papers were doing stuff on the school they expected him to go to. During the day, he fell over [at Chequers], banged his head, so they called NHS Direct who suggested he go to Stoke Mandeville Hospital [Buckinghamshire]. He got the all-clear very quickly but we were back into another potential PCC situation.[1] TB felt we shouldn't push it, while CB told Fiona she felt we should. TB called me as his guests for dinner at Chequers were arriving, including Chris Meyer [former UK ambassador to Washington], Peter Hain, Ben Kingsley [actor], Richard and Judy [Madeley and Finnegan, TV presenters]. Chris Meyer was being touted as the leader of the Olympic bid, presumably by himself as he was very busily not denying it.

Watched GB on *Frost*. The reality was that he was not very warm on EMU. He said he would fight in a referendum as hard as TB if there was one, but the constant emphasis was on the tests. It was an odd performance all round. He was very but-but, his legs stuck together making him look tight and unrelaxed, and he had this odd habit of putting both hands on the arm of the sofa. He was also

---

[1] The Press Complaints Commission editors' code calls for respect for private and family life, including health.

dropping in references to Raith Rovers [Scottish football club] in an obvious attempt to give himself a touch of man-of-the-peopleness. When I briefed TB on it afterwards, he said it sounded like a real wasted opportunity. He felt the problem was that whatever the issue, GB was obsessed with idea of winning or losing. He can't just be part of a team making the right decisions. He has to win, and be seen to win, in the decision-making process.

Fiona spoke to Peter M re CB. Fiona felt Cherie was in something of a state of denial. She just didn't want to live a normal life really. Peter was broadly sympathetic to Cherie, but the cumulative effect was negative. He also said *en passant* that he thought GB got the best of me in the joint euro statement because it still meant he had the lock on the process through the tests, which in the end were not scientific but a mix of economic and political. He sounded pretty down about his life, said in terms that he had another busy but ultimately meaningless week ahead of him.

Monday, May 19
The euro was pretty much back where we had started a few days earlier with GB 'reasserting control' via the economic tests. The issues were conflating in the Eurosceptic papers which was deeply irritating. We weren't really motoring on public services either. Also unhelpfully, someone had briefed Colin Brown [*Independent*] yesterday that TB would do a press conference on Thursday on better asylum figures, and the right-wing press were gearing up to undermine all that in advance. On the euro, we had the first round of Cabinet trilaterals and that plus the IGC was the main news of the day. We were not in the right place on the IGC. And on the euro, there was still a lack of unity.

At the party meeting with Hilary A, Ian McC and David Triesman, TB was very open. He said that on Europe and on the public services, the party felt division. 'If GB and I were united on this, there would not be a problem. We have to sort it.' Ian McCartney said the party was feeling more and more remote, partly from TB but also from the whole government. It was partly about Iraq but it was also about the way we spoke and the claims that we made and the way we made them. The values didn't come through power-fully enough. TB kept telling me that the EMU stuff was moving our way but there was very little sign of that from GB and his lot.

Jeremy sat in on all the trilaterals. Hilary was clear they could be read either way. So was Ian, who said that on the basis of what he had read, he certainly wouldn't rule it out. JR was more sceptical, Patricia and Charles more pro and Jeremy said that on a number of specific detailed points, Patricia got the better of GB. Giscard [d'Estaing, chairman of the Convention on the Future of Europe] was due in for dinner with TB to discuss the Convention, but Danny Pruce [press officer, foreign affairs] and I proposed against drawing attention to it. Europe was suddenly right back at the top of the agenda again and I didn't feel we had a proper strategy for it. Even though he was mainly focused on the euro, in the chats we had in between, he was banging on about reform again. 'I know I'm right about this.' If we don't take on reform the Tories will rebuild around it, and win their way back by promising to do things that we should be doing. It was just crazy to stand in the way of reform. Wrong for the country, wrong for the party.

Sally having told me he was in denial about me leaving, I wrote him a note setting out why I was going. Also, Godric was going to announce at the four o'clock that he was moving on. Then just before, bizarrely, Ari Fleischer announced he was leaving. I had David Hill in for a chat, and asked him, if I moved on, whether he would take on my job. He said he feared he was too old at fifty-five. He had got himself into a nice position [in commercial public relations] and didn't know if he had the energy to get up for another massive job. He was clearly tempted, said he felt it was probably a no, but he would think about it.

Tuesday, May 20

In for a meeting on the Convention [on the Future of Europe], trying to get a grip on overall strategy and message. We were not in a good place on the euro, or on Europe more generally. Ian McCartney came to see me, said he was really worried about the party, that the sense of division had definitely driven through. TB said the euro trilateral with Andrew Smith [Work and Pensions Secretary] in particular, and to a lesser extent with Alistair Darling, was comical because they were totally on the Balls script. Most of the others were pro. Some in particular were clear that if the judgement was not now, we had to be clear we would be going in before too long. TB was convinced GB was moving a bit, but his CBI speech was pretty sceptic, and was emphasising all the obstacles.

Then we heard that Peter M had done a lunch with the women's lobby and had said, off the record, that TB had been outmanoeuvred by a 24-hour political obsessive, and that because GB had won that battle, we were in danger of making the wrong decision for the country and the government on EMU.[1] Of course the chances of it staying off the record were zero as Peter must surely have known, and for once it gave GB the moral high ground. Even though nobody seriously believed we would have put Peter up to do it, it allowed GB to present himself as victim. TB was furious at Peter's stupidity. He said it also made it much more difficult to bring him back.

Wednesday, May 21

Peter M all over the press. TB up the wall about it. GB was on to him, Ed was on to me, saying that unless we denounced and disowned Peter, people would think TB supported what he said. TB was up in the flat on his own working on PMQs. He was looking more isolated, or maybe that was just my guilt at the thought of leaving. PMQs was clearly going to be EMU division and/or the latest education fuck-up, namely schools sending kids home because of lack of funds.[2]

Peter M was not in a mood to back down. He said he believed in the euro, he intended to carry on fighting for it, and as he was a backbencher, he should be allowed to behave like one. He did not believe there was any chance of him coming back to government and he therefore intended to speak out more freely. He said he did believe we were making the wrong decision and it was because TB had been outmanoeuvred. Then in his ultra-haughty voice, he said he was about to do a doorstep for ITN and then sit down to write an article for the *Guardian*. TB just shook his head and rolled his eyes when I told him.

PMQs was OK-ish but we didn't have a good answer to the question 'why not a referendum?' and we needed one fast. TB didn't really dump on Peter M or defend GB so afterwards GB came in, TB called me in and said Gordon felt he had not been firm enough. I had to agree. GB said unless you put him down he will do this every day, day after day, because it's a campaign to divide and undermine the government and it has to stop. It was of course an exact mirror of

[1] Mandelson was quoted as saying 'Gordon Brown is a politician right down to his fingerprints, twenty-four hours a day, seven days a week. Tony is not. If he was as obsessed with politics he would not have let himself be outmanoeuvred by [his] Chancellor in the way that he potentially has.'

[2] Edenham High School in Croydon, South London, had unilaterally decided to send 720 pupils home because wages for temporary staff could not be paid. Changes to schools funding from government had been cited as the reason for sudden budget deficits in some schools.

what Peter, and from time to time we, said about him. TB was pretty meek about it. Jonathan said that the trilaterals he had been at had been OK, but then when the two of them were together, there was a rhythm of low murmuring followed by explosions. 'It's like watching a marriage fall apart.'

I had lunch with Phil Stephens to discuss his book on TB [*Tony Blair: The Making of a World Leader*, published 2004]. He told me he had extensive notes of all my previous lunches with him. I was trying to tell him that TB was basically the same person. He seemed almost as interested in Cherie as TB, which for someone from the *FT* was a bit odd. [David] Bradshaw and I were working on a script for TB's press gallery [bicentenary] dinner, which was annoyingly at the same time as Celtic's UEFA Cup Final tonight. David and I went to discuss it with him, and afterwards I said to him 'You do understand that I'm leaving don't you?' I could see he realised I was serious. I went through some of the arguments – that I had lost enthusiasm, that my relations with the media were bad and I didn't much care, too many groundhog days, too much pressure that I felt others ought by now to be taking. He was very nice about it, I think finally realised it was going to happen, said he agreed that if I wasn't really motivated I couldn't really do it. He said he still wasn't sure if he would fight another election. I said if he didn't, maybe all the more reason why I should go now, and if he did, I could come back.

I wasn't the only one feeling down about things. Peter M came to see me, said he was planning to move to the country, that he really wanted out of the [Westminster] village. I told him about my intentions, and reasons, and he said I would be mad to go. Life outside is not that great. What I do now matters. In the end the media doesn't matter that much. And also there's the question of duty. [Major General] Tim Cross came in for a chat re ORHA and I got TB to come round to see him too. He felt there was a lot we could do to grip it if they let us. I was quite impressed by Cross. I liked the fact that he said he couldn't do *Frost* because he said he had to go to church. He was very clipped, smart. He said that if he ever heard anyone say the Americans were involved in a conspiracy he wouldn't believe it, because they weren't capable of organising a conspiracy. We were at a bit of a disadvantage though. The Americans were a bit worried about us taking over. There was still something holding me back from sending TB the note setting out fully my reasons for departure, but I was eighty-five per cent there. I didn't much enjoy the press gallery dinner. In a way it was our two lives coming together, and though I stayed in for TB's speech,[1] I sneaked out to a bar in the [Hilton London Metropole] hotel to watch Celtic's extra-time defeat against Porto [Porto 3, Celtic 2].

Thursday, May 22

TB was very worried about the *Times* stuff on schools based on an NAHT [National Association of Head Teachers] survey on teacher sackings. Overnight, the *New Statesman* broke the story of the Attorney General's advice, which we assumed was leaked by Clare. At Cabinet, JP asked Jack to say who had received it, so he read out the list of copy addressees which ended 'Secretary of State for International Development', at which point JP just said 'Next business.' Asylum was running fine, with much better than expected figures, but TB was keen to press home the advantage by saying there would be further legislation to deal with other abuses.

After Cabinet TB saw Charles and warned him to be careful that we didn't simply sort out schools funding at a technical level but still had schools laying off teachers around the country. Cabinet was mainly Iraq. There was a hilarious moment when Gareth [Lord Williams, Leader of the Lords] was going through Lords business and said they had all been up till 2.25am on sexual offences. 'They love it in there!' roared Blunkett, who said people ought to read their Hansard, especially when they were recommending 'delete genitalia and insert penis'. TB did fine on the euro, then GB presented a short paper on the benefits and the possible steps we need to take to get there, and he was a bit warmer than usual. TB said some ministers had been honest enough to admit they hadn't read all the documents before their trilateral meetings with him and GB. What was clear was that everyone was in favour of setting a direction towards entry, and he urged them all to ignore what he called 'noises off'.

Patricia [Hewitt] spoke first after GB and was very good, said there had to be part of the assessment which set out the costs of staying out which she believed were growing, in terms of falling share of foreign investment, possible loss of trade. She felt the longer we stayed out, the higher the economic price. JP said he felt much clearer about the economics, JR that there had been a coming together of the political and the economic. Nearly all of the speeches had been in favour. TB summed up by saying he felt a clear strategy as reflected by the

[1] Blair described making his maiden speech in the Commons with a single reporter in the gallery. Afterwards, he recalled, 'I saw her later in the corridor and asked her what she thought of the speech. She said: "I'm a Hansard reporter. I just transcribe speeches. I don't listen to them."'

discussion would release energy within the party and elsewhere to start making and winning the case. The press conference was fine, TB very confident, pushing back hard on Europe, and strong on asylum. On the euro, the question that worried me most was whether the Cabinet could change the assessment but he didn't really get pressed on it. I had a meeting with Ian McCartney and Douglas [Alexander]. Douglas felt we needed a strategy for reconnection with the party along the lines of the one we did for TB last summer.

Friday, May 23

I went in for TB's meeting with John Sawers. TB wanted a note of all the things he would need to get Bush to deliver on. He popped round to my office later and said that on Europe, it would be a total disaster if we turned our backs, that he was glad the right wing was out there campaigning on the referendum and the IGC because he felt we were going to have to take on the whole argument. Alistair Darling called me about a piece in the *FT* saying that Number 10 were not impressed with him. 'If it's what Tony thinks, I'd rather know and I can go and do something else.' He said he had seen this happen to other ministers and it wasn't going to happen to him. I said I could honestly say that neither TB nor I had ever expressed such a view. I told TB who said he would speak to him. It was pretty clear they were all getting a bit jittery pre-reshuffle.

Saturday, May 24

Geoffrey Levy and Gordon Rayner had a big piece in the *Mail*, 'Carole the Conqueror', saying that Fiona was going to leave and it was a victory for Carole [Caplin]. Fiona called Cherie and said to her she was worried that CB was 'sleepwalking to disaster'. I told TB it was perfectly clear she had a link into the *Mail* and the paper was just toying with her, building her up, in the hope of using her to create a huge splash later. TB called ostensibly re Europe – again – and his continuing worries on education funding, and then raised Carole. She does Cherie's clothes and personal training. So what? He said he had seen her five times since Christmas. I said the problem was that he didn't think there was a problem, and I did. Relations between CB and Fiona had effectively broken down and it was too late to sort it out. He said it was vital that we do not let this kind of stuff take over the agenda. I said we haven't, they had. I had been warning about Carole for years and neither of you have listened. The whole thing was demeaning and belittling.

He called me again later, said he hadn't been able to speak freely because he had been in a car, but I had to understand Carole was barely involved at all any more. I said I just didn't believe it, and nor did Fiona. He said if we left now, people would think it was about this, which was belittling for everyone. Fiona spoke to Cherie a couple of times during the day but the lack of trust was pretty obvious. She asked Cherie outright if she had told Carole about her leaving. 'She said no, but I didn't believe her.' I took Rory to the South of England Championships up at Watford, and got in an hour-long run myself.

Sunday, May 25

Big pieces in the Sundays on Fiona to quit. TB called and said we had to put a lid on this. He said it was becoming dreadful for Cherie because the coverage was making her look crazy. I said it was bad for all of us. He said we had to make clear it was nonsense. I said there was no way we could deny Fiona was leaving, because she is. He was now very irritated by the whole thing, and when he was irritated with this kind of issue, he could become very irritating. It was as if this was all terrible for him when in fact they had created this madness by allowing her in so close. I gave the press office a line that Fiona had not left and that it was absurd to see this as some kind of power struggle with Carole, the usual flimflam. The problem was a number of journalists now already knew she was leaving. Philip was in the States and Georgia [Gould] needed a lift to the QPR vs Cardiff play-off finals at the Millennium Stadium, so I went down with her and Calum. She was a bit upset when they [QPR] lost, and we could see [Cardiff supporter] Neil [Kinnock] going crazy in the directors' box. The Israeli Cabinet endorsed the road map, which dominated the news. TB said he found that even at weekends now, he was working pretty much all the time, and it never stopped.

Monday, May 26

The latest Giscard [d'Estaing] draft [European constitution] appeared to the usual insane cacophony from the sceptic press. Work-wise, it was a fairly typical quiet bank holiday. I made a few phone calls whilst watching Calum play tennis, trying to get some of them off the ceiling about Giscard. We went out for dinner with David and Louise Miliband who had decided to adopt a baby and had us down as referees. David felt we were drifting politically. I agreed but somehow I lacked the energy to respond to it in a way that I would have done a while back. Meanwhile, the situation re Fiona was being made to look like the end of the Camelot show, and she was starting to get hit in the press unfairly.

Peter M called me later and said that he felt I would know for sure when I wanted to go. So did I, and it wasn't quite yet but it wasn't far off. Fiona felt TB and I worked so closely, and ninety-five per cent of the time in a pretty good spirit, so that by now I was in many ways TB's closest friend and he mine, and she understood why that made it harder to leave, because I felt I was letting him down. There was something in that, but I also felt I was letting him and myself down in not being up for the job in the way that I used to be. I had a dreadful cold but went out for a run in the afternoon and got a phone call to say that Mark Gault [close friend from university] had dropped down dead. I was pole-axed. I tried to call Susie [his wife], eventually got hold of her and she was pretty much inconsolable. He had literally just conked out sitting in a chair.

Tuesday, May 27

TB was at Chequers and I was supposed to go down for a meeting but in the end didn't as I was dealing with the fallout from Mark's death. Peter Hain gave us a problem by appearing to say that European elections would be seen as a [euro] referendum, so we had to weigh in on that a bit. I got Jack Straw to do a *Times* article on the Tories fighting old battles. GB, unbeknown to us, was doing something in the *Wall Street Journal*. It almost looked co-ordinated, but the truth was that, as so often, we had no idea what GB was up to. His piece was mainly to emphasise his European economic reform credentials for the US audience and Murdoch in particular. TB saw Adams and McGuinness and told them he thought it might be time for him to meet the IRA guys that they kept going back to see. Adams seemed keener than McGuinness. TB felt they had to give something. I took a couple of meetings on Europe. The Europe coverage showed once more the need for better rebuttal and proactive communications. As ever, the press was setting the agenda for the broadcasters.

Wednesday, May 28

The car came at 7.15 to take me to the airport, where we waited for TB. We sat down to work on his speech for Poland on Friday. He was up for a big pro-European message. He had not really read the papers so I briefed him on just how mad the *Sun/Mail/Telegraph* had been. He said they were going to have to be confronted on this. The heavy thing to do would be to say that this was a campaign headed by three people – Murdoch, an Australian living in America, [Conrad] Black, a Canadian [*Telegraph* proprietor], and [Paul] Dacre [*Mail* editor], an extreme right-winger. They thought it was fantastic that he faced down public opinion over Iraq, but terrible that he could possibly disagree over this. I was worried that we had missed the time at which it might have been possible. But he seemed up for it and was very firm when we went down the plane to see the press. After a good run around the block on Iraq, he engaged with Cabinet on Europe in a pretty robust way.

Rumsfeld had not helped set up the visit to Iraq with a statement that we may never find WMD, or that he may never have had them, which was a pretty dreadful backdrop to the visit. But TB was pretty firm, strong on both Iraq and Europe. We had breakfast together on the plane to Kuwait and as we were just chatting away over his current list of concerns – Europe and the IGC, the assessment, GB, the press, whatever – it was very hard to imagine not being on these kinds of trips, having these kinds of conversations in future. Despite everything, he was still very engaging, very funny and hadn't fundamentally changed at all. We always had a laugh on these trips, which was good for us, but also I think helped build a sense of team with everyone else, from the cops to the policy wonks.

In Kuwait we were almost in hysterics when the deputy prime minister [Sheikh Sabah al-Ahmed al-Sabah, also foreign minister] started lambasting us over our asylum and immigration policies, saying we were too soft on the Kurds and we gave too many benefits to asylum seekers. It was a pretty bizarre event, a bilateral where none of us could hear the conversation, so we sat muttering amongst ourselves while just looking over at the line of princes sitting playing with their worry beads. TB and I kept exchanging looks and we just stayed on the right side of laughter.

The news was leading on TB and Rumsfeld. What a clot. The cuttings came through to the residence where I once played the bagpipes with my namesake [Colonel Alastair Campbell, defence and military attaché]. Linda Lee-Potter [columnist] had a ghastly piece about me and Fiona in the *Mail*, obviously written to order. While TB had a bath, Kate [Garvey] and I went over what pictures we wanted from the visit to Iraq, then out to a pretty sumptuous dinner at one of the palaces. Chirac's people came on with an interesting suggestion. He wanted to do a joint article about Africa with TB and Schroeder. Schroeder was less keen than we were. TB was saying again that he found the workload really heavy at the moment.

Thursday, May 29

Up at 5, UK time. The press was dominated by WMD and Rumsfeld's comments, which was really irritating. When I thought of what we could do to fuck them up in the same way. We then heard, though we couldn't get it substantiated, that Paul Wolfowitz had said that WMD had been a bureaucratic convenience to get us into the war. Some of the top British military told us that the American top brass loathed Rumsfeld, found him impulsive, interfering, making the wrong decisions for the wrong reasons. The local Kuwaiti paper had a picture of TB and a group of sheikhs all in traditional headgear, with the caption helpfully pointing out that TB was 'second right'. I was working on a political strategy paper and planning upcoming events.

We boarded the Hercules flight to Basra. TB was up in the jump seat, David Manning and I behind. We flew over Umm Qasr, burnt-out tanks all over the place. It was very hot and arid, and a few oil wells were burning. We landed at Basra airfield to be met by [Paul] Bremer and [John] Sawers. TB afterwards was very clear that we really had to press the US to get better engaged. It was just not moving in the way it should be. I had a meeting with Bremer. He had read my earlier note and said he basically agreed with it, yet was still waiting for a replacement for [Margaret] Tutwiler. He was falling into this classic US thing of waiting for these mythical figures who were never quite delivered. He asked if I could provide someone, and I agreed to provide John Buck [FCO] to help draw up a plan. He also agreed to the idea of more of our people going out there if we got a plan in place. So it was useful but I could sense he was feeling pretty overwhelmed by the whole thing.

John Sawers was as tiggerish and enthusiastic as ever in his light suit and white shirt looking every inch 'our man in a hot country' and revelling in the machine gun-toting close protection squad. We then drove off to a visit to a school. Nice kids, lovely reception. He did a little speech in the playground while I talked to General [James] Conway [Marine Expeditionary Force], who said how impressed he was by how light we travelled compared to GWB. I told him about Rumsfeld's WMD comments and he didn't seem too surprised.

Our military had accommodated brilliantly to what was going on. The recurring theme though was that the Americans were not quite getting it right. TB had a fairly long briefing on how Basra was won, and then on to the speech to the troops. It was by a river under an awning, hot, but with a breeze, and his words were OK without being brilliant. He was full of praise for the troops, said it was a defining moment for the country, which the press felt was OTT. But he said afterwards he really believed it changed the way people in the region thought about the future, as was clear from the discussion with the

Kuwaitis last night. I hung round talking to the press about a ghastly Gilligan story [aired that morning on the *Today* programme] claiming that the spooks were not happy with the dossier, which was clearly a repeat of the stories at the time.[1] We left for the flight to Umm Qasr by Chinook [helicopter], then down to see the army and navy in a very well-organised session. Several soldiers asked me my marathon time. Some of them had been following the *Times* column but hadn't seen the result. They were a nice crowd. One came over and said he had never been much of a fan of TB or the government but both had grown on him and he felt that went for a lot of them. We went on to the minehunter, [HMS] *Ramsey*, where he did a Forces Radio interview.

TB clearly got a charge from the positive response, though earlier there had been no applause for his speech, which was a surprise, but then it was pointed out to me they had been told to be quiet. On the way back to the chopper, the Number 2 in the base said they had just heard that someone who worked in a photo shop had sent the police pictures of soldiers maltreating Iraqi PoWs. Bad. The reception he got was warm all day but General [Peter] Wall [1st UK Armoured Division, responsible for security in Basra] said that at night there was a lot of criminality. On the dockside, bizarrely, given I was spending so much time thinking about my own future, one of General Wall's protection team asked me whether I had a lot of pressure. I said yes. You wouldn't miss it for the world, he said. I'm not sure about that, I said. 'You just hang in there.' Odd. He was from Stirling.

We flew back to Kuwait and the relief of a cool, air-conditioned place. TB had to get changed into a suit for the official send-off and called me in for a chat. He said he found our troops really terrific, easily the best, and he was glad that we came. On the plane, we both worked on the Poland speech. He felt he needed a harder political strategy based on public service reform, Europe and the poverty agenda. He felt that post EMU, what we needed most was Number 10 and Number 11 working far more closely together on policy. I said I didn't think it was possible. He felt GB allowed himself to be influenced too much by his inner circle. He thought Balls was clever but got too many backs up, which would not help him once he entered Parliament. There were two things that might shift GB to be more

[1] Andrew Gilligan, had alleged on the *Today* programme that Downing Street ordered the transformation of the September 2002 dossier on WMD in the week before it was published. He claimed it had been 'sexed up', including via the insertion of information Downing Street 'knew to be untrue' and against the wishes of the intelligence agencies.

co-operative. The first was that he now genuinely believed TB might move him. 'He's already said to me if I try to move him to Foreign Secretary, he will go on the back benches.' Second, he was very worried about being portrayed as anti reform. He said that though DFID offered the most extreme picture of GB influence over minister and department, there were other parts of departments where things only happened if he said so. The Civil Service often talked of ministers being lazy. In truth, often they were just doing what they were told, or not doing what they were told not to do. TB said the real nightmare is that he is head and shoulders above the rest, which is why it is always better to try to work with him. He said he had always been sincere in saying to him that he wanted to hand over to him at some point, but he made it very difficult.

I was keen to get to Mark's [Gault] funeral in New York, and mentioned it to TB, who said he would prefer it if I stayed for the whole trip but would understand if I didn't. Over dinner on the plane TB, AC, DM, Tom Kelly. Serious stuff on Iraq. TB said it reminded him of FMD [foot and mouth disease] before we gripped it and the military sorted it. People knew what problems needed to be solved, but nobody was gripping it. Paul Bremer was impressive but looked like he was overwhelmed. David and I explained to him that the problem was the US. His critics looked at Bush, said he'd won his war and now seemed less interested. Rumsfeld fired off orders the whole time. The State Department was marginalised. Bremer spoke to Rumsfeld and the Security Council were out of the loop. There was not much we could do to make it better.

Alarmingly, TB said what he felt it needed was for me to go out there and be his person totally gripping it, alongside someone who was GWB's person. I said I was not keen, but he clearly was. He said he would speak to GWB, Russia and France and make them realise it could go belly up. I felt that the US had an electoral strategy that meant they just kept moving on to the next bold thing. He said we shouldn't see it as a conspiracy, it's just that they had a bigger and more difficult bureaucracy.

Overnight we had a telegram about the US warning that there could be two Brits among those at Guantanamo Bay that could end up being executed. I said to TB it would be dreadful and it couldn't be allowed to happen. He said he didn't think they would go through with some of this tribunal stuff, but I wasn't so sure. He then turned to Chirac. Giscard [d'Estaing] had said to him that Chirac was a man of strong but changing emotions. TB said he only really understood strength. Since we turned on him over Iraq he had become much nicer and treated TB with much more respect. TB believed Chirac would try hard to get back onside with Bush, but another telegram was saying that Bush was only in the mood to tolerate, not to forgive. David M suggested we try to get Jeremy Greenstock to go to Baghdad.

TB was worried about [visiting] St Petersburg [EU–Russia Summit]. He wanted to be low-profile and felt it would be a disaster for Putin if the whole thing was over the top because people would think he was suffering real *folie de grandeur* and possibly becoming corrupt. We had a nice enough dinner on the plane and I was in a reasonably good mood, which ended as we approached Warsaw [tour taking in Warsaw, St Petersburg and the G8 summit in Evian, France]. I gave him the note I had done setting out a plan for my departure. He read it, gave me a quizzical look and then said 'Keep it, don't put it in my box, don't copy it round.' Meanwhile Fiona had told her staff she was going, so it was all going to be a bit messy. Part of me felt I couldn't let Fiona down but part of me felt I would be a real loss to him. I had grown very friendly with David Manning, who I liked, for his seriousness and commitment. He said he felt TB would be bereft and I should probably fix on the general election and make clear I would be going then. We arrived at the hotel in Warsaw and TB was pretty much doing the speech himself now. I went for a run then tried to work out how I could get to Mark's funeral.

Friday, May 30

WMD firestorm was getting worse. I told TB the papers were really pretty grim as he woke up, and he was worried that the spooks would be pissed off with us. He felt that in part the attacks coming now were about Europe. 'It's another attack to go to the heart of my integrity,' he said. We decided we would have to hit back at the press conference even though it would take away from the Europe speech. He said he was happy with the speech. He was a bit jumpy about the spooks [September dossier] stuff and said we had to get him all the facts on it. I said the facts were that it was the work of the agencies and the idea that we would make these things up was absurd. I spoke to Julian Miller [Cabinet Office intelligence and security official] in the car, and then to John Scarlett during TB's meeting with the Polish PM [Leszek Miller].

John S said he was emphatic in saying to people that it was not true that we pressured them, and they were saying that. But he stopped short of agreeing to do a letter about it. He was very much up for helping us but only so far. As TB's meeting went on, I did a very strong line of rebuttal and when the press conference came up, he hit back hard on it. The meeting with the Poles was excellent. Though the prime minister and the president [Aleksander Kwasniewski] were different sorts of people from different parties, they were on the same agenda. They were pro NATO, anti Chirac, determined to protect the transatlantic alliance. The president was really concerned about the neocons in the States and TB didn't go that far to placate, though he did say he sometimes felt the analysis was right but the way they secured their objectives was all wrong.

On the Polish referendum [on entry into the EU], the president said the Pope [John Paul II, a Pole] had helped in saying vote yes, but a lot of the priests were saying vote no. He said turnout was a problem and they really wanted TB to do a big vote-yes pitch, which he did. They also asked him to offer support to Ukraine and to get Russia to be nicer to former satellites. The press conference was a bit of a shambles and I rather childishly enjoyed the sight of two burly Polish women manhandling Trevor Kavanagh and others out of sight. We went for a break at [UK ambassador] Michael Pakenham's residence and sat out in the blazing sunshine. TB's speech [at the Royal Castle] had gone down well.[1]

I eventually decided to go to the funeral, and arranged to meet Jeremy Greenstock while I was out there to put the idea of him going to Baghdad. Cherie joined us on the plane for the flight to St Petersburg, which whizzed by with lunch and a bit of work. They had the papers from the last couple of days. TB had a rare look at the *Mail* and said it's not just vile, it's evil. On my future, he said don't do anything yet, you must distance it from all the Carole stuff. I said fine, so long as he understands we are serious about leaving. He said he understood that but it required careful handling.

We arrived and were driven to a specially built complex of so-called cottages for the leaders attending the anniversary celebrations [300 years since the foundation of St Petersburg]. The cottages were grand, ornate identical homes built for the purpose of this event. It underlined TB's worries about *folie de grandeur*. Marble of dubious quality all over the place. Huge en suite bathrooms, lavish but rather tacky furniture, gyms and pools. Yet the overall effect was pretty horrible and the people working there were not much less surly than during the Communist days. TB went off for a ceremony and then we went to the Mariinsky Theatre concert to join the leaders. I had been

[1] Blair said 'For Britain and Poland the lesson is the same: accept the European Union as a modern reality, join it wholeheartedly, fight to make it, economically and politically, an instrument of future strength and prosperity for the nations within it.'

dreading it but actually quite enjoyed it. Chirac, TB and wives were seated together. The body language was OK. By the time I got back to the cottage, I was trying to work out what I had really added today. I had sorted our response on the [September] dossier, helped out re the funeral, done a note on forward strategy, talked to Fiona a few times but that was about it.

Saturday, May 31

TB away at a stack of different events and ceremonies. I met up with him at the EU–Russia summit. He said they were all wondering why they were there. Lots of the other leaders had been rolling their eyes around at the nature of the event. He said Chirac had been very warm to him and had sent him a note thanking him for what he said about France in the Warsaw speech. He was being very fulsome with TB in front of all the others. Chirac asked me if I enjoyed the concert. He said it was too long, and that music events should never be longer than forty-five minutes.

At the summit, TB was taken into the leaders' room while the rest of us were taken to what must once have been a dungeon. I had a long chat with Bela Anda [Schroeder's spokesman]. He said Schroeder was getting fed up with all the stuff coming out of Condi Rice's mouth and might fight back at some point. TB came back to the cottage after what he said was the most extraordinary fireworks spectacle he had ever seen. Both he and Bush said neither of them could have got away with something like it. He had obviously been talking to some of them about the nature of opinion in Britain. He said we had to do something about the press on Europe, and we may have to take them on properly. I said I have been saying that for years. He said I know, but you have to pick your moment and your issue, and you may be right, but this is it. He said it may be that we have to do it even if we lose because ultimately we should do the right thing.

He was also musing on the 'prophet in his own land' phenomenon. You didn't have to be at an event like this for long to see how the other leaders, particularly those from the accession countries, saw the UK as perhaps the best place imaginable, and TB in the very top league. Even the French and the Germans were clear that Bush would not be moving in the way he was on the Middle East without TB's influence, but all we got from our media was total shit. GB sent through a forward strategy note for TB that happily was similar to mine in the way he saw the dividing lines. I did a long run with Rod Lyne [UK ambassador] out on a trail near the sea. We had a bilateral with [Atal Bihari] Vajpayee [Indian Prime Minister]. Kashmir, Iraq,

MEPP, Nepal, Peter Bleach.[1] He was more fluid and talkative than usual, but very frail. He walked very slowly now and his hearing aids were clearly very powerful. We were still being hit hard on WMD and the Sundays were going to be doing it even bigger with a lot of the focus on me.

Sunday, June 1

With DM to the airport, had a readout of the papers, pretty grim. On the plane I told TB and he was a bit down about it all. Also, he and Cherie seemed to have had a row and she was really lip-quivering. TB went down the plane to see the press, again pushing back on WMD. He was fine but the WMD issue was now digging into us. TB kept saying 'What are the allegations?' I said it's that we made them do something they didn't want to do. But it's ridiculous, he said, and so it went on. At Geneva, he left for Evian and I stayed on the plane to come back with Cherie, Alison etc. The Sunday papers were on there, and were even worse than media monitoring had said. The *Sunday Times* had a story about an email showing I'd discussed the dossier with John Scarlett and there was a suggestion that I had tried to get JS to write a conclusion. In fact John had drafted one and I'd said I didn't think that it worked. There was an account in the *Observer* of meetings with TB, JS, C, Jack Straw and complained it wasn't right. There would be grains of truth in all this but it was just crap. Indeed I'd bent over backwards not least because I was fearful this kind of thing could happen.

Gilligan had a big piece in the *Mail on Sunday* having a go at me from the alleged source that he had, with descriptions of meetings there had never been and things I was said to have done that I never did.[2] But it was grim, and grim for me, and also for TB with huge stuff about trust. It was definitely time to get out. I called John Scarlett when I got back and he remained, at least to me, very supportive, said he'd always been happy to do the dossier, had always insisted it was his work, and would only release it if happy with it. Maybe there were some people lower down who were not happy at the idea

[1] Bleach, a British-born mercenary, was serving a life sentence for involvement in the Purulia arms-drop case. In 1995, a large consignment of unauthorised weapons had been dropped by aircraft in West Bengal. He would be pardoned by the Indian government in 2004.
[2] Gilligan had written 'I asked him [Gilligan's then unidentified source] how this transformation happened. The answer was a single word. "Campbell." What? Campbell made it up? "No, it was real information. But it was included against our wishes because it wasn't reliable."'

of a dossier because of the need to preserve secrecy and because of the fear it would be politicised, but that was not the case for the people at the top. He was emphatic that the agencies were pushing back and denying all this, but there was precious little sign of that in the Sundays.

He said he was minded to set everything out in a note to ministers, which they could then draw on themselves. He said we were being made to accord to our stereotypes – you are the brutal political hatchet man and I am the dry intelligence officer. It's not very nice but I can assure you this is not coming from people at the top. He was clear I had never asked him to do anything he was unhappy with. I said before long, once the left was bored with WMD they would be on to the idea that we were victims of what security services have always done to Labour governments. TB didn't believe in that stuff but he was clear that there was something going on here. John S recalled the various stages of the dossier process; how we said we would present the evidence, then how we retreated last Easter because we feared it would raise the stakes too high and it was not a great document. Then how more and more intelligence came in, then how we agreed to go for it at the time we did. Then on to the production through Julian Miller. I said it was really bad, all this stuff.

Monday, June 2

In early, WMD still raging and it was going to be the big build-up to Wednesday, PMQs and the G8 statement, then hopefully some kind of catharsis. TB was still in 'it's ridiculous' mode and getting more and more irritated by what was essentially a media-driven thing. The main problem of course was that there were no WMD discoveries beyond the two labs, and no matter how much we said that there were other priorities now, the public were being told as a matter of fact that we had done wrong. We had Clare S, Robin C and a lot of backbenchers on the rampage now. So it was difficult. I did the morning meeting which essentially I used to get together the briefing for Wednesday. Meeting with Jonathan to try to get a sense of where to go on the WMD story. ISC [Commons Intelligence and Security Committee] inquiry or a letter from John S to TB saying there was no improper interference in the process. [Andrew] Marr was back from holiday and decided to peddle the line that AC would be the scalp the Commons was looking for. So here we go again, Black Rod, Cheriegate, all over again.

On the flight out to New York, I did a bit of work and then read [Harold Wilson's former press secretary] Joe Haines' book [*Glimmers of Twilight: Harold Wilson in Decline*]. Pretty grim reading and the problems with Marcia [Falkender, Wilson's former political secretary] worse than anything we had. His section on the BBC of today was brilliant. I was met by Jeremy Greenstock's driver Gary and his Bentley and taken to the residence. I did a bit of paperwork, then out to meet friends from university who were over for the funeral. Rebekah Wade [*Sun* editor] was over for a News Corp meeting and I had a drink with her and Sarah Murdoch [wife of Lachlan, Rupert Murdoch's elder son] at Soho House and gave her a hard time over their coverage of Europe, and made-up stories.

Later I sat down with Jeremy [Greenstock] and explained that TB was looking for someone to go to Iraq effectively to be his man, and we would be urging Bush to do the same. Jeremy wasn't keen. He said he was an Arabist not far from retirement and desperate for a break and not sure he really wanted to keep doing government work. He also felt that unless and until the Defense Department moved over and let the whole bigger operation take over, it was not going to work. He really admired David M for the way he worked with Condi but said he found it quite alarming that what was basically happening was that David was almost tutoring the American president and his team. He felt TB had much more influence over Middle East policy than on Iraq and he was clear TB had to stay close to GWB. But he felt sometimes they just didn't care sufficiently either about the way things blew back on us or actually, whether things got better or not.

The impression was almost of a country-by-country war strategy and they were far less focused on what happened after the fighting stopped. It was brought home to me later when Rebekah and Les Hinton dragged me out to Langan's [restaurant] and the *New York Post* editor [Colin Allan] said 'WMD just isn't an issue here. Nobody cares.' So we had to be careful. I said to Jeremy G I was worried that TB was setting himself up for too much of the blame if it went wrong. He said that Bush didn't really grip these guys at all, but Rumsfeld was off the leash and out of control. He said the other reason why he was hesitant was because the American system knew that he thought very little of Rumsfeld.

Tuesday, June 3

Godric called just before his briefing, said the frenzy was going apace and was obviously going to keep going up to Wednesday. I spoke to Jonathan and we agreed a way forward was for the ISC to trail an inquiry before TB formally announced it and John S to make clear nothing improper took place. I wrote a long note for TB re what we

June '03: WMD not an issue in the US

should try to do in rebuttal of the continuing WMD allegations. Defensive and offensive, give context and explanation, inquiry, defend ourselves re agency interference nonsense, and also hit back in that the people who were saying there would be no WMD were the people saying this other stuff too. Five pages or so, culminating in MEPP and they said we would never do that either but we are, GWB is there etc. We had to fight back but also put over a more subtle message. But there was no doubt we were in trouble on it, and the trust thing was back, which was partly about trying to undermine him on the euro. I felt it was an OK piece of work though and hoped it helped him. He was going to be feeling the heat on it, although the Beeb would try to deflect it to me.

I finished my speech for the funeral and then dictated a long note to TB by telephone. I guess the main point was that he needed to give a sense of process, show understanding of the concerns but also make clear we did the right thing because of the better things now happening. Met up with some old friends in a bar before the funeral, then up to the church. I read my speech over the phone to Fiona and was worried I wouldn't be able to hold it together. Susie [Mark Gault's widow] was in a bad way and the boys just looked out of it. The speeches were fine. His brothers [Philip and Hugh], me, two good friends and a McCann-Erickson [advertising company] executive. I just about got through without breaking down. The worst bit was when the boys told me that Mark was still their best friend.

The event afterwards was pretty dreadful. A series of corporate speeches, one of which seemed to be saying that what he would want was for the company to use this to go out and pitch for business. It really was the worst of corporate America. I got a lot of nice plaudits for the speech, certainly got the most laughs. Mark's dad [Jim Gault] said he didn't get the impression that some of the people speaking at the wake really knew him at all. WMD still raging at home. I spoke to TB, who said it was grotesque. There was no story here at all, but it was being driven by the BBC as a huge crisis for us. He said he liked my note. I got on the plane and slept all the way back with the help of a sleeping pill.

Wednesday, June 4

I arrived back and the big story was John Reid saying rogue elements in the security services were out to get us. By the time I landed, Switch[board] called me to say that C, John Scarlett and [Sir] David Omand [permanent secretary and security intelligence co-ordinator, Cabinet Office] had all called for me. I called Richard [Dearlove, C] who said there would be a bad effect on the staff if they felt ministers couldn't trust them. I said I'm sure Reid would not have meant to attack them as a whole but clearly someone was stirring it. I said TB would be very supportive at PMQs. Scarlett said he was pushing back the attacks on me and my integrity. I'd asked for all my notes to be dug out on the dossier and I was provenly in the clear. I'd done a long three-page process note on Sept 9 last year making clear it must be one hundred per cent their product and there must be nothing in it they're not happy with. And there was also a long note I made with detailed drafting suggestions.

I went to a TB meeting re what to say about it all with Omand, Scarlett, David Manning, Sally M, Clare Sumner [private secretary], Jonathan. Scarlett was fine re what we were going to say, namely we did not override them. TB was pretty cool with me and the truth was he wasn't taking much advice. I had a chat with Bruce [Grocott, Lords chief whip] about my future and he said he was worried the operation would fall apart if I went. Then a better than usual meeting with Balls and Mike Ellam [head of communications, Treasury] to lay the ground for a euro statement. It was all about the body language. We really had to go out of our way to show a united front. Peter Hyman was trying to push towards a referendum in this parliament, or a change of gear to the next steps, but Ed was not having any of it. It was an OK meeting but I suspect they felt they had got their way. Fiona was really fed up with Cherie. It transpired she hadn't sorted the finances of the Bermuda trip. Fiona also discovered CB had agreed to a *Harper's Bazaar* [fashion magazine] interview.

Thursday, June 5

The main focus of the day was the euro Cabinet. TB and GB had had literally dozens of meetings and TB remained convinced that something had moved in GB, that he wanted to be in a pro position but he also wanted to keep the anti press on board. Ed Balls had revealed that yesterday when I said the best way to signal a gear change was for the *Sun* and the *Mail* to say this was getting serious and there was a real fight on and Ed said yes, but we don't want the *Sun* to go for us next week. WMD still raging on and I sent a long letter of complaint to the BBC re Gilligan, pointing out factual inaccuracies e.g. the fact that he said the JIC [Joint Intelligence Committee] was a Number 10 committee.

TB seemed pretty clear with me that he was thinking of standing down before the election, but I couldn't be sure that he wasn't just stringing me along a bit. He had made no mention of the note I showed him last week about my departure, and was clearly hoping it would just go away. The euro Cabinet started with TB making quite a long exposition of where we were, then GB, as usual in rather more dense form but not too bad. The discussion was OK, though nobody openly said what I suspected most of them thought, namely that the assessment was more negative than the earlier discussions had led them to believe. GB was pleased with the process, as were we all, as there had been no real leaks on this for weeks, ever since we took the decision to involve them all. Patricia H and Charles C were both very strong on the costs of staying out. Peter Hain was very pro, Margaret Beckett far more pro than I thought she would be. Helen [Liddell] and Tessa [Jowell] were very pro. JR, DB and Jack S a little bit more sceptical, Darling and Andrew Smith more so. But it was a good discussion and the mood was definitely 'yes but' rather than 'no but', with a lot of focus on the steps to get there.

The discussion ended with a barnstorming JP performance in which he said that when TB and GB were united, and the Cabinet involved properly, there was nothing we couldn't do. So the mood was good. But then GB went out in the street and did his usual 'nothing to harm the national economic interest', so we ended up with the usual headlines, facing both ways. We had also agreed a joint TB/GB letter which I drafted and sent over but it came back with lots of changes that made it more dense and Brownish. Even the little things were difficult with them. We were going right up to the statement knowing that it would all be in the body language and the briefing.

Reid's comments had upset the spooks and Jack said to me they should have been told straight away about what he had said. But at the same time, there was some stirring going on somewhere and they needed to grip it, surely. I left for the ballet with Fiona and David and Janice Blackburn [friends]. I didn't like ballet at the best of times, and these weren't the best of times. I have never been so stared at in my life. I felt like I was an exhibit in a zoo. It was a mix of 'He doesn't look too evil' and 'What on EARTH is he doing here?' I wondered myself.

Friday, June 6

Iraq meeting with ministers and officials, TB wanting to get fully briefed on how bad it was, for example reconstruction work going too slowly, what the military really thought. He was due to speak to Bush later. Jack was scathing re Rumsfeld, said 'Let's be honest Tony, he has no affection for you or the government and couldn't care if we survive. He just wants his troops home.' TB was looking pretty fed up with this. He realised that WMD was one thing but if we didn't grip this it would give us problems for the future. [General Sir] Michael Walker [new Chief of the Defence Staff, succeeding Admiral Sir Michael Boyce] was much less friendly than [CDS preceding Boyce, now General Lord] Guthrie.

The Bush call began with lots of congratulations re the MEPP summit. GWB was sympathetic re the way we were getting hit on Iraq and WMD which was still running today because Blix had criticised our intelligence. There was a fair bit of the usual friendly banter but TB was getting a little exasperated at the Pentagon's seeming lack of grip. At the office meeting, we had yet another discussion on strategic message. TB and GB had been discussing it and they wanted to go for a message based around 'choice and equity'. I didn't like it at all. I also felt we needed less new policy and more focus on seeing existing policy through, and with far greater drive on message. There was a lot of reshuffle talk in the press. Derry [Irvine] was in a terrible state because of all the talk of him being for the chop. DB was fretting on all the suggestions that he would lose out [as Home Secretary] with the creation of a new Ministry of Justice.

TB wanted Ann Taylor [chair of ISC] to do a quick investigation into the 45-minutes stuff.[1] TB was telling us that we had to get back on domestic politics but then also saying he wanted to make more speeches on Europe, wanted better rebuttal on Afghanistan and more of our people into Iraq. I can't say I blamed him wanting to avoid domestic because it was such hard work dealing with GB at the moment.

Saturday, June 7

Lots of pick-up on yesterday's *Guardian* splash on a briefing note Peter M did re TB and GB during the '94 leadership contest, on which GB had scribbled 'change'. It was not much of a document but such was the media interest in TB/GB chemistry that it was reproduced in most papers with various interpretations. Peter M was adamant he wasn't responsible and if there was a gainer out of this, it was GB,

[1] Taylor would chair the Commons Intelligence and Security Committee Inquiry into the published intelligence assessments of Iraqi WMD capacity, including the claim made in the September 2002 dossier that WMD could be launched within forty-five minutes. The committee's eventual report would describe the 45-minute claim as 'unhelpful', lacking context and assessment. Though the ISC would conclude editorial changes had been made within Number 10, Campbell would be exonerated from Gilligan's charge of having 'sexed up' the document.

because it showed him both as Mr Fairness and Mr 'I'm in charge'. TB was worried about the euro and I briefed the *Observer*, based on TB, JP and GB interventions at Cabinet, to the effect that the idea of a referendum in this parliament was still on the agenda. I told Neil [Kinnock] that the line would be 'yes but not yet' and he was happy enough with that. I also told him about leaving, and he said I should leave if I wanted, but he was worried about it.

WMD was still rumbling on with the BBC driving it as hard as they could and we were bracing for more Sunday stuff, a lot of which basically directed at me, e.g. David Clark [former special adviser to Robin Cook] in the *Mail on Sunday*, AC must go. The *Sunday Times* went back to the old dossier and why we didn't publish it. The *Sunday Telegraph* led on a so-called apology from me to Richard Dearlove re the [February 2003] dodgy dossier, the *Indy* talked of the spies recording all the pressure put on them, and so it went on. I felt I was being royally set up for a fall.

The Sundays arrived, ghastly, full of absolute shit about me, which would keep the story going. Also I'd been invited by FAC [Foreign Affairs Committee] and ISC to give evidence so it was going to be a grim few weeks. I worked out a line with Danny Pruce re the *Sunday Telegraph* – it was not the case at all about an apology, but that I had made clear to those who produced the [February 2003] dossier they should have acknowledged the author of the article [Ibrahim al-Marashi] and I assured agencies that greater care would be taken about anything that impacted on them or their work or their reputation. Of course, the BBC just took that as a green light to say that we had said that we had abused the intelligence.

Sunday, June 8

Ludicrously, my 'apology' to SIS was leading the news and being conflated into a sense that it was an apology over the main [September 2002] WMD dossier rather than – the reality – that it was about the so-called dodgy dossier [February 2003] about which I'd accepted mistakes were made, sent a letter to the system about it, and on which Omand suggested new procedures. But it was an outrage the way the BBC was twisting this. Anyone listening to their bulletins would think I'd apologised – all I had done was give assurances – and that I'd admitted we abused intelligence material – I didn't. We were going through a totally mad phase.

The first call of the day was from GB who wanted to know what to say on *Frost* and we agreed it was best to get on to the bigger theme of WMD and why we did the right thing. I explained the line and the fact that this was the second dossier they were talking about. In the event there was very little about it, mainly Europe and the euro, he was pretty good, very strong and confident, pushing a pro-European line and the effect was pretty good. I called Richard Dearlove on the way to Calum's tennis match, said I was really dismayed that our exchanges were leaked and twisted in the *Sunday Telegraph*. He was in Cornwall, said he could not recall an apology, not at least a letter, felt there may have been something verbal. Then he said that he may have told the ISC he had had an apology. I also told him that some of the papers said he and Eliza [Manningham-Buller, director general of the Security Service, MI5] had threatened to resign. He said that was totally untrue. He was actually more concerned at news that he was going to be Master at Pembroke College [Cambridge] was going to break. I agreed with Richard that he would deny the resignation story and re the apology we just had to put out the line that we had not had major rows but that somebody was stirring it.

JR, Hilary A and Tessa all called during the day, just to say they would do anything they could to help. Hilary said Dennis Skinner [Labour MP] had called offering support but also saying 'Don't trust spies, they're treacherous.' JR said whenever ministers got into trouble, I would organise operations to help them, and did I want him to get one organised for me? Hilary said much the same. Then a call from Margaret Beckett who was doing media in the afternoon and who said that it was an accolade that they kept coming at me, and it was because I did the job well that they went for me. I said I had been interested to see how pro EMU she had been, far more positive than she used to be. She said it was partly the views developed at the DTI. She felt the assessment was more negative than the tests.

The *Mail on Sunday* had done a story that CB was going for an Olympics job and TB wanted her to go to the PCC. The trouble was there was something in it. He put her on to me, and she was very defensive, just said 'What's the problem?' I said we just needed to know, because we were asked about it. We agreed to say she was not interested in running the bid but others had been keen that she would help as appropriate.

Monday, June 9

Most of the papers were reasonably low-key on the AC 'apology', apart from the *Mail* which splashed on it and was its usual vile self. Blunkett said on *The Politics Show* [BBC] yesterday that we shouldn't have done the second dossier and called for an apology. I was reasonably curt, said it was obvious he had to find a use for some

Sheffield steel. Hilary A and Sally said the PLP were virtually solid for me and that Dennis Skinner had been going round the place saying 'Who do you trust? AC or a spy? He is one of ours.' The euro was obviously leading the news and we had set it up OK. The *FT* had done 'GB sells advantages of the euro'. Mike White [*Guardian*] talked of a change of gear.

The statement was still a bit ambiguous though and the Q&A revealed the tensions between them. TB felt the statement had come along but he was still worried. He called Jonathan and me up there at 8, both of us in running or cycling gear. Jonathan was his usual jovial self. 'Surprised you are still here,' he said. TB said he was not yet sure GB was going to go for this. Jonathan said how do you guarantee he won't just do the same thing again next year? TB said he would know in a matter of weeks if this was serious or not, and if it wasn't, he would have to move him. We talked a bit about the reshuffle and TB was dreading having to sack Derry, who he was sure would take it very badly. I was working with Ed, Jeremy and Peter H on a Q&A and material for the press conference tomorrow.

I saw Jonathan to tell him I was definitely leaving now. He said TB had mentioned it, so maybe he had accepted it. Jonathan felt sure I would regret it. He said he knew that he would. He reckoned I would have a long period of decompression and he was sure the business appointments people would be very difficult. He said he had always felt I was like an extra battery for TB, and he would lose extra power. I spoke to David Omand who, like everyone else, was feeling that DIS [Defence Intelligence Staff] were probably responsible for the briefings. I said to him the only thing that could be seen as an apology were my exchanges with him re the handling of intelligence post the dodgy dossier.

C called later to say he had been through all the correspondence and there was no apology. He was glad he had denied the resignation story. I was of course not sure who would be at it, but somebody was. I went over to the Commons for the GB statement on the euro, which was OK-ish but the Tories seemed to unsettle him and he wasn't clear. [Shadow Chancellor Michael] Howard was strong. TB called me straight away and asked me what I thought. I said it didn't work. No, he said, it didn't. He just wasn't clear. He was pointing both ways and people picked up the tension. The pro columnists and commentators were very dismissive. Ed Balls and I agreed it hadn't gone terribly well. It had been a big day, but we had not really taken the big step forward that we planned. IDS wrote to TB saying that I should appear before the ISC and the FAC, underlining that this was now a political campaign. Sally felt the more obvious that was, the more support I would get.

Tuesday, June 10

Press pretty grim. The pro press were very disappointed, the *FT* scathing, while the antis remained aggressive. As GB said, we don't have a single newspaper supporting us on the position we set out yesterday. I ran in, up to see TB and Jonathan in the flat. TB was in shorts and a T-shirt, making toast, though at least with marmalade rather than the usual olive oil. He said the problem was lack of clarity. It just wasn't clear where we were going [on EMU policy] so people felt we were saying the same as in '97 or '99. GB was also throwing in all this stuff about the housing market and TB couldn't see how it was going to be possible to move on it before an election. We went through likely difficult questions. I said what do you say to the question – 'how long will it take to remove the obstacles to the euro?' 'The best way would be to get out a gun, shoot the obstacle and then have a reshuffle,' he said. He was no longer in any doubt that GB was still slowing it down deliberately. 'It's the dead hand, the paralysis of progress.'

We discussed the requests from the FAC and the ISC for TB and me to go to their inquiries into WMD. TB was clear that I shouldn't go, and that he should only go to the [select committee chairs] Liaison Committee. Then a chat with him and GB on the euro. You could tell from his confident body language that GB was where he wanted to be. He was also making clear that if we wanted to make the necessary housing-market changes, that could include a tax on housing, and lots of other things that would not be palatable. TB was sitting behind his desk asking perfectly reasonable questions and GB suddenly got up and stood over him. 'We have to stick to the language of the statement.'

I was saying that we, i.e. Number 10, had got too focused on 'referendum possible this parliament' and had therefore set ourselves up for defeat in the eyes of the media. GB was saying we should get back on to a message about Europe as a whole. I said the day after a statement on the euro, that would be seen as a retreat. GB was being very warm to me which meant he felt confident and at the press conference he was much more relaxed than TB who was twiddling with his pen too much, though afterwards he felt it was worth doing. *The Times* came in for lunch and Sally and I were passing each other notes about how bored we were.

TB spoke to Jeremy Greenstock who agreed to do the Iraq job, despite his reservations. News broke that Manchester United were prepared to sell [David] Beckham to Barcelona.[1] Alex [Ferguson] called later from the south of France and said he had definitely played his last game, and that his people had been in negotiation with Real Madrid for months. As far as he was concerned, the sooner they got the money for new players the better. He said even in France, he was picking up how much they were throwing at me at the moment. He said the one thing you and I both appreciate is pressure and it looks to me like they want to go for you till they've got you. He said the important thing was still to stay in control over when and how I went. I watched the news for once and Andy Marr was basically a television columnist now.

Wednesday, June 11

Things just hadn't worked on the euro and TB was pretty fed up when we went up for the PMQs pre-meeting. He was confident though we could get into the Tories on 'in or out' of Europe. But in terms of a gear change, it hadn't worked, and the judgement was settling that GB had basically thwarted him. TB feared we were making the wrong decision for the wrong reasons. He thought the Tories would come at us today on trust/WMD and/or trust/division/euro. We discussed the reshuffle. Alan Milburn had been to see TB on Monday and told him that he was going to leave. He had spoken to Sally first, who also told him I was thinking of leaving and during the day I had various conversations with him. He said I may think he was the last person to say this, but he really thought I shouldn't go. He said everyone knew the stuff about me was bollocks but he really didn't think I should go at a time I was under pressure. He had told very few people about his own situation and asked me what I thought he should say. I said that he should say that he faced a choice between career and family and chose family, that it was not political but personal. He said he was sad but convinced it was the right thing. Alan's decision was going to be a big talking point and it would be presented as a blow to TB. Alan said he felt wretched doing it now but he felt he had no choice. TB said he felt it made it a bit more difficult for me to go straight away. I suggested Hilary A for the job.

I decided to go for a letter of apology from the *Sunday Telegraph* over the 'apology' story at the weekend. John Scarlett said it had been a real eye-opener to him how newspapers could write whatever they

[1] Though the two clubs announced a possible deal, Beckham subsequently went to Real Madrid for a transfer fee of £25 million.

wanted. PMQs was fine, and TB/GB did OK at the PLP, with people feeling they were up for it, though Peter M seemingly embarrassed himself by doing a long apology to GB re his recent comments. TB said afterwards it was a real lapse of judgement. Greenstock said yes to TB to go to Iraq after John Sawers. TB went off to Paris for dinner with Chirac.

Thursday, June 12

TB reckoned the Chirac dinner last night went well. He had found him much warmer than usual, wanting to put Iraq behind them and work together closely. TB felt it should be possible to reshape Britain's future in the EU but we had to seize it. Jonathan, Sally, David Hanson, Hilary A and I were going through the list pre reshuffle. Through the day we had all the usual stuff. Sorting out the big changes first, then going through the list, endless discussion. Messages coming through, for example, about [junior minister in the Lord Chancellor's Department] Yvette Cooper's very high expectations for herself. For health, we had been thinking of Hain – Simon Stevens and Alan both opposed. Hewitt – Hilary A opposed. Reid – but the problem was his Scottishness [health being a devolved matter in Scotland]. TB though felt that wasn't insurmountable, and he wanted a Blairite moderniser in there. The changes at the Lord Chancellor's Department, not least to the courts, took up a lot of discussion, and I knew TB was dreading the Derry discussions.

TB saw JP who told us he had just been with GB who was pushing for a big job for Douglas [Alexander] and also for Michael Wills [junior Home Office minister], though not in the Treasury. TB then saw GB, who was pretty thunderous about the whole thing. After he had left, TB said that despite everything, he was still prepared to help him become leader, but he had to work with him on the euro and public services. If he didn't, he would fight another election and eventually put him out. He didn't really want to fight another election, and as things stood, only GB could make him.

I spent part of the day drafting resignation letters. Cabinet was pretty surreal because everyone knew there was going to be a reshuffle. Several people now knew about Alan, pretty much everyone knew about Derry and yet on they went with a discussion about Europe, the Middle East, Congo, Iraq. TB said the UK European Convention team had done a brilliant job. *Le Monde* had been running the line that we had pretty much bulldozed our way to getting everything we wanted. Afterwards, Alan came to my office and we finalised the letter. I said there would be all manner of conspiracy theories, political, financial, sexual, you name it. He said it was none of that, he would be full of regrets but it was the right thing to do. He had another go at persuading me not to leave. I had actually been thinking about whether to do my own announcement today. I discussed it with Sally and she seemed upset about it. We got the Milburn announcement out for the lunchtimes. He did interviews while we had another session on the reshuffle.

TB saw Derry. He and I had a perfectly amicable discussion re families before he went in. Previously, TB had argued he needed to shake things up and put an elected MP in charge of the new department, so when he told Derry it would be Charlie F [Lord Falconer], he was particularly pissed off. 'You are getting rid of me and putting in another peer, that's not exactly what I expected.' As he left, he looked pretty miserable.

He then saw Helen Liddell, then Reid who was not immediately too keen on health, wanted to think about it. These reshuffles were always awful. During a break, I asked TB why we didn't announce my departure at the same time. We were out on the terrace. He asked why I was so sure I wanted to go. I said I wasn't really working as hard or as well as usual. Most days I woke up feeling depressed and didn't think it would improve. For ten minutes or so, he seemed almost up for it. Then he said it wasn't a sensible day to do it, because it would give another boost to GB. He was also not convinced that I was one hundred per cent sure, and said he thought I would get a second wind before long. He sacked [Michael] Meacher [environment minister] by phone, who made clear he would be difficult. He didn't do Nick Brown [minister for work] because he was on *Question Time* tonight. We finished by 7.30, with another day of it ahead tomorrow. Eight-mile run.

Friday, June 13

The Milburn announcement seemed to be taken at face value. Despite all the crony attacks, the Charlie appointment seemed to be OK. But there was a sense of things being a bit of a mess re Scotland and Wales.[1] I was in for eight then out on the terrace with the others to go through the list again. We needed a few more sackings to make room – Lewis Moonie [defence], Barbara Roche [social exclusion and equality]. Tessa Blackstone [higher education] as well. TB wanted to

[1] The offices of Secretary of State for Scotland and Wales were combined with other portfolios, Alistair Darling taking Scotland and transport, and Peter Hain taking Wales and Leader of the House of Commons

promote Kim Howells [culture, moving to higher education] and wanted Des Browne [junior Northern Ireland minister] to do asylum but Blunkett came in and argued for Bev Hughes [Home Office minister] to stay with him. David could be very difficult and egotistical at these reshuffle times.

GB, who for years had been a nightmare at reshuffles, was relatively quiet. His attempts to protect Nick Brown were pretty half-hearted. He did his usual appeal for Douglas to go into the Cabinet – 'Don't be ridiculous,' said JP – and he was of course arguing for the promotion of Michael Wills. Hilary A and Sally were regaling us with stories of how Michael would not even sit with his officials on the same part of a train. TB said to GB 'If he's so good why not take him to the Treasury?'

GB said it was 'Not appropriate I'm afraid.' We spent most of the morning going through the lists again and again, making sure there were no glaring mistakes, Jonathan keeping tabs on the numbers. We finally got Estelle who said she would think about the arts minister job. We had a hiccup with [Baroness] Patricia Scotland who wasn't sure about the job [minister for the criminal justice system] with Charlie but he persuaded her. Lewis Moonie was difficult. Meacher made a few threatening noises. Barbara Roche very unhappy.

We shifted Yvette [Cooper] to ODPM [Office of the Deputy Prime Minister] and she had learned from last year, in that she didn't complain. He sacked Nick Brown by phone. Nick said he would 'continue to support him and the government' – joke. Then getting people with new jobs to come through the door – Margaret Hodge [minister for children], Malcolm Wicks [minister for work and pensions], Chris Pond [junior work and pensions minister], Hazel Blears [Minister of State, Home Office] – all fine, real freshness and enthusiasm. Hilary A was an absolute brick throughout all this, softening people up when she knew they were on their way out, keeping in touch with all the Cabinet ministers about who they did and didn't want. Sally also had a real toughness about her in these situations. Then another hiccup re Tommy McAvoy [government pairing whip] threatening to walk re Bob Ainsworth [Home Office minister] being made deputy chief whip. Then Melanie Johnson [moving from minister for competition and consumers to public health] wanted a long conversation with him about this and that concern, and he was starting to get frazzled, asking if they all thought he had nothing to do but listen to their outpourings.

By the time we started doing the bulk of appointments by phone, he had got it down to a very curt 'I'd like you to join the government as X. You should call Y minister and get the drill. There you are, well done.' The Tories went on a line that he was a dictator because there had been no consultation about changes at the Lord Chancellor's Department. They felt they were on to something with it being a bit of a constitutional mess, while we were trying to get it pitched as a dividing line of privilege vs modernisation and change. I had a bad phone call with Dominic Lawson [*Sunday Telegraph* editor] who was refusing to apologise over the spooks story. Then talking to various incoming and outgoing ministers. I felt Alan Johnson to universities [minister for higher education, having left school at fifteen] was the best move. Brian Wilson [former energy minister] was very down. 'What do you need to do? Do you have to creep and cause trouble like some?' He said he had always been supportive. I said I think TB would admit man management was not his forte. Brian was also of the view that until TB sacked GB, he would never get the government he wanted.

Saturday, June 14

It was now pretty much a given in the media at least that the reshuffle had been 'botched'. Ian McCartney was out and about defending it but the general feeling was we had fucked up. TB called, clearly pissed off. The truth was the press was in total kicking mode. There was no debate about whether the reform of the LCD was a good thing or a bad thing, it was all about the handling. TB said of course if Alan [Milburn] had not gone we wouldn't have needed the other changes, but we hadn't remotely prepared the ground. I was feeling ground down and fucked off. I tried my best with the Sundays but they had written us off on it. I asked TB if he wanted me to work on Tuesday's [Fabian Society] speech to try to get things back on an even keel and he said no, they'll just say it's all spin. We now had a press who could only operate at the level of hyperbole, frenzy and venom. Every story had to be bigger than the last one.

Neil and Glenys were round for lunch. I walked in and Fiona said 'bad news'. She said did I remember a couple of years ago when she had sent an email to the wrong address, and the *Mail on Sunday* seemed to have it. We tracked it down and in it, she was absolutely vile about Anji [Hunter], her influence, her undermining of Fiona and Sally. Judging from what the *Mail* were putting to us, my impression was they didn't have the email as such, but knew of the content, but it was another piece of soap opera we could do without. Anji was pretty upset about it when I told her. Dealing with it meant I didn't really have a proper chat with Neil and Glenys.

Neil said he thought I should be the next European commissioner, which I thought was pretty crazy. He felt I would do it better than any of the other names being touted, but I felt it was a non-starter. Glenys felt the problem with the reshuffle was that it felt like we weren't gripping things in the way we used to, and she thought that was because I was fed up with it. Peter M called, said much the same and added that the problem was not just the presentation but the substance of the reshuffle and he blamed 'Baroness Morgan of Huyton' [Sally Morgan]. He said her main talent was to undermine and she had poisoned TB against his return and got others to do so. I said TB had been thinking of bringing him back but he felt that both his speech to the women's lobby and his 'apology' at the PLP made it very difficult. I suggested to him he still had a judgement problem about himself.

Charlie Falconer was on *Frost* tomorrow. We agreed things had not been well handled but we had to get it back on to some proper dividing lines. The Sundays were on to the theme that the reshuffle shifted the balance to GB but it overlooked the fact that Clare had gone. Charlie asked me what my own intentions were. He said he was very worried that if I left, there would be a new template created by the media for the government, namely TB fucks up after AC's gone, and creates more space for GB.

Sunday, June 15

Charlie fine on *Frost*. TB was pretty down though, felt the media was vile at the moment. It was just one of those periods of malaise and we had to get through it. Jack Straw called re the dossier Q&A for the FAC, which was going to be the next big dumping on me. There was a lot of shit coming my way again. George Pascoe-Watson [*Sun*] called and asked me outright if I was planning to leave in the next few months. I dodged it. I had decided I was just going to pick a day soon, and go for it. The consensus in the Sundays was that the wheels were starting to come off a bit. TB said 'They'll go into total hysteria when they know you're going.' Maybe.

Monday, June 16

The reshuffle was still rumbling on. GB's people were briefing that he had secured positions for Scotland and Wales in Cabinet. Hoon, Hewitt and Tessa were all saying to Sally that it was a dreadful mess, but she took that to mean they had all wanted health. But the truth was that we hadn't really thought it through and now we had problems of definition. We also had the PLP getting a bit jumpy re competence. Whatever else they said about the centre, at least they thought we usually ran a pretty efficient operation. TB seemed a bit down at his morning meeting and was asking what he could have done differently. Anyway, it was done and now Charlie F had to make the thing work, and Reid [replacing Milburn as Health Secretary] had to establish himself for competence and leadership.

What we had really lacked was political narrative and momentum which was why I was arguing for a proper political speech [to the Fabian Society] tomorrow. Peter H and Patrick Diamond [policy adviser] had done what everyone thought was an excellent draft. Everyone, that is apart from TB, who felt it risked sparking a reaction similar to the [September 1999] forces of conservatism speech. He felt it was too simplistic about left and right. We argued about it on and off through the day, using a draft of my speech-briefing note. It started with us talking about closing the progressive deficit and ended with a top line that he was holding firm to reform, which was kind of heard-it-all-before territory. He never wanted to go for the right in isolation. Through the afternoon, the draft went backwards. Peter and Patrick had based it on the progress made on the themes of his '94, leadership acceptance speech, but he wanted the basic argument to be all about commitment to future reform.

As I was about to leave for home, I bumped into TB who had just seen a group of MPs. We went into his office. He said he was really worried about the reshuffle because we had mishandled it and it was really unsettling the troops. I felt he was overdoing it, and exaggerating how bad it was. He said he was feeling very discombobulated, about me going, about Peter M – they had dinner last night – and by the constant feuding with GB. He felt tired and couldn't get focused. Tessa had also warned him that there was a feeling he didn't really look after his own in a way that GB looked after his people, the same point Brian Wilson had made. He looked pretty ground down. I felt really bad now about leaving, but I still knew it was the right thing to do.

Tuesday, June 17

We had managed to get TB's Fabian [Society conference] speech up as a lead story but inevitably they were seeing it as a post-botched reshuffle attempt to get back on the front foot, and with Robin and Clare giving evidence to the select committee we were never going to get an easy run at it. I kept trying to assure TB that it was all a bit of a frenzy that would pass, but he seemed really worried. The PLP was definitely edgy. Hilary [Armstrong] told him that if he didn't bring back the Hunting Bill for a third reading soon we would not have a hope in hell of winning the foundation hospital vote. TB said sane people just will not understand how we can put at risk our whole public service agenda over hunting. Hilary said he had to understand that hunting went deep, and was symbolic, also that even with it we couldn't be sure of winning on foundation hospitals. She was very straightforward with him, and a very solid citizen. She was one of the few people I knew who seemed able to combine being close to the end of her tether with total niceness. Even Jack Cunningham [former Cabinet minister], who called me for some briefing for interviews, said we looked really ragged, that it felt like 'the opposite of the Midas touch'. He said we had to get a grip pretty damn quick. Mark Mardell [BBC] even talked on the news about 'a whiff of decay'.

TB said he wasn't clear about a way forward at the moment. The atmosphere was about as bad as it could be for the speech he was making. Rory got his first byline doing work experience at *The Times* on a story about Gaddafi's son and was enjoying winding them all up about the fact he had known in advance Milburn was leaving. I had a flare-up with Rebekah [Wade] because Trevor Kavanagh, absurdly, was trying to run the line that the speech was a warning about future tax rises.

We set off for the speech. 'I suppose "Blair relaunch backfires" will be the headline,' TB said. Probably. I watched the speech but I could tell it was going to get a bad press. The most important thing now was that we get IDS on the floor tomorrow, paint them as the people who resist all change that benefits the many. TB was very down, and hinting again it was because of me going. He called again later. Even if we had fucked up the reshuffle, the reaction was totally overblown. He said the press has become a real drag on the country, but I'm not sure what we do about it. It sometimes feels like living in the reverse of a police state. Anything the government does it automatically bad, anyone who attacks us automatically good. Tomorrow was going to be tough. He had to wipe the floor with IDS or we could be in a bit of trouble.

Wednesday, June 18

The speech coverage was pretty crap, tax being the line in several papers, ludicrously. TB was pretty fed up with it all. We all pretty much accepted the reshuffle had been fucked up and we now needed to get into a good old-fashioned tribal war with the Tories about it. He looked pretty nervy before we went over [for PMQs, then a statement on changes to government functions caused by the reshuffle] but he did fine. IDS was dreadful so the focus was on him in the end. I had a bizarre email exchange with Richard Desmond [*Express* proprietor]. I complained about the *Express* splash on the speech – Blair knifes the middle class – and sent him the speech, asked him to read it, and tell me how they get that headline out of it. He sent an email saying he totally agreed and signed it off 'Fuck editors, fuck Brown, yes to Tony and Alastair.' I had a meeting then with David Hill, Hilary C [Hill's partner] and Fiona to discuss whether he would do my job.

Then up for a meeting with TB. Peter M was there, and said when you boiled all our problems down, they went to the TB/GB fault line. TB said you either had to manage it or use the nuclear option but we had to realise the nuclear option had the potential to be disastrous for all of us. He felt in the end he had to manage him, get him to agree to his strategy. He certainly felt the ground had shifted a bit and that the Cabinet was different post reshuffle. Peter also felt we had to separate out the total oppositionalists from the malcontents. Above all, Blairites had to get a sense he still had energy and policy worth fighting for. Peter felt there was a lack of project, a lack of politics, a lack of communication strategy. Party and government were too much in silos. He was right, and what I felt in myself was that I lacked the energy to do it all again. Got home in time to see the news on GB's Mansion House speech. Back to square one re the euro.

Thursday, June 19

TB got a fairly good press out of yesterday's reshuffle statement but there was no doubt there was something of a sea change going on. TB set off [for Greece, EU summit at Porto Carras], pissed off that neither I, nor Sally, nor Jonathan, who was in Belfast, was going with him. The morning meeting was focused on Greece and the coverage of Beckham was massive after his transfer to Real Madrid. Just before Cabinet, David Hanson told me that his intelligence was that the FAC were looking to clear TB and Jack but have a go at me, particularly over the dodgy dossier. He said he feared an all-party whack at me would be really bad news. I had a bad feeling about it, sensed they were really going to go for me.

I talked to Neil [Kinnock], said I was ready to go and felt instinctively that I had to do it soon. He said I should ride it out. But when I told him my worries about the FAC, he changed his tune, said maybe do it sooner because 'with our ridiculous media they will treat it like a mini Nagasaki near the Thames' and it will wipe everything else out. He said if he was TB, he would be shitting himself. He said his feeling was always that I should have been doing Jonathan's job and overseeing somebody else doing mine. He felt me leaving was bad for TB but right for me. 'You're taking too much shit and you don't need it or deserve it.'

Cabinet was dull and short. We were facing difficulties putting legislation through because of the Lords. Gareth Williams kicked off by saying 'I bring you greetings from the men in tights.' But GB wasn't in the mood for joking, as he was still raging at them trying to get more powers over his taxation. Jack briefed on the European Council issues. He described [Romano] Prodi as 'a rampant federalist' who seemingly had said 'I want to kill myself' when he saw the draft Convention, because it wasn't federalist enough. There was quite an interesting discussion about how we counter, via patriotism, their attempt to use Euroscepticism to hit the patriotic buttons.

I had a good long meeting with Peter M and we agreed an outline plan based on the policy ideas coming forward. He felt TB had slightly lost the values part of our big arguments. Andy Marr called to warn me the Sundays were doing a story that I was planning to leave. I said nothing. Then he called me again later and said he had been told by a member of the government that I was definitely going to go. I said nothing had been finally decided. Meanwhile the FAC, because some Labour MPs were missing, voted to summon me because Gilligan said he'd seen documents showing that I'd asked for changes, and also re the second dossier. I called Tom Kelly who was with TB in Greece. TB said to hold firm, get Andrew Turnbull to reply to the committee and say that I should not go. TB said we should co-operate with the ISC and that was that. I meanwhile had done a note to Jack S re how to handle the dossier issue. I told TB of the rumours doing the rounds that I was going to go in July or September. He said 'Why can't you deny it?' I said that's difficult and clearly people are talking. Very curtly, pretty cool, he said 'I'm afraid that's what happens.' Both Fiona and Godric were of the view that some of us were being bugged by someone flogging stuff to the media, or by the media per se. It was extraordinary how many private conversations were getting out.

Friday, June 20

Just when we thought things might be calming down a bit, I woke to the radio news leading on Peter Hain saying that we should look to raising the top rate of tax. He had briefed the *Mirror* in advance of his Bevan lecture and they had splashed with 'tax the rich'. He had also briefed the *FT* on his continuing support for PR [proportional representation]. Why do we fucking bother? If there is one thing we didn't need right now, it was disarray, on an unnecessary debate about tax. I called Hain, who was still in bed and I said this thing was raging, leading the news and [Michael] Howard was out saying it showed Labour red in tooth and claw. He sounded a bit detached from it all, said he was just trying to get up a debate about inequality and he was amazed it was going so big. I said we should call *Today* and offer to go on, make absolutely clear we are not going back to tax and spend and this is all part of the problem of a political debate conducted constantly in the media at the level of frenzy and hyperbole.

He went on and pretty much regurgitated the same message. The problem was he was relying on the offending paragraphs that had been pre-briefed and I told him we would have to rewrite the speech making clear no minister can undermine HMG tax policy in this way. I agreed with Balls and Austin that we would have to turn it into a story about process and discipline. I spoke to TB who was about to do a doorstep. He was not happy. Our top line was a clear commitment not to raise the top rate, and TB said he had not spent ten years changing the Labour Party to go back now. The problem was it just looked like another dent in TB's authority. Then the frenzy got worse when Charles Clarke seemed to say – though in fact he didn't – the same thing. Pat McF's view was that Hain never said anything without thinking it through whereas Peter M was more of the view that it was stupidity.

I did a long note for TB setting out what we needed to do in the next few weeks up to conference. He was aware of how bad things were but clear that he could see a way forward. Philip's view was that we had lost any sense of political project and that the party was getting silly and complacent because there was no sense the Tories could get anywhere near us. By the time we had finished with Hain's speech, all of the difficult stuff on tax and PR was out. There was a bit of talk around that he was trying to position himself as a possible future leadership challenger from the left. I was pleased with the note, eight pages, emphasis on values, the need to reimpose strategic themes, tying in existing and future policy and events. TB got back late, though he left the summit before it finished. The Europe stuff had gone well but Hain gave us a problem we could have done without. For once the phone was going infrequently, though the Sundays were still chasing me re departure.

Saturday, June 21

I hadn't slept well. I was avoiding answering the phone other than to the office because by now all the broadcasters and half the Sundays were trying to ask me if I was going. Now was probably not the right time. It would be seen as bad for TB and bad for me if I went under a cloud. The *Independent on Sunday* had a story with quotes from Eric Illsley [Labour MP on FAC] that they were going to go for me personally re the Iraq dossier and I felt the best thing for me to do was to go to give evidence and get my retaliation in first. I was sure of my ground, so why not? I did a note to Jack saying that when he gave evidence, there were two central points that needed to get over re the dodgy dossier. One, I was unaware of the plagiarism. Two, that it had nothing to do with the people named in the email about it, like Alison [Blackshaw]. We desperately needed to reposition on this and I was thinking the best way was for me to surprise them by saying I positively wanted to give evidence.

Sunday, June 22

I did the Hampstead 10k in forty-six minutes. Tough, but really enjoyed it. I had been up early to do a note to Jack S on the *Independent on Sunday*, and called re the same. I spoke to TB, first re the general scene, on which he felt we had been here before and we could get out of it. I said we had to keep going on the long term and ignore the media. I also said I was worried about the FAC and thought I should go. I sent him a note explaining why, and copied it to Jack. I said to TB I feared none of the questions and that we had to get to a point where they accepted we did nothing wrong regarding the first dossier, made mistakes re the second. I said I was confident, really felt I should take the heat on it and get it into a better place. If not, the report would come out the day before the Liaison Committee and that would be a real problem for him as well as me. I thought the best thing to do was a note to TB, which I did, giving the reasons why we should break the convention and then give it to Donald Anderson [Labour MP, FAC chairman] as a letter. Jack S agreed with me I should appear because it was clear that a lot of the evidence given so far related to communications issues. TB was persuaded first by me and then by Jack that it was the right thing to do. Jack spoke to Donald Anderson and we agreed a process, that he'd write to Donald, and I subsequently gave him a memo.

TB sensed that me going to the FAC would go very big, but I was in no doubt I had to do it, try to get my reputation in a better place and I felt more confident if I could do that myself. Melanne Verveer [Hillary Clinton aide] came round for tea, advising Fiona she should get out because Cherie had made her position untenable, advising me to get out and get going on memoirs. She thought I could do well on the US speaking circuit. She said Bush was still getting away with murder because he had brilliantly hijacked the security issue and the Democrats didn't really know how to handle it. Clinton's view was that Bush was a far better politician than people gave him credit for. There was an intruder at Prince William's twenty-first birthday bash which gave us a massive news sponge.[1]

Monday, June 23

The William situation was still the main attraction but by the time of the eleven o'clock, it was clear I would be a strong second. I had redone a memo and Jack's letter to the FAC. At the office meeting, TB looked dreadful and there were long pauses as he went through his weekend note, the usual list of the usual subjects, the usual hits on departments. He was getting more and more frustrated at what he called the lack of radical policy direction in the public services. Andrew Adonis would say that we were doing this, trying that, pushing on this, but TB was irritated. Geoff Mulgan [policy adviser] had meanwhile done an excellent note, which was a brutal assessment of our lack of long-term strategy on policy. He said we had lost authority at the centre, that Number 10 had got bigger but less effective, and that our overall narrative was no longer clear. He gave lessons from other midterm governments around the world, and said that they sometimes got renewal through brutal changes of personnel.

As I read it, eight pages of pretty good stuff, I noted Jonathan could hardly keep his eyes open, I was moving on in my mind already, and the contributions around the table were pretty rambling and anecdotal. It was pretty dispiriting. Towards the end I said to TB 'For God's sake try not to look so miserable. It's not as bad as all that. When we have an agenda and we just get on with it and ignore the press, we are always strong.' But he just kept asking if the overall plan was OK. Pat and I were arguing that we needed a clearer message – it was not about choice but about our values. Then I said: are you OK for us to announce me going to the FAC and he said he was not so sure any more. Someone had got at him, but I enlisted Andrew Turnbull, who persuaded him it was the way to avoid the Liaison Committee being about me/WMD/trust.

So Jack and I then finished the letter to Donald Anderson and got it in time for the eleven o'clock briefing. TK briefed on it, and it ran

[1] The intruder, Aaron Barschak, self-styled 'comedy terrorist', had gained easy access to Prince William's twenty-first birthday party, dressed as Osama Bin Laden in a ball gown.

for most of the day. We had a party meeting, TB again casting around for support and Hilary A being very clear about problems in the PLP. I was now totally focused on FAC, reading lots. Clare Sumner and Catherine Rimmer [Number 10 Research and Information Unit] were doing lots of work for me. Then to a meeting with Michael Jay and Dickie Stagg [FCO official] to go through what MJ would say tomorrow when he appeared with Jack, then back to see John S, Clare Summer, Tom and Godric to begin to go through the difficult questions.

Alison [Blackshaw] was back from holiday and getting me out all the files and I was beginning to work out all the answers to the difficult questions, for example [Ibrahim] al-Marashi's claim [as the plagiarised source for the February 2003 dossier] that his life had been put in danger. Hilary A said some of our members on the committee were worried. They felt I could easily deal with Gilligan, but al-Marashi was not so easy. Clare had established who in the CIC was responsible for not telling people where it all came from, but we agreed I would take responsibility at the FAC.

Tuesday, June 24

Fairly big coverage of me going to the committee. Vile in the *Mail* needless to say but not bad overall. I spent most of the day with Clare and Catherine, who were terrific. Clare had got to the bottom of the whole [February 2003 dossier] thing. I spent several hours going over and over again the text of my memo which we eventually got to the FAC by 6.15pm. Jack S was keen that I apologise upfront. I agreed, but later came to the view that I should not and said it was because I was worried it would leak. My strategy was to apologise to Dr al-Marashi for the mistake and then demand an apology from the BBC not just for me but for the PM, etc. John Scarlett was getting my memo put through the agencies.

I saw TB, whose main interest seemed to be how the FAC would impinge on him. He gave little advice at all. At least Jack was suggesting changes and improvements. Jack also came over, very friendly, said the most important thing was that I was nice and polite and didn't go for them. Then to a series of TB meetings on political strategy. He was infuriating me going on about our lack of plan, and I could tell he was as infuriated with me as I was with him, because I was constantly banging on about values, saying he was too technocratic on reform. TB said we had alienated the left on Iraq, the right on Europe, the party on public service reform. Yet he felt on all three we were in the right. Our problem was we weren't explaining it properly – blah – we didn't have a proper communications plan for it – blah – so on and so forth, blah blah blah. I was pretty heavy with him, and he with me. Peter M was very good at seeing all the points where actually we agreed and by the end we kind of knew what needed to be done, by way of changing the draft plan from the weekend.

I then spent four hours with John Scarlett and Dickie Stagg to go over all the questions, etc. Meanwhile, six UK RMPs [Royal Military Policemen] were killed, which was really grim. I discussed with Neil [Kinnock], with Fraser Kemp [Labour MP] and a few others how to approach it. They all felt go for the BBC but be clinical and be forensic. John S was keen that I didn't include the agencies in any general attack on the BBC. Jack's evidence didn't go brilliantly. He said I had commissioned the paper, and the BBC said that undermined me before my appearance. But I felt confident.

Wednesday, June 25

Jack had set me up badly by saying that I had commissioned the dodgy dossier and it was 'a complete Horlicks'. He called me while I was preparing for the committee with Clare and Catherine. I said I didn't want to speak to him but I would see him at the House before PMQs. There was quiet a lot of build-up in the news, full of the usual agenda stuff. TB asked me up to the flat. He said he really wanted me to stay calm at all times and treat the committee with respect. We had worked out the right strategy, concede the apology to Dr al-Marashi, be as detailed and as full as possible, go on the BBC, broaden it, demand an apology and get up the big-picture message about the cynicism of people who say that the prime minister would go to war on the basis of this. TB and I agreed that the media were a real democratic problem, but he didn't really want to do anything.

It was an odd feeling to go out from Number 10 with lots of good wishes and with the media there for me, not TB. PMQs was pretty low-key. Afterwards TB had another private word. He said look, this is the reverse of the usual. I am telling you that you have to be calm and not get peevish. Clare S and Catherine R were brilliant in preparing me, going through the difficult questions again and again. Meeting with John Scarlett, Godric, Tom, etc. Over at the House, feeling not bad, long walk to Boothroyd Room, there were crowds outside the room, and I had to wait around the corner. I got in, slow start with [Sir] John Stanley [Conservative MP] before a break for a vote at 4. Three hours in total. I picked up after a while. I got most of my lines in, and it went pretty well. I thought the Labour MPs were reasonably helpful, I think they were glad I apologised and they went for the BBC thing pretty well. I cut my hand on the sharp object in my palm (a paper clip). It was gruelling, and I walked back exhausted, followed back by cameras, but there was a nice round of applause when I got back. I felt a lot better. Flank opened on the BBC.

Then to the Leukaemia Research reception and we got the cameras in, partly to get coverage for the charity, partly to give fresh pictures of me looking a bit more normal and less wound up than I was at the committee. The kids were brilliant. I did a good speech, and they gave me a great cartoon as a present for having raised so much. David Davis [Shadow Deputy Prime Minister] came, which was nice of him. By the time I got home, I was totally shagged out. There was loads on the news. It had been live on the news channels plus CNN. I felt the tactic of going myself had worked. TB called late, said 'Everyone was saying you did superbly, which you did. There is no Cabinet minister who could do that as well.' Audrey [Millar, Fiona's mother] called, said she liked [LBC radio talk show presenter] Nick Ferrari's line, that I don't pick fights I can't win.

Thursday, 26 June

Huge coverage in the papers and some great cartoons. Generally I was thought to have done well, though the BBC were still focusing on dissent and opposition to me. During the morning we put together a letter following [BBC director of news, Richard] Sambrook's interview in which he made further contradictory statements. I put together a letter, and got Clive Soley [Labour MP] to do a letter saying that the source should speak to Donald Anderson and, if not, Gilligan should be recalled. We were on a roll, all right yesterday and today, we had good messages of support coming through. I was up at 5 to work on the letter that I was to send to the committee to deal with their extra requests. It took hours and hours and hours. I went through all the different exchanges of correspondence with John Scarlett. It took hours for me, John, Clare and Catherine to get it sorted. I also wrote to [Greg] Dyke [BBC director general] and to Sambrook and put the Sambrook letter out to the press. I was going to nail Gilligan completely, and then the *Mail*.

Pre Cabinet, Jack S came up to me and I was very short with him and did not engage. Later I told Michael Jay I took it very personally, felt betrayed, that the FCO had basically been interested only in protecting JS and the FCO. TB called me in before Cabinet. 'You did brilliantly.' 'No help from ministers,' I said. 'You have to understand these guys are not as used to pressure as we are,' he said. 'They panic.'

June '03: Applause for AC after FAC appearance

I said I'd taken a lot of shit for these people and got very little back. I'd thought JS was a bit different.

At Cabinet, I was working on my supplementary letter to the FAC. They were mainly discussing Iraq and TB talking about the general situation. Ian McCartney did me proud, said that yesterday I had shown passion, values, conviction and humility and an awful lot of ministers could learn from that. He said he had watched it on the news and he hoped every party member had seen it because it showed that we believed in something. JR said something similar and then had a real whack at Peter Hain for 'launching a debate' on tax. Putin was in for lunch, which was OK as was the press conference, though it didn't really fly. The media were still obsessing about me the whole time, though we were doing pretty well. The BBC letter went well though and I felt it was turning our way a bit. TB's demeanour about the whole thing had changed. I had never had so much coverage as in the last few days but TB said it was the right thing to do, I'd have been hung out to dry if I hadn't done it. We had a farewell dinner for David Manning [moving on to be UK ambassador to Washington]. I had a nice chat with John Scarlett and his wife. Condi was over, which was quite a tribute to David. He was such a nice guy, and TB rightly paid him a very warm tribute.

Friday, June 27

Ran in, thirty-one minutes. I had been going through the FAC memo until late last night. Early in to go through it again. John Scarlett had a lot of cuts and a few changes and he was really good. We had a long discussion about whether we should be specific that I had previously pointed out an inconsistency between the text and executive summary of the 45-minute description. I decided to put in a general line in relation to the ironing out of inconsistencies. I had to leave for a speech meeting with TB, at which Peter H and I were trying again to tilt the balance towards values and away from the technocratic side of reform. TB was keen to get back on public services but we had to cut short the meeting because Derry arrived to see TB. They had bumped into each other at a state banquet recently, where Derry completely blanked him. He looked totally forlorn as he waited outside and I chatted to him for a minute or two before he went in.

Clive Soley and Phil Woolas [Deputy Leader of the Commons] were doing media defending me. There weren't that many ministers out but I don't think that meant they weren't behind me. Audrey [Millar] did however remind me of the observation that if you want a friend in politics, get a dog. I did the final memo with the last changes then sent it to Clare Sumner to get ready to send while I went with Calum and Charlie [Calum's friend] to Wimbledon. I lost my rag in the morning watching Jack's live evidence, where he was umming and aahing and when asked whether the 45-minute claim was in the first dossier, looked shifty. He did not just say yes. I had even talked to him about that point in the morning when I spoke to him at the request of John Scarlett to let him know that I HAD probably made a point to John S re forty-five minutes but it was not a request. So what the fuck was going on?

I suggested to Danny Pruce to get a note to Ed Owen [Straw's special adviser] saying that the answer was yes, and why didn't he say that? I said that I felt badly let down and this was what happened when a department cared about itself, not the government. John Williams [FCO] left a hurt message on my mobile saying it was not deliberate, though I was not so sure. But I sent him a softer message back. At Wimbledon, C called me to say he thought I'd done brilliantly at the FAC, that I'd moved the debate on and people in the agencies felt I'd done well. He said we had to win this because it was so unfair and wrong. We went for lunch at Wimbledon. Julie Kirkbride [Conservative MP] was at our table. She said she was totally supportive of me re the BBC and she agreed with pretty much everything that TB said. I said I was determined to get an apology. We watched Andy Roddick and Venus Williams [US tennis players], but I was constantly being called out.

Jack S called me after his private session at the FAC, said it went well. He asked me to understand that he'd not done it deliberately. We went in for tea when news came through that Sambrook had replied. It was real sophistry. Their line now was that it was OK to report a source even if you didn't know what he said was true. He said I had a vendetta against Gilligan and that I was intimidating the BBC. He also had a line that they would express regret if story turned out to be false. So they were both blustering and on the run. I wrote a very angry response, probably too angry. 'Weasel words, BBC standards debased beyond belief,' I really went for it. Once it was drafted, we had a conference call to discuss it.

We drove back and I listened to the BBC *Six O'Clock News* in the car. It was a total PR job on the BBC letter, and a straight hit at me. I got in to the office and Jon Snow [news anchor] had asked me to go on *Channel 4 News*. Hilary C had said no but I was tempted because I knew the story inside out. The office was split, half in favour, half against. Jonathan feared it would make me the story even more. I spoke to TB, who said do you really want to do it or don't you? I said I do. OK, be calm and be careful. The important thing is you do what is appropriate and don't go over the top. I got into the car and headed there gathering my thoughts. I was taken straight to the studio. Snow seemed not to be expecting me, but there I was. I felt I won it re the words and was able to pick him up on fact a couple of times, but I did get a bit too angry. The clips used in later bulletins were good though.

Lots of calls of support came in, including John Reid, Neil and Glenys, Philip. The office was OK, but TB said he felt I was too angry and Fiona was livid I'd done it at all. She did one of her 'you never listen, never acknowledge anyone else's views' numbers. Peter M called and said get a strategy for the weekend, keep calm, get friends and don't lose it. The Tory line on *Newsnight* [BBC] was that I'd flipped my lid and was a liability. But we kept going and I was sure we were going to win. I had the idea of calming it down by saying that we would go to the BBC Complaints Unit. Tom Kelly said it would suit their purposes, not ours.

Saturday, June 28

I was up at 5.50 and did a note to Fiona apologising that I had sent the kids home on their own and gone on. I felt it was the right thing to do; but if she thought it was a mistake, please understand the pressures, and the need I feel to be vindicated, and understand that I'll get out as soon as we are through this. I listened to Ben Bradshaw [fisheries minister, former BBC journalist] on the *Today* programme who was excellent. [John] Humphrys [presenter] was getting very childish and petulant and Ben got him to say that Gilligan DID check it with MoD. The MoD press office told us that he didn't, that all he had said to them was that he was on talking about an interview with [Adam] Ingram [Armed Forces minister] re cluster bombs, said he had a WMD story but it would not bother them. So we got Ben Bradshaw to put out a statement plus a letter to Sambrook, which was running later and kept them on the back foot.

I got some very supportive phone calls through the day. Rory answered the phone to Nick Soames [Conservative MP], who before realising it wasn't me went off on one – 'You sex god, you Adonis, you the greatest of all great men' – before Rory said 'I'm his son.' Soames was totally supportive, said keep going, these people are total shits. He said in part we had created this monster, seen it as a beast and we fed it well. But it was now out of control and we had to get the control back. He said bad journalism is like pornography. Every time you fail to check it, it gets closer to being the norm. 'Do you think my grandfather [Winston Churchill] had a spin doctor? Course he fucking did.' He said we had to win but he would be happy to speak up for me at any point. He was in great form. 'Tell the prime minister that the next time I'm called at PMQs I intend to say "What is a lifestyle guru and do I need one?"' He said he had once said that the Royal Family was like a great tree and if you hack at the roots hard enough eventually the tree will die. That is what's happening to politics thanks to our wretched media. Keep going, because they don't like it up 'em.

I spoke to Robin Oakley [CNN European political editor, formerly BBC] who said the same, that he had always considered I was straight and what was happening was wrong. Geoff Hoon called saying he wanted to be out there supporting me. John S called to say he was a bit worried about my interview. He felt I'd done so well on Wednesday, maybe I should have quit while ahead, but he also said he had spoken to C and they were all really pleased they had such a loud champion of the spooks. I told him of the extraordinary moment yesterday, like something out of a film, when I was dictating my response to Sambrook from the marquee at Wimbledon and who should walk by but a spook I recognised.

I felt we were in a much better position. I did the Sunday broadsheets. I spoke to Neil [Kinnock] and got some nice words out from him, also Alex F, Soames and Oakley. John Reid called, keen to do something, ditto Bruce Grocott. Letter from Blunkett saying don't quit. Ben Bradshaw was brilliant on the media and I told him so. He said he felt it really strongly and we really had to make this stick. TB said keep going hard for another day or two, then we leave it to the committee.

Gilligan called the MoD press office in a bit of a flap to say that the call to the press office of May 28 was indeed the only one he made. We had media outside the house the whole time but I decided to go out for a run anyway. Home for dinner with the Goulds and the Kinnocks. Neil was in one of his wonderfully over-the-top, often comic rages – at the BBC over me, at Glenys over Iraq. His big rage was at the idea of Peter M going to Brussels. The papers came. They were mixed. Some of them had MPs saying I would be cleared, others that Gilligan intended to sue. Fiona seemed a lot happier. I felt very lucky that I had friends like Neil and Glenys, Philip and Gail [Rebuck], Alex, the handful of others who were calling the whole time to help me through. I did a conference call for the Sunday broadcasts with John Reid, Margaret B, Douglas, Valerie Amos, Geoff H. JR did most of the talking. The agreed top line – one month in, one question remains, is the story true? This was getting clearer.

Sunday, June 29

TB wanted to work out an exit strategy. John Birt [former BBC director general] had suggested that I put it in the hands of the FAC and say I'll do nothing until after that, which was probably the right thing to do. He said it was important that I didn't let my emotion come into this too much. Birt drafted my letter to Sambrook, which we got out by 4pm. By then Sambrook digging in deeper by saying that they never said TB lied – what the fuck do they think saying something whilst knowing it to be untrue means? Sambrook said we'd acknowledged their source was right (!) and that the real question was where are the weapons. They were beginning to look silly and defensive.

Monday, June 30

The BBC were trying to move the goalposts to the 'dodgy dossier'. Peter M said [Greg] Dyke was personally masterminding it and had written parts of Sambrook's letter to me himself. Peter said they'd got themselves on a hook, whereby they felt their independence was under attack but they'd parked on very weak ground. I went up to see TB who said he didn't want it going beyond next week. His rationale was that he didn't want every single media organisation against him. I said we had to get it absolutely proven that we were right and use that to force a rethink of the political journalism culture. I could see he was up for suing for peace. He/Peter M wanted to get it stitched up in advance.

TB wanted desperately for us to get back on the domestic agenda. At the office meeting we had a decent enough discussion of the plan I put forward. The message he felt most comfortable with was that we were doing things that would make us unpopular in the short term but deliver results in the long term. I still felt we were too short on values. I did a revised version on the next four weeks and resubmitted it later. I talked to a few editors and commentators to try to explain this was about BBC journalism not WMD. Dennis Skinner called on his first day back in Parliament after his illness. He said keep at it. He thought I was brilliant on Channel 4, the MPs were totally behind me and 'I'll tell [Andrew] MacKinlay [Labour MP on FAC] he has to back you because TB needs you. I'll tell him he's worth ninety-nine Roger Liddles [special adviser] and TB is surrounded by twats whereas AC is fine and probably against the war anyway.'

[Peter] Kilfoyle was the only Labour voice apart from [Bob]

Marshall-Andrews, who I didn't count as Labour, to be offside. I spent the rest of the day with Clare S, Catherine R and David Bradshaw trying to agree lines re next steps. The BBC guidelines were shot to pieces by this story. Gilligan issued his threat to sue. I had been quoted as saying: If that guy sues, I'm a banana. Tony Parsons [columnist] had a supportive column in the *Mirror*, attacking the Beeb. Ben Bradshaw was piling it on to Sambrook and did a letter to the BBC governors about where guidelines were broken. I had a sense of it motoring. I hoped that Scarlett might send a letter of support to the FAC, or maybe C. The jury still out on Channel 4. I got some good feedback, but both [John] Birt and Scarlett thought it had been a bad idea. Mum phoned and said she had lost half a stone in the last few weeks. A friend from Ayrshire had called her to say the vicar yesterday had said a special prayer for me because I was standing up for truth against lies. Seven-mile run.

Tuesday, July 1

Hunting was the main story after the government had to bow to MPs' pressure and the story was that we were heading for a total ban. Gay marriages [proposed same-sex civil partnerships] were going big. I got good feedback from Peter M, Philip and Jonathan who all felt the forward-plan note I had done was strong. *The Times* had stuff on Dyke being in charge. The *Guardian* said the BBC would offer an apology for what was inaccurate if it was accepted they were justified in the broader context. The *Telegraph* had an Alan Cochrane [Scottish editor] piece pro me, a leader [column] on the fence. There was a vile piece from Hugo Young [*Guardian*] who said the BBC had behaved impeccably. Defending the indefensible.

I sent a letter to Charles Moore [*Telegraph* editor] re his leader. Lots of letters were coming in in support of what I was doing. Nice one from Joe Ashton [Labour MP]. Letter to Dyke re his letter to TB that 'if we make mistakes we will admit we were wrong and apologise'. The intelligence from the BBC was that they were going to fudge the two dossiers in their response to the FAC report, and say there was sufficient concern re abuse of intelligence to justify the story. Meeting with TB. He asked where it was going. I said Birt told us yesterday – a defeat for BBC. I put to him a plan to use this to isolate small parts of the BBC and the *Mail* as the real cancers in our media. 'How are we going to get back on to domestic politics?' TB asked. I said this was part of the answer. We had to change the media dynamic and this was part of it. Get back to honest public service broadcasting, etc. He was not totally against it.

I gave him a plan which I thought would help him get into a better place. One, we get through the FAC. Two, we brief that TB has asked AC to put together a new A team of fresh blood including a new policy head and a replacement for me before I work myself out of the job. Three, I leave but we say I will come back for the election in a different position. He seemed up for that. I said to him that I sometimes felt he hadn't really defended me properly and I had to do a lot of this myself. Yes, he said, and I've let you! He said 'You're motoring again, which is good.' I was clear though I was still going. He said he felt there were two problems with the media and GB, but they were better problems to have than a recession or a national crisis. Re the BBC, Peter M was asking me not to get too heavy with Greg Dyke. Rebekah Wade came to see me and said Murdoch had asked why the *Sun* wasn't doing the story properly. Research [and Information Unit] was going through the worldwide coverage of it all so that we could show just how far the original story had gone round the world. I had a meeting with David Omand. He said he was worried re Gilligan saying the source was clearly someone fairly high up.

Wednesday, July 2

The BBC row was lower in temperature. Then news came from Westminster of a very bloody meeting of the FAC yesterday, the Tories going very political, Richard Ottaway [Conservative MP] saying he wouldn't endorse anything that exonerates me, [Sir John] Stanley putting down lots of amendments and saying they may do a minority report. It was clear it was going to go line by line and was difficult. Also I didn't realise Ottaway had replaced [Sir] Patrick Cormack [Conservative MP] who was much more with us on this.

At the PMQs meeting, TB was clearly unhappy with our position on hunting. The PLP really wanted the ban, but TB didn't. It was tough though. Meeting with John Scarlett and Clare Sumner. John S had agreed with Jack S that Jack would send a note, also cleared by C, that made clear the intelligence for the second dossier was cleared. I argued strongly that it would also help if they said the attacks on me were an attack on their integrity too because it suggested they connived and colluded with me. John was worried, felt that really was him moving the JIC tanks out in front of me. John was being helpful but didn't want to be political support. Ditto C, who put his name in support of a Straw letter that introduced the thought that if the allegations persisted they were also aimed at the agencies. The MoD were putting out a letter of complaint re Gilligan claims that he had checked his story with the MoD press office. We were still on top but if the committee split on party lines it was going to be very difficult for us. This was taking up too much of my time.

PMQs was OK. IDS hopeless, [Charles] Kennedy did a bit on me – crap – and then back for a meeting of the Iraq Communications Group. The guy from the DIS was just back from Iraq and said things were getting worse not better. Gerard Russell [Islamic Media Unit, FCO] was really worried about the Arab media operation. I had a meeting with Gavin [Millar, QC, Fiona's brother]. He said the BBC had broadcast a libel but that I wasn't named at first. It was the *Mail on Sunday* that did the libel. I could sue the BBC for aggravated libel because of all the other media who supported the story. He felt I could go for Gilligan but though the BBC would not want to litigate he felt the *Mail on Sunday* probably would. He undertook to read all the papers, felt it would be OK but I had to be clear what I was getting into. They could mount a wider defence. On balance he felt probably don't do it, but the most important thing was to be cleared by the inquiry.

Meeting with Peter M. He was worried it would be really bad for TB/trust if I did not get vindicated. It was not going to be easy and everyone said it was getting tribal. I spoke to [Nicholas] Soames, who said he would defend me and attack the Tories for undermining the intelligence agencies. Peter M felt that we had to get some kind of deal with the BBC, but Gavyn Davies [BBC chairman] had gone into his shell and would do nothing to – allegedly – undermine BBC journalism! Peter M felt I had to get victory without humiliation for the BBC.

Thursday, July 3

The *Guardian* splashed on my memo to the FAC. They did it dead straight, quite helpful to me. Greg Pope [Labour MP, FAC member] decided to confess that he leaked it. I had no idea he was doing it. I thought it was a disaster but Hilary A and Bruce [Grocott] said it would be fine and not to worry. Soames had called me late last night to say he had run into C and asked him straight out if the story against me was true. C said no, and Soames said can I say so? Yes, said C. He was a bit pissed when he phoned and basically said he would do anything to help me, adding 'Especially if you stop TB using the Parliament Act on hunting.' He wanted to go on the media, called the *Today* programme and seemingly told them 'You are dozy, dishonest cunts and I am coming on your programme to say so.' He was, though, serious that he wanted to go on and make the point that this was an attack on the intelligence agencies as well as on me.

[Andrew] Marr did the interview and was now redefining the allegations as us having given 'undue prominence' to the 45-minute point. Total bollocks. C called me after the interview to say he was surprised Soames had gone public, that he thought he meant he was going to speak to Tory MPs on the committee. But he added 'Secretly, I'm pleased that I've been outed.' I said 'We will keep your pleasure secret, C.'

Then to a strategy meeting with TB, GB, JP, Douglas Alexander, Ian McCartney and David Triesman. TB said he would give the Cabinet next week a political sitrep and then have a polling and political discussion. JP said we needed a lot more than that, and there followed a positive and good discussion. JP's main point was that we didn't do enough to promote what we had done and talk about our values. The party felt itself on the defensive because that's how we came across to them. GB said we had to think forward to the election, the issues, big choices and values dividing lines, and then think back, then plan from here to then. He felt there was so much focus on reform that we were losing sight of values, that the messages were too technocratic. It was exactly what I had been saying. But TB was worried it was a bit of a JP/GB stitch-up to block some of the reforms. He said if we didn't have reform we would not be New Labour. We would look like we were running out of steam.

I said I still felt we could put together a clear single strategy based on the establishment of delivery, motivation of the party through values and dividing lines, then the next steps on future reform. What is the point of suddenly launching ID cards or LEAs [local education authorities] reform on an unsuspecting world? The ground work has to be about the values. GB made the point that the stuff running today on Lottery reform was fine, OK on its own, but not remotely strategic. Jonathan felt afterwards it was a hopeless meeting but I felt it gave us the right parameters of a better strategic approach.

Then Cabinet, during which I was only half listening because I was rewriting Pat McF's draft of TB's speech for tomorrow [in Liverpool, on public service reform], trying to reassert values and politics. I got a call from Hilary A around 12 to say the committee had agreed the report, with some amendments from [John] Maples [Conservative MP], but [Sir John] Stanley had been seen off. She felt it would be OK on the BBC issue, and that I could say that I was in the right, even if they didn't want to say that the BBC were in the wrong. So it felt fine and I felt we were back on top. But the BBC reporting then moved either on to the second dossier or whether the select committee system could be fair as it was run by the parties, etc.

Long chat with Peter M re strategy. He felt we should not reveal tactics, keep our powder dry and see what happened. The BBC was panicking according to everyone now. JP came to see me for about an hour, first re politics, saying TB had to stop dropping massive reforms on us that we hadn't had a chance to think through. He really felt we should get rid of some of his policy people. He also wanted to discuss the plan for him and Pauline [his wife] to come out with Pauline's child from way back.[1] He was a bit nervous but I assured him it was the right thing to do and agreed the plan he had worked up with his kids and Pauline.

TB called a couple of times from the North-West where he was doing a Granada TV special on the NHS. We were mulling over the debate on how to respond to the FAC. Jack S wanted to do a Commons statement, which I didn't think was very clever. I felt we had to get it all pinned on the BBC story and go for that and that meant it could be better that I did the media on the day. There was of course a worry that if I did it, the story would become me/spin rather than HMG.

Off to [broadcaster] David Frost's party, people generally supportive, including Frost. I avoided Dyke and Davies. I had a good chat with [General Sir] Mike Jackson who wanted me to kill Gilligan. At the Hillary Clinton book launch at the Orangery [Kensington Palace], Jim Naughtie [BBC *Today* programme presenter] was urging me not to do a big attack on the BBC generally, saying it was not the majority view that we were anti war, etc. I said I had a very good case in having a go at them. Chatted with Bill and Hillary Clinton a bit, both still very supportive. It was a nice enough evening but I was getting very down at Fiona's constant portrayal of me as having brought all these problems on myself. Peter M called to say BBC were trying to shift the terms of the story in all their reports and we had to lodge that.

Friday, July 4

Got Ben Bradshaw to do another letter to Sambrook pointing out how they were changing their story, and at the 11 Godric did the same, also pointing out that Hoon had been refused an appearance on the *Today* programme. I spoke to Robert Jackson [Conservative MP who later defected to Labour] who had called saying he wanted to help. We eventually agreed he would do an article for the *Sunday Telegraph*, getting out the line that I was not totally opposed to the BBC but to this strain of reporting that was anti politics and anti public life. I had a series of long chats through the day with TB and Jack re how

[1] At the age of sixteen, Pauline had given birth to a son. The boy, given up for adoption, had been identified as Lieutenant Colonel Timothy Paul Watton OBE.

to handle Monday. JS wanted a Commons statement. I said it was crazy because it put the onus on the Tories rather than us. I said we had to get it all on to the BBC/forty-five minutes.

I spoke to Hoon who said that a man had come forward who felt he was possibly Gilligan's source. He had come forward and was being interviewed today. GH said his initial instinct was to throw the book at him, but in fact there was a case for trying to get some kind of plea bargain – say that that he'd come forward and he was saying yes to speaking to Gilligan, yes he said intelligence went in late, but he never said the other stuff. It was double-edged but GH and I agreed it would fuck Gilligan if that was his source. He said he was an expert rather than a spy or full-time MoD official. GH and I agreed to talk tomorrow.

I was meanwhile doing my letters re BBC behaviour as well as a bit for TB. TB [public service reform] speech went OK but low-key. I was talking to TB, Peter M, Ben Bradshaw and later John Scarlett. We needed to work out our strategy for Monday. Godric said there was a case for us simply saying we had been cleared, the ball was now in the BBC court, and wait for their response before further action. Peter said we should be nice about the BBC and get ready to go for them on Monday. TB wanted closure. Peter M was being extremely helpful at the moment, and I was grateful that he was turning his mind to it. Ben Bradshaw ditto. Soames was in a bit of a panic after his interview and saying nobody must know that I helped him set it up, because I was such a bête noire for the Tory Party. Meeting on EMU, in which I was falling asleep the whole time.

Saturday, July 5

The BBC story seemed to be moving our way. The governors were to meet tomorrow to discuss it. The BBC started briefing aggressively that they would stand by their story and warn the governors it would be the end of BBC independence if they backed down. I spoke to TB and we agreed I should send a fairly emollient letter to the governors, and a file, to set out our side of the story vis-à-vis the BBC, and say it was not about attacking independence, or a broader attack, but dealing with one specific set of allegations.

Jack called a couple of times to say he felt he should do the bulk of Monday's media, and I should be low profile. I was not so sure. He later called to say the FAC was going to be in Rome on Monday, so no point in a Commons statement, but we had to work out a line. I agreed with Jack that it had to be about the BBC story because that was where the focus was. There was a case for saying nothing and going up to do discussion stuff, e.g. do we do a phone-in or discussion with BBC. Catherine Rimmer went into the office to put together the file for the governors. Meanwhile I was dealing with the car, which had been broken into, then took the boys to various sports events, then saw Gavin [Millar] again, who having read through everything felt I had an open-and-shut case for libel but that we should wait and see what the BBC said on Monday.

I was out running when Martin Sheehan [press officer] called to say the *Sunday Telegraph* were doing Dyke presenting new evidence to the governors to justify the story, the *Observer* saying that C met [John] Humphrys and [Kevin] Marsh [editor of *Today*] shortly before the *Today* programme story. I organised a conference call with C and a colleague of his. C said – and I knew this – that he met them a few weeks before this story, but when Humphrys recently said in his interview with John Reid that he had sources too, C's colleague got on to Humphrys to be assured he did not mean C. We agreed that they call the Press Association and BBC – or get the FCO to – and say they discussed nothing that would add to Gilligan's story and they should stop digging. It was a big So What. C agreed we should say it added nothing to the story. It looked like the last desperate throes, but it was possible the governors would go for it and back Dyke. C wanted to get Humphrys to deny the story.

I ran home, exhausted, and got the papers. They were pretty tricky. It was also still not clear whether the FAC would clear me or not, or had split on party lines. Alex F called from the women's final at Wimbledon, said he had been at the same table as Gavyn Davies, who seemed pretty out of sorts. Later I did a conference call with Tessa and Ben Bradshaw to go over their interviews tomorrow. Tessa called later to say she had really tried to speak to me but I never returned calls or messages. It was true that I was to a large extent trying to rely on my own resources.

Sunday, July 6

Ben Bradshaw did well on *GMTV*. I called Hillary Clinton before she did *Frost*, so that she had the full picture. TB's *Observer* words on the BBC and me were leading the news.[1] I spent much of the weekend

---

[1] In an interview, Blair had told the *Observer* 'The idea that I or anyone else in my position frankly would start altering intelligence evidence or saying to the intelligence services "I am going to insert this", is absurd. There couldn't be a more serious charge, that I ordered our troops into conflict on the basis of intelligence evidence that I falsified. You could not make a more serious charge against a prime minister. The charge happens to be wrong. I think everyone now accepts that that charge is wrong.'

talking to TB and Geoff H re the 'source', the man who felt he was the source because his colleagues said he sounded like what Gilligan was saying. He had come forward earlier in the week to confide that he'd seen Gilligan in a hotel, that he'd made some of these comments, but not others, for example about me. GH, like me, wanted to get it out that the source had broken cover to claim Gilligan had mis-represented him. TB and I had a long chat about it and TB was worried, felt that he or GH ought to tell the FAC about this. His worry was that it could lead to them reopening the inquiry. I wanted, as GH did, to get it to the BBC governors that we may know who the source was, that he was not a spy, not involved in the WMD dossier and was a WMD expert who advised departments. TB was fine about that but backed off after speaking to Omand, who felt the guy had to be treated properly and interviewed again. GH and I felt we were missing a trick.

I suggested to GH to speak to TB to try to persuade him we should do this and maybe GH should speak to Sambrook and tell him that he was a nobody re the dossier. GH said he was almost as steamed up as I was. TB said he didn't want to push the system too far. But my worry was that I wanted a clear win not a messy draw and if they presented it as a draw that was not good enough for us. We were getting the files to the BBC and when the governors arrived, the BBC put out a line that they never said we lied, so we hit back on that. Michael Howard on Sky said I was the most malevolent influence ever. TB felt that we should not push [MoD permanent secretary] Kevin Tebbit/David Omand too hard, and could maybe bring it out tomorrow if we needed it. TB was also feeling that we had to have something for the ISC to go for and that could be this. Jack – who'd spoken to Donald Anderson – said that the Tories had not supported the report so it was going to be split on party lines, and unclear and very messy.

As the governors met, it was clear we were heading for a bad day tomorrow. TB said we had to get it on to the issue of the UK media culture. 'It is a disgrace the BBC are behaving like this, it really is.' He said to me how are you feeling about it? I said fed up about the whole thing. He said don't be fed up. It's important and we have to keep to it. All this media stuff is really important and we had to stick to it. I was suddenly feeling stressed, exhausted, deflated. Tom Kelly was briefing and said the press were bored with the story. The problem was I'd felt we were going to win and it was going to be a messy draw at the FAC.

Source idea went nowhere as he had to be interviewed again by Martin Howard [deputy chief of Defence Intelligence], DIS and

Personnel. TB called to tell me not to worry. Martin Sheehan called after the BBC governors broke up and I listened to Gavyn Davies' statement. Dyke had got them on to the same line, defending the story, extending it to general issue of coverage. It was pretty poor, but clear they were all going along with the BBC line, if not defending the story. TB and I agreed the line that would put the focus on the claim that they never said we were lying, and we made clear what the central allegations still were.

Monday, July 7

There was a demo outside the house. I slept badly. Endless FAC blurb on the radio. I spoke to Peter M before going out, and did a good clip before getting into the cab. I felt it could go any way really. I was feeling a bit under siege, and very tired. Up to see TB. We were not clear what it was going to say, but he said we should make clear that we were not going for BBC independence, but they had to correct the story. TB's feeling was that we had to press ahead with it and be robust, but also look for a way out with the BBC. We met in my office – Jack, his officials, Clare Sumner, Godric, John S – to wait for the [FAC] document to arrive. A first reading seemed fine for me but less brilliant for the government as a whole re WMD. It was pretty clear-cut re me, but with Tory amendments. But even those did not support the BBC story. I did a quick skim read, some good, some bad.

Then round with Jack and John S to see TB who was meeting Kevin Tebbit, Omand and others re 'the source'. He was an ex-inspector, who advised the government, was aware of information going into the dossier but not involved in drawing it up. He'd once sat next to Jack as an expert at a select committee. Kevin said the guy claimed he never mentioned me. He was a bit of a show-off though. Felt that maybe Gilligan just put in the stuff about me. It was agreed he should be interviewed again, and then we should get it out that the source was not in the intelligence community, not involved in drawing up the dossier. Agreed we should be saying the source was misrepresented by Gilligan. TB was keen for Tebbit and Omand to be in control of the process. I watched the FAC press conference. Donald Anderson very clear re me. [Sir John] Stanley said I was a sideshow, Bill Olner and Gisela Stuart [Labour MPs and FAC members] were supportive. Tories and Andrew MacKinlay not too bad for me, and overall the impact was pretty positive.

TB said we have to be forensic about getting up the main points about the BBC allegations. Just before Jack [Straw] was due to go out in the street, John Stanley said the BBC was 'wrong' re the central allegations against me, so we put that into Jack's clip and he added that they must apologise. Sambrook was up defending the BBC, saying the report justified the decision to broadcast the story as the parties were split, etc. Everyone at our end said he came across as pathetic, but the problem was that the public probably believed them. TB was wanting to calm things down. For example, I wanted to do a discussion programme with Sambrook, but TB said do a letter instead. Then, when I did the letter, I got good advice from John Birt, who said claim victory and don't rejoice. He said the BBC would not apologise and therefore there was no point pushing it. I should be magnanimous. He said they look ridiculous, they can't answer the question if it's true or not. Birt said he knew what it was like to be on the receiving end of injustice, which is what this was, but you have to live with it. He said the biggest worry was where these wretched weapons were. TB rewrote my statement to be a bit more emollient. It was not strong enough for me or the team. Hours of coverage all day. I felt it was OK for me but others thought it was too muddy.

Several chats with MoD, Pam Teare [MoD director of news], then Geoff H re the source. I felt we should get it out through the papers, then have a line to respond and let TB take it on at the Liaison Committee. TB felt we had to leave it to Omand/Tebbit judgement and they didn't want to do it. We had to go for natural justice. GH said there was a problem that the source once gave evidence alongside Jack Straw. We were briefing that the BBC would eventually apologise. Wall to wall all day, source issue not moving. More calls for public inquiries. All went fine for me, but there were lots of difficult questions for the government as a whole. Jack was at home with food poisoning. Tessa good, Margaret B good on the media. The story was moving from me to WMD issue generally, on which not so good for us. TB was working up for the Liaison Committee tomorrow. I called my mum to tell her it was all going fine. She said she had not watched or listened to any of the news all day.

I was beginning to think I should say I'm going soon, maybe even this week. Source going better but not necessarily him. We were OK. John Scarlett was a bit worried that people felt I was running intelligence meetings. The agencies didn't come out great. Lots of unanswered questions. The problem for TB was the Iraq WMD were not found. GH wanted to get up the source, Tom and Godric felt it was best to wait until tomorrow, we had to do it right. The story on the FAC report was the whole of *The World at One*, ten to fifteen minutes on news, thirty minutes on *Newsnight* – Donald Anderson was strong.

The papers were disgraceful. Even for me, though cleared, they managed to muddy the waters, e.g. the *Telegraph* saying they would constantly call for my resignation. *Mail* vile, and left press not that great. It was even worse for TB, and of course the issue was moving quickly on to WMD rather than BBC. Up to see TB in the flat who was preparing for the Liaison Committee. He said the papers were unbelievable, 'It is truly Orwellian the world that we live in, I just don't know what to do with this constant rewriting of history and moving of goalposts.' Meeting with TB, JS, Scarlett, DM, etc. to go over the Liaison Committee. It was still not clear how we were going to handle the case of the MoD official.

Halfway through the TB evidence, I called Geoff Hoon. He was not remotely on top of the case. He said he had not checked out where we were on it. Also admitted he'd been crap on *Today* programme when asked who wrote the dossier and he hadn't seemed to know it was John Scarlett. Said he should get going on the source issue, TB clear that we should leave the bureaucracy to deal with it. Scarlett on good form as ever. TB off to the House, did pretty well. Gave no quarter on Iraq/WMD/kitchen Cabinet. He was a bit dozy on the issue of Europe, didn't push on the euro, OK on the reshuffle, overall a bit tired but OK. He came back and continued to try to sort the source issue. He met Scarlett and Omand and agreed to try to resolve it through a letter to Ann Taylor [ISC chair]. Word then came back she didn't want a letter on it. That meant do it as a press release.

Jonathan, AC, Tom and Godric, John S and Kevin Tebbit went to Godric's room and wrote a press release. Tebbit drafted a letter from GH to Gavyn Davies offering to give him the name of the source. Martin Howard had interviewed [Dr] David Kelly [government scientist and weapons expert], and was pretty convinced that he was the source, though of course we could not be sure. Tebbit took the draft away to the MoD and had to clear it with David Kelly, who was on a motorway. Then out by 6 and briefing mainly on the fact that the BBC put out a non-denial denial within two hours.

I told TB I still wanted to leave and why not now? Said he was really against it, it was the last thing he needed, and at the moment there would be meltdown in Parliament and that we should wait until Commons was not sitting. I said but I've only got two weeks left. Political strategy meeting with TB, GB, JP etc. PG presented the latest poll, which was bad. TB felt we had to get up delivery, get an acceptance of progress made. But he was tired and unfocused and GB's response was pretty brutal. He said we had no strategy to deal with the right-wing press, no clear plan for the election, no decision on election dividing lines. TB then asked him to circulate the strategy paper he had sent to TB, which he said he agreed with. GB said he wouldn't circulate it until he had the raw polling – to which he always had access anyway if he wanted it. It was one of those meetings in which whatever TB said, GB then said something slightly different. JP pitched in with a warning about putting too much new policy out there. It meandered on for about half an hour but got nowhere.

Wednesday, July 9

The BBC story was going away because they were refusing to take on the source idea. There was a big conspiracy at work really. The biggest thing needed was the source out. We agreed that we should not do it ourselves, so didn't, but later in the day the *FT*, *Guardian*, and after a while Mike Evans [defence corrrespondent of *The Times*] got the name. It was going to be difficult to keep it going and of course the politicians really wanted out of it. The story was moving away and as the source row grew, I felt I'd lost. Brendan Foster [former Olympic runner] came to see me, and he said TB was still the best there was. He said he would be amazed if I ever left the job until TB went because there couldn't be a better job and in many ways he was right.

TB went to the PLP and everyone said he did well. Then PMQs. I wanted him to turn the heat on the BBC but he wasn't really up for it and IDS and he ended up with some pretty vicious exchanges about WMD. Strategy meeting. Stan [Greenberg] went through the polling detail and though we were still ahead, it was a gloomy picture. Peter M, Philip and I put forward our tired responses and it all felt a bit jaded. TB felt WMD/Iraq was hurting him personally very badly and of course it was. Re GB, he said there was no point pretending that we would ever get back to being one big happy family, so we had to work around him as best we can.

By the time I got home, I felt really tired. Heat, pressure and stress, the problem of knowing when to leave, it was all pretty grim really. TB was not really engaging with me re my departure. Andy Marr led the news, massively ramped across all channels, with a story about senior sources saying we were unlikely ever to find WMD. It transpired the source was Jack Straw. JS apologised to me later saying he thought he was just chatting for background, not that Marr was going to do a big story. It was an outrage the way the BBC was now using its reporters and outlets to promote its line on the issue.

Marr WMD story still going big. [Robin] Cook on *Today*, John Major at 8.10. TB said the BBC coverage was actually a scandal. It was like dealing with the *Mail* on this, not the BBC. It was like Orwell's *Nineteen Eighty-Four* and all that. I got Ben Bradshaw on to TV re the WMD story saying this was a BBC diversionary tactic re the source. The FAC met and agreed publicly to call Dr Kelly [to the committee] and privately they were writing to Gilligan, so this was still moving in an uncertain direction. Geoff Hoon got a letter of apology from Sambrook about the claim they'd put the allegations to us.

Political Cabinet at 3. TB did an OK introduction but once Philip's polling was done they had what Douglas [Alexander] called 'a meeting of government by anecdote' designed to promote views we already knew they had. Alistair Darling on the Libs, Andrew Smith on local campaigning methods, Pat H on targets, DB wanting more ASBOs, Charles Clarke on green issues, Hain on the need at least to think about tax. Not a good discussion. JR was the only one who really said anything worth taking on board. GH also spoke quite well, echoing John in the line that we needed to keep on with reform as a way of holding the middle ground but do it according to our values. GB was not as impressive as usual, started well with his line about working back from the election, then seemed to run out of steam a bit. JP was very passionate, defended TB saying that he alone must not take the blame for Iraq, because it was a decision we all took and we all had to stand by it.

TB spoke better summing up and he was very open about the conundrum – that we needed reform to make change but the individual changes could always be unpopular till they got through and made an impact. It was a tired Cabinet and a tired meeting and we were going to have to raise our game. TB looked tired. Both JP and GB had big bags under their eyes. There was no real drive or energy in there. TB felt the coming fight would be a very traditional left/ right one. Asylum, immigration, Europe, tax and spend. We have to get to acceptance of a minimum basis of delivery. But we have to show we have the only viable long-term strategy for the future. We must not concede the intellectual and political dominance we have in the political debate. But the values must be clearer. On the issue of trust, WMD – lack of – is obviously a problem. But trust is best addressed by reconnecting with people on the issues they really feel strongly about – crime, antisocial behaviour, health, education. It is through the values that we get the dividing lines and through detailed policy that we highlight them.

Charles C agreed with the analysis, but said the party as a family feels ill at ease with us and we have to make the party feel more involved. Alistair Darling was on his usual worry re the Libs, said he would relish a traditional left/right fight but we needed to be clear about how to handle the Lib Dems within that. In Scotland tactical voting was now common. We must not underestimate the Lib Dem threat in some areas. The argument has to be that they are not risk-free. Jack S felt the position was more difficult than PG's polling suggested. He felt we were kidding ourselves if we thought trust was just policy-based. We are delivering a huge amount of what we promised, but a lot of people don't like us. Part of the problem was that too often we defined ourselves against the party. We alienated our own people. We sometimes win the vote without being clear about winning the argument. He said he was all in favour of being at our best when at our boldest, but there was no point picking fights for the sake of it. Jack was being pretty tricksy at the moment and TB was very deliberately raising his eyebrows and making sure people clocked his reaction. Andrew Smith said people on the [social housing] estates felt we were pursuing Middle England at their expense. Pat H said values not management were the key. It goes deeper than the language we use. All people hear is targets, efficiency, all fine but limited. They need to hear values. Talking about users of public services like they were customers was also alienating. There were too many confusing initiatives, too many targets, not enough willingness to listen and engage. GH was clearly worried about the general drift. He said it would be a disaster if we in any way abandoned the middle ground. Both the traditional working class and the middle classes are better off and 'I'm worried that if we listen too closely to party and unions, we get pushed to making a false choice.' TB nodding.

Bruce [Grocott] said the party was not so much rebellious as moribund and he felt that was worrying. Peter Hain – music to my ears – said we had to generate a bigger debate about the future of politics and the dire impact of the modern media. Hilary A was cogent and intelligent as ever. She said to TB 'You warned the PLP that division was the death of all previous Labour governments. But you have to realise they feel the only way they get listened to is by being difficult, including voting against the government.' She was worried it was becoming habit-forming. She said to be fair TB spent a lot of time every week talking to backbenchers and he is the busiest of all of them. Yet a lot of ministers just don't bother.

There was a coffee break and TB was not terribly happy at the general tone and tenor, felt they were all conceding too much and also in some cases coming up with the wrong answers. JR spoke first, and said though TB 'took the trust issue on your own shoulders' it was about all of us and they had to do more as a group to address it. He spoke well, if for too long, about the need for themes rather than policy initiatives to drive our politics. He felt the strategic audit should force us to agree the overall priorities, and we should not just be fighting our own departmental corners. He also said we should not get too despondent. We were six years into government with a massive poll lead. We had made mistakes but we were basically seen as competent and delivering. Nor should we be amazed at the forces ranged against us – the right-wing media hate us because we're in power. The ultra left hate us because we're moderate and sensible. Sacked ministers have their own grievances. We have to build the alliances to defeat them in argument.

GB agreed, said it was an amazing success story that we had stayed dominant for six years. We know how we did it and we have to carry on with the same rigour and discipline. He felt the Tories were following a Bush strategy – try to shut down debate on the traditional right-wing issues. Try to get people to forget the Tory past. Try to get the economy taken for granted. They want to spread disillusion in public services and then move to tax cuts and privatisation. He felt we had to work back from the next election, agree the themes and dividing lines and then plan back. He felt on the economy it should be stability and enterprise. We need a strong public services dividing line. Another on the nature of progressive change. Families. The state of Britain and national identity.

JP did his usual speaking up for TB. Through some of the contributions TB had been drumming his fingers. JP seemed pretty irritated too, maybe not because of the content but the lack of balls being shown by a fair few of them. He said TB had 'done a very noble thing' in accepting responsibility for the trust issue. But it was not just his problem. Trust was the responsibility of the whole Cabinet. He felt Iraq would, long term, be seen to be the right thing to do. 300,000 people in mass graves – never let people forget it. He said in the PLP we had nearly fifty people there permanently trying to poison fifty more, plus they could always call on the Lords, lots of our own people included, to damage us. We had ex-ministers feeding it all the time. We have to fight back harder, get into the kind of mode we're in for elections. It was good rousing stuff and lifted the mood.

TB said he had listened carefully. He said that being in government did not fit easily with the party's culture, which prefers to campaign than to govern. We have done a lot but we are not the government of the party's dreams. No government ever will be. But they need to know if we divide, if we go back to the ways of the past, we will be out again. Also if we lose the capacity for renewal, we will go out. New Labour is not a finite thing. It means a Labour Party constantly renewing to meet the challenges of a world of change. He said '97 to '01 was all about establishing credibility to govern. We did some terrific things – but a national minimum wage does not transform the country. We did the basics well. But in a second term we are challenged more. The country and the party want more. But in meeting the party's demands we must not yield up the middle ground because that is where the country is. It is not just about what Middle England wants, but the challenges of today are best met in the middle ground. There are some policy solutions that neither party nor government will like. But we have to do what we think is right for the long term.

He said the unspoken message from some – and he was looking at GB – was to go easy on reform because it would anger people. GB said 'I'm not saying that,' but TB ploughed on – 'There is no division in my mind between the need to reform and staying true to our values. It is not inconsistent. We are being true to our values in making the reforms needed to improve life for the people we represent.' He said he wanted people to think over the summer about how that applied to their departments. Think long term. We could avoid a bit of political pain by opting out of difficult policy decisions. But it would be a mistake for the long term. I was left thinking he was the only one there who could speak like that. JP had warmed it up well but the bulk of the contributions had been either tired or timid and distinctly lacking in leadership.

Douglas [Alexander] was good on the new politics. If he didn't look so boyish, he would make so much more of an impact because he talked a lot of sense. But listening to them, I did feel that a lot of our problems about lack of strategic capacity were caused by the fact that for a while now I had not been fully engaged. Also on policy, as Bruce G pointed out, most of the good things we had done were from the first term. Dan Bartlett called me later from Air Force One, said his sense was we were winning.

Friday, July 11

Still a lot of focus on Iraq and intelligence and whether it was poor, or wrong. Fiona and I went to the unveiling by [Nelson] Mandela [former President of South Africa] of a blue plaque at [South African politician] Joe Slovo's old house in Lime Street in Camden. The Milibands were there and I had a nice chat with Ed about how much he enjoyed his time out in America. I shared a car with him to the office and he agreed there was very little direction and strategy.

To the Ritz where I was having lunch with Clinton, with Peter M and Philip. Mary McCartney [photographer] was taking some pictures. BC had had just two hours' sleep after getting in from Greece. He was dressed in golf-type clothes. He was a lot thinner than the last time I had seen him. Doug Band [Clinton aide] had organised lunch, which seemed to be a succession of different meals, and Clinton was eating a lot of them. First a plate of eggs, then bacon, then hamburgers. First we talked about Bush. We talked a bit about the US scene. I asked why he never stayed in embassies when he travelled. He said Bush had some mean people round him. 'I could, but I'm not sure about the welcome.' He said he was not much for having things named after him but there had been a Clinton Fellowship for Israeli and Palestinian students and at first the Bush administration changed the name and then they took away the money. 'These are ruthless people you are dealing with.' On Marc Rich [indicted in 1983 for illegal oil deals with Iran and tax evasion] and the controversial pardon [by Clinton on his last day in office], he said that Cheney's chief of staff [Lewis 'Scooter' Libby] had testified for the guy. 'You have to understand that what they care about is power. They control the press, they control the agenda and they hoard power ruthlessly.' They were changing the law to allow the White House to be more secretive. He said the view in DC was Bush had put all his [Texas] governor papers into his father's presidential library because that meant they couldn't be got at.

He said Bush liked TB because he stayed with him but if somebody came along they thought would help them more, they would go for them. He was speaking very slowly, calmly, matter-of-factly, probably conscious that we were on the lookout for signs of bitterness, but there was precious little of that and it was pretty compelling. He felt Bush had lost an election and having 'won' it he was now behaving as if he had walked it. But they were clever, and so was Bush. He was good at dealing with opponents. I asked him what Bush would do with the BBC. 'If he could kill the governors, he would. But he can't, so he would do a deal.'

On Iraq, he said the Bush lot had never been keen on Blix. He said Powell was the one who really wanted to let the inspectors work, and now it was looking bad for them, but because they still had control of the media, Bush was not yet under pressure. September 11 had changed the American people's psychology. Bush understood that and the Democrats had not worked out how to respond, how to fight it. He was angry about Bush, philosophical about the campaign [Al] Gore fought, hopeful for Hillary.

Peter M had to leave to do an interview. Philip, BC and I went over to the sofas and out poured something of a masterclass in political strategy. He followed our politics closely, and I asked him what his remedy would be for our problems. He said he was touched that we trusted him so much that we could openly lay out the problems we had. He said first, you have a weak Opposition. Keep them weak by coming up with the forward policy positions and push them where you want them. Second, TB is about as good as they get. Keep reminding everyone of that. Third, on the press, he said you need a strategy to get back credibility. He said he'd followed my troubles and was sympathetic. He said that I'd always been the number two target after TB and that I'd taken a lot. I'd been right to fight for myself and I did a great job, but now move on. Don't keep digging the hole. Let others do it. Go back to the media and say I didn't lie, but maybe I missed something. I always strove to tell the truth but I've thought deeply about it all. I've got a job to do and so have you, and it's best if we can do it without regarding each other as subhuman. He said the problem was they felt it was a pattern of behaviour – manipulation and bullying – and that I had to show them I was real again. He said they don't like me in part because I was one of them and now I'm not.

Next, a strategy for the PLP. Understand their lives and reach out to them. They have shitty lives. You guys go to DC. You have real power. They get a weekend in their constituency. Give them some romance. They think you guys have gone Hollywood and they want more local. It's about their psychology. It's the same with the press. Some you will never win but others you will if you are nice to them, involve them. Your MPs know TB is better than them but that doesn't mean they are nothing. Fifth, you have to reconnect. People are falling out of love with Tony because they think he has fallen out of love with them. He's a statesman and that's great but their world is here and now and they are paying him to sort out their world, here and now. They know he has to do this other stuff but they want to know he cares about them, here and now. Sixth, the Third Way is fine, but it has to be a third way with liberal values. Don't just push a reform message. He has to have good old-fashioned left causes too, for the poor, whatever. It's about values not reform.

It was the same argument I had been having with TB. I said so, and he said yes, but maybe he thinks you are just beating up on him. It's all about balance. He has to balance the Third Way message for his new coalition with the liberal message for the party. You have to balance frank advice with real support. On TB himself, he said he had to rediscover his joy in politics. He needed new stimuli without throwing everything out. He had to keep change with continuity. He came to the point about me not beating up on Tony. He could see for example why I thought Carole [Caplin] was a problem, but other people's emotions and psychology are not always the same. 'My brother was a cocaine addict and the word to remember for addicts is HALT. Yes, it means stop. But it also means I'm Hungry, I'm Angry, Lonely and Tired. You usually find the reason in one of those.' Clearly talking now about Monica Lewinsky [White House intern with whom he had had an affair], he said 'I wasn't hungry but I was angry, lonely and tired. I was being beaten up by everyone. Ken Starr [Independent Counsel, prosecutor] was trying to put me in jail. Friends were leaving me and enemies were killing me. Hillary was angry with me. This ball of fire came at me as I felt H, A, L, T.'

He said he sometimes thought Tony wanted a blue ribbon and a gold badge for the work he does, 'but the ribbon and the badge are the JOB. It's a privilege. It's a great job he's got and yes it's tough but who says it shouldn't be? Get his juices flowing again.' So he summed up. Keep the Tories weak. Get back credibility with the press, remembering that you are the best and that's why they judge you so harshly. It's the same with Tony. You've got to show you're real. Get your troops back in shape by loving them a bit. Reconnect with the public by showing it's about them. Get TB to rediscover his joy in politics. He told a story about the first woman he ever loved, how he left her and drove her into the arms of a friend and she ended up hating both of them and it always bugged him. Years later when he was president he made contact with her and they talked it over, and he felt happy that he had resolved an important thread in his life. Another story about a friend he fell out with but then when he became president they rediscovered that friendship. So keep your friends, get some joy back into your politics, get a left liberal cause.

Philip then asked him what he thought I should do, whether he thought I should leave the job. Again, he was terrific on the analysis. A long pause, then said these are the factors: 1. Is it hurting you more than you're getting out of it, especially for Fiona and the family? 2. Is it hurting Tony more than you are putting in? 3. Can anyone else do it? 4. If you stay can you deliver a new strategy? Only you know, but remember it's a great job and I don't like to think what could have happened if you had not been there. He also thought in some ways Fiona would blame herself for having let Carole take Cherie over, but she shouldn't. Really warm and friendly. He took me to the door and said 'Hang in. There are three centres of power in your politics. You guys, the Tories, the press. You have an affirmative programme. The others don't. Their job is to stop you doing your job. Don't let them. Raise your eyes above them, and stay with it.'

As we left, both Philip and I observed that he was about as near to being a political strategic genius as we knew. Philip asked if it made me want to stay and it did but I wondered if TB was up for the change needed. I told TB later what Bill's analysis had been and he agreed with most of it, apart from some of the liberal stuff. We finished the [Third Way conference] speech and then headed for the Metropole [hotel]. Lynn Forester [Lady de Rothschild] told me she had been at a dinner recently where C had really stuck up for me during a row with Lord Carrington [former Conservative Foreign Secretary]. Bill C said he had really enjoyed our lunch, hoped he had helped, but on my own situation, he said only I could know.

TB's speech was OK without being brilliant. He told a very funny story about an early experience canvassing and asking a woman in Hackney what she thought about getting rid of nuclear weapons and she said 'I don't have nuclear weapons, I have rats and I want to get rid of them first.' Bill gave a terrific speech, very hard on the Republicans, strong on why our values were right for today and said that we had to fight the resurgent right. Think. Feel. Fight. We had to understand that there was indeed a Fourth Way, namely aggressive conservatism. These people want real change and we should be the ones resisting it, winning the argument for our own agenda for change. They want more power for people at the top. They want America and her allies to dominate everything. He told about how they ran smears against people who even asked questions of e.g. their policy in Afghanistan. He said the Third Way worked and we had to stick with it and fight for it.

It was a really good speech, easily the best I had heard for a while. I don't know why TB was so reluctant at the moment to do the values. I loved Bill's line about the Fourth Way. He was also very funny in parts, like when he told of how he had to cut into a meeting with [Viktor] Chernomyrdin [former Prime Minister of Russia] on nuclear arms control because Turkey and Greece were about to go to war over an island with 200 sheep on it. In the car later, TB said he agreed with Bill's analysis in many ways and on some of it we should act. Re me, and the four questions BC had posed, TB said three answered themselves. He said his one worry was about whether he could get a real replacement.

Saturday, July 12

The *Guardian* ran a piece on the front about me maybe leaving. There was also a lot of coverage on the theme that TB's position was becoming perilous. Clare Short did a pre-record for *GMTV* saying TB should go. There was a lot of noise from the unions digging away at the Third Way conference. We also had the bizarre resignation of Michael Wills, who resigned in interviews without actually telling TB or anyone at Number 10.[1] The BBC row was weakening but would come back on Tuesday with the FAC.

Sunday, July 13

TB called a couple of times. He had spent a fair bit of time with Bill C who had given him pretty much the same analysis.

Monday, July 14

WMD was still going big. The BBC were operating a news blackout on the source issue. The *Scotsman* had a page 1 story about GB preparing to take over. The drums were definitely beating. GB was getting marked up the whole time, and TB marked down. GB was making clear he wanted to visit Murdoch in the States during the holiday. TB press conference in Surrey went OK, but it showed up further evidence of the BBC simply driving their own agenda. They cut away from initial questions and instead ran a commentary alongside saying all the UK media was interested in was WMD/Iraq. Guto Harri [BBC] was claiming that TB didn't answer the question about whether he backed the intelligence. He did. I got John Sawers to call Trevor Kavanagh who was doing a two-page spread on Iraq being better than everyone says.

TB came back, and had a meeting with John Scarlett, DM, Clare Sumner, Jonathan re his upcoming session with the ISC. Then to the den to discuss what TB would say at the reception for [former Labour leader] Michael Foot's ninetieth birthday. I said to him that I felt he needed at some point to make clear what his plans were for himself in the future because people were making assumptions about him going, and were therefore starting to peel off and take licence. Michael Foot arrived around 6 and although physically he wasn't in great shape, mentally he was all there, and determined to have a good time. Speeches were fine. I had an interesting chat with John Cole [former

---

[1] Wills resigned as a junior minister (for information technology in the criminal justice system), vowing to campaign for the abolition of the EU Common Agricultural Policy. He claimed every UK family paid £70 per year to support Europe's cattle.

July '03: BBC news blackout on source issue

BBC political editor] about the BBC. He felt BBC journalism was not in good shape, but didn't really want to get involved.

Tuesday, July 15

Ran in, forty-five minutes. We were looking forward to [David] Kelly giving evidence to the FAC, but Godric, Catherine Rimmer and I all predicted it would be a disaster and so it proved. Despite MoD assurances he was well schooled, a mix of the MPs' malice – Tory – and uselessness – our people – was going to give us a bit of a headache. By the end of the day, we were down as usual. I tried to have another discussion re a successor with TB. We had both spoken to David Hill again and it was clear he would come. There was a slight problem in that a lot of people were urging me to stay, but I had pretty much decided. Gerard Russell showed me a two-page spread on me in an Arab newspaper. There was even stuff in the press today about my haircut, so it was getting more not less ridiculous.

There was a good atmosphere at the office summer garden party, where I played the bagpipes on the balcony, much to the amusement of GB and the people he was entertaining at Number 11, including John Edmonds [GMB general secretary]. The FAC, despite a big row on the committee today, were saying that Kelly was probably not the source, thereby spectacularly missing the point. I had an hour or so with John Scarlett and Clare Sumner to go over ISC inquiry issues. TB did it this morning and all was fine, but Clare was a bit worried because TB said that he wrote the foreword [to the dossier] when in fact I did the draft.

Wednesday, July 16

I got a cab in and the driver had also done the marathon, so we chatted away about that. We thought the Tories would do a mix of FAC and NHS and TB/trust at PMQs but when it came to it IDS went for me, as did one of their backbenchers. IDS quoted the *Mail on Sunday* made-up story of me saying TB couldn't cope without me. I bumped into Rod Gilchrist [deputy editor, *Mail on Sunday*] at a party for Michael [Foot] later, and thoroughly enjoyed telling him he was scum.[1]

TB was pretty down today. PG, Sally, Pat McF, Peter M and I had

---

[1] The next Sunday, Gilchrist wrote of the encounter: 'Campbell, his newly cropped convict haircut – which gives him all the charm of Magwitch – on public display for the first time, thrust his face within an inch of mine and declared: "You're scum." I said I wasn't, but why did he think I was? His response came quickly. "And your paper's scum, too."'

a long meeting specifically to discuss TB and how to get him back in shape. We were all a bit tired and the whole operation needed a blood transfusion, new energy. I did a note based on the discussion and later saw TB in the flat. It was ragingly hot. He looked a bit ridiculous in a sleeveless grey vest, matching shorts and flip-flops with 'Bermuda' emblazoned on them. Unlike me, though, he loved the heat.

PMQs had been fine, but he agreed the whole operation was a bit tired. He felt on policy, on media strategy, and on systems for reaching out to the party, we had to improve. GB was motoring in the party and there was a danger that we were leaving the field to him. We had a pretty tired meeting with Ian McCartney and the party people. We went round in circles. We were pressing TB to focus more on progressive causes, but he felt he really had to be the one constantly emphasising the hard edge of New Labour.

I had a long chat with Dan B who said Bush was finally taking a bit of a hit on Iraq. He had picked up on the fact that the Tories were calling for my head and said Bush was unimpressed at the way the Tories had behaved. At Michael's ninetieth at the Gay Hussar, which Fiona had pretty much organised, there were a lot of the Old Labour people urging me to stay. Bostock [AC's GP] had said earlier he was worried I would crack up again if I suddenly went from all-out activity to doing nothing.

Thursday, July 17

In for a meeting with Clare Sumner and John Scarlett, before my ISC appearance. Clare discovered that I'd said to the FAC that I did see JIC assessments so we had to agree a line on that. John was concerned I had to make clear that I was not chairing intelligence meetings. I was due to give evidence from 8.30 to 9.45. I went over with Clare and Catherine Rimmer. I went in with Ann Taylor [chair], who joked that I had two minders, whereas TB had only had one. It was more relaxed than the FAC. I got them laughing telling them the story about how John Sergeant didn't want the PM to come down the plane to see the press because he was watching a film.

Michael Mates [Conservative MP] was very friendly, made a joke about a bet we once had and also said he had no doubt I did not put the 45-minute point in the dossier and he hoped the committee would say so. Gavin Strang [Labour MP] was interested in whether we should use intelligence publicly at all. Ditto others, but I felt it went OK. Mates put to me that C had said that no intelligence should be used with other material but I was not aware of that and said so as it didn't accord with my memory. It was over in just an hour. The clerk asked me via Ann T if I thought Gilligan should go to jail. I said don't get me going.

We then left for the airport, and on the plane [to America], TB was working on his speech [to Congress, where he was being awarded the Congressional Gold Medal]. He was very keen for it to be a pro-US as well as pro-EU speech. We didn't bother seeing the press on the way out. We flew over Guantanamo Bay, and agreed it was best to play it low profile but argue for change. The speech was strong and between us we made it stronger.

Cherie was in friendlier than usual form but meanwhile back home John Burton [Blair's constituency agent] had got a tip that 'enemies of CB' were going to meet at the Hilton Olympia in Kensington, and Fiona asked Mark Bennett [Labour press officer] to check it out covertly. It turned out to be a meeting in the bar between Ian Monk [PR] and Paul Dacre. Mark somehow got close enough to hear them, make notes and he reported back a lot of detail re their discussion about Carole [Caplin]. I did a note to TB which also included the fact that Monk sent a statement to PA re Cherie's clothes in Washington. I felt bad that I was going to be leaving him when things were getting tougher not easier. Also GB was really motoring now.

We landed and straight away I had a rash of messages re Gilligan's evidence to the FAC. Basically Donald Anderson went out with John Stanley and Andrew MacKinlay and then said that Gilligan was an unsatisfactory witness, that he had changed his story re me, and there was a danger of unfairness to me. So we were pretty happy about that. We had a discussion about whether I should say something. Godric and I thought maybe but TB felt it was better that I stay out. We went up to Congress, where we had a discussion and then a conference call about it. It was clearly the best news we'd had for ages, and Tom K in London said it was running very much for us and against Gilligan and I should stay out. TB got an amazing reception at Congress. It was interesting to watch which parts of the speech went down particularly well with Democrats, and which with Republicans. It was a good speech though. Our press were obsessing about his line 'if we are wrong' re the WMD/terrorism link, and saying it was moving the goalposts.[1]

Then up to the White House. As we walked into the Oval Office, Bush was very friendly, said 'Hey, congratulations, you took on the

[1] Blair said, 'Can we be sure that terrorism and weapons of mass destruction will join together? Let us say one thing: if we are wrong, we will have destroyed a threat that at its least is responsible for inhuman carnage and suffering. That is something I am confident history will forgive.'

bastards, and you did great.' He said he had seen some of my testimony and that Dan [Bartlett] had kept him informed. 'You did great. You showed that if you are in the right, if you believe it, and you give no quarter, you can prevail.' He kept coming back to it during the meeting, almost embarrassingly so. Cheney was as impassive as ever, [Colin] Powell was chirpy but looking tired, while Condi was more subdued than usual. At the press conference Adam Boulton gave TB a full toss on the BBC but TB didn't really hit it to the boundary.

We went out for a drink on the balcony overlooking the lawns. The mood was pretty relaxed. They did a bit of substance on Iraq, but not much. They agreed that [Paul] Bremer needed a lot more help. On the [Guantanamo] detainees, Bush said his big worry was that one day one of them got out and killed someone. TB at one point asked him about Libya and it was clear from the answer that Bush thought he meant Liberia. GWB was now smoking a massive cigar and producing huge amounts of smoke. I was also struck by his shoes, which looked phenomenally expensive. At the dinner, I was seated between Powell and Dan. Apart from a fairly interesting discussion on Africa, it was mainly small talk. I had enjoyed the trip, but was also glad that I was now heading home rather than going on with TB to the Far East. I headed to the airport with Sally and Alison, who had a selection of very good cuttings about Gilligan from the first editions. There was a Tory MEP at the airport who said he was proud to be British listening to TB's speech to Congress.

Friday, July 18

We landed at Heathrow about 9am, and we sat there for ages. I turned on the phone, and got a message from media monitoring that Kelly had disappeared. Then a message to call the Number 10 duty clerk, very urgent. I was told Kelly had gone for a walk yesterday and his wife [Janice] had reported him missing this morning. I felt sick. I called Tom. It took ages to get off the plane and when we did I felt dreadful. I told Sally and Alison, who were both shocked. I could sense a juggernaut moving my way. Terry [Rayner, Number 10 driver] drove me home. I spoke to Hoon who said [Kevin] Tebbit would handle it initially but he would go up on the media if needed. He said he felt it had to be properly handled from the start. I then spoke to JP in Cyprus. He said he felt he should come back, and I was grateful. In part it was about himself. He said he was worried that with TB out of the country, they'd come looking for him on a beach, and he also said he could be back to steady things. He felt GH and

JS were a bit too close to it all and I should stay out of it. I said what will Pauline think about it, and he said don't worry, I'll sort it.

Then Tom told me that a body had been found. This was getting more and more grim. Tom did the eleven o'clock. Then TB came on from the plane. I said I'd really had enough. He said we should announce a judicial inquiry now. I said I really wanted to go and felt I should do it now. I had been determined to clear my name, I was always going to go now, it may not seem the time to do it, but it's exactly the time to do it because I was clear it had all gone too far and we needed to step back and think. Philip came round to the house and was in two minds. He felt wait until tomorrow. TB said it would be a disaster for me if I did that. Charlie Falconer [Lord Chancellor], who called me re the inquiry, said I would be mad to do it. All people would remember is Dr Kelly killed himself and AC went. They would not hear your arguments and they'd think you were making it about you. TB called a couple of times and said we have to be really strong about this. I said I'm fed up being strong, I want to get a life back. There was a mass of photographers outside by now.

I called Neil [Kinnock] who clearly didn't know about Kelly and was telling me that Gilligan was done for. I told him re Kelly and he said Jesus H. Christ. I said what to do. He said hold tight, be strong and don't let the bastards take you as a scalp. He said he would support me whatever but felt I had to do that. Peter M came on, said I must not go, now or in the future, because that was what they all wanted. You must hang in. John Scarlett called and we had a long chat about the whole thing. He was very supportive, said that even though he'd had a bit of flak, he felt fine. Charlie F said I'd be mad if I quit, Peter M said I'd regret it, TB thought it would be really bad for me, Godric that it would look like my fault.

Jonathan called from the US, said he felt physically sick, and should he come back to help? I said no, he said don't do anything rash. Rebekah [Wade] sent me a nice message, you've done nothing wrong, told the truth, more principles than these other people. Just hang in and don't give them the satisfaction. Piers [Morgan] was not totally unsympathetic but felt there was no escape for me or for Tony. He felt the mood had just turned, and people would keep going on it. I was the story and that was that even though it was unfair. Fiona was desperate for me to go. So was I now. But I wanted some honour and dignity. Things quietened down but then I wept because of the pressures I was under, and the sadness I felt for Kelly's family. JP called after his return and said he would be around to help if needed. The rolling news was relentless and really grim. Everyone feeling grim about it all. I said to journalists who got through on the phone that I was shocked and felt dreadful, it was about our media culture, but I had done nothing wrong.

Saturday, July 19

The papers, as expected, were totally grim, the *Mail* needless to say the worst, pictures of TB, Hoon and me and 'Proud Of Yourselves?' Lots re me and suggestions that I would get the blame. The *Mail* was disgusting, the *Telegraph* less so. The only person who came out well was Kelly. There was not nearly enough directed towards the BBC. Cameras started gathering outside at 6 and by 9 there were four or five film crews and a dozen or so photographers. We had to go through the elaborate charade of getting the kids and Fiona out first and then being driven to meet them. I got Mel [Cooke, a neighbour] to drive me away, and she said she had always had a fantasy about being a getaway driver. The mood of the hacks was reasonably sombre but they still asked if I planned to resign, and later that cunt Jonathan Oliver [*Mail on Sunday* reporter] asked TB if he had blood on his hands.

During the day, lots of people called with messages of support. John Reid, who said his secretary was really angry and hang in. Kim Howells – don't let the bastards get you down, because lots of our people love you. Margaret Beckett said she was really angry the media could blame me when this was about the media. Blunkett – solidarity and support. Bruce Grocott of course, Syd Young [former *Mirror* journalist], Richard Stott, [Roy] Greenslade [both former *Mirror* editors] who all said this was about the curse of modern journalism.

But the most important conversation was with JP. He'd come back yesterday and did a little doorstep at the Policy Forum. I asked him what he thought I should do. He said I hope you stay because you're a vital part of the team and I think TB still needs you. But everyone will be giving you advice because of what THEY want, not what's best for you. You've been under massive pressure for years, paid a big price and so has Fiona, who has lost her sparkle. I've noticed you've been a bit detached and so has she and you should do what you think is right for you. I asked if he thought I could go before the inquiries were completed and he said no. But then as with David Mills [husband of Tessa Jowell], he came round to it being possible. Everyone I spoke to felt I was in the right, but maybe that was because of the kind of people who phoned me. JP and I also discussed TB/

July '03: TB asked if he has blood on his hands

GB and he said it was bad on both sides. He was pissed off that TB wanted Douglas and Hazel Blears on the NEC rather than GB. TB had complained GB had not even discussed it with him, but JP felt they were as bad as each other. TB did the press conference in Tokyo and looked dreadful.

Clive Hollick [Labour peer and media businessman] called me, said he'd been to a BBC do last night and they were all very bullish, behaving arrogantly like it was their duty to bring down the government. He said Dyke was defensive and non-apologetic, but did say they were thinking of making clear Gilligan's only source was Kelly, and they wanted to know what we would do about it. I said we would not make any comment, and TB later said we must not cause them any mischief. TB was looking haggard and unshaven as they arrived in Japan.

The body was formally identified, Clare Sumner was checking out what kind of an inquiry it would be. She spoke to the secretary [to the Hutton Inquiry, Lee Hughes] who said it would be MoD people first, then the BBC. I said it was important we send them our side of the story and try to get the facts clear early. I was feeling very down by now. Much of the press gunned at me. Brendan Foster called and said he felt TB should do more, be more human and emotional, make clear nobody wanted this to happen. He told me the story of a journalist who killed himself, and at the time a colleague got the blame but in fact it turned out the guy's wife had left him with their four children. He said the point is that people who kill themselves are disturbed, and they say things in suicide notes and final conversations that can haunt other people forever. He felt strongly that I should not do anything rash and hang in for now.

Philip said Peter M was spooked about me going because of something GB said to him once, namely that TB was a weak person with two strong people – me and Peter – propping him up. He felt that once we were gone, TB was gone too. The Kelly family issued a statement which basically said everyone should think deeply about the fact his life had been made intolerable. This would obviously be a hard time. TB called. It was 5am there. He said he couldn't sleep, he felt grim and was about to do an interview with [Adam] Boulton, which he didn't want to do. He said I had to stay and we had to fight this through.

Sunday, July 20

I didn't read the papers but by all accounts they were pretty grim. The main focus was on the Kelly family statement, alongside lots of commentary about us, very little of it nice. I went for a run and felt myself moving towards saying something about it. I went through my argument and the various scenarios. I had a long chat with JP. He said he was glad he came back, said he'd thought about my position. He felt I'd done my bit for TB and the government and should be allowed to decide the next part for myself. I said maybe long term it was the right thing for Tony because he'd be able to reorder things for the future. JP said you've obviously decided to go. I think you deserve to do what you want. We discussed the call from Clare Sumner a few moments earlier that the BBC were about to make a statement that Kelly was the source. JP agreed I had a window and should seize it and go for it if I felt it was the right thing to do. The BBC statement went out. Sky really going for the BBC, but the BBC's own coverage was like *Pravda*.

I spoke to Godric on the flight from Korea to China to tell him I wanted to make clear publicly that I was going to go very soon, say that it was agreed with TB ages ago, and the family had had enough. I said to GS that I would quite like to do it tomorrow, with the BBC on the back foot. TB called from Shanghai on the way from the airport to the hotel, and said it was a mad idea. I said it was not. It was a good thing for me and a good thing for him. He said don't do it. I know what you're worried about, you're worried that it's not going to happen, that you'll go at a time not of your choosing, with them hounding you out. But it's a big moment this, and if you don't do it properly, it will be a real problem. It's just mad. They're on the defensive, let the stuff about the BBC sink in and then do it when I get back. If you do it when I'm out of the country it will be even worse. It will look like I was not involved and you bounced me. If you want to do it, fine, but I promise you it's not a good idea. I said I really had to know I was getting out on my terms. I said I was confident about the inquiries but I was also confident about FAC and a fat lot of good that did me. He said don't forget that in the end we're all in this together and we have to help each other. He said 'When you leave I want to be able to say that there are two ACs, the one parts of the media portray and the one I know who is a great person.' He said it was better we do that at the end of the week or after you go on holiday. I said OK but I wanted a guarantee. Sky was really going for the BBC though Boulton was still being a total cunt, e.g. in saying I was not totally exonerated because I was chairing intelligence meetings, etc. ITN was OK, but the BBC was like a house magazine. Geoff H called, said he was determined to go to the [British] Grand Prix because he was not having his life dictated by the worst excesses of the British media. Quite right. Once the dust settled I would have to deal with the BBC etc. and I would have no stomach for it all. I hated these people. The BBC/*Mail* link was now beyond the pale.

We went for dinner at the Goulds', joined by Charlie and Marianna [Falconer] and Peter M. Charlie felt I now had a window to go. Marianna was not sure I really wanted to go and said I should just take a holiday to think about it. Peter felt I was the one person in Number 10 who gave TB muscular advice which he listened to. I still felt I could do a fair bit from the outside. Peter M was unconvinced. He said three things will happen: 1. the media will rejoice; 2. champagne will flow in Number 11; 3. there will be panic in the PLP and ministers will become even more useless. I found it hard to see how I could stay in a position related to the media when I had such total contempt not just for a few of them, but for most of them, and certainly for the media culture and prevailing style. Charlie was clear that once I went, though I would still be able to help, I would not be able to pull the levers and that was a problem for TB, though he completely understood why I wanted to go. What was important was that we gave TB good replacements quickly.

Monday, July 21

The papers were finally turning to the BBC, but the *Mail* was vile and Robert Harris [author, former journalist] had a vicious piece in the *Telegraph*. I had to fight my way through a [media] scrum to get into the cab. I was feeling shit and keen to go. I had a nice cabbie who was basically onside, and felt the thing was moving towards the Beeb. Bruce, who had been persuaded that my leaving was the right thing to do, came back and said don't do it because 1. you are TB's last line of defence, and 2. they'd say it was an admission of guilt. [David] Bradshaw, Peter H were saying much the same thing. Jonathan came back from the States and he, Sally and I met discuss how to do it and what I would say. Jonathan said he probably agreed it was the right thing, but we needed a replacement sorted first.

The day was largely taken up with going through the Clare Sumner/Catherine Rimmer file. [Lord] Hutton was announcing his plans at 10.30 and it was clear he would go as wide as he wanted and do most of it in public.[1] He looked far too Tory for me, though as Fiona said, that might mean he was pro war whereas a left-wing

---

[1] Lord Hutton, former Lord Chief Justice of Northern Ireland, would chair what was formally known as the 'Inquiry into the Circumstances Surrounding the Death of Dr David Kelly CMG'.

judge almost certainly would not be. Peter M was terrific on *Today*, skewering Humphrys on what he said on May 29 about the Gilligan story and Humphrys was very defensive. Clare Short came on with her usual whine. Geoff Hoon was page 1 of the *Mail* for being at the Grand Prix. He said to me last night he didn't really want to do the job if his family had to live life according to the morals of the immoral *Daily Mail*.

The first big meeting of the day was with Jeremy and Jonathan, Sally, Catherine Rimmer – Clare now away – and John S to go through chronology. It was very hard to remember all the comings and goings and toings and froings about the whole thing. CR had dug up all the emails and the ones that caused possible problems, one from Jonathan asking me or Sally to speak to Ann Taylor. Also one from me that the ISC should delve into the source, Gilligan and me. But it was OK really.

Omand came over at 3 for another meeting at which he was much more formal and said Hutton would want us to send a consolidated account but each person would have to give evidence on their own account. There was a real possibility of this going in any direction and of course the BBC were clearly now going to suggest that Kelly did say all these things. Clive Hollick called to say would it be sensible for me to see Greg Dyke for a private chat. I felt probably not. The press was trying to put the focus on who put the name in the public domain and going for the fact that the MoD said they would confirm the name if it was put to them.

Tom Kelly did the eleven o'clock with a fairly straight bat. Meetings for two hours or so. Omand setting up a little team to work full-time on the inquiry while we were on holiday. It was going to be tough. The BBC were trying to maintain that the Susan Watts [BBC *Newsnight* journalist] story was the same as the Gilligan story. It wasn't. It was a softer version. Ditto Gavin Hewitt [BBC journalist]. I had a long chat with Graeme [AC's brother] in Poland who said that every time he turned on a TV channel, I seemed to be on it, whatever the country.

Tuesday, July 22

Fiona has a real downer on me at the moment. I said surely you can understand the pressure I'm under at the moment. She said a lot of it was of my own making because I went from one obsession to the next and she feared I would never change. She was ducking out of the decision re timing of departure though. Neil, Sally, Charles Clarke, Mum, Godric, lots of others I spoke to, pretty much all felt that if I

July '03: All concerned to be called by Hutton

went on Friday it would be taken as an admission of guilt of some sort. Neil said I should wait till September, maybe go after the ISC.

Godric called me after TB's Q&A in Shanghai. TB was not happy with the positioning of the media on the inquiry after Tom's briefing which was being taken as a hit on GH. TB said we had set up the inquiry and now had to shut down on all this, stop commenting, stop engaging with the media on it. But then, later in the day, he went down the plane to talk to the hacks, despite me warning Godric no good would come of it. And he said he did not authorise the leaking of the name. He had been caught on a classic 'When did you stop beating your wife?' type question and rose to it. But it meant more pressure on me and Geoff Hoon. I could not believe he had done that. I was pissed off with him, and with the people with him for letting him talk to the hacks. There was just no point in the current atmosphere. He should do the formal press events and nothing else.

I also felt it would make it much harder for me to leave on Friday. JP called. He said he had been thinking about my situation. It was obviously a case of when not if I was leaving now and he just wanted to say I should make that judgement in my own interests. He said I had given a phenomenal amount to the government and the party and I was owed that at least. I should decide how and when to depart, and he would be around to speak up for me whenever that was. He also called Fiona with the same message. I called GH, said I couldn't believe TB had dropped us in it like that. I don't think he meant to, but they were all taking his statement as HE didn't authorise it but someone else – GH or AC – did. I saw Bob Phillis [chief executive, Guardian Media Group] and told him I would be leaving. His view was that it was good for me, a tragedy for TB.

Later came news that Uday and Qusai [Saddam's sons] were dead. Charles Clarke called. He said you should not leave. There is a lot of respect for you out there, even among the people who attack you, and I think you will regret going. I set off for King's Cross then off to Retford. Mum looked really bad. She had lost half a stone in the last few weeks and was clearly worrying herself silly about me. I said I'm not losing sleep or losing weight so there's no need for anyone else to. But she was finding it tough. She said every time she turned on the telly news or the radio, someone was having a dig. She said she wouldn't be happy till I was out of it. She wouldn't have that long to wait. TB called from Hong Kong. 'Well, you dropped a bollock today,' I said. He said I know, I should never have gone down the plane. Paul Eastham [*Daily Mail*] had said 'Why did you authorise the leaking of the name?' And he got provoked.

It was leading the news, a great frenzy unleashed around it. The atmospherics meant it was terrible if anyone ever suggested the name should have been out there. Truth was there was a case for it being said – what WAS Kelly doing talking to journalists? Did he in fact say more? TB said the whole thing felt Dreyfusian. I felt it was a cross between Kafka and Orwell. He couldn't work out what the public really made of it. It wasn't good but he felt they would know there was something wrong about the media reporting of it all. He agreed it was impossible for me to resign on Friday now. He felt at the end of the holiday, or around publication of the ISC report, or maybe announce in August, and go at conference because I was still popular in the party.

He intended to go ahead with the public service delivery press conference on Wednesday. He felt it was important the public saw we were still focused on the business of governing. He had spoken to Charles Powell [former adviser to Margaret Thatcher, brother of Jonathan] recently who told him of the day they told Thatcher the Tories had slipped to third in the polls during the Westland helicopter scandal. You just have to keep going. I put him on to Mum and they had a nice little chat. He said people underestimated the toll on families when someone was going through the media mill. She said she had lost half a stone with worry but he was doing a great job and keep going. It cheered her up a bit and she was telling everyone that he'd been talking to her. It was an odd irony that Paul Eastham had inadvertently postponed my departure. Shame I couldn't let the silly fucker know.

Wednesday, July 23

Had a really bad night because Grace was up with asthma and hay fever. Mum seemed better and Dad was looking stronger too but they were both worried about everything. I read some of the papers and now everything was being recalibrated away from the notion that it was inevitable Kelly's identity would become public, to the sense that anyone who spoke about him to anyone else was effectively responsible for killing him. It was all part of the new hysteria. I did a note setting out the need to reframe the debate by getting people to see events through the eyes of then not now. I talked to Charlie F who said he felt it was very hard for a judge not to be influenced by the one-sided nature of the media debate. He said that even he, after TB's ridiculous outburst on the plane, assumed it meant that what he was saying was that HE hadn't authorised leaking the name, but Geoff or I had via a strategy put together without TB's knowledge.

I was genuinely shocked. I said 'Christ, Charlie, don't tell me you actually believe it?' He said what he knew was that we were losing the PR battle. That was because the media framed the debate the whole time to suit the BBC line. It was also because we had announced the inquiry and then vacated the field, whereas the BBC were at it the whole time. He felt we should be explaining the broader context – Kelly's fear it would come out, his worry about a cover-up, suicide not something anyone ever imagined would happen. Jonathan said there was no way Tebbit would do that kind of statement. He felt we just had to trust the judge. He felt there was a chance the judge would be getting irritated because it was so obvious what the media were up to.

I was worrying about whether me having told *The Times* that the other papers had the name would become a problem, whether it would be thought to contribute to the outing. I knew I'd done nothing wrong but in the frenzied atmosphere it could so easily be misinterpreted. The BBC briefed that Susan Watts had Kelly on tape and we were able to say we thought that would be good for us because her story had been very different to Gilligan's even though the BBC spin machine was trying to make out something different.

It was all getting nasty though. Fiona was getting letters saying what's it like sleeping with a murderer. Liz [Naish, AC's sister] was getting abusive phone calls. I was getting letters with fake blood on the envelopes. And they wonder why I get angry. I was working on the overall narrative note Catherine Rimmer was co-ordinating. Geoff Hoon visiting Mrs Kelly was the main story. The media were on autopilot, presenting it as her having a go at him over the way the MoD handled him. He called me later and said they had had a really good chat, she was very friendly and very strong. He said she wanted to get a message to me that the way I was being hounded by the press was an outrage. I was really touched by that. I thought again about writing to her but worried about how she would feel about that now the inquiry was on its way. Geoff said he found the meeting really moving. She was friendly, the family was nice and he left feeling a lot better than when he went in. Not that that would remotely be reflected.

Thursday, July 24

In to finish my various notes to send to the Hutton Inquiry. Catherine R had put together a huge folder and was working away. TB called me up to the flat and said he felt pretty chirpy, that apart from the press they had a good trip. He was in two minds about whether I should go now or a bit later. He was clear it had to be planned properly, and seen to be as much about the nature of the media as about us. He said what the media had managed to do was define me as the epitome of a political culture that they represent and which I had spent my career fighting – distorting, manipulating, lying, spinning control freaks. He felt they had to be challenged on that basis.

Both he and Godric felt that once I had gone there was a chance of getting the debate on to that basis. TB said his and my interests on this were convergent – I wanted to be able to go in a position where people felt I had something to say that was significant, and he wanted me to be able to do that too, and give him the space to make change and challenge the culture. He said to me later that there was a part of him that felt I WAS being driven out by the media, or at least by the state of my relations with them. He was a bit gobsmacked at how offside Fiona was. He was perfectly nice but a part of him was obviously calculating how to use my departure while at the same time keeping me on board should he want to call on me. He said he would be very surprised if we didn't end up speaking most days, and most weeks that he would hope I would put something down on paper. He saw Geoff H, told him he had no worries about his future, that we would tough this out.

Geoff came to see me afterwards and I told him I had agreed with TB back in April I would go and nothing had happened since that made me want to change my mind. He said if I went, he felt it would be a disaster. TB was great, so were lots of people around him, but 'one thing that people know about you is that you give good advice and you're never afraid to say what he doesn't want to hear'. He felt TB was becoming a bit remote and he was worried if I wasn't there everyone else would be telling him he was the emperor and one day he'd be left standing with no clothes. I said that my mind was made up and I was telling him because I knew the media would try to up the pressure on him without me there. He was pretty much a total Blairite, a decent bloke. I felt I was dropping him in it a bit.

On Kelly though, he said he was absolutely confident of the outcome of the inquiry. I then did a ring-round of the people in the know to get their views on us doing this tomorrow. Fiona said yes, Tony said yes. I called Neil, who said everything in him said no. I called in Godric and Tom. They said no, that it would be seen as an admission of guilt to go right now. I had a chat with Phil Webster [*Times*], who felt the same. Then to a TB meeting with Omand, Scarlett, Jonathan, Jeremy, Matthew Rycroft [private secretary, foreign affairs], Catherine R, Tom and Godric.

There were mixed reports of what Hutton was like. Jonathan said [Gerry] Adams and [David] Trimble were united for once – in saying he was dreadful. Scarlett said he was an Ulster puritan, but nobody knew if that helped or hindered. He was a conservative with a small c. It was a fairly sober meeting, because the truth was none of us knew where or how this would end, and it was fraught with risk. We went over all the background material we would need, and the areas we would need to prepare on. I called Ann Taylor as she was about to board a ferry in Newhaven and told her in confidence I was going to leave. I was thinking about when, and felt that if the ISC report was going to clear me, that might be the time to do it. She said she was hoping to publish during the two weeks in September when Parliament was sitting. She couldn't go into content but we could speak nearer the time.

Dennis Skinner called to tell me that the NEC had turned on Tony Robinson [TV actor and NEC member] who had said we should be nice to the BBC. Skinner said they had to support AC 'because he's probably against the war anyway' and the party should support him against all the lies and distortions against us. He'd also had a pop at Mark Seddon [editor of *Tribune* and NEC member] for writing for the *Mail*. 'I'm not listening to anyone who writes for the fuckin' enemy.' My own mailbag was running around 6 to 1 in my favour though there were some pretty unpleasant ones among the antis. I knew Mum would be getting upset, called her and she said she'd been losing weight again. Truth be told she didn't have that much to lose. She said she wouldn't sleep well again until I was out of there. She said every time she turned on the radio or the TV someone seemed to be having a go. I said it was fine, that I was doing fine and in in any event it is not going to go on for ever. Joe Ashton [Labour MP] called, said the PLP was strong for me. He said it pissed him off how the papers liked to say the party was against me. He said the party knows you do a great job for Tony, and they know that your enemies are your enemies because you do their job better than they do theirs – and that goes for Tory MPs having a pop as well as all the journalists doing the same. I got a similar message from Dale Campbell-Savours [Labour MP]. He said he was sure I could convince myself that I actually wanted to leave, but I needed to think about who would be happiest about that – our enemies.

Bruce [Grocott] popped in for a chat, and said something similar. He said he didn't know what my plans were, and he knew he couldn't believe the papers, who were probably speculating about me going because that's where they wanted the story to go, but he really hoped I stayed. He said it must be hard at the moment, but it has always been hard, and you can get through this. He said he knew I could convince myself that actually it was in my interest to go, but it wasn't. He said it was what our enemies want and they would be the happy ones if it happened, not me. Bruce had always been such a strong support and I felt like I was letting him down, as well as Tony, in even thinking about going right now. He said he had seen day in day out how much TB relied on me, how much the whole operation did. He said there are going to be real storms ahead and I needed to be there to help him through them. 'You are strong. I can see how horrible this is but just don't give your enemies any satisfaction at all.' I said I thought I was too far gone. The family was very clear they'd had enough and after all they had done for me, I owed them this. My relations with the media were also now pretty poisonous and I felt there had been times when I had done TB harm as well as good. He said that was nonsense – which is pretty much what TB had said, saying we conceded too much on the whole fuss about spin. He said I think it will be bad for TB and the government if you leave, and therefore bad for the country. 'These people going on at you don't think about things like that. I'm the last person to try to persuade you not to listen to arguments from your family, but if you go, it is a victory for people who actually don't care too much about the country, but about the next story or the next attack.' I said it meant a lot to me that he said all this, but I had pretty much made my mind up about it. I confessed it had felt pretty lonely and brutalising at times but it helped to have people like him giving such strong support.

The FAC put out a statement saying that at Gilligan's request they would not be publishing a transcript of his evidence in the private session but sending a copy to Hutton. I bumped into Gisela Stuart. She said it would be terrible to publish it now because it showed both Gilligan and Kelly had got it wrong, though Gilligan was worse. I got home and Fiona was walking down the stairs as I walked through the door. 'I've been fired,' she said. 'What?' She said CB had called and said she felt she ought to leave soon. She accused Fiona of briefing against her, which Fiona said was ridiculous though she accepted there had been a breakdown of trust between them. Fiona said she did believe Carole was a menace but it was not true that she had ever briefed against her, let alone against Cherie. She was really upset that CB could think as she did. She was due to go out to the ballet and I said just try not to worry about it, Cherie will regret what she said. I watched the [BBC] *Ten O'Clock News*, and Marr opining that a world without me – i.e. post spin – would be the best thing for both the media and Number 10. Not a word about the Gilligan transcript. Marr had become a PR man for the Beeb, nothing else. So the news was basically GH not commenting, followed by a tendentious two-way about me.

Philip called and said don't fight it any more, you know you are going so just think of that, and don't fight. Get out ASAP. I was being inundated with nice messages, ninety per cent from party people, a small number from hacks. JR and DB called, saying don't go. Darren Murphy [special adviser] said don't give the *Mail* and GB the pleasure. He said I was the ONLY person GB feared – and that included TB and JP – and he would rejoice at this.

Friday, July 25

As part of their continuing obsession, *Today* led on the story that I was planning to leave. We had the 'wishful thinking' line in the mix but it was clearly true and though they got details wrong – e.g. saying I would not go till Hutton reported – I was baffled as to how they got hold of it. Peter M called. I asked whether he thought I should do a clip on the way out. He thought not. Audrey [Fiona's mother] was staying with us, said don't give them any satisfaction at all. I walked out, said simply 'Dream on' and went on my way. I went up to Les Hinton's house. Though I didn't go into timings I told him I would not be there much longer. We discussed a few options with News International. I was most interested in doing something on sport for a bit. He of course was most interested in books and political columns.

I went in and told TB about CB's call and said it was unforgivable that she spoke to Fiona like that after all she'd done for her. He said people were too fraught at the moment and Cherie was feeling under pressure. I said she needed to apologise, otherwise there would be badness between them that helped nobody. He said the problem at the moment is that the public will begin to wonder whether we are governing the country. All they hear is all this stuff about personalities, process and the rest and they start to wonder if that's all we do. There was a case for me going right now, but I was tired and I needed a holiday to marshal the arguments and get things in a better place first. He said he was still finding it hard to imagine life without me being around the whole time. I said I would be available to help, but in a different way. He once thought he needed Peter around the whole time, but he didn't, provided he could call on him. It would be the same with me.

Peter M joined us and he and I were chatting away while TB was just looking out of the window, a bit vacant. After a while, he said 'I can't see the way to rebuilding trust unless we find WMD. And at the moment I don't see how we regain momentum.' Peter and I said things would look very different after a break, also that he needed to get focused on conference, where we always seemed to get things back on an even keel. We agreed that for Wednesday's press conference he should say the focus was public services and anything at all re Iraq he should just say wait for Hutton. Peter M was being very helpful and supportive, albeit in his usual spiky way. He said it was poignantly ironic that he should be helping me plan my departure when I had so spectacularly been responsible for his 'defenestration'. It was to his credit though that apart from the odd joke, he'd never really shown bitterness at his second resignation, and still helped when I was the one needing support.

I drafted an email to put round the building telling people what was going on but TB, Charlie F and Jonathan talked me out of sending it. They felt it might leak and thought it best just to let the media say what they want but not fuel it. Catherine R was doing a great job getting the materials together for Hutton. David Omand seemed a bit too laid-back, saying everyone should go away and have a good holiday. The BBC were still spinning away madly and of course would carry on using their output to help shape their case. It would take a very strong mind not to be influenced. Dyke wrote to TB claiming a Cabinet minister had told Marr there would be 'revenge'. TB drafted a pretty rough reply which Peter felt we shouldn't send.

Peter M asked if I was going to conference. I hope not, I said. 'Who will write your speech?' he asked TB. 'Alastair and I will,' he said. 'He'll have more time if he's not doing everything else.' TB went off to Chequers and I called in all my staff. I said that they'd all have been hearing and reading all this stuff. I wanted them to know I was going to use the holiday to decide what to do. I said whatever decision I took, I was proud of the team I had built and grateful for the phenomenal support they gave me, but ultimately a decision like this had to be for me and the family, and a holiday was the right place to make it. I could tell that they knew where it was heading.

[David] Bradshaw came to see me later, and seemed close to tears. He said people in here would be devastated if I went, that I underestimated how much of what they all did they did for me, because I made it a great place to work, and I took all the hits for them, and let them take risks. He said nobody ever understood how I managed to do the job the way I did, but he was worried if I stopped doing it, the place would collapse. Gone was his usual mickey-taking Scouse humour, and in its place an impassioned plea to stay. But I think he knew it would fall on deaf ears, though I was really touched by his warmth and trust.

We went for dinner at the Blackburns' [David and Janice]. Peter M there too and we were really going for a couple of people there who were close friends of Tom Bower and Veronica Wadley [husband and wife, *Mail* journalist and *Evening Standard* editor]. They seemed shocked by the strength of our hatred of Dacre. I said your friend Wadley works for the most poisonous influence in British life. He and his papers are evil. They add nothing of good to the world whatever. I was confident of being cleared by Hutton but wish he'd had the *Mail on Sunday* in there too. They hid behind the BBC. David Blackburn got the plot re the BBC, had followed it closely and could see all the holes in their arguments. He said he felt it was possible that I would be vindicated but also that Gilligan would not be condemned. I felt relieved it was more out in the open that I would be going. Catherine MacLeod [*Herald*] had done a piece making clear I had agreed with TB on May 28 that I would go. I felt I would be free to do lots of different things but also stay involved in a different kind of way, less intense, less demanding, with less contact with the media.

Wednesday, July 30 (holiday, Puyméras, Provence)

Writing by Philip and Gail's pool. Everyone has gone to Vaison to get bikes. Feeling a pretty big sense of foreboding. Catherine Rimmer just texted me to say the first question at TB's press conference was about me and my future. No doubt they're going to try to keep me as a big issue for him. JP very nice about me on the *Today* programme apparently. Michael Barber [head of the Prime Minister's delivery Unit] did his delivery slides presentation at the press conference, and did it well by all accounts, but it was unlikely to get much coverage. They couldn't give two tosses about the public service agenda. CR said the public services slide show had been excellent punishment for the hacks. The other major soap event was Carole C who had done a big picture spread in *Hello!* magazine, which the press were going big on. Sally called me, said she had been to see TB yesterday and told him 'that woman' is going to destroy you if you do not sort it out. She said TB went mad at her, saying it was ridiculous how we were all against Carole. I think TB just liked her, and liked the fact she had been a help to CB, but there wasn't one of us who didn't find it a bit odd. I was feeling fairly detached. I was moving on psychologically and there were plenty of options to consider. News International were pressing pretty hard. I wrote I was keen to do sport before politics and based on a few chats with the boys I started to work up an idea for a series on how to decide who the greatest sportsmen of all time were.

TB called me the day I left but then we had radio silence for a while. Peter M called for a few chats, not least re the *Sunday Telegraph* when Gavyn Davies wrote a piece on how we were allegedly threatening BBC independence. This followed the letter from Dyke to TB claiming Marr had received a call from a Cabinet minister warning that we planned to get revenge. Marr's behaviour in all this had been disgraceful, and he had just become part of the BBC's lobbying and PR operation, which was going on relentlessly. I spoke to Tessa [Jowell] before she did *The World at One* and also did a note saying we had to make clear there was no link between the row and [BBC] Charter review.

Meanwhile there was more coming out about Kelly and his contacts with the press. The BBC were successful in keeping things focused on how Kelly's name came out, and pretty much ignoring other more relevant issues. On the drive down through France I'd had a worried call from David Hill. He said someone was getting to TB over the Order in Council issue [the ruling allowing AC and Jonathan Powell to direct civil servants]. It was probably a mix of senior civil servants, who would be keen to use my departure to rein back, and Peter M who was keen to use it – for the right reasons – to give a sense of a post spin era. Bruce Anderson [*Independent*] was already on to the theme that we were now spinning non-spin as the new spin. But I was worried a change would weaken DH in the job. I told him I felt it was imperative that he keep it, particularly as the [Bob] Phillis [review] team was split on the issue and Bob needed support.

PG meanwhile was worried we were nearing a tipping point re TB. He had just been to the US with Ian McCartney, Pat McF, Douglas and Alice [Cartner-Morley, pollster] and came back both awestruck by the professionalism and ruthlessness of the Republican operation, but also alarmed at how people had started to talk of TB almost in the past tense, and focusing more on legacy than forward agenda. We drove down via a stopover in Paris to see John and Penny Holmes [UK ambassador to France and his wife]. Penny was very alarmed at the CB/Carole situation. John [Blair's former foreign policy adviser] said of TB. 'You must do something to try to distance himself from Bush. Nobody here believes Tony will do anything that Bush doesn't want and he is seen as even more right wing and unpopular here than he is in the UK.' He felt TB gave Bush very strong support early on and Bush has exploited it. He does not get enough back in return and his European policy is paying a price. He felt the two GBs were Tony's big problems – his foreign policy was foundering on his closeness to Bush. His domestic policy was stalling because GB kept his foot on the brake the whole time. Also, he said the thing I managed to give him – grip and good presentation – was now likely to weaken. He felt TB didn't grasp the scale of the challenge at the moment. He had let things drift – never tackled Gordon properly, never really worked out a proper euro strategy, never dealt with Carole and the lifestyle image issues. He was paying the price and there were the beginnings of a feeling of decay. Philip felt the same.

We had a more or less painless journey down and the kids were on good form. I had meanwhile decided that I would pretty much leave as soon as we got back from holiday, the reasons as per the note I had done earlier. I felt I could continue to advise from outside on strategy and maybe do election planning. I would make speeches to make a living, write on sport and politics after a while, also do more on the leukaemia fund-raising front and motivational stuff for the party. I had a vague notion of getting involved with the ad agency. Maybe do a chat show but it might be difficult because part of the public argument I intend to make is how awful modern TV has become. I was thinking a lot about the media culture and its impact on the health of democracy. The balance had gone from being a good check-balance to just creating a culture of negativity.

I spoke to Richard Desmond in Majorca at one point. He said 'You can't go because Tony needs you too much.' I said people always underestimated Tony. I told him I might do a film on Dacre and [Lord] Rothermere and he was very up for it. 'How much do you want? We'll do it.' I was not going to be short of offers but I had decided no to the consultancy and lobbying route. Just not my thing. PG felt I needed to strike while the iron was hot re the US speaking scene. Nice call from Jonathan Prince [Democrat strategist], who was working for [Senator John] Edwards [Democrat presidential hopeful]. He said there was a fair bit of coverage of my travails in the States. 'Just hang in there. They only hate you because you're too good for them.' I was getting a lot of 'hang in' messages, but my mind was set. I was clear I had to go.

On the Saturday I had a long chat with Alex F who was out in the States, raving about the Nike training centre. I told him I was definitely leaving now. 'Give my congratulations to Fiona,' he said. 'Maybe I gave you the wrong advice. Maybe you should have left when you first thought of it, but the one thing nobody can ever take from you is that you know you've done a great job, and you should now do what is right for you and the family. You've given enough.' Fiona was still detoxing on the CB stuff, still angry about Carole but the more there was about her in the press in a way the better it was for Fiona as she tried to shape a new professional future too. Catherine Rimmer was keeping me in touch with the Hutton team. It now seemed Hutton would read himself in, then take witnesses from the 11th to the 18th, first the MoD, then the BBC, then others, then reflect, maybe re-interview, report maybe in October. So it was definitely going to be another interrupted holiday. Also the whole conference season would have Hutton as the backdrop.

I was now reaching a settled feeling about leaving – I felt excited at the prospect of new and different things to do. It would be nice for the family as a whole that I travelled less, saw them more, and could earn decent money. I sometimes felt I had been pressured by Fiona, but equally I knew she had my interests as well as her own at heart. But I also knew I would need to stay involved in some way, not least because I still felt at my best I was the best, and could make a contribution. It's just that I hadn't been at my best for a while. I also felt sad at the thought my team would break up. As I whirred things round in my mind it was clear for the first time I was thinking more about my own future than TB's. I would help if I could but he would have to help himself.

The weather was beautiful and I was pretty much running every day, including a couple of big ones. We didn't see that many papers. Philip felt the combination of no WMD plus Carole would get the party unnerved. I was getting into my stride on the sports series and by the weekend had written four or five articles. The *Mail* were still going at me hell for leather according to Catherine R. Sad fuckers.

Thursday, July 31

Catherine Rimmer kept the faxes coming thick and fast. Matthew Lewin [journalist neighbour] did a piece for the *Press Gazette* about the press in the street outside the house and general BBC standards. Bill Hagerty [editor, *British Journalism Review*] did a piece attacking the BBC. The Hutton hype was winding down in advance of him saying tomorrow how he intended to proceed. I had a long chat with Jonathan who said TB had finally seen the light re Carole. 'I know we've heard it before but *Hello!* was the last goodbye.' After the call

Catherine R called again to say that Hutton wanted to see me and Jonathan on August 21.

I had been hoping to be able to see out the holiday but no luck. We now had to work out how best to get myself fully briefed and also properly psyched up. It put a real dampener on things and Fiona was even more pissed off now. Ross [Kemp, actor] and Rebekah [Wade] came over and we had a nice enough time with them. They, along with Gail and PG, felt I was on strong ground but I felt Hutton would feel he had to make some criticism of everyone. Philip felt TB had panicked in calling an inquiry. Kelly killed himself because he killed himself and we should have held our nerve. He was pretty down on TB at the moment.

Ditto Rebekah who felt public services were going backwards, though as I kept telling the News International lot, they tended not to use them. She and I discussed a number of News International options going from occasional columns up to a deal across titles. TB felt the *Sunday Times* was the paper to do a column in. PG felt the *Sun*. The Hutton traffic was fairly steady, with people calling regularly. Tom K and Catherine both felt the order of witnesses was good for us – MoD, then BBC, then us, then TB, then Geoff H and then John Scarlett who I felt sure would be a very strong witness.

Friday, August 1

Catherine R called again re flights as we felt there may be a case for her coming out to brief me. She was very happy with *The Times* which did a big number, and the *Guardian* had the Gilligan [FAC hearing] transcript which did not do him much good and suggested he was backing off the central allegations against me. John Stanley and Eric Illsley [FAC MPs] gave him a very hard time on it. Rachel Kinnock was due out so I was getting a new package of briefing material to come out with her. Truth was the holiday was pretty much going down the Swanee but hopefully it would be the last to be like this. Also I was pretty desperate to be cleared and so I had to keep my focus the whole time. I needed to be at my best when I reached the witness stand and a lot of the preparation had to be done now.

Hutton was doing his stuff at 11 and it would dominate the media all day, plus everyone was saying it was important I stay hidden away on the day of the funeral. I was finding it easy, and quite therapeutic, to do the sports series and had done the concept and the first few drafts in a matter of days. But I was not plugged into the political scene apart from re Hutton though I suppose that was about the only politics going at the moment. Neil was hilarious on the sports greats idea. I told him about the idea over dinner on the evening they arrived and for pretty much every sport he had a Welsh name to suggest. He was adamant John Charles [Wales and Leeds United striker] was better than Pelé or Maradona. He had a Welsh boxer better than Muhammad Ali.

By now I had a huge Hutton file to read. Hutton did his opening statement which seemed to be pointing heavily towards the BBC but it was also clear the manner in which Kelly's name came out was going to be a big part of it. I felt the weight of it all building again. Catherine felt the statement would worry the BBC more than us. PG felt Hutton came across as clear and strong and it was important I came over as being clear and strong. Later I spoke to Omand and Charlie F. CF said he felt there was no need to be too nervous but Hutton was not someone to be pushed around. Omand felt GH was the one who might be in difficulty and said they were all getting a bit jumpy at the MoD. I'd felt the name should come out and that Kelly should appear before the FAC and ISC and that it was important we knew what was what. I felt comfortable in that position but it may be others would see it very differently. I told Neil I was very nervous about it all. He said there was no need because if I told the truth it would be fine. He felt Hutton would just want facts.

Saturday, August 2

Neil was being very supportive, though he was also in a rage re a few EU situations. I was working on a witness statement which meant going over the whole thing again and again. I wasn't sleeping well. I called Joe Haines [Harold Wilson's former press secretary] for a chat. He felt I had to maintain control of my own exit, don't go under a cloud or looking like I've been harassed out. He said what had happened was awful, that Gilligan should be ashamed. The coverage of the Hutton statement was OK but there was still an awful lot being pointed at me.

Sunday, August 3

I read the Kelly MoD interviews, which were pretty good for our case. I had had another night waking up, tossing and turning. I then just lay there waiting for the church bells to ring, and every time came the thought that they'd toll for me. Fiona was being very supportive and keeping the kids' spirits up but it was like we had a big dark cloud over us the whole time.

Tuesday, August 5

Peter M in the *Sunday Mirror* had said TB was clear we would be OK. I sent a message round the system saying we should all just shut up. The *Indy* yesterday splashed on Number 10 describing Kelly as a Walter Mitty character.[1] I told the office we had to disown it very forcibly at the eleven o'clock, which Anne Shevas, who hated doing the briefings, duly did. But it emerged that it was Tom who had said it, when chatting to Paul Waugh [*Independent*]. He had been going over the questions Hutton would want to look at, had not remotely intended it to run as a story and now it was the latest frenzy. I said he should apologise and drop a line both to Mrs Kelly and to Hutton. PG and Gail thought it was a bad idea to involve the widow because we had no clue as to how she would react. I had earlier drafted a letter to Mrs Kelly myself and discussed with JP whether he thought I should send it. He felt the sentiments were fine but you could never tell how people in grief and shock would react. He said he would take it to the funeral and make a judgement then as to whether to give it to her. There was no other major story around at the moment so several of the papers splashed on Tom on the Tuesday. He was feeling wretched and I called him to say not to worry too much about it. I got a message through to TB to call him too.

Jamie Rubin [former US State Department chief spokesman] called to offer support. He said he assumed that I knew the BBC were in the wrong but they got into a 'won't back down to him' situation and it all got out of hand. Pretty much. Even out on holiday, Philip was doing notes for me. He was seeing and reading more of the media than I was, I having pretty much given up on reading the papers. He felt that what came through, even in the ones who hated me, was a sense of really deep commitment and professionalism and work ethic and it was important that side of me was what came over to the judge. He felt I should strive to de-personalise, de-emotionalise my own role. Be focused and professional.

The office sent through my ISC evidence which I had to sign off. Again I felt confident in the facts. Neil could tell though how nervous I was. He said I could not bottle up something like this and if I wanted to talk to him at any time, he was there. He was very warm and supportive and also lifting a lot of the pressure on the family too. Even though Fiona and the kids were still doing all the things we do on holiday they were clearly feeling the tension a fair bit. Philip felt

[1] From a 1939 story by James Thurber, *The Secret Life of Walter Mitty*, dealing with the imagined adventures of a mild-mannered dreamer.

the problem was that the media were effectively running this as the government on trial. The press were helping the BBC to reframe the debate in their favour, without vacating the field, so that they were both player but also 'neutral' spectator. Not. JP went to Kelly's funeral and called me afterwards. He said Mrs Kelly had been fine with him, had not been seeking to blame the government for his death, which made me feel a lot better. I was starting to work on my own statement. I was not impressed with the advice we were getting from the Cabinet Office about lawyers.

Thursday, August 7

We had dinner in Malaucene with Ian and Andrea Kennedy [personal friends]. I was looking forward to getting some hard-headed and objective advice from Ian about how to approach it. His chairing of the Bristol babies inquiry [into baby heart deaths at Bristol Royal Infirmary, begun in 1998] had been seen as pretty good, and he was always very good on problem solving generally. He felt, based on what he had read in the press, that I was fine on the substance. But he was amazed that I did not already have my own lawyer, and he was really pressing me to get my act together, or get the Cabinet Office to get theirs together. He said he had advised everyone involved in Bristol to have their own lawyer.

What would happen, he asked, if the nub came down to a difference of opinion between, say, me and Geoff Hoon, or me and John Scarlett? Was I really saying there would just be one government lawyer representing everyone? He thought it was ridiculous. I was already feeling pretty sick, having heard from the inquiry team that the judge wanted me to give him my diaries, or at least any relevant extracts. The request came as a real shock. Sandra Powell [secretary] had called me to read through all the various areas he wished to ask me about, and as she ran through them, I felt absolutely fine. It was only when she faxed through the letter that I noted at the end this request to see anything from my diaries. Ian thought it was probably just a fishing expedition but now not only was I worried – as I said to Fiona, Christ knows what I've written in there – but I was also beginning to panic a little about what Ian had said re the need for my own lawyer. I was very pleased Ian would be around.

Friday, August 8

Ian got hold of Alan Maclean, who had been one of his legal team for the Bristol inquiry, and made arrangements for him to come out next week. I called the Cabinet Office and asked for a list of lawyers

August '03: Hutton wants to see AC's diaries

to choose from. Rosemary Jeffreys [Treasury Solicitor's Department] gave me a list but of course what we didn't know was who was available and this was the worst time imaginable to be trying to find one. I put a call into James Goudie [QC] for his advice, also Charlie F and Derry, and TB. Charlie in particular thought I would not get on with Jonathan Sumption [QC], who was the one Alan Maclean and Ian were recommending. The general view was that he was right wing, a bit quirky and someone who would want things done his way. Charlie felt we were both strong characters who would get on each other's nerves. Ian was strongly of the view that if Alan was saying he was the best, and also as his reputation was so strong, we should try to get him.

Alan got on to his clerk. It transpired Sumption was staying at his place in France, and had indicated immediately he was keen to do it. I was also trying to sort the shipping out of my diary for this year. The summer holiday is the one time of the year where I don't take it with me, and instead just scribble a few notes every now and then when I feel like it. Poor old Audrey had to get into the house, root around under the bed and then get the book to Number 10. Originally the plan was to get it shipped out with books that were being sent out for Gail but her stuff was coming out late so Number 10 had to sort it out. I was now finding it really hard to sleep. The request for my diaries felt like a hostile act to me. I suspected I was the only one being asked to do this. And why – because the papers had said I kept a diary. Why isn't everyone asked if they keep a personal diary, and to provide any relevant bits?

Sunday, August 10

I had received the request for my diary on Thursday and now, finally, this year's was being flown out by Peter Howes [duty clerk]. As I left the house, and said goodbye to Fiona, I did actually wonder momentarily whether it would be the last time I saw her, whether what I discovered on reading my own diary would be so awful that I would want to top myself. It was only a passing thought, but it was there, and it came back several times as I drove down to Marseilles. I knew I had done nothing wrong, but in this climate, things had gone beyond reason, it was like a drama or a novel, and nobody had control of events. I tried not to be in a panic on the drive down, but I was. I couldn't remember what I wrote in my diary the minute I wrote it. On the few occasions I ever looked back, I was always surprised at things that happened, things I said, things other people had said. I just didn't know.

I met Simon Lever [UK Consul General in Marseilles] as we waited for Peter to come through. I managed to hide any nerves I had from Peter, who was dressed like he was just having a nice day trip to an airport on an aeroplane. But inside I was feeling sick. He handed me the package and I set off back to the car. I put it on the passenger seat, thought about opening it there and then but the car was hot and I wanted to get away from the airport. I drove for maybe half an hour and then pulled into a service station. It was now unbelievably hot. I opened the envelope slowly and then pulled out the diary, put it down again and just stared at it. What I had written in there, or so I felt, had the capacity to deliver vindication or destruction. One bad word, and who knows, for me, for Tony, for the whole bloody government.

When I thought of some of the things I've said in there about ministers, about colleagues, about the press, about the BBC. By the time I finally started flicking through it, I was sweating. It was now so hot that even in the shade of a few trees, the sweat was falling down my face. I found the various sections on the dossier. At first glance, it seemed fine, and I started to feel a bit better. There was certainly nothing I could see that would mean I would have to resign straight away. A few bad bits, a bit too colourful in parts, but overall manageable. The best thing was that in terms of all the facts in there, they supported what we had been saying about events.

It then suddenly dawned on me I had made a terrible mistake. I had been so focused on Kelly's death, which was after all the subject of the inquiry, that I had only got this year's diary sent out when of course it was last year that the dossier was put together and it was clear from the inquiry team's letter that was absolutely central. I felt sick all over again. What an idiotic thing to do. As I sat there, feeling a mixture of relief that my cursory flick through had revealed nothing terrible, and anger at my own stupidity in not getting both diaries sent out, the phone went.

It was Number 10 with Godric. When I told him what I was doing, he was horrified. He said he thought it was unbelievable that he [Lord Hutton] was asking for my diaries. Like me he saw it as a hostile act. Maybe, he says, it shows he basically buys into the media line on us. Godric was so principled and proper, and a believer in playing fair, that he seemed if anything even more shocked and upset than I was. He made the same point I had – why hasn't everyone been asked if they keep a diary? But anyway, we were beyond that. He then got more and more anxious as I told him what I was organising on the legal front. He said that he had heard nothing from the Cabinet Office other than the fact he would have to give evidence. He had had the same conversation I had had with Omand on the day Hutton set out his terms, namely take a bit of a break and see what happens. It was, as Charlie F had also observed, a bit Heath Robinson.

Godric was asking whether I thought he should go back straight away. I could tell that I had ruined his holiday, if it wasn't already ruined. I got home, and we went out to Villedieu for the evening. Ian [Kennedy] said he really thought I should put my fate in the hands of a good team of lawyers now, stop trying to make all the decisions myself, stop relying on the government or the Cabinet Office. He said Alan was terrific. Sumption was now on board and he described him as having 'a brain the size of a planet'. I also now had Adam Chapman from the Treasury Solicitor's Department. After Fiona and the kids had gone to bed, I went back through the diary, read it all more slowly and in more detail. The thought of it all being put before the inquiry did not exactly fill me with joy, but it wasn't the disaster I feared. I was kicking myself though re not getting 2002 sent out. I wasn't even sure where it was, so poor old Audrey was going to have to look around the house and we'd have to go through the whole process again.

Wednesday, August 13

Ian had really acted as a fantastic catalyst in getting a proper legal team together. Alan Maclean was staying with the Kennedys at Faucon and I met him briefly last night. He said he, Sumption and Adam Chapman had read the papers on the train from Toulouse to Avignon, where the other two were staying overnight. He said they had concluded that there were only two fundamental questions for me: 1. did I play around with the dossier on the 45-minute point, and 2. did I play a part in a conspiracy re Kelly? He said they all three of them felt, based on all the material they had read, that the answer was no to both. He said Sumption was very clear about it. 'He has pretty much decided that you are the cowboys and the BBC are the Indians.' He said Sumption was reflecting overnight on how we handle the issue of the diary request. I went over to the Kennedys' this morning. Alan and Andrea were getting the printouts on the inquiry from the Internet.

We were into the third day and the BBC case appeared to be falling apart. Gilligan by all accounts a poor witness, Susan Watts to her credit refusing to toe their line and so making things worse for the BBC. The MoD seemed to be doing OK in stressing that they did what they could for Kelly. Sumption and Adam Chapman arrived a bit late. He was not at all what I expected. I'd expected someone rather overbearing, tall, smooth. He seemed a bit shy and nervy, as though a comfortable holiday home was not really the place for this kind of thing. He had a mass of all-over-the-place grey hair. His clothes didn't quite hang together. He was carrying a biography of [John Maynard] Keynes [economist]. We got down to business straight away and I took to him fairly easily, despite all the warnings. He was sharp, to the point, and very clear. He repeated the view Adam had expressed, about the two main questions, and said matter-of-factly 'I don't think you have to worry about that.'

He was also very direct about my diary. He said the prime minister has established an inquiry, Lord Hutton has been appointed, the PM has said he and his staff will co-operate fully, and this is an example of the judge asking for full co-operation. He felt it would be a very bad move to refuse to provide it, or to seek to frame an argument as to why I should. He said the judge would not appreciate it, so I should just accept I would have to do it, and take whatever heat came from it. It was what I had been expecting to hear, and in any event I had already gone through the pain barrier on that one.

On the draft statement I had done, he felt it was fine, in that all the relevant facts were in there, but both he and Ian felt it was too personal and too emotional. All the judge would want is fact. Adam and Alan worked on my statement while Jonathan S and I sat at the dining room table and went through my diary. He felt that he would have to be the judge of what Lord Hutton would deem to be relevant to the inquiry. In terms of what went in, and what stayed out, even though we did not know what Hutton intended to do with this stuff, and even before Sumption knew what I had written, he was at the broader end of the margin. I was sort of hoping that his attitude would be 'when in doubt, keep it out'. It was the opposite. He clearly felt that the more open we were, the fairer the judge would be. I read through page after page, putting pencil marks through the bits he felt were irrelevant, but also making notes in the margins of the vague subject matter to show he had been through it.

Occasionally he would have a doubt but would usually say 'No harm including it.' Some days there was nothing relevant at all, on other days a line or two. At other times, virtually everything would go in. Obviously TB, other departments and the agencies were going to have to see this, and that would maybe have its own problems, but I had now pretty much decided that I was going to take Ian's advice to take this guy's advice, unless it clashed with TB's interests, and as the day wore on, that seemed less and less likely. I found the whole experience really stressful though, going over all the same ground again, not just Iraq, but the other big policy nightmares, TB/GB, Cherie and Carole, also some of the rows with Fiona, some of the guilt at not being there enough, some of the other political stuff, the hatred of some of the media, the pressure, the agonising at my own situation.

When the kids came round later in the day, I also felt a growing sense of injustice that I was the only witness having to do this, when I wanted to be having a normal holiday with the family, and after they went down to the pool, I just started sobbing. 'I'm sorry,' I said to Sumption, whose expression didn't really change. 'It's all right,' he said. 'I totally understand why this is difficult.' I said I don't understand why this is happening to me. He said 'If I were you, I would feel that too. It is dreadful that you are being asked to bare your soul when in my view you have done nothing wrong. But the prime minister set up the inquiry and you have to co-operate with the judge when he asks for this. If he thinks your diary may contain something which helps him, he is entitled to ask for it, warts and all.' I composed myself pretty quickly, and we went back to the task in hand.

It took five or so hours, and I felt totally drained at the end. 'So how was that voyage of discovery for you?' I asked him. 'It was certainly a discovery. I have read so much about you. Now I think I know you. In fact I don't think I've ever learned so much about someone so quickly.' He writes books on medieval history and he said 'I wish there had been people keeping records like this in those days. It would make my life so much easier.' He felt there was something 'wonderfully Victorian about it'.[1] He said it would one day be an amazing service to historians, 'but I can see why that does not hold much appeal to you right now'. It was an odd experience, to have sat down with a total stranger, and gone through so much detail of my own life and work, and at the end of it to be talking as though we had known each other for ages. I noticed he hadn't shaved properly, and as the day wore on his clothes seemed to get scruffier, but I felt by the end of the day that I was with someone who knew what he was doing.

In the ensuing days, first Jeremy [Heywood] – on TB's behalf – and then TB himself came on to say they didn't agree with Sumption's

---

[1] Sumption's vast multi-volume *The Hundred Years War between England and France* would be described by journalist Allan Massie as 'an enterprise on a truly Victorian scale'.

strategy re the diaries. They felt it was unfair, but also wrong, to ask someone to submit a private diary to a public inquiry. I could tell TB was really worried about it, not least by the number of times he told me not to worry. But Sumption resisted the pressure. TB's argument was that we should fight harder for me not to have to do this. Sumption was adamant that would backfire badly with the judge – on me, but also on the government. Although he did not articulate it in this way, I saw his strategy was maximum openness for minimum disclosure.

We now had to work out process. I was thinking I should probably go home, but Alan felt I should stay here for as long as possible, that if I went back, I would be miserable without the family, would follow the inquiry the whole time, which at the moment I was managing to avoid, and he felt I would do better on the stand if I stayed here than if I went back. I called Alison [Blackshaw] and asked her to come out and join us, so that I could get the diary extracts properly typed up. She arranged to come out tomorrow. We went for dinner at the Goulds' and I felt so much better. Sumption went off again. I don't know if it was a joke or not but according to the others he 'owned a village' somewhere in the south-west of France. As he left he said I could call him at any time, but he really believed I had nothing to worry about on the substance. I was really worried about the fact I had told *The Times* two other papers had the name but on my first meeting with Sumption, he said it didn't matter.

Though I felt more at ease with the process, and more confident now I knew I had some decent lawyers involved, I was still not sleeping well, and was feeling real stress not just about the obvious, but also the idea that Fiona and the kids weren't really having much of a holiday with all this going on around them. Every morning now, I was waking up at 4 or 5, waiting for the next ringing of the bells at the village church, and from time to time the old 'ask not for whom the bell tolls . . .' lodged in there. It was impossible not to imagine the worst. The kids kept me going really – the thought that eventually we would get a proper family life back again, and the knowledge that no matter how bad it was, apart from the occasional fleeting moment, I did not think of doing what Kelly had done.

Thursday, August 14 – Friday/Saturday, August 15/16
TB was calling regularly now, and was clearly getting more and more anxious re my diaries. At first he had been dismissive, saying it was a fuss about nothing, but I sensed that was him trying to make sure I didn't get too worried. Now he was getting more agitated and angry,

and strongly disagreed with the Sumption strategy. He felt we should be fighting harder for non-disclosure. I explained Sumption's strategy as I saw it – maximum openness for minimum disclosure and on the substance he thinks on balance that, whilst there are difficulties in there, it helps our case. Yes, said TB, but you are dealing with lawyers and we are politicians in a political situation. I said yes, and part of the politics is that he set up an independent inquiry and promised full co-operation and we cannot now be seen not to co-operate. What is more, if we refuse and it becomes known, then all hell will break loose again and a lot of it around me. I said I was confident that Sumption's strategy was right and I thought we had no choice. He asked me several times 'What's in these things?' I explained that I was getting Alison out to help me transcribe, but that in Sumption's view there was nothing catastrophic. There was a fair bit of bad language. 'How much?' A fair bit. 'Fuck?' Yes. 'Cunt?' Probably, can't remember. 'Bloody hell, Alastair.' He asked if there was anything disparaging about him, or about ministers. Nothing too bad re him. Lots of criticism of Clare [Short], yes, one or two others. Bits and bobs re him and GB. Me thinking of leaving. Fiona and Cherie. 'What?' Yes, but Sumption did not think any of that needed to be put in. We ended up swapping notes on the extent to which our respective holidays had been ruined. He also said I shouldn't worry, that the diaries sounded more embarrassing than damaging, though by now he was back in 'let's keep AC calm' mode.

He called every few hours now, chatting over various things, and eventually I said please let me get on and finish the transcription, and then we can make a judgement as to how bad or not it all is. But he was generally reassuring in these circumstances. He said it was horrible for me, and horrible for all of us, but I should take strength from the fact I had done nothing wrong, and he was confident we would come through this. He said 'What is the worst thing that can be said against you – that you went over the top? But you had every right to, because these were allegations made directly against you, not just me, and you had every right to defend yourself.' He felt that there was a chance Hutton would decide this was as much a story about our rotten media culture as the nature of government.

The inquiry was certainly not going well for the BBC, no matter how hard the media tried to spin it their way. But none of us could really gauge which way Hutton was going. We just had to get on and make our case as best we could. Alison arrived, bringing with her my 2002 diary, and a quick flick through that also reassured me, in that it showed how much care we had put into the September dossier, and it showed in terms how I tried to ensure the agencies were happy with every word and every part of the process. Alison and I started to go through the stuff I had gone over with Sumption. It was not as bad as I feared, though there were one or two points where she winced, usually when I was swearing or saying something derogatory about someone, though it was all stuff she had heard before.

We set up in the dining room/lounge bit of the house and worked on it most of Thursday night, all day Friday, when the lawyers went back to London, most of Saturday, as Alison and I travelled back to England by train, and I finally got a full typed version to Sumption at his house in France by Sunday pm, well ahead of the Monday 5pm deadline, though a lot of people would want to see them before then. He had initially secured a delay to my deadline because of the work required transcribing the diaries but then they came back and said no, the original timetable stood, so we had been working flat out to get through it. Thousands of words and he was trying to reach a deal with the inquiry that it would not be submitted as evidence as such, which would then have to be published along with everything else, but as a supplementary statement.

Fiona and the kids had adapted pretty well considering, and were just carrying on doing everything around us, while I was trying to grab a half-hour here, a half-hour there. It was great having Alison out at the house. The kids liked her and once we got going, I realised it was not going to take quite as long as I feared. When I left for home, and my appearance at the inquiry, Fiona was pretty cold with me, said good luck, but with a 'if you'd listened to me, you wouldn't be in this mess' look on her face. 'Sorry for ruining the holiday,' I said. She smiled, shrugged and just said do your best and get back as soon as you can. She was understandably angry that the holiday was being so disrupted. Grace was crying, and later apparently asked the boys if I could go to jail. Rory went off on a bike ride, I guess to avoid saying goodbye, though he and I had had a good chat earlier. Calum was putting on a brave face and playing the hard man. 'Never forget you're a Campbell, and nobody messes with our family.'

On the train, we had a table to ourselves and so were able to carry on with the transcription, but it meant me whispering into Alison's ear as I dictated and I am sure there were people on there who thought I was at it with her. Then some creep from the *Daily Telegraph*, who I don't think could believe his luck that I was on the train, came up and started to make small talk, pretending to be an ordinary passenger. He was not very convincing. 'Which paper are you from?' Er, the *Telegraph*, I wondered if I could do an interview about your coming appearance at the inquiry, blah blah. 'I'm busy.' Alison had typed for hours and hours on end, God knows how many. Her view was that it wasn't great – particularly the language – but that it did show the kind of pressures we were under and also that we were most of the time just trying to do our best. I had not been seeing the papers at all, had been binning the media briefs, but the impression I got from Philip, who was following it more closely via the Internet, was that it wasn't going well for the BBC. Ian K emphasised to me again and again that I should trust Sumption, who would be focusing on one thing only – the judge. I had decided to do just that, and though Sumption was happy to argue over a point, and accept my view on things, equally I was happy to listen to him and trust his judgement.

I arrived home and decided to go in through the Farthings' [Michael and Alison, neighbours] back garden so that the press in the street didn't know I was there. Audrey was looking after me, and had been reading every word. She felt it was not going well for the BBC. But they were really gearing up for me, and they were desperate for me to fail. Peter M called, and said did I have any idea how much the media wanted me to be a disaster in the witness box? TB was calling more regularly from Barbados now. Before the diaries got out to him, he kept asking me the same questions re content. All I could do was give him Sumption's view. He felt they were neither good nor bad. But on the positive side, they underlined our side of the story. They showed I did nothing wrong re the dossier. They showed I got very angry re the BBC, and made very clear why. They did show I wanted to put out Kelly's name, but didn't and instead did as I was told by him. As for the bad language and the loose language, Sumption's view was that the judge would not take it amiss. This was a private diary and he would understand.

The point of substance I was worried about related to where it looked like Geoff Hoon was suggesting a kind of 'plea bargain' [see July 4]. It was becoming clear to me that my lawyers were very much trying to get me to think of myself rather than the government as a whole, and particularly GH. If he had said that, and I recorded it, and it was a problem, it was a problem for him, not me. But I found it hard to think like that. I saw this still as the government under attack, me included, but also the government as a whole. They felt GH could use a 'cut-throat defence', and go for me, and therefore it was better I go for him, but I was not comfortable with that.

I called him on the Thursday or Friday, not sure which, and warned him about the line in my diary that they were calling the 'plea bargain point'. He was in the States on holiday and said he felt a lot better having gone away, despite the advice to stay. I felt he was under similar family pressures to my own. He said he had indeed been intending to throw the book at Kelly when it became clear he was Gilligan's source, but then calmed down and felt his honesty was to be commended and even rewarded in some way. He said he was grateful for my call and did not give me the impression he was worried about his own position. The only journalist I was talking to at all really was Phil Webster. *The Times* were about the only paper left covering the story from all sides so far as I could see. Most of them were totally with the BBC, but my sense was their case was falling apart.

Sunday, August 17

I was into the office early to go through a mass of material prepared for me by Clare [Sumner] and Catherine [Rimmer], who were both absolutely brilliant. They were so on top of the detail, and so driven by a belief that we were in the right. The diary extracts were circulated internally and also to a few in other departments. TB thought they were fine, though was worried about one or two observations made re him. Jeremy was still passionately of the view that it was just wrong that I had to do this, and we should have fought harder to stop it happening, but things had really moved on from that. I was trying to avoid adding to the big build-up to Tuesday at the inquiry, so I got back home via the neighbours' garden network again. I guessed if they had no new pictures they would give less space.

Had they had a camera in the garden they would have got a nice shot of me ripping my trousers, and cutting my leg, on the Farthings' trellis fence. I decided as well that tomorrow I would stay in Number 10, let the press continue to think I was at home, in a hotel, or wherever, just avoid being seen until I have to be. I had a nice dinner with Audrey, just chatting away about the whole thing, what Bob [Millar, Fiona's father] would have made of it, the effect it was all having on my mum and dad. Audrey was a hundred per cent full-on supporter, didn't believe a word against me, hated the BBC for what they'd done, and was not that sympathetic to Kelly, felt he should never have got involved with Gilligan in the first place.

Monday, August 18

I felt OK but reckoned I had now averaged three hours' sleep a night since I got that wretched letter re my diaries. I was going to have to rely on a mix of real preparation, nerve and adrenaline to get me through. TB was working on his own witness statement and remained confident. Catherine R had collated all the various comments from departments about the diaries, and the requests for further redactions from some, including TB. She and I then did a conference call with Sumption, and went through them all. Some he accepted but the bulk he didn't, and he was absolutely clear he was not taking something out just because the prime minister wanted it. Jonathan [Powell] was back to give evidence, and I got the feeling he had very deliberately not allowed it to ruin his holiday. The downside meant he was not terribly well prepared and I was worried he was a bit cavalier.

He had also grown his usual summer holiday beard and I was urging him to shave it off as it looked a bit ragged. Hutton did not strike me as a beard man. But Jonathan was adamant he was not changing anything just because he had been dragged back for this. He was nervous though, as was I. I noticed at one point a slight shake in his hand, and when the two of us were alone, without the lawyers and researchers around, he let the front down a bit and seemed really quite anxious. He went off and by all accounts did fine, though he rather dropped Tom Baldwin [*Times*] in it by indicating that Baldwin was the one who briefed me re the Sambrook lunch. I said I would have to find a way of rebutting when I gave evidence tomorrow.

Stephen Parkinson [government lawyer] came back with Jonathan and then sat down with me for a really helpful, but quite gruelling, Q&A session. I felt by now that I had every word and every argument just about right, and there were no questions I absolutely dreaded. I felt on top of the facts. It was still not clear how the judge or the QC [James Dingemans, senior counsel to the inquiry] intended to use my diaries which was still a bit of a worry. But there too, I felt confident I could defend myself, even though there was the odd embarrassment or difficulty in there. I was getting a lot of Good Luck messages coming through, and there was definitely the sense on the media that after TB, I was the one they were really waiting for. In fact for some of them, I was a tastier target than he is, because the thing was coming over now as being about government vs media. I was impressed by Parkinson, very calm, very clear, tested my answers well.

I was getting lots of advice, not least from TB, re how to deport myself. Always answer the question, not the question you want to answer. Make your answers short answers. Do not waffle or lecture. Don't be worried about pausing, or asking for time to reflect. If you cannot remember, say so. Call him 'My Lord' regularly. Look at him even if he is not looking at you. Be polite to all the lawyers. Above all, do not get riled. I remembered him saying the same thing before the [Rupert] Allason trial. 'And you won,' said TB. Yes, but not before the fucking judge gave me a sideswipe.[1] I called John Scarlett and made sure he was OK about the various references to him. He said he was fine. It must be dreadful for someone whose entire life has been about secrets, and dependent on staying low profile, now to be so out there in the public domain. He said he wouldn't have wanted it that way but he was sure we had done nothing wrong and it was important we were vindicated. He wished me luck. I said when the lawyer or whoever first uttered the words 'your diary', the press would get out their todgers and have a great collective wank. I went out for a quiet dinner with Gavin [Fiona's brother], Alan Maclean, Clare and Catherine. By the end we were the only people in the restaurant and we had a good laugh, but I was now as nervous as hell. The Number 10 staff had made me up a bed in John Birt's old office. It was fine, but slightly surreal. I got a message that there were people queuing outside the court [Royal Courts of Justice] overnight to try to get in. The thing had become a bloody circus.

Tuesday, August 19

I woke up to the sound of Big Ben. I heard four chimes but looked at my watch, and saw it was 5. I knew I wouldn't get back to sleep. It was so quiet now. I thought of Fiona and the kids asleep in Puyméras. I thought of Mum and Dad, and wondered whether Dad would see out the year. I thought of all the people who had been such a help in recent weeks. I thought about Mrs Kelly, really wished I knew what she really thought about all this. I was nervous but I had gone over everything fully, I was confident there wasn't a single difficult question we hadn't thought of, and I was confident my answers would withstand questioning. I scribbled a few thoughts – push hard on the dossier, express depth of anger at the BBC without getting angry, admit I wanted Kelly's name out, but emphasise I did nothing to make it happen.

I got up and went to TB's gym for a run on the treadmill. I just wanted to work up a sweat, without getting too tired, so ran for twenty minutes. I went down to the press office. The TVs were on and on both news channels there were people outside my house

---

[1] Campbell had been sued by Allason for malicious falsehood in 1996. Mr Justice Drake, the judge in the trial, said of Campbell 'He did not impress me as a witness in whom I could feel one hundred per cent confidence', had not been 'wholly convincing or satisfactory' and had been 'less than completely open and frank'. The comments were resurrected by the media in advance of Campbell's Hutton Inquiry appearance.

saying they were expecting me to leave any minute. I called Audrey, who was so proud of herself that we'd managed to go through the whole three days without any of them seeing me. There were snappers covering every exit from Number 10. I had a shower and got dressed in the office and as I came out the first person I bumped into was Bill [Wells] the messenger, who had also been the first person to wish me luck on the day of my FAC appearance. There was something wonderfully Dickensian about Bill. The conspiratorial wink, the little smile that was always there, the walk that wasn't so much a walk as a shuffle. He said to me 'Whatever happens, whatever anyone says about you, you're a good man and that's a fact.' I found it very comforting. I felt almost that it was a positive omen of some sort, he having lodged in my mind from the FAC day too. Everyone was supportive. Bill making tea, Felicity [Hatfield, secretary] making toast, Alison sorting my flight to Marseilles, Catherine R and Clare S coming in, their arms as ever full of huge, perfectly ordered files and folders, just going over the same old Q&A material.

Adam Chapman and Alan Maclean arrived. Alan had unsettled me a little at dinner when he said that my diary extract re 'we didn't do it ourselves' ['We agreed that we should not do it ourselves', July 9], could be read as saying we got others to do it. We went over how to deal with that. He knew it was innocently meant but said it was the one part he would zone in on if he was looking for a bit of a forensic challenge. Finally we left. Dave Borritt [Number 10 driver] drove us down there. I didn't want to arrive with an entourage so CR, CS and Alan got out early and went ahead. I drove up as close as we could get to the court entrance.

The demos were far bigger than we had been led to believe but I was glad we had turned down the chance of going in the back. I walked straight through. They were shouting and screaming, some through loudhailers, but I had got the blinkers on, got into my best Roy Keane mode and just walked on, Adam at my side. There was a bank of cameras to the right, and I ignored them too. I caught sight of the odd placard, one saying 'Ban the Campbell, ban the bomb'. I reached the door and CR looked like she was crying. I was taken by the cops and an usher to a little room upstairs. Within seconds, text messages were coming in. It had clearly gone out live. 'Entrance the stuff of legend' from Martin Sheehan. The court official said she had never known anything like it. People had been queuing since 1 to get into the marquee. She said there were journalists in there from all over the world. I bumped into Harry Arnold [ex-*Mirror* colleague] on the stairs. Another lucky omen. I looked out of the window and saw a group of journalists I knew. It dawned on me that the little group was made up of people I actually liked. Another one.

I was feeling OK. I was pacing up and down this tiny little room, making a few black-humour jokes about executions, drinking tea, when someone from James Dingemans' team came to see me. He said that Dingemans intended to refer to my diaries but not read from them. He would refer to them in questioning and if I wanted to read from them, I could, or I could paraphrase. I was fine with that. I was taken through by the usher, who was really looking after me. There were dozens of hacks around and I made a point of not looking at any of them, not letting any of them catch my eye, just talking to the usher and getting to my seat. Once I was there, I looked around at the lawyers, all chatting away to each other, and the people in front of the judge's bench, including a beautiful young woman just a few feet from me. She smiled really warmly and I smiled back and decided whenever I felt my hackles rise I would just look at her.

Hutton came in, everyone stood until he had settled himself, and away we went. Dingemans went through things very carefully and methodically. After the first couple of answers, I felt I was OK and that I just had to relax now and rely on my knowledge of the detail of everything. Listen to the question. Answer it. I had the file in front of me but I was really relying on the short list of points I had made to myself, and also the witness statement. We focused on the dossier right up to lunchtime. Hutton came in at several points and it took me a while to work out that didn't necessarily mean he was probing or trying to catch me out. On the contrary, on one occasion it finally dawned on me that if I looked at my diary extracts I would see the answer I was searching for. Dingemans was very clear and polite and helped my nerves settle quickly. I later thanked him for handling the diaries so sensitively. There were a few lighter moments, e.g. when I said [press officer] Danny Pruce's comments were above his pay grade, or that I didn't always respond to Jonathan's emails, and when I said at one point TB's comments were not taken on board. But I felt totally confident on the dossier and the overall impression was surely one of very good working co-operation with the spooks.

On the BBC again I felt Dingemans was fair in the way he took me through the correspondence with Sambrook. Here I think it helped that Hutton had my diaries because he had the full picture about the reasons for my rising anger and frustration. It was also clear that this was not some rampage for myself but for TB and the government. On Kelly, I felt comfortable with what I was saying. I was clear and straightforward, said it would have been much better if we had been clearer at the start rather than put in place a process that allowed the press to control when he was identified. I said in a way I was pushed to the margins of that decision and so did not really say, in the way I normally would perhaps, what I thought, because others involved may think I had a clear vested interest. Hutton was interested in why we didn't just batten down the hatches, why did he have to appear at the committee, to which I said it was inevitable and it would have been better if we had all faced up to that at the start.

By the time we broke for lunch I felt I was in good shape. The lawyers and CR/CS came to see me and said the tone was spot on, just keep going as you are. I had a coffee and a sandwich with CR and CS and was now worrying that my evidence would take us into another day. But we whizzed through the second half of my statement and the second session wound up fairly quickly and I could head back to France. There was an interesting moment when Dingemans, referring to a point in the diary where I said Gilligan would be fucked [July 4], where I answered in a way designed to convey the meaning without using the word, and I could see a little smile at the corner of Hutton's mouth. So he didn't mind the occasional in-joke. I felt that he and Dingemans had both been fair. However, they hadn't raised the admission I had thought about briefing the press (re Kelly's name) before TB appeared at the Liaison Committee. That meant when Godric got in there tomorrow, it was a problem for us. At least it was there in my statement, so it would not be news to the judge, but it would be new to the media. I felt it went OK and that was what all the talking heads seemed to be saying by the time I got back to the office.

There was a very warm reception as I got back in. I felt pretty tired and was desperate to get back to the family. I saw Tom and Godric before I left for Gatwick. I think my doing well had given them a bit of confidence too. I said the most important thing was to remember it is not a lobby briefing. They are not out to get you. Unlike the lobby, they actually want the truth. The only dramatic moment had been when they showed me an email that Gilligan had sent to David Chidgey [Liberal Democrat MP] re Kelly which I said was 'unbelievable'.[1] Dingemans said 'Don't make a speech on that,' but the fact the BBC had not disclosed this meant Gilligan was in big trouble now.

[1] Gilligan's email named David Kelly as Susan Watts' source for a BBC *Newsnight* story.

When I was on the train, TB called. He said everyone seemed to think I had been the perfect witness. He said that after the initial panic – in which I had shared in spades – the diaries had actually worked in our favour. He said he had said a prayer for me this morning. So had Cherie, who sent me a note saying well done, and how sad she felt that she and Fiona had fallen out, and was there anything she could do? TB said he felt confident re the outcome. He also felt Geoff Hoon would be OK too. He had been reading up more of the background from the inquiry so far. Hutton would not be impressed by the way the BBC handled it all. He would probably also think Kelly was a bit at fault – something I had picked up from the judge as well. TB had felt throughout that the fact I lost it at times was OK, in that the judge would see why, because he would understand the seriousness of the allegations against me, when maybe those who made them did not. I had lost count of how many times TB had called in recent days, particularly about the diaries and his worries about Sumption's strategy. He now accepted it had been the right strategy. I had been totally open. Sumption had redacted parts he thought irrelevant to the inquiry. But when we had finally handed them in on Monday at 5pm, nobody could say we were not being open. They had been gentle with me in the way they questioned me on them. There had been no reference to my bad language and only the phrase 'plea bargain' was specifically picked out.

I called Sumption from Gatwick, as I sat in the departure lounge bar, with the news blaring away, endless coverage of my evidence. He said he had been following it on the website all day and I did well. He sounded genuinely pleased. I thanked him, said I could not have had better advice and support. He said the next part of his plan was not to push for lots of cross-examination of the other witnesses. It was tempting to want to tie the BBC people in knots, but he reckoned Hutton would have probably made up his mind by now. I said it seems an age away that I was sitting crying my eyes out at Ian and Andrea's dining room table, going through the last days of July in my diary. I watched ITN and *Channel 4 News* in the first-class lounge. The general view was I did fine. It had been a pretty extraordinary holiday so far. The first few days great. Then starting to get stressed as I worked on my witness statement. Then the dire sinking feeling when that letter came through with the list of areas to cover – fine – and then the bombshell request for my diaries, and suddenly feeling like I was in some awful Kafkaesque nightmare. Neil trying to assure me it wasn't a hostile act. Then Sumption and the lawyers coming on the scene. His legal advice clashing with TBs political instincts, and me backing the lawyer. Then Alison coming out, then home for the final preparations, and now all done, and on a plane back to France.

Wednesday, August 20

I finally got to Puyméras at midnight. It was fantastic to see the kids, and Fiona and I seemed to get on for the first time in ages. I was trying to switch off now but the message coming from London was that both the broadcasters and the press were overwhelmingly positive. As expected we had a problem when Godric went through his evidence and he was asked about the idea I had had for briefing before TB went to the Liaison Committee that someone had come forward and even though it was in my witness statement, I had not been asked about it yesterday; he was, and so the media went off on one about me having misled the inquiry. Of course Hutton knew that was balls but it meant more crap in the press. The Tories were also on to me re what they claimed was a discrepancy re forty-five minutes in my evidence to the FAC, and now this. Also, the Chidgey email was going big as a problem for Gilligan, but Catherine R was worried because she had done research for the whips. The BBC case having been poor, and us having so far thought to have done well, they were now working up the line that Kelly was caught in a mincer between the two of us. Philip had a load of the cuttings sent out and I did seem to have done OK. Even the *Mirror* and the *Independent* were not that bad. I had prepared better than for the FAC, partly because more was at stake. Also, I was more nervous and that had helped. On the diaries, Dingemans had been particularly kind in that he gave the impression I had volunteered them. I went to see the Kennedys to thank them for all their help, then sent a stack of thank-you letters. PG was worried that Peter M was moving in to fill the vacuum that would be there when I left. He felt it would kill stone dead any chance of using my departure to put spin to rest as a problem.

Thursday, August 21

I called Geoff H in the States. He had read my evidence online, felt I did well and accepted that contrary to what some of the media tried to say, I did not drop him in it. He felt able to deal with the 'plea bargain' point. I was somewhat suprised to hear Kevin Tebbit had said he couldn't recall saying that Kelly didn't want to be named in the first wave of publicity. He also apparently gave a little soliloquy at the end which people didn't think was very clever.

David Hill called me, said TB now seemed seized of the need to get rid of the Order in Council. Clearly people were getting at him. I was pretty sure Peter M was on that track. I felt very strongly that it was a mistake, that my departure would be enough to signal some change, but that he should not allow his central operation to be further depoliticised. PG was increasingly of the view that TB was a bit out of touch and remote.

I was struggling to pack a whole holiday into a few days, and failing. TB called. He said he had read the transcripts of everyone's evidence to the inquiry. He thought I had been 'brilliant'. He said he honestly felt it was word-perfect and he was sure the judge would have been impressed. 'I think you just put it so much clearer than everyone else.' My worry was that Hutton, based on some of the interventions he had been making, seemed to think it would have been possible for Kelly's name not to come out, and we didn't. TB said he was going to have to use his own evidence to be clear with him the nature of the media world we have to deal with. His worry was that Hutton may in the end just feel he has to have a balance of blame, rather than just state the truth, which is the whole thing stemmed from the *Today* programme broadcasting what they did and then refusing to back down. Though I was still getting an OK press for my own evidence, the focus re me had moved to what Godric said. It was irritating, though if Hutton was reading the press, it would give him another example of how they worked. Some of them were saying he looked amazed to hear what GS said re me. It had been in my own bloody statement.

TB and I discussed when was the best time for me to leave. He said if I was totally decided, it was probably better to go sooner rather than later. We discussed the Order in Council. He said he was not sure it mattered as much as my note suggested. In the end people in the system would know David Hill was his person. Yes, but the Order in Council makes explicit that he can instruct them. This weakens him from the start and that therefore weakens you. It was an important symbol and symbols should not be underestimated. He said he felt he had to signal change. I said my leaving would be the change. Yes but though David may not be you, he is still a Labour spin doctor.

He said he hoped I would continue to advise him informally, and that we would be able to speak regularly and go over things. He said there were not many people who were both good at strategy and good at tactics. Re conference he now accepted Hutton would over-shadow it but he still felt we had to get back on to the domestic agenda. Philip felt he had to explain Iraq better than we had so far because that was the source of most of the negativity about him. I felt he had to make the affirmative case for progressive politics. He said he had had a good meeting on holiday with Murdoch, Elisabeth [Murdoch], Les [Hinton] and Irwin Stelzer [Murdoch adviser]. He said he knew most of us had had a crap holiday but he had enjoyed himself despite everything and felt rested. But he knew the knives were sharpening for him and once I was gone he would have lost his main lightning conductor.

Tuesday, August 26

I had managed to get in a couple of nice and reasonably relaxing days, Fiona and I getting on well, but it was still on balance a pretty grim holiday. I had hoped to have time to think through what to do after I left, but the Hutton business really put paid to that. We set off for Troyes today to break the journey back. TB called when I was in the hotel gym. He was now back in the UK. He felt that whereas my evidence was good, Jonathan's was a bit loose in parts. John Scarlett was up today and I had called him last night. He was very calm, very proper, focused but anxious. He said he was sure he had done nothing wrong and would be fine. He felt we had a good story to tell but he would rather that he didn't have to be there to tell it. His evidence, needless to say, went well. So did Omand's.

TB felt having looked at all the interventions by the judge that he was closer to our arguments than the BBC, whose evidence had been poor. He felt if there was one area where Hutton may have problems with the government it was over whether the MoD took sufficient care of Kelly. He was moving towards a line on Thursday of saying he accepted responsibility for everything as PM. He really hoped Hutton would draw a line and we would regain the space to get back focused on the domestic agenda. It was far from certain that would happen. PG told me the groups done recently were dreadful. I'm not sure TB got the scale of how bad public opinion was in parts. Philip and Peter H were both worried now that Peter M was TB's main influence re strategy and communications, and also responsible for reorganisation of the office. TB felt I should get a column, make money speaking and basically keep helping him but in a different way. There was big coverage of the memo I wrote him from New York [June 3]. It was actually a good piece of work, but they were using it to show I was pulling the strings etc.

Wednesday, August 27

Scarlett got a terrific press. Hoon did badly, gave the sense he was trying to blame everyone but himself. We got home about 6 so that Rory could watch Man U vs Wolves [1–0]. I spoke to Alex [Ferguson] who said he was now sure it was the right thing for me to leave. He had followed the whole thing and felt I would be fine. TB was being briefed by the lawyers and seemed fine. He felt he should go big on the seriousness of the allegations and how those making them failed to see that and make sure he took responsibility for difficult decisions.

Thursday, August 28

Geoff H got a dreadful press; now it was TB's turn to take the stand. I missed his first briefing meeting, felt it far better he see the lawyers first and then work out what if any thought we needed to give re the media. He asked me what the desired headline would be. It was somewhere in the area of TB taking responsibility (which GH had not done) whilst defending the decisions we took. It was also an opportunity to lay out what it is like making some of the decisions he has to. People felt GH did very badly, and gave himself some real problems. We had done well so far because everyone had been clear about the facts, even where they were difficult. But Geoff had opened us up. I felt he had ensured that more of us would be called to the second phase of evidence-taking than might otherwise have been the case. John Scarlett and I were already pretty much settled to the notion that we would certainly be called back. David Omand then said he thought I did really well. Re the diaries he said 'I hope you have all your diaries safely locked up somewhere – otherwise the men in black might come looking for them.' I was not entirely sure whether he was joking or not. Probably not.

TB set off and everyone, including the media, said he did well. He said on his return he had felt totally robust, and the facts didn't frighten him on this. No doubt his legal experience helped a bit too, and he felt that even though the inquiry team were in the driving seat, they were conscious of the fact that he was, when all was said and done, the prime minister. There were no attention-seeking histrionics, just more of the same fairly painstaking probing. He was clearly pleased it had not gone badly. I said that my evidence had gone well, his evidence had gone well, and I felt I should go tomorrow. It is the right moment. He looked really taken aback, but when I said we had agreed it would happen soon, why not now? Everybody is expecting it soon, but nobody is expecting it this soon, so why not? I was keen, within the limited room I had, to maintain an element of surprise which would help me shape the mood around it. He then started to warm to it. He said I should use it to get up a big argument about the nature of the media. I felt not yet, that I should just do it, be very nice about him and the government, make the case for progressive politics, but then be pretty low-key until Hutton was over. I had agreed with Jeremy Heywood that when Fiona and I left we would have five weeks' notice to work out. I told very few people what was happening – Godric, Tom, Anne, Alison – who all seemed both shocked and not shocked. My real desire was to keep it all quiet till tomorrow.

We had a meeting with Sumption and team in the Cabinet Room to go over the plan for the next stages, and in particular Sumption's note re what we should aim to get from the inquiry. Again, he made an interesting strategic call. He did not think we should press for lots of cross-examination. Nor did he think we should be saying to Hutton that the BBC should be criticised. All we would ask for was an acceptance that the story was wrong and that we were justified in challenging it. Also on Kelly, he obviously thought it would be wrong to attack him, but equally he hoped to steer the judge towards accepting that Kelly did wrong. TB was as near to deferential towards Sumption as I had seen him with anyone for ages. He knew his reputation for being very clever if a bit awkward, and we had all been saying how good he had been so far. It was interesting how much the legal side of this was actually about presentation too. A lot of the points made by the lawyers were tactical presentational points, but with the audience the judge, not the press or public. What I liked about Sumption most was that he didn't seem to care what the press or public were thinking about all this. He was totally focused on the judge.

Friday, August 29

I slept in a bit, having had a bit of asthma through the night. In to finalise my statement. TB didn't want any sense in there that he kept persuading me to stay. He thought it would be weakening. He wanted to write his own words about me, that there are two ACs, the one he knows and the one the media likes to portray. I left him to it, put changes into my own statement and then made a few calls. I told JP, who was very supportive, thanked me for everything and said he would like to do the media on it once we'd made the announcement. I called Margaret B, DB, JR, Tessa, Charles C, Ian McC, Pat H, GH and a few others. I decided not to call GB because I didn't trust his operation not to get it out ahead of me. Later – once it was out there and loads of messages were coming in – there it was on a long list typed up by Alison. 'The Chancellor's secretary called to say he wanted to thank you for everything you'd done for the party.' He couldn't even bring himself to call.

MB was very nice, said she really valued the way we had always worked together, that I had done a great job but there was a limit to what anyone could take. JR said he had been at a party meeting at the weekend and when he did a big defence of me, he got a great response. Ian McC put out some really nice words. So did Robin C. JP said his main line on the telly would be that I had decided I wanted a change, spend more time at home, that I was steeped in Labour and would be badly missed. I got a message to Hutton as I didn't want him to hear it on the media first. I told Dan [Bartlett], who said Bush would be disappointed because he was 'one of your biggest supporters', and I told Clinton and thanked him for his recent advice.

Once I finished my statement I got Alison to send out a message that I wanted to see all my team and anyone else in the building who was around. They knew what was coming so they weren't exactly shocked, but there was a lot of sadness in there. I said they knew I had been thinking about going and today was the day. I had had a great time and it had been an amazing privilege and one of the things that meant most to me was the team I had built up. I could not have done any of it without them and certainly in recent weeks I could not have asked for more by way of support. I said everyone was replaceable, I would leave with nothing but good memories of them, but Fiona and I desperately wanted to get a life back for ourselves and the children.

I suppose I knew it would go quite big but it was ludicrous just how big it went. Someone told me PA gave it the same Priority tag as a royal death or prime ministerial resignation. For several hours, once they did the breaking news Whoosh, they did literally nothing else. They had some so-called intelligence expert in the studio when it broke and they had him blathering away without knowing what on earth he was talking about. Matthew Doyle and Mark Bennett [Labour press officers] organised JP in Leeds, JR for later bulletins and some good backbenchers. The Tories put up Ann Widdecombe [former minister], Theresa May [Conservative Party chair] and eventually IDS. They looked shrill and ridiculous, trying to make it a disaster day for TB.

I gathered my thoughts again before doing a round of interviews with the broadcast political editors. They came in one by one and I used pretty much the same messages – great privilege, downside all taken by family, big on values, make the case for politics. It was also going big in the States and across Europe. Graeme [AC's brother] said he had been channel-hopping in Poland and found me simultaneously on Russian, Polish, French and Portuguese telly. The news channels were going with it hell for leather in the outer office and the endless two-way blather reminded me why I had got fed up dealing with them all. They just went on and on and on until another talking head was found. It underlined how out of hand the whole thing about me had got.

TB said even he was surprised how big it was going. He said I was a big personality and even though some of them hated me, they knew it was a big personality leaving the centre of the stage. Some of the hacks were trying to build it as a huge blow to him – could he cope blah? – which must have been a bit galling. Peter H was now also talking of leaving. He was worried Peter M was moving into the gap and it would not help us. My worry was more that there would be a concerted Civil Service retrenchment effort. All in all, things went fine today. Lots of nice messages, most media people saying I did well, even if I had become a problem.

The announcement re Fiona was in there though buried in all the avalanche of coverage re my leaving. It was a real sadness to me that she was leaving on bad terms with CB and with Tony too. But she was clearly happy we were on the way, and maybe surprised I had brought it to a head so quickly. They were straight on to what would I do in the future, and making assumptions I would make a fortune. The truth was I didn't really have a clue what I would do. I didn't speak to many journos. It was all kind of on autopilot. Boulton was pretty sour as ever, Marr OK, [Nick] Robinson [ITN] a jerk. Andy Bell [Channel 5] and Gary Gibbon [Channel 4] pretty straight. After a while they started to cover the coverage – the fact that it was so big abroad, that so many foreign hacks came into the street when the statement went out, the Trevor McDonald [ITV] special, US network websites doing it as number one or two and Boulton et al. saying they couldn't think of any official who would ever have sparked this kind of interest by announcing his departure. Catherine Colonna [Chirac's spokeswoman] called and said '*Tu es un star mondial, tu sais. Il faut saisir le moment.*' [You are a global star, you know. Seize the moment.] She said the president '*te salue*' [salutes you]. It was all a bit weird. Twenty minutes on ITN news, fifteen on the BBC, hours on Sky, the Sundays preparing to do pages and pages on it.

I cleared my desk. Went on a last walk round the building to say a few thank-yous and goodbyes, met Fiona and then we walked out together. I didn't look at the hacks and I didn't bother to listen, let alone answer. I just wanted to get out, and get home. There was a horde of media waiting in the street when we got home, more than I think we'd ever had. We parked at the top of the road, then walked down and we were swarmed as we tried to walk down the pavement.

Fiona got left behind a bit and I kept looking back and she had virtually disappeared. I stopped and yelled at a few of them and she caught up for a bit. The live reporters were describing what was going on, others shouting, snappers falling over each other. Ridiculous.

We got it and Audrey was very upset I had gone. She felt it was the right job for me and I should have stayed with Tony to the end. I was cheered by a message from Hutton. I had earlier asked Clare Sumner to tell Lee Hughes [secretary to the inquiry] what was going on and that I was keen he understood I would be doing interviews but would not talk about anything being investigated by him. The message came back now that he was very touched that I took the trouble to tell him in advance. I was probably reading too much into it but I had felt giving evidence that he felt I was an OK personality and I felt the same from the tone of his message today. I also thought that if he had watched any of the coverage, he would see once more what a nightmare culture we dealt with. I had a hunch that the diaries will have had a similar effect. TB felt the same, that the diaries gave an insight into what it was like trying to handle these big decisions surrounded by the 24-hour media trying to trip you the whole time.

Neil, Glenys, Rachel [Kinnock] and the Goulds came round for dinner and I think shared some of the relief. Rachel had been one of the first suggesting I leave ages ago, feeling it was time I stopped taking hits for others. Neil and PG were ambivalent but agreed it was the right time for me. TB called a couple of times. He had seen some of the news and couldn't believe how much coverage it was getting. He felt it was partly about the size of my personality but was also a reflection of their obsession with themselves. Philip had been following it all day and said I should get the tapes of the live coverage. 'You'd have thought the Pope had died.' We had a nice evening and Fiona was definitely more relaxed and I sensed the kids, though annoyed at all the bollocks in the street every time they came and went, were feeling a change for the better was happening. My asthma was bad though, partly the air, partly the current stress, also maybe a bit of anxiety about the total lack of certainty about what I would now do with myself. People were telling me I could make a fortune on the lecture circuit, but I can't say it held that much appeal. The most important thing was to try to get things at home on a better keel, rest, and then take stock. As I left, TB had said 'You do realise I will phone you every day, don't you?' I said yes, and I hope you realise sometimes I won't be there.

To be continued . . .

Index

Aaronovitch, David 140, 512
Abbas, Ali Ismaeel 548 *and n*, 549
Abbas, Mahmoud *see* Abu Mazen
Abdullah, Crown Prince of Saudi Arabia 151
Abdullah II, King of Jordan 75–6, 83
Abdullah, Abdullah 90, 134
Abu Mazen (Mahmoud Abbas) 496, 499, 511
ACAS 380
Adams, Gerry 44, 61, 325, 413, 540, 584, 659
Addis, Rose 147–8, 149
Adie, Kate 45
Adonis, Andrew (AA): on billions wasted on GB's projects 138; as Head of Policy Unit 252, 351; and CSR figures 263; at brainstorming session 265; and foundation hospitals 310, 320; and TB 328; attacked by Dobson 351, and student finance 366, 423, 464; and Roy Jenkins 407; against euro referendum bill 529; irritates TB 615
Advani, Lal Krishna 131
Afghanistan xii; and OBL 8, 12, 16, 36*n*, 86; Allied invasion 12–13, 15, 33–4, 35; humanitarian issues 43–4, 46, 57, 58, 89, 103, 348; battle damage assessment 48; lack of strategy 56; support for NA 56, *see* Northern Alliance; battle for Mazar-e-Sharif 57, 58, 59, 61, 62, 66, 70–71, 83, 84, 86, 95, 135; Muslim poll on war 88 *and n*; liberation of aid workers 89; and diplomatic problems 90, 91; UK/US split over future 91, 92; fall of Kandahar 103; TB on its future 106; TB's visit (2002) 133–6; US 'wants out' 187; British troops in 191; AC meets journalists 267; al-Qaeda documents seized 425; *see also* Kabul; Omar, Mullah; Taliban
Agence France-Presse (AFP) 344
Agyepong, Kwabena 162
Ahern, Bertie 324, 428, 539, 540
Ahmad, Asif 323
Ahmed, Kamal 402
Ahmed, Naji Saberi 304
Ahmed, Lord Nazir 113
Ainsworth, Bob 376, 606

Alexander, Douglas (DA) 182, 233; 'snappy' 238; TB solicitous about 238; and TB/GB rift 239, 245, 401; and London's special problems 265; impresses AC 277, 331; on New Labour 300; and euro debates 342, 348; and GICS review 350–51; drafts asylum communications plan 428; semi-permanent in war room 531; on need for reconnection with party 582; and reshuffle 604, 606; conference call with AC 622; at strategy meeting 627; on political Cabinet 636, 639; TB wants on NEC 651; in US with PG 664
Al Jazeera: impact of 75, 369; TB interview 43, 44; OBL video 68, 71, 72, 74, 75, 76, 83–4, 85; visits BBC 414
Allan, Colin 594
Allan, Tim 209
Allason, Rupert 682 *and n*
al-Qaeda 8, 38, 45, 110; and OBL 4, 21, 36 *and n*; and New York air crash 87*n*; and Mullah Omar 102, 103; tape on 9/11 104; and Richard Reid 122*n*; Guantanamo Bay prisoners 140; Leicester suspects 143; and Iraq 285, 414, 448 *and n*, 449; and WMD 356*n*, 411, 425; No. 3 arrested 473; Riyadh bombings 571
Amanpour, Christiane 305
American Airlines Flight 587 87 *and n*
Amos, Baroness Valerie 570, 622
Ancram, Michael 255, 389
Anda, Bela 591
Anderson, Bruce 664
Anderson, Clive 374
Anderson, Donald 614, 615, 618, 631, 632, 633
Anderson, Dr Iain 218, 273, 277
Andrew, Prince 241, 254
Angola 476*n*, 483
Annan, Kofi 22, 26, 183, 278, 291, 302, 471, 501, 503, 504, 506, 525, 526 *and n*, 550
anthrax 55, 56, 63, 64, 65, 450
antisocial behaviour/orders (ASB/ASBOs) 152, 186, 211, 220, 223, 230, 347, 348, 349, 352, 358, 381, 398, 636
Anti-terrorism, Crime and Security Bill (2001) 110

and NI 279, 287; at the end of his tether re GB 280–81; worried about Iraq 282, 286; invited to 9/11 commemorations 283; profoundly affected by Milburn 284; critical of Policy Unit 286; wants more formal way of working 286; and IGC negotiations 287; hoping to direct US down UN route 285–6, 287, 288–9, 290, 291, 293, 294; in Mozambique 287–9; at Johannesburg summit 285, 287, 289–91; decides to publish dossier on Iraq WMD 291–2 *and n*, 293; against recalling Parliament 293, 299, 300; meets with Blix (*q.v.*) 293–4; Camp David discussions with GWB 294–7; at Balmoral 297; TUC speech 297–8 *and n*, 299; and Iraq dossier 299, 300–1, 302, 303, 306, 308 *and n*, 309

September 2002–January 2003
and US/UNSCR difficulties 300 8 *passim*; 'poverty' speech 303 *and n*; and Estelle Morris/A-level row 303–4, 309–10, 318, 320; prays for Schroeder to win election 305; does well at NEC 308–9; and GB's attack on foundation hospitals 310–11, 312; Conference and speech 300, 303, 305, 310, 311, 312, 313–14, 316, 319; further difficulties with Americans on UN route 316, 317–18, 319; endures *Mirror* lunch 317; and press reports of GB's jealousy 320; on GB and euro 320–21; obsesses about GB 321, 322; and NI negotiations 323, 324, 325, 332 *and n*; clashes with GB over foundation hospitals 323, 324–5; discussions with Putin 325–7; persuaded to swap coat for photocall 326; relations with GB worsening 329; PMQs (October–December 2002) 330, 336–7, 346, 354, 369, 381, 399; and UNSCR 331, 355; and military options 331; pressures GB to discuss euro 334, 344 5; does not want Chirac credited with 'sorting' GWB 334; plans reshuffle 335, 336, 337, 338–9; further rows with GB 339, 346, 348; clashes with Chirac at Brussels summit 339–41, 342, 344, 345, 346n; makes funny speech 343; disappointed with Schroeder 346, 355; and AC's marathon sponsorship 349; and CB's book project 350, 354; and Dobson's attack on Andrew Adonis 351, 352; on relations with GB 352, 356–7, 362; and new 'board meetings' 353; on reform 357, 358, 389; Mansion House speech 359, 360; on GWB's disinterest in different concerns 361; and FBU strike 336, 360, 362, 364, 365, 366, 367, 371, 372, 373–4, 375, 376n, 377, 379, 380; Queen's Speech/debate 328, 333, 345, 348, 359, 361, 362, 363; sends radio message to Saddam 362–3, 364; *Mirror* interview 365; ITN interview 366; accepts that GB is a 'malign force' 367–8; and GB's NHS strategy 368; and Chirac and GWB at Prague summit 369, 370; and CB and Caplin 375–400 *passim*, 461, 466; on GB as cause of Labour's

problems 379, 380; discussions with Assad 396–7; almost caught out in House 399; not on sparkling form 400; schism with GB growing 401; New Year message 402, 404 *and n*, 405; his problems the same as a year ago 405; decides to sack GB 406, 409, 411; and Roy Jenkins' death 407

January–April 2003
on likelihood of war 408, 409, 411, 412; angered by Derry Irvine (*q.v.*) 409–10; and Israel and Palestinian conference 409, 414; and need for discipline in Cabinet 411, 412, 413, 414; clashes with GB over tuition fees 413, 418, 423, 424, 425; on GB's game plan 415, 421, 423; on need for real changes 414–15; 'holds firm' on Iraq 415, 16; and imminent war 418–19, 420; and UN inspectors' discoveries 421, 422; worried about US declaring war without UNSCR 423, 426, 427, 430–31, 432–3; Liaison Committee appearance 424, 425; at launch of AC's marathon appeal 426; PMQs (January–April) 427, 436–7, 468, 493, 512, 531, 542; does deal with France over Zimbabwe sanctions 427, 428, 444; on lack of international support over Iraq 430; and press reports on situation with GB 432; their dysfunctional relationship 433–5, 436, 467; and Blix reports 435; on need for second UNSCR 437, 438, 439–41; Camp David talks with GWB 441–3, 450; on Saddam's non-cooperation 445 *and n*; and Chirac at Le Touquet summit 445 8; at 'shock and awe' presentation 449; sees weapons inspectors 450–51; angry at Irvine's pay rise 452–3; and Franco-German plan 454, 455, 456; and Heathrow security 455; on need for more emphasis on humanitarian side in Iraq 458, 459, 461; worried about Iraq 459–60, 463; gives conference speech on Saddam 460 *and n*; and Chirac at Brussels summit 461, 462, 463; has dreadful meetings with GB 462, 467; and 'last push for peace' 463, 464, 465, 466, 467; sees John Paul II 465; angry at the departments 465–6; his statement to the House 467 *and n*; angry with Blix 468, 471, 472, 475; and possibility of no second resolution 469–70; at Madrid summit 470, 471–2; Welsh Labour Conference speech 470–71, 472; and UNSC votes and vetoes 472, 473, 474, 475, 478, 479, 480, 482, 488, 493, 495; in NI 474; and need for Mexico and Chile to come over 475–6, 483, 484, 486, 487, 493, 496, 500; conversations with GWB 475–6, 477–8, 483–4, 486–7, 490–91, 493–4, 496–7, 499, 500–1; MTV interview 477 *and n*; and CS's Rawnsley interview 481, 484–5, 488; and ITV programme 485–6; and Attorney General's opinion on legality of war 488, 489, 495; feels close to contempt for GB 490; angry with

Rumsfeld 490, 494; and Murdoch 490, 492; and Saddam's six tests 492 *and n*; and Commons vote 497; and the French 497–8, 499; and Palestinians 499; at Azores meeting 502–5; Margolick interview 505 *and n*, 563; and RC's resignation 507; speech in the House 509 *and n*, 510; praised by GWB 510–11; doesn't rule out a deal with GB 513; and invasion of Iraq 513, 514; and Chirac at Brussels summit 514–16; and deaths 515; gives BFBS (forces) interview 517; and progress of war 518, 519, 520, 521–2, 523; writes note to GWB explaining US unpopularity 523–4, 528–9, 538; at Camp David with GWB 524, 525; sees Kofi Annan at UN 526; and propaganda effort 527; and need for communications and media plan 527–9
April–August 2003
discussions with GB on euro 532, 533, 551–2, 553, 566, 567, 569, 572, 573, 596, 597; on need for counter-plan on future of Iraq 532; visits troops 532, 533; his letter to Iraqis 532, 534; keen for US to rebuild relationships 536; in NI for GWB's visit 536–40; speaks to FM 542–3; a key player in Iraq aftermath 543; and IRA 543; sponsors AC 544; at a loss re GB 544, 549; at Sandhurst 545; in *The Simpsons* 545; sees troops in Scotland 549; with Schroeder 550, and Prodi 550; and reshuffle 552; rift with GB over foundation hospitals 553, 560, 561; a 'diplo-disastrous' discussion with Putin 555–9; PMQs (April–July) 560, 566, 610–11, 635, 646; and NI 560; meets Rumsfeld 562; and need for radical domestic policies 563–5, 568; still making mind up re GB 565; and foundation hospital vote 567; and press reports about CB 569, 582–3; and CS's resignation 570; and euro statement 575, 576, 577; open at party meeting about division with GB 577; angry with Peter M over comments re him and GB 578–80; press gallery speech 580, 581 *and n*; confident at press conference 582; wants to meet IRA 584; in Kuwait 585; visits Iraq 585, 586–7; hopes for more co-operation from GB 587–8; Polish speech 584, 587, 589, 590; in St Petersburg 590–91, 592; and WMD dossier allegations 589–90, 594, 595; thinking of standing down 597; wants to be fully briefed on Iraq 597–8; arranges ISC inquiry into 'forty-five minutes' claim 598 *and n*, 602, 612; and GB statement on euro 601, 602, 603; dinner with Chirac 604; dreads sacking Irvine 601, 604, 605, 619; and reshuffle 604, 605–6, 608–9, 611; and Hunting Bill 609–10; Fabian Society speech 609, 610; and Hain's comments on tax 613; frustrated at lack of radicalism re public services 615; and AC's FAC appearance

617, 618, 619, 623, and on *Channel 4 News* 621; wants closure on FAC and to get back to domestic agenda 623, 624, 625, 629, 630 *and n*; on need for reform 627, 629, 636; and the 'source' 631, 632, 634; and the BBC 631, 632, 633, 635; and Liaison Committee 602, 614, 634; and strategy meetings 634, 635; clashes with GB over lack of strategy 634–5; at Political cabinet 636, 637, 638–9; Third Way conference speech 643; speaks at Michael Foot's 90th 644; at ISC inquiry 644, 645, 646; 'down' 645–6; Congress speech 647; with GWB at White House 647–8; and Dr Kelly's death 649, 650; in Tokyo and Shanghai 651, 652, 655; and leaking of Kelly's name 655, 656; on WMD/trust issue 662; and Caplin's *Hello!* magazine spread 663–4, 666; is talked about in past tense 664; and relations with GWB 665; worried about AC having to submit his diaries to Hutton Inquiry 675, 676–7, 679, 686; works on witness statement 680–81; and AC's appearance at Inquiry 681–2, 686, 688, 689; takes the stand 690–91; deferential to AC's barrister 691; and AC's departure 688, 693, 694

Blank, Sir Victor 317, 394, 463
Bleach, Peter 592 *and n*
Blears, Hazel 147–8, 606, 651
Blitz, James 318
Blix, Hans: and TB 293–4, 300, 317, 411; conciliatory at UN 304; making progress 316; goes back to Baghdad 366; disliked by GWB 370; felt by US to be a problem 392, 396; and FCO briefings 399; goes to UNSC 400–1; and Iraqi weapons inventory 401; to do 'minor' UN reporting 412; 'cat and moused' 413; finds shells and nuclear papers 419, 420, 421 *and n*, 422 *and n*; given more time 430, 431; and Saddam's non-cooperation 433, 435, 439, 440, 441, 444; report covers banned missiles 438; TB feels he is the key 439, 440, 448; cagey at Cabinet 450; has found nothing 450; in Baghdad 453; given more time 456; delivers report to UNSC 459, 461, 463; on Saddam's decommissioning of al-Samoud missiles 471; angers TB 468, 471, 472, 474, 479; his clusters document 475, 476, 477, 484; and GWB 483, 640; and TV address 494; criticises British intelligence 598
Blunkett, David (DB): post 9/11 4, 9, 10; and asylum seekers 17, 215, 322, 423; has hopes of being deputy leader 17–18, 19; rants at Civil Service 28; and civil contingencies 29, 31; angry with BBC 31; and the police 45, 174, 183; worried at lack of strategy 57–8; blamed by Balls for TB/GB split 100; writes to IDS on Tory policy 103, 104; worried about race 'debate' 105, 106; on loss of confidence in politics 109; on Tories and IDS 137; as next Chancellor 139; on Civil Service

138–9; paranoid about Milburn, CC and Hain 152–3; article on Commonwealth Education fails to mention TB 159; angry with TB over 'NHS day' 175; and new *Times* editor 180; respected by permanent secretaries 181; 'looms large' 182, 184; looks odd 184; and Budget 186, *see* Budgets; NHS speech eclipsed by crime meeting 191, 192, 268; pro graduate tax 193; appearance 197, 200; makes public Liam Fox's unwise comments 206, 208; and NHS campaign 207, 208, 210, 211; and child benefits 217, 218, 230, 231; 'boorish' 224; on crime 220, 230, 231, 245; his team 235; opposed to reshuffle 237, 238; impossible at strategy meetings 245, 247, 248, 249; constantly plotting against TB 245–6; against CC's attack on press 246; Mansion House speech 258; goes back on commitment to Africa 258; and unions 262, 277; CSR and his counter-strategy 263, 264, 266–7, 278, 270; his public image 263–4; gives CSR statement 271–2, 273, 274; at Kemp/Wade marriage party 274; and Iraq war 289–90, 301, 306, 360, 367; against foundation hospitals 310–11, 312, 313, 318, 319, 322, 323, 324–5, 348, 553, 560, 561; Conference speech (2002) 312, 313; on pay awards 331; not consulted over reshuffle 338, 339; and EU rebate 339; unamused by TB's speech 343; becoming impossible 346; and antisocial behaviour agenda 348, 358; his left-wing strategy 352; against reform 357, 358, 366, 368; and university funding 366, 367, 368, 381, 398, 413, 418, 420–25 *passim*; and FBU strike 371, 373; gets bad press 375, 379, 380; has 'non-arguments' 399; openly 'organises' against TB 411; and tax credits 73, 417, 418; ahead of TB in polls 419; and Olympic bid 423, 572, 574–5; incapable of laughter 429; on tax rises 429; 'encouraged' by AC/Balls meeting 436; on unions 438; gives divisive speech 444; nervous of being moved 448; and Irvine's pay rise 453; on *Frost* 453, 454; considers TB's article Tory 467; and PLP 490; and Iraq 492, 495, 501, 502, 506, 509, 510, 514; more engaged on policies 497, 500; and CS 510, 512, 549, 570–71; critical of War Cabinet meetings 520; vile to Tessa Jowell 423; and Peter M 532, 578–80; and TSC report 554–5; on *Frost* on EMU referendum 576–7; CBI speech 578; presents paper on benefits 581; *Wall Street Journal* article 584; and press leak on briefing note 598–9; good on *Frost* re WMD dossier 599–600; and Peter M's apology at PLP 604; and reshuffle 604, 606, 609; rages at the Lords 612; on lack of strategy 627, 634–5; at political Cabinet 636, 638, 639; wants to visit Murdoch 644; amused by AC's bagpipe playing 645; resigns as prime minister xxii

Brown, Jennifer Jane 123, 130, 132, 134, 135; funeral 136, 138–9, 175
Brown, Nick 218, 234, 235, 236, 268, 275, 277, 605, 606
Brown, Paul 98
Brown, Sarah 123, 161, 274, 433, 560; *Magic: New Stories* 249
Browne, Des 606
Browne, John 426
Brussels summits: 2001 25–6; 2002 254–5, 339–41; 2003 461–2; *see also* Laeken
Buck, John 586
Buckby, Simon 572
Buckeridge, Anthony 329
Buckland, Chris 272
Budgets: and PBR (2001) 44, 92, 94, 95–6, 97, 98; 2002 186, 188, 200, 205, 207–8, 209–10, 211, 212, 213, 214, 230; 2003 429, 529, 532, 541–2, 543
Burgess, Charlie 328
Burnley 194; elections 215, 217, 222, 562
Burnley Football Club 18, 48; vs Norwich 26, 180; vs Crystal Palace 63, 99–100; vs Wolverhampton 72; vs Watford 88, 160, 480; vs Coventry 91; vs Millwall 121, 122; vs Barnsley 163; vs Preston 190; vs Coventry 214; vs Stoke 301; vs Leicester 333; vs Tottenham Hotspur 355; vs Man United 359, 380–81; vs Gillingham 401; vs Brighton 402, 403; vs Grimsby 406; vs Brentford 432; vs Fulham 468; vs Wimbledon 564
Burrell, Paul: trial 349, 350, 359–60, 361, 362, 401
Burton, John 174, 647
Bush, Barbara 297
Bush, George, Sr 23, 204, 205, 295, 297
Bush, George W., US President (GWB) xv–xvi, 259–60; relations with TB xiv, xv, xx, 19, 640; post 9/11 7, 8–9, 11, 12, 13, 14, 15, 17, 19; and British press 18; with TB in Washington 23–5; gives powerful speech 26; on security 30; lacks strategy 31; and Putin 37; ready for war 41; statement on Afghanistan 41, 42; and OBL 48 *and n*, 50; sends out mixed messages 50, 51; discussions with TB 56–7, 82, 87, 88; and British opinion 64, 291, 425; and bad PR 64, 65; grateful to AC for going to US 72, 74; visits Washington CIC 79; 'axis of evil' speech 152, 154, 155, 158, 203; and MEPP 199–200, 201, 202, 204, 295–6; with TB at ranch 202–4, 205; chats with AC on dog, drink and running 202, 203; on Arafat 202, 204, 205, 257, 258, 259; likes Schroeder and Putin 205; Middle East speech makes waves 257; at G8 summit 258–60; on Africa 259; appreciative of TB's support 272; and Iraq 285–6; White House speech 292; and TB's US visit 283, 288, 294, 295–7; UNGA speech 286, 291, 300, 301; and UN route re Iraq 302, 317–18, 320, 334, 337; lays out case for disarming Iraq 323 *and n*; wins election 355; uninterested in different concerns

Charles, John 668

Chat magazine 279

Chater, David 540

'Chemical Ali' *see* Majid, Ali Hassan al-

Cheney, Dick xvi, 24; gives mixed messages 55; 'bullish' 66–7; *Sun* interview 81, 84; and run-up to Iraq war 186–7, 199, 284, 285, 286, 288, 294, 295, 296, 297, 300, 301, 306, 316; and Sunday shows 499; and aftermath issues 519, 526; 'menacing' 534; impassive as ever 648

Chernomyrdin, Viktor 643

Chidgey, David 685

Chilcot Inquiry xiv–xv, xvi–xvii

child benefit 217, 218, 230, 333, 361

Chile 473, 475–6, 477, 482, 483, 484, 486, 487, 491, 496; *see also* Lagos, Ricardo

Chiles, Adrian 103*n*

Chinook helicopter crash (1994) 153, 159

Chirac, Jacques xvi; post 9/11 5, 14, 15, 20; meeting with TB and Schroeder 57, 58, 59–60, 71, 77; and CENTCOM 111, 113; on good form 111; against food agency being in Finland 112; wins election 223; attacks TB on NATO 236; dines with him in Paris 255; anti-American 260, 298, 446; warmer than at Johannesburg summit 290; and Iraq 294, 318, 320, 322; and UN resolutions 332, 333, 334, 337; clashes with TB over CAP 339–41, 342, 344, 345, 445, 446; his actions explained by French ambassador 342–3; shakes TB's hand 369; offers TB summit date 377; against invasion of Iraq 426; and sanctions against Zimbabwe 428; full of 'blather' 436; TB on 439, 440; at Le Touquet summit (2003) 444, 445, 446, 447–8, 454; and Iraq/UN resolution 446–7, 455, 462–3, 483–8 *passim*, 493, 495, 497–9, 499, 501, 503; visions for Europe 471; 'pained and shocked' at being misrepresented 511; behaviour at Brussels summit 514–16; GWB on 538–9, 540; causes trouble on Iraq and ESDP 550; wants to do Africa article with TB and Schroeder 585; TB on 588–9; at St Petersburg summit 591; warmer towards TB 604; and AC's departure 693

Chissano, Joaquim, President of Mozambique 288

CHOGM *see* Commonwealth Heads of Government Meeting

Chowdhury, Badruddoza, President of Bangladesh 127

Chrétien, Jean 26, 227, 248–9, 258, 291

Christiansen, Sabine 226

CIA 49, 59, 71, 428

CIC *see* Coalition Information Centre

Civil Service 28, 29, 110, 273, 286, 424, 564, 588, 593; and special advisers 44, 185; TB on 185, 408, 427

Clark, David 247, 599

Clark, Helen 291

Clark, General Wesley 77

Clarke, Charles (CC) 15, 26; on CS 26; on NHS 95; gives 'silly' interview 99; blamed by Balls for TB/GB split 100; on need for more political and ideological debate 106, 110; criticised by Kinnock 112; not happy 140, 141, 144; PG's view of 150; Hyman's view of 151; at meeting on PG's groups 182; and MEPP 183; and Budget strategy 207–8; visits Burnley 215; and the media 221, 244, 246; focused on 'new politics plan' 227; 'hyper' 229; backs Levy's *Times* interview 232, 233; meeting with TB over unions 262; admits to hating the job 266; and recall of Parliament 298–9; worried about relations with AC 303; on mood of party 307; and the Tories 330; becomes Education minister 335, 338–9, 342; 'starting to motor' 354; excellent on reform 358; on CB 400; and student finance 412, 413, 420, 421, 422, 423, 428; pro Olympics bid 439; discusses schools with TB 551; and schools funding 563, 566, 581; and PLP 572; and euro 597; misreported on tax 613; at political Cabinet 636, 637; advises AC not to leave 654, 655; mentioned 114, 228, 347, 578

Clarke, Kenneth 355, 409, 428

Clarke, Victoria ('Torie') 81, 114, 141, 142

Cleaver, Magi 37, 121, 127, 129, 202, 313, 326, 539

Clinton, Bill (BC) xvi; and Kosovo 11; post 9/11 21, 22; worried about GWB 108; taken round No. 10 by AC 108; gives AIDS speech 108; advises TB 182, 194, 276, 301, 644; writes article on TB 222–3; at Third Way conferences 243, 643; at Labour conference (2002) 310 *and n*, 313, 314–16, 317, 318, 321; on GWB 313, 316, 317, 320, 640–41; at Chequers 387; and GWB 431, 499, 615; his *Guardian* article 502, 507; at Frost's party 628; Ritz lunch with PG and AC 640; gives political masterclass xvi, 641–3; on TB 641–2; AC thanks for his advice 692

Clinton, Chelsea 22, 108

Clinton, Hillary 51, 315, 443, 614, 628, 630, 642

Clwyd, Ann 247, 469

CNN: TB interview 14, 15, 19

Coalition Information Centre (CIC) 73, 74, 78, 79, 80, 81, 82, 83, 107–8, 114, 187, 292, 302, 323, 332, 374, 422, 462, 616; 'dodgy dossier' (February 2003) 451–8 *passim*, 479, 599–600, 608, 611, 612, 614, 616, 617, 623, 624, 625, 627

Cobra meetings 6, 7, 9, 10, 255, 273, 333, 361, 378, 410, 454

Cochrane, Alan 624

Cockerell, Michael 90, 293

Coffman, Hilary 32, 34, 116, 121, 384, 388, 389, 399, 414, 533, 554, 611, 620

Cole, John 644–5

Coleman, Jonno 104

Collins, Tim 254

Colonna, Catherine 20, 58, 344, 345, 369, 444, 445, 447, 693

Delhi (2002) 130–21
Dell'Olio, Nancy 212, 214, 323, 324
Delves, Lt General Cedric 198
Denham, John 362, 509
Dennis, Steve 401
Department for International Development
(DFID) 54, 92, 127, 128, 136, 461, 544,
570, 588
Department of Trade and Industry (DTI) 10,
164, 182, 372, 600
Department of Transport, Local Government
and the Regions (DTLR) 5, 96–7, 98, 145,
146, 167, 168, 171, 173, 174, 217–18, 231n,
235; see also Mottram, Sir Richard;
Sixsmith, Martin
Desmond, Richard 104, 105, 176, 212, 225,
226, 227, 228, 231, 251–2, 367, 611, 665
Dewar, Donald 85, 223
DFID see Department for International
Development
Diamond, Patrick 402, 609
Diana, Princess of Wales 162, 163, 195, 196,
349, 360n, 384
Diego Garcia 43, 278, 489
Dimbleby (ITV) 176, 177, 178, 530
Dimbleby, Jonathan 176, 265
Dingemans, James, QC 681, 684, 685, 687
Diogo, Luísa Dias 288
Dobson, Frank ('Dobbo') 122, 140, 227, 350,
351, 352, 468, 482, 553, 562
Donaldson, Liam 356
Dondo, Mozambique (2002) 289
Donoughue, Bernard 206–7
Dos Santos, José Eduardo 483
dossiers: WMD (September 2002) xvi–xvii,
xviii, 292, 293, 297, 299, 301, 302, 303,
304, 306, 308 and n, 309, 325–6, 587, 589,
591, 592–3, 596, 614, 624, 634, 645, 646,
672, 677, 679, 684; and 45-minute point
598 and n, 619, 620, 627, 646, 673; and
Kelly 631, 632; 'dodgy' dossier see
Coalition Information Centre
Douglas-Home, Alec 219
Downing, General Wayne 82
Doyle, Matthew 427, 692
Doyle, Vera 224
Drake, Mr Justice 682n
Drummond, Stuart 222n
DTI see Department of Trade and Industry
DTLR see Department of Transport, Local
Government and the Regions
Dunwoody, Gwyneth 243, 247
Durkan, Mark 324
Dyke, Greg 45, 512, 618, 623, 624, 625, 628,
630, 632, 651, 654, 662, 664
'Dynamite, Ms' 404
Dzurinda, Mikulas 546, 547

Eastham, Paul 655, 656
Ecclestone, Bernie 260
ECHR see European Convention on Human
Rights
Economic and Monetary Union (EMU) 79,
94, 128, 165, 175, 286, 320–21, 529, 533,
554, 575, 602, 629
Edenham High School, Croydon 579 and n

Edmonds, John 3, 322, 645
education: TB on 193, 194n, 267; A-level row
303–4, 309–10, 311, 320, 330, 419–20;
maintenance allowances 263; schools
funding 563, 566, 579 and n 581;
university funding 193, 333, 341, 342,
345, 346, 347, 351, 366, 368, 369, 374, 381,
398, 420–21, 423, 424, 425, 489
Edwards, Senator John 442, 665
ElBaradei, Mohamed 446, 450–51, 453
Elizabeth II: and Princess Margaret's death
163, 164; and Queen Mother's death 195,
196, 205; at Golden Jubilee media
reception 216–17; at No. 10 dinner
218–19; TB's speech about 241; Leo Blair
sings to 297; and Burrell trial 349, 350,
360; and TB 490; message to the troops
509
Elizabeth, the Queen Mother 86; death
195–6, 199; lying-in-state and subsequent
furore xx, 200, 201, 205, 208, 209, 212–17
passim, 228, 230, 238–50 passim, 252, 253,
254; funeral 203, 204, 206
Ellam, Mike 596
Elliot, Larry 209
Elton, Ben 241
EMU see Economic and Monetary Union
Ennis, Jeff 478
Enron 152
Enstone-Watts, Charlie 432
Erdogan, Recep Tayyip, President of Turkey
487, 504
Eriksson, Sven Göran 104, 212, 213, 214, 224,
323
Errera, Gérard 342, 344, 444–5, 493
Ervine, David 540
ESDP see European Security and Defence
Policy
Eskew, Lisa 115, 186
Eskew, Thompson 186
Eskew, Tucker 80, 84, 87, 88, 89, 110, 115,
121, 146, 147, 172, 186, 320, 321, 427,
535
euro/single currency xx, 17, 34, 46, 79, 94,
99, 111, 126, 229, 246, 260, 280, 281, 312,
328, 329, 334, 342, 344–5, 354, 380, 529,
532–3, 551–2, 560, 567, 569, 572–8 passim,
581–2, 597, 599, 601, 602, 604
European Convention on Human Rights
(ECHR) 431, 432, 433
European Parliamentary Labour Party
(EPLP) 255
European Research Institute, Birmingham:
TB's speech (2001) 94 and n
European Security and Defence Policy
(ESDP) 343, 550
Evans, Alun 546
Evans, Huw 356
Evans, Mike 635
Evening Standard 84, 145, 147, 157, 184, 208,
209, 240, 274, 320; see also Reiss, Charles
Eyre, Richard 284

Faber, Lady Caroline 219
Fabian Society: TB speech 607, 609, 610, 611
FAC see Foreign Affairs Committee

Hutton Inquiry xvii, 649, 651, 653, 655, 660, 666; AC's preparation for 654, 657–9, 662, 663, 666, 667–8, 669, 670– 82 *passim*; AC's appearance at 682–5, 686–7; and MoD 651, 666, 667, 668, 673, 689; *see also* BBC; Hoon, Geoff

Hyman, Peter: as TB's speechwriter 3, 31, 32, 310, 312, 609, 619; on TB 138; on CC 151; and Byers' resignation 177, 180; wants Budget strategy meetings 205; and TB's conversion to spontaneity 213; and the euro 246; appalled at Cabinet 257; on importance of Queen's Speech 322; critical of CC 335, 338; thinks party is complacent 367; sees CC re student finance 423; and euro referendum bill 529, 596; against AC's departure 653; worried about Peter M's influence on TB 689, 693; mentioned 220, 265, 414

IAEA *see* International Atomic Energy Agency
Illsley, Eric 614, 667
immigration 161, 162, 215, 216; *see also* asylum
Independent 28n, 140, 158, 241, 242, 243, 271, 318, 416, 599, 664, 669, 687; *see also* Grice, Andy
Independent on Sunday 105, 614
India 35, 38–9, 41, 124, 126, 133, 137, 555, 556, 557; TB's visits 39–41 (2001), 125, 128–32, 136 (2002)
Inge, Field Marshal Lord Peter 159–60
Ingram, Adam 621
Inkster, Nigel 456
Institute of Contemporary Arts (ICA) 547
Intelligence and Security Committee (ISC) inquiry 334, 593, 594, 598 *and n*; and AC 599, 601, 602, 645, 646–7, 654, 669; and Dearlove 600; and TB 602, 612, 631, 634, 644, 645; report 655, 656, 659
Intergovernmental Conference, EU (IGC) 287, 563, 577, 582, 585
International Atomic Energy Agency (IAEA) 294, 446, 501
International Committee of the Red Cross (ICRC) 142, 544, 548
International Institute for Strategic Studies: report 299
International Security Assistance Force, UN (ISAF) 115, 126, 127, 135, 145n, 154, 199
IRA 27, 61, 63, 67, 273, 325, 428, 543, 584
Iran xiv, 5, 21, 30, 152, 279; JS in 24–5, 28, 92–3
Iraq march, anti-war 455, 458, 459, 450 *and n*
Iraqi National Congress 536n
Irvine, Alastair 85 *and n*, 86, 282
Irvine, Alison 85
Irvine, Derry: and press reports on his son xix, 85, 86, 282; and Byers 178; advises on Black Rod/PCC affair 238, 249; not a natural politician 270; clashes with DB on asylum 322; hosts Queen's Speech reception 363; angers TB re sentencing 408, 409–10, 411, 415–16; and AC's appeal for sponsorship 425; and pay rise

452–3; on second resolution 507, 509; and reshuffle 552, 598, 601, 604, 605; blanks TB 619; AC asks advice from 671
ISAF *see* International Security Assistance Force
ISC *see* Intelligence and Security Committee
Islamabad: TB's visits 37–9 (2001), 132–3 (2002); CIC 65, 68, 72, 83, 90, 95, 96, 99, 101, 124, 132, 146
Israel: and terror groups 6–7; and JS 28, 29; not helpful 42; and Palestine/Arafat 49, 53, 54, 60, 206, 224, 251, 409, 414; TB in (2001) 73, 74, 76–7; and US 59, 66, 107, 202, 259, 266, 496, 501; suicide bombs 224, 559 *and n*; endorses road map 583; mentioned 46, 62, 266, 307, 522, 556; *see also* Sharon, Ariel
ITN 355, 517, 652
Ivanov, Igor 475, 486
Ivanov, Sergei 36

Jackson, Glenda 469
Jackson, General Sir Mike 522, 544, 548, 628
Jackson, Robert 628
Jaish-e-Mohammed 40n
James, David: report 115, 116
James, Howell 406
Janvrin, Sir Robin 163, 164, 195, 196, 205, 214, 215, 216, 219, 305
Jarvis, Sian 142
Jay, Margaret 207, 315
Jay, Sir Michael 145, 165–6, 354, 455, 564, 616, 618
Jay, Peter 207
Jay, Tamsin 315
Jean, Al 545
Jeffreys, Rosemary 671
Jenkins, Roy 407, 408
Jenkins, Sue 171
Jiang Zemin 17, 480
JIC *see* Joint Intelligence Committee
Johannesburg: summit (2002) 285, 287, 288, 290
John Paul II, Pope 465, 590
Johnson, Alan 607
Johnson, Boris 209, 217
Johnson, Melanie 606
Joint Intelligence Committee (JIC): report 334, 441, 596, 646
Jones, Hugh 409, 428, 431, 528
Jones, Ian 173, 176
Jones, Kevan 560
Jones, Michael 267
Jonsson, Ulrika 104, 212, 213, 323
Jordan 57; TB visits (2001) 74, 75–6
Joseph, Tanya 72, 95, 132, 163
Jospin, Lionel 6, 15, 59, 108, 214, 216
Jowell, Tessa: and 9/11 victims 10, 17, 44, 69, 72; in Cabinet 109; and Wembley Stadium 115–16, 119; asks AC for advice on her image/profile 158; wants media control 189, 191; against AC leaving 247; and Treasury letters 271; and Estelle Morris's resignation 335, 337, 338; on GB 339; and sports policy 364, 374; angry with CS over Zimbabwe/cricket

controversy 403; and student finance
412; supports AC 416; and Olympic bid
423, 425, 430, 439, 573; at AC's marathon
sponsorship appeal 426; on Iraq 450; on
euro 597; offers to help AC 600; on
reshuffle 608, 609; interviews 630, 633,
664; mentioned 27

Minister for Education 236, 237; helped with speech by AC 240, 241; missed in Policy Unit 252, 264, 351; supportive of AC 254; works on TB's conference speech 312; and Estelle Morris's resignation 334, 337, 338; writes script for CC 339; on top-up fees 342; feels government is losing its way 403; on backbenchers and Iraq 469; and schools funding 563

Miliband, Ed 182, 193, 209, 220, 230, 274–5, 401, 583, 639–40

Miliband, Louise 123, 583

Millar, Audrey 53, 432, 618, 619–20, 661, 671, 673, 679, 680, 683, 694

Millar, Bob 680

Millar, Fiona (FM): and 9/11 7; wants AC to quit xx, 31, 36, 68, 155, 497, 513, 576, 649; complains about his absences 25, 41, 160; and security review 46; TB's advice on 68; AC afraid of losing 69; rows with AC 73, 91; and GB's Frost interview 100; sees Yelland 102; at Desmond party 104; and CB's image 121; wants AC to make Burnley film 122; a happy birthday 125; and GB's baby 130, 138, 154; on need for new people 138; at the end of her tether 146; on Anji Hunter 155; 'nice as pie' to TB 157; in Devon en famille 195; visits Holloway jail 209; at No. 10 dinner for Queen 219; buys AC a pedometer 233; and AC's depressions 234; against AC leaving now 246; at book launch and Thomson dinner 249; at the ballet 251, 597; angry with DB 256–7; praised by TB 261; and Roger Bannister 265–6; and Jan Taylor 269; spots reporter 274; discusses GB with Ed Miliband 274–5; and TB's departure date 276; in France (2002) 282, 283, 284; and CB/Cate Haste book project 289, 309, 330, 350, 354; on TB's TV image 290; at Independent dinner 318; against AC's sponsored marathon 343, 347; and Caplin/Foster affair 375, 377, 380, 382, 383–4, 386, 387, 388, 389, 390, 391, 392, 393, 397, 398, 403, 461; 'down' 404, 405; a pleasant birthday 406; and AC's FA job offer 406, 408; and article on AC 414; dinner with DB 424; at AC's sponsorship appeal 426; feels TB's on kamikaze mission 470; pizzas en famille 482; rows and unhappiness 511, 512, 524, 528, 531–2, 535, 552, 558, 572, 654; discussion with TB 542–3; at Marathon finish 547; in Majorca en famille 551; and Alex Ferguson 553; definitely leaving job 561, 589; and Iraq 562; bad relations with CB 568, 569, 570, 577, 582, 583; her leaving reported in press 582, 583; understands AC's difficulty in leaving 584; fed up with CB's behaviour 596; old email causes problems 607; suspects bugging 612; advised to leave by Hillary Clinton aide 614; angry with AC for going on Channel 4 News 621; thinks he's author of his own problems 628; at

plaque unveiling by Mandela 639; BC's views on 642–3; organises Michael Foot's 90th 646; on Lord Hutton 653–4; receives abusive letters 657; fired by CB 660–61, 666; and AC's Hutton Inquiry appearance 668, 669, 671, 678; gets on well with AC 687, 689; leaves job with him 693–4; more relaxed 694; mentioned 102, 161, 200, 213, 230, 237, 359, 414

Millar, Gavin 100, 190, 626, 630, 682

Millennium Dome 234, 438, 573

Miller, Julian 186, 293, 301, 303, 355, 589, 593

Miller, Leszek 589

Mills, David 27, 443, 650

Mills, Jessie 27

'Mind Out' mental health campaign 94

MI6 297

Mittal, Lakshmi 163, 164, 165–7, 168, 176

MMR vaccinations 120–2, 123, 156, 158, 159, 160

Mohammed (Prophet) 6

Mohammed, Khalid Sheikh 473 and n

Mombasa, Kenya: Paradise Hotel bombing 376 and n

Monde, Le 604

Monk, Ian 376, 377, 380, 384, 647

Monks, John xiii, 4, 157, 184, 190, 298, 372, 373, 374, 380

Moonie, Lewis 454, 605, 606

Moore, Charles 250, 624

Moore, Jane 401

Moore, Jo xix, 44–5, 46, 51, 52, 53, 56, 58, 60, 61, 98, 142, 156, 167, 168–9, 170, 187

Morgan, Piers 73, 98, 139, 148, 153, 155, 160, 173, 247, 250, 274, 309, 317, 372, 399, 412, 463, 571, 649

Morgan, Sally (SM) 28; and GB 110, 231, 245–6; on TB and Anji Hunter 155; and Byers 177, 237; worried about TB's Iraq article 182, and his health 212; and diary meeting 220, 221; and Dobson 227; on TB becoming a lame duck 245, 276; TB suspects of protecting him 290; on US trip 294, 296; at TB/Piers Morgan interview 309; and Estelle Morris's resignation 334, 336, 337; on TB/GB relations 367; and TB 378, 409, 414, 574, 578; and CB and Caplin 382, 388, 391, 396, 663–4; and Iraq 426, 427, 474, 501; at TB/GWB joint press conference 442; in Glasgow for conference 459; and TB's Commons speech 509; and FM 511, 514, 531–2; on GB and euro 533; on support for AC 602; and reshuffle 604, 606, 608; and AC's departure 603, 605, 654; at meeting re TB 645–6; mentioned 33, 102, 187, 233, 247, 490, 602

Morris, Bill 312, 553

Morris, Estelle: demoralised 28; 'a real star' 89; on Labour caution 109; 'opting for a quiet life' 138; and child benefit 218; worried she's going to be sacked 237; and A-level exams 303–4, 309–10, 311, 320; afraid to do ministerial briefing 333; resigns 334–5, 336, 337–8,

Smith, Jon 168
Smith, Paul 181n
Snow, Jon 620, 621
Soames, Nicholas 73, 159, 621–2, 626–7, 629
Social Democratic Party (Germany) 233
Solana, Javier 78
Soley, Clive 618, 619
Sopel, Jon 214
Southgate, Gareth 224
Spacey, Kevin xvi, 315
Spears, Britney 404
special advisers (SpAds) 32, 44, 46, 77, 80, 100, 142, 161, 170, 179, 182, 303, 338, 347, 349, 356, 369, 599, 620
Spectator 206, 209, 212n, 247, 264, 265, 274
Spiegel, Der 456
Squire, Air Chief Marshal Sir Peter 522
SRA *see* Strategic Rail Authority
Stagg, Dickie 323, 532, 616, 617
Stanley, Sir John 617, 625, 627, 632, 647, 667
Starr, Ken 642
Stelzer, Irwin 689
Stephanopoulos, George 443
Stephens, Phil 46, 396, 552; *Tony Blair . . .* 580
Steven, Stewart 95
Stevens, Sir John 8, 9, 45, 174, 192, 457
Stevens, Rachel 122
Stevens, Simon 310, 324, 563, 604
Stewart, Jackie 256, 260–61, 426, 444
Stinchcombe, Paul 384
Stockton, Alexander Macmillan, 2nd Earl 218–19
Stoiber, Edmund 233, 290, 305
Stothard, Peter 180, 485, 563
Stott, Richard 42, 650
Strang, Gavin 646
Strategic Rail Authority (SRA) 191
Straw, Jack (JS): post 9/11 4, 6, 7, 8, 10; and US belligerence towards Iraq 12, 13; on *Today* 15; sent to Iran 25, 28; in diplomatic row with Israel 28, 29; thinks he's being briefed against 29; and Musharraf 35; questions Lander re British suspects 45; agrees with AC on Arab opinion 53, 59, 63; on TB 62, 173, 182, 471; on GB 62–3; shines AC's shoes 63; on Washington trip with AC 62–3, 64, 66, 67; *Frost* interview 71; visits Iran and Pakistan 92–3; worried about cynicism in politics 109, 110; on euro 111; and bugging scandal 113; worried about TB overreaching himself 125; and Byers 137; on people's rising expectations 142; and Guantanamo Bay 144; and Mittal affair 165, 166, 167; on sanctions on Iraq 183; and Monks' attack on TB 190; worried about WMD 191; thinks TB looks ghastly 210; on French elections 216; in 'wind-up mode' 217; on Gibraltar 229; happy to defend AC 251–2; and sale of HUDs to US 266; on Iraq 278, 279, 284; and dossier 293, 297, 304–5; with Michael Martin in New York 299; and RC 302, 307; and UNSCR 306, 316, 331, 355, 420, 435, 437; does clips on

WMD 308, 309; conversations with Colin Powell 317; and Bali bombings 327, 328; spat with CS at Cabinet 331; AC helps with statement 333; agrees to CC being Education minister 338–9; and CAP 340, 348; horrified by GB's behaviour 360; a key communicator 374; FPA speech 374; conflicts with TB over dossier 399; on chances of war 408, 409, 412; angry with CS 403; does deal with French over Zimbabwe 427, 428; on Labour popularity 429; on Blix report 438; and Olympic bid 438, 574; spat with Geoff Hoon over DIS leak 449; 'on form' 456; blames AC for dossier 458; and second UNSCR 458, 461–2, 463, 469, 475, 506; worried by Colin Powell 464; and parliamentary debate 463–4, 468, 469; impresses AC 476; UNSC speech 478; annoys AC 479; wants a day off 479; and CS 481, 483, 537, 543, 554; on Rumsfeld's comments 491, 492; talks with the French 498; irritates TB and JP 505–6; on Chirac 514, 515; on Powell 523; worried about TB 523; defends UN to GWB 525; on US 'loonies' 527; and ORHA 531, 554; in NI 537, 538, 539; works on the Americans 539; and the euro 597; on Rumsfeld 597; on Prodi 612; and FAC 614–20 *passim*, 625, 628, 629, 631, 632–3; has food poisoning 633; tells Marr WMD will never be found 635, 636; being 'tricksy' 637; mentioned 18, 26, 31, 42, 54, 232, 318, 387, 499
Straw, Will 381
Strozzi, Prince Girolamo 257
Strozzi, Princess Irina 257
Stuart, Gisela 632, 660
Stubbs, Sir William (Bill) 310, 311
Sugar, Sir Alan 394
Sumner, Clare: and Queen Mother's lying-in-state controversy 208, 212, 213, 215, 239, 240, 242, 250, 254; and AC's FAC appearance 616, 617, 620, 624, 625, 632; and AC's ISC appearance 644, 645, 646; and Hutton Inquiry 651, 653, 680, 682, 683, 685; mentioned 596, 652, 654
Sumption, Jonathan, QC 671, 673–6, 677, 678, 679, 681, 686–7, 691; *The Hundred Years War . . .* 675n
Sun 73, 81, 94, 97, 98, 99, 100, 105, 115, 153, 160, 211, 249, 291, 297, 394, 404, 561, 562, 667; *see also* Kavanagh, Trevor; Yelland, David
Sunday Express 243
Sunday Mirror 669
Sunday Telegraph 84, 85, 163, 229, 263, 301, 387, 599, 600, 603–4, 607, 630, 664
Sunday Times 85, 113, 175, 176, 180, 225, 262, 283, 354, 365, 366, 385, 403, 503, 592, 599, 667
Sunil (Indian valet) 39–40, 41
Sylvester, Rachel 232
Synnott, Sir Hilary 68, 132
Syria 527, 548; *see also* Assad, Bashar al-

Illustration
Acknowledgements

Picture research: Amanda Russell

p. v   Picture of Philip Gould by Adrian Steirn

Section 1

p. 1   top: Marty Lederhandler/Press Association Images; centre, left: Getty Images; centre, right: Chris Ison/Press Association Images; below: Getty Images

p. 2   top: Getty Images; centre: Getty Images; below, left: Getty Images; below, right: Sipa Press/Rex Features

p. 3   below, left: Getty Images; below, right: Getty Images

p. 4   top: Getty Images; inset: © Chris Ridell, New Statesman, 12 Nov 2001/British Cartoon Archive, University of Kent, www.cartoons.ac.uk; below: Press Association Images

p. 5   top, left: Fiona Hanson/Press Association Images; top, right: Richard Gardner/Rex Features; below: Getty Images/Terry O'Neill

p. 6   top: Press Association Images; below, left: Rex Features; below, right: Getty Images

p. 7   top, left: Antony Jones/Press Association Images; top, right: Stefan Rousseau/Press Association Images; below: Author's private collection

p. 8   top: Nick Danziger/nbpictures; centre: Nick Danziger/nbpictures; below: Sipa Press/Rex Features

Section 2

p. 1   top: Nick Danziger/nbpictures; centre: Nick Danziger/nbpictures; below: Nick Danziger/nbpictures

p. 2   main: Rex Features; inset, above: Press Association Images; inset, below: Rex Features

p. 3   top, left: Author's private collection; top, right: Author's private collection; below: © Jonathan Pugh

p. 4   top: Sipa Press/Rex Features; below: Stephan Rousseau/Press Association Images

p. 5   top: Author's private collection; below: Morten Morland/NI Syndication

p. 6   top, left: Getty Images; top, right: Press Association Images; below, left: Rex Features; below, right: Press Association Images

p. 7   top, left: Topfoto.co.uk; top, right: Stefan Rousseau/Press Association Images; below: Topfoto.co.uk; inset: Priscilla Coleman/Topfoto.co.uk

p. 8   main: Rex Features; inset: Reproduced by kind permission of PRIVATE EYE magazine www.private-eye.co.uk